D1597007

# THE HERITAGE

# THE HERITAGE

The Education of Women
at St. Mary's College,
Raleigh, North Carolina
1842–1982

*Martha Stoops*

MARTHA STOOPS

To My Husband

# CONTENTS

# PREFACE

This project grew from an observation made by North Carolina historian Hugh Talmage Lefler in 1972 when he said, "The fact that St. Mary's does not have a documented history leaves a gap in the written history of this state." I saw, from the beginning of the research, the institution as a part of a larger picture, which included the history of women's education.

The absence of early records at the college forced a search for other sources of information. As I read the students' letters and diaries, major sources for the chapters on the nineteenth century, I realized that those young women were relating a social history and, also, the story of women's changing perceptions of themselves.

Yet there were elements of the St. Mary's story that, when augmented by the fuller records of later eras, remained unchanged throughout 140 years. Original buildings remained in daily use, giving a sense of continuity. But, more than that, it was the spirit of the school that remained unchanged—that indefinable sense of family combined with a strong sense of purpose.

# ACKNOWLEDGMENTS

Many persons contributed in many ways to make this history possible. From the college administration came initial encouragement by Frank Pisani and Jane Rabon and continued encouragement by John Rice, Henry Read, B. W. Conrad, and Margaret Burgwyn.

It was Sarah Dawson Davis who brought the project to fruition and who for over a decade gave moral support. Through her efforts, funding was secured for the leaves of absence from my classroom duties granted by the board of trustees. The college is grateful to those friends of the institution who provided the funds:

Mr. and Mrs. John Bratton, Jr. (Michelle Telfair), Mr. and Mrs. Godfrey Cheshire, Jr. (Elizabeth Silver), Mary Pride Cruikshank Clark and William E. Clark, Margaret Clements, Frances Cheatham Cooper, Mrs. C. C. Dawson, Margaret Highsmith Dickson and family, Mr. and Mrs. David St. Pierre DuBose, Frances Venable Gardiner, Elizabeth Lay Green and the late Paul Green, Margaret Pou Parham, Bennett Perry, Mr. and Mrs. James Poyner, Mary Wilson Stoney, Mildred Lee Stout, the late Elizabeth Gold Swindell, Sallie Lee Walker.

The interest shown by alumnae of all ages and the evidences of their devotion to St. Mary's provided inspiration. The endnotes document the hours that dozens of alumnae spent with me. The notes also acknowledge the importance of the diaries and reminiscences lent by alumnae or their families and of the centennial volume, *Life at Saint Mary's*. And always the memory of the late Mary Swann Carroll of the faculty of Mary Baldwin College spurred me on.

New friendships with other women writers were unexpected gifts. Elizabeth Reid Murray, Frances White Saunders, and Mary P. Coulling generously shared research for their books in progress. Helen Dugan Allen, Catherine W. Bishir, and A. Elizabeth Taylor also shared their research.

I am very grateful to a number of my colleagues at St. Mary's who read chapters and contributed criticism and insights. Dean Emeritus Mabel Morrison was especially helpful.

The alumnae should know that the original work consisted of two volumes; that manuscript is in the college archives. When it became apparent that publication of two volumes was impractical, the college engaged Fannie Memory Farmer Mitchell to cut the manuscript. That she did with such skill and perception that the work is considerably stronger for her editing. Our decision to adhere to modern usage concerning titles and to use inconvenient abbreviations in the notes was made with reluctance.

I thank the staff of the Southern Historical Collection for many hours of gracious and efficient service. Also, indispensable tasks were performed efficiently by Doris Barwick Parker, Anne Young Gregory, and others, and their interest in the book was an incentive. Joyce Kachergis Book Design & Production designed and produced this volume; their work always speaks for itself.

Those closest to an author become bearers of the burden. I am blessed with my husband Bob, my sister Caroline, and dear friends Mary Lib and Bob, who constantly heartened me.

Martha Stennis Sprouse Stoops
RALEIGH, N.C.

# THE HERITAGE

Aldert Smedes as a young man.

The James Hart portrait of Bishop Ives confirming students—1845.

ST. MARY'S SCHOOL.

The grove—1881. The facade of the main building was later remodeled and named Smedes Hall. Photograph courtesy of N.C. Division of Archives and History.

Drawing by Elsie Liddell of St. Mary's Chapel—1864. Photograph courtesy of N.C. Division of Archives and History.

The Chapel— c. 1977. Drawing courtesy of Jerry Miller.

Smedes Hall—c. 1977.
Drawing courtesy of Jerry Miller.

Language-Art Building, erected in 1887, also served as the library.

Holt Hall, built in 1928, was the home of the seniors.

# "IN A GROVE OF
# STATELY OAKS"

On May 12, 1842, carriages rolled into the circular driveway of a new school for girls in Raleigh in response to the following advertisement that had been circulated widely through southern newspapers and Episcopal periodicals:

The Rev. ALDERT SMEDES, of the city of New York, designs to open a School for Young Ladies, in the City of Raleigh, N. C., on the 12th day of May next.

This institution is to furnish a thorough and elegant Education, equal to the best that can be obtained in the City of New York, or in any Northern School.

The School Buildings, situated in a beautiful and elevated Oak grove, furnish the most spacious accommodations. The Dormitories are separated into alcoves, for two Young Ladies each, of a construction to secure privacy and at the same time a free circulation of air.

Every article of furniture is provided by the School, except *bedding* (beds will be *furnished*) and *towels*.

TERMS.—For Board (including washing and every incidental expense), with Tuition in English, Latin, &c., $100 per Session, payable in advance.

The Extra charges will be for French, Music, Drawing, Painting and Ornamental Needle-work, at the usual prices of the Masters. *There will be no other extra charge.*

Pupils will be admitted at any age desired.

No pupil, except by a WRITTEN request of the Parent or Guardian to the Rector of the School, will be allowed to have an account at any Store or Shop in the City. A disregard of this prohibition will be followed by an immediate dismission from the school.

Day-Scholars will be received from such Parents or Guardians as reside in the place.

The Reverend Aldert Smedes, D.D., founder and rector, 1842–1877

Sarah Lyell Smedes, wife of Aldert Smedes

The year will be divided into two terms of five months each. The former commencing, after the FIRST term, on the 15th of May, and terminating on the 15th of October. The latter commencing on the 20th of November and terminating on the 20th of April.[1]

Each young lady was met on the steps of the large main brick building by Smedes and his wife. Smedes bounded down the steps and greeted each new arrival with that special manner of his—an irresistible mixture of gallantry and fatherly concern. At 32, he was tall and handsome with blue eyes, regular features, and wavy brown hair. Fond of puns and a great tease, as well as a demanding teacher, he received lifelong devotion from most of his pupils.

Sarah Smedes, 29, seemed to the new girls a young surrogate

mother. On that first day she wore "a blue dress with appropriate lace and ribbons." Her auburn hair, parted in the middle, was "braided around her head, curls falling softly behind her ears";[2] finely arched brows accented her hazel eyes. At once the school that Smedes had decided to call St. Mary's seemed almost like home to those first students, some of whom—the youngest—would remain for as long as ten years. St. Mary's was to be home to Aldert and Sarah Smedes for the rest of their lives together.

## "THE ORIGINAL THIRTEEN"

St. Mary's tradition has it that 13 students arrived on that first day. Although there were at least 20 boarders[3] and a number of "day scholars" by the end of the opening week of school, the first-day arrivals always called themselves "the original thirteen." Only a few fragmentary records of the school are extant for the period before 1879. Fortunately, however, the names of many of the first St. Mary's students were listed in 1906 by one of their number. Known to be among the 1842 girls were Martha Hinton, Lucy Williams, Kate Badger, Sallie Badger, Harriette Borden, Molly Cameron, Mary Long Daniel, Olivia Daniel, Lizzie Davis, Margaret Dudley, Annie Freeman Gales, Mary Guion, Kate Hanrahan, Annie Haywood, Bettie Haywood, Jane Haywood, Mary Kinsey, Cora Manly, Jane Miller, Madeleine Saunders, Sarah Saunders, Adriana Tucker, Laura Washington, and Eleanor Williams.[4] Many descendants of those first students later were educated at St. Mary's, sometimes unto the fifth and sixth generations. The list of early students reads like a roster of prominent North Carolina families, for Smedes, a successful clergyman and schoolman, educated as a lawyer, also possessed business ability. He had consented to go south only after the bishop of North Carolina had assured him that he could secure the patronage essential to the success of a large school for young ladies in antebellum North Carolina. Aldert Smedes had a vision of great things to be accomplished to the glory of God and the betterment of mankind through the lives of educated women. That vision was shared by the Right Reverend Levi Silliman Ives, bishop of North Carolina, and by Judge Duncan Cameron of Raleigh, who owned land and buildings that he was willing to rent.

This account of the journey to Raleigh, written by a student of the 1850s, survives:

We drove to Salem in our carriage. Then we took the stage, a large three-seated coach for nine passengers—their luggage stowed away in "the Boot" as it was called. We traveled day and night, changing horses and getting the best meals at the regular stopping places, our arrival being heralded by the lusty notes of

Duncan Cameron, purchaser of defunct Episcopal School of
North Carolina, which he rented to the Smedes family
(Photograph courtesy of N.C. Division of Archives and History)

the horn, which also called together those who wished to hear the news or to
meet friends. . . . On our arrival in Raleigh we went at once to St. Mary's in the
. . . omnibus, which was very long and drawn by four fine horses.[5]

A St. Mary's-bound girl, having survived the trip to Raleigh, either
by way of the new railroads from eastern North Carolina or by stage,
was not particularly reassured to hear the driver of the omnibus offer
to take her to the "cemetery" (seminary).[6]

Compared to the journey, Raleigh itself probably was disappointing.
Raleigh's population numbered only 2,244, and its unpaved streets
were carefully laid out within a forest. Nevertheless, an air of prosperity had pervaded the place since the 1840 completion of the new
railroad and the new Capitol. There were hostelries, and the shops ad-

vertised "extensive, rich, and fashionable" goods from New York and Philadelphia including "rich cameo and mosaic pins and rings, silk purses, silver salt and mustard spoons, Spanish guitars, polished steel spectacles, pantaloon stuffs, vest patterns." Raisins, figs, French cordials, and fancy candies were readily available, as was "ice from Boston sixteen to twenty inches thick by the pound or by the bushel." The North Carolina Bookstore featured Sir Walter Scott's novels and Jane Austen's *Emma*.

Handsome mansions were appearing along Raleigh's tree-lined streets, and the pace of social life was almost giddy by North Carolina standards, especially during legislative sessions. Young William Hooper Haigh, in Raleigh from Fayetteville to read law, wrote in his diary in 1844, "squeamish, fashionable foolishness characterizes most of the Raleigh people who ape city manners" with much "moving to and fro and *bustling* about which they call promenading." He found Gov. John M. Morehead's parties "dull and tiresome like all conversational parties," despite the facts that "the beauty and fashion of the city were there as usual, and the sideboard was as usual adorned with sparkling liquors." [7]

Whig Governor Morehead, under attack for extravagance, was defended by editor Weston Gales of the *Raleigh Register*:

He is extravagant, say they, because out of 3 or 4,000 dollars appropriated by the last Legislature to improve the dilapidations of the Governor's House, and Premises, he has used 75 dollars to build an Ice house, a few dollars for a hencoop, and . . . perhaps the enormous amount of 25 cents for constructing a— pig pen! [8]

No, Raleigh was not yet a real city.


A TIME FOR DREAMS

To Bishop Ives, Judge Cameron, and the Reverend Mr. Smedes, 1842 seemed a promising year for making their particular dream a reality. America was in the mood for new beginnings. The optimism of the Jacksonian period, dissipated for a time by the financial panic of 1837, again dominated the national mood. America was "in ferment" and "nothing seemed finished. 'Improvement,' both personal and collective, was a national preoccupation." [9]

In 1842 the population of the United States numbered a little over 17 million people. Humanitarian causes—world peace, temperance, the abolition of slavery, labor reforms, public education, women's rights— were popular, but liberal causes did not interest everyone. In fact, southerners in general were conservative on all issues. Many of the men were interested mainly in profits and the possibility of expanding cotton and slavery into the Southwest. A few southern women crusaded for various reforms; but most of them, along with most women everywhere, tended their babies and kitchens as usual. Nonetheless, liberalism was abroad in the land, and change was inevitable as a young and vigorous nation looked forward confidently to a glorious future.

Eighteen forty-two proved to be the best of years for beginning a new "school for young ladies," for the doors of St. Mary's have remained open ever since. And Aldert Smedes's conviction that educated women can make a difference is still a basic tenet there.

Optimism and a shared vision would not have been enough to insure the success of the new school. It was the happy conjunction of three essential factors—the right man, the definite need, and the perfect place—that made it possible for St. Mary's to become more than just another short-lived southern academy.

The perfect place for a school for young ladies stood vacant in Raleigh in 1842 because a decade earlier Bishop Ives had dreamed a dream that proved to be beyond the capacity of his diocese to bring to realization. From the beginning in 1831 of his episcopate, Ives was determined that a diocesan school would be established to train future clergymen. The bishop, born in Connecticut and reared in New York, was convinced that few northern men would endure for long the climate and living conditions in North Carolina. To have "a *permanent* clergy" his diocese would have to "secure a *native* clergy." [10] He felt that a diocesan school was necessary to protect the young men of Episcopalian families from "the prevailing errors of the day" so that they would not "be tossed about *by every wind of doctrine.*" Bishop Ives held high church views, as had Bishop John Stark Ravenscroft before him, and he wanted to make sure that the young people of his diocese were provided with "*an anchor, sure and steadfast,* in the Scriptural Liturgy and Scriptural views of the Church." [11]

The 1832 convention of the Diocese of North Carolina appointed a planning committee, and the 1833 convention passed a resolution locating the Episcopal School of North Carolina in Raleigh. Bishop Ives delivered to the convention a ringing charge on the importance of combining secular and religious education; this charge was circulated in pamphlet form. Thus, as early as 1833 the Diocese of North Carolina was committed to the cause of Christian education. [12]

Plans for the Episcopal School of North Carolina proceeded rapidly, and the *Raleigh Register* reported that the institution's first session began on June 2, 1834, "under the most flattering auspices." Most of the school committee members became trustees, including Duncan

The Jacob Eichholtz portrait of Bishop John Stark Ravenscroft, first
Bishop of North Carolina

Cameron, who was later to save the diocese from financial disaster.[13] The school prospectus, largely the work of the bishop, projected an ambitious program—an English and classical education to prepare boys for the learned professions and a liberal English education for those entering business or farming. It was understood, of course, that this was to be a school for males only. Students did not have to be Episcopalians.

The school committee decided against renting space in downtown Raleigh for fear of encouraging the boys in "nocturnal irregularities"[14] and bought from Col. William Polk a magnificent oak grove west of town, signing a note to him for $1,619.17.[15] That was a large tract, 159.5 acres, and certainly a bargain at about $10 an acre. The plan was to set aside some of the land for a future residence for the bishop of North Carolina.[16] In the early years the grove was called Ravenscroft Grove after the first bishop of North Carolina.

A fortunate coincidence enabled the school committee to erect the first two buildings at a considerable savings. By the time the committee was ready to build, "the most elegant State House in the nation" was under construction in Raleigh. The first State House, built in 1794, had burned in June, 1831, and all of North Carolina was interested in the progress of its fireproof replacement.

Someone on the committee for the Episcopal School had an idea. The undersize blocks of gneiss rejected for the Capitol were being given to citizens who would haul them away. Perhaps it was Duncan Cameron, member of the committee and for a time chairman of the Capitol Commission, who concluded that the school should be built of that surplus stone. The first building for the Episcopal School, later known as East Rock, was constructed in 1834 from the random-size stones for about $4,000. The school committee in its report to the diocesan convention described this structure as "a stone building . . . 56 by 36 feet, two stories high, and covered with tin; designed to serve at present as a Dormitory, but ultimately for Studying Rooms."[17] The exterior walls of East Rock were built two feet thick.

No sooner had the first "Rock House" been completed than the school committee authorized in June, 1834, "the erection of another building of the same dimensions and materials . . . reserving interior arrangements there for future decision."[18] West Rock was completed by early 1835 when the committee decided that the growing enrollment at the school necessitated the placing of a large brick main building between the two rock houses. In March, 1835, construction began on a four-story house 85 feet long and 60 feet wide. It was "divided from bottom to top by two partitions" of stone and brick separated by halls 14 feet wide. The ground floor was divided into a dining room on the west and three utility rooms on the east. The next floor had one large school room in the western half and a chapel and three "recitation rooms" in the eastern half. The third story contained a comfortably large apartment on the east for the family of the rector (headmaster) and on the west a library, a "sick room," and other smaller rooms. Ceiling heights were 9 feet on the lower floor, 15 feet on the second floor (making it ideal for the formal parlor in later years), 12 feet on the third floor, and 10 feet on the top floor. Behind the building were a separate kitchen, a laundry, and servants' quarters. The main building, when completed in 1837, was an impressive structure; it cost about $15,000,[19] and it helped push the Episcopal School into bankruptcy.

The men responsible for the Episcopal School were neither naive nor careless. They were, in fact, successful men of large affairs—planters, bankers, the state's chief justice, a congressman, a future governor, two future bishops.[20] They had every reason for optimism after Bishop Ives persuaded Joseph Green Cogswell, former coproprietor of the prestigious Round Hill School in New England, to become the first rector of the new school in Raleigh. Cogswell's reputation and the recruiting efforts of Bishop Ives drew so many applications that when the school opened on June 2, 1834, it overflowed into rented quarters at nearby Elmwood, the spacious house owned by Judge William Gaston.[21] By the time West Rock was completed, 103 students were enrolled, 83 of them in residence. The highest enrollment the Episcopal School attained was 135.[22]

Unfortunately, Cogswell found life in Raleigh uncongenial. Also, the trustees, while building, had failed to view realistically the narrow base from which they operated. There were in 1832 in the Diocese of North Carolina only 809 communicants, despite the arduous efforts of Ravenscroft, the first bishop of North Carolina (1823–1830) to overcome the effects of the American Revolution upon the church. Fifteen clergymen served the scattered parishes.[23]

Joseph Cogswell, sometime lawyer and merchant, had been librarian and professor of mineralogy and geology at Harvard. In 1823 he had established with George Bancroft a successful school for boys near Northampton, Massachusetts. They ran Round Hill with a rigorous daily regimen of religious devotions, study, and physical exercise, and the academic standards were high enough to admit the graduates to the junior year at Harvard or Yale. When Bancroft left Round Hill in 1831,[24] Cogswell, who had little talent for management, grew discouraged; in 1834 he closed the school.[25] Bishop Ives had been favorably impressed when in 1833 he had visited Round Hill and its imitator, Flushing Institute on Long Island.[26] Professor Cogswell needed a job when Bishop Ives approached him, and the academic standards proposed for the Episcopal School pleased him.

Cogswell began his work in Raleigh with high hopes. Since the trustees gave him full control, he established a truly Cogswellian system: rising bell at 5:00, school at 5:30, no Saturday holidays, no communication with town, no pocket money, no smoking. Clearing brambles, cutting up stumps, and going fishing did not provide enough diversion. Wholesale expulsions became routine because the students deliberately broke the rules and then refused Cogswell's orders to testify against one another.[27] Furthermore, the rector and his faculty disagreed on discipline. Cogswell was beginning to despair of producing either Christian gentlemen or scholars, although the performance of the boys during the customary public examinations was praised by the local press.

The members of the faculty (Joseph H. Saunders, John DeBerniere Hooper, Nathaniel Richardson, Frederick W. Shelton, George Hand) were competent, as their later careers testified,[28] but they were terribly overworked. By the fall of 1835, nearly everyone at the Episcopal School was unhappy, and the members of the school committee were uneasy because pledges were coming in so slowly that the trustees were lending personal funds to keep the institution solvent.[29]

In April, 1835, Joseph Cogswell resigned, citing poor health as his reason and dealing what proved to be the fatal blow to the Episcopal School. He had never found congenial intellectual companionship in Raleigh. The abolitionist movement was discussed in Raleigh during the 1830s in "language a little too strong for Yankee pride."[30] Although he was received cordially, even lionized, by Raleigh's social leaders, he remained a lonely middle-aged widower. He wrote back to Cambridge that dinner parties in the capital were fine, except for "a superabundance of ham and great titles." There were always several supreme court justices, governors, and legislators present, but often "*no ladies,* except the lady of the house." He described Raleigh women as "southern pretty . . . soft, delicate and languishing. . . ."[31] Cogswell never taught again except as a private tutor, although he considered teaching "the highest of all occupations."[32] He owned and edited the *New York Review* briefly before beginning his long association with the Astor Library.

After Cogswell's resignation, Bishop Ives, always inclined toward optimism, managed to persuade the Reverend Adam Empie to leave the presidency of William and Mary College for that of the Episcopal School. Dr. Empie was well known in the diocese and had been secretary of the organizing convention in 1817.[33] He faced a nearly empty treasury and a declining enrollment. In less than a year Empie left to become rector of St. James's Church in Richmond, Virginia.

The Reverend Moses Ashley Curtis, who had joined the faculty, ran the school almost single-handedly while the bishop made desperate

efforts to raise funds. Ives pleaded for increased pledges from Episcopalians within the diocese and throughout the country. Although
enough money was obtained to keep the school open, the diocese
found itself in dire straits. It had spent about $30,000 on the school and
still owed $14,508.81 of that amount. Sarah Hawkins Polk, widow of
Colonel Polk, had been paid neither the purchase price of the land nor
the interest. The school had borrowed $7,400 from the Episcopal Fund,
and the bishop's salary was in arrears because part of it was derived
from that endowment.[34] To make matters worse, the commissioner of
public buildings had suddenly demanded $200 in payment for the sup-
posedly free stone used to build East Rock and West Rock; eventually,
he decided that payment would not be collected so long as the buildings were used for educational purposes.[35]

The Episcopal School of North Carolina was closed in December,
1838. Curtis returned to the parish, spending most of his career at St.
Matthew's Church in Hillsborough. He became a respected botanist as
well as an influential clergyman.[36] The school buildings were rented to
individuals for private schools, while the bishop tried unsuccessfully
to persuade the Diocese of South Carolina to join North Carolina in
founding a theological seminary in Raleigh, and the trustees tried
unsuccessfully to sell some of the school's land.[37] Edward Geer and
John A. Backhouse, two young clergymen who had taught at the Episcopal School, ran a day school for boys in East Rock until June, 1840,
while West Rock was rented to a family.[38] The buildings were leased
briefly for two other ventures, a music school taught by Mr. and Mrs.
Peter LeMessurier and Robert Gray's Raleigh Institute for Boys.[39]

Finally, the 1840 convention ordered the sale of all property belonging to the Episcopal School; however, no buyer appeared.[40] Hoping to
recoup at least some of the losses, the next convention authorized the
sale of the property at public auction.[41]

## "A SCHOOL FOR YOUNG LADIES"

All the while, Bishop Ives was determined to find a way to retain the
property. He altered the details of his dream and turned to the one
man in the diocese who could help him realize the new vision. The
bishop recounted the following sequence of events to the diocesan convention in May, 1842:

Tuesday, 29th, [Nov. 1841] I returned to Raleigh, and immediately applied myself to the work of devising some plan by which to prevent the sacrifice of the
Episcopal School property [which was advertised for public sale on the following Monday], or its passing into the hands of some other communion. God
heard my prayers, and blessed my efforts in this hour of the Church's danger
and humiliation. Just as every project seemed to fail, the Hon. Judge Cameron,

ever the able and active friend of the Church in her need, came forward, and by an arrangement which secured the buildings and adjacent grounds to the purposes of a FEMALE SEMINARY of the highest order, so greatly needed at the South, restored the funds which the Diocese had invested in the property, and saved the Church the deep dishonor of suffering it to pass irrevocably from her control.[42]

It may be that it was Duncan Cameron, not the bishop, who caught the first glimpse of the new vision. Bennehan Cameron wrote in 1910 that his grandfather had decided as early as 1838 to establish a school for girls in Raleigh and had asked Ives to help him to find the right headmaster.[43]

Duncan Cameron, as a member of the school committee and a trustee, had from the beginning wrestled with the educational and financial problems of the Episcopal School. At the public auction he was the only bidder. First, he reimbursed the other trustees for their personal funds paid to Sarah Polk.[44] Then on January 1, 1842, Cameron paid the exact amount owed by the school to the Episcopal Fund ($8,866.66),[45] thereby acquiring for a little over $10,000 the school's buildings, which were rented until 1897 to the Smedes family to house St. Mary's School, and valuable acreage for later development.[46]

Business acumen was not the only reason for Duncan Cameron's purchase of the property. Cameron, wealthy planter and president of the State Bank of North Carolina, was a leading churchman with an abiding interest in Christian education. He had in 1821 chaired the joint committee that persuaded the General Convention to agree to the union of the New York Diocesan School and the General Theological Seminary.[47]

Bishop Ives returned from the General Convention in November, 1841, with more than a plan to save the campus. In New York he had run into Aldert Smedes, a young man eminently suited for the job in Raleigh, who was seeking a position in the South.

Eighteen forty-two was a promising year to be opening a school for girls, for there was great interest in education, especially in "female education." North Carolina had no provision for public education until 1839, but private schools existed for the children of the privileged. Often several families hired a tutor for their own children and advertised for a few more pupils. The subscription, or "old-field" schools,[48] often operated sporadically. Academies chartered by the legislature and controlled by trustees were usually superior to the "old-field" schools, although many lacked proper equipment and well-educated faculties. Most were day schools whose nonlocal students boarded with nearby families, and many were short-lived. Between 1800 and 1860, the North Carolina legislature chartered 287 academies, 12 of which were in Wake County.[49]

Before the public school law of 1839, fewer than 3,000 children per year were in schools of any type, according to estimates made by Calvin H. Wiley in 1853 after he had become the state's first superintendent of common schools. Some 40,000 pupils were enrolled in the state system by 1853,[50] but many families still patronized the academies. The new interest in female education led to "a marked tendency" in the coeducational academies "to make the studies for girls similar to those for boys" as Latin, physiology, and chemistry were added for girls.[51]

Southerners preferred church-related and segregated schools over the commercial coeducational schools. Parents felt safest when they had deposited their daughters in a boarding school run by a well-educated clergyman and his wife with the aid of cultured women teachers, for patrons expected careful in loco parentis supervision.

By 1840 academies for females had been chartered, Asheville, Louisburg, Milton, Shocco, Charlotte, Lincolnton, Hillsborough, Nashville, Northampton, Hannah More, Salisbury, and Randolph among them. At least 22 more female academies were chartered in the state by 1860. "Female departments" were added to the Warrenton, Fayetteville, Hillsborough, Salisbury, and Raleigh academies for boys.[52] The female academies tended to substitute French for the Greek and Latin taught in the academies for males, and they added to their curricula art, music, and other "accomplishments." The most prestigious boarding school for girls in North Carolina in 1842 was Salem Academy, which had grown out of the coeducational day school established by the Moravians in 1772. The popularity of the best academies and the lack of public schools in North Carolina indicated to Cameron, Smedes, and Ives a definite need for another excellent boarding school for girls.

By the 1840s the question of higher education for women was under discussion throughout the land. There was fairly general agreement that women needed more than the rudimentary education they had received during the eighteenth century and that many of the academies offered a smattering of too many subjects with showy, but superficial, results. But there was sharp disagreement over the kinds of educational opportunities that should be offered to women because there was disagreement over the role of women in American society.

Although the belief that women were innately inferior was not so widely held as it once had been, conservative opinion was still strong. The more popular view of the period held that the intellectual capacities of women, while not inferior, were different. Those mid-nineteenth-century women who thought about it at all mostly accepted the view that theirs was a crucial, but secondary, role in society. However, as historian Anne Firor Scott points out, the wives of southern planters were caught in a double paradox.[53] They were expected to maintain the illusion of fragility, but they often worked as hard as their slaves and were expected to manage smoothly quite complicated households. Most of them accomplished miracles, despite almost perpetual pregnancy, and they mothered their large families lovingly and efficiently.

The most popular feminist writers of the 1830s and 1840s bombarded women with articles and books extolling the perfect housewife-mother-teacher. Although feminists all, they were willing to wait for the educational process to bring about reform in the legal status of women. Catherine Beecher, daughter of theologian Lyman Beecher and sister of Harriet Beecher Stowe and Henry Ward Beecher, used the proceeds from 50 years of writing to encourage higher education for women, especially teachers. She established two female seminaries and was instrumental in the organization of the American Woman's Educational Association in 1852.

Interestingly enough, during the week that St. Mary's School opened, the *Raleigh Register* published an extract from a Beecher article decrying the physical inactivity of American women, especially

the young ladies of the wealthier classes who are sent to school from early childhood, and neither parents nor teachers make it a definite object to secure a proper amount of fresh air and exercise to counterbalance their intellectual taxation.[54]

Catherine Beecher believed in the total education—intellectual, moral, and physical—of women for their specific and limited role. She did not believe that the vote was necessary to the fulfillment of that role.[55]

Few mid-nineteenth-century American women were ready to demand even their property rights. Only the most radical agreed with transcendentalist Margaret Fuller, who wrote, "We would have every barrier thrown down. We would have every path laid open to women as freely as to men."[56]

It was decisive action early in the century by Emma Hart Willard that had first generated the public interest in the education of women so evident by the 1840s. In 1819 she published a well-reasoned and forceful plea to the New York legislature in which she outlined the defects of the traditional education of women and requested funds for a female seminary. The conservatives were appalled, but Gov. DeWitt Clinton was interested. Former presidents John Adams and Thomas Jefferson liked the idea. Eventually, the New York legislature granted a charter and a share of the literary fund to the Waterford Academy for Young Ladies. That was a landmark law, the first legislative measure to recognize women's *right* to better education. Emma Willard had accomplished that by persuading the men that her desire was not to challenge the system, but only to make it work better by improving woman's contribution to her special sphere. And indeed, she was not a crusader for equal rights, although she pointed out the law's inequities. When her students showed excited interest in the presidential campaign of 1824, Emma Willard announced sternly that she would have "no hyenas in petticoats." She told her girls that men should be the oak trees and women the apple trees, each beautiful and useful in its place.[57]

By the time of Willard's retirement in 1838, her seminary which had moved to Troy, New York, in 1821, had an enviable reputation both in the United States and abroad. Her graduates were much sought after as teachers. Although Willard made no collegiate claims, her school certainly provided higher education than that dispensed by the very best of the academies.

By the 1840s a number of institutions calling themselves female seminaries had appeared. Some were mere academies; others were glorified academies; a few were nascent colleges. It is difficult to sort them out because usually an institution developed slowly from one state into another. The early New England schools such as Mount Holyoke, established by Mary Lyon in 1837, are well known, but the South, too, had its early institutions for women. In 1844 Salem Academy added an advanced class of 12 girls.[58] Franklin Academy (now Louisburg College), chartered in 1787, had organized a Female Department in 1813, but it was not called a college until 1857. Greensboro Female College (now Greensboro College) was chartered in 1838 and opened in 1846. Chowan College opened in 1848 as Chowan Baptist Female Institute and Mitchell College in 1856 as Concord Female College. Queens College was founded in 1857 as Charlotte Female Institute.[59] In Virginia, Augusta Female Seminary (now Mary Baldwin College), and Valley Union Seminary (now Hollins College) opened the same year as did St. Mary's.

Wesleyan Female College in Macon, Georgia, chartered in 1836, claims to be the first regularly chartered degree-conferring college for women in the world.[60] In 1855 *The American Almanac of Useful Knowledge* listed Wesleyan as the only college for women in the United States, thus specifically denying all claims of the female seminaries to higher status.[61]

The really radical educators of the 1840s advocated coeducational colleges. From its opening in 1833, Oberlin in Ohio admitted women; however, most chose the nondegree "ladies course." Only 79 women had received the Oberlin degree up to 1865.[62] When the University of North Carolina was chartered in 1789, "the rising generation" it was to educate did not include women. Not until 108 years later were women admitted to the regular session at Chapel Hill.[63]

It is difficult to determine the exact position of St. Mary's in the educational hierarchy of the times. Aldert Smedes called his institution simply "St. Mary's School." Yet it was more than an academy. A student of the 1860s said of Smedes, "He recognized that a woman who could, and would, should pursue higher studies, and he taught higher mathematics to one girl with as great care and time as to twenty."[64] Some of the work done at St. Mary's was certainly of the caliber required at the female seminaries and colleges, and historians are inclined to list St. Mary's among the nineteenth-century institutions of higher learning in North Carolina. However, the definition of "higher" education for women was still in the process of determination.

## "BISHOP, I AM YOUR MAN"

The philosophy of education held by the founder of St. Mary's was his own blend of the current ideas of the true rights of women. Because he was rector of the school for 25 years, Aldert Smedes determined the character of St. Mary's. Fortunately, he was a man uniquely fitted by training, experience, and philosophy to head a school for girls that could operate within the framework of southern tradition without embracing entirely southern provincialism.

Perhaps Aldert Smedes was God's chosen, as Bishop Ives firmly believed him to be. Smedes, giving an account of his decision to move south, wrote:

In the fall of 1841, the present Rector of St. Mary's met the Bishop of North Carolina in the city of New York, when the following colloquy ensued:
"Bishop, what sort of place would Raleigh be for a school for girls?"
"The best in the United States."
"Have you any buildings there?"
"The best in the United States."
"Why don't you open a school there?"
"I am now looking out for a man."
"Bishop, I am your man."
"The very man I want."[65]

Prospective patrons of the new school liked everything they heard about the young rector and his wife. The rector came from an old Knickerbocker family,[66] and his wife's father and grandfather were prominent Episcopal clergymen. Sarah Smedes's English ancestors had settled in colonial Connecticut.[67]

Aldert Smedes was the eldest child of Elizabeth Sebor Isaacs (1793–1883) and Abraham Kiersted Smedes (1780–1835). "Aldert" was a Kiersted family name. After their 1809 marriage, the couple settled at a country place on Bloomingdale Road, now in Central Park. Aldert was born on April 20, 1810. Abraham and Eliza Smedes had eight other sons and three daughters.[68] About 1825 business reverses led Abraham K. Smedes to move his family to Lexington, Kentucky, where he grew hemp. He was a leading churchman, being a vestryman of Christ Church and a member of the standing committee of his diocese.[69]

Young Aldert, who had entered Columbia College at 13, moved with his family to Kentucky and completed his classical education at Transylvania University. He also read law and was admitted to the bar in Lexington.[70] Soon Smedes felt called to the priesthood and was back in New York studying at the Protestant Episcopal church's General Theological Seminary. He was graduated from the seminary in 1832 at the age of 22. On September 16 of that same year in St. George's Church in Newburgh, New York, Smedes was ordained deacon by the Right Reverend Benjamin Tredwell Onderdonk, bishop of New York. He was ordained to the priesthood by Bishop Onderdonk on April 27, 1834, at Christ Church, New York City.[71] It was that church that Aldert Smedes served from 1832 to 1836 as assistant to the longtime rector, the Reverend Thomas Lyell, D.D.

On July 18, 1833, in Christ Church, the young curate and Sarah Pierce Lyell, daughter of the rector, were married by Bishop Onderdonk. Sarah, at 20, was well educated and comely. She was the perfect mate for a priest, for she knew what to expect. Her father, a Virginia native, served Christ Church for almost 50 years.[72]

Aldert Smedes's experience, as well as his training, had prepared him for the rectorship of St. Mary's. His association with the congregation of Christ Church and with his father-in-law was exceptionally happy, but by 1836 he was ready for a parish of his own, and he accepted in July a call to St. George's Church in Schenectady. He was a popular preacher, and soon enlargement of the sanctuary became necessary. The additional burden of supervising the expansion and the rigorous climate caused a chronic throat ailment that was to become incapacitating. In the fall of 1837 he asked for a leave of absence in order to seek relaxation and recovery in travel through Europe and the Holy Land. Smedes stayed abroad almost a year without recovering sufficiently to endure the Schenectady winters. He left St. George's in May, 1839, deeply disappointed to be giving up his parish. Besides the building program, his brief pastorate resulted in the addition of 48 members, almost half of whom were young people.[73]

The Smedes family moved back to New York City. There were two young sons, Lyell born in 1835 and Bennett born in August, 1837.[74] Little information is available concerning the Smedeses between their Schenectady years and their arrival in Raleigh. Aldert's mother, widowed in 1835, had returned to New York. The *Evening Post* (New York City) carried in August, 1839, this advertisement:

Mrs. Eliza Sebor Smedes will open on the first of September, a Boarding and day school for young ladies in the large and eligibly situated house No. 168 Duane Street, opposite the Park. . . . Mrs. S. will be assisted in the care and education of her pupils by her son, the Rev. Aldert Smedes, and by her daughters Mrs. Sarah P. and Miss Mary A. Smedes.

Eliza Smedes did not live at the Duane Street address, but apparently the young couple did. City directories for 1839–1841 list for that address: Smedes, Rev. Aldert, Seminary. When in later years the Raleigh newspapers described Aldert Smedes's career, they often referred to his "large and fashionable school in New York City."

Aldert and Sarah Smedes had found their calling. That felicitous situation did not change New York's climate, however, and Aldert felt that he had to move south for his health. At that point in his life came the providential meeting with North Carolina's Bishop Ives.

The extensive travel abroad was an important factor in Aldert Smedes's preparation for his career. In journals mailed to his wife, he described the court of Louis Philippe where he found "the Queen ablaze with diamonds" but "the ladies to be presented dressed about as we do." He observed Queen Victoria at close range and reported to Sarah that "Her face corresponded with her attire—simple . . . pleasing . . . but not striking." He found the pope less imposing than expected, having seen him take a pinch of snuff. He collected a few pieces of sculpture and a number of paintings, some of which are at St. Mary's today.[75]

In addition to his broad education and experience, the young rector's personality and his attitude toward women fitted the Raleigh situation perfectly. His mother, a pious and indomitable woman, seems to have been the guiding influence in Aldert Smedes's life, and it was doubtless his affection and respect for her that caused him to treat all women with "a marked deference and chivalrous grace of address."[76] Eliza Smedes was a favorite among the St. Mary's girls when she visited the school. At 75 she was still "very handsome" and "enjoyed the parlor receptions and music nights as much as any young person."[77] She died in her 91st year, having endured blindness for nearly a decade and having survived nine of her twelve children.[78]

Sarah Smedes was not only her husband's "dearest treasure" but also his right hand. She handled much of the correspondence with parents and when her husband was away ran the school. One of the St. Mary's teachers wrote:

To aid her husband in his great work, Mrs. Smedes brought all of the resources of a brilliant and cultivated intellect, an unflagging cheerfulness and a quaint humor that revived him in hours of weariness and depression, and a wide-reaching and never-failing sympathy with the young . . . and an unfaltering faith in the doctrines of the church.[79]

## CHAPTER TWO

# NO UNCERTAIN TRUMPET

$B$y the time he founded St. Mary's, Aldert Smedes was well along in the process of evolving his philosophy of education. As the years progressed, he became absolutely sure that the St. Mary's way was the best way to educate the young women of his time and place. In 1875 in a magazine article about his school he wrote, "Our trumpet gives no uncertain sound."[1]

Smedes hoped to transform society gradually through the influence of educated, Christian women. His goal was the same for which Catherine Beecher pleaded so eloquently, the education of women to fulfill their traditional roles—in the home, in the church, in the school—better than ever before. He did not consider those roles to be subordinate. He deplored the customary superficiality of women's education, and he felt that women were best educated in separate institutions.

## "THE TRUE MISSION OF WOMEN"

Smedes was well aware of the fact that he was educating the daughters of many of the leaders of the state who would be the wives of the leaders of the next generation. In a stirring sermon entitled "She Hath Done What She Could," he noted that society had made "a radical error." He said:

The true mission of woman has not been generally felt and understood. The controlling and sanctifying influence she can exert has not been appreciated; what she can do to refine and elevate and bless mankind has not been properly estimated, and she has therefore been sent forth on her high vocation, too often entirely ignorant of her responsibilities, and utterly unfit to discharge them.[2]

How he must have inspired his students when he told them that educated Christian wives, mothers, and teachers could actually change the world. He said of the Christian woman:

> If she *will* do what she *can* . . . , she *can* do almost what she *will* for the moral and spiritual welfare of the world. But to accomplish this, she must understand her high and heavenly mission.
>
> For this purpose, she must be trained . . . in the knowledge and love of her duties towards God and man. . . . With persuasive accents—with . . . love—with unwearied explanations and illustrations—with consistent and holy example must it be enforced, until it is received into the heart, and there sustained by the habitual endeavor to practice what has been enjoined.
>
> In secular knowledge, after the necessary elementary study, a broad and deep foundation must be laid in those departments of study which strengthen and establish the mind, and improve the reasoning faculties; nor should the lighter accomplishments of Woman . . . be without their share of diligent attention; and this course should be pursued . . . under wise and authoritative direction, till its effect on the pupil's mind is evident to all, and she has acquired both a taste for profitable knowledge and the ability to appreciate and digest her studies.[3]

The education provided at St. Mary's was much more than a veneer, but, in most cases, less than a collegiate course. Few of his students lived up to their rector's best hopes for them academically, but those who took advantage of his willingness to tutor them in advanced subjects left St. Mary's having achieved far beyond the rank and file of students there. The first to do advanced work was Catherine DeRosset of Wilmington, who was well prepared when she enrolled. Smedes called her his first "evident graduate." He wrote her father that he had hoped to institute some elements of the English university system at his school. "But," he wrote, "the difficulty has been to get graduates; most of my pupils leave before they have completed respectable courses."[4] Because no diploma was offered, the fathers of most students considered them "finished" at St. Mary's when they turned 17 or 18. Kate DeRosset, after she was widowed during the Civil War, returned to St. Mary's as teacher and lady principal.

It was the practice for the best upperclassmen to help "hear the recitations" of the younger students, thus acquiring some experience in teaching. Training of teachers was a stated goal. Smedes urged his pupils, when they had returned to their homes, to teach Sunday school and to do volunteer secular teaching in their communities where many were growing up in "ignorance and vice." He added, "And the exercise of patience and forbearance—in a word, the self-discipline required of a teacher, is the best possible preparation of a woman for the peculiar duties of her after years."[5]

In his 1859 brochure describing the school, Smedes wrote:

The rector has seen so many instances in which the acquirements and accomplishments that wealth has purchased for children, have proved to them, in a reverse of fortune . . . their only support, that he often urges upon his pupils as a powerful motive to diligence, the certain and honorable means of independence here within their reach, and endeavors to make the standard of attainment among them the fitness to become teachers of others. This indeed, is the vocation of a woman in the most important and interesting relation which she sustains in life. SHE MUST BE A TEACHER—of children, whose minds receive from her their first and most durable impressions—impressions that stamp them for eternity, as good or evil, happy or wretched.

Smedes always insisted that his institution be called simply "St. Mary's School." He wrote, "There is significance in its name. It is not an Institute, nor a Hall, nor a College. It is simply a school for discipline, for training for good, honest, hard work."[6] He eschewed the public examinations then in vogue; faculties often primed students for those public performances, thus prompting the *Raleigh Register* to label them "an attractive but false test."[7] Smedes wrote:

St. Mary's School . . . offers no medals, or prizes, or stimulants of any kind to rivalry or emulation. It expects and secures from its pupils zeal in their studies and order in their conduct, from motives of duty to their school, to themselves, to their parents, and to their God. . . .[8]

In his school *Manual*, which began with "My dear child" and was signed by their "preceptor and friend," Smedes detailed the strict rules, but added:

You should look upon your school as an affectionate, and therefore, vigilant and faithful mother. . . . O think not . . . her eye too vigilant, her hand too severe. Every provision she makes for you . . . has originated in the warmest affection for your person and desire for your welfare. . . .
For the improvement of your mind you will find here a course of study carefully arranged, and patiently and faithfully taught. If you pursue it earnestly and perseveringly, you will become an intelligent young woman, an ornament of the domestic and social circle.[9]

St. Mary's students spent at least five and a half hours daily in classes and music practice and at least two hours in supervised study hall. But not all subjects could have been studied every day. An 1858 monthly report for one of the younger students shows grades on 15 subjects: spelling, reading, Bible, poetry, geography, grammar, history, composition, natural philosophy, arithmetic, writing, French, piano, guitar, and sewing. The grading scale was one through nine, nine being the highest grade. Besides the written abstracts of the chapel lectures, longer compositions were required every other week. There were weekly assignments of scripture verses and long passages from Shakespeare and Milton to be memorized and recited perfectly. Diligent indeed were the girls who moved up to "the good bench." One of the busy ones wrote home in 1846:

If I don't improve it will be my own fault. . . . I know it is my last opportunity and I am resolved to improve every hour. . . . The girls here have no time to be *Idle* if they attend to their duties. . . .[10]

The armloads of textbooks, protected by homemade black cambric covers, that girls carried to class were largely the same texts used by the academies, the female seminaries, and in the "collegiate courses" for women at the time. The younger students took their preparatory work at St. Mary's. The curriculum for the older students (as clearly as can be determined from the textbooks listed in bills, on report cards, and in the students' letters) seems to have paralleled closely the three-to-four-year courses in the female seminaries throughout the nation during the period. It also seems much like the 1855 curriculum of Spartanburg Female College in South Carolina. Everyone took English grammar, composition, English literature, geography, and history. At St. Mary's the Bible and religious courses were always required. For several generations, one of the texts was a 600-page tome by William A. Paley entitled *A View of the Evidences of Christianity*, a book also used at Mount Holyoke and at Spartanburg Female College. The number of collegiate texts included in the St. Mary's booklists implies a curriculum much stronger than that of an academy.

A student could go as far as she was willing to in the study of mathematics and languages. Greek was never required at St. Mary's, but Smedes occasionally tutored a student or two in the language. In 1855 he wrote to the father of a promising student:

I've hinted Greek to Victoria, but she says she has not time this term. As she is not very robust . . . I have not pursued the matter. . . . If I thought her lazy, or physically capable of being hard pressed, I should decide differently.

I think Victoria a very sincere and honest girl, and, therefore, have less hesitation in allowing her some voice in the estimate of her studies.[11]

Advanced courses in Latin were taken by many; German, Italian, and Spanish were offered whenever teachers were available. French was "almost a second language throughout the school," for fluency in French was nearly as important an "accomplishment" as musical proficiency for refined ladies. From the opening of the school, the French teachers were natives of France, and assignments in French literature were long and difficult. The older students also took logic or moral philosophy.

Smedes took advantage of the special opportunities for enrichment that Raleigh afforded. His girls heard famous lecturers, and they saw most of the incumbent presidents of the United States. Regularly they visited the state legislature. After the hospital for the mentally ill, then known as Dix Hill, become operative in 1856, the students went there annually for a tour and lecture.

An account of the end of school at St. Mary's in the fifties appears in *The Old Plantation* by James Battle Avirett:

This is Commencement week at St. Mary's, and those carriages filled with youths are just down from Commencement at Chapel Hill. These young gentlemen *en route* home from the university, have stopped over—some to witness the graduation of their sisters and sweethearts, others to have a good time generally. . . . Wilmington, New Berne, Edenton, Washington, Fayetteville, Charlotte—in fact nearly all of the larger towns and most of the counties of the State are represented, as well in the young ladies of the school as in the many guests. . . . In that large parlor, perhaps the largest, and certainly the most beautiful in the whole South, what an assemblage of beautiful maidens and handsome men. . . . How proud is their old bishop [Thomas] (Atkinson) of them all—his dear children, most of whom he has confirmed—you may see, as his loving eye lights up with admiration of those lovely, tidewater girls who glide over the stage to their places at the piano, harp and guitar! . . . How broad and full the course of study in this school, the admirable essays, read so modestly and effectively by the young ladies, set forth, as the noble face of Dr. Smedes lights up with pleasure at some singularly fine sentence. . . .[12]

Aldert Smedes realized that a competent faculty was vital to the success of his school. Kemp P. Battle said of him, "Having accurate insight into human Nature, his mistakes in the selection of teachers were of the rarest. . . ."[13] Unfortunately, information about the early faculty is meager.

It is certain that Madame Clement was a member of the original St. Mary's faculty, but it is not known when she left her native France for the United States. Madame was "very French, quick, impulsive" with a "commanding personality." She scolded the girls and servants alike and was "a terror to wrong-doers."[14] Even the students realized that Madame was fiercely zealous for the school and its reputation for excellence. A student of 1848 wrote to a former student, "Madame is just the same, I hear her now urging some tardy servant to labour; indeed I think she gets an undue proportion of crossness . . . awarded her. 'Tis nothing but the interest she takes in the welfare of St. Mary's, and all connected with it."[15]

The girls found Madame Clement fascinatingly French. She was, however, a devout Episcopalian. When they asked, "Madame, do you say your prayers in English or in French?" she unhesitatingly replied, "Mes enfants, je ne sais pas." She usually wore silk dresses with bright ribbon trim. The gardens and the "sick-room" were her responsibilities. Madame presided majestically over the French table in the dining room and over her classes on the lower floor of the main building—"the brick house" as it was called then. Hour after hour, the girls droned their French verbs until Madame would begin to nod. Awakened by a wave of tittering, she would rap sharply for attention, and the drill would resume.[16]

In late 1845 Madame's only child, Eleanor, who was about 12, arrived from Paris. Though unhappy initially, Eleanor grew to love St. Mary's and, after spending several years in Paris to complete her education, returned to teach French.

In the late 1840s Madame began to plan for a school of her own. Smedes, in his usual generous spirit, wrote to a former student:

With her energy and talent, she will no doubt do well. . . . I do not like the idea of parting with the old lady, at all. . . . *I have fought so many battles with her & for her*—that I shall feel . . . as if a main spoke of the wheel has gone. . . . She is a most sterling woman, and deserves to prosper.[17]

Madame Clement's Classical Institute for Young Ladies was located in Wilmington, North Carolina. Later she and her daughter operated Madame Clement's School in Germantown, Pennsylvania; it was sold after Madame's death in 1878.

Frances O'Connor, known as "Miss Frank," went to St. Mary's early in its history to teach the younger girls. "Tall, handsome and dignified, with a smile which took away all fear from the most timid . . . she kept perfect order without seeming to exercise any authority. . . ."Along with her teaching and dormitory duties, she helped Sarah Smedes supervise the wardrobes and shopping for the little girls. She left St. Mary's to teach at Clement's school.[18]

Eliza Evertson became the "main spoke in the wheel" after the departure of Madame Clement. Tall, slender, and aloof, she made the girls "walk a chalk line." She never laughed, possibly because her health was so wretched that she was often in pain. Her pupils recognized that she was an excellent teacher and a just disciplinarian. An upperclassman wrote home about her three-student botany class, "Miss Evertson makes it so interesting. She has a microscope and we get flowers and young plants every day and analyze them."[19] She also taught history and mental philosophy. Unapproachable as she was, she had her favorites among the youngest girls, sometimes allowing them to climb upon her knee.

Eliza Evertson led a missionary society that met weekly to make clothes for American Indians attending a mission school and to work on other projects. A student of 1855 wrote later, "My first lessons in making clothes *myself* were learned there, and they stood me in good stead when the war times came on so soon."[20] After leaving St. Mary's, Eliza Evertson became a deaconess and served in a church school and orphanage in Mobile, Alabama.

Little is known of the educational background of those early mem-

Madame Clement

bers of the St. Mary's faculty. Over the years, various well-educated members of the Smedes family, both male and female, taught at St. Mary's. Passing references in the letters of students would seem to indicate that Smedes got some of his teachers from the Willard school, but it has been impossible to verify this assumption. Smedes liked to secure his music and language teachers directly from Europe, and it is known that he used his New York connections to recruit faculty. Nearly everyone at the school took lessons on at least one musical instrument. Piano, organ, violin, harp, and guitar lessons were offered for extra fees of about $30 a semester.

Gustave Blessner, pianist, violinist, and composer, presided over the music department from 1844 to about 1849, succeeding a Mr. Brandt and his wife. Mrs. Blessner was an accomplished harpist and organist as well as a painter. The Blessners, who were referred to by the Raleigh press as "celebrated *Artistes*," added considerable luster to North Carolina's cultural scene. A number of Blessner's minor compositions had been published in New York, Boston, and Philadelphia before he moved south. In 1844 he composed "The Grand March of the University" for the University of North Carolina commencement program. Blessner's students were inspired to special efforts when he dedicated a new composition to a promising student who would then play "her" piece at a soiree. In 1845 a Baltimore company published "a collection of characteristic waltzes for the piano" by Blessner. Entitled "The Flowers of the South" and dedicated to "the young ladies at St. Mary's School, Raleigh, N.C.," the pieces were descriptions of "Lavinia's" school days at St. Mary's.[21]

Mrs. Blessner designed the covers for her husband's published music. For "The Flowers of the South" she sketched the arrival of the omnibus taking new students to St. Mary's. The lithograph was reproduced in folio; a letter written on the heavy paper by Tempe Neal of Louisburg to her mother and dated September 5, 1844, read in part:

as Mr. Smedes received the picture of the school I thought I would write to you on it and give you a description of the place in order that you may understand the picture better you will see under it Drawn by Mrs. Blessner the lady and gentleman nearest it is Mr. and Mrs. Blessner and their lap dog running on before them the stage is coming with some of the scholars and the driver is blowing his horn the porch ought to be full of girls for we always run out when any of the scholars are coming You wil see a few persons walking with parasols I expect they are intended to represent visitors for the girls never use parasols when they exercise and besides there are not enough for the girls there are most too many gentlemen about.[22]

Blessner was a fervently patriotic Frenchman, and sometimes he and Madame Clement disagreed so violently that he would "erupt like Vesuvius," spouting French and German expletives. After such a scene, Madame would stalk off muttering that *her* French, unlike that of some provincials, was pure Parisian. Mrs. Blessner, a gentle English lady, could "always quiet the storm." The professor, a bit of a dandy, was kind and patient with his students, and they were fond of him.[23] Mrs. Blessner, in addition to playing the organ for chapel and teaching piano and harp, gave free voice lessons to some of the girls.

Prof. Louis Mendelssohn went to St. Mary's in the winter of 1849 soon after his arrival in America. Master of the piano, flute, violin, harp, and guitar, he had been the first music teacher of his gifted young cousin, Jakob Ludwig Felix Mendelssohn Bartholdy (1809–1847). One day during a music lesson, Mendelssohn pointed to his treasured photograph of the composer and remarked with pride, "The pupil excelled the teacher." Mendelssohn's struggle with the English language amused his pupils. Despite the fact that he always carried a dictionary, he was often perplexed. He complained to Smedes that the servants brought his "vood" (wood) when he wanted his "voots" (boots).[24]

Another music teacher at St. Mary's during the fifties was H. I. I. Solomons, organist at Christ Church and organizer of the Raleigh city band. He was also a composer, writing music for his St. Mary's students and for his band. He went to Raleigh in 1849 on a concert tour with a group of musicians and decided to stay.[25]

Still another music teacher was Stella V. Shaw. Sometime during the 1840s, when she was about nine years old, Stella was taken to St. Mary's by her mother. The well-dressed woman explained that she was about to take a long journey but that she would remit the tuition as it fell due. The little girl was simply abandoned at St. Mary's. Aldert and Sarah Smedes reared her as a foster daughter, and she remained at St. Mary's as chapel organist and music teacher until her final illness. When she died in 1890, she was buried in the Smedes family plot in Oakwood Cemetery, Raleigh.[26]

Drawing and painting were taught in the early days by a succession of women, most of whom were from New York City. The extra fee for art lessons was $15 a semester.

The heart of the curriculum at St. Mary's was the study of the scriptures. Aldert Smedes had for some years the aid in the classroom of another Episcopal clergyman, Richard Sharpe Mason, rector of Christ Church in Raleigh from 1840 until his death in 1875.[27] He taught to the juniors and seniors the rational nineteenth-century approach to Christianity expounded in Paley's *Evidences of Christianity*. Ellen Brownlow, who enrolled in 1845, wrote of him:

I could never decide which I loved best, Dr. Mason or Dr. Smedes. . . . They were so entirely different except in their deep and true devotion to the Church, their unfeigned humility as Christian men, their powers of mind and soul, devoted to the Master and His cause. . . . Entirely different types in personal appearance, Dr. Smedes with his clear-cut features illuminated by his gracious smile, Dr. Mason, rugged of feature, near-sighted eyes, and some traces of the years he had passed. He rarely smiled; when he did it was a burst of sunlight, and when he gave us some rare words of approval, we were most happy and uplifted.[28]

Smedes, in addition to his administrative duties and his preaching, taught at various times Bible, chemistry, mathematics, philosophy, and sometimes Latin and French. He possessed, according to his students, "a marvelous gift for impressing the essential points of the lesson and rejecting the less valuable ones." It was his habit to use practical illustrations to elucidate a point. He would, for example, explain a mathematics lesson by showing how his paid-up life insurance policy was providing him dividends.[29] He gave science lectures, and periodically he invited professors from the university at Chapel Hill to lecture at St. Mary's to his students and to interested townspeople. Smedes enjoyed his "chemical and philosophical apparatus." The girls particularly liked the "shocking experiments" with the galvanic battery and his "*real* little engine" that "whistled and puffed and then finally started—just like a large one."[30] The rector was much interested in astronomy, and he illustrated his lectures by calling the girls outside on clear nights to look through his telescope. Especially exciting was the "look at the comet" on September 17, 1858.[31] It seems that the science courses were superficial by today's standards but that the school owned more than the normal "apparatus" for the period.

It was Aldert Smedes's lectures on the Bible and on church doctrine, however, that St. Mary's women remembered most vividly. Mary Johnson Iredell, a student of 1847–1855 and later a member of the faculty, wrote of him:

As a teacher Dr. Smedes excelled. He had a strong way of putting things in simple words which clung to the memory. . . . In its epigrammatic character his words often had the force of a proverb. . . . I do not doubt that many of his pupils could use his very words in the explanation of some passage from the weekly Bible lesson, and in his teaching them to give a reason for the faith that was in them. . . .[32]

Soon after a lecture, the students were required to write from memory an abstract of its salient points. In "writing half-hour" every Tuesday and Thursday each young woman tackled the "dreaded abstract." That practice was continued during the rectorship of Bennett Smedes. The writing of the abstract was no mere exercise in mental discipline. For years each one was carefully graded by Aldert Smedes; later, the teachers helped with the chore. The highest mark was "v.v.v.w." for "very, very, very well done." At the end of the month the marks were translated into a grade on Bible for the student's report card. That was before the practice of using letter grades.[33]

Aldert Smedes had no tolerance for indolence. The school *Manual* put it plainly enough:

In your classes you must be punctual, regular and attentive, honestly depending upon yourself for your answers, and eagerly drinking in the instruction of your teacher. You must disdain the little tricks by which idleness and ignorance seek to evade the responsibilities of a recitation. Be assured such tricks are seen through by your teachers and your fellows. . . . Such devices, indeed, mortify your teachers; they cruelly defeat the purposes and desires which led your parents to place you here; and they are a bad example to the class; but their most injured victim is yourself.[34]

The desire to please their rector seems to have been the prime incentive for many St. Mary's students. Speaking at the school in 1910 at the observance of the centennial of the founder's birth, the Right Reverend Robert Strange, bishop of East Carolina, spoke of his mother and other relatives who had been educated under Aldert Smedes. He said:

Though I did not have the privilege of knowing in person him who under God made St. Mary's, I have been taught from childhood to honor and revere Dr. Aldert Smedes. So it has been—the coming here today and preparing to come—a labor of love. . . . [35]

As academic head of the school, Smedes personally interviewed and "classed" each of the approximately 1,900 young ladies educated at St. Mary's during his 35–year tenure. He questioned each new girl until he could decide what her schedule should be. Whenever a student wished to change her schedule, she consulted with Smedes. He also performed some of the duties customarily assigned to a "lady principal," for the students had to go to him for special social permissions. He handled the relatively few disciplinary cases; his impeccable sense of justice did not allow him to overlook misconduct. After "a little talk" in the rector's study, the penitent was sent away, always with a prayer and, sometimes, with a little gift of candy.[36]

His duties as rector included those of recruiter and business manager. He combined recruitment with trips to Mississippi and Louisiana to visit his brothers, often escorting a bevy of new girls back to Raleigh "on the cars." Smedes made rather frequent trips to New York to buy supplies and interview teachers or to Chicago, where he owned property, or to Wisconsin to visit his mother and sister.

St. Mary's School was a financial success during a period when many similar institutions failed.[37] Smedes was not only an unusually able business manager, but he also handled his personal finances so well that he enjoyed an income from wise investments.[38] The charges at St. Mary's were relatively high for the times and the South. When the school opened, tuition and board were $200 a year or $100 for a five-month session. Music, drawing, foreign languages, and dancing were extra; some pupils took three kinds of music lessons. Day scholars under 13 paid $50 per year, the older ones $75, plus the fees for extra subjects.[39] The charges remained about the same until the Civil War years. The teachers were paid about $40 a month in cash and were provided room and board on campus.[40]

Smedes carried the accounts with local merchants and physicians for his pupils, and he also advanced travel money at vacation time. It was not unusual for the total for school, books, clothing, medical care, and travel to be over $400. Both the rector and his wife were careful to keep a pupil's expenses within the limits prescribed by parent or guardian. Patient with his patrons, Smedes occasionally carried over bills as high as $1,000. He made it clear, however, that he expected payment as soon as arrangements could be made; he did not charge interest on overdue accounts.

Smedes paid his own bills promptly, and it was a matter of pride with him that he patronized Raleigh merchants whenever possible.[41] Apparently, he lent money to friends, for his few surviving account books show that he kept considerable sums out at interest. That proved a profitable practice until the years during and after the Civil War. Then some of his friends found themselves insolvent, and Smedes took their losses.[42]

Prudent though he was in business affairs, Smedes did not hesitate to take into his school each year a number of promising students whose parents could not pay his charges. Contrary to the popular conception, St. Mary's was not a school for the privileged only. Aldert Smedes's generosity was dispensed quietly; but according to those who knew him, it was "almost boundless."[43]

The financial success of Smedes's school was due in part to the impressive buildings and campus that he rented from Duncan Cameron. The judge was so eager to have a female seminary in Raleigh that he had offered to assist financially,[44] but that was not necessary. In fact, during his first year as rector, Smedes wished to purchase the campus. Cameron, however, dissuaded him from taking so great a risk so early in the venture. In November, 1842, Smedes wrote from New York to his landlord saying that as he had been unable to collect notes due him there, he would defer to Cameron's judgment and withdraw his purchase offer.[45] In later years, the Cameron family was unwilling to sell. When Duncan Cameron died in 1853, the school passed to his two daughters. Therefore, over the years the expense of the maintenance and improvement of the campus was borne by the Camerons, and the rent of approximately $1,500 was adjusted as new buildings were added. In 1856 the three original buildings were insured against fire in the amount of $6,000.[46]

After the initial remodeling of the old Episcopal School dormitories, no major changes were made in the buildings until 1849. That summer Smedes persuaded Cameron to add a porch with second-floor entrance steps to the main building and covered walkways from that building to the two rock houses. The rector wrote to the judge, "Say but the word, and a porch shall grace our front, that will make us as classic in appearance as we are in profession. Speak, and our little girls will get to their dormitory without apprehension from November blast, or Southern rain."[47]

And so St. Mary's, operated by Aldert Smedes on Cameron property, prospered. On the eve of the Civil War Smedes reported a full house of 78 boarders and 30 to 40 day scholars.[48] He felt that North Carolina and "sister states of the South" had given him "generous support";[49] others labeled St. Mary's as "perhaps the most popular school in the South."[50]

## "WE BUILD OUR SCHOOL ON THEE, O LORD"

The philosophy of education and the Christian faith of Aldert Smedes were so inextricably bound together that the educator was indistinguishable from the priest. That he considered himself first the priest is evidenced by his explanation of his choice of a name for the school:

Its title, "St. Mary's," designates it as an institution of the Church, a school of Christ, whose chief desire and care are to instill into the minds of its pupils the wisdom that is from above, and to form in them habits of obedience, industry and piety that will make them blessed and a blessing here, and meet for the inheritance of saints in the light hereafter.[51]

That was not a controversial choice, for education and piety had gone hand in hand in America since colonial days. From its founding Smedes made his school such an integral part of the life of the Diocese of North Carolina that St. Mary's was regarded by everyone as the diocesan school, although it was privately owned. During 55 years the Episcopal church bore none of the responsibility but reaped untold benefits from the school. It is true, on the other hand, that much of the success of the institution was due to the endorsement of successive bishops, the patronage of Episcopalians, and the excellent quarters built for the Episcopal School of North Carolina.

The strength of St. Mary's lay from the beginning in "the continued service of prayer and praise whereby the common life of the school became the life of common prayer." Tribute to that pattern of life in the school was offered by the Right Reverend Joseph Blount Cheshire, fifth bishop of North Carolina, in 1910 upon the occasion of the observance of the centennial of the birth of Aldert Smedes. Bishop Cheshire said that in establishing that pattern "Dr. Smedes did a work here not only for us of this particular household of faith, but he set an example which has borne fruit in many institutions since that day."[52]

On the very first day of school in 1842, Smedes held an opening service in the parlor. Soon he had prepared a chapel that occupied most of the first floor of East Rock house and could seat about 150 worshipers. The young rector described that first St. Mary's chapel in his 1844 report to the diocesan convention:

This is a room some 30 by 45 feet, furnished with pews, an organ, a chancel and altar, and exclusively appropriated to religious instruction and worship. Here the solemn Service of our Church is performed, and her Sacraments and ordinances are administered, in the presence only of our pupils, their teachers, and our domestics, with a freedom from interruption and distraction most favorable to devotion and their spiritual improvement.[53]

Thus, from the beginning the chapel was "the heart of St. Mary's."

The chapel in East Rock was used for 15 years. Then, during 1856–1857, the Cameron family built in the grove a Gothic Revival chapel.[54] The first confirmation service in the new chapel was held on April 5, 1858. The Right Reverend Thomas Atkinson, third bishop of North Carolina, reported to the convention:

April 5, P.M., I preached in St. Mary's Chapel, Raleigh, and confirmed sixteen persons belonging to the school. It was the first time in which I had taken part in the worship at the new Chapel, and I was gratified by its beauty, its appropriate arrangements, and its adaption to its purpose.[55]

The new chapel, customarily referred to in the Raleigh press as a "gem of architectural beauty," was designed by Richard Upjohn (1802–1878), the architect for a number of fine American churches, including Trinity Church, New York City, and Christ Church, Raleigh. Upjohn, in November, 1847, wrote to Christ Church's Richard Sharpe Mason, "I hope the erection of our church will be the means of introducing a new style of church architecture in the South."[56]

Letters from Aldert Smedes to Richard Upjohn during the spring and summer of 1856 indicate that the architect drew original plans for the St. Mary's chapel. However, the porch and "some of the ornamental work prescribed for the rear wall" were omitted in order to keep the cost to about $1,600, which was the most that Smedes thought the Camerons would want to spend to erect a chapel. The first intention had been to build for about $900, using plans in Upjohn's 1852 book of drawings and specifications. It appears that the architect selected in New York the octagonal stained glass window that was placed over the front door.[57] The other original windows (probably of plain glass) were eventually replaced by stained glass memorial windows. (See appendix A.)

The simple board-and-batten structure with a steep gable roof was originally a rectangle 53 feet by 24 feet. It was painted brown and remembered by St. Mary's girls as "the dear little brown chapel." When the transepts were added in 1905, giving the chapel its present cruciform shape, most of Upjohn's plan was left unaltered.[58]

One St. Mary's woman wrote:

And the heart of St. Mary's was the chapel; small, brown, not especially beautiful to the stranger, but filled for us with the holiest of memories. The orderly reverent daily services, the glorious strains of the music of high festivals, the beauty of holiness which illuminated the minister are influences for good which will abide with us forever. The yellow and white chrysanthemums, the glory of autumn leaves, the sound of the All Saints Day prayers and praise of those feast days of the church come to us now deepened and made more sacred by the memory of the services of long ago, the services in the small brown chapel that we loved.[59]

In his sermon entitled "She Hath Done What She Could," preached to each school generation, Smedes described the educated Christian woman:

to a good husband she will prove a wife including in herself all joys; to his children, a mother who will fulfil all that the sacred name imports, to his household a mistress in whom authority will be graciously tempered with love, to society an ornament and a blessing. . . . [60]

Under such tutelage the typical young St. Mary's girl suffered no serious identity crisis. She expected to become a wife and mother; if, however, the Lord failed to provide a husband, she expected to become a teacher or missionary or both. Her rector urged each young woman to consider carefully the moral qualities of a man *before* marriage since she would "be consigned to his authority and mercy." He quoted scripture in reminding his charges that "one of the first conditions of the married state is, that the desire of the wife shall be to her husband, and that he shall rule over her." A good wife, he said, "is patient, humble, meek, heavenly minded." She makes "the home of her husband, a place of rest from the toils of business, of comfort amid the disappointments of life, of cheerful recreation amid its cares. . . . " The doors of such a happy home would be closed against "anger, clamor, . . . complainings . . . while for meekness, gentleness, resignation, forbearance, hope, peace and joy, there should be an abundant entrance and a perpetual welcome!" Such a woman could turn even an unreligious husband to God. Such a wife, their pastor assured them, was "the richest prize, the dearest treasure this earth contains for man."[61] He reminded his students that many of them would be living on plantations where the burden of their children's early education would fall upon them when he said,

what physical endurance, what exhaustless energy, what triumphant patience, what wise economy of time and resources, must that mother exercise, who amid all her other duties, yet considers every day lost, of which a part is not devoted to the education of her children.[62]

He acknowledged that the "high and holy mission" was a difficult one, but he confidently expected his young ladies to measure up to his and the Lord's requirements of them. To that end, they should, he said, use their leisure hours in school, and afterward before marriage, for mental improvement so that they could "discharge with grace and intelligence the engrossing duties" of wife and mother.

His pupils considered Smedes's sermons quite superior to those of visiting clergymen that "generally amounted to nothing in the end," as one wrote home. Smedes "turned their thoughts to God."[63] Usually his sermons were direct, short, and very personal. He would ask, "Have you sinned? Have you grown in grace? Do you realize that you have been consecrated to God?"

After church, the young ladies walked around the grove discussing the details of the sermon in order to be ready, if asked, to give a synopsis at evening prayers. A student of the 1860s said that three truths were impressed upon her mind by Aldert Smedes's sermons: belief in an overruling Providence, the duty of the young to their superiors, the danger of presumptuous sins.[64]

The "life of common prayer" was pervasive at St. Mary's. In the school *Manual* the rector urged each student "to enter upon the great work" of her salvation. He cited the aids she would find: the daily morning and evening prayers "of the family," the daily chapel services, the daily study of the Bible and prayer book, "the lectures and exhortations of the chapel" during the week, the Sunday services with "hymns and catechising at night," and the good examples of teachers and companions. Each week the passages of scriptures to be expounded in the daily and Sunday services were announced and then "pondered" and memorized by each student. The *Manual* included questions to be used as guides for the "daily reflection and self-examination."

At night after prayers in the parlor, the rector often gave his "little talks." When he began, "My dear children," the girls knew that he was about to praise them; but when he began, "Young Ladies," they all knew that a lecture was forthcoming.[65] His pupils took their priest's admonitions seriously, as is shown by the following set of resolutions written by Lou Sullivan in 1864:

It is Sunday night & sitting in the school room surrounded by a crowd of cheerful, chattering girls, I will essay to draught a few resolutions with the firm trust that they may be of much benefit to my future course. 1st that each Sabbath may be spent as near to God as my frail nature will admit & in each one may I approach near that perfect image to which I hope at last to be changed. May I begin each day with thoughts of my Divine Protector & thanksgiving for his continued mercies. May I be cheerful, corteous, amiable, forgiving towards all with whom I may be connected. Oh, that I may continually grow in grace and in the knowledge of our Lord and Saivor.

In appreciation of Gods past care & goodness to me I will try to trust him & submit myself with more resignation to His will. Oh! that I could always feel that He does what is best for me. May I do nothing that I would not willingly submit to be held up to scrutiny.[66]

It was considered important in mid-nineteenth-century America for a woman to have settled her religious future before her marriage. Each year from 10 to 20 of the St. Mary's girls were ready for confirmation. Smedes prepared them carefully. After they had studied his published booklet, *Hints on the Rite of Confirmation*, he took his communicants' class to his study and "talked as a father would to his own children, then took each separately and gave us advice that he knew we needed . . . ," a student recalled.[67]

Not all the women educated at St. Mary's under Aldert Smedes were from Episcopalian families. Those of other communions often grew to love the Episcopal service, influenced perhaps by Smedes's beautiful reading of the scriptures.[68]

It was not enough for a St. Mary's girl to be an exemplary wife and mother; she also had to be a blessing to her community. She should aid and teach "the poor, the ignorant and the distressed," and she should teach Sunday school. Bennett Smedes said that the object to which his father devoted his life was "so to educate those who were committed to his care that they might go forth into the world, devoted daughters of the Church."[69]

Training for generosity in the service of the church began at St. Mary's. The congregation, officially an unorganized mission because there was no permanent parish group, was included in the annual assessments; St. Mary's regularly gave as much as many of the small organized parishes in the diocese, the assessment during the 1850s being $150. In addition, there were always special projects. The voluntary missionary societies, to which both faculty and students belonged, sent barrels of books and clothes to mountain churches in the western part of the diocese. (The entire state comprised one diocese then.) In return, the churches sent by covered wagon bags of chestnuts and apples as a winter treat for the school.[70]

Their rector encouraged the students to make personal sacrifices in order to help those less fortunate. At the beginning of Lent one year during the 1840s, Smedes spoke at prayers of a poor family sadly in need of a new roof. He said that anyone wishing to help could volunteer to make such sacrifices as doing without butter during Lent and that he would keep account of the total savings. The family got the roof.[71]

Aldert Smedes was called "the chief missionary of the church in North Carolina" because St. Mary's alumnae became church workers and missionaries all over the South, and some served in foreign fields. In 1890 the bishop of Northern Texas wrote to Bennett Smedes for details about his father's methods of teaching. "I find," he wrote, "all over my diocese the beginnings of Sunday Schools and churches, the work of St. Mary's women; and I am determined to establish a church school for girls as the best means of building up my diocese."[72]

Aldert Smedes set his pupils an example. From his arrival in Raleigh he was active in diocesan affairs. Smedes was received cordially from the start by his fellow Episcopal clergymen of whom there were about 30 in the diocese in 1842.[73] His patron, Bishop Ives, was delighted with his protégé and with the school. To the 1844 convention he said of St. Mary's:

Its prosperity and promised benefits to the Church, while they call for our prayers and encouragement, go far to show us God's ways are best. That while we were mourning over the failure of the Episcopal School He designed in the failure a greater good to the Diocese.[74]

Apparently the bishop and Mrs. Ives made their headquarters at St. Mary's during the early years of the school. In February, 1842, the bishop wrote to a friend in Mobile to tell her of the proposed "first-rate" school for girls to be opened soon in Raleigh by the "highly accomplished Mr. and Mrs. Smedes," adding, "Mrs. Ives and myself are to live in one of the wings of the school buildings."[75] His close association with the school confirms the fact. Bishop Ives recorded for May 29, 1842, "Preached to an interesting assemblage of young ladies, at St. Mary's School, Ravenscroft Grove, Raleigh."[76] From 1844 the bishop of North Carolina was listed in the school brochures and in the *Journal* of the diocesan convention as "Visitor" to St. Mary's. In that same year, Smedes in his report to the convention expressed his "grateful sense of the benefit" his school derived from the services with which it was favored by the bishop during the winter session.[77] Writing in 1849 to a former student, Sarah Smedes listed the 16 girls confirmed and continued, "The Bishop gave us a delightful sermon. . . . He says he always does feel a confirmation service at St. Mary's to be peculiarly solemn and impressive. . . ."[78]

Tangible evidence of the high regard in which Aldert Smedes held Ives is the confirmation painting in the St. Mary's parlor. The following description appeared in the *Raleigh Register* of May 2, 1845:

"How fine,
The power to fix the hue of beauty's cheek.
The sparkling of the diamond eye—the look
That speaks without a tongue, yet speaks the soul
Quicker than tongues e'er uttered?"

The above statement of the Poet involuntarily occurred to us as we gazed with unmixed admiration at the magnificent Painting just finished by Mr. James Hart, and elegantly framed, representing Bishop Ives in the act of administering the rite of Confirmation. The painting, with the frame, is 6 1/2 feet wide, and 9 1/2 feet high. It contains the Bishop, and four female figures the size of life. The likeness of the Bishop is most striking; the attitude admirable and expressive; the kneeling figures graceful and exquisitely proportioned; and the whole calculated to preserve a vivid recollection of our beloved Diocesan in the performance of one of his most interesting duties. This splendid Painting is intended, we learn, to grace the spacious Hall at St. Mary's School—a room well calculated to develop and set off all its beauties and excellencies. It was painted expressly for the esteemed Rector, Mr. Smedes, who desiring in some way to express and perpetuate a sense of his own and the Church's obligation to the Bishop for his constant and unremitted care of this valuable institution, happily thought of this mode.

It is impossible to be certain of the identity of the four St. Mary's students in the confirmation painting because at least five students were named by their schoolmates of 1845 as models for Hart. The only known account written by one of the models is that of Madeleine (Mittie) Saunders, who was a close friend of Claudia Wingate, a relative of the artist. One afternoon as the two girls walked in the grove, Hart rode by on horseback and stopped to chat. Soon afterward, Mittie and Claudia were summoned to the artist's studio near the Capitol. In 1906 Mittie, by then the widow of William J. L'Engle, told the story in the St. Mary's alumnae magazine. She wrote:

Mr. Hart told us that the central figure was to be a fancy sketch, two other figures Dr. Smedes was to choose, but he had been offered by him to select any girl he desired from the school-girls, and he had chosen me.

I was placed in the picture kneeling next on the right of the middle or fancy figure. I do not remember the dress, but I do remember my hair done up in a funny little knot at the back of my head. . . . I simply wore it that way for convenience . . . for no day was ever long enough to accomplish all that I desired to do.[79]

Madeleine Saunders, Sarah Crawford, Eugenia Hinton, Laura Washington, and Lucy Raegon were identified by their schoolmates as being in the confirmation painting. One classmate positively identified the girl shown in profile as Lucy Raegon, instead of an imaginary figure. Another said Eugenia Hinton was the girl of the long curls. Both Sarah Crawford and Laura Washington were identified as receiving the laying on of hands.[80] Perhaps there were many young models; perhaps the artist painted more than one composite.

American Episcopalians were already in disagreement over the issue of evangelicalism when the Oxford Movement of the 1840s intensified their differences. Although the leaders of the Diocese of North Carolina, Smedes among them, were "old fashioned High Churchmen,"[81] they were shocked when Bishop Ives turned his mission school and model farm at Valle Crucis into "a feeble . . . imitation of monastic institutions of the Church of Rome."[82] After several years of controversy, the bishop was granted a leave of absence. On Christmas Day, 1852, before the pope in Rome Ives formally embraced Roman Catholicism. A few North Carolina Episcopalians accepted at face value Ives's statement that his prolonged doubts "had grown into clear and settled *convictions*";[83] he had changed those convictions once before, having begun life as a Presbyterian. Most of his former flock, however, chose to believe that his "unhappy fall" was the result of a mental derangement.[84] Even the St. Mary's students were aware that the bishop's apostasy, as it was always referred to, placed a strain upon the Smedes family. One pupil wrote home wondering what Smedes would do since he had "a very handsome painting" of Ives and a son who might find that he had been "named for a Romish saint."[85] Ives wrote to Smedes from Rome, "Whatever you may think of me, I still love you and yours with a love which at the Mass of each early dawn agonizes for your salvation."[86] Episcopalians tried to forget the "unfortunate" Ives affair, but Roman Catholics honored Levi Silliman Ives as an outstanding lay leader in the field of Catholic charities.[87]

The Diocese of North Carolina returned to normality with the election of Thomas H. Atkinson, D.D., as its third bishop. Bishop Atkinson arrived in Raleigh in November, 1853, and on the evening of his first Sunday in his new diocese preached at St. Mary's, where he confirmed 12.[88] Atkinson was ever a staunch friend and supporter of the school and a great admirer of Smedes. They worked closely together because the rector of St. Mary's was reelected annually to the standing committee of the diocesan convention. Smedes served some 30 years altogether on that committee that conducted the business of the diocese between conventions. Smedes possessed such a keen sense of professional propriety that he refused to officiate at the wedding of any former pupil, no matter how dear she was to him and Sarah, unless she happened to "be a lamb without a shepherd."[89]

The founder of St. Mary's envisioned yet another service to his church when he opened Trinity, a high school for boys in July, 1847. That venture was under the patronage of Ives but was financed entirely by Smedes, who bought a large house on beautiful high ground about eight miles west of Raleigh.

Boys could be "fitted for entrance into any class in college" or "carried through an entire collegiate course." The dates of the sessions were coordinated with those at St. Mary's, and a discount was offered to parents who placed students in both schools.[90] Despite the efforts of the first rector, the Reverend Fordyce Hubbard who had taught at Round Hill, and of others, the school closed after about five years. Smedes had kept it open at a loss because he "could not bear to give up this last hope of a church school for boys in North Carolina.[91]

Aldert Smedes had been a resident of his adopted state for only 12 years when, at the 1854 commencement, the University of North Carolina conferred upon him the honorary degree of doctor of divinity in recognition of his contributions as educator and churchman. From time to time, Smedes was mentioned as a possible bishop. However, the response usually was, "He already has two or three missionary dioceses since St. Mary's girls come from the whole South—from Virginia to Texas." [92]

Truly, the "St. Mary's School Hymn," although written many years after the death of Aldert Smedes, reflects the spirit of the founder of the school:

> We build our School on Thee, O Lord;
> To Thee we bring our common need:
> The loving heart, the helpful word,
> The tender thought, the kindly deed.
>
> We work together in Thy sight,
> We live together in Thy love;
> Guide Thou our falt'ring steps aright,
> And lift our thoughts to heaven above.
>
> Hold Thou each hand to keep it just,
> Touch Thou our lips and make them pure;
> If thou are with us, Lord, we must
> Be faithful friends and comrades sure.
>
> We change, but Thou art still the same,
> The same Good Master, Teacher, Friend;
> We change; but Lord, we bear Thy Name,
> To journey with it to the end. AMEN. [93]

## "A GREAT AND ENTIRE FAMILY"

The common life at St. Mary's was as much like that of a happy family as was possible in so large a household. By December, 1844, there were 46 boarders at the school; by July, 1846, enrollment had climbed to 71 boarders and 40 day scholars. Soon there was nearly always a full house of about 80 boarders, and during a few sessions the school was reported by students in their letters to parents as being "full to overflowing" with almost 90 beds occupied. [94] There were usually 40 or more day students.

In 1849 seven pupils from South Carolina were enrolled, and Sarah Smedes wrote to a former student, "I am glad to have an opening in that State, as they have not there a Church School." [95] By the next decade there were students from Texas, Mississippi, Louisiana, Arkansas, Florida, and Virginia, as well as an occasional student from "more northern latitudes." [96] The enrollment remained fairly constant until the war years, when St. Mary's received girls from occupied areas until not another cot could be crowded in.

The school was customarily the recipient of extravagant praise in the local press. The *Raleigh Register* in 1846 said of the school, "Its superior cannot be found in the United States."[97] A Mississippi visitor to St. Mary's, upon returning home, wrote in 1851 to the *Vicksburg Sentinel* about the school "in the hope that more from our State may participate in its benefits."[98] Such praise was not quite universal. At least one dissatisfied parent of the 1850s found the situation at St. Mary's "rather commonplace" and quite lacking in "finish & polish."[99]

Nonetheless, happiness seems to have pervaded St. Mary's in those early years. A student of 1854 reported, "There are ninty [*sic*] odd of the happiest young ladies I ever saw, & if I may judge from appearances, they are mostly of the first class. . . . St. Mary's cannot be surpassed by any in America, and it has more intelligent girls."[100]

It was Aldert Smedes's personality that made St. Mary's work. Somehow, each year he managed to meld the school into a real family. Robert Treat Paine, Edenton lawyer and shipper (and later, United States congressman), was in Raleigh for the legislative sessions, 1844–1846. He was often invited by Smedes to Sunday dinner at the school and to visit his young student sister. He wrote to his wife:

Mr. and Mrs. Smedes are both young . . . and dedicated to the care, improvement, and happiness of their students. . . . The more I see of Mr. Smedes and his school, the more I am pleased with both. . . . I find that the girls are kept under great restraint, and what is admirable not one of them seems to know it. It is in fact a great and entire family & the girls are managed exactly as they should be by kind yet careful and anxious parents. . . . I was perfectly delighted with the joyous freedom with which the girls converse with each other and with their teachers. Mr. Smedes would when the conversation became too loud, give a rap on the table & say young ladies some of you are interrupting the conversation of your neighbors. The conversation would then be lowered to a proper tone, but deprived of none of its cheerfulness.[101]

Another visitor to the school observed that Aldert Smedes must have been the happiest of men,[102] possessed as he was of the respect of his peers, the adoration of most of his pupils, the devotion of his wife, and enough money to carry out his plans.

Life within the St. Mary's family was strictly regimented. From the rising bell—a large handbell rung by a servant who ran up and down the halls at 5:30—until evening prayers at 9:00, the day was filled. Roll call and morning prayers in the parlor came at 6:30. After breakfast came "walking hour" followed by an hour of study; those were reversed during the dark winter months. Daily chapel services were held at 9:15. Immediately thereafter each student wrote "the dreaded abstract" if a Bible lecture had been given. On other days this time was devoted "to exercises in vocal music." The rest of the morning was taken up with classes and individual music practice.

Dinner was served at 1:30. Recitations were heard from 3:00 to 5:00, followed by study or music practice until tea at 6:15. Next came an hour of group recreation, or in spring and summer another walking hour, after which the student was free until 9:00.

As the roll was called at evening prayers, intense soul searching was the custom. The school rules stated:

. . . each young lady reports herself for the day. If she has faithfully performed her duties during the day, not failing in a single particular, through wilful neglect or carelessness, she takes, as her mark 5. For every failure this number is diminished, till, if it disappears entirely, a cross is substituted for it, which is the severest penalty known to our Statute Book.

A monthly report will be made to each Parent or Guardian of the standing of his daughter or ward.[103]

In 1846 a chagrined student wrote, "My darling Pa: Oh! I lost my mark the other day for not getting down in time in the morning. . . . All of the girls in our dormitory were too late, but it was on account of there being some mistake about carrying water up. It was right hard that we had to lose our marks for no fault of ours."[104] Another tried to convince her father that only two failures in 36 days indicated good behavior, especially since one of them was for writing letters in study hall after all her lessons were done. The other failure was for a more serious matter—laughing in chapel. She wrote that although only one person witnessed her merriment, she "took four because I knew I ought not to laugh in church."[105]

The daily exercise requirement was a discipline that many parents would not have required of their daughters, but the school *Manual* made the daily exercise an imperative:

In the pure and invigorating air of these ample grounds, and in the innocent amusements of this large family of which you have become a sister, you will find such exercise and recreation as will secure the health and vigor of your body. These you must remember are the gifts of God which it is your duty to preserve and to improve. . . . In the glorious open air, you must walk and *leap* and run!, and when the weather will not permit out-of-door exercise, you must avail yourself of the resources of our large house, for that relaxation of mind, and lively action of body, which are essential to your health and happiness.

It is a duty, as imperative as any in the school; and failure in it will be visited with displeasure and censure.[106]

About five turns around the grove were considered sufficient for the morning exercise. Each girl kept her "walking shawl" on a handy peg in the basement hall of the main house. The paths were kept leveled, but even so, a student of 1847 wrote home asking if anyone had time to knit her some stockings, complaining, "I have to walk so much I would wear out iron if I had it."[107]

On many a sunny afternoon the exercise consisted of games played in "the circle," as the circular driveway was called even then. Hoop rolling was the rage in the late fifties. At first the girls rolled barrel hoops; then Smedes brought iron hoops from New York.[108] Almost every night during recreation hour there was dancing. Older students played the piano for the dancing in a large room on the first floor of West Rock. Sooner or later, nearly every girl took lessons from one of the dancing masters in town who taught at the school. Smedes sometimes joined in the play during recreation hour at night.

The importance of physical exercise for women was becoming more generally accepted during the forties and fifties because of a widely held belief that the health of American females was declining to the point that they would soon become "unfit to bear the succeeding generation."[109]

The school was, as the rector wrote in his 1843 circular for prospective patrons, "remarkably favored in the health of its pupils." Raleigh was considered an excellent location because of its elevation. A few girls from the East arrived each year with malaria and dutifully took quinine. Sometimes outbreaks of more serious illnesses occurred. A smallpox scare in the spring of 1846 caused some parents to request that their daughters be vaccinated, but apparently there were no cases in the school.[110] Periodically there were epidemics of scarlet fever in the state. The resumption of classes after Christmas in 1854 was delayed for a week because of a case of scarlet fever among the students who had remained at the school over the holiday.[111] There were the expected sieges of measles and chicken pox. One of the teachers presided over the "sick-room," a large and airy room near the Smedes apartment. Sarah Smedes also kept a close watch and wrote detailed letters to reassure the parents of the ill.

It was inevitable that over the years a few girls would die while in attendance at St. Mary's. A moving description of the funeral of Eleanor Williams is recorded in the diary of William Hooper Haigh. Eleanor, one of that first group of 1842 students, lived with the George Badgers of Raleigh. She died after an illness of only two days. Haigh sat all night with Eleanor's young "lover" beside her bier. On April 1, 1844, he wrote:

the young ladies and teachers from the seminary followed in the procession, with their badges of mourning. The scene in the Church was impressive, the music plaintive and solemn; Being one of the pall bearers at the funeral of her I loved as a sister, was a painful, melancholy duty. . . . she was full of life and animation . . . her face lit up with smiles . . . a bright and merry heart. . . .[112]

Death was less a stranger to the young in those days than now. Private correspondence was filled with the news of illnesses and deaths, both among family and slaves, and with the haunting fear of epidemics. Even young girls wore mourning for close relatives. In 1854 a student wrote home, "There is quite a number of girls in black this session."[113]

Overall, however, the students were healthy. Emphasis upon fitness and exercise in the fresh air made for ravenous appetites. The kitchen, which had served also as the kitchen for the Episcopal School, was a separate brick building with brick floors behind the main house. Students, teachers, and the Smedes family ate together at long tables. The published rules of the school made it plain that pupils were "required to be punctual at their meals, and must not leave the table without permission." French students ate at "the French table" headed by Madame Clement. Because not one word of English could be uttered at that table, many a beginner in the language might have gone hungry had not Smedes, who often ate there, kept a watchful eye upon the younger ones.[114] Mrs. Smedes also found time to give special attentions, and sometimes she would arrange a treat to celebrate a birthday.[115]

Naturally, some students complained about the food at the school; however, it seems during the antebellum years to have been surprisingly good. Letters home contained such reports as: "Mrs. Smedes keeps an excellent table. I never sit down to better at home unless we have company; girls who have been to other schools say it is the best food they have had; we have light bread every meal; we have corncakes, bread, coffee, tea, and water during regular session for breakfast, and batter cakes during vacation."[116] Madame Clement's close supervision of the vegetable gardens produced ample supplies. Fresh fruits were abundant in season but were not served at other times. Camilla Cash of Surry County wrote that she enjoyed the daily peach pies. Her sister, however, felt that *daily* was rather too often to have her "attention called to squash."[117] The meat served at St. Mary's was likely to be either pork or poultry. Smedes bought bacon and lard in quantity and hams by the hundred from the Cameron plantations. He was not above a bit of sharp bargaining with the judge over whether the current price of hams should be 8 1/2 or 9 cents a pound.[118] Sometimes fresh fish arrived from Norfolk. The school's cows pastured behind the buildings provided milk.

Most day scholars had their lunch baskets delivered by the young sons of their family cooks. One girl refused to drink the well water at the school although it was considered to be good, so a second youth carried a pitcher of ice water from her home. Sometimes a third little boy brought a watermelon as a special treat for the day scholars' "spread" in their room on the lower floor of the main building.[119]

The St. Mary's family during the early years always included a Smedes baby or two. There were six boys before the first girl was born in 1853. Until just before they began to think of St. Mary's girls as more than sisters, the Smedes boys attended classes at St. Mary's or at Lovejoy's, an excellent academy for boys established in Raleigh the same year that St. Mary's opened. Each son was packed off to boarding school at a rather early age, a sacrifice for Sarah Smedes. She wrote to her son Edward, "Ben always said he was sent away too soon. If we had been living a more private life I would not have parted with Lyell and Ben so young."[120]

Bennett was a handsome boy with "rosy cheeks, curly hair and blue eyes." He sat next to his father at the French table and was extremely shy with the girls.[121] After he went to boarding school, he was at home only on one Sunday a month, except for an unauthorized visit in the dead of one night when his rowdy classmates at Trinity School forced him to ride into town and steal some chickens from the St. Mary's coops.[122]

Lyell was at the University of North Carolina by 1852 and "thought himself quite a gentleman"; yet "he deigned to play hide and seek or any game the girls may propose" when he was back at St. Mary's for Christmas.[123] The other Smedes sons were Edward Sanford, born in 1841, Ives (named after Bishop Ives and usually called "Bish"), born in 1843, Abraham Kiersted, born in 1845, and George Mancius, born in 1850.[124]

At last, on June 27, 1853, Aldert Smedes had a daughter of his own. She was named Eliza Sebor for his mother and was called Bessie. Two more daughters were born to Sarah and Aldert—Annie Beach in 1855 and Sarah Lyell in 1859.

The early teachers understood their position as surrogate parents within the school, the surrogate family. There was general agreement by the mid-nineteenth century that a prime objective of education was character development, but there was disagreement among educators over the nature of the relationship between the pupil and the teacher. At St. Mary's no such confusion existed. From the beginning, the institution was built upon the absolute commitment of dedicated teachers.

During the Smedes era, nearly all teachers lived in the dormitories in order "to promote the cheerfulness and social improvement of the family." They provided daily opportunities for their young charges to choose the better way. Indeed, the strict dormitory rules eliminated undue temptation. The rector's exhortation in the 1857 edition of the school *Manual* read:

Perfect silence must be observed in the Dormitory from the time of entering in at night, until the prayer bell rings in the morning. The same order is observed on Sunday after dinner.

No romping, running, dancing or noise of any description can be allowed at any time in the Dormitories.

Every young lady *before* leaving the dormitory in the morning must have her bed *properly* made, and everything in her alcove in perfect order.

On Saturday every young lady is expected to employ at least two hours at her needle, under the care of her teacher.

No works of fiction are to be read, excepting on Saturday, after the *duties* of the day are over, and then, only those that are approved of.

The ladies of the faculty saw to it that the daily life at the school provided constant training for the accepted role of women in antebellum society. The *Manual* read:

As a part of your discipline of body and mind you will be called upon to correct what is amiss, and to study what is graceful in gait, posture, bearing, and manners. . . .

To a woman soft voice, and gentleness, and grace of manners are especially becoming. Indeed, without these, she has nothing of her sex externally, but the dress; and it is much feared, that within, there is an equally lamentable deficiency of feminine qualities.

Despite those stringent rules (which were not a great deal stricter than those at the contemporary colleges for women), the St. Mary's girls sent home such reports as: "I am well and happy, yes happy as I can be away from *my dear Ma*," or, "I long to finish at St. Mary's and be at home, but then I would never see Mrs. Blood [a music teacher] again. I think she is the dearest, lovliest creature . . . so patient and mild and gentle," or "Mamma please send me a nice little pound cake and ice it for my darling teacher." [125] Some friendships between teacher and pupil were lasting, and it was not unusual for teachers to visit the homes of students and former students as cherished family friends.

The common life of the school family was very much a shared life in the dormitories. The only major remodeling done by Duncan Cameron to turn the Episcopal School buildings into a school for girls was in the dormitories. Small dressing rooms called "alcoves" were built in West Rock, the top floor of the main building, and on the second floor of East Rock. The long dormitories were divided into five alcoves on each side with a half window in each, except for the choice corner alcoves with a full window each. The spaces were about 8 feet by 8 feet; the partitions stopped several feet short of the ceiling. An alcove was usually shared by two girls. On one side of the cubicle was a closet, on the other a low washstand shelf with holes cut for two bowls and two pitchers. Those glazed pottery utensils, made from the dark red native clay of Wake County and considered quite unattractive by the students, were the bathing facilities. Each night servants filled two large tubs which stood on low stools in the dormitories. The girls filled their pitchers from the tubs and took the water to the alcoves to be ready for their morning ablutions. Sometimes on a dark, winter morning there would be a thin skim of ice over the filled bowls. Hot water was available only from the kitchen, where a huge caldron of water hung over a wood fire.[126]

It was fun to "alcove" with a good friend and to arrange the little place with a mirror and family daguerreotypes on the wall, a scrap of carpeting from home on the floor, and a plant on the window sill. White or blue curtains served as doors for the alcoves. They were tied back each morning before the students left for prayers so that the dormitory teacher could inspect for the required "perfect order."[127]

In the open floor space in each dormitory stood plain, wooden bedsteads, one on either side of the entrance to an alcove. Innocent of springs, each was equipped only with a mattress and a pillow. Students were required to bring with them homespun linens and heavy quilts. No one expected the woodburning stove in the middle of the dormitory to keep the place comfortable, and sometimes on the bitterest of nights it was permissible to push two beds together for warmth.[128] On at least one chilly night, a chimney caught fire and everyone "came tumbling out in nightclothes and barefoot, some praying."[129] Each girl kept her trunk at the foot of her bed; it was fashionable to decorate one's trunk. The dormitory teacher usually lived in a small, cozy room, but some had only enlarged alcoves.[130]

Students from distant states sometimes lived two or three years at St. Mary's without going home, spending their vacations at the school. The extra charge was $2 or $3 a week. The school calendar fluctuated over the years, but usually there were two five-month sessions beginning in July and January with June and December as vacation months. Those spending their vacation months at school were given reading, music, and French assignments under faculty supervision, and their social activities were as closely regulated as during the session. Special festivities were planned for those staying over Christmas.

The campus family, in fact, enjoyed frequent parties. Every holiday was celebrated with a frolic planned by teachers and students and anticipated for days. Some years Washington's birthday was celebrated with "a fancy ball." The holiday from classes was spent in the contriving of costumes, the excitement scarcely diminished by the fact that no boys were invited. Other years, charades and tableaux provided entertainment on the February holiday. "Making April Fools of one another" was considered great sport. Even the servants joined in the jokes; one year they served cotton-filled fritters for breakfast.[131] Easter Monday was a gala holiday with an outing or dance planned. Mary Jane Jarratt described the "rare times" on Easter Monday, 1854, to her mother:

Some of the girls dressed as boys, some as fine ladies and some in their bloomers and we had a rare dance and frolick. Ma I know you think we are a miserably wild set and you are not much mistaken some of the girls are remarkably good sedate young ladies but the generality of us are tolerably wild.

(Actually, the wildest escapade reported by Mary Jane was skipping evening prayers in order to remove the slats from a classmate's bed. That she related to her brother, not her mother.)[132]

Each year Smedes "showed his magic lantern," and scenes from the Holy Land and Europe seemed to materialize in the St. Mary's parlor. The day scholars stayed for tea and the show, and sometimes "a great many ladies and gentlemen from town" attended. There was a St. Mary's May Queen at least as early as 1856. The coronation was "quite a pretty scene" witnessed by many. After an elegant supper and "all sorts of nice cake and ice cream," the girls danced in West Rock until 9:00.[133]

The really "royal day" was July 4. The Independence Day celebration of 1846 was described in detail in a letter written by Kate DeRosset of Wilmington to her father. The rising bell rang a full two hours later than usual. After a leisurely breakfast came a solemn morning service where "everything that could be was chanted." Soon thereafter the cavalry "came up and rode around the circle firing three salutes, and went off amid the shouts and cheers of the girls." A band arrived about noon and played for dancing (without boys, of course) in West Rock until suppertime. Supper was a picnic just at sunset. The July 4 picnic was always the most memorable meal of the year—platters of roasted fowl, fried chicken, bowls of succotash, and "the delight in watching for the big wagon which came laden with . . . ice cream freezers, each full to the brim," a day scholar of 1842 recalled. As darkness fell, "a beautifully lighted" service was held in the chapel in East Rock.[134]

The young ladies at St. Mary's were not quite so sheltered as the published rules of the school implied. "Visiting Saturday" was "a great day" each month. Nearly everyone had a relative or a friend of her mother in town, or a special friend among the day scholars with whom she could spend Saturday afternoon. Invitations had to be specific and approved by Smedes, and under no circumstances was the student to stay out after sundown. So popular were his young charges that in June, 1843, Aldert Smedes, in order to make the serious purpose of his new school clearly understood, placed the following announcement in the *Raleigh Register*:

The Rector of St. Mary's School, respectfully informs his friends, that it is against the rules of his Institution, for his pupils to accept invitations for the Evening during the Session; or, to accept invitations for the day, except on the first Saturday of each month.[135]

Always there were at the school a number of the daughters of legislators and other state officials, and they were permitted to attend special functions under parental supervision. Parents of the students often stopped at the elegant Yarborough House on Fayetteville Street after its 1852 opening.

Fortunate indeed was the girl who had a brother at the University of North Carolina or a relative living in Chapel Hill who would extend holiday invitations. In his memoirs, Kemp Plummer Battle remarked that his mother's home was always open to their young relatives and that "the high reputation of students [at the university] for gallantry attracted young ladies." The "fun and frivolity" consisted of group activities such as singing ballads and spirituals around the piano in the parlor or enjoying lemonade parties on the porch.[136]

A Chapel Hill student of 1844 wrote his sister that she was "to spur up" the girls he knew at St. Mary's to write to him. He had time to answer because his sophomore class of 54 was "very large . . . so each is taken up to recite quite seldom and tis glorious."[137] Letters between Chapel Hill and Raleigh were carried on a heavy stagecoach drawn by four horses. The round trip was made three times weekly unless the roads were impassable. After Valentine's Day in 1853, a St. Mary's student wrote her brother, "There has been quite a number of Valentines flying this year."[138]

Some of the youngest St. Mary's girls had their doubts about Chapel Hill. One wrote in 1858 to her mother:

The Chapel Hillians are the students at a college called Chapel Hill. They are a very wild set, and we are very much afraid of them, for when they get intoxicated we don't know what they might do.[139]

Raleigh swains made the most of their infrequent opportunities to catch a glimpse of the St. Mary's belles. In December, 1855, a cousin of the Camerons noted from his vantage point at the Cameron home across the street from the campus:

St. Mary's School has broken and detracts very much from the attractiveness of this part of the city; besides leaving some poor fellows very sorrowful from being parted from an occasional sight of their sweethearts.[140]

Sometimes the more boisterous young fellows took matters into their own hands. In October, 1854, a student reported to her mother:

Yesterday morning a passel of town boys dressed in masquerade and as soldiers rode round the circle on old mules blowing trumpets and keeping an awful noise. They stopped in front of the building and took a good look at the girls.[141]

Most of the unofficial encounters must have been mere glimpses. St. Mary's girls did not attend church in town except on the few Sundays a year when Smedes preached at Christ Church. A teacher always accompanied the pupils on shopping trips. On July 4, 1844, according to a student's letter to her mother, "The gentlemen of Raleigh invited the young ladies of St. Mary's to a dance." She added, "But of course we did not go."[142] *Ladies*, said Smedes, were never seen at public dances. Dating nights had not yet been invented. A young suitor could call only after Smedes had received from the girl's father permission for a closely chaperoned visit. There were ways, as there have always been ways, to bend the strict rules. Aldert Smedes said that he had observed over the years that whenever a bona fide brother went to see his sister at St. Mary's, he soon began to claim cousinship with one or more of her friends because male relatives were allowed to call. Most of the young ladies managed to become engaged before they were finished at St. Mary's or soon thereafter. Many married Raleigh men and stayed in the city to contribute much to its cultural and religious life.

The most exciting of all occasions for the St. Mary's girls were the music evenings or "soirees" when the place swarmed with young men. There were several of those faculty and student recitals each year. On an appointed evening, carriages swept into the circle to discharge "ladies dressed in silks and satins . . . their heads loaded with flowers," as one young pupil described them.[143] Their escorts led the ladies up to the parlor declared by a Raleigh editor to be "one of the most notable rooms in the State . . . scene of many rare and refined social and intellectual entertainments. . . ."[144]

William Hooper Haigh, who had escorted a St. Mary's day scholar, wrote in his diary after the affair of September 6, 1844:

After making our debut there—bowing here and there to teachers (because *etiquette* requires it)—then to pupils—the grand promenade was commenced. Soon however Blessner gave his musical signal. . . . the first piece was *magnificent*, capable of thrilling even the most *souless*. . . . It was a composition of Blessner's dedicated to Misses Borden and Washington, who performed it as a duet on the piano—accompanied by Mrs. Blessner & Miss Hundley on the harp & Blessner on the violin.

After a number of vocal solos and "Vive la Compagnie" sung by everyone as a finale, there was more time for visiting and refreshments. Hooper complained, "These soirees gratify the head & heart—but do not *satisfy* the stomach."[145]

The soiree was the one occasion when emphasis upon dress was not frowned upon at St. Mary's. The announced purpose of these evenings was that "the pupils may have opportunity of seeing their friends, and acquiring ease of manner in society. . . ."

Simplicity in dress was a matter of principle at St. Mary's and was so stated by Smedes in his advertisements, a signal to all that his was not a fashionable finishing school.

Extravagance in dress is contrary to the principles and practice of the School, and Parents will confer a favor, by providing their children, only with the plainest attire. Jewels and Lace are forbidden. The dress of the Pupils in Winter, for Sundays and special occasions must be a *mouslin de Lain* or *Merino*, of a dark-blue color; the Bonnets, of Straw, trimmed with dark-blue ribbon. For their ordinary apparel, they may wear dresses of *Calico, Gingham,* or such other available material, as their wardrobes well furnish.[146]

The summer uniform for all public appearances was a light blue or white dress trimmed with pale blue ribbons. Most of the girls seem not to have resented the uniforms. They agreed with the student who wrote home in 1845, "I wish you could see all the girls dressed in our blues. I think it looks beautiful."[147] It is no wonder that Aldert Smedes beamed with pride whenever he walked the student body to the Capitol and back. If a boarding student made the mistake of appearing in public in her calico, she was called into the rector's study to make her explanation. Uniforms—uniform more in hue than in cut—were worn until the exigencies of war ended the custom in the sixties. The uniform did discourage rivalry and snobbery; that was one of its purposes.

The youngest pupils, who sometimes were 12 or younger, asked their mothers for permission to tuck up their hair and to let the tucks out of their dresses "because all the girls wear long dresses here." Some girls employed local dressmakers. Sarah Smedes supervised every detail of their wardrobes for any number of motherless girls over the years, keeping careful records of their accounts with seamstresses. Many mothers forwarded finished garments; others sent materials or requested that fashionable materials and patterns be sent from Raleigh. More often, the wardrobe was a cooperative project, the garments being completed by the pupil during the Saturday morning sewing sessions. Dormitory teachers supervised the required sewing and mending sessions every Saturday, except on visiting Saturdays.

Teachers supervised shopping trips to Tucker's, McKimmon's, or Stith's dry goods establishments and allowed no bills except with parental consent. Many of the girls made the comfortable high-necked, long-sleeved dark calicoes that they wore to class except in the hottest weather. Summer school dresses were of gingham, and summer uniforms for public appearances were of muslin, lawn, or swiss with appropriate ribbons. Aprons, worn to protect school dresses, were made by the girls from their old ginghams and calicoes.[148]

The older girls developed a great interest in fashion as they prepared to enter the real world. Letters home began to be peppered with requests for "a mantilla cape to wear to Chapel" or for "light blue kid gloves" or even for earrings. From 1830 until 1868 the bell-shaped, or hoop, skirt dominated the American fashion scene; the skirt of an elegant ball gown sometimes measured 10 yards in circumference. "No sign," Agnes Brooks Young, fashion historian, wrote, "of the feminist movement is visible" in women's garments of the period. Even the construction of the sleeve restricted movement, the shoulder line "being sloped more and more until women achieved the slightly wilted appearance so much in keeping with the fashionable pose of anemic helplessness and so out of keeping with the dynamic and pioneering spirit which underlay Victorian mannerisms."[149]

Although the St. Mary's girls usually did not wear the various devices contrived to hold out the voluminous skirts, they did wear petticoats to make their uniforms billow properly. In the warm first week of April, 1845, a student wrote to her aunt that although they were still in their merinos, "scarcely a girl in school would leave off one of her petticoats for the sake of comfort" on Sunday.[150] The older girls wore stays to achieve the tiny waistlines in fashion.

St. Mary's girls wore their bonnets abroad but not to the chapel services on campus. Their plain straw bonnets, known as Gipsy hats, were tied under the chin with wide blue ribbons. The silk lining of a bonnet and the ruffle, or skirt, at the back could not be noticeably fancy. A student of 1847 from New York decided to sacrifice "the very beautiful blue satin bonnet" sent by her mother, since it was against the rules to wear it, for half price ($4) to a girl who was finishing that spring.[151] The fashionable shoe of the period was the gaiter, a soft shoe of morocco with a cloth top. Shoes were known as gaiters or half-gaiters, depending upon how high the cloth portion laced; gaiters were more popular at St. Mary's. (One student of the fifties wrote home for shoes because she had lost hers as she helped push the omnibus out of a mudhole en route to St. Mary's from the train depot.)[152] Stockings were of black cotton. In winter requests were likely to be, "Send me my flannel boddies and a pair of draws," and in summer, "Please send me a loose callico gown. I kneed it very much."[153]

Laundry presented problems. Until the early 1900s, black laundresses from town picked up and returned the laundry of their customers, and each student's account was kept with the school, the washerwoman being paid in cash by the school. At least one St. Mary's student of the 1840s solved the laundry problem by taking her slave to school. Sarah Anne McClennehan of Pittsboro took Carrie to St. Mary's with her because the slave, who threw spoonfuls of pepper into every pot on the stove, had proved unteachable as a cook. Carrie was allowed to live in the servants' quarters; she "did for" her young mistress and performed assigned chores around the place.[154]

The common life of prayer, study, and play nurtured deep and lasting friendships among Smedes's "family of sisters" living in the grove. In summer there were nightly gatherings at the well back of the main building. On winter nights and during recess on cold days, students and teachers huddled around the two large brick kilns on the lower floor of the main building from which heat was piped throughout that building. There was the occasional pleasure of sharing with friends a box of "eatings" from home. Such boxes were discouraged and certainly never allowed in the dormitories, but it was possible to visit one's goody box from home where it was stored in the pantry.

It was the joy of joys to share one's treats with an admired upperclassman. Reminiscing in 1906 about her schooldays at St. Mary's, 1853–1858, Lucy Catharine Moore Capehart wrote:

> I know not if it is the custom now for school girls to have sweethearts among their own sex, but it was in those days; such devotion you cannot imagine. . . . Every delicacy possessed was reserved for the adored one; she was waited upon as we by our slaves; no exertion was too great in her behalf. I remember one case where the tables were turned by some tale-bearer who overheard slighting remarks made by the loved one. Then the once beautiful one's every perfection was changed to imperfection. . . . My sweetheart was Ellen Brent Pearson; to get a smile or glance from her . . . made me supremely happy. She was at the time engaged to her future husband, later Governor Fowle, who was permitted by Dr. Smedes to visit her occasionally.[155]

As each school year drew to a close, the friendship albums began to circulate. Verses, tender sentiments, and sometimes delicate drawings penned in them were to be treasured for generations. Eleanor Williams wrote in Sarah Covington's 1844 album:

> The violet droops its soft and bashful brow
> But from its heart, sweet incense fills the air.
> So rich within so pure without art thou,
> With modest mien and soul of virtue rare.

A popular offering was:

> May the roses of Happiness
> Ever bloom in the garden of your Destiny.

The teachers were likely to write personal messages or to copy long religious poems. Professor Blessner penned verses in French in an ornate script. A student of 1847 wrote to her friend who had finished at St. Mary's:

> the breaking up of so many very happy associations . . . separation, and forever from those with whom during long years, we have mingled in working, and in play, sharing equally our joys & our griefs. These . . . will make us sigh so tenderly that we must for liberty give up these.[156]

After many tearful embraces, the "finished" student went home, escorted by a father or brother. If they traveled "on the cars," the young lady heeded the advice given in *Miss Leslie's Behaviour Book* and rode with her back to the engine so as to "be less incommoded with flying sparks."[157] If the railroad did not serve her community, she left St. Mary's by the public stage or more stylishly ensconced in her family's rockaway. In most cases, she left forever a part of her heart at St. Mary's, and she forever thought of herself as "a St. Mary's girl."

CHAPTER THREE

# "A SAFE REFUGE"

Life was good at St. Mary's during the prosperous fifties, as it was throughout the state. With the reputation of his school and his own respected place in the community firmly established, Smedes had every reason to look forward to the sixties with confidence. And his young ladies expected life to continue as happily as ever. There were, however, disturbing political developments. Although St. Mary's was "a little world in itself," a few of the students took an interest in politics because their fathers were in public life. The rector subscribed to several papers and made them available to all in his study on the third floor of the main building, which served as the school library. However, most of the girls were content to get current events from the day scholars or from Smedes, who made a point of imparting the news he gathered on his daily walks into town.

Because they were in Raleigh, St. Mary's students witnessed a number of stirring occurrences, including "the great Whig festival" of April, 1844, when 10,000 people[1] "tossing high their hats and welcoming with a hearty hurrah the greatest statesman and patriot of the age,"[2] heard Henry Clay. Pres. James K. Polk was welcomed to his native state in 1847 with a "magnificent display of fireworks," the "hilarity of the evening" culminating in "the ascension of a large Balloon, which mounted in gallant style Ether's fluctuating element, and wended its way majestically in the direction of the Federal City."[3] When James Buchanan visited Raleigh in 1859, Emma and Lizzie Kimberly wrote home that Smedes "carried the girls" to see the president who "was paraded through the streets in an open carriage," and that the girls who went that night to the reception "at Colonel Yarborough's hotel . . . were introduced one by one" to the president.[4]

Political celebrations could not disguise the fact that trouble was brewing in the late fifties. The Mexicans had fought over territory, as Henry Clay had feared they would, and the victory of the United States had made the status of slavery in the vast new lands, and in the old territories, the burning political issue. At the root of the controversy lay the struggle for control of national economic policy. The intransigence of the abolitionists, who made slavery a moral issue, made old solutions impossible. Old leaders—Clay, John C. Calhoun, Daniel Webster—were dead. The best hope among the younger leaders, Stephen A. Douglas of Illinois, had alienated North Carolina Democrats by reiterating in Raleigh on August 30, 1860, his belief that popular sovereignty should settle it in the long run.[5]

Southern Democrats left their party and nominated John C. Breckinridge of Kentucky, and many former Whigs went into the new Constitutional Union party that nominated John Bell of Tennessee. The Republican party, only six years old, captured the majority of the electoral vote (but not the majority of the total popular vote). The Republican party was not on the ballot in North Carolina in 1860.

By November even St. Mary's students were aware that the election was a momentous one, although they were vague about issues such as the tariff, the national bank, and popular sovereignty in the territories. On November 6, Emma Kimberly wrote to her father, a native of the North,

This week is elections; such excitement! I never did see among people before. The girls talk as if they were the greatest politicians, but ask them the difference between whig and democrat they say they do not know; neither do I. I have tried to find out, but in vain. . . . Today at intermission the schoolroom was the sound of the tower of babel . . . for there was such a noise about politics. . . .

They say Lincoln is elected. I am sorry. I have just been reading the papers; the old Black Republicans are running down the southerners. All of us are like tigers about Lincoln's election. Some of the southerners run down the North, but I will not and I hope I never will. There is one girl in school who is a northerner and the girls say she is a Lincoln man.[6]

For North Carolina, the election of Abraham Lincoln was not the signal for immediate secession. An analysis of the state's vote for presidential electors shows that "the overwhelming majority" of the voters were unionists, although they divided their votes among Breckinridge, Bell, and Douglas.[7]

The events that precipitated North Carolina's secession were Lincoln's decision to provision Fort Sumter and his call for troops after the outbreak of hostilities there. The call for troops was refused by Gov. John W. Ellis, who stated categorically, "I can be no party to this wicked violation of the laws of the country, and to this war upon the liberties of a free people."[8] The governor's call for 30,000 troops to defend the state caused a flurry of anticipation at St. Mary's because a training camp was set up in Raleigh. One of the girls reported that men were arriving on every train and that

the Captain said, that as soon as, they were drilled a little better, he is going to ask the young ladies of St. Mary's out to see them; that will be charming, will it not? I wish they would make haste and learn.[9]

RAISE THE FLAG!

North Carolina was the last of the southern states to leave the union, but even before the state ratified the provisional constitution of the Confederate States of America on May 20, 1861, Confederate flags were appearing. St. Mary's girls displayed at least three. Kate Curtis, the daughter of Moses Ashley Curtis, wrote to her brother on April 22:

The most intense excitement prevails both in town and up here among the girls. The tales we hear are enough to make one's hair (*braids* and all) stand on end; but of course they cannot be relied on. We have now three flags of the "Southern Confederacy" waving from our windows. Saturday morning some people from town rode by here with their flags, and their cries of "secession." That first made us think of displaying our zeal, and all hands were immediately at work. . . . By the time the men repassed, in the evening, our three flags were raised on the front gate where all the girls were assembled; at a given signal, one of them rang the school bell (you remember how very loud it is?), and the noise of that and the men cheering and clapping us was almost deafening. I say "us," but . . . I took no part whatever in it, not considering it the most delicate work that a lady could do. My description sounds . . . as if it was just child's play . . . , but the reality was very different. . . . They seemed totally to forget themselves and where they were. . . . There are still a great many unionists about, as we could see from the number of hisses our flags received from those riding by.

In June "the stalwart men in red shirts," Ellis's Flying Artillery, marched to St. Mary's School "and received with appropriate remarks from its Rector, a beautiful flag prepared by the fair and patriotic hands of the young ladies. . . ."[10]

From those first tumultuous weeks Aldert Smedes took the moderate approach that carried him through the war years. Kate Curtis wrote, "Dr. Smedes is very much alarmed at the state of affairs. . . . There is no danger of his breaking up the school; he says he believes in the verse, dwell in the land and do good, and verily thou shalt be fed!"[11]

Cover for a group of waltzes composed and published by Gustave Blessner, director of music, 1845
*(Lithograph executed by Mrs. Blessner)*

Aldert Smedes was "strongly opposed on the grounds both of principle and expediency" to secession. When secession became a fait accompli, he simply "continued . . . in the assiduous and exclusive discharge" of his "proper duties" as rector of St. Mary's.[12] Writing in May, 1861, to refuse an invitation to serve as a member of the examining committee at the General Theological Seminary, Smedes said:

I fear the troubles of the time will compel me to stay at home.
What terrible condition we are in, brought about by the folly and wickedness of both sides.
I, of course, take the Southern view . . . and wonder at the folly of the government in not letting us secede quickly. If they conquer us we shall be no more a united people. Our old political relations can never be restored.
But they cannot conquer us. They may inflict and receive infinite harm; and, after all, a treaty will be made conceding all we ask, the right to govern ourselves, and live peaceably with all the world.
Why not then make the treaty at once? But politicians are mad.
Happily I don't find my affections for my old friends in the least diminished by the national disruption.[13]

Apparently, the Smedeses were fully accepted in their adopted state. Both had southern connections.[14] In later years the press referred to Dr. Smedes as "one who became in sentiment and in purpose and spirit a genuine Southerner."[15]

Aldert Smedes had two slaves, an elderly couple who had begged him to buy them because their master planned to separate them. They lived for years at St. Mary's, performing light tasks. "Uncle Tyler" so idolized Smedes that he imitated his every mannerism. He had one habit Smedes did not have; Uncle Tyler drank too much. One night when he fell into a ditch on front campus, Tyler called piteously, "Please, come help po' ole Dr. Smedes out of the ditch!"[16] Smedes encouraged his servants to buy their own homes, sometimes lending them money for that purpose.[17]

As their teacher and priest, Smedes felt responsible for preparing his students to do their Christian duty toward their slaves. In his published sermon on the Christian woman, he emphasized her duty to teach the scriptures to slaves:

in a community like ours, where we are surrounded in such numbers by servants born in our own houses, and looking up to us for the supply of every want, surely the pious daughter need not go far . . . to find suitable objects of her benevolence, whose tender years, without transgressing any human law, . . . she might imbue with those lessons of piety, and those sound words of scripture, and of prayer, which, while they would make them more faithful servants of their masters upon the earth, might also invest them with the freedom of the skies.[18]

The divine law had to be obeyed by drilling slaves in memorizing the scriptures because human law forbade teaching them to read.

Although the fighting did not reach the vicinity of Raleigh until the spring of 1865, the war had immediate effects upon life there. After Lincoln declared a blockade of the Confederate ports on April 19, 1861, wild rumors circulated among the St. Mary's students. Kate Curtis wrote home:

There has been such a panic in the school about *the times*, that many of the girls have written home, entirely misrepresenting the state of affairs here, and some have been sent for. . . . Dr. Smedes said he'd been to town . . . and secured a quantity of everything we could need. We might "be obliged to forego *some of our luxuries*," but we wouldn't be pinched for want of food. The girls have been anxiously inquiring what the luxuries are, so that they can enjoy them before they are taken away.[19]

During April Raleigh women were "so pushed with war work," preparing the new training camps, that St. Mary's girls petitioned for and received a two-and-a-half-day holiday from classes. They made 167 mattresses and hemmed 118 towels, and two of the teachers made a Confederate flag "for the governor's house." There was general agreement that those days were "no holiday," faculty and students alike being in a state of patriotic exhaustion.[20]

But there were compensations. During the June vacation, the few students who stayed at school watched the Flying Artillery carry the flag made by St. Mary's students. The soldiers "threw up their hats and caught them" as the girls "waved them out of sight." Afterward, there was "a splendid ride all around town" to wave at "ever so many camps of soldiers" and to watch a dress parade. That exhilarating excursion ended at "the ice cream saloon."[21]

After the first Battle of Manassas (or Bull Run) of July 21, 1861, Smedes, preaching in the St. Mary's Chapel on "The Hand of God" described the battle, concluding with the words, "We will not have the presumption to say it is for our righteousness; nor will we say it is for their wickedness. But we do say it is the hand of the Lord. . . ."[22] The students agreed. One wrote, "The South is certainly right in everything . . . Providence is certainly on our side."[23]

After Fort Hatteras fell in late August, 1861, St. Mary's seemed the safest haven for girls from the coastal regions; a few of them stayed at the school throughout the war. Richard B. Creecy of Cloverdale plantation near Elizabeth City wrote to Smedes:

sustain Bettie as well as you can . . . her mother wanted her home. . . . I regard your situation as much less perilous than ours, and I have full confidence in your parental care, kindness and watchfulness. So far as you can do not let her be distressed, as it is her first absence from her family.[24]

In his 1861 Thanksgiving sermon Smedes enjoined his pupils to be thankful for "our comparative immunity from the consequences of war" with "as yet no houses burnt, no fields destroyed." That autumn Edward Smedes, who had enlisted in July, was home from Virginia on sick leave. His father, seeing him "from afar, ran down the walk to meet him, threw his arms around him, and kissed him, as if he had been a child," while the students watched and shared his joy.[25]

By late March, 1862, the union forces controlled Roanoke Island, Edenton, Elizabeth City, New Bern, and Washington. In Raleigh rumors were "as plentiful as blackberries and the people were in a state of depression," many packing to leave the city.[26] Josie MacRae of Fayetteville wrote to her father:

The girls are terribly frightened. Dr. Smedes has told us to hold ourselves in readiness to leave at any moment. Poor Dr. Smedes is much distressed, he says that if his school is broken up, he is a ruined man. . . . Wilmington will certainly be the next place of attack. Let us put our trust in God, for what is the use of having a God, unless we trust in Him.[27]

Creecy wrote his daughter that her box of clothes had been burned at Elizabeth City, so she must take good care of the clothes she had at St. Mary's, especially her shoes. He would get news and money to her via a friend in Norfolk. Her family was safe in their country home, so she must "be a good girl and attend to your business as usual, and don't be distressed at not hearing from us regularly." He wrote, "God's hand is in it all! . . . It is an extreme condition, which in the nature of things must exhaust itself. . . . Tell Dr. Smedes that he must take good care of you, and if he has to run he must take you with him or leave you with Dr. Curtis [Moses Ashley Curtis in Hillsborough]."[28] By April the state of military affairs was, indeed, cause for alarm in the South. After the battles of Shiloh and Island No. 10, the possibility that the Confederacy would be split in two became a real one. In the east, Richmond was threatened by Gen. George B. McClellan, Fort Macon was under siege, and Savannah was endangered.

In the spring of 1862 it seemed that St. Mary's, also, was in immediate danger. In late March, the mayor of Raleigh received orders to seize the school's buildings for a Confederate hospital. Hattie Harold, who taught penmanship and arithmetic, wrote:

it met with so much opposition, the order has been countermanded. Dr. Smedes went down to Goldsboro . . . to see General Holmes . . . who has agreed to take Wake Forest College. . . . Breaking up just at this time would be terrible. There are many here whose homes are threatened, and they have sought refuge here, and there are many who have no homes, and poor dear Dr. Smedes would be a ruined man. . . . He has had so many trials this last year, but he bears them all so patiently, so cheerfully—no one but a perfect Christian could be so resigned to God's will.[29]

As it turned out, Smedes's visit on April 2 to Gen. Theophilus Hunter

Holmes resulted in the eventual decision to use the unfinished building at Peace Institute.[30] Dr. Thomas Hill, sent to Raleigh by the Confederate government to open a general hospital, decided that the building at Peace "would be more suitable and cause less dissatisfaction."[31]

By the second year of the war there was "not a house for rent in Raleigh,"[32] and Smedes offered shelter to the First Lady of the Confederacy. Pres. Jefferson Davis decided in early May that McClellan's Peninsula Campaign made it imperative that his wife and their four small children leave Richmond. Varina Davis first established her family at the Yarborough House in downtown Raleigh. In June, little Billy (William Howell), who was less than a year old, lay so ill that President Davis brought the family physician to Raleigh (June 15–18).[33] Billy, whom the president called his "angel baby," recovered.

Apparently Varina Davis moved to St. Mary's in early July and stayed until late August when Richmond was deemed safe again after the Second Battle of Manassas. At the school with their mother were Margaret, Jefferson, Joseph, and the baby. The St. Mary's girls had mixed feelings about Varina Davis. They admired her beauty and the air of distinction with which she wore her simple but fashionable clothes. She possessed "a flashing intelligence" but was subject to "mercurial shifts of mood." She "spoke beautifully in a well-modulated voice" but was inclined to sarcasm and was a compulsive talker. Varina Davis enjoyed people and spent much time with the students, especially in the art studio on the first floor of East Rock where she liked to copy pictures and to watch the students at work. A doting but strict mother, she demanded from her children perfect manners, punctuality, and tidiness.[34]

Varina Davis had pleasant memories of her stay in North Carolina. In 1895 she recalled:

dear old Raleigh. . . . When I rented a part of Dr. Smedes' house, and took board in his school, I was greatly depressed and heavy with anxiety—but in him and his, and in the dear people of hospitable Raleigh I found friends whose regard made a home feeling which I am sure would now come back to me if I should revisit that dear and well beloved town.[35]

For the first years of the war, daily life at St. Mary's remained relatively unchanged. Best friends still "alcoved" together. A few of the old girls still teased the most naive of the new girls. A favorite joke was to remark while walking through the covered way, "This is fine in summer, but in winter it is divided into cow stalls and how I hate it when it comes my turn to milk!"[36] There were the usual minor upsets over alcove-mates and teachers, the tearful or indignant letters home, and the parental advice to "be patient, forbear, be a lady." There were the secret dormitory parties when occasional boxes of "eatables" arrived from home and the legal "candy stews" with sorghum substituted for sugar in wartime.[37] Students still enjoyed dividing with a corset stay a melon smuggled into the dormitory.[38] A favorite recreation-hour diversion was the roughhouse game of kickball played by two teams using "a large India rubber ball about the size of the top of a keg." When the ball rolled out of the circle into the grass "a screaming mob of forty girls pursued it."[39] Katie McKimmon, who was to become a longtime St. Mary's teacher, was known as "Little Kim, the most *extinguished* kicker."[40]

There was, however, evidence of wartime. The youngest girls sometimes played soldier. The popular decoration for the alcove was a little handmade Confederate flag, and the Saturday night tableaux assumed a patriotic theme. Descriptions of impromptu "serenades" by military bands, passing through Raleigh or stationed nearby, appeared frequently in students' letters. One young one wrote:

We had a delightful serenade a few nights ago from a band from the Twenty Ninth N. C. regiment. We were all in study hour when they came but teacher let us on poarch. Dr. Smedes came out and asked them into parlough and they played a long time.[41]

Even the Saturday holidays from classes—"sweet, lovely Saturdays," as one student called them—gradually changed. Saturdays had always been special. In the 1860s just as the old rising bell (its lost clapper replaced by two brass keys) was rung, the washerwomen arrived to deposit bundles of clean clothes. The students, after "a hurried toilette and a precipitate dash to Rollcall, repaired to the antique looking little Chapel" for morning prayers. Following a "smoking breakfast of hash and hominy" came "the mending hour" when clothes were repaired and shoes "blacked."[42] Saturday afternoons were free for reading, daydreaming, a walk in the woods with a teacher, or a chaperoned trip to town. The published rules of the school, as had been the custom since 1842, provided a monthly "visiting Saturday" when students could visit approved hostesses in Raleigh during the daylight hours. The students spent many a Saturday afternoon reading. Frivolous reading was not encouraged, but approved novels could be enjoyed "*after* the duties of the day" had been performed. The rector's library, always open to the girls, contained the works of Dickens, Thackeray, Cooper, and Irving. Smedes had the complete set of the Waverley novels in multiple copies, for the students were particularly fond of Scott's romantic tales. As the war wore on, the girls wrote home about long Saturdays devoted to war work; they sewed fatigue suits and shirts, knitted scarves and socks, and rolled bandages.

The Saturday shopping excursions revealed that even in the South in 1862 economic conditions were not yet desperate. Food and fashionable clothing were readily available in Raleigh. In April the City Emporium had 50 boxes of oranges and 50 boxes of lemons at $4 the box, ten boxes of French candy at 45 cents each, and 20,000 Havana cigars. H. L. Evans advertised "for the ladies plain gaiters, kid, morocco, and calf bootees, white kid and satin slippers" and "heavy Dutch bootees for servants." He had "a large lot of ladies dress goods" including poplin and mohair, black mitts, and kid gloves. Pescud's drug store offered a shipment of "new and splendid extracts," perfumes "put up in elegant style." Young officers called at St. Mary's in handsome uniforms. The Civil and Military Clothing Manufactory of Raleigh advertised that it had both "Confederate gray" and "sky blue" cloth and plenty of gold lace.[43]

Raleigh's stores were able to offer such an array of goods because the Federal blockade of Confederate ports was relatively ineffective during the first two years of the war. On March 5, 1862, the *Register* reported that "The saucy Rebel steamer *Nashville*" had once again "escaped the toils spread for her proving Lincoln's blockade a thing of straw, a sheer humbug." In 1862 only one of every eight blockade-runners was captured,[44] but as the United States Navy was enlarged the Confederacy's trade was slowly paralyzed.

Interest was added to daily life during the Civil War years because there were at St. Mary's, as a student wrote in the winter of 1863, "a good many who are daughters, or near relatives, of distinguished characters." She noted with surprise that a niece of Union general Ambrose E. Burnside was there.[45] Nancy Haywood Branch, daughter of Lawrence O'Bryan Branch, a former United States congressman and a Confederate general, attended the school during the war.[46] Mary Gale, step-granddaughter of Leonidas Polk, Episcopal bishop and Confederate general, was placed at St. Mary's during 1861, "that being a good school and a safe place." Lucia, the general's daughter, joined her there in 1863, but she left soon after her father was killed in June, 1864.[47]

The rumor that Gen. Robert E. Lee had decided that St. Mary's would be a safe refuge for his daughter, Mildred Childe, caused "quite a flutter among the girls" until Eliza Evertson, in whose dormitory she would live, observed matter-of-factly, "Suppose she does come; she's no more than an ordinary mortal like the rest of us." Mildred Lee was 16 and described by a classmate as "a slender girl, with a prominent nose and gifted with a good voice, sweet and clear, but not very strong."[48] Mildred entered the school either in the late summer or in the fall of 1862. Having arrived late, she was unhappy at first because she found the girls less friendly than those at the small boarding school she had attended. Furthermore, she was heartbroken over the death of her older sister in October.[49] Mildred stayed at St. Mary's over Christmas because her father feared that she might fall into enemy hands while traveling.[50]

By spring Mildred was happier and decided to return for the session beginning in July, 1863. She studied astronomy (her father's favorite subject) with Smedes that spring, and the rector wrote "a very complimentary letter" to the general concerning his daughter's progress and deportment.[51] Her father advised Mildred, his youngest and favorite child whom he always addressed as "My Precious Life" or "Life," to "read history, works of truth, not novels and romances. Get correct views of life and learn to see the world in its true light."[52]

When Mildred left St. Mary's, her father regretted that she was no longer in school, but he wrote:

you are now prepared by diligence and study to learn whatever you desire. Do not allow yourself to forget what you have spent so much time and labor in acquiring, but increase it every day by extended application.

Once he sent a song composed by a French soldier and asked Mildred to send a reply in verse because she was "so learned in the language."[53]

## "STRICTER AND STRICTER EVERY WEEK"

Smedes, although extremely busy with the added burdens of the war and the increased enrollment, showed his genuine interest in each pupil. He was never too rushed to stop for a small joke. It was his custom to take the girls to ride about Raleigh in his two-passenger buggy. He would sit up front and drive while the two pupils chosen (alphabetically) for that day rode proudly as his passengers.[54] For holidays during the war years, the Smedeses planned all kinds of special treats for those who could not get to their families. During the Christmas holidays in 1861, there were "glorious times" with dancing and "elegant, magnificent charades" in the parlor. No boys were allowed, but no one had expected that they would be. Everyone sat up until midnight "almost every night," and on Christmas Eve eggnog was served. Christmas dinner was "splendid," and one night the girls gave an oyster supper for the teachers. All agreed that "we spent a merry Christmas."[55]

Along with extra efforts to preserve the happy home atmosphere prevalent at St. Mary's, every effort was made during the confusion of the war years to adhere to the normal academic schedule and standards. The major problem, the scarcity of textbooks, was met by urging students to bring used books from home and by an appeal to alumnae to send their old texts to St. Mary's.[56] The list of texts became more flexible as a variety of acceptable books used in academies and colleges appeared at the school. The girls believed that more than ever was required of them and that Smedes got "stricter and stricter every week."[57] Not a moment was to be wasted, and those who "trifled" in class were denied permission to visit in town.[58] The requirements for the regular compositions were so exacting that one desperate student begged her professor father to "take pity" and send her "at least one" of the compositions he had written as a student.[59] One week the assigned topic for the "big girls" was "Our Opinions of the Present War"; that for the little girls was "On Leaving Home."[60]

Perhaps Smedes *was* requiring more of his students in the sixties; he realized that times were changing. Writing to his daughter at St. Mary's, one father advised, "Be diligent . . . for the times will cause great neglect of education and those who are well educated will be more highly valued than before." Although well pleased with his daughter's progress, he held the traditional view of "a woman's place." Writing about a healthy new baby brother, he commented, "You ought to feel quite independent in having five brothers to lean upon in the journey of life. If this little fellow lives to be a man, he will be your protector."[61]

Aldert Smedes's Bible lectures were, as always, well organized, comprehensive, and accompanied by appropriate scripture passages and poetry to be memorized by the pupils. The "dreaded abstracts" were required, as always. The French lessons then were presided over by Madame Gouyé. She was "gentle and elegant." One of her students wrote that "to know her was a liberal education." By the war years she was a semi-invalid, and her classes met in her bedroom.[62]

Eliza Evertson, who had left Raleigh in 1853 to set up a school in Milwaukee,[63] returned and lived in "a cozy room at the head of the stairs in West Rock."[64] She and Mary Johnson Iredell, an alumna who began teaching at St. Mary's a few weeks after her husband was killed at Gettysburg, were close friends. Mary Iredell never forsook her widow's weeds, and she rarely smiled; but she was much admired, and her services to the school for the remainder of the century were invaluable.[65]

The music department was presided over by Prof. George F. Hansen, a native of Germany. When in 1860 he became the volunteer director of the newly organized local musical association, the *Raleigh Register* referred to him as "an accomplished and successful instructor in music, as has been demonstrated by his long service at St. Mary's School, one of the most successful and popular female schools in the South."[66] The professor's daughter taught singing and piano. Stella Shaw continued to teach piano. "Sweet and plump," always wearing "a dainty dress," she was in her thirties by the war years. The students found quite intriguing the story of her abandonment at St. Mary's as a child.[67]

Even more thrilling was the story of Penelope ("Pensie") Wright's short hair, shorn for a daring rescue attempt. Penelope Wright's father, a prominent physician of Norfolk, was sentenced to death by the occupying Federal authorities. While visiting him in his dark cell, Pensie managed, despite the presence of a guard nearby, to exchange outer garments with her father and to arrange herself in his boots on his cot. Wright actually walked out of the prison and had almost reached the waiting carriage when a sentry noticed the unusual height and stride of the departing "woman." After Wright's execution, his widow and daughter went through the Federal lines to Raleigh, and Penelope taught at St. Mary's in 1864.[68]

The story of Margaret Walker Weber was typical of Smedes's hospitality and of the continued attention to academic standards during the war years. A member of the Mallett family, Margaret Walker had married German-born Heinrich Weber, and the couple had taught in Tennessee at Columbia Institute and in Nashville. When Nashville fell, Margaret Weber was visiting relatives in Alabama. Eventually, she with her two young sons and their nurse arrived in Raleigh. They all lived at St. Mary's for two years, where Margaret Weber taught. An older stepdaughter, who was a fine musician, joined them to teach music.[69]

A number of such refugees lived and taught at St. Mary's at some time during the war. Because Smedes's compassion and generosity were known far and wide, those in need of shelter felt confident that he would find a place for them. Apparently, he always did. By 1864 every nook and cranny in the dormitories was filled with beds. Sarah Smedes remarked that St. Mary's could be renamed "Liberty Hall" because it was "free to all!"[70]

One of the wartime teachers had been for a decade professor of rhetoric and logic at the University of North Carolina. While John Thomas Wheat was awaiting an eye operation, he and his wife lived at St. Mary's for over a year during 1864–1865. The "amiable Wheat," as he had been known in Chapel Hill, taught history at St. Mary's. The girls found him amiable, too, and vied for the honor of helping him about campus. His wife was known to be a bit eccentric, and she enjoyed the role. Someone sent her some cereal, which she passed around the breakfast table. When a student asked the identity of the new dish, Mrs. Wheat replied brightly, "Like me, cracked wheat." Following a successful operation, Dr. Wheat was able to accept a church in Memphis, Tennessee.[71]

Thus during the war years, Aldert Smedes continued as usual his business of educating young women. A senior of 1864 wrote to her mother, "My only regret is that I did not come sooner. It certainly works greater improvement in the girls than any school of which I have had any knowledge." She vowed that when at home again she would spend "a large portion" of her time "reading, studying, and practicing and the rest in keeping house for you."[72] Their years spent at St. Mary's were preparing Smedes's young ladies to meet far greater adversities than anyone had imagined would be their lot.

Tragedy had touched the St. Mary's family a few months before the war commenced. Lyell, the eldest Smedes son, was 25 when he married Susan Dabney of Burleigh plantation near Raymond, Mississippi. Their wedding was cause for rejoicing in both families. But 11 weeks later, Lyell lay dead of "a swift disease," probably yellow fever. His father mourned Lyell deeply; he wrote in his meditations of his son's unselfishness, of the joy his honors at the University of North Carolina had brought to his parents, and of his "reverence for sacred things."[73] But Aldert Smedes was able to accept Lyell's death, and he wrote to Kate DeRosset, "My only consolation . . . is that our loss is the infinite gain of our darling boy."[74]

Sarah Smedes, however, would not be consoled. Aldert said of her, "My poor wife . . . cannot resign her treasure even into the hands of Him who lent it. . . . It is most painful to see her wasting away with grief. . . . But I trust to the gentle hand of time, and the omnipotent hand of grace. . . ."[75] The students, also, were terribly worried, and one wrote, "Poor Mrs. Smedes will grieve herself to death."[76] When portraits of Lyell and Susan arrived in April, 1861, Kate Curtis wrote that they were "exquisitely done" but that "the continued sight of them" hanging in the parlor was bad for Sarah Smedes, who was in "dreadful condition."[77] Lyell's widow remained a favorite with the Smedes family and visited St. Mary's frequently.[78]

Although life at St. Mary's during the early part of the Civil War had proceeded as normally as the rector could manage, the effects of war were felt more and more. And there were reported in the newspapers disturbing, but unadmitted, indications that perhaps the South would not be able to gain its independence. Everyone wondered how long Raleigh would remain a safe refuge.

By the winter of 1863 the war had become a grim reality rather than an exciting adventure, even to teen-aged girls. Many of their brothers and sweethearts who had not enlisted were drafted under a law conscripting white men between the ages of 18 and 35. After major engagements, the casualty lists in the Raleigh papers sometimes filled two or three columns, and the papers regularly published guides to the Richmond hospitals so that relatives could locate their wounded.

On May 6 Aldert and Sarah Smedes received word that Ives, who had enlisted in February and was serving in the Seventh Regiment as adjutant, had been wounded at Chancellorsville on May 3. Arriving in Richmond at the same time as the trains carrying the wounded, they found their son in a hospital that night. Smedes telegraphed Eliza Evertson that his wife would stay to nurse Ives, whose condition seemed favorable, and that he would return to St. Mary's. Instead, the grief-stricken parents arrived home with a flag-draped coffin. His colonel, in Raleigh recuperating from his own wounds, told the parents that he had never seen "such coolness and courage on the battlefield, or such unselfishness after he was wounded," as Ives had displayed.[79]

The death of his bright 20-year-old son was a severe blow to Smedes. Ives had planned to prepare for the ministry. But Aldert Smedes remained "amidst all his trials . . . the same patient hopeful Christian man." That spring he also had lost a student at the school and a brother in Mississippi.[80]

Sarah Smedes was inconsolable. She wandered about the campus, her melancholia increased by the fact that many of the finest trees in the grove were in the path of the fortifications around Raleigh. She would wring her hands, moaning, "My boys are gone, and now they have taken the trees."[81] Her husband wanted her to risk the trip north to see her family, but she was not able to undertake such a venture.[82] Sarah Smedes retreated into a shadowy world of grief from which she never fully emerged. The trials of the later war years were, therefore, doubly difficult for her husband.

As the war wore on, more and more of the girls suffered personal losses. They were allowed to go home, if possible, when a brother or a father returned on furlough. All too often the students went home for funerals. Heartbroken, they penned in diaries and notebooks entries like this one by Kate Curtis, "Alas, my gallant, brave, soldier brother, shall I mourn you in tears and bitterness all my life, and never be comforted."[83]

Raleigh felt under constant threat. On June 5, 1863, a legislator wrote to his wife, "There is another panic here about the Yankees. . . . They are making for Fayetteville or Raleigh."[84] Fortifications for the capital constructed during the summer of 1863 passed across the western edge of St. Mary's grove just beyond the chapel. On sunny afternoons the girls would fulfill their exercise requirement by walking atop the earthworks to Dix Hill (later Dorothea Dix Hospital) and back.[85]

In the first week of July the Confederacy suffered two calamities— Gettysburg and Vicksburg. On July 15 the editor of the *Register*, John W. Syme, who had not heard from his own son at Gettysburg, wrote, "The news which we give today from the ensanguined field of Gettysburg will fall heavily on the ears and hearts of many persons in the State." At the beginning of the three-day battle the Twenty-sixth, a North Carolina regiment, numbered 880 men; when it was over, 708 were killed, wounded, or missing. Thirteen North Carolina regiments were among the 27 regiments sustaining the heaviest losses at Gettysburg.[86]

Also published in the *Register* that second week of July was a long extract from a sermon sent in by "Mary Ann." The preacher exhorted the women of the South to gird their men for the conflict "with words, looks, glances, and smiles" and to write letters that would set their men ablaze "with a martyr's courage and zeal for home and country."[87] Suddenly, thousands and thousands of the women of the Confederacy had found that *they* were the ones in need of courage. Alone and responsible for children, slaves, and land, they somehow devised ways to cope.

One St. Mary's alumna did infinitely more than write letters. Helen Johnstone was instrumental in organizing and equipping three companies of infantrymen. One, a part of the Twenty-fourth Regiment, Mississippi, and known as "The Helen Johnstone Guards," she equipped and maintained at her own expense throughout the war. When blankets became unobtainable, she cut up the carpets from Annandale, her plantation home near Canton, Mississippi.[88]

## "FROM HAND TO MOUTH"

From 1863 on, such serious food shortages plagued the Confederacy that President Davis and Congress urged that tobacco and cotton lands be planted in food crops. No one at St. Mary's ever went hungry, but it was a constant struggle for Smedes to feed his "large family of nearly 150 persons." The fare was plain, and naturally the girls grumbled. It was, however, considered unpatriotic to complain unduly. There were small luxuries—molasses three times a week (despite the price of $10 a gallon) and sometimes cookies on Sunday nights.[89] Always there was meal for making corn dodgers, but the excellent "light rolls" disappeared. Two years later, flour was quoted at $400 to $450 a barrel, but the market was "entirely bare," making the price of flour hypothetical. Coffee sold for $12.50 a pound in the winter of 1863 but later became unobtainable even at $100 a pound.[90]

There were enough vegetables in season from the school's garden, but Smedes scolded any pupil caught pulling a turnip or carrot for munching during afternoon walking hour.[91] A new breakfast dish introduced in the summer of 1864 inspired a student to write to her mother, "You have no idea how nice it is. Try it." It was fried okra.[92] In wintertime vegetables were incredibly expensive, cow peas selling for $30 a bushel and Irish and sweet potatoes for $40 a bushel. Eggs were $10 a dozen.[93]

It became virtually impossible to find meat to feed 150. In his circular dated March 14, 1864, Smedes informed his patrons that

Six thousand pounds of meat engaged for me, were taken by the enemy on the way to Tarborough. Three thousand pounds were lost to me through the failure of a letter to reach me in due season. Other disappointments have occurred and have reduced me to the necessity of living . . . from hand to mouth.

Fresh pork was sometimes brought into town "sparingly" and sold from carts at $5 to $6.50 a pound. Chickens sold for about $10 apiece and turkeys for $25. By March, 1865, inflation was so rampant that the *Daily Progress* estimated that a basket of groceries costing $3.80 in Raleigh in 1860 would sell for $205 that month.[94] Until the last year of the war, Smedes was usually able to procure ham, turkeys, corned beef, and lard on contract by paying exorbitant prices. He paid $900 for a barrel of lard in 1864.

Despite inflation, the charges at St. Mary's were not raised until the second session (July–December) of 1862 when an additional charge of $1.25 weekly was made for board and laundry. Tuition remained at $100 a session plus the extra fees for music and art. In January of the next year, Smedes notified his patrons that the experience of the last session had convinced him that he had to raise his charge for tuition and board to $160. Fees for the various extra lessons were raised minimally.[95] In June, 1863, Smedes announced that tuition and board at St. Mary's would be $225 a session.[96] He wrote to the father of two of his pupils, "My charge last term was too low for the times. I have increased it, but I fear, and my friends fear, not enough."[97] Smedes found it necessary to write a number of letters, gracious as always but plain enough, to patrons owing him old debts. "I am gathering up fragments to reimburse myself for heavy losses sustained in keeping my school open during the war," he wrote. "But I do not wish to aggravate the troubles of any of my friends by an unreasonable demand even of a small amount. I shall await, therefore, with patience their convenience. . . ."[98] Some of the amounts owed were not "fragments" as the charges at St. Mary's skyrocketed with the depreciation of the Confederate currency. Tuition and board were $500 a session by 1864 and $1,000 each session by 1865,[99] and Smedes was carrying some patrons on his books for as much as $3,000. Board for pupils staying at the school over vacations was $3.50 daily, about the weekly rate for the 1840s. Textbooks sold for about $10, instead of $1.50, but most students used tattered texts from other days. Slates at $4.50 each became indispensable as the shortage of paper became acute. Lead pencils sold for $3 and drawing paper for $2.50 a sheet. Smedes's account book indicated that he was paying teachers about $70 in cash, instead of $40, plus room and board.

At the end of 1864 Smedes was still solvent. However, the problem of feeding his students was more than a financial one. He was forced to postpone briefly the opening of the January, 1864, term in order to procure "indispensable supplies" so that his students would return to "a larder not empty." [100] There were 120 to 125 boarding students during 1864 and 1865, the largest number ever. [101] (There were not to be that many students in residence again until after 1900). [102] The usual number of day scholars during the war years was 40 to 50.

In January, 1865, Smedes resorted to barter. He announced in his circular for the session beginning on February 1, "Satisfied that it will be impracticable to purchase provisions for a large family, I am compelled either to close my School or to require payment for the board of pupils in provisions." The charge for board was $50 payable in gold or in provisions *at the 1860 prices.* The allowance for flour was $8 a barrel, for bacon, about 17 cents a pound. The food was to be delivered to Raleigh, freight prepaid, and parents were asked "to state the kinds of provisions it will be most convenient to them to furnish." On the back of one of his circulars, Smedes wrote, "I hope to see Miss Sullivan next term. If her quota could consist of bacon and lard, she would be especially welcome." [103]

The tuition and other charges, payable in Confederate currency, amounted to $700 or more. It was estimated that the laundresses would charge at least $100. The circular stated, "For lights, we rely on the gasworks, whose operations and charges depending on the supply and cost of rosin, are uncertain. An assessment of the actual cost of lights will, therefore, be made on each pupil at the close of the term." Pupils were asked to bring a mug, a plate, knife, fork, and spoon, and any "slates, pencils, pen-holders and music which their elder sisters have accumulated." It was not uncommon for from three to five sisters to have been educated at St. Mary's, for "going to St. Mary's" quickly became the thing to do in Episcopalian circles in North Carolina.

The sharp rise in charges necessarily had an adverse effect upon enrollment, although there may not have been so drastic a curtailment as one letter from Fayetteville would indicate. A St. Mary's girl wrote to her classmate, Kate McKimmon, that she could not return in February, "since Dr. Smedes requires gold or provisions," but that she hoped to return for the following session. In the meantime, one student from Fayetteville would "have to answer for the host that was there last." [104]

The necessary produce arrived in Raleigh, and St. Mary's remained open. Smedes's acount book contains entries showing that bills for Mary Skinner of Louisburg were paid in cash and 20 bushels of corn, for Harriet Nixon of Hertford in cash and a $500 state bond, and that Katharine Russell Clements of Wake County was entered in the fall of 1865 "on a bale of cotton." [105] Payment "in kind" had become common practice by the last year of the war. Confederate currency depreciated rapidly as the military situation deteriorated; $500 in Confederate currency was worth only $10 in gold in 1865.

While the head of the school was scouring the countryside as far away as South Carolina for food and the faculty was teaching from an assortment of frayed textbooks, the girls at St. Mary's were learning to make do with improvised wardrobes. No longer did a new girl arrive with a trunkful of poplins, calicoes, and merinos, plus a silk or two. Before the end of the war, the girls wore homespun and calico for classes and a merino or an old silk for church. Although few students possessed more than three or four dresses, Eliza Evertson saw to it that the proprieties were observed. One Sunday she sent Lizzie Wilson back to her alcove to change from her school-day calico, even though it was a new one costing $30 a yard.[106] The requirement of blue dresses as the school uniform was suspended in January, 1863, and was never reinstated. Mothers cautioned their daughters not to give away any of their clothes,[107] but sometimes favorable trades could be arranged. In the spring of 1864 one student proudly informed her mother that she had sold her piece of gingham goods for $10 a yard and had bought a beautiful piece "like silk" worth $25 a yard for only $21 a yard. She asked her mother to rip to pieces an old muslin apron and to send in her next letter a starched strip of the material "for ruffles." She also begged a piece of black silk left from her mother's dress so that she could make "a fashionable waist with a high neck . . . like the other girls."[108]

Some of the girls and their mothers knew that Paris dictated that hoopskirts be of immense proportions. However, only women who bought goods brought in by the blockade-runners wore the newest crinolines. Occasionally a student would attend the wedding of a "finished off" St. Mary's girl in finery borrowed from several classmates. At school, the students dressed even more simply than usual. Their hoops, if worn at all, were small. They still wore plain straw bonnets, but the skirts of their bonnets were shorter and narrower than in past days and often were made from the silk linings of old coats or even of cambric.[109] Some of the girls made sunbonnets for "walking hour" from plaited straw and trimmed them with cornhusk plumes.[110] The high walking shoes laced up the front, known as Balmoral boots, were the latest in footgear although gaiters were still worn. St. Mary's girls solved the shortage of shoelaces by dipping string in black ink.[111]

Social life at St. Mary's during the war centered on simple schoolgirl diversions as it had during the two decades before. There were still the musicales to which guests from town were invited, but they were, of necessity, less glittering affairs than the soirees of prewar days.

There was considerably less traffic from Chapel Hill to St. Mary's than before because enrollment at the university was down as students went to war.[112] There were always soldiers in Raleigh. Letters from one student to another reveal that the girls usually knew the approximate count, not that such information did them much good. Smedes was stricter than ever in granting social permissions, for the protection of his charges from unacceptable suitors was an added burden placed upon him by the exigencies of war. A soldier, no matter how dashing, did not come calling (even under the scrutiny of chaperones) without the express approval of the young lady's parents. Quite a stir was caused one visiting Saturday during the war when one of the older students went with her hostess's daughter to take tea with officers at the camp near Raleigh. After his anger had subsided, Smedes decided not to expel her; but everyone understood the seriousness of the offense.[113]

St. Mary's girls always knew enough acceptable young men, friends from home or friends of brothers and cousins, to make life interesting, and their alcoves were decorated with tintypes of soldiers. Mail call, after the rector's daily trip to the post office, was a time of dreadful suspense. Because the mails were erratic (one pupil complained that she had received no letters because the "males" from Virginia were so unreliable),[114] a different means of communication became popular for a brief time.

A group of privileged seniors lived, without a dormitory teacher, in "the long room." That was a much coveted location on the west side of the second floor of the main building, the only room used for students on that floor. An alumna recalled:

One diversion we gave ourselves, very stealthily, as we knew intuitively Dr. Smedes would not approve it, and when he found out that the turning of the tables was in constant practice, he gave us a serious talk and peremptorily forbade it. . . . We would hang a shawl before the window, light the gas for an hour, on Saturdays, cluster around the table. We soon found out a medium and through the moving of the table, in reply to our calling over the alphabet, we asked many questions and thought we gained satisfactory replies. . . . The sweetheart of one of the girls had just been killed on the battlefield of Virginia. . . . he was wild and dissipated, and utterly fearless. The table spelled out that he wished to communicate with her, and the message that followed . . . , "Remorse," caused a panic and we left off table turning for some time.[115]

## A SON RETURNED, A SON LOST

In the spring of 1864 Bennett Smedes went home to St. Mary's to assist his father, who was beginning to show the strain of his heavy responsibilities. For a time, the Reverend Frederick FitzGerald assisted Aldert Smedes in the chapel and taught chemistry while also serving as temporary editor of the new *Church Intelligencer;* soon he entered military service as a chaplain.[116]

Bennett Smedes really had returned home. He was not quite five years old when he moved with his parents in 1842 to St. Mary's. His college degree was from the College of St. James, a diocesan institution near Hagerstown, Maryland. He took his theological training at the General Theological Seminary and was graduated in 1860. He was ordained deacon in July of that year. Bennett Smedes, while a deacon, remained in the North serving for about two years as assistant at Grace Church, Baltimore. He decided to return to the Confederacy and apparently was captured while passing through the Federal lines; however, details of that incident are unclear.[117] Once back in North Carolina, Bennett enlisted on July 16, 1863, just a few days after the death of his younger brother, Ives. He became chaplain of the Fifth Regiment.[118] On July 26, 1863, he was ordained priest at Christ Church in Raleigh by Bishop Atkinson. The elder Smedes, visibly haggard from grief but proud of Bennett, assisted in the laying on of hands along with Richard Sharpe Mason.[119] The bishop of Maryland, not recognizing the Protestant Episcopal Church in the Confederate States, had refused letters dismissory, but Bishop Atkinson had decided to receive young Smedes without them.[120]

Because army life was detrimental to his health and because of his father's desperate need for help, Bennett Smedes resigned his commission on April 22, 1864, and returned to St. Mary's.[121] He spent the rest of his life there. "Mr. Bennett," as the students called him, taught the science classes and assisted in the chapel. He was listed as assistant to the rector in advertisements for the school. At 27 he was still shy almost to the point of diffidence, but this trait only made him more interesting to the girls, who considered him quite handsome and teased one another about being "in love with Mr. Bennett."[122] One student wrote of him, "He is extremely handsome, and yet I think his good looks proceed more from expression than any faultlessness of feature." In describing his ordination she wrote, "As he rose and bowed his head, I thought I had never seen a more divine expression. . . ."[123] That was also the impression of a member of the legislature, who wrote to his wife that Bennett looked "angelic in his robes." He added, "He preached a very good sermon, too."[124] In his sermons young Smedes avoided direct reference to the war, but he spoke often of the continual presence of God during perilous times; and he assured his young listeners that God would give them the strength to face an uncertain future. "Rejoice in the Lord" was a favorite theme with him.[125]

Sundays during the sixties were described by Lizzie Wilson Montgomery, who wrote:

The Chapel was the center of life at St. Mary's. . . . we met Sunday morning in the parlor, an hour later than our usual hour. . . . Dr. Smedes sat at a square table just at the upper entrance from the hall. He read or repeated a few verses of Scripture bearing on the Sabbath Day, with short prayers, then gave us the Bible lesson for the week. . . . After breakfast we walked an hour. At eleven we assembled in the Chapel for the Morning service . . . Miss Stella Shaw being the organist, with the girls who took "voice" as the choir. The girls did not wear hats except on the first Sunday when the Communion Service took place; the Communicants then wore them.

Sunday afternoon was a quiet time devoted to rest and reading. All novels taken out for Saturday reading were returned to the rector's study the first thing on Sunday morning, and "suitable" Sabbath reading was selected. *Bessie Melville, Little Episcopalian, Mothers' Recompense,* were all "suitable" titles. Evening prayers were held in the chapel about sunset.[126]

The missionary societies were active; about $35 each month was contributed by St. Mary's to the diocese mission fund. Confirmations numbered, as usual, about 20 a year. A highlight of any month was a visit from the bishop. When Bishop Atkinson was present at dinner, the linen tablecloths, replaced by oilcloth during the war, were produced.[127] He could sympathize with those of his flock who had suffered greatly during the war because he had been held at gunpoint while Federal soldiers looted his Wadesboro home.[128]

It was during the Sunday morning service at St. Mary's in May, 1864, that Aldert Smedes received news that his son Edward had been killed at Spotsylvania Courthouse. Years later, a student recalled the day vividly:

It was a lovely Sunday. . . . we knew on Saturday that a fierce battle was raging and many of the girls had near and dear relatives in the army. Dr. Smedes's son Edward was with the forces engaged in battle, so when Sunday morning dawned, cloudless and bright though it was, the girls moved quietly, and even nature seemed to wear a hushed and expectant air. We were assembled in the Chapel, the service nearly over, when a messenger appeared at the door. Madame Gouyé went out and Dr. Smedes in a trembling voice pronounced the benediction and knelt at the altar. We quietly withdrew and then Madame sent his little daughter to him with the telegram. . . . we did not see our beloved Rector again that day, but the morrow found him at his post of duty, pale and sad, but as brave a soldier as the sons who fell in battle.[129]

The engagement known as Spotsylvania Courthouse, May 8–21, was at the beginning of the yearlong final assault upon Richmond. Twenty-three-year-old Edward Smedes, a second lieutenant, was shot through the heart on May 12 as he led his men after his colonel was killed. He was buried on the battlefield by two of his Raleigh neighbors, William Ruffin Cox and Seaton Gales.[130] Educated at St. James, Edward never had a chance to begin a career. He was a thoughtful young man of gentle Christian character. When in the winter of 1866 the federal government ordered the removal of all graves from the Virginia battlefields, Smedes sent his younger son, Abraham, to claim Edward's body. Abe, too, had served in the war. Enlisting at 18, he was promoted from the ranks to second lieutenant; his regiment was the North Carolina Seventh. A girlhood memory of the return home of Edward's remains was recorded:

The mournful cortege passed through the grove on a Friday afternoon; the body was placed in the Chapel till Sunday. On Saturday the ladies from town came up with flowers to place on the casket. . . . Dr. Smedes, always considerate of others, was anxious to know how the girls would feel about having the usual morning Service in the Chapel where lay the body of his son. After being assured of their warm sympathy and affection, he conducted the service, as usual, with only an occasional break in his voice denoting his suffering.[131]

After Edward's death, Aldert Smedes seemed older and quieter, and Sarah was described by the neighbors as being "in a dreadful state."[132]

## "SHERMAN WILL HAVE HIS WAY"

The war shifted into high gear during the spring of 1864 after a lull since the preceding fall. In March, Lt. Gen. Ulysses S. Grant assumed command of all of the armies of the United States but kept his headquarters in the field with the Army of the Potomac. Morale in Raleigh was high. In May legislator Frank Shober wrote his wife that the town was "filled with good news from Petersburg . . . our independence is thought not to be far off."[133] Optimism was dampened somewhat by the news of the fall of Atlanta in November, but the people of Raleigh had no way of knowing that Sherman's march would end on their doorsteps. The air was so full of rumors during the winter of 1864–1865 that the Daily Progress carried a regular column headed "Richmond Gossip."

After Sherman presented to President Lincoln his "Christmas gift" of Savannah, Georgia, and 25,000 bales of captured cotton, North Carolinians realized the gravity of their own position. The editor of the Daily Progress predicted that Sherman would be in Raleigh "if not with the April showers, certainly with the buds and blossoms of May" and that Sherman would "have his own way." The editor endorsed the idea of an immediate peace conference.[134] The Hampton Roads Conference of February 3 was a failure because President Lincoln insisted upon the recognition of national authority and the acceptance by the southern states of the Thirteenth Amendment abolishing slavery; that amendment was then in the process of ratification. As tension mounted in Raleigh, the mayor closed all bar rooms[135] and the Home Guard, made up of men above the draft age, patrolled the streets at night.[136] In late February the cadets from the Hillsborough Military Institute marched into town equipped for service and were quartered at the Town Hall.[137]

A week after Lincoln's "with malice toward none" second inaugural address, General Sherman's army was in Fayetteville, having left the capital of South Carolina in smouldering ruins. Once over the border, Sherman kept a firm rein on his men, ordering his officers to "deal as moderately and fairly by North Carolinians as possible." [138] However, the normal destruction and foraging of war seemed anything but "moderate" to the people of North Carolina.

Although the Battle of Bentonville, March 19–21, ended with General Sherman in possession of the field, Gen. Joseph E. Johnston's strategy had been both bold and skillfully executed against overwhelming odds. [139] After the encounter, Sherman went into camp at Goldsboro to rest and refit his some 90,000 troops. Johnston's ragged force of about 20,000 [140] camped outside Smithfield waiting to see whether the Federals would choose the Weldon or Raleigh route to Richmond.

Meanwhile, in Raleigh there was "such a stir," as a Wake County woman wrote on March 20, that some people were moving out while others were preparing hiding places for their families, and everyone was burying valuables. She wrote, "All of the Hospitals, and Churches, and a good many of the stores and private residences are full of the sick and wounded." [141] There was a frantic rush to convert Confederate currency to tangibles. At St. Mary's, Smedes and his teachers did their best to see that life went on as usual despite the fact that the girls from the eastern part of the state were frantic for news of their families.

The morale of Johnston's men, encamped near Smithfield, was high although supplies were so low that one of their own number described the review of April 4, witnessed by Gov. Zebulon B. Vance and "many ladies from Raleigh," as "the saddest spectacle of my life." When on the next day "the shades of sorrow" began to gather as rumors of the occupation of Richmond reached them, [142] Johnston's men deserted in such numbers that as many as five roll calls daily were ordered. [143] By then, Raleigh was so crowded with wounded from the battlefields of Virginia and North Carolina that some of the older day scholars at St. Mary's quit school to nurse. [144]

On April 10 Sherman's jubilant troops began their march toward Raleigh "with great enthusiasm and good cheer." [145] On that same day Johnston's army began to move ahead of them in what Susan Collier at St. Mary's described with emphasis in her diary as "the *honorable* fallback from Smithfield to Greensboro." [146] On Tuesday, April 11, the long lines of ragged and half-starved Confederate soldiers began to pass through the capital. As if by magic, wagonloads of cooked food appeared, according to eyewitness accounts written by St. Mary's alumna Harriet Cobb Lane and by Mary Bayard Devereux Clarke of Raleigh. With one mind, the women of Raleigh and Wake County had decided that Sherman's foragers were not to have their precious last stores of food. Both sides of Fayetteville Street were lined by women holding out baskets of food to the passing troops. Behind each woman stood a servant who kept her basket filled.[147] The bands played "Dixie" and the whole "fall-back" began to take on a rather festive air. The news of Appomattox had not yet reached the troops although there were disturbing rumors from Virginia.

When the first lines began to file by St. Mary's, Aldert Smedes refused to allow the girls to run to the fence. However, after two of the soldiers and "Mr. Bennett" interceded, he gave his consent. Eighteen-year-old Susan Collier recounted in her diary the excitement:

We had a charming time feeding the soldiers. We gave them our dinner. They were so *grateful*. I was quite exhausted carrying great tubs of water. . . . All of the girls seem wild with joy though we know tomorrow at this time we will be left desolate. . . . One of the dearest of the dear soldiers gave me a cartridge to kill one Yankee with. . . . All of the girls seemed to regret the sudden appearance of darkness. After supper several soldiers came after food, . . . but they came rather to see the girls. We took two of them into prayers. We girls were quite carried away with them. Dr. Wheat made us come in much to our disgust.[148]

The next day the excitement continued. Some of the troops had camped nearby, and other regiments were coming into the city. The girls were out in the grove again giving out food and tiny bouquets of flowers, which the soldiers stuck in their caps. Some saw relatives and neighbors; Mary Scott found both her father and her brother. Sue Collier resumed a flirtation of the day before and walked to the stile with a young man to see Gen. Joseph Wheeler's horse, captured from Union Gen. Judson Kilpatrick.[149]

Some soldiers also recorded their "big times." The April 11 diary entry of Bromfield Lewis Ridley read:

Camped three miles west of Raleigh on Hillsboro Road. . . . As we passed the female seminary . . . the beautiful girls greeted us warmly. Each one had a pitcher of water and a goblet. We drank took their addresses and had a big time. It was a terrible task . . . to get the staff away from them.[150]

Col. John Hinsdale, writing in 1901, recalled how on April 12, 1865,

we marched through Raleigh . . . past St. Mary's . . . in a beautiful grove on the right. . . . How the fair girls trooped down to see us pass! How one tall, beautiful damsel exclaimed: Why girls, these are all *young* men; and how one of our saucy sargents replied, "Yes, ladies, and we are all looking for wives!"[151]

While his army was passing through Raleigh, General Johnston was answering a summons to meet with President Davis and his cabinet in the temporary Confederate capital, Greensboro. The general rejoined his troops at Hillsborough with authority to negotiate surrender terms.[152]

Meanwhile in Raleigh, the decision had been taken to surrender the city rather than risk its destruction. The peace commissioners[153] spent the night of April 12 at Sherman's headquarters where they were treated with friendly courtesy.[154] But word reached Raleigh that the peace commissioners had been captured, and Governor Vance and other state officials left the capital taking along the state's records.

Early the next morning (Thursday) a Raleigh delegation carrying a surrender flag met Sherman's cavalry commander, young General Kilpatrick, who promised to protect lives and property and also vowed to "pursue with relentless fury all traitors in armed opposition to the integrity of the Union."[155] The entrance of the Union troops came so close upon the heels of the departure of General Wheeler's Confederate troops that Susan Collier actually spoke to two Yankees, before she noticed "the hateful blue blouse," because they went into the grove carrying captured Confederate flags.

The scene in Raleigh and at St. Mary's was quite different from that of two days before. All businesses were closed, and the people were shut in their homes fearfully awaiting their fate. Smedes kept the girls close by the buildings, but from their windows they could see the flames and hear the exploding of shells at the nearby railway depot.[156] The Confederates' last act had been to fire the food and ammunition stored there. To add to the general gloom, a downpour turned Raleigh streets to mire.

General Sherman set up his headquarters in the governor's mansion at the foot of Fayetteville Street; he found the house emptied of all its furniture. Gen. Oliver Otis Howard, who commanded the right wing of Sherman's army, encamped some of his men in the grove at St. Mary's School. There had been no little excitement before the situation became stabilized. The last of the rebel stragglers were driven off at pistol point, making Sue Collier's "blood boil *cold.*" The housekeeper "talked up" to the "vandals" who demanded brandy. Mrs. Wheat insulted a Yankee, who chased her with fixed bayonet and threatened "to burn the school down," and the grounds were thoroughly but fruitlessly searched for "hidden treasures." Sue Collier noted in her diary that one of the pirates "put a pistol" to Smedes's head and threatened to blow his brains out if he did not get into the house, and that "the Dr. was glad to get in the house." As a crowning insult, "a scoundrel came into the parlor and read the capitulation of General Lee's army to some of the girls."[157]

The officers camped in the circle. The students, who could see into their mess tent, wondered where "all that gleaming silver" came from.

They saw one soldier in the tent "kissing a photograph." There was much noise and confusion in the grove as the bands played loudly and late. Some of the girls became disturbed because Smedes, realist that he was, invited the "plague-taked Yankee" officers in and gave them "ham, potatoes, pickles, and everything" and even called them "my dear fellow." Some of the pupils and all of the servants stayed outside to hear the music, but many of the girls closed their windows "and would not hear a note of it." The most ardent rebels gossiped about "the shocking conduct" of the girls and teachers who talked to the "plague-taked" Yankees. Eventually, things calmed down and Smedes held prayers as usual. Most of the girls were afraid to undress, but they were "protected through the night by merciful Providence."[158] April 13 had been a tumultuous day.

Next morning the officers' tents had disappeared from the circle, although the men remained camped in the grove. General Howard stayed with Mr. and Mrs. R. S. Tucker near St. Mary's until he left Raleigh on April 30. He wrote his wife that the Tuckers "are young people like you and me. I have been treated with marked cordiality and have acquired a great friendship for them. There is No More War!"[159]

On Sunday morning, which was Easter, General Howard's men "had the impertinence" to send coffee for breakfast. Smedes, some of his family, and some of the students drank it "with greatest pleasure." But six-year-old Sadie Smedes, who was fond of coffee, announced firmly, "I don't take Yankee coffee!" Most of the girls followed Sadie's example. Bessie Cain of Hillsborough wrote an account of that Sunday to her alumna mother, Sarah Jane Bailey Cain:

This morning O horrors, the United States flag was hoisted in the grove. We went to Chapel for the first time since the arrival of our enemies. We had a few flowers in Chapel and seven Yankee Officers came in, But thus far they have treated us with the greatest possible kindness and respect. . . . after dinner the band and about two hundred yankees came up and had preaching in the grove. . . . the service commenced with a hymn played by the band. It was perfectly exquisite. . . . the teachers asked Dr. Smedes if we could go for a walk, we had been cooped up in the house so long. . . . we enjoyed our walk so much. We have been hearing the worst news. . . . what will become of us.[160]

On Easter Monday, just as General Sherman and his staff were about to board the train for Durham Station to meet General Johnston, the news of Lincoln's assassination arrived. After sternly ordering the telegraph operator to tell absolutely no one the contents of the coded message, Sherman proceeded to the rendezvous. The two generals had never met, but each had respect for the other's ability. They borrowed the small log house of James Bennett nearby and there Sherman told Johnston of the assassination. The southerner, who did not attempt to hide his distress, responded that Lincoln's death was "the greatest possible calamity to the South."[161] Hurrying back to Raleigh, General Sherman planned his measures for protecting the city from the vengeance of his troops, who would surely blame the South for the president's murder.

In the grove at St. Mary's all was orderly. General Howard told Smedes that "nothing was to be feared from his troops."[162] Raleigh historian Moses N. Amis later wrote that crowds of soldiers were to be seen standing on street corners "open in their declarations to have vengeance for what they termed 'the rebel murder.'"[163] Bessie Cain described that night at St. Mary's in a letter to her mother:

We knew that on the least provocation the Yankees would do anything they wanted to us. . . . we were frightened to death. The officers thought they could restrain their soldiers, but they thought if the news about Lincoln spread . . . they would set fire to houses, and have a tremendous uproar; the noise would be heard here and then St. Mary's would be set on fire. We all slept in our clothes having filled the pocket of our dresses with anything we particularly wanted to save. Nothing however happened . . . we have no news of Johnston yet, oh what has become of Buddy [her soldier brother]?[164]

Sue Collier noted in her diary on the morning of April 18, "We are all safe, much to our surprise. Our movements are all watched though. The girls do not mind it very much."

Among the St. Mary's girls, as among the people of the entire South, opinion was divided. Some called the death of President Lincoln "A Great and wonderful surprise"; others called it "the dreadful news."[165] Many an "unreconstructed rebel," St. Mary's faculty and alumnae among them, would forever lay the entire blame for the Civil War upon "that black Republican Lincoln."

On April 18 Generals Sherman and Johnston met again at James Bennett's. Sherman wrote out surrender terms providing for a general amnesty, the guarantee of constitutional rights, and the recognition of existing state governments. These terms were rejected outright by the cabinet and the new president, Raleigh-born Andrew Johnson. On April 24 General Grant arrived in Raleigh. When he showed Sherman his own orders of March 4 from Lincoln warning him not to make political terms with Lee, Sherman realized his dilemma.[166] Finally on April 26 the shaky armistice became a peace on the same terms that Lee had received. The next day rations for ten days were issued to Johnston's disbanding army from Union supplies. When General Johnston divided among his men the $54,000 in silver left, each man got less than $2.[167]

Although the official policy of the forces occupying Raleigh was one of conciliation, the residents of the city suffered personal indignities and property losses. Most of the pillaging was done by Sherman's undisciplined fringe, known as "the bummers," or by Wheeler's stragglers during the confusion of the Confederate evacuation and the Federal occupation. There was hardly a horse left in town. Some houses were burned, and many families lost their jewelry and silver. Bennett Smedes lost his favorite heirloom ring to a Federal soldier. He had gone to protect a near neighbor and St. Mary's alumna, the wife of Gen. William R. Cox, and he saved her jewelry by giving up his.[168] The food shortage became acute in Raleigh as large numbers of blacks left their plantations and crowded into town, the plantations having been literally stripped by Sherman's men.[169]

The women of Raleigh and the schoolgirls at St. Mary's had some difficulty deciding on the proper conduct under prevailing conditions. Some realists elected, as had Aldert Smedes, to accept the situation with the best possible grace. Some bitterly refused to recognize the sad facts. The younger ladies of Raleigh were sorely torn between southern patriotism and their desire for some excitement. Many shut themselves behind closed blinds for all of April and ventured forth on necessary errands with uncurled hair and wearing their oldest faded calicoes, according to Mary Bayard Devereux Clarke. Others dressed in their best and walked out with the Yankee officers, insisting all the while that they "did it to save their homes."[170] Sue Collier recorded that a classmate had "felt it impossible to refuse" the bouquet sent by a Federal officer. That was the day of Johnston's surrender, and Collier lamented, "Oh God why hast thou forsaken us in our adversity?"

The St. Mary's students incurred the wrath of General Howard with their daily demonstration of drawing their curtains as the United States flag was raised in the grove. Howard finally stopped that overt hostility by threatening to close the school; the girls enjoyed their martyrdom. His successor, Gen. Gordon Granger, ignored the fiery little rebels. "Let the little doves flutter," he said, "they cannot hurt the eagle. If I desired to punish them, I should rather order that the school be kept open during vacation."[171] Smedes lectured his "little doves" so sternly that when General Sherman called a few days later he was "charmed with the polite reception" he received. "So charmed," Mary Bayard Clarke reported, "that after saying adieu he must needs turn at the bottom of the steps for a parting bow." Unfortunately, the girls were making ugly faces, and some were shaking their fists. The general was so amused that he told the story himself.[172]

On the evening of April 26 the official announcement of General Johnston's surrender was made. On the St. Mary's campus two nights later, the troops still camped in the grove sent up fire rockets until "the whole face of the earth seemed to be luminated." Soon a torchlight procession and a band arrived and "formed a circle at the front gate." Some of the students could not help enjoying such a "splendid, beautiful sight" despite their "sad, sad hearts," while others viewed the spectacle as "mocking the fate of our beloved country—its funeral." [173] Actually, the display was in honor of General Howard, who was to leave Raleigh the next morning.

As the long lines of Yankee troops left the city on their march to Washington for the grand review before disbandment, Raleigh's citizens stayed in their homes. Although orders against foraging had been issued, a band of soldiers thought to be "bummers" appeared in the grove at St. Mary's. As riders circled the buildings, the rumors spread that the school would be confiscated for barns. [174] All day in the distance the girls could hear the sound of firing—21 guns at sunrise and at 30-minute intervals, and 36 guns at sunset—to honor the murdered president. [175] On May 23 the army passed in review down Pennsylvania Avenue. And it was over at last.

Aldert Smedes, on the eve of the expected fall of Richmond, had called the St. Mary's family together in the chapel. He spoke of the evils of war and "the fierce and dreadful passions it inflames." After talking at some length of the destruction, the waste, the terrible loss of life, and God's punishment of His errant children, he said:

Alas, that a country once so favored, so envied, so admired as ours should present to the world a spectacle so sad, so horrible—"the bloodiest picture in the book of time". . . .

We mourn, we ought to mourn. We are summoned to the sanctuary of God to . . . spread our hearts before him . . . to supplicate His pardon. [176]

## CHAPTER FOUR

# "POVERTY IS A BADGE OF HONOR"

The departure of Sherman did not end the long ordeal for the people of North Carolina, for the bitter years of Reconstruction lay ahead. Gen. John Schofield was placed in command of the occupying troops in the state. The Tenth and Twenty-third Corps and Kilpatrick's cavalry remained in Raleigh, but there were no troops quartered in the St. Mary's grove after May 11.[1] Despite the Federal presence, Sue Collier confided to her diary on May 11, "Proud am I to be called a Reb. . . . it is only a smothered flame. . . . It will take only one puff to revive it." The "flame" was soon quenched by the news that Jefferson Davis had been captured on May 10.

Mourning the lost cause did not impede flirtations with the "Johnnie Rebs" who gathered at the front gate of the campus to ogle. Sometimes the boldest would wrap a poem around a rock and toss it over. Their verses were mostly patriotic, running to lines like, "Oh weep for the South" or "God bless our Southern girls." There were "Confeds" in the parlor nearly every night that May with permission to call on one or more of the students, but a "Billie Yank" who dared to kiss his hand to the girls was frigidly ignored, and they "could have caned him well."[2]

Classes continued until the normal vacation date in June.[3] St. Mary's was one of the few schools that remained open throughout the Civil War. Pupils from the eastern section of the state, some of whom had not been home in many months, began to leave school as soon as it was safe to travel. A father or two went to Raleigh to escort home the group of students from a particular area. Smedes himself left in mid-May to see about his property in the North, and Mrs. Smedes was able to go with him.[4]

Many a St. Mary's student returned home to a devastated plantation and the prospect of near starvation until the next crops were harvested. Harriet Cobb Lane wrote for her children recollections of the return to her Wayne County home. As soon as women were permitted to ride the trains, she left Raleigh with her uncle. At home, Harriet learned that Sherman's men had "destroyed literally every useful thing" on the plantation and found her home wrecked, except for the room in which Mrs. Cobb lay ill. In addition to the wagonload of their own corn, returned by a Federal officer, their diet consisted of the hardtack, fatback, and brown sugar issued by the government. They still had some of their wartime "coffee" made from dried sweet potatoes and parched rye, wheat, and barley ground together. Almost the only cash available anywhere during the summer of 1865 was made by selling to the occupying troops. The Cobbs sold mulberries at $2 a gallon.[5] Mary Bayard Clarke wrote in 1866, "Poverty is a badge of honor now."[6]

Much of the rebuilding of the shattered economy of the South fell to the "Southern ladies" who found themselves alone and responsible for families or married to men who returned home broken either in body or spirit. Emily James Putnam, the first dean of Barnard College, writing in 1910 on the lady throughout history, observed, "The Southern lady was forced by war and ruin to make in a day the transition the rest of the world had taken several centuries to effect."[7]

During the 1860s and 1870s the public schools became women's domain. When the war began only 25 percent of the nation's public school teachers were females. By 1880 the figure was 60 percent; by 1910, 80 percent.[8] Only 7.5 percent of North Carolina's public school teachers were women in 1859. By 1863 40 percent were women,[9] and it became socially acceptable for "society ladies" to teach in the public school system. Prewar society had considered teaching respectable but had been inclined to pity the woman who "had" to teach. The average salary paid a woman teaching in public schools in the South was $25 a month, the equivalent of 64 cents in gold in 1865.[10] Any woman who completed the course at St. Mary's was well prepared to teach in an academy or public school of the day, and many of Smedes's former pupils became teachers.[11] Some alumnae taught a few students in their own homes or offered music or drawing lessons to support themselves during and after the war.

A career was thrust upon many, as in the case of Katie McKimmon, who was 18 and still a student at St. Mary's when in 1868 her brother wrote her that there were no more family funds. He suggested that she "board with Dr. Smedes and render any assistance possible."[12] She became an assistant in the French department and later had charge of the primary department. "Miss Katie" remained at St. Mary's for over 60 years.

The sudden need for women teachers provided new momentum to the movement for higher education for women. Between 1865 and 1890, Vassar, Smith, Wellesley, Bryn Mawr, Barnard, Radcliffe, Goucher, Sophie Newcomb, and Agnes Scott were founded. North Carolina's first public institution for the education of women was the State Normal and Industrial School (later the North Carolina College for Women and now the University of North Carolina at Greensboro), which opened in 1892.

Some southern women became writers instead of teachers. One of the most popular of all southern writers was Frances Christine Fisher Tiernan (1846–1920) of Salisbury, who wrote over 40 books under the pseudonymn of Christian Reid. Her only boarding school experience was a brief stay at St. Mary's.[13] The war opened other vocations to women. Nursing was more popular in the North than in the South because many southern families considered it an "improper" profession for young, unmarried women.[14] Sewing and painting china at home were occupations of talented gentle ladies. Some venturesome women went into offices, retail stores, and even into factories.

In spite of the opening doors, women did not get the vote; giving the vote to black men was controversial enough without including women. However, the war did lead to another wave of reform movements— movements for temperance, for birth control, against prostitution, and for improved educational opportunities for women.

Even though the opportunities for educated women were expanding, the economic realities of the postwar South denied education to many of them. When the fall session of 1865 opened at St. Mary's, enrollment was down to about 50 boarders compared to 120 in 1864.[15] It was 1876 before total enrollment again reached 120 students.[16] Smedes was able to weather the lean years of that decade by using income from investments and by offering scholarships to fill the school. Regular tuition after the war was $130 a session or $260 a year. That was only 1/3 higher than prewar charges but still a little higher than tuition at most southern schools. When Peter Evans Smith's friend was "put out" with him for persuading him to send his daughter to expensive St. Mary's, Smith wrote to his daughter Lena at the school, "If he can't appreciate a good school, I hope his daughter can, and I feel sure of her thanks . . . if she remains there a year."[17]

# St. Mary's School,

The desolation which the war has brought upon the South, is felt, perhaps, in no department, more keenly, than in that of Education.

In some of our States the free schools have been suspended; and, in all, parents who formerly were able to pay liberally for the education of their children, are now embarrassed to provide for them food and clothing.

My position, as the head of a school for girls, has brought under my notice many touching instances of an ardent desire for literary advantage, without the ability to pay for them.

In the present depressed state of the country, the School yields only a support. But, that support being secured, there are in our ample buildings many vacant places, which, without pecuniary loss, I could fill with pupils, paying for their board, and their tuition in Latin, French and English, seventy-five dollars, a term of five months; or one hundred and fifty dollars, a year.

The benefit would be administered to those who are of gentle breeding and nurture, once the possessors of affluence, now the victims of poverty; and it would be so administered as not to wound the most delicate sensibility.

To any congregation or individual, disposed to aid me in this endeavor to extend the usefulness of my school, and to alleviate a pressing want in our community, I pledge myself to use my best exertions to make their bounty a blessing to its recipients.

Our next term will open on the 17th July.

Communications addressed to me at Raleigh, N. C., will receive prompt attention.

## ALDERT SMEDES.

Announcement sent in 1867 to parents of current and prospective students by Aldert Smedes

In June, 1867, Smedes published a circular stating his situation frankly and offering dozens of personal scholarships. He wrote:

In the present depressed state of the country, the School yields only a support. But that support being secured, there are in our ample buildings many vacant places, which, without pecuniary loss, I could fill with pupils, paying for their board, and their tuition in Latin, French and English, seventy-five dollars, a term of five months. . . .

The benefit would be administered to those who are of gentle breeding and nurture, once the possessors of affluence, now the victims of poverty; and it would be administered as not to wound the most delicate sensibility.[18]

Smedes invited any congregation or individual to assist him in providing scholarships. In their letters home St. Mary's pupils of the post-war years inquired anxiously, "Will I be able to come back next session?" Raleigh historian Moses Amis wrote that the benefactions of the rector of St. Mary's "in the way of free tuition and board on credit, at all times liberal, were in those days princely."[19]

Kemp Plummer Battle wrote of Smedes, "He gave as largely in proportion to his means as any man within my knowledge. He endeavored to keep his charities secret, but it was impossible to conceal from his friends that they were abundant to the verge of danger to his financial status."[20] Eventually Smedes began requiring definite security for the loans made to his businessmen friends.[21] He was hoping to use his remaining assets to purchase the St. Mary's property so that Bennett Smedes could continue the school indefinitely. The future of St. Mary's was very much on the mind and heart of Aldert Smedes during the last decade of his life.[22] The Camerons, however, remained unwilling to sell, so the lease was renewed for about $2,000 annually. The postwar economic problem in the South was the absence of cash. Smedes husbanded his resources very carefully, acting personally as the school's steward. He prided himself upon dealing with the local merchants insofar as possible, saying that they were his patrons and he theirs.[23] Raleigh businessmen marveled that a clergyman should possess such financial acumen.[24]

Smedes's response to the political chaos of the period was as practical as his approach to the financial problems. He promptly applied for and received his presidential pardon. Pres. Andrew Johnson added to the list of those excluded from the general amnesty, and therefore required to make personal application for a pardon, "all persons who have voluntarily participated in said rebellion and the estimated value of whose taxable property is over $20,000."[25] Smedes fell under that clause regarding property. He enclosed the required oath of allegiance "which I have taken cheerfully and which I intend religiously to fulfill."[26]

North Carolina ratified the Fourteenth Amendment and was back in the union by July 20, 1868. Only 18 carpetbaggers and 15 blacks were elected to the state's constitutional convention, which was dominated by the newly organized Republican party. The progressive constitution written by that convention reformed the public school system, but the necessary taxes were never levied. Therefore, a real need remained for the private schools that had survived the war.

Although political chaos and corruption lasted longer in many southern states than in North Carolina, there was turmoil enough with the railroad scandals, the impeachment and removal of Gov. W. W. Holden, and the Ku Klux Klan indictments. Letters of St. Mary's students reflect an awareness of the political tumult on both the state and national levels. The few daughters of southern Republicans found themselves ostracized as "scalawags." One of these, Mary Devereux Clarke, who was at St. Mary's in 1868 or 1869, described her plight to her brother. She wrote, "We have 68 scholars now and some of the ugliest and worst girls that it was ever my fate to meet with. I did not know how bad girls would be till I came up here." [27]

## "WE ARE HIS CHILDREN AND GRANDCHILDREN"

Despite the political, social, and economic confusion of the Reconstruction years, life within the little world of St. Mary's remained relatively unchanged. Smedes was old enough to be a grandfather figure, but he continued to supervise every detail of his "large and entire family." Mary Ferrand Henderson wrote to her mother, "He takes good care of his girls. He seems to think we are all his children and grandchildren." [28] Writing years later in the alumnae magazine, Nellie Jackson Mason described Aldert Smedes as he appeared at 60, "his cheeks as pink as a baby's, his eyes as blue as the summer skies, his silvery wavy hair and the sweetest smile ever seen." [29]

By the 1870s the Smedes children, except for Sadie, who was still being educated at her father's school, were adults. Abe was practicing law in Goldsboro and George in Raleigh; George also taught at St. Mary's. Although an able lawyer,[30] George Smedes took a carefree attitude toward his practice. He posted his office hours as "from hell to breakfast," and when away left a card that read "will be back." [31] Bessie Smedes in 1874 married Moreau Pickette Leake of Wadesboro; they had no children. In 1876 Annie Smedes and Charles Root of Raleigh were married; they and their descendants contributed much to the community. During the 1870s there were, as usual, various Smedes nieces and cousins being educated at St. Mary's under the watchful care of Aldert Smedes.

Academic life during the postwar years led the girls to complain more than ever about how hard they were compelled to work. One wrote to her mother listing her courses and said of Smedes, "Yet don't you believe he asked me the other day if I had enough to do . . . since I have stopt music." [32]

There was a new emphasis upon science after "Mr. Bennett" joined the faculty. Extra lectures and demonstrations were scheduled at night and on Saturday mornings so that the whole school could attend. Student reactions were mixed. One wrote enthusiastically, "I am going to take every opportunity I get of seeing such things, for I think you can learn a great deal more by seeing than reading. . . . the burning of phosphorus and zinc in oxygen was perfectly beautiful. . . ." [33] Another student was less impressed and thought the required chemistry lectures "one of the greatest afflictions anyone could suffer," especially the Saturday morning lectures that kept her from reading one of the new "Saturday" books, *The Last Days of Pompeii*. [34]

French, still an essential "female accomplishment," remained "almost the language of the school," according to a student of the 1870s. Josephine LeGal presided at the French table where a cash fine was levied for every word of English uttered. Fortunately, "Aunt Amanda," the waitress, being Louisiana-born, spoke French. When mademoiselle's student niece roomed with her for awhile, visiting pupils were not permitted a word of English. [35] "A lady of learning and elegance," Josephine LeGal was "highly thought of, although a Romanist." [36] She taught at St. Mary's from 1869 until just six weeks before her death in the spring of 1882.

Nearly all of the faculty continued to live on campus. The women formed close, often lifelong, friendships. The teachers customarily gained a brief respite from duty by taking the light lunch in their rooms, and special friends formed "lunch clubs." One widowed teacher of the 1870s, Nora Devereux Cannon, and her three young daughters lived in a large room in the main building. She described her circumstances to a relative:

I do not mind running up the stairs fifty times a day. The room is heated by pipes from the furnace in the basement and is very . . . pleasant. I have . . . pictures . . . several pretty brackets with flower vases etc. and the promise of a hanging basket for my window so that in spite of the plain and shabby furniture my room is a pretty looking place. My children are delighted to be at school . . . and I am delighted to know that I am paying for my children's education as well as my board. So why should I not be happy? [37]

At St. Mary's during the Reconstruction years the academic habits of the pupils were supervised even more carefully than ever. The report card advised, "Parents will confer a favor by aiding with their exhortations our efforts to promote the health and improvement of our pupils, and by measuring, in some degree, their indulgencies to their children by the character of their reports."[38]

Lizzie Jones in 1873 confided to Mollie Nixon that she had "three or four cries" over her report and advised her friend never to take rhetoric. She was unhappy with "Mr. Bennett's science grade" as well but had resolved not "to let angry passions rise." She had never had to study so hard in her life and considered Smedes "the crosses ole' critter I ever saw." But by the end of the school session, Lizzie's grades and her morale were greatly improved, and she hoped that her father would allow her to complete her education at St. Mary's.[39] Many of the students wrote to parents and friends, "I am studying harder than ever I did."

By the 1870s the dormitories had changed little—the prettily decorated alcoves, the hospital-narrow beds in neat rows, the dim gas lights, the giggling girls. And there still were the homesick ones like Mary Ferrand Henderson, who during her birthday week wrote home, "I don't see why children and their parents should have to be separated. . . . I think an education is dearly bought even excepting the money cost. . . . Have my plate and chair set as if I was there."[40]

The postwar food at the school was rated "excellent" by the students brought up during the lean war years. They wrote home of "mutton and beef, and chicken once or twice a week." Because desserts were seldom served, except for fresh fruits in season, gift boxes were highly prized. Sometimes as many as 20 friends were "invited to a box down in the storeroom."[41] It was permissible to buy sweets and fruit in town or from the several servants who were allowed to sell at the school. Sometimes supper parties were put together like that described by a student of 1876. It was an oyster stew for six with two girls bringing the oysters, one butter, another crackers and pickles, and another apples and candy.[42] Food was not allowed in the dormitories, but the implication was that the stew was cooked on the dormitory heater.

If feasting, legal or otherwise, landed students in the "sick-room," Sara Cade Smedes, widowed sister-in-law of the rector, provided loving care. The girls of 1867 discovered at the patent medicine counter a cough syrup that was recommended by Lucy Warren to her mother as marvelously beneficial. It was, she wrote, "made of hops."[43]

"Five times around the grove" was still the daily exercise requirement. For playtime jumping rope was the rage with "all the girls large and small doing it" in 1867.[44] Trees in the grove were older and more stately then, and in 1867 Smedes "had arbor vitae set out."[45] The year before, a plain board fence had been erected to give protection from the townspeople who had made "a thoroughfare of the grove."[46]

Amusements were simple and largely within the campus family. A monthly newspaper made its appearance in 1869. Called *Embryo*, it was "published" by the *Utile Duci* Society. That society of about 40 members seems to have been unofficial, but both Bessie and Annie Smedes were members. The newspaper related events in "Smedesborough," where Smedes was the "Mayor," the dining room "City Hall," and Mary Iredell's dormitory "Iredellton Square." Read aloud to the whole school, the short-lived paper reported "crimes," the most heinous of which was that of leaving the front gate open "against the Mayor's orders." [47] More serious offenses were committed occasionally. In 1870 a student actually "met her suitor behind the breastworks." She was promptly sent home to New England. [48]

Most of the girls amused themselves with chorales, tableaux, and the minor diversions of "visiting Saturdays." A surprise holiday, granted in 1866 because "Mr. Bennett begged for it" and because the students had been "such good girls," was spent in preparing for the three elaborate tableaux presented that night to the assembled school. They depicted "Joan d'Arc," "The Three Graces," and "The Intercepted Love Letter." The next year the "little children got up the chorales," and the rector "was delighted with them." [49]

The highlight of the fall of 1873 was the arrival of the circus. Mary Ferrand Henderson described the excitement when "about half past nine we heard the music and Dr. Smedes sent us word to put on our hats and come down street." Later that week Smedes took a number of students to see the animals, but they were not to attend the performance. Although he saw no harm in a circus himself, "the other denominations would never get done talking about it" if he allowed such frivolity. Unable to resist temptation completely, the girls "all stood before the door of the tent looking at the performance" but refused to enter, even at the manager's invitation, "to see the little dogs act." Smedes, joining the students at the door, found the performance "splendid" and decided to let the "other denominations" think what they pleased as he led his happy group into the circus tent. [50] Almost as exciting as the circus were the "baseball matches at Mr. Lovejoy's school" witnessed by Smedes and his pupils over the years.

Christmas of 1876 was "an event to be remembered," according to Kate DeRosset Meares of the faculty. "Shut in by snow from the outside world, the girls made the best of it" and were "real merry." A path was shoveled to the chapel, which had been "dressed beautifully" for the Christmas Eve Communion service "with full chorale." After the midnight service, a student costumed as Santa delivered gifts and "there was great jollification in the different dormitories" until all hours. On Christmas day breakfast was delayed until 9:00, and the late afternoon Christmas dinner was such a feast that it "almost set the girls wild." [51]

In the postwar years the soirees at the school continued to be leading events of the Raleigh social season. For the soiree in November, 1867, Bessie Cain wore the required "white dress with high neck body" because, as she wrote to her grandmother, "low neck is frowned upon by the young ladies at St. Mary's." After the musicale, "the girls and a few of the young gentlemen danced a little while."[52]

Although elaborate clothes were, as always, forbidden, St. Mary's girls showed, as always, considerable interest in fashion. Quantities of goods were available in Raleigh stores, and calico was only 18 cents a yard in 1867. "Bismarck brown" was the most fashionable shade for a fall outfit. Lucy Warren planned to have her Sunday dress of that hue made of "beautiful Empress cloth" and "with a sacque, as they are much worn now," and trimmed in velvet in the same shade.[53] For class the girls continued to wear calicoes, and ostentation was unpopular. One of the students was thought "to put on a good many airs" because she possessed a watch which she "sported very extensively."[54] Nonetheless, the cut of the calicoes was important. A student of 1873 asked for two calicoes "made in the latest fashion" and instructed, "Be sure to have them open in front and to touch the floor." Her plain dresses without overskirts looked "rather queer," she said.[55]

By the 1870s the fashionable hair style was an arrangement of braids pinned close to the back of the head. Often a cluster of curls hung over the braids or one long ringlet fell to the left shoulder. St. Mary's girls gave a great deal of business to a woman in town who made braids of real or "false" hair.[56]

## "A HIGHER AND MORE BINDING DUTY"

So life at St. Mary's changed little during the upheavals of the Reconstruction era. In 1871 a father who had spent a week at the school sent an almost rhapsodic account of his impressions to the *Maryland Church Record*. He was perceptive, for he wrote:

The chapel is the core; the central life of the school; the holy offices of prayer and praise, the clear and reiterated instructions in the Word of God and the doctrines of the church, the honest and faithful enforcement of vital, inward devotion and practical holiness, as a higher and more binding duty *on them*, because of their great and peculiar advantage—these things, as I saw and heard, helped me to understand why the graduates of St. Mary's so generally adorne [sic] the doctrine of God . . . by a content and holy life. . . . They have occupied . . . no mean place in the world's eye and exercised no slight influence for good.[57]

Aldert Smedes continued his active participation in the affairs of the diocese; also he served as trustee of the General Theological Seminary and of the University of the South, and was deputy to the General Convention. Episcopalians had managed an amicable reunion almost immediately after the war because their bishops approached the matter as old friends. There was controversy until Bishop Atkinson won a change in the prayer of thanksgiving for peace so that southerners gave thanks for unity without reference to defeat or to slavery.[58] The Episcopal church set about the task of helping to educate the some 4 million freedmen in the South. Aldert Smedes was one of the incorporators of the St. Augustine Normal School and Collegiate Institute established in Raleigh in 1867 by the Freedmen's Commission of the Protestant Episcopal Church to meet the demand for black teachers and ministers. When the first principal of St. Augustine's died suddenly in 1872, the Reverend John Esten Cooke Smedes (younger brother of Aldert Smedes), who had operated a school in Mississippi, went to be the temporary principal. He remained as head of the school until his resignation in 1884 to return to the pastorate.[59] The presence of his brother and family in Raleigh was a great joy to Aldert Smedes. They lived at St. Mary's while quarters were being built for them on the campus of St. Augustine's, and J. E. C. Smedes often preached in the chapel— sometimes in verse, as he was a poet.

As Aldert Smedes approached old age, the future of his school became a matter of concern to the Diocese of North Carolina. A committee appointed by the 1873 convention "to take such steps as may seem to them expedient toward securing properties to be owned by the Diocese as a school for girls" inquired about buying the St. Mary's campus from the Camerons. The committee reported to the 1874 convention that "the owners did not desire to dispose of it in any manner" and recommended that "in the present state of the Diocese and of the country" no further action be taken.[60]

At the convention of 1873 Bishop Atkinson in his annual address paid Smedes the highest praise. After describing his "unwearied labors, singular tact and judgment, firmness tempered by gentleness and affection, and his large-hearted liberality," the bishop went on:

If I were called upon to say what individual has exerted for many years, and is now exerting, the most beneficial influence upon the people of this State, I should be bound to express the Conviction that it is not this or that statesman . . . or soldier . . . , but the man who has successfully trained up so many maidens . . . to be themselves useful and happy in their respective spheres and to diffuse around them the incalculable benefit of womanly intelligence, refinement and piety.[61]

During the winter of 1876, Aldert Smedes suddenly began to suffer fainting spells. When the diagnosis of Bright's disease was made, Smedes "seemed determined to ignore the inevitable" and continued his daily round of duties even when in great pain.[62] Forced to preach his last sermon while seated, he finally relinquished the pastoral duties to his son.[63] On the Sunday before his death, Smedes was strong enough to attend the chapel service. Afterward, he told Mary Iredell that he had "never enjoyed a service so much . . . its power for comfort, its wonderful grandeur."[64]

On April 24 Smedes taught a class and then "tottered to his bed."[65] At breakfast the next morning the St. Mary's family knew that Aldert Smedes's condition had worsened when Bennett Smedes, visibly distraught, did not realize that he had pronounced the benediction instead of saying grace. Classes were canceled, and "soon the pianos were hushed and everything was perfectly quiet" as the girls and teachers "sat and waited for the news." Their rector died at 11:00 on Wednesday morning, April 25, 1877, just five days after his 67th birthday.[66]

A letter written by Annie Bitting, a student of 1877, describes the next two days:

Dr. Smedes had requested to be laid in the Chapel. . . . Of course we all went to the funeral at Christ Church, the little girls dressed in white and black led the procession, the tallest ones coming up behind. We were all dressed in black, and had black crepe badges tied with white ribbon on our arms. . . . Each of us took a bouquet of flowers, and, when the grave in Oakwood Cemetery, Raleigh was covered up, we went up and put our bouquet down. . . . so that when we came away, the grave was covered entirely with exquisite flowers. . . . six ministers, in their surplices, followed the hearse. . . . Friday night we were told the bells would be rung the next day as usual, and we would have prayers in the Chapel . . . the girls all came out of the Chapel crying. . . . and Mr. Smedes had utterly failed to command his voice during the service and afterwards when he tried to thank us for being so quiet and orderly. . . . I do feel so sorry for him. He told us to tell our parents that the school would go on just the same until June. Nothing has been decided about next year.[67]

Sarah Smedes remained calm, receiving friends "with perfect composure."[68] Tributes to the memory of Aldert Smedes poured in from all over the South. So many people, especially St. Mary's alumnae, remembered the man—his inborn gaiety, his gracious manner, his fatherly affection and his quick sympathy with their joys and their griefs.[69]

Others remembered Aldert Smedes the educator. Emilie McVea summed up the first 35 years of education at St. Mary's when she wrote in 1904:

the characteristics which from the beginning distinguished this school, have been simplicity, sincerity, a regard for tradition, an open-mindedness to the demands of new conditions, and a belief in the value of service. In the earlier years the standards of education for women required only a cultivated taste for literature, an acquaintance with the stories of history, and some accomplishment in music or art. Girls of that period left school at the age of seventeen and were considered fully equipped for life. St. Mary's fulfilled those demands and more. She succeeded in implanting in her students an appreciation of culture which enabled them to discern true values in literature and art, a love of truth which carried them far in intellectual development after they had left her halls, a reverence for sacred things which made them a power for good in their church and in their community.[70]

The editor of the *Observer* (Raleigh) called the death of the rector of St. Mary's "an irreparable loss" and "a most afflicting calamity . . . fallen upon the Christian Church, the course of education, and the State at large. . . ."[71] His fellow clergymen passed resolutions of praise;[72] and Bishop Atkinson, "who always weighed his words carefully,"[73] flatly declared, "Dr. Smedes accomplished more for the advancement of this Diocese and for the promotion of the best interest of society in its limits than any man who ever lived in it. . . . His work remains, and will remain from generation to generation."[74]

## CHAPTER FIVE

# "A MOST SACRED TRUST"

For 35 years Aldert Smedes had *been* St. Mary's. Upon his death every-one wondered what the future held for the school. On the day after Smedes's funeral, the *Observer* (Raleigh) carried on its editorial page the announcement that there would be "no interruption in the conduct of the school. . . . The corps of teachers so well and so favorably known will remain . . . and there is every guarantee that the utmost care and attention will continue to be paid to the pupils. . . ." The edi-tor expressed his hope that the institution which had "fixed itself in the affections not only of our city and state, but of the South generally" would "live for generations to come as a memorial of its distinguished founder."[1]

Undoubtedly that was the hope of all who knew St. Mary's. But Bennett Smedes, feeling unsure of his ability to fill his father's place, made no decision beyond the immediate future. Mary Iredell wrote to an alumna who was considering returning to teach that although "the girls were much subdued" everything had gone on "as usual, not one single School exercise being omitted." She added:

Mr. Smedes has endeavored to discharge his father's responsibilities as he him-self would have done, and he has justified all I told you of his ability to do so and more. He would like to go on with the school and nothing would prevent him if the means to do so were forthcoming. But so far he does not see how it can be done. . . .[2]

Bennett Smedes, a gentle and scholarly man, was ill-fitted to cope with the financial problems of the Reconstruction era. Dynamic Aldert Smedes had overshadowed his retiring son completely, thus depriving them both of what could have been a strong partnership. The son real-

The Reverend Bennett Smedes, D.D., rector, 1877–1899

ized this. He wrote on July 3, 1877, to Catherine (Kate) DeRosset Meares:

You well know to what extent Father took upon his shoulders the labors and anxieties of the School. He classified all the girls, attended to the accounts of everyone connected with St. Mary's, kept the house, catered for the establishment. . . . He had no clerk, no steward. . . . Time and time again I made the attempt to get between him and his overwhelming work; but . . . so completely was his method . . . peculiar to himself . . . that it only worried him when I attempted to interpose. Consequently, though I have taught my classes here for thirteen years I am as much a novice in the matters of organizing a school in its various departments as when I first began.[3]

Because of Smedes's reluctance to head the school, Bishop Atkinson began a search for a clergyman with teaching and administrative experience to work with him. The most likely candidate proved to be in such "flourishing circumstances" in Wisconsin that he decided not to accept the position.[4]

For weeks Bennett Smedes wrestled with his disinclination to assume full responsibility for St. Mary's. In the end, he could not bring himself to refuse to accept what he considered to be "a most sacred trust."[5] He decided, "In order to keep up this work *for the Church* I shall try to conduct it myself."[6]

Once he had steeled himself, Bennett Smedes began to make plans for improvements both in the equipment and the curriculum. But first he took a wife. In October, 1877, a faculty member reported, "Mr. Smedes is going to be married to a sweet little woman. . . . She is very thoroughly educated, is a fine housekeeper, and we all think him very fortunate. Miss Etta Harvey is her name. . . . They have known each other for years."[7]

Henrietta Harvey had moved to Raleigh when John E. C. Smedes became principal of St. Augustine's Normal School and Collegiate Institute. An orphaned cousin of John's wife, she had become, by informal adoption, an older sister and teacher of their five children. "Miss Etta" was 26 and Smedes (she always called him "Mr. Smedes") was 40 when they were married; but he appeared so young that he grew a moustache and beard to make himself look the part of the rector of St. Mary's. He was somewhat shorter than his father, standing about 5 feet 10 inches.[8]

His fiancée was petite—"a titian beauty with brown eyes and a heavy suit of auburn hair," according to her foster sister. Emilie Smedes Holmes described the excitement at St. Mary's as the wedding date approached:

Mr. Smedes kept the girls on the anxious bench by announcing frequently his intention of being married during the ten-minute noon recess, so they would lose no time from their studies. However, nine o'clock on the morning of No-

Faculty, 1893–1894. Left to right: Albert Mack, Lizzie Battle, Kate McKimmon, Florence Slater, Bennett Smedes, Mlle. Rensch, Kate Shipp, Martha Dowd, Nancy Stone, Alice Dugger, and Emilie McVea

vember 20, 1877, found the girls present in a body at Christ Church with the assurance of ice-cream and a holiday ahead of them. The ceremony was performed by the rector of Christ Church, Reverend Matthias M. Marshall, assisted by Bishop [Theodore Benedict] Lyman.[9]

Henrietta Smedes was quiet and modest in public, but at home she was more vivacious. Her parties were highlights of the school year. The girls liked to hear about her life on her family's Louisiana plantation before its devastation by the Yankee soldiers.[10]

## "NOTHING FOR SHOW"

Having arranged his private life, Smedes, no longer the reluctant rector, took steps to raise the academic standards of his school. Although the assistant bishop of North Carolina, Dr. Lyman, had called St. Mary's "undoubtedly the best female school in the whole South" presenting "advantages of the highest character,"[11] Smedes realized that the best women's colleges in the country had attained the same standards as the men's colleges. He also realized that they were under fire for being too much like the institutions for men.[12] During his 22–year tenure, he made just enough changes to keep up with the demands of new situations but not enough to disturb his southern clientele, for he agreed wholeheartedly with his father's philosophy of education and religious convictions.

In his first sermon of each school year, Smedes gave his definition of education:

that *all your powers* may develop . . . to the best advantage. That your *bodies* may be cared for so as to secure for you one of earth's greatest blessings—health. . . . That your *intellectual faculties* may be developed so that you may have confidence in them by many a difficult exercise . . . may use them for your support or entertainment when the work for which you were sent into this world opens full to your view. And above all that your *moral* character may be trained . . . so that you will naturally turn toward those things which are true, honest, just, pure, lovely—of good report.[13]

The popular conception of the educational needs of women was changing, as evidenced in an 1877 series of Raleigh newspaper articles on the institutions for the education of females in the Carolinas. The editor said he fully recognized that "the proper education of the female youth of the land is as essential to the well-being of the state as that of our male youth . . . an educated woman is worth as much to society, in a politico-economico point of view, (to say nothing of refining influences) as an educated man. . . ."[14]

That Smedes expected southern women to continue in traditional roles is revealed in his comments in an 1879 letter to Ellen Tew, one of the first full graduates:

whatever you may be will be for good. Don't expect to do anything very conspicuous. Nothing very great as the world counts greatness; but in your own little way, as you say, . . . do *all* that you can in your proper sphere as sister, as companion, as a traveller with many others . . . to make Earth brighter & better & happier by your presence.[15]

Most St. Mary's women saw themselves in traditional roles, as evidenced by a review in 1882 in the school literary magazine of an article from the *New England Educational Journal*. It gave "many new ideas on the education of girls," ideas that sounded like those of Aldert Smedes:

Women make society, and it rests with them whether society shall raise or lower our country. . . . Thus in the kitchen, the home, the school, society and the church, the influence of woman is paramount; and the subject of Education for Girls is one of the greatest of the century.[16]

Over the next decade, however, horizons were to be broadened for the brightest of St. Mary's students under the influence of the truly excellent teachers Smedes employed.

Once he had decided to raise standards, Smedes spent lavishly from his inheritance for immediate improvements. He bought new furniture, "Baltimore heaters" to replace the wood stoves, laboratory equipment, maps and globes, several pianos, and a pipe organ for the chapel. He also purchased books for the new school library on the third floor of the main building. Eventually, there were over 2,500 volumes plus those in the rector's private library.[17] Upon Bennett Smedes's death in 1899, the newspapers noted that "he had been always a student and . . . kept his library supplied with the best books as they were issued, without regard to price."[18] It was also said of Bennett Smedes's administration that the equipment was "very fine for the day . . . nothing for show—everything for use."[19]

Smedes reorganized his school to meet the needs of his patrons and the times at all levels from the first grade to "higher" education. The Civil War so depleted the state's permanent school fund that public education was left to local governments until 1869.[20] High schools were so slow to develop that there was no provision for a public high school in Raleigh until 1905. To meet demand, a primary department was opened at St. Mary's in January, 1879, with eight pupils. A day scholar could go to St. Mary's for the first four grades, stay on either as a day student or a boarder for three years in the preparatory department, and continue for five or six more years to earn a diploma. It was recommended that she plan to spend an extra year in the academic department, if, in addition to the required subjects for graduation, she wished to study music or art seriously.

It was possible for a good student to enter the system at any point, to absorb so much as she could from the faculty, and to leave with at least the equivalent of a junior college education, although the term had not yet been invented and no degree was granted. Few chose that rigorous course. Most St. Mary's girls saw life from about the perspective of the 1869 student who, having just passed her seventeenth birthday, declared, "Mama is going to carry me home as a lady."[21] The largest graduating class of the eighties numbered seven. Most students were "partial graduates"; they took the same academic courses taught by the same teachers but not enough of them to earn diplomas. By the nineties attitudes were changing, and more students were taking advantage of the full academic course. A few alumnae, in fact, were interested in what later was known as "continuing education." The school

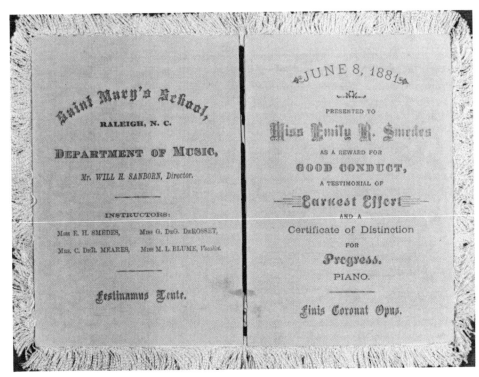

Music Certificate, 1881

catalog announced, "Liberal arrangements will be made with *old scholars* who wish to review their studies or to take lessons in any ornamental branch with a view to preparing themselves for teaching." They were warned, however, that special boarders under 20 would "be subject, in every respect, to the general rules of the School." [22]

The academic course leading to the St. Mary's diploma required grammar and rhetoric as well as five years of literature, and parents were requested "not to urge upon their daughter so many 'extras' as to hinder their advancement in a solid English education." American, English, and general history were required; art history and music history were optional. Mathematics through trigonometry was essential, and science requirements included geography, biology, botany, zoology, physiology, and a smattering of chemistry, physics, and astronomy. Logic, mental philosophy, and Paley's *Evidences of Christianity*, a knowledge of the catechism, Bible history, ecclesiastical history, and the prayer book were still necessary. The stiff requirement of five years of Latin could be reduced by one course by "demonstrated *proficiency*" in either French or German. One did not drop a course without permission, and attendance rules were stricter than in earlier days. New students were "classed" by the authorities who gave what the girls called "a right close examination" before placement.[23] The catalog stated of the preparatory department, as well as of the academic department:

Special attention is given to English composition. Beginning with abstracts of informal lectures on familiar objects, the pupils are taught to express themselves correctly, and encouraged to put on paper their own opinions and fancies. We esteem this branch of study of such importance, that *no young lady is excused from it* until she can dispense with it.[24]

## A LADY PRINCIPAL

As part of his reorganization plan, Bennett Smedes created the position of lady principal to provide administrative assistance. Alumna Catherine DeRosset Meares was employed in 1877 to fill the post. Her husband, Col. Gaston Meares, had been killed at Malvern Hill. Paul C. Cameron, who handled the St. Mary's property, wrote his sisters that he thought Kate Meares would do well. He added, "I think it should be made known who she is,"[25] for the widow of a war hero had special status then.

Kate Meares could stand on her own reputation. She had taught in several schools, including the excellent one run by her old French teacher, Madame Clement. In 1876 Aldert Smedes finally had convinced her that she should return to his school to teach music. He wrote, "I want you for the influence you will exert as a church woman; and an earnest Christian; and for the help you will give us in our Chapel Music."[26] Almost immediately, however, a family emergency called her home. Upon her return as lady principal, she was greeted joyfully. Plump and middle-aged, she always wore a white muslin cap trimmed in black ribbon, and the students looked upon her as a mother.

Bennett Smedes and Kate Meares made a good team. She was, he wrote her, to give advice and to devise a scheme whereby everything "would be conducted in decency and in order."[27] She was principal only a few short years before family obligations called her away again. She had, however, helped St. Mary's weather the school's second crisis (the Civil War being the first), a fact that Bennett Smedes gratefully acknowledged when in June, 1881, he wrote her, "You were sent in my extremity to give new life to the work; and right nobly did you fulfill your mission!"[28] Aldert Smedes would have agreed.

Marie Elizabeth Josephine Czarnomska, a faculty member since 1877, became the second lady principal. The students among themselves invariably referred to her as "the Czar." The best students loved and admired her, but most feared and admired her. Emilie Smedes Holmes described her as "tall and slender and of queenly bearing, with steel-grey eyes and jet black hair worn in a French twist, in the coils of which the red rose she affected seemed naturally to belong." [29] Of Polish and English parentage, she was a native of Long Island.

There were those who felt that a southern woman would have been a better choice, [30] but Smedes knew what he was doing. During her eight years as lady principal, Elizabeth Czarnomska made academic excellence important at St. Mary's. She gave much of herself, and she expected much of her students. She taught English literature and botany, and the girls thought her classes "interesting" and "inspiring." [31] The finest result of her efforts was the seven-member class of 1884. So gifted were they that their grade averages for their last three years at St. Mary's ranged from 98.4 to 96.1, and "each one stood first in some subject." Yet, reported the school literary magazine, "They have walked in love." [32] Three of the seven returned to St. Mary's to teach. Martha Dowd taught music and eventually headed that department. Both Elizabeth Battle and Emilie McVea served as lady principal. A fourth member, Belle Graves, became principal of the church school at Valle Crucis.

In 1888 Elizabeth Czarnomska went to Smith College as professor of English literature. She later taught at the University of Cincinnati and at Sweet Briar College. When, after 55 years as an educator, Czarnomska retired, her students from Smith and St. Mary's contributed to a fund to augment her pension from Sweet Briar. At age 78, she completed a two-volume anthology, *The Authentic Literature of Israel.* [33]

Under Elizabeth Czarnomska's direction of academic affairs at St. Mary's the usual reports were sent to parents and honor rolls were published in the local newspapers and announced at commencement; there was also "the reading out" every Friday afternoon. "At this most solemn time" everyone assembled in the large schoolroom across from the parlor, teachers on the first rows, Smedes and the lady principal on the rostrum. Those who had for the week "perfect marks" and "good work" heard their names read out, while the others suffered "extreme mortification" from the implied threat of being "moved down" in a subject. The grading scale was first, 96; second, 91; third, 86. An average of less than 86 on the monthly report was considered less than satisfactory, and pupils making below 75 were "either incapable or hopelessly indifferent to any incentives to study," according to Smedes. [34] Grades were generally high, perhaps because of the "reading out," but some dismal report cards have survived.

The Friday afternoon "reading out" was mild compared to the final examinations. Written papers were made available for public inspection at commencement, but the orals were closed. The catalog mini-

Catherine
DeRosset Meares,
first lady principal

Marie Elizabeth
Czarnomska,
lady principal
The Archives,
Smith College

mized the ordeal of examinations, noting that "No 'cramming' is necessary . . . they are but the continuance of the year's work, and without them the work is not complete and the pupils cannot be properly advanced." The catalog urged parents not to have their daughters exempted from examinations and warned, "There is a marked difference in the character of the work done by those excused and by those who are not excused."[35] The girls took a dim view of the experience. A student of 1884 described her oral examination in every harrowing detail:

> Well the examinations are all over, and you can't imagine how light-hearted I feel. . . . the literature was the most exciting the Czar came in with a crowd of teachers and after they were all seated . . . said, "Mrs. Iredell, suppose we let Carrie Freer be the first victim. . . ."
> The Czar asked me about Milton and I recited a whole chapter on him, and part of one on Scott, and I broke down and just cried.

Lady Principal Czarnomska sent for a glass of water and her own smelling salts for Carrie, but it was three days before she recovered fully. However, later that week she sang so beautifully at the musicale honoring the wife of Gov. Thomas J. Jarvis that the lady principal requested an encore, thus restoring completely Carrie's self-confidence.[36]

The *St. Mary's Muse* received special attention from Elizabeth Czarnomska. It was first published in 1879 as an eight-page monthly pamphlet edited by "Euterpe," who was Will H. Sanborn, the director of music. He was assisted by "a corps of editresses" known as the Pierian Club and made up of members of the senior class. Kate Meares wrote under the pseudonym "Calliope." The early *Muse* contained brief comments on world events of cultural interest and was "rather the little newspaper in St. Mary's than the little St. Mary's newspaper."[37] In 1881 it became a quarterly magazine. The Pierian Club apologized for a slight delay in publication: "We wish to have our work intrinsically good, and acceptable to more than the indulgent home-circle. All of this will take time, and time, to school girls is a precious commodity."[38] Under the direction of Czarnomska, a demanding critic, the magazine was worthy of senior college students, presenting original pieces, essays in French, book reviews, and abstracts of articles from the leading magazines. It was sold locally and by mail for 15 cents a copy. Raleigh merchants and sometimes out-of-state music companies and other schools advertised in the *Muse*.

Czarnomska and Smedes took advantage of the interest in current events created by the *Muse*. Its student editor, noting in June, 1882, that a professor at Smith College intended to teach "a class of current topics and then the art of discussing events and books intelligently," remarked, "*We* had a class of current topics over a year ago."[39]

Unfortunately, after the class of 1884 graduated, the *Muse* was published only sporadically until 1899 when a 100-page volume was published. Edited by Minna Bynum, it was both a yearbook and a memorial to Bennett Smedes.

When Elizabeth Dancy Battle succeeded Elizabeth Czarnomska, she was called "principal assistant to Mr. Smedes" instead of lady principal because she was still in her twenties. "Miss Lizzie" was considered distinguished looking and a little apart from the ordinary world. Her reprimands began gently, "Now, young ladies," but she had no tolerance for indolence. She ruled "justly and admirably," although severe headaches forced her at times to teach her Latin classes in her darkened bedroom. Her weekly reading evenings for the seniors were popular, and it was said that "Miss Battle could make even arithmetic sound delightful." [40]

A devout churchwoman, Lizzie Battle held early morning prayers in her room for a little band who formed the Society of St. Chrysostom, the purpose of which was "the avoidance of slang" and the cultivation of purity of heart as well as of speech. [41] Four years after leaving St. Mary's in 1895 to head the mathematics department of Sachs's school for girls in New York City, Elizabeth Battle died, a week before her 34th birthday.

### "THE SOUL-ABSORBING DESIRE"

Bennett Smedes's great strength was his ability to gather about him some extraordinarily able teachers. Emilie McVea wrote:

Real motive power is not always discernible at close range, but looking back . . . with the clearer view of mature years we know that the centralizing force was the unswerving nobility of Dr. Bennett Smedes' ideal of and for women, his entire merging of self in the purpose of his work and his unsurpassed reverence for spiritual things. His teachers responded nobly to his confidence in them; almost without exception they worked for love of St. Mary's; they gave largely of their hearts as of their intellect, and unconsciously the girls realized this and so our teachers were our warm friends and advisors. [42]

Smedes, in his message to the faculty at the beginning of school in 1878, spoke of his hope that "our daily work and conversation might be the result of . . . the soul-absorbing desire to educate." [43] Smedes's faculty numbered about 15, usually all women except for the rector and the director of music.

Perhaps the most notable of those women was Emilie Watts McVea, who returned in 1888 to teach and later served as lady principal. The niece of Mrs. John Esten Cooke Smedes, she had entered St. Mary's at the age of ten. [44] During the course of her career she became dean of the women's department at the University of Cincinnati, president of Sweet

Briar College, the recipient of two honorary doctorates, and a nationally recognized educator and advocate of women's rights.

Perceptive and witty, "Miss Emmie" was one who "made things come alive." She was a large woman who seemed "to be working all of the time" despite the fact that she suffered from chronic anemia. Her extracurricular classes in cooking and current events were popular. She taught history and literature, usually lecturing without notes and reading from great literary works to illustrate her points. Scholarly and deeply religious, she was also forthright and toughminded—an inspiring teacher whose intense ambition was that each of "her girls" should glimpse the larger world.[45]

Another alumna, Catherine Cameron Shipp, returned in 1886 to teach mathematics; she had taught in the public schools of Raleigh and Charlotte. A large and imposing woman "who moved in a slow and stately manner that was not so much a walk as an advance," she inevitably was dubbed "the Ship of State" by her pupils; but she was quite jolly outside of class.[46] She chaperoned small groups of the girls to Europe during the summers. Kate Shipp left St. Mary's for three years in the 1890s to teach at the Charlotte Female Institute (later Queens College) where she also was associate principal, but she returned to St. Mary's 1894–1897. Her widowed sister, Anna McBee, also an alumna, taught in the primary and preparatory departments. They resigned to open the Mary Wood School in Lincolnton, but they later returned again to St. Mary's.

Alumna Mary Florence Wells Slater joined the faculty in 1883, the year after her graduation, to teach calisthenics. Smedes had made it possible for her to study in Boston with Avon D. Burnham, then "America's finest gymnast."[47] The St. Mary's gymnasium occupied half of the first floor of the art building. The primary children annually delighted the townspeople with their commencement programs when, dressed as sprites or flowers, they performed graceful maneuvers with hoops, balls, and Indian clubs to the music of Chopin. Florence Slater also assisted with the chapel music and was known as a wise counselor in spiritual matters.[48]

In her physiology classes for the older students, Florence Slater actually spoke of the biological differences between the male and the female, with the result that at least two girls were withdrawn from school by their scandalized parents. While teaching botany and natural history at St. Mary's, she fell in love with science and determined to take her bachelor's degree at Cornell. She received the degree in 1900. She taught in the Flushing, New York, schools for years, becoming a well-known special lecturer and a leader in the fight for equal pay for women and for a retirement system. Always loyal to St. Mary's, she bequeathed $4,000 to the biology department.[49]

Bennett Smedes taught Paley's *Evidences of Christianity*, logic, chemistry, and physics. Mary Iredell shared with him the Bible classes. The students realized that Smedes gave them "a peep into things we had never known existed." His classroom performance, however, they considered less than dynamic, although they regarded him as a kind friend and a handsome gentleman. He would sit at his desk on the platform in his classroom (a moth-eaten stuffed wolf on the platform beside him) and lecture with his eyes closed. But let a student whisper so much as one word and Smedes, eyes still closed, would quietly name the culprit and send her from the room. Neither would he tolerate slipshod preparation for class.[50] He kept "the philosophical apparatus" up to date. In 1885 he added "a large binocular microscope"; and in 1896 the science laboratory, then located upstairs in the new art building, was "greatly enlarged and refurbished." The rector had just bought two fine compound microscopes and 400 slides, and "everyone" was collecting bugs, according to the *Muse*.[51]

Bennett Smedes's classical and theological attainments and his outstanding service as an educator were recognized by the University of North Carolina when in June, 1892, it conferred upon him the degree of doctor of divinity. Even the authorities at Vassar recognized that Smedes's school had kept abreast of the times. The 1895–1896 catalog of St. Mary's School announced that Vassar College had "extended the privilege of admission by certificate," thus eliminating placement examinations in subjects certified at St. Mary's.[52]

The music department at St. Mary's continued to attract favorable notice. Bennett Smedes invested heavily to make his "the best equipped musical department in the South." His 1880 circular advised that he had 19 pianos "including the only pedal piano south of New York," a cabinet organ, and "a magnificent new pipe organ of two manuals and twenty stops—the largest for school purposes in the United States." He felt justified in offering a higher course of study to teachers who considered their musical education to be "defective." In 1882 Smedes bought two new grand pianos for the parlor so that in the ensemble playing that was just coming into vogue "both performers would have fair play."[53] The grand concert of commencement week was attended by standing-room-only crowds.

Will H. Sanborn was a good music teacher and was also a help to Smedes in business affairs.[54] Sanborn had studied in Leipzig from whence he called Fraulein Blume, who joined his faculty in the fall of 1879. She was only 18, but her "glorious" voice was well trained. They resigned during the summer of 1881, and the reason became clear when Will Sanborn's prize pupil, Eliza Smedes, en route to Europe for further study, encountered on shipboard the honeymooning couple.[55]

After two years of study in Germany, Eliza Smedes returned to St. Mary's to teach.

Auguste Kürsteiner was the director of music during the 1880s.[56] A native of Basle, Switzerland, he taught piano and organ and conducted the chorus. The music department was then located in East Rock, and he and his wife also lived in that building. In 1882 Dr. Kürsteiner assumed additional responsibility as conductor of Raleigh's new Philharmonic Society.[57]

Albert Mack presided over the music department during the nineties. The girls "liked him extravagantly"; and his wife, who taught grammar and geography, was also a great favorite.[58] Trained at the Stuttgart Conservatory, Dr. Mack taught music "not only as a pleasing accomplishment, but as a serious and noble art."[59] About 1900 he went to Hollins and from there to Syracuse University, gaining recognition as a composer before his untimely death in 1907.[60]

The study of the violin was popular during the last decades of the century. There was a St. Mary's orchestra composed of about a dozen violins, the cymbals, drums, and triangle. Sometimes several male musicians joined the orchestra.[61] Nannette A. Stone taught voice (1881–1896), and Martha Dowd remained on the music faculty throughout Bennett Smedes's administration.

Smedes's "soul-absorbing desire" to have the best school in the South led him to begin an art library and to announce in his catalog for 1880–1881, "No expense will be spared to make the study of Art practical, thorough and successful." In the early eighties china painting was "all the rage"; the *Muse* reported in 1881 that the pieces being sent north to be baked were "just too utterly utter." By mid-decade painted screens were in vogue.[62] A few students were more serious artists. Paintings by Mary Lyde Hicks, who studied with Dora Hyde, hang in North Carolina's state buildings and in the Confederate Museum in Richmond, Virginia.[63]

In early January, 1885, Dora Hyde and her students moved into the art building that Smedes had persuaded Margaret Cameron, then owner of the campus, to build. A two-story wood building about 60 feet from East Rock, it was described by the Raleigh papers as "perfectly adapted" to its purpose with gothic arches of oil-stained heart pine, skylights, and "immense windows." Aldert Smedes's famous bronzes had been moved from the parlor. Also in the building were two classrooms, the calisthenics room, and the science laboratory. New equipment was moved in, and the student art work was arranged in anticipation of holding the best of all of St. Mary's celebrated "art evenings" the moment the water system was installed.[64]

Then disaster struck. Early in the morning of January 6 the building burned to the ground in a spectacular fire. The rainy weather and "the chemical engine" saved East Rock although the surrounding trees were damaged heavily. Nothing was saved from the new building. Smedes felt that the gas furnace had been the cause of the fire. He told the seniors that "to their obedience and steadfast example" was owed "the perfect order of the school in time of danger." [65]

The art department immediately set up in the empty dormitory on the top floor of the main building. Desks were borrowed from Peace Institute for the primary and preparatory classes. By June, 1887, the new brick building "of gothic design" erected on the site of the burned building was in use, and the *News and Observer* advised its readers that the new studio was in itself worth a visit to St. Mary's. [66] (In 1982 the art department and the foreign language department shared this building.)

Clara I. Fenner, a graduate of Maryland Institute, School of Art and Design, became director of the art department in 1888. She remained on the St. Mary's faculty until 1926 (except from 1898 to 1902 when she taught at her Baltimore home).

Kate McKimmon faithfully saw to it that children in her primary classes learned what the school catalog promised—that they could read with accuracy and expression, could cipher through short division, and could write legibly. Other members of the faculty taught those youngest pupils calisthenics, choral singing, elocution, and freehand drawing. Great care was taken with the primary children because Smedes believed that "the success of all higher study depends largely upon the character of the training . . . received in childhood." [67] Most years a few boys attended primary classes. Kate McKimmon's commencement-week entertainments were major productions, often including a play given in French as well as the usual songs and recitations.

McKimmon's classes in American history were remembered vividly by her former pupils. Unreconstructed, she refused to teach certain pages of the history text. She would set her lips firmly, close the book, and remark, "We shall skip that part." It was her habit to write on the blackboard important historical events of that day's date. On February 12 she might ask, "Whose birthday is today?" Without waiting for the reply, she would snap, "Lincoln's. There, I've told you. *Now, forget it!*" [68] Exceedingly straitlaced, Kate McKimmon was at the same time "the sweetest person in the world" and scrupulously fair. The "primaries" thought she *was* St. Mary's, and no matter what she required they would chorus, "Yes, Miss Katie." [69]

McKimmon's senior dormitory in West Rock was a merry place, although rules were enforced strictly and fairly. The seniors of 1894 organized "McKimmonsville," with a government and a weekly newspaper "laboriously printed on an ill-behaved duplicator." They held a memorable picnic and crowned Miss Katie their May Queen. [70]

The daily routine of the school under the second Smedes remained much the same as always—the 7:00 roll call and prayers in the parlor, the big southern breakfast, the study period in the large schoolroom across from the parlor, the "brisk walk" around the grove before chapel at 9:00. After chapel on three days a week came the Bible lecture with "the dreaded abstract" required afterward. On the other two days of the week, there was choral practice for everyone in the parlor. Classes preceded and followed the 11:00 snack. After dinner at 3:00 until another study hour at 6:00, there was time for all kinds of recreation to satisfy the daily exercise requirement. The short evenings were devoted, after supper at 7:00, to various planned activities, meetings, and study. Always someone played the piano for dancing in the parlor before everyone in the household gathered there for evening prayers. (The punishment for tardiness at prayers, either in the morning or at night, was an assignment of poetry to memorize.)[71]

Its stability was the great attraction of the institution. It was customary during the nineteenth century for young ladies to go from school to school before they were "finished off," and many schools were short-lived. At St. Mary's, however, some pupils stayed as long as ten years; they had known exactly what to expect from hearing about their mothers' and grandmothers' school days at "dear, old St. Mary's."

It was only natural that Bennett Smedes should continue to run the school as "a great and entire family." St. Mary's had been his home since memory began. And it became the home of his children. Four daughters were born to Henrietta and Bennett Smedes. Eliza Sebor, named for her paternal great-grandmother but called "Bessie," was born in 1878. Just before her eighth birthday, Bessie died from fever probably contracted during a vacation at the beach. Henrietta Smedes wore black for years to mourn her firstborn.[72] Bennett Smedes also felt keenly the loss of his eldest, although by that time there were three younger daughters. Margaret Harvey, the second daughter, was graduated from St. Mary's in 1889 with first distinction in piano and was listed on the academic honor roll. When the twins, Helen and Mary, were born at St. Mary's on July 25, 1883, someone broke the news to Smedes by saying, "Your girls have arrived!" He, thinking that some new students had just come, replied, "Send them on up to the dormitory." Life was never quite the same at St. Mary's after the lively, inquisitive twins were old enough to walk. Mary identified with her father so completely that when he received his honorary degree, the eight-year-old began to sign her arithmetic papers, "Mary Sherwood Smedes, D.D."[73]

Because all three children loved animals, there was always an assortment of pets. Runt Harvey, the dog, celebrated his third birthday in style in the children's dining room. A parrot, having learned to talk

Faculty, staff and students, c.1892. Bennett Smedes is wearing a white hat and his wife Henrietta is to his immediate right. Sitting in the goat cart are the Smedes twins, Helen and Mary.

elsewhere, was dispatched after swearing at a local clergyman. Pet goats pulled two custom-built carts. Later, the twins acquired ponies, which they rode bareback "down Hillsborough Street like lightning" to the dismay of Raleigh's proper ladies. Their father encouraged tomboy antics, even teaching Mary how to handle a gun and his hunting dogs.[74]

That carefree life ended abruptly for the Smedes twins when they turned 12 and were required to attend all classes regularly at St. Mary's. Heretofore, their mother had taught them all subjects, except mathematics. Miss Etta taught piano to her daughters and a few of the younger students, and she usually had several of the slow readers from Kate McKimmon's class under her tutelage.[75]

Etta Smedes loved all children. She gave an annual Christmas party for children of the servants at the school. There was a tall tree and presents for everyone—sometimes for as many as 50 children. Over 80 years after the event, Mary Haywood Fowle Stearns, a day scholar at St. Mary's, remembered Etta Smedes's love. When Mary's father, Gov. Daniel Fowle, died suddenly in 1891 leaving her orphaned, Etta Smedes put a cot in the family sitting room so that she could live with the Smedes family until she felt ready to move into the dormitory.[76]

Bennett Smedes was a devoted husband and son as well as the most loving of fathers. Every fair afternoon the Smedeses strolled downtown and back arm in arm—she in a black silk dress and black silk coat, he in his Prince Albert and off-white, high, felt hat. Except for those daily sallies, Etta Smedes was most retiring. The poor of Raleigh knew her better than did the leaders of the capital's society, for her kindness to the poor, white and black alike, knew no bounds.[77] After the daily walk with his wife, Smedes invariably went across Hillsborough Street to his mother's home for tea. Sarah Smedes lived very privately until her death on April 11, 1887. She had outlived five of her seven sons.[78]

Bennett and Etta Smedes succeeded in making their home a second home for most of the students. A new arrival in the autumn of 1882 reported that on her first night at school Jennie Coffin (then in charge of the "sick-room") brought the little Smedes girls into the dormitory "and kissed us all good night & it seems very home like."[79] A careless or lazy student who had received demerits was required to appear before the rector. Smedes sat behind the big desk in his book-lined study puffing on a Cuban cigar and, with his usual "ahem-ahemming," gently told the errant one that duty *must* be served. Then he invariably reached into his desk for an orange and handed the culprit this treat, saying, "Run along now."[80] His gentle, fatherly approach did not mean that he tolerated serious misbehavior. Extant are stern letters to parents and stories of a few expulsions.

Bennett Smedes was as careful as his father had been in his oversight of the health of his young charges. The traditional emphasis upon exercise remained. Each pupil kept her knitted or crocheted "walking shawl" hung on her peg in the hall behind the parlor. The penalty for not wearing one's shawl was one "disorder" on a chilly day and five "disorders" on a really cold day.[81] Tennis became the "prime favorite afternoon recreation" at St. Mary's in the 1880s. Smedes provided courts on the front campus. An article in the 1883 *Muse* described the game, "fairly new to the South," mostly in terms of the proper attire— "a shorter, bright skirt, a blouse waist, and shoes of white or colored canvas, with corrugated rubber toes."[82]

By the nineties bicycling had become a national craze, and the St. Mary's cycling club enjoyed "the most exciting spins" after they had taught enough faculty members to ride to provide the necessary chaperonage. The lessons, given "on the secluded path from the kitchen to the infirmary," went poorly at first; but eventually the teachers' "valiant and persistent efforts" were successful. The *Muse* noted that the teachers' perseverance in learning a new skill "might serve as an example for us in our school work." The fashionable costume for "a spin" featured a jaunty, shorter skirt for safety's sake.[83]

## "HEARTY GOOD TIMES"

Smedes was particularly solicitous that his young ladies be well fed. Often after the students had left the dining room, he would make the rounds of the tables to determine which foods were unpopular.[84] His sister-in-law, Annie Harvey, supervised the dining room. She visited St. Mary's in 1885 and stayed for 14 years. The Harvey sisters, orphaned by the Civil War when Etta was ten and Annie five years old, were thereafter separated. Annie, reared by her Roman Catholic former governess who had married her older brother, was "a Romanist," a fact that caused comment in Raleigh.[85] She had been a kindergarten teacher and was especially good with the youngest students.

The school's kitchen remained located in the large, airy brick building behind the main house, connected to it by a covered way. In 1882 a new "Paris range," featuring two ovens with dampers, was acquired.[86] Most of the kitchen staff and their families still lived over the kitchen or in a wooden building nearby. A smokehouse filled with hams, the large barn, the extensive vegetable garden, and the cows pastured beyond it all gave the campus almost a plantation atmosphere as late as the 1890s. The garden kept the school practically self-sufficient during vegetable season. Smedes noted in 1884 that he needed few cows since the students had "in large measure given up drinking milk."[87]

Food at the school was wholesome but plain. The girls called the daily bowl of soup "the substance of things hoped for, the evidence of things not seen." There was a brief food strike during the 1880s when the students boycotted the 11:00 snack. Their grievance was as much the ignominy of being lined up and "treated like puppies" as the meagerness of the snack, usually three crackers and an apple. The strike was simply ignored, and by the end of the week hungry girls again stood docilely awaiting their turn.[88]

There were special treats—an orange or tipsy cake for dessert on Sundays, gingerbread on Tuesday nights, and another dessert on Thursdays. In the spring there were "strawberry days" when a box of fresh strawberries was allotted for every two girls and chattering groups sat under the oaks capping and eating the fresh berries.[89]

Several times a year everyone was invited to one of Etta Smedes's famous suppers. The dining room was rearranged, and a festive air prevailed as the girls arrived dressed in their Sunday best. Chicken salad, beaten biscuits or crisp, buttered toast, pickles and olives, and assorted fruits were passed by the girls selected to help with the party. The drink was always hot cocoa.[90]

The 1880s version of a hall party was the birthday "box of eatables" from home. Those "invited to a box" gathered in "the box room" to partake of homemade delights. The recipient had first shared with her favorite teachers, carrying to their rooms little plates of goodies. The party in the "box room" often ended with songs and laughter or with illegal cooking by the bright fire of the nearby furnace.[91] The administration did not really approve of boxes. The school catalog each year stated firmly, "Boxes of eatables are entirely unnecessary. . . . A large part of the little sicknesses among the pupils is directly traceable to 'Boxes from home.' Parents will confer a favor by keeping this in mind. . . . Boxes will be disposed of by the lady in charge." Smedes, however, could never bring himself to enforce that harsh edict, and "rare times" continued in "the box room."

Those affected by "little sicknesses," whatever their causes, were still cared for in the "sick-room" in the main building. The victims of contagious diseases were isolated in the new infirmary, a frame cottage built in 1881 some distance behind the chapel and called "the pest house" by the students. During the measles epidemic of the winter of 1884–1885, a large portion of the school experienced "the horrors of darkness and flaxseed tea" there.[92] The "horrors" of illnesses were mitigated a great deal by Anne Saunders, who returned to her alma mater in 1894 to care for the sick. A thoroughly unreconstructed southerner, she clung to the styles of a bygone era, even to her bonnet.[93]

Dr. Peter E. Hines, the school physician for over 30 years, began his ministrations under the rectorship of Bennett Smedes. In December, 1882, St. Mary's "went in a body" to Christ Church to attend the wedding of Dr. Hines and Fannie I. Johnson.

Times had changed enough to allow young people more freedom. The "good ones" who had accumulated no "disorders" could go downtown just for fun with teachers as chaperones. Little groups walked or waited in the octagonal, wrought-iron summer house near the front gate for the streetcar, horsedrawn from 1886 until 1891 when electric cars came in.[94] St. Mary's girls were expected to know how to manage the ascent onto the cars without revealing so much as a shoe top. Downtown, the group always visited Royster's Candy Store, and an indulgent chaperone would allow a lengthy visit to one of the drugstore fountains.

During the school session, the boarders had fairly frequent contact with the townspeople. Because by that time the second and third generations of many families were attending St. Mary's, every year there was a round of teas and "spreads" given by the classmates of mothers and grandmothers. Day scholars entertained their classmates at tea, and Smedes was lenient in granting permission for overnight visits in the homes of Raleigh students during holidays. Popular indeed was the day scholar with brothers.

The girls realized that Smedes was an indulgent headmaster. Every year he tried to plan enough outings to keep his boarding students happy away from home. The student editor of the *Muse* reported in November, 1882:

so many pleasant things happen in the fall, when school-girls are home-sick and their duties are new and difficult. And at St. Mary's there are a greater number of real, hearty "good times" than anywhere else, we think. First, Mr. Smedes always sends the new girls out to see the city, and every afternoon five happy girls go on their pleasant drive. Then . . . our Rector has not the heart to stop the fun till every member of the household, old and young, has had her turn. Then, when we have worked hard for just one month, and sent home our first reports, comes Fair-week. And then comes Hallowe'en![95]

Campus entertainments were more elaborate than in earlier days. Masquerade "balls" were popular, despite the total absence of young men, there being no Smedes sons. The parlor as it appeared in 1885 was described by Alice Dugger Grimes in *Life at Saint Mary's*. The teachers watched the fun seated around large round tables in each corner of the room. The upholstered benches still lined the walls. A handsome horsehair sofa was placed under the large mirror, and two console tables stood under the portraits of Bishops Ravenscroft and Ives. The portrait of Aldert Smedes hung over the north mantel and that of his wife over the south mantel. The walls were still lined with the Smedes art collection, and a curio cabinet held other treasures.[96]

The Halloween parties were noisy affairs held on the lower floor of the main building. The day scholars attended, too. By the late nineties, the Halloween entertainment was more sophisticated than in earlier days; the older students spent days preparing in great secrecy several short dramas for presentation before all joined in the usual games.[97] Etta Smedes always made refreshments for Halloween.

The Smedeses did everything possible to make Christmas very special for the few who could not go home for the holidays. Before school was out, the dormitories "vied with each other in their ornamentations," and there was a Christmas musicale. Those left behind moved into the main building. There were games before a roaring fire in the parlor and gifts for all.[98] The Christmas of Christmases was that of 1879. That was the year Fraulein Blume introduced the German custom of the Christmas tree. Emilie Smedes Holmes described that wondrous tree: "When the parlor doors were flung open on Christmas night, and we marched in singing a carol, we beheld a holly tree reaching from floor to ceiling ablaze with lights and hung with gifts for everybody."[99]

One of the good times ended in near tragedy. Known as "the great switchback accident," it occurred on Tuesday, April 4, 1893. For the school's Easter outing that year, Smedes had planned a picnic at the fairgrounds and as many rides as the younger students could desire on the switchback railroad he had engaged along with its usual operators. The switchback, or "gravity track" railroad, was designed so that the momentum of a car's descent would send it bounding up the grade to a platform where the car was switched to the parallel track for the return trip. The St. Mary's girls were having a hilarious time, and both cars were loaded to their capacity of 12 when it became apparent to the horrified teachers and the Smedeses that both cars were on the *same* track and would meet at the track's lowest point. Etta Smedes had had her daughters wait for that trip to sit in the front seat because they "should not be selfish."[100]

A Raleigh newspaper headlined the story "Terrible Disaster—Young Ladies Cruelly Injured" and described the splintered wreckage and how "the maimed little girls lay helplessly upon the ground and touched the stoutest hearts." A courier had run into town, there being no telephone at the fairgrounds off season, and half a dozen doctors had arrived "in an incredibly short time." Students from the State Agricultural and Mechanical College (later North Carolina State University) carried the injured on stretchers to St. Mary's.

About a dozen pupils were hurt seriously, but everyone recovered. Helen Smedes had both legs broken, one being so badly mangled that the doctors discussed amputation. The whole city had shown such concern that Smedes published "a card" in the newpapers expressing gratitude.[101] And in the chapel at St. Mary's a brass Communion rail was inscribed "To the Glory of God in thankfulness for a great mercy, *4th* of April, 1893. 'He will give his angels charge over thee.'"

In the nineties it was still difficult for would-be suitors to get near St. Mary's girls. The campus was then enclosed by a few strands of barbed wire to keep out cows and pedestrians, and the girls were instructed to ignore the A&M students who liked to happen by during "walking hour." Smedes once expelled a girl who deliberately displayed a few inches of a shapely "limb" before the gawking college youths.[102] Of course, no young man was "received" in the parlor without the express permission of the young lady's parents.

Sometimes young men visited the faculty. Kate Meares's sons enjoyed holidays at the school; and after a Christmas there, one wrote of loving "the dear old place . . . with such sweet cousins."[103] At one

Christmas dance there were three visiting boys; but when some town boys crashed the party, the dancing was stopped until they left. The public receptions and soirees were a different matter. The girls knew the exact number—85—of boys attending the dance during fair week in 1883. They were probably "the Binghamites" from a boys' school, who after drilling in the circle that afternoon, "threw up their hats and cried, 'three cheers for the young ladies of St. Mary's.'" The young ladies "were allowed to wave their handkerchiefs" in acknowledgment of the compliment.[104] Kate Meares reported to her son that the girls had "a splendid time" at the soiree in October, 1879, and that in attendance were "lots of Binghamites, and a few snips from Wilmington . . . all have good society manners and are at home with the girls."[105] Sometimes Smedes and the teachers escorted the girls to "a football match," especially when "the Chapel Hillians" played. The *Muse* of 1879 acknowledged publicly "the courtesy paid us in the musical tones of a delightful serenade" because "stern dormitory rules" had forced the excited girls to listen in "unmitigated darkness." They fell asleep again to dreams of "moonlight, music, love and flowers."[106]

Dreams often had to suffice. The school catalog for 1880–1881 plainly stated, "Correspondence with the home circle is freely encouraged; but beyond that, *there is no time*, even were it otherwise desirable, for letter writing, and letters to and from young gentlemen are positively prohibited." Probably that harsh edict, like the one against "boxes of eatables," was not enforced, since reminiscences of the period frequently mention how eagerly students awaited the distribution of the mail after Smedes's daily trip in his buggy to the post office. The one telephone on campus was installed on the wall of the rector's study and was never available to the students. Nonetheless, Cupid won out. A student of 1890 actually went "directly from the schoolroom to the altar"; she was married in the chapel during commencement week.[107] The brief Spanish-American War seems to have made little impact upon the mores of courtship despite the fact that the only United States Army camp in North Carolina, Camp Bryan Grimes, was located a few blocks out Hillsborough Street from St. Mary's.

Dress at St. Mary's was still demure. The catalog announced, "Extravagance of dress and fashion is opposed to the principles of the school. Parents will confer a special favor by consulting simplicity and economy in the attire of their daughters, and by giving them a limited supply of pocket-money."[108] In reply to a parental inquiry, Smedes wrote, "There is not distinctive dress worn by the pupils. We desire, however, an absence of silks and velvets. . . . All pupils will be expected to wear white muslin dresses at Commencement and at all public entertainments given by the School."[109] The lady principal decreed the day each autumn when *everyone* was to don flannel skirts. After steam heat replaced the open fires and stoves in the 1880s, the girls complained of cold feet, and everyone bought "thick hose" for 25 cents a pair.[110] By springtime daughters would begin negotiations with their mothers for new clothes. In the spring of 1880, Rebecca Collins rejected the sample of material suggested by her mother "because stripes are used here only for trimming." She thought "a solid lilac lawn" would do nicely. She calculated that she would need 8 1/2 yards of material.[111] By the spring of their senior year, the older girls began to acquire real finery, such as black silk dresses.

A creamy complexion was a necessity. A student of 1884 assured her mother, "I am wearing my sunbonnet faithfully, & my gloves too so that I will look at least decent when I get home."[112] Another anxiously inquired of her mother, "How do you take Sulphur? I think I will take some to take the bumps off my face."[113]

The nineties brought a new sense of freedom in dress. The gored skirts swept out in the back and, although slightly shorter, still concealed the ankles. A skirt was worn with a plethora of petticoats and a shirtwaist. Sunday dresses were elaborately trimmed with fancy braid, the effect both of the sewing machine and the war in Cuba. The fashionable hairstyle was the pompadour, and schoolgirls wore enormous hair bows. The latest rages were a bracelet made from a lock of one's best friend's hair and a pin-on watch with a four-leaf clover pressed inside.[114]

A student writing of "Fashion and Follies" in the *Muse* of June, 1899, noted:

now a woman's glory is her hat. We have sailor hats, violet hats, rose hats, feathered hats, upturned hats, downtilted hats. . . . health and exercise have become the fashion. . . . tennis, golf, cycling. . . . our girl rather likes bright, joyous colors; red caps, pretty ties and gay trimmings on her blue or white yachting suit. . . . We have lost the stateliness and perhaps some of the dignity of the olden times . . . but we have rosy-cheeked, strong, capable looking maidens.[115]

For all public appearances a St. Mary's girl was required to pass a rigid inspection by her dormitory teacher. As had always been the custom, the entire student body during the last two decades of the nineteenth century was marched downtown to witness major public events. In October, 1883, the girls were present when the remains of over 400 Confederate soldiers removed from Arlington Cemetery were brought for reinterment in Raleigh.[116]

Most of Raleigh's population of 13,000 and thousands of visitors turned out a decade later on May 30, 1893, when the funeral train carrying the mortal remains of Jefferson Davis stopped in Raleigh. The former president of the Confederacy had died on December 6, 1889, but his widow had delayed making the decision that Richmond, Virginia, should be the final burial place. Bessie Henderson wrote that "all Saint Mary's had to march in the procession." The eight-car funeral train was met by a funeral carriage, and riding upon it, two in front and two in the rear, and carrying folded Confederate flags were "four fair young ladies." Upon arrival at the Capitol rotunda, they "took up their positions, one upon each corner of the catafalque, where they remained holding their furled Confederate flags over the casket." The "four fair young ladies" were Mary Armistead Jones, Frances Burton Hoke, Ellen Devereux Hinsdale, and Addie Boylan Snow, all daughters of veterans and all then students at St. Mary's.[117]

The most thrilling of public occasions were those of commencement week at St. Mary's when the concerts and other entertainments drew crowds. The *Muse* reported that during the "dramatic soiree" of commencement week in 1884, "Crowds of grown-up gentlemen stood on the roof of the covered way . . . while eager hands tore away the scaffolding from the new art building and dragged it to the parlor windows."[118]

Commencement day (usually a Thursday) was a more solemn occasion. The opening exercises were held in the parlor from a platform decorated with "floral gifts." The graduates, wearing long white dresses, read their senior essays; usually several essays were in a foreign language. There were minor mishaps. A member of the first graduating class in 1879 "fainted from excitement and was carried to the lady principal's room where she was quickly revived with whiskey."[119] Jennie H. Pescud, the valedictorian of 1892, completed her speech in broken voice, not so much from emotion as everyone assumed, but because she had swallowed a fly.[120]

After the exercises in the parlor, the whole school and the visiting clergy proceeded to the chapel singing "Ten Thousand Times Ten Thousand." There Smedes read the honor roll and distinctions and gave a brief talk to the graduates. Nearly always the main address was given by the bishop of North Carolina, an indication that he considered St. Mary's the unofficial diocesan school. After receiving their diplomas tied with blue and white ribbons, the graduates knelt before the bishop for the benediction. The recessional hymn was the stirring "Jerusalem! High Tower Thy Glorious Walls." And then, as a graduate of 1895 wrote, "It was all over but the parting and the tears and the love that we will always have for our Alma Mater."[121]

## "SAVED FOR THE CHURCH"

When a St. Mary's girl relived in memory her years at the school, it was often to the chapel that her thoughts first turned. A graduate of the nineties wrote, "There can be no real recollection of St. Mary's apart from the chapel. When it is called, 'the soul of St. Mary's,' everything is said." [122] The second rector would have agreed, for his catalog stated: "The school deems the training of its pupils in the nurture and admonition of the Lord to be the most acceptable service it can render to them, to their parents, and to God." [123] Certainly, the school's patrons accepted that premise, for as Bennett Smedes told the diocesan convention of 1892, his pupils had been "for the most part, the children and grandchildren" of those taught by his father. The chapel remained essentially unchanged for generations although a transept had to be added when the pipe organ was installed in 1879. There were "about 200 sittings," according to the school catalog. Emilie Smedes Holmes wrote, "Easter was always the supreme day of the year for us, with every thought centered upon the Chapel and its glorious services. . . . the whole school was trained to sing the full choral service." [124]

Bennett Smedes's sermons carried essentially the same messages of love and duty as those his father had delivered. Somewhat more scholarly and a little less fatherly in his approach than Aldert Smedes had been, he spoke often of "the cords of love binding those who labor here together in our little world," and of the beauty of holiness and "the quiet of the soul" attained by the virtuous. Each year in his sermons he reminded his pupils of their duty to parents who had "at great expense in tears and money" sent them away to school. He told the girls that they must be "gentle . . . considerate and loving—Christ-like." [125]

The "fitting for God's service" was a continuous process; and Sunday was, as Kate Meares once said, "the busiest day of the seven." Before church the girls studied the scripture and the collect and rehearsed the music for the 11:00 service. There was afternoon Sunday school followed by 5:00 evensong. On Sunday night the confirmation classes and other special study groups met. [126]

The gifts to others—the poor of Raleigh, St. John's Hospital, various mission churches—made by St. Mary's amounted to about $400 each year of the last quarter of the century. The Aldert Smedes Scholarship to the mission school in Shanghai was the special project of the missionary society. The society raised the $40 annually through sewing and fancy work. Fines for "delinquencies in table manners" helped fill the mite chests for other projects.

In 1880 the *Muse* ran a series of articles on St. Mary's women giving extraordinary service to the church "in order to stir up others to recognize their responsibility." Pattie Hicks Buford, working among blacks of Virginia, saw the establishment of a school for 200 pupils and 27 Sunday schools teaching 1,400 children. The three Dabney sisters of Mississippi, one the widow of Lyell Smedes, although "utterly poverty-stricken" after the Civil War, organized a training school for divinity students and managed to get built a church and rectory. Cecilia Dabney Foster, after being widowed, joined the Sisterhood of the Good Shepherd and organized in Wilmington the first deaconesses' work in the Diocese of North Carolina.[127] It was the devotion of St. Mary's women that kept many a parish active. An article in the *Observer* of 1877 noted "the irradiating influence" of the "ex-St. Maryites" who seemed to be united by some indefinable "sign of recognition."[128]

When Bishop Atkinson died, he was succeeded by Dr. Theodore Benedict Lyman, who had been the assistant bishop since 1873. Bishop Lyman inherited a growing church, for during Bishop Atkinson's tenure (1853–1881) the number of communicants had increased 300 percent (from 1700) while the population of the state had increased by only 40 percent (from about 1 million).[129] Bishop Lyman had long been interested in Christian education, having been a cofounder of the College of Saint James in Maryland. He frequently recommended St. Mary's "because it has no superior in any department in our Southern states."[130] The school catalog continued to list the bishop of North Carolina as "Visitor."

Bishop Lyman each year gave one of his travelogues at St. Mary's. Having lived abroad for a decade, he had fascinating stories and pictures. Sometimes the bishop's visit was official. In the spring of 1884 he confirmed 22 persons, believed to be the largest number ever confirmed at once at the school.[131] The students were so moved one year by the bishop's description of "the waste places within our own borders" that each girl in Kate Meares's Bible class pledged $3 to a fund for a chapel in the mountains. They sewed for months and gave a "fair" (bazaar) to raise the $100 pledged by the class.[132]

Bishop Lyman, speaking of the school's jubilee in 1892, said of St. Mary's, "May it long continue sending forth as from a perennial fountain, those pure, and Christian, and ennobling influences which shall make it an enduring blessing to generations yet unborn."[133]

The celebration of the 50th anniversary of the founding of St. Mary's was a memorable week. The semicentennial observance began with a service in Christ Church on June 5, 1892 (Whitsunday). A procession of some 200 students, teachers, alumnae, and clergy passed down the two main aisles singing "Ten Thousand Times Ten Thousand."

The Monday night reception honoring the alumnae was described by the press as "the greatest gathering of her daughters ever yet witnessed," taxing the streetcars and livery stables. The front lawn "ablaze with Chinese lanterns" was soon filled with carriages. In the hall, "the butler, with his silver waiter, received the cards." In the parlor, the Phalanx Band played as "the mass of people" went down the receiving line. Refreshments were served in the art building where the exhibition included some of the drawings of the 1842 art students. Tuesday night's concert was described as "so brilliant that St. Mary's surpassed itself." Representatives of 49 classes attended commencement exercises. As usual, senior essays were read in the parlor and diplomas were presented in the chapel. There were six full graduates.[134]

After the graduation exercises, the alumnae met. The alumnae association, organized in 1879, had been sporadic in its activities. At that meeting the association decided to place in the chapel a memorial to Aldert Smedes and to publish an account of the semicentennial celebration. Over 150 former students had signed the guest book during the week, including several men who had attended the primary grades at St. Mary's.

The diocese considered all to be well with St. Mary's. The committee on the state of the church reported to the 1893 convention that St. Mary's was "so well known as to require no further notice on the part of this committee." Fortunately for the school, Joseph Blount Cheshire, Jr., who became the fifth bishop of North Carolina when Bishop Lyman died in December, 1893, was a St. Mary's friend.

When Bennett Smedes became rector in 1877, the economic situation in North Carolina was anything but propitious. Raleigh's merchants were advertising "fresh arrivals" at "prices to suit the dull times"—calico at 8 1/3 cents a yard and linen "for dresses and travelling suits" at 20 to 40 cents a yard.[135] Smedes wrote to Kate Meares as soon as she had accepted the position of lady principal saying, "I have commenced by cutting off every superfluous appendage, and I think that by close economy we may get through without overwhelming debt."[136] However, his desire to raise the standards of the school to meet the new needs of southern women and to replace equipment worn out during the war years led him into lavish expenditures.

Enrollments did not justify major outlays. Because of the months of uncertainty as to who was to run St. Mary's, enrollment for the 1877–1878 session was down to less than 50 boarders.[137] By 1880 there were about 120 students, 55 of whom were day scholars. Normally there were a dozen part-time "specialists" in music or art, some of them alumnae. Since pupils were allowed to enroll any time during either the first semester (the Advent session) or the second semester (the Easter session), there was more coming and going than the teachers liked; but some pupils from a distance continued to board and do some supervised study at St. Mary's in the summer; the charge was $40 for the 12-week vacation.[138]

By the mid-nineties, the enrollment was up to between 175 and 200, with almost half of the student body made up of day scholars.[139] The day scholars seem to have had mixed feelings about St. Mary's. They danced in the parlor during part of the afternoon dinner hour, and on rainy days they accepted Smedes's invitation to go downstairs for something hot.[140] Some of them, however, felt that they "didn't count, except to pay the bills to keep the school going."[141]

Student fees did not bring in enough to pay the bills. The 1881–1882 charges for boarders for each 20-week session were $115 with a discount of $15 for paying the entire year's charges at the beginning of an academic year. The extra fees for music lessons were from $35˙to $40 each session and for art from $15 to $20. Latin was included in the regular tuition, but Italian, French, German, or Greek cost $10 to $15 extra each session, and French in the primary grades cost $5. Day scholars paid from $25 to $30 per session for the college course and $15 to $20 for the preparatory program. Interest at 8 percent was levied on overdue accounts.

In addition to the decreased enrollment and spending for equipment, Smedes always gave scholarships beyond his capacity. In his report to the diocesan convention in 1879, he spoke of the many scholarships provided by his father "without a penny of endowment or extraneous help" and then offered even more generous aid, saying, "Having carried on the work successfully during the past years of financial distress, we feel encouraged for the future to offer the daughters of the clergy of the South free tuition in every department."[142] Henceforth, he charged the daughters of Episcopal clergymen only for board at a reduced rate. In actuality, Smedes would write to a fellow clergyman, "Name your own terms," and, in the end, some of their daughters attended "entirely free." Smedes wrote to Bishop Lyman, who was the only person aware of the extent of his generosity, "It has been the greatest satisfaction of my work that I have been able to help our brethren in this way."[143]

Bennett Smedes could not bring himself to insist firmly enough upon the payment of old debts. His account book for the 1880s shows that he was forever having to wait for someone to get a higher price for cotton or having to accept a small parcel of land of questionable value as tuition. The final inventory of his estate showed over 200 uncollected accounts.[144] The panic of 1893 was, as Richard H. Battle said later, "especially hard on the patrons of St. Mary's and those who would naturally become its patrons."[145] Smedes kept his basic charges at $230 but raised his fees for extras; he worried about competition from public institutions and schools and colleges of other denominations. However, he continued to pay his faculty well for the times, as his father had before him. Most of the women were paid between $300 and $350 a year and room and board; two who were "full graduates of Vassar" were paid $450 and maintenance. The director of music, the only man on the faculty in addition to Smedes, was always paid about three times the salary of the women teachers and twice that of the lady principal. This differential was the custom of the time.

The school buildings became an increasing expense, for as additions and improvements were made Smedes paid higher rent. In 1885 he requested steam heat for all of the main building. (Radiators had been installed in 1880 in East Rock and the parlor.) He wrote to Paul C. Cameron, "You showed great faith when you urged me to undertake the work at St. Mary's in the first instance. If you go to the expense of putting in steam heat, I will do all within my power to pay the interest on the money." [146] Cameron had steam heat installed, and it was as unsatisfactory from the beginning as it remained for almost 100 years thereafter. By the early 1890s there was running water in all the buildings.

The new art building had in 1887 increased the value of the campus and thus the rent. When the 1885 art building burned, Smedes bore $3,000 (the value of his uninsured furniture and equipment) of the $12,500 in uninsured losses. [147] By 1896 Smedes was paying $2,600 annually in rent. [148] It appears that he never took advantage of the Cameron offer made in 1877 of "some abatement of the rent if the school did not make expenses." [149] Rather, Bennett Smedes paid deficits from his own resources until he had spent about $30,000 of his personal funds and had borrowed against his insurance. [150] Finally, in 1896, Smedes turned to the Diocese of North Carolina to save St. Mary's.

Bishop Cheshire had, as he had told the diocesan convention only the year before, "from earliest childhood been brought up to look upon St. Mary's . . . as the most valuable of our church institutions . . . in North Carolina," [151] and he had called it "a quasi-diocesan school." [152] He readily agreed that "the Church should not throw away what had been by the labors of so many lives . . . built up." Having practiced law before entering the priesthood, the bishop understood Smedes's argument that the school had grown over the years into "a sort of corporate entity . . . with a tradition and life of its own, in the minds not only of its pupils and graduates . . . , but of the people generally." [153]

The St. Mary's Alumnae Association organized itself to exert pressure. In May, 1896, the association sent to the convention of the Diocese of North Carolina a memorial signed by the president, Annie L. Patterson Harris, and "numerous" others. The memorial appealed to "the three dioceses either to endow the school or to erect for it suitable buildings in Raleigh or elsewhere." It stressed the untiring and faithful service to the church of the alumnae and noted that the diocese would too late realize the value of St. Mary's should it "be called upon to feel its loss." [154] The convention by unanimous consent then heard Mary Iredell make the first of her many effective talks on behalf of the school.

The 1896 convention adopted Bishop Cheshire's resolution assuring the alumnae that the church in North Carolina would "not be found wanting in this emergency" but would "do all in its power to place St. Mary's School upon permanent foundation as an institution under the charge and patronage of the Church throughout the entire State."[155] In his address the bishop said, "If St. Mary's is to remain the glory of the Diocese . . . , the Churchmen of North Carolina must rally to the support of the faithful and generous man who so worthily occupies the place of his noble father. . . ."[156]

The memorial was referred to a special committee consisting of the bishop and five others empowered to buy new buildings for a diocesan school for girls or to purchase a new site and build.[157] That special committee was able to report to the convention only a year later that a board of trustees then controlled St. Mary's School, which was continuing business as usual on its own campus. The new board of trustees reported that:

by an Act of the General Assembly of the State of North Carolina, ratified March 2, 1897, Jos. Blount Cheshire, Jr., Alfred A. Watson, Francis J. Murdock, Julian E. Ingle, Charles E. Johnson, William A. Erwin, Robert Strange, Wharton J. Green, McNeely DuBose and Theodore F. Davidson, their associates and successors, were constituted a body politic and corporate, under the name of "Trustees of St. Mary's School," with power to increase their number so that the total shall not exceed sixteen, exclusive of *ex officio* members, and were granted all powers usually granted to school corporations, and amply sufficient for the purposes of St. Mary's School.[158]

The act further provided that the corporation could buy and sell personal and real property. The corporation was to be "under the jurisdiction, control and direction of the Protestant Episcopal Church in North Carolina," and all bishops exercising jurisdiction within the state were trustees ex officio. The school could "be located in Raleigh or in such other place in North Carolina" as the trustees determined. The charter provided, however,

that in case for any cause said trustees shall determine to abandon the trust imposed on them, all property belonging to them shall be devoted to such religious, charitable or educational purposes, as may be determined upon by the several representative bodies entitled to elect said trustees . . . having respect, as far as practicable, to the proportions in which several dioceses or jurisdictions have created said fund.

The 1897 charter was not changed substantially, except to include South Carolina, until 1968. The original charter granted the right to confer degrees, but until 1970 graduates received diplomas only.

By the convention of May, 1897, the board had organized itself with Bishop Cheshire as chairman and Charles Root of Raleigh as secretary-

Class of 1896. First row: Susan Marshall, Columbia Munds, Elizabeth Cheshire. Second row: Margaret Jones, Mary Pride Jones, Lucy Cobb, Nannie Skinner. Third row: Harriet Bowen, Ann Barnes, Bertha Stein

treasurer. Of the 16 members, eight were from the Diocese of North Carolina, four from the Diocese of East Carolina, and four from the Jurisdiction of Asheville. After the expiration of their staggered terms, this first board, which was elected by the incorporating trustees, would be succeeded by trustees elected by their conventions to three-year terms.

The trustees retained Smedes on salary to run the school. After some difficulty, agreement was reached with the Cameron family to buy "the St. Mary's Tract" (25 acres and all buildings) for $50,000, one fifth of which was to be paid in cash.[159]

The Diocese of North Carolina at the 1897 convention approved all of those actions of the St. Mary's trustees and placed certain diocesan funds at the school's disposal in return for scholarships.[160] The convention then passed a resolution expressing to Bennett Smedes "its sense of obligation for his unselfish work for the good of the Church in this and other southern dioceses during the last twenty years."

The trustees decided to reduce the basic charges at St. Mary's from $230, where they had stayed for over a decade, to $200. The daughters of all clergymen "of the Ecclesiastical bodies represented on the Board of Trustees" were to pay only for board and "extras." The trustees maintained that a church school "should not be a school for the benefit of the daughters of the rich,"[161] and the charges for many years remained slightly below those of some of the comparable private schools.

Bishop Cheshire, convinced that the school, in order to survive, needed a $50,000 endowment in addition to a debt-free campus, set out to raise $100,000. He proposed to raise half of that amount "from our people generally" and half through a St. Mary's Alumnae Association Fund. He organized two gift societies: the Patrons of St. Mary's, women who gave $500 each, and Daughters of St. Mary's, who gave $100. Mary Iredell, president of the alumnae association, was employed by the trustees as their agent to organize St. Mary's guilds in as many parishes as possible; each guild made a pledge to the fund.

By the next convention, all of those efforts had brought results. Cheshire reported that $10,000 had been paid on the property and that there was "good hope of another $10,000 soon." There were 60 boarders at St. Mary's, but 80 were needed to fill all beds. Despite his valiant efforts, the bishop was not to see St. Mary's debt free until 1906, and the endowment was to be postponed from decade to decade as the acute need for new buildings took precedence.

Bishop Cheshire's efforts to include the Diocese of South Carolina in the St. Mary's enterprise brought more immediate success. Cheshire had not realized until 1896 the extent of the school's longtime patronage from South Carolina. The two representatives from that diocese who were invited to commencement and the board meeting in 1898 went away "highly delighted with the school," according to the *Muse*.[162]

In August of that year an informal meeting at Saluda between representatives of the school's trustees and the Diocese of South Carolina resulted in a resolution placing St. Mary's "under the control and patronage of all Carolina Dioceses." After Cheshire addressed the South Carolina convention in May, 1899, that convention unanimously adopted the Saluda resolution.[163] Cheshire had been so sure that South Carolina Episcopalians had "much the same feeling of attachment to St. Mary's" as North Carolinians that he had the charter amended in January of that year to permit their participation. The amended charter provided for a board of trustees of 30 members with six-year terms.[164]

Also in May, 1899, came approval by the Diocese of East Carolina of all actions of the Board of Trustees of St. Mary's School and the first election of East Carolina's trustees, their original trustees having been chosen by the incorporating board. The Right Reverend Alfred A.

Watson, D.D., bishop of East Carolina, who had worked with Bishop Cheshire since 1896 on the St. Mary's question, reminded his convention of "how great a blessing this school had been in times past to this Diocese."[165] Dr. M. M. Marshall, rector of Christ Church in Raleigh, said in a commencement address that the "dear old nursery of the daughters of the Church" would go on "in its glorious career of untold usefulness with accelerated pace. . . ."[166]

Life at St. Mary's went on as calmly as possible, but the teachers were dismayed to find their salaries lower than expected. The trustees were "regretful" but "found it necessary to cut expenses" in order to keep the school open.[167] Emilie McVea, as lady principal, kept academic standards intact. A major innovation was the business department established in 1897 under Lizzie Lee, who presided over it for many years. She also acted as secretary to Smedes. In 1897 the trustees opened a kindergarten for children from four to seven. For $2.50 a month, Louise T. Busbee, a St. Mary's alumna who had a diploma from Miss Pollock's training school in Washington, D.C., gave "practical lessons in form, color, numbers, modeling in clay and sand, animal and plant life, songs, games, and physical culture." By the 1898–1899 academic year there was once again a full enrollment of 233 students, of whom 80 were boarders.

The winter of 1899 was Raleigh's worst since 1857. In February "the great snow" fell, with almost 18 inches accumulating over a three-day period and the temperature falling to 2 degrees below zero.[168] A student wrote home, "One night . . . Raleigh was the coldest place in the United States, and St. Mary's is *the* coldest place in Raleigh."[169] One afternoon Smedes, knowing how disappointed his young charges were not to be receiving their mail and unwilling to ask one of his workmen to brave the storm, decided to walk downtown to the post office. He made it home only with the greatest difficulty and by the next day was ill, although he continued to teach and preach for two days before taking to his bed. He seemed to be improving, but on February 22 Bennett Smedes died at St. Mary's of pneumonia.[170]

As the news of Smedes's death spread, "the community was painfully stirred."[171] The *News and Observer* headlined his obituary "A Prince Among Men." A memorial service conducted by Bishop Cheshire, M. M. Marshall, and J. E. C. Smedes on the afternoon of February 23 in the St. Mary's Chapel was attended by the students, all in white dresses, and many others. The music included the favorite St. Mary's hymns—"Ten Thousand Times Ten Thousand," "Hark the Sound of Holy Voices," "Tarry with Me, O My Saviour," and "Jerusalem! High Tower Thy Glorious Walls."[172]

Next morning a great throng of "all classes, races and creeds" attended the funeral at Christ Church. In his address Dr. W. M. Clark of Richmond, Virginia, said, "Because Bennett Smedes lived, you and I obtain a better idea of the glory of God." [173] The women (almost 3,000 of them), who had studied at St. Mary's under Bennett Smedes, remembered "his unwavering kindness, his wise counsel," his "earnest instruction in things spiritual," and "his gracious presence pervading the whole school." [174] The inscription on the stone marking the grave of Bennett Smedes, in the family plot at Oakwood Cemetery, seems eminently fitting: "Blessed are the pure in heart, for they shall see God."

CHAPTER SIX

# "ENCOMPASSED BY SUCH LOVE"

It was Emilie McVea as lady principal who saw to it that life went on at St. Mary's after Bennett Smedes's death. Henrietta Smedes and her daughters moved away from the campus. The trustees bought from her the school furniture and equipment,[1] and she gave the chapel pipe organ as a memorial to her husband. She later spent some time in New York where the girls studied music before their marriages.[2] Henrietta Smedes eventually returned to Raleigh where she lived until her death in 1929.

The board of trustees through its executive committee made the necessary decisions during this interim period, the remainder of the 1898–1899 academic year. The board lost the services of Charles Root when he resigned to administer the estate of Smedes, his brother-in-law. Kemp P. Battle, Jr., who had longtime associations with the school, succeeded Root as secretary and treasurer of the board.

## "THE RIGHT MAN IN THE RIGHT PLACE"

By the spring of 1899 the trustees had in mind a successor to Smedes, and Bishop Cheshire had a plan to secure him. Richard H. Battle had told the bishop about the Reverend Theodore DuBose Bratton, whom he had come to know in 1895 when they were fellow deputies to the general convention of the Episcopal church. Knowing that it would be difficult to lure Bratton away from his church and his college profes-

The Reverend Theodore DuBose Bratton, D.D. rector, 1899–1903

sorship in his native South Carolina, Bishop Cheshire had suggested him as a trustee of St. Mary's from the Diocese of South Carolina. Within a few days of his election Bratton attended his first meeting of the St. Mary's board at Tarboro, where it met during the convention of the Diocese of North Carolina. To his surprise, the main business of that meeting was to elect him rector of St. Mary's.[3] Encouraged by the board's enthusiasm and his own bishop's desire to see St. Mary's prosper, Bratton accepted the election; he took up his duties in Raleigh during the summer of 1899.

Theodore DuBose Bratton was born in 1862 at Roseland, his grandfather's plantation near Winnsboro, South Carolina, and grew up at Farmington, his father's plantation nearby. His father, John Bratton, was a physician who became a Confederate general and later served a term in Congress. His mother was Elizabeth Porcher DuBose.[4] Theodore was educated at home until the age of 12 when he was sent to the preparatory school of the University of the South at Sewanee, Tennessee. He next studied civil engineering there before entering divinity studies, also at Sewanee. In 1887 he received the degree of bachelor of divinity. That same year he was ordained deacon and assigned to mission work within his home diocese. The next year he was ordained priest and went as rector to the Church of the Advent in Spartanburg, South Carolina.[5] In 1888 he had married Lucy Beverly Randolph, the daughter of a physician of Tallahassee, Florida.[6] The Brattons spent 11 years in Spartanburg; the parish was congenial, and he enjoyed his teaching as head of the department of history and political science at Converse College. He was, according to the college historian, a popular and influential figure during the formative years of the institution.[7]

The new rector moved quite a family to St. Mary's. There were his wife and four young children—William, John, Randolph, and Marion—Lucy Bratton's mother, and Isabel Bratton, his sister, who would teach at the school. Because the Bratton family needed more space than that in the rector's apartment over the parlor, and because the trustees wished to enlarge the enrollment by housing students in that area, a two-story frame rectory was built just west of the chapel in 1900. It served for almost 70 years as the home of the head of St. Mary's. Both Bratton and his wife spent their first weeks at the school "getting the buildings and premises in the best condition our limited finances would warrant." They found, in fact, so many repairs needed that the new rector suggested that he relinquish $500 of his first year's salary; his cash salary was $125 per month. The offer, refused by the trustees, confirmed that they had "the right man in the right place."[8] Lucy Bratton's devoted efforts were recognized when the trustees appointed her "the school mother." The office of lady principal had been abolished when

The Bratton family in 1901. Photograph taken on the steps of the then new rectory

Emilie McVea left in the summer of 1900 for George Washington University to obtain the bachelor's and master's degrees. The rector assumed the academic duties, and Lucy Bratton supervised the daily living. As school mother, she always had time for the students despite the fact that she gave birth to two girls, Mary and Isabel, while she was at St. Mary's.

Although Theodore Bratton found St. Mary's in 1899 rather marking time, he did not propose major changes immediately. He agreed with the basic philosophy of Christian education at St. Mary's, and he did not disapprove of its conventional "southern lady" atmosphere. In his report to the trustees in May, 1900, the rector, himself a member of Phi Beta Kappa, pronounced the academic work "good, but not as good as we can do" and proposed to differentiate clearly between the preparatory and college departments. The trustees voted "to establish the College in which the study of the Liberal Arts and Sciences might be pursued at St. Mary's on an equal standard with other colleges for women." The plan to raise standards went into effect for the senior class of 1902. Bratton felt that reorganization of the curriculum could "be managed without friction" because the faculty would "help develop the wisdom to do it properly."[9] His experience at Converse and the catalogs of other institutions gave guidance.

Under the new system a student could still attend for as many years as she desired, from the first grade through the second year of college, and could receive certificates for all subjects satisfactorily completed. The St. Mary's diploma was awarded only for completion of all required subjects in the new four-year course comprising the last two years of high school and the first two years of college. The four years, renamed the college department, were organized into three curricula—the classical, the English, and the science—and each student in the college department, regardless of whether or not she planned to get her diploma, was required to choose a curriculum in order to prevent "that vascillating course which puts an end to serious work." The classical diploma required the completion of four years of Latin, four of French or German, three of English, and one of ethics, plus three terms of mathematics, two of history and political economy, two of science, and four of gymnastics. Greek was offered, but few were interested. The English course required four years of English and four years of either Latin, French, or German. It required more mathematics, history, and science than the classical course. The science diploma required four years of science, three of English, and two of mathematics, and either French or German. The four classes of the college department were designated as freshmen, sophomores, juniors, and seniors.

The preparatory department was organized like a four-year high school. It prepared students for college or for the business course at St. Mary's. As the preparatory department was also organized into the classical, English, and science curricula, a student could enter the diploma program her third year in high school. "Preps" were not allowed to live on campus until they reached the third year of high school. The reorganization raised academic standards considerably, and Bratton was strict in enforcing class attendance.

The trustees admitted in their 1901 report to the Diocese of North Carolina that there had been some apprehension among them as to whether "an old institution can pass into a new phase . . . without losing much of its . . . influence." However, St. Mary's under Bratton, they noted, had adjusted to "the pressing demands of the times" without losing its unique identity.[10] The University of the South conferred the honorary degree of doctor of divinity upon Theodore DuBose Bratton in 1901 in recognition of his contributions to Christian education.

The success of the transition from the Smedes era can be attributed to the fact that Bratton was so completely gracious. Among the students of his day, there was universal agreement that "all the girls worshipped him" and that "he was the handsomest and sweetest man we ever knew." The girls privately called him "T. D." Like Aldert Smedes, Bratton was said "to have a wonderful way of bringing out the best in everyone."[11] Even Bratton's magnetic personality could not ease all the burdens of change. There were only four 1902 graduates who had "aspired to mount the difficult but honorable hill of seniorship,"[12] and some of the nine graduates in the class of 1903, which called itself "the reconstruction class," had to stay in school two extra years. Apparently, the times, the influence of Emilie McVea, and Bratton had nudged St. Mary's into the twentieth century. The trustees reported that the new curriculum brought the school "nearer to what the Diocesan School of the Carolinas should and must be,"[13] and serious students welcomed the rigorous curriculum.

The trustees of the University of North Carolina had in 1897 recognized, albeit inadvertently, the college work taken at St. Mary's. The trustees of that institution had passed a resolution "that the postgraduate courses at the University be opened to women, under such regulations as the faculty may prescribe." Pres. Edwin A. Alderman chose to regard graduates of the female seminaries as "post-graduates," making them eligible to enter the regular junior class at Chapel Hill. (Women had been attending the normal school summer sessions at the university for some years.) The handful of young ladies at the university during those first years proved their dignity by wearing hats and gloves to classes. Nonetheless, their pictures were omitted from the yearbook, and their diplomas were presented privately.[14] The only female member of the class of 1905 at the university was Julia Hamlet Harris, salutatorian of the class of 1903 at St. Mary's, who later earned a Ph.D. degree from Yale and headed the English department at Meredith College from 1922 to 1952.[15]

The third rector of St. Mary's inherited a small corps of dedicated and competent teachers. Martha Dowd continued in the music department and Kate McKimmon was the primary teacher. Florence Slater had returned with a degree from Cornell. Another alumna, Margaret Mordecai Jones, valedictorian of the class of 1896, had returned in 1897 to teach mathematics. "She inspired us by making us think we could do mathematics, so we did it," her pupils said of her.[16] Margaret Jones spent a year during Bratton's tenure continuing her studies at Chapel Hill, and returned to St. Mary's until 1905 when she went to Columbia University to earn her bachelor's degree, and later returned twice more, once as a teacher and finally as president of St. Mary's. Imogen Stone, a friend of Emilie McVea's who for three years taught the English literature courses, was a Chaucerian with a degree from Cornell. She left St. Mary's in 1901 for graduate work and a teaching career at the H. Sophie Newcomb Memorial College. After Imogen Stone's departure, the literature classes were taken by Eleanor Walter Thomas, who had arrived the previous year to teach mathematics just after taking her master's degree at the College for Women in Columbia, South Carolina. Petite and vivacious, "with sparkling brown eyes that could look right through you," she was a strict and excellent teacher.[17] She was to be an important influence on campus life during three tours of duty spread over 17 years.

The art department was once again under Clara Fenner, who returned in the fall of 1901. For the three years of her absence Virgina Blanchard, who had studied at the Art Students' League and at the Posse Gymnasium in Boston, taught art and physical culture classes (for an extra $100 in salary).[18] Clara Fenner usually had about 25 art students, and she gave a free art lesson weekly to the primary class. In the studio her method was to set up models and then to leave her students to work while she painted also. A number of her pupils later studied in New York and Europe, and Clara Fenner studied further at Pratt Institute and in Paris during her St. Mary's tenure. Her lectures on art history were famous. She would pound the table as she exhorted her students to think about what they saw. "Use your ounce!" she would say. There were stiff cram sessions for the chosen few invited to take the summer grand tour of European art museums.[19]

Bratton, during the first year of his administration, had found that the music department, although made up of strong individuals, "was not in complete harmony." He thought the work of the students "surprisingly good" considering the conditions under which the music students practiced.[20] The acute need for a separate building for the music department had been apparent for decades; the situation was alleviated when, during the winter of 1901, 20 tiny practice rooms were built along the short covered way leading from East Rock to the art building. John Wynn Jeudwine, an Englishman who was both a barrister and a fine musician, was director of music from 1900 to 1902. He standardized the music courses and gained recognition of music as part of the academic curriculum, a step forward of which the rector highly approved.[21] However, the two men disagreed strongly over discipline when Jeudwine gave "ten disorders" and suspended social privileges for a long list of girls delinquent in music practice. The rector, considering the withdrawal of privileges to be his prerogative, countermanded the list. Jeudwine resigned despite the fact that he was reelected with an increased salary. Soon he retired to England to write several historical works.[22] Will Sanborn and his wife returned to teach music at St. Mary's with their daughter Gertrude, who taught voice.[23] Enrollment in music was over 100 each year during that period. Each year at least one musician of national reputation performed at St. Mary's.

The total enrollment of the school was given a considerable boost by the success of Lizzie Lee's business department, for it consistently attracted about 20 students. Juliet B. Sutton, who went in 1898 to assist Lizzie Lee, remained at St. Mary's in various capacities for 42 years. The business department had been established in 1897 "to meet the growing demand for instruction in the commercial branches, which are more and more affording women a livelihood."[24] Although the typewriter was invented in 1868, the process of the feminization of clerical positions did not proceed rapidly until the 1890s.[25] The business course at St. Mary's, which could be completed by the diligent student in one academic year, included grammar, spelling, mathematics, and penmanship as well as stenography, typewriting, and bookkeeping. A student who chose to master only one or two skills could finish sooner. In 1903, "scarcely a business student was present to take her diploma," nearly all having completed the course and accepted jobs before June.[26]

Louise Busbee's kindergarten, which had been moved to the campus when it became associated with St. Mary's in 1898, was moved during 1901 back to her home in the center of town to avoid the expense of transporting the children to the campus. "Miss Lulie" retained the St. Mary's name for some years although her school actually was autonomous. There were always about 25 kindergartners, boys and girls. (A few boys attended the primary grades on the St. Mary's campus.)

Revenues from increased enrollment made possible the replacement of equipment in use since the early 1880s. In his first report to the board, Bratton said, "We have absolutely nothing up to date in our science school, and the ingenuity of the teacher is sorely taxed to supply the deficiencies," but by the spring of 1902 he was able to say, "We are well prepared for the year before us." He was not able to obtain adequate support for the library, which had been moved in 1899 from the main building to the first floor of the art building because the Brattons needed the living space until the rectory was built. The library of about 2,500 uncataloged volumes was managed by Elleneen Checkley and an assistant, who also had other duties. Elleneen Checkley was principal of the preparatory department and taught history. Every year in his report Bratton noted the dire need for furniture and additional books.

The library subscribed to several newspapers and the leading current magazines but was adding no more than 40 books a year.[27]

Intellectual activity outside the classroom was stimulated by the continuation of the traditional lecture series on campus and by the new literary societies. The 1899–1900 lecture series included 11 visiting professors. The literary societies were organized in April, 1900, when Imogen Stone, at Bratton's suggestion, divided her college literature classes into two societies "to promote and cultivate literary interest." The girls regarded the societies as rival "sides," and the annual debates engendered great excitement. The names finally agreed upon were the initial letters of two southern poets—Sigma Lambda for Sidney Lanier and Epsilon Alpha Pi for Edgar Allan Poe. Colors, mottoes, flowers, and pins were selected, and several teachers were made honorary members. In 1902 E.A.P. challenged Sigma Lambda to a debate, held before the whole school amid great fanfare, which Sigma Lambda won by proving that "Poetry had done more for the development of mankind than prose." The next year, Sigma Lambda challenged and won by proving, to the surprise of no one in 1903, that "Man has done more for the world than Woman." The quality of the presentations on both sides impressed the judges, distinguished men from the community. The societies' practice debates in preparation for the great contest revealed an awareness of current issues—the protective tariff, the regulation of trusts, and the governing of the Philippines.[28]

## "THE LARGEST EPISCOPAL SCHOOL FOR GIRLS"

By the end of Theodore Bratton's first year as rector, the trustees not only felt that they had "the right man in the right place" but also that it had been a wise decision to remain in "the venerable buildings" about which clustered the fond memories of "long lines of alumnae."[29] The buildings, however, being overcrowded and in need of repairs, presented constant problems. Because the full board met only at commencement, the school was run by the rector and the executive committee of the board chaired by Bishop Cheshire. All members of the committee had intimate connections with the school through the women in their families.[30] They gave a great deal of time to the institution, but they recognized the rector's control over daily discipline although patrons were inclined to write to Bishop Cheshire concerning details. The students recognized the commitment of the men who had wrestled with the problems of transition and reorganization when they dedicated their Christmas issue of the *Muse* in 1900 to the trustees.

During the last year of Bennett Smedes's administration the dormitories had been filled to their capacity of 80, and the total enrollment including the kindergarten and special students had been 233. The uncertainties of the months following his death led to a decreased enrollment (156) for the next year. The total number of students by 1900–1901 was up to 201, and the trustees rented the William Augustus Blount house nearby for the overflow until the rectory and the new senior dormitory were completed. The seniors moved into their new quarters in December, 1901. Called north dormitory, it was a two-story frame house quite near the art building, but the seniors called it "the far countree." (It was to be known later as faculty house.) The trustees had hesitated "to build in wood," but funds were limited. Enrollment for 1901–1902 was 244 with 127 boarders—the largest number ever, rivaling the 125 of the Civil War years.[31] There was a waiting list despite the fact that the new Baptist Female Seminary (later Meredith College) opened in 1899 and attracted St. Mary's Baptist clientele. St. Mary's was by then the largest Episcopal school for women in the United States.

With a note of pride, the trustees reminded the 1901 convention of the Diocese of North Carolina that the board had decided to reduce the charges at St. Mary's "to such a rate as would provide for the running expenses . . . upon an economical basis with only a small margin of possible profit towards the payment of interest on the debt. . . ." The board felt that there was not another school in the country where the same advantages could be enjoyed at such moderate cost.[32] That decision proved to be of debatable wisdom for an institution lacking a large endowment. The increased enrollment did not pay for the changes necessary to provide for the 40 extra students. By 1901 the basic charges had been raised to $220. There were only two sizable scholarships, the alumnae association scholarship and one given in 1903 by Lucille Murchison, a Wilmington alumna, in memory of her father, David R. Murchison. There were six other scholarships worth about $50 apiece, and three students worked in the offices and library.[33] The fund-raising efforts of a great many—the bishops, the alumnae, Mary Iredell and the Reverend Alfred A. Pruden as traveling agents, and the workers for the special offering for St. Mary's in each parish—by the spring of 1901 had reduced the $50,000 purchase debt to $17,000. In addition, about $9,000 had been raised and spent for permanent improvements. Bishop Cheshire was well pleased, but he knew St. Mary's needed an endowment.[34]

Bratton took particular interest in the buildings and grounds at St. Mary's. In addition to the rectory, the music practice rooms, and north dormitory, he built an infirmary. Unfortunately, that small frame cottage burned in January, 1903. No one was hurt, but most of the furniture was lost.[35] A new brick infirmary (used in 1982 as a dormitory and called "1903") was built immediately. During the Bratton years, the

Senior class, 1901. Officers were Eliza Drane, Deas Boykin, Betsy
Montgomery, Ellen Faison, Janet Biggs, Allie Welsh, Julia Parsley, Lena
Dawson, and Sophie Wood

Board of editors of the *Muse*, 1902. Marie Brunson, Louise Venable,
Jennie Trapier, Mary Weeks, Katherine Meares, Annie Root

dining room on the ground floor of the main building was enlarged; the rest of that floor was used for classrooms. East Rock was arranged to contain the rector's office, the faculty sitting room, and the business school on the first floor, and rooms for teachers and students on the second floor. West Rock was remodeled, and the school then assured its patrons that it had "complete sanitary arrangements." It seemed to the rector that expensive maintenance problems appeared constantly. The grove of stately oaks suffered severe storm damage when 19 trees were lost in the autumn of 1896 and 16 in the summer of 1899.[36] Each year Bratton planted large areas of the grove in "assorted grasses," being determined to have eventually "an even green sward." He kept four cows, a few pigs, and a five-acre vegetable garden. All of those projects not only helped to provision the table but altogether netted a profit of over $350 in 1903.[37]

## "THE LOVING ATMOSPHERE OF THE PLACE"

Most girls enjoyed life at St. Mary's. One "forlorn little new girl," Louise Manning Venable, described in her journal her first unhappy days at school: "I wished that I had never been stuck in this awful, horrible hole. . . . There were bells about every five minutes . . . and that horrid little cubby hole of an alcove. . . ." But by her graduation in 1902 Louise wrote, "I nearly wept myself to death," continuing with a description of the many parties given for the seniors, and the gifts, and flowers.[38]

Life at St. Mary's was as carefree as possible. The strict rules were still on the books, but it was "the loving atmosphere of the place" that "encompassed" one, as Imogen Stone put it.[39] "Disorders" were still meted out for minor infractions, but the rector was likely to send a note with the report explaining that the demerits were not held against the student as any great offense, having been given "for little noises" made at the wrong times.[40] Jeudwine, several years after his departure from Raleigh, wrote to Bishop Cheshire predicting direly that Bratton's successor would "have to do a great deal of building up of discipline." The British gentleman remembered the following scandalous behavior: "a very heavy snow, and a young girl standing on her head, with her garments all over her head in the front of the Main building. . . . No one interfered, and no one dared tell Mr. Bratton, because as they said, he would only say he liked it and have it repeated for Mrs. Bratton."[41]

There were not many opportunities to stand on one's head in the snow in Raleigh, but nearly everyone danced in the parlor as had always been the custom during the free time before study hall at night. The pianist was likely to be playing "Under the Bamboo Tree" or "In the Good Ole Summer Time." (When the last surviving member of the class of 1903, Kate Herndon, returned to St. Mary's for her 75th anniversary, she exclaimed upon entering the parlor, "Oh! I feel just like dancing!"[42]) The two german clubs, Tau Delta and L'Etoile, organized about 1900, gave one or two formal dances a year. The idea was to practice for the real thing in anticipation of an invitation to Chapel Hill, where there were then 527 men.[43] At the St. Mary's germans all of the etiquette of a formal ball—programs, gold pins as favors, even a stag line—was followed. The "beaux," however, were those girls who could "lead," dressed in white shirtwaists with stiff standing collars, black bow ties, and their black skirts.[44]

On Mondays St. Mary's girls literally covered Fayetteville Street. There was always the tantalizing possibility of running into a beau from A&M where, in 1901, there were 301 students.[45] It did not take long "to go dead-broke" downtown. Boylan-Pearce offered velvets, silks, and "gloves and little fixings." Heller's Shoes sold "patent kid oxford ties—the shiney kind"—for $2 a pair.[46] Shopping for school clothes was easy, for everyone wore a sort of uniform consisting of a dark, floor-length skirt and a white shirtwaist with a tight collar and tight, long sleeves. One of several styles of ties was usually added. The girls spent their allowances mostly at the soda fountains, or at Royster's for candy, or at the California Fruit Store. The purchase of the makings of a feast was the real purpose of the Monday trip to town. Late night feasts—still officially forbidden—were frequent and could be as simple as crackers and dill pickles or as elaborate as chicken salad, fruit, and homemade candy. (The rector thought that it was the good bread made in the St. Mary's kitchen that caused students "almost without exception to gain weight while under the strain of literary work.")[47]

The best feasts of all were the sorority banquets. The first Greek letter sorority at St. Mary's was organized in 1900 "under the kindly fostering auspices of the beloved rector."[48] Alpha Kappa Psi was founded at St. Mary's in 1900 and became national in 1904 when its Beta Chapter was organized at Virginia Female Institute (Stuart Hall) in Staunton, Virginia. Its purpose was to express "the highest ideals of Christian womanhood," and three esteemed faculty women were included on the charter roll. Gamma Beta Sigma was founded at St. Mary's in 1901 and granted a charter by the state of North Carolina in 1904. Three other chapters were organized in 1904.[49] Upsilon Delta, founded at St. Mary's in 1902 and chartered in 1904, later became a chapter of Phi Mu. Kappa Delta was represented at St. Mary's by the Phi Delta Chapter.[50] It was a time, as the *Muse* noted, when women were experiencing "the advantages of organizations binding them together and enforcing . . . mutual loyalty and protection."[51]

Not many girls received bids to the sororities, but everyone had a chance to play team sports. By 1900 there was an athletic association to supervise the activities of the sports groups—the walking, tennis, and cycling clubs, two baseball teams called the "Sunny South" and "Dixie," and the Sigma and Mu basketball clubs. The 1902 yearbook pronounced bicycling "a worn-out fad." In 1899 everyone had "gone crazy" over the new game of basketball introduced by Imogen Stone, who had played at Cornell. Bratton usually refereed the games on the outdoor court just east of the art building. The uniform for basketball was a middy blouse and a full skirt that covered the knees and was worn over bloomers and black stockings. The excitement over basketball became so feverish that "T. D." decided that the game was too strenuous for young ladies and called a halt in 1902, whereupon the girls grumbled that their beloved, easygoing, pipe-smoking rector was behaving like "an old maid."[52]

## "THE HANDMAID OF THE CHURCH"

That it truly was "the same old St. Mary's" under the rectorship of Bratton is attested to by the description of the primary department in the catalog for 1901–1902: "St. Mary's having been always the handmaid of the Church, the children of the school are taught from the first day, both in the school-room and the Chapel, the things which are for their eternal interest." The Sunday school class taught by the rector was "organized for instruction designed to prepare for confirmation and to strengthen the newly confirmed." Because nearly all students were from Episcopalian families, Bratton reported the 1902–1903 enrollment by diocese. Of the 242 students, 149 were from the Diocese of North Carolina and 28 from that of East Carolina. Eight were from the Jurisdiction of Asheville, 27 from South Carolina, 11 from Virginia, and 10 from Georgia. Florida, Maryland, Mississippi, West Texas, Illinois, and Colorado were represented also. That same year Bratton told the trustees, "I have noted a deeper spiritual tone in our devotions, due in large measure I think to the older average age, 17 1/2, of our students, and that the Auxiliaries have increased their contributions materially and enlarged the area of their benefactions." [53] Most of the faculty had for years been organized into an active woman's auxiliary. There were then five junior auxiliary chapters which "under Miss McKimmon's leadership and largely through her indomitable religious energy . . . maintained their work with zeal." [54]

The celebration in 1900 of Katie McKimmon's 50th birthday gave an opportunity for recognition of her services to St. Mary's as a member of the faculty for 32 years. Bratton declared a holiday, and after chapel the students marched around the grove waving banners and singing. There was a feast and a cake in the evening and the presentation of a watch given by a number of her former students. Four of the young teachers, all alumnae of St. Mary's, had arranged the best of all possible gifts, a bundle of letters to Miss Katie from "her girls" who over the years had lived in West Rock. [55] The 1902 yearbook was dedicated to her.

"The Chapel," said Bratton "is the centre round which everything revolves at St. Mary's, and I believe it is true to say that its influence is by all odds greater than any other in our school life." [56] A student of the period wrote many years after her schoolgirl days, "Chapel service was as natural a part of our daily life as good or hard work, and we took it so. . . . However much we may have loved the rest of the school life, that is the part that abides with St. Mary's girls." [57] The service on All Saints' Day had always been one of particular significance. The members of the auxiliary decorated the Chapel with autumn leaves and chrysanthemums, and "the day scholars were especially asked to be present at the Eucharist feast." [58] Bratton, realizing that the St. Mary's Chapel was hallowed by the memories of Aldert and Bennett Smedes, instituted Founders' Day as part of the All Saints' observance. He asked R. H. Battle to give the address on November 1, 1902; on that occasion Battle gave an account of the school's first half century. [59]

Bratton's sermons, as well as his classroom lectures, were interesting and instructive—not especially eloquent, but never pedantic. He was, according to a fellow clergyman, possessed of "a remarkably beautiful voice," and the effect when he preached was enhanced by his "open countenance" and his reverent manner.[60] His messages as their priest to the St. Mary's girls were much like those of Aldert Smedes. Bratton loved St. Mary's, but on April 30, 1903, he was elected bishop of Mississippi.[61] In his letter of resignation of May 25, 1903, he characteristically included only the positive aspects. Bratton wrote: "I shall always look back upon these years with the sweetest sentiment of gratitude, and thank God that, as near as human recollection can be, the recollection will be unalloyed, for in receiving so much, I am sure that Mrs. Bratton and I have honestly tried to give all that is in us to the blessed work."

Lucy Bratton died in 1905 after a brief illness.[62] The St. Etheldreda's chapter of the junior auxiliary at St. Mary's, of which she had been the first directress, changed its name to the Lucy Randolph Bratton chapter to honor her memory.

Bishop Bratton founded "his own St. Mary's," All Saints' College (later All Saints' Episcopal School), in Vicksburg in 1908. For many years he served as the president and board chairman of All Saints' in addition to his other duties.[63] He was chancellor of the University of the South from 1935 until his retirement in 1938.[64] He died on June 26, 1944. Theodore Dubose Bratton probably was described best by one who said of him, "He had more personal religion than any other man I ever saw and annoyed you less with it."[65]

## CHAPTER SEVEN

# "NONE HAS LABORED
# MORE FAITHFULLY"

The fourth rector of St. Mary's School, the Reverend McNeely DuBose, had considerable prior knowledge of the institution and a deep commitment to its ideals, for he had been a trustee representing the Jurisdiction of Asheville since the incorporation of the school. Theodore Bratton, his close friend and first cousin, had suggested him.[1] On the day that he sent his letter of acceptance to Bishop Cheshire, DuBose also wrote to the Right Reverend Ellison Capers, bishop of South Carolina, saying, "I most earnestly beg your official and personal sympathy and prayers, that God may help me to carry on this most important work."[2] His use of the word "sympathy" indicated that DuBose understood the magnitude of his new task.

McNeely DuBose was born in 1859 at Roseland, the family plantation near Winnsboro, South Carolina. His father, Cowan McNeely DuBose, died the next year. His mother, Margaret Ann Boyd DuBose, eventually moved with her two sons to Sewanee, where her late husband's brother, Dr. William Porcher DuBose, was on the faculty of the university, and McNeely DuBose was educated from grammar school there. He received from the University of the South the B.S. degree in 1881 and the B.D. degree in 1884. He was ordained deacon in 1884 and priest the next year. Before going to St. Mary's, he served the Church of the Nativity in Union, South Carolina, and Trinity Church, Asheville.

In 1885 Mac DuBose had married his boyhood sweetheart, Rosalie Anderson. She was the daughter of Henry Mortimer Anderson, a phy-

The Reverend McNeely DuBose, rector, 1903–1907

sician who went from Rome, Georgia, to be the first treasurer of the University of the South, and Julia Isabella Hand of Georgia. The Andersons moved with the DuBose family to the St. Mary's rectory.[3] There were five DuBose children—two daughters, Margaret Rosalie and Rainsford Fairbanks, and three sons, McNeely, David St. Pierre, and Marion St. John.[4] Margaret, at St. Mary's when her father became rector, continued to live in the dormitory; she taught in the preparatory department for two years after her 1905 graduation. The other children were young enough to attend the lower grades at St. Mary's. Rosalie DuBose was appointed "school mother," and the rector announced when school opened in 1903, "The School Mother will be found at the Rectory whenever needed. She is always glad to welcome either teachers or pupils."[5] The students wrote of her, "She is as the sweet presence of good diffused."[6]

## "FROM PLUMBING TO PREACHING"

Because DuBose went to a school ready to open with a full enrollment, he had only a few weeks to learn his new duties, which would be, he said, "to carry on the work so wisely managed for the past four years." But as he reported to the board, the carrying on seemed to consist of "anything from sawing wood to teaching Ethics, or from plumbing to preaching."[7] A meticulous man, he always insisted upon checking every detail. Furthermore, Bratton had left with the trustees some major recommendations consisting of more than just carrying on. It was necessary to pay off the debt on the property, to enlarge the chapel, to erect new buildings, to increase the library's collection, to strengthen academic programs, and to foster a more active alumnae association. He set about accomplishing his goals as quickly as possible. The students seemed to sense his commitment, for the seniors of 1904 wrote in their yearbook, "Of course we missed Dr. Bratton, but we daily grew fonder of his successor, as he, with his quiet dignity, worked with us, showing the great interest and love he entertained for St. Mary's and all connected with it."

DuBose, in addition to his plumbing and preaching, was giving much thought during his first year at St. Mary's to academic standards. He realized that southern institutions, always lagging some years behind those of the North, had to come to terms with the changes that had occurred since 1890 in the philosophy of the education of women. His predecessor had been strongly of the same mind. In his first report to the board DuBose said, "I can join unhesitatingly with Dr. Bratton in saying that we must lose no opportunity to make St. Mary's wholly collegiate. . . . the Bryn Mawr, Smith, or Wellesley of the Southeast."

Bishop Cheshire agreed in part. He told the 1904 convention of the Diocese of North Carolina: "Twenty-five years ago such successes as the school has now attained would have left nothing to be desired. But the world has changed, and its demands have changed. . . ." The bishop, however, wanted to make sure that St. Mary's retained its unique characteristics. It needed, he said, "no violent revolution," but just enough financial support from the church for its "natural growth and development."[8]

The clientele of the institution was not ready for any revolution. Southern women, in general, felt that being a woman was good; most were still content to be mothers, teachers, and church workers operating behind the scenes of visible power. But times were changing. About 100,000 women were enrolled by 1900 in institutions providing some kind of higher learning,[9] and some St. Mary's women were taking graduate degrees or going into professions other than teaching. A clever sketch published in the *Muse* in 1908 depicted an incredible world of 2808 A.D. run by women, complete with meals "of two small tablets" and vacations on the moon.[10] Some American women during the first decade of the twentieth century were wondering about change and progress; soon many would be taking action to bring about both.

The first St. Mary's catalog prepared under the DuBose rectorship, that of 1904–1905, presented a college curriculum requiring 15 hours each semester but allowing a few more electives than before within the student's chosen emphasis upon Latin, modern languages, English, or science. Everyone was required to take Bible. Those not specializing in one of the fine arts were encouraged to take some courses in either music, art, or elocution. Freshmen and sophomores had almost no time for electives, being required to take a course in reading and also to spend an hour a week "overcoming defects in spelling, composition, and letter writing." It would have been out of character for St. Mary's to institute a system of free electives because the idea, although introduced in 1825 at the University of Virginia and popular after Harvard's acceptance of it in 1869, remained controversial.[11] The new St. Mary's catalog was organized by departments, although a department in several cases was one teacher.

That the new rector understood the philosophy by which St. Mary's had always lived was evident in his first annual report to North Carolina's Diocesan Council when in 1904 he wrote, "The whole idea of St. Mary's is to foster the Christian family life rather than to develop a mere scientific school plant; yet in the family as well as in the machine, order and system cannot be ignored, and so there is always the effort to have just enough of quiet discipline to make life run accurately and also smoothly." He soon decided, however, that more of the family rules should be spelled out, and he published a pamphlet to prevent misunderstanding. The school operated, as always, under an unwritten honor system whereby each girl reported her offenses at roll call. As always, the dormitory teachers noted down offenses when necessary. The 1904 rules sounded too much like those of 1842 to the girls: "absolute order during school hours . . . no walking or talking in the grove or in and around the buildings during school hours. . . . There is *only one proper place* for each pupil during each hour. . . . pupils who take extra holidays, even with parental permission, lose any chance to be on the Honor Roll. . . ." There was a late afternoon study hall during recreation time for minor offenders as well as one for the "unstudious."[12]

The serious students responded by working very hard "in our humble way to help our new rector." The student editor of the *Muse* wrote: "We are always responsible for our actions, whether or not someone calls us to account for them. A higher duty—that of doing right for its own sake—should guide us in our conduct in class as in our general relations with others."[13] The grade average of the 13 members of the graduating class of 1905 was 93.46, with valedictorian Margaret Rosalie DuBose and salutatorian Anna Barrow Clark both averaging almost 98.[14] By 1905 many more of the St. Mary's alumnae were continuing their educations, mostly at southern institutions for women. The commencement speaker of that year, Dr. Charles Martin Niles, then rector of Trinity Church, Columbia, South Carolina, was so impressed that he made arrangements for a gold medal to be awarded for the highest grade average made in the school each year.[15]

## "THE LONG TASK—THE PRECIOUS PRIVILEGE"

DuBose had inherited in 1903 a small faculty with several strong members. The trustees were willing to grant unpaid leave for study, and the younger teachers took further work as they were able to afford it. In each generation several unusually competent faculty members gave their lives to St. Mary's. Bratton's great parting gift had been to secure two able men, Ernest Cruikshank and William Enos Stone, whose contributions were beyond measure.

A rare glimpse into the heart and mind of a teacher was offered in an article written in 1904 for the *Muse* by Elleneen Checkley:

In dear old St. Mary's the yearly opening service always brings some solemn moments to those . . . who are taking up again all the grave responsibilities and all the varied opportunities of the sacred charge of young souls that the Church has seen fit to commit to their care. . . . As they look and listen in the throng of fresh young faces, of which more than half are new and yet unfamiliar in the halls of St. Mary's, . . . it is but natural that there should be a moment of shrinking from the long task . . . which might be overwhelming if it were not that some hymn or psalm, some prayer . . . leaves a strengthening message that becomes a promise for the coming year . . . of the precious privilege and the pure happiness. . . .[16]

Students recognized those truly dedicated to teaching. The 1905 valedictorian said, "Every month of our Senior year has made us realize more than ever before what the teachers are to the girls and what the girls can be to the teachers."

One of those master teachers, Kate Shipp, returned to St. Mary's in 1904 after two years in England with a degree from Teachers' College, Cambridge University. That year she taught English; the next year she went back to the mathematics department while Margaret Jones, her prize pupil from her years at St. Mary's during the 1890s, was on leave for further study. Kate Shipp once again enlivened the campus considerably by her wit outside the classroom and her scholarship within it. A leading lawyer once remarked that with her qualities of leadership— a forceful personality, a highly trained intellect, discriminating judgment, business ability—she could have made a great governor of her native state.[17] In 1907 she opened Fassifern, her own school for girls. Over the years several teachers and alumnae went from St. Mary's to teach at Fassifern, which was located in Lincolnton and then in Hendersonville.[18]

When Eleanor Thomas left in June, 1904, for a year at Columbia University, the editor of the *Muse* lamented, "An important part of St. Mary's life seems to be missing. . . . Her influence for four years pervaded the entire school."[19]

Towers of strength during the DuBose administration were Kate McKimmon, Lizzie Lee, and Clara Fenner carrying on as competently as always in the primary, business, and art departments. In Fenner's department "the rage" in 1906 was textile design—"the new effects in stenciling on curtains, tablecovers, and pillows"—while little interest was shown in the course in architectural and mechanical drawing that Bratton had wanted because he heard that jobs were opening for women in drafting.

Martha (Mittie) Dowd of the music department, with her perpetual air "of delicate wistfulness—of chasing a shadow," as Imogen Stone described her, seemed almost as young as when she had gone to teach at St. Mary's in 1886. She possessed an extraordinary gift for teaching, and students and faculty praised her as a pianist. The small group of women who had taught at St. Mary's for long years remained a close-knit group, and Martha Dowd was the one especially treasured for her "genius for friendship."[20]

For some years the music faculty had consisted of about six persons.

The requirements for the certificate in music were rigorous, including an examination and recital before all of the music faculty. The department had never been considered a separate school at St. Mary's, and those wishing a diploma were required to take the regular academic courses. The violin teacher of the DuBose era was Charlotte Hull, a graduate of the University of Chicago and a native of that area. She went to Raleigh in 1902, studied in Prague in 1907, and returned to St. Mary's before going to Sweet Briar. Her St. Mary's orchestra of about 16 pieces was popular. Chelian A. Pixley taught piano, 1902–1907, studied in Berlin for a year, returned to St. Mary's for a year, and then taught at Fassifern. She was the niece of Emergene C. Schutt, who taught piano at St. Mary's and then at Winthrop College. For two years Prof. Almon W. Vincent, a graduate of the Royal Conservatory at Leipzig, was the director of music, and his wife taught in the department. The joint recitals of the St. Mary's music faculty were still considered cultural events in Raleigh despite the fact that nationally known artists by then included North Carolina on their tours.

DuBose taught ethics and Bible and performed many of the functions of an academic head. As the administration of the school became increasingly more complicated, he called for help from the faculty. A committee advised students in the selection of courses, and gradually William Enos Stone and Ernest Cruikshank assumed various administrative duties.

Ernest Cruikshank was only 24 when he went to teach Latin and science at St. Mary's. He had heard stories about the school since childhood from a favorite aunt.[21] Until 1921 he kept the routine of the school running smoothly and was a vitalizing force in campus life. He was born in 1879 at the family home in Elkton, Maryland, where his father, George Washington Cruikshank, was a lawyer and editor of the *Cecil Democrat*. Young Ernest entered Washington College in Chestertown, Maryland, at 14 and took both his bachelor's and master's degrees there. After serving briefly as principal of a public school in Virginia, he spent 1900–1901 taking graduate work at Johns Hopkins. He taught two years at Shenandoah Collegiate Institute in Dayton, Virginia, before going to Raleigh in 1903.[22] Cruikshank taught with such casual competence that his students were likely not to realize until years later the brilliance of his lectures.[23] By 1906 he was teaching fewer classes because he was the librarian and also, as secretary of the school, doing the work of business manager and registrar.

There was considerable educational activity outside the classrooms. In addition to the traditional lecture series, informal morning "Thursday Talks" were added. Collier Cobb of the University of North Carolina was a favorite with students and townspeople alike because of "his

Waiting for the streetcar at the summer house on front campus, 1905

West Rock glee club, 1907

happy manner of imparting information."[24] R. D. W. Connor of the State Department of Public Instruction lectured on "Some Women of North Carolina," not a lecture on women's rights but one about women who had served.[25]

A popular topic for lecturers during the first decade of the century was the glories of the lost cause. The centenary year of Gen. Robert E. Lee, 1909, saw commemorations in every southern town, and January 19 was observed as a holiday at St. Mary's. Kate McKimmon, recording secretary of the North Carolina Division of the United Daughters of the Confederacy since its organization in 1897, was as unreconstructed as ever. She felt exceedingly honored when Gen. Fitzhugh Lee paid an informal visit to the campus in February, 1905, while in Raleigh to promote the Jamestown Exposition. And she was so deeply humiliated on October 19, 1905, when all of St. Mary's turned out to cheer Republican Pres. Theodore Roosevelt that she retired to the chapel to pray for "her beloved Southland which, in her mind was capitulating to the enemy" on that day.[26]

Student interest in the world outside St. Mary's was generated by a current events course, literary club debates, and lectures by their history teacher, Harvard-educated William Stone. For Democrats, as well as the ten admitted Republicans on campus, the presidential visit to Raleigh for the state fair was a great excitement. Stone, who had known T. R. at Harvard, taught the girls the Harvard yell—just in case they had the chance to please the president. The *Muse* described that day:

We gathered in force near the summer house about eleven. . . . The procession with its host of marshals and military display, was quite imposing, but of course the centre of attraction were the President and Mrs. Roosevelt. As the marshals passed, they halted for a moment and cheered us heartily . . . and when the President came, led by Mr. Stone we saluted him with the Harvard "Rahs." He seemed much pleased . . . and bowed most graciously.[27]

The cheering girls could not have known on that October day in 1905 that they stood upon the threshold of a new era when presidents would fly in planes (T. R. did) and women would vote in North Carolina, for little seemed to them to change.

Daily life at St. Mary's rolled along about as merrily as ever with new clubs springing up yearly. The serious students managed heavy academic loads and numerous activities. By then the seniors could have lights until 10:30. They were especially close because some years all of them could fit into senior hall. The continued sense of family at St. Mary's was remarkable because many girls attended only for the two college years; only two of the 13 members of the graduating class of 1905 had been at the school for four years. Lizzie Lee's room in the senior dormitory was a popular spot, especially just before bedtime when "her girls" liked to stop by just to visit for a few moments. She truly loved the students and considered them "her friends for life." That gracious lady, who always presided over the tea table at public receptions, personified St. Mary's.[28]

Life was not quite so serene on the third floor of the main building where presided Juliet Sutton, keeper of many loose ends on campus. That area was still a dormitory with alcoves and one small bathroom "that had to be dated up about a week ahead to get the tub." Sometimes it was late at night before Juliet Sutton completed the post office and bookstore accounts and climbed the stairs to quiet her giggling charges. She was genuinely interested in the details of the lives of her girls. Alumnae, when writing postcards to friends still at school, were known to note in the middle of the message, "Hi, Miss Sutton!" because they knew that she would be keeping up with the news on the incoming postals. She was one of St. Mary's traditions, for she was there from 1898 until 1940.[29]

Faculty and students alike enjoyed the traditional holidays. The first holiday of the school year was the afternoon spent at the state fair. The students assembled in squads, each with a teacher, and took the cars to the fairgrounds. In 1905 the big event, in addition to President Roosevelt's visit, was the successful ascension of a balloon; in 1906 the thing to do was to have one's picture taken in an automobile. The students, though not allowed to go to the circus, always watched the parade. At St. Mary's own grand parade around the parlor each Halloween, more elaborate costumes than ever were exhibited. The students particularly enjoyed the antics of the faculty men. Because students did not go home for Thanksgiving, many boxes arrived, and the cry rang up and down the halls, "Bring a hat pin, and let's cut the cake!" A pleasant surprise awaited returning students in the fall of 1907 when they discovered the new "grill room" on the ground floor of the main building, where cooking was permitted.

In 1905 Juliet Sutton's St. Anne's chapter of the junior auxiliary presented as an extra November treat *The Grasshopper Cantata*, the first known presentation of this classic that was revived periodically over the next 70 years. By the DuBose era, the Christmas party was held in the art studio with dime store presents for all piled high under the tree. The little gifts, arranged by a drawing of names, were called "knocks," and much care went into the selection of the gift and into the writing of a ridiculous verse to accompany it. The Christmas plays were started in 1902 at the suggestion of Ernest Cruikshank. Two plays—one secular and one religious—were presented each year by the senior class. As a Christmas surprise for the students in 1904, the faculty gave *Alice in Wonderland*. The production required some ingenuity because rehearsals had to be held secretly after 10:00. The performance was such a smash hit that it was repeated for Bishop Cheshire, at his request.[30]

School spirit was rampant, even at schools for young ladies, by the first decade of the twentieth century. Athletics were so popular that in 1905 the athletic association was reorganized under the control of a student-faculty committee. The athletic field behind the new auditorium was ready for use by the fall of 1907. Everyone was expected to be outside from 3:30 to 4:30 on school day afternoons, and games were more popular than "five times around the grove." In the spring of 1907 the *Muse* noted, "Riding parties have become quite the thing. There are not so many that indulge, but there is always a goodly assemblage to witness the start."[31]

School spirit meant school songs. There was "Hail, St. Mary's" adapted in 1899 from Margaret Mason Young. Its stirring stanzas still rang across the campus in 1982. In 1905 Herbert E. Hodgson, with aid from Margaret Jones of the faculty, wrote the alma mater to be sung to the tune of "Believe Me If All Those Endearing Young Charms."[32] The first of the three stanzas proclaimed:

> St. Mary's! wherever thy daughters may be,
> They love thy high praises to sing.
> And tell of thy beauties of campus and tree
> Around which sweet memories cling.
> They may wander afar, out of reach of thy name:
> Afar, out of sight of thy grove,
> But the thought of St. Mary's aye kindles a flame
> Of sweet recollections and love.

Herbert Hodgson, owner of an organ building firm in Norfolk, Virginia, began making his regular visits to the school in the 1880s to care for the organ and pianos, continuing until 1914. A man of many talents, Hodgson was a watchmaker, an inventor of specialized engines, and the composer of two operas. For the St. Mary's girls he wrote whimsical verse and songs for their parties.[33] The 1910 yearbook contained a section honoring him, and the 1914 yearbook was dedicated to him.

The seniors of 1905 revived class day (the first one was held in 1899) and sang the alma mater for the first time in public. The commencement of 1906 was the last held in the parlor using the decorated temporary platform. The seniors, as usual, received "scores of beautiful bouquets." After the ceremonies in the parlor, there was the traditional processional to the chapel for the remainder of the ceremonies. The students wore white, and the student marshals were attired in the regalia of their positions—the white sash for the chief marshal and the blue sashes for her assistants.[34] The literary clubs elected the marshals in the spring. To be elected marshal was the highest honor that could be given to a junior, and the literary clubs took turns choosing the chief marshal.

By the DuBose era sororities, which certainly strengthened the bonds of friendship among the few but which the trustees were beginning to consider detrimental to morale on the whole, had become a thorny issue for the administration. By 1906 the german clubs had been abolished, and there were "dark hints" that the sororities would follow suit.[35]

The frequent letters written to Alpha Kappa Psi by Elleneen Checkley, despite her hectic days as principal of a mission school in Cuba, revealed a deep concern for the sorority even after "her girls" had graduated. She wrote of the importance of impressing upon new chapters the very highest ideals of fraternity life:[36]

I am sure that you must know something of the current criticism of Fraternities, . . . objections often only too well founded. But I have always trusted that our fraternity would eventually evolve an exceptional type of the Fraternity bond, . . . especially in Church or distinctly religious schools.[37]

That the sororities' influence was "to a high standard of deportment and scholarship" was acknowledged in the 1904–1905 college catalog. Nonetheless, there were the problems of exclusiveness and of the elaborate sorority functions. The *Muse* of the era recorded luncheon tables that were "a dream of beauty" laden with "all the delicacies of the season" and catered banquets with hired orchestras. While visiting churches in the interests of the school, DuBose began to hear complaints about the excessive personal expenses of St. Mary's students. His reply was, "If the parents . . . will only help, St. Mary's will try earnestly to 'call a halt' in these matters. . . . it is a fault of the age in which we live." He added, "The Rector earnestly begs the help of all parents and the sympathy of all friends, for the girls will be against him."[38]

Rivalry among the sisterhoods became acute despite the inter-sorority rules. One sorority member described the fall of 1907:

When St. Mary's opened . . . , there were only three Alpha Kappa Psis who returned to battle against two Kappa Deltas, five Phi Mus, and twelve Gamma Beta Sigmas. The last of October we were joined by one of last year's girls, Nell Wilson, from Princeton, N. J. It was so hard for us to be in a dozen places at the same time and to be nice to everybody.
The principal form rushing takes up here are trips down town, ball games, strolls around the grove and dancing. We four danced, walked, shopped and went to ball games religiously. Our last year's girls stood by us nobly. At times we would get blue and write the most doubtful letters. . . .
We knew Alpha Kappa Psi would come out on top . . . and it did.[39]

The sorority sister from New Jersey was Eleanor Randolph Wilson, daughter of Woodrow Wilson, president of Princeton University. She went to St. Mary's because her mother, Ellen Axson Wilson, and Rosalie DuBose were longtime friends. Nell, who entered a month late in the fall of 1906, considered the rules "abominable" and was unhappy, despite the efforts of "Aunt Rose" DuBose, the DuBose girls, and relatives in Chapel Hill.[40] Soon, however, her letters to her sister Jessie were filled with descriptions of "perfectly glorious" times. For the Muse Club's play, Nell in a military jacket borrowed from an A&M student "looked just like a boy" (except for her black skirt), but she giggled when the college boys on the back rows laughed uproariously. When selected to speak for the affirmative in the 1908 literary society debate on the question, Resolved: That Robert E. Lee did more for the Confederacy than Jefferson Davis, Nell was "petrified to a peanut" until her father sent a long letter of advice. Nonetheless, the affirmative lost. After the debate, Kate McKimmon accepted Nell as almost a southerner.[41] Because her father insisted that she take Greek and because of her high grades in English, Nell was voted the most intellectual in her class.

Social life off campus for most of the students still consisted of little more excitement than the Monday trip to town unless they had connections in Raleigh or Chapel Hill. Sometimes a day student would have a card party—"cards in the school" were forbidden.[42] For a trip off campus, pompadours were piled higher than usual and topped with enormous hats anchored by long hat pins with ornamental silver heads. Gloves were required, and the daring peek-a-boo waists with open work embroidery were frowned upon. The girls had to endure Juliet Sutton's tart comments on extravagance in order to obtain money from their accounts.[43] Ice cream was a nickel a cup and oysters six for a quarter. The students bought sheet music frequently; "Why Did I Pick a Lemon in the Garden of Love?" and songs from *The Merry Widow* were popular choices.[44]

Saturday night for one hour under the watchful eye of a chaperone continued to be the arrangement for gentlemen callers. Even so, Nell Wilson reported that one girl had "a real suitor." Hand-holding was considered almost tantamount to engagement. Because of the rule that each male caller had to present written permission from the young lady's parents before seeing her, many were left standing in the hall disappointed. Their friend and champion was Anne Saunders, who loved the A&M boys as well as the St. Mary's girls. Having returned to the campus in the 1890s to supervise the infirmary, she was made the rector's assistant in 1901. Her favorite job was the Saturday night hostess duty. She died during commencement week of 1906.

## "MANY CARES AND WORRIES"

McNeely DuBose took his multiple responsibilities so seriously that by the winter of 1904 he was obliged to leave Raleigh for a month's rest. When he returned looking much stronger, the girls (he always called each one "daughter") gave him a rousing cheer as he entered the parlor for evening roll call.[45] DuBose had made an effort to utilize his staff and faculty efficiently by assigning announced routine duties to assistants, but it had been the habit of generations at St. Mary's to take almost every matter directly to the rector. The school really needed a dean of students and an academic dean, although Ernest Cruikshank was performing informally many of the duties of both.

Besides keeping the students reasonably happy while raising academic standards, DuBose faced the eternal problem of keeping up the property and balancing the budget. Enrollment remained about 20 students below the "crowded school" of the preceding years. It was encouraging that 34 South Carolinians were enrolled in 1905, twice as many as the year before. By careful management, expenditures were kept just within the school's receipts, despite a drastic rise in food prices. For example, flour sold for $4.25 a barrel in March, 1903, and for $6.65 a barrel in March, 1904.[46] By 1905 the trustees reluctantly had raised the general charges at St. Mary's to $225 plus $25 for laundry, library, and laboratory fees. The extra charges for art were $30 to $50 a year and for music $50 to $60. In addition to the routine responsibilities of the rectorship, DuBose during the four years of his tenure helped to mount a fund drive and supervised three building projects—the enlargement of the chapel and the erection of the auditorium and the steam laundry.

Bishop Cheshire always regarded the welfare of St. Mary's as one of his major responsibilities. In February, 1904, the bishop's family moved into Ravenscroft, the handsome residence built on the corner of Hillsborough and St. Mary's streets on an acre of campus land conveyed in 1900 to the trustees of the convention by the St. Mary's trustees. The school was paid $1,000. Almost immediately the bishop had a large paneled room added for the diocesan library, known as the Lyman Memorial Library.[47]

Cheshire, reviewing in 1903 the first decade of his episcopate, named the acquisition of St. Mary's as a church school the greatest achievement.[48] He urged the convention of 1904 to do everything possible to liquidate the remaining $15,000 of the school's mortgage. Enrollment should be doubled, he said, because "we have deliberately chosen to become a general institution for a large section of our Southern country, instead of a mere diocesan school. Having chosen this sphere, it is our duty to fulfill it worthily."[49] To that same convention DuBose made a very positive statement:

St. Mary's, as the church school for the Carolinas, is no weakling begging help to keep her alive; but that she may grow stronger and more useful, she needs the loving consideration and cooperation of every Bishop, Priest and Church-

The Clement Strudwick portrait of the Right Reverend Joseph Blount
Cheshire, which hangs in Smedes Parlor

man. . . . Give her, therefore, your prayers; send her your daughters; so shall you and she do the Church's work.[50]

After 1901 the trustees, believing it within their power to be responsible for the operation of the school, no longer made detailed financial reports to the conventions. As early as 1905 Cheshire, as chairman of the board, suggested that there should be two regular meetings of the entire board each year, but such a step was not taken until many years later. The burden of decision still fell heavily upon the members of the executive committee. That committee, immediately after the 1904 convention of the Diocese of North Carolina, took action toward raising the $15,000 by engaging William E. Stone to canvass the two Carolinas during that summer. Stone subsequently spent many summers during his long tenure either recruiting students or raising funds. Through the efforts of many, the school's debt had been reduced within a year to $10,000 and an additional $2,000 had been spent on long-deferred improvements. In addition to that good news, Bishop Cheshire was able to announce at the 1905 commencement the Eleanor Clement legacy of an immediate scholarship fund of $5,000 with the residue of the estate expected at a later date.[51]

An unsolicited gift of $13,000 had come to the school in the fall of 1905. Under its provisions a perpetual scholarship was to be established[52] and an auditorium built. The will of St. Mary's alumna Mary Eliza Battle Pittman of Tarboro provided for a memorial to her daughter, Eliza Battle Pittman, who also attended St. Mary's. She died in 1889 at 21. Because of the Battle family's long connection with St. Mary's, the memorial was established there. The Eliza Battle Pittman Auditorium, a two-story brick neoclassical revival building, was dedicated on May 29, 1907. Described as graceful and acoustically superior, it seated, including the elliptical gallery, over 600 persons. A handsome skylight added illumination. The architect probably was Charles E. Hartge of Raleigh, who was designing other buildings on the campus at the time.[53]

At a special meeting of the trustees of the college in December, 1905, Bishop Cheshire outlined his dreams for St. Mary's. He was determined to see the institution debt-free by the 1906 commencement. After that, he wanted an endowment of $100,000 in celebration of the 10th anniversary of the acquisition of St. Mary's by the church. He told the trustees,

We must be able to maintain our departments without reference to whether they pay for themselves or not, and we must be able to retain our teachers when they have by their achievements shown that they are entitled to increased salaries.[54]

When on March 27, 1906, the final payment on the mortgage was made, St. Mary's "became the unencumbered property of the church." As the bishop delivered that good news to the convention, he said that no one at the time of incorporation would have believed it possible to obtain $90,000 within nine years. Only the initial cash payment of $10,135.53 to the Cameron family was from the diocesan treasury, but as the bishop noted, "A large proportion of personal subscriptions and donations" was from "the laity within the Diocese of North Carolina . . . not from the few, but from the many . . . , mostly of small means, in all parts of the Carolinas."[55]

Having delivered those positive reports, Cheshire presented his dreams for St. Mary's—the $100,0000 endowment, a new dining hall, and a new dormitory. The convention decided nothing more definite than that it was "most thankful" for St. Mary's, that steps should be taken to raise funds, and that "it should be a pleasure to rally to the support" of the school.[56] The board soon voted to secure estimates on a dining hall and "passed over" the matter of the endowment that was to have given the school "scope and stability."[57]

McNeely DuBose, understanding the enduring strength that an active alumnae association can bring to an educational institution, encouraged the St. Mary's guilds and the alumnae chapters as he made his rounds among the churches. The guilds, revitalized under his rectorship, included women friends of the school as well as alumnae; their purpose was "to urge the claims of St. Mary's upon the church people." Mary Iredell, who continued as president of the alumnae association and also as agent of the trustees, was responsible for gifts. She had grown accustomed to traveling alone and to addressing male audiences.[58] The alumnae through the monthly *Muse* felt themselves more than ever a part of the extended St. Mary's family. Edited by the senior class under Ernest Cruikshank's supervision, the *Muse*, although still the vehicle for the students' creative writing, contained alumnae news and details of daily life at the school. In 1906 the *Muse* presented two issues (in April and December) filled with fascinating reminiscences of a number of the oldest alumnae. There began to be talk of the importance of preserving records against the day when "a full history of the development of the school" would surely be written,[59] but record keeping remained sketchy.

In the spring of 1904 the alumnae association at last completed its first project and turned over to the trustees $4,000 to support their scholarship, renamed the Smedes Memorial Scholarship Fund to honor Aldert, Sarah, and Bennett Smedes. Fourteen candidates stood the competitive examinations.[60] Immediately the association turned with enthusiasm to its long-planned second project, the enlargement of the chapel. By their June meeting Mary Iredell reported $1,750 "in reach," $300 of it contributed by the student organizations. As the estimated cost of the project was $2,000, it was decided to go ahead over that summer. The students marched downtown for services for a few weeks in the fall, but the Founders' Day service was held in the enlarged chapel.

The original chapel was left almost intact as the nave of the enlarged building, thus preserving the integrity of Richard Upjohn's design. Two transepts were added, arched and open to make the chancel visible from all parts of the church. An organ chamber and robing rooms were added. Care was taken to preserve the furnishings and memorials that "had been hallowed by long years of worship and consecrated by the love of those who had placed them there." The Jurisdiction of Asheville gave the chancel, and the alumnae through a number of gifts, augmented by one from Bessie Smedes Leake, gave the new altar and reredos dedicated to the memory of Aldert and Bennett Smedes. The handsome pulpit was given by Annie Ruffin Cameron in memory of her grandson, Paul Carrington Cameron.[61] Several memorial windows were added during that period. (See appendix A.)

By the spring of 1907 the alumnae association had paid all it owed for the chapel improvements that had cost about twice the original estimate. The St. Mary's Chapel, being "the full unencumbered property of the Church," could for the first time be consecrated. Technically, it had been a private chapel when the Camerons owned the campus, and since the incorporation there had been a school debt. The impressive consecration service was held on May 29, during commencement week. The trustees had four marble posts placed to mark the corners of the churchyard. It seemed wonderfully appropriate that 1907 was the 50th anniversary year of the original chapel building. A Raleigh paper was quoted in the *Muse*:

The consecration services were impressive and beautiful, and were followed by a deeply spiritual sermon preached by Bishop T. D. Bratton, of Mississippi. . . . The clergy opened the procession, followed by the lay trustees acting as a vestry . . . followed by the bishops. . . .

Rev. McNeely DuBose . . . read the petition for consecration on the part of the trustees, after which Rev. J. E. Ingle, Secretary of the Diocese of North Carolina, read the sentence of consecration for Bishop Cheshire, the latter then reading the formal prayer of consecration. . . .[62]

It was fitting that the consecration of the chapel at St. Mary's should have come under the rectorship of McNeely DuBose, for he believed that "the education of 'a divine and eternal life,' for which we shall, in large measure, be responsible to God, is too serious to treat lightly or to leave undone, however small the detail may be."[63] The students recognized the spirituality of the man, for they wrote of him, "With loving fervor he has worked for the spiritual welfare of those entrusted to his care."[64]

Commencement of 1907 was DuBose's last commencement as rector of St. Mary's. He had announced his resignation in January because he longed to return to the pastorate. There was no friction between him and the board; to that Bishop Cheshire attested.[65]

It was appropriate that the St. Mary's Alumnae Association celebrated its 25th anniversary during the rectorship of McNeely DuBose, who devoted much time and energy to encouraging and visiting the local chapters. The history of the association, organized on June 19, 1879, was reviewed. Mary Kinsey Boylan of Raleigh, one of "the original thirteen," by virtue of her seniority among those present was elected the first president. Kate McKimmon, elected secretary and treasurer in 1879, held that office for many years. On May 14 of the next year, "in pursuance of a call through the morning papers," about 50 alumnae assembled at Christ Church to hear an address by Bishop Lyman and to make plans for the first annual meeting of the association to be held on Thursday of commencement week. They planned the alumnae scholarships, which they hoped to support by the annual membership dues of $1.[66] Actually, Bennett Smedes underwrote the scholarships partially for many years. Penelope Bradford Cox, the second president of the alumnae association, died in office in December 1880, and was succeeded by Kate DeRosset Meares. (See appendix C for alumnae association presidents.) There were about twenty local chapters during the early years of the association.

McNeely DuBose left St. Mary's, at the close of its tenth year as a church school, free of debt and with a hopeful future. The board considered his resignation "a matter of deep distress to all."[67] The *Muse's* tribute, probably written by Ernest Cruikshank, read in part,

None of those who have labored for St. Mary's . . . has worked more faithfully for the school than has Mr. DuBose. From the moment of his administration he gave every energy to the advancement of St. Mary's. . . . He leaves behind him evidences of his tireless zeal here that will live long.[68]

The fourth rector of St. Mary's continued to work for the school as a member of the board of trustees, a delicate feat that few could have managed so well. His successor said that he found in DuBose his best friend and helper in all he wished to do for the school.[69]

After leaving St. Mary's, McNeely DuBose tackled another strenuous assignment when he became rector of Grace Church, Morganton, and priest in charge of the associate missions. With the help of an assistant priest and seven teachers he ran seven day schools with 200 children enrolled.[70] He had returned from an effective rest and had just accepted a new post at Saluda when on April 15, 1911, he met a tragic and untimely death. The *Carolina Churchman* reported that "he was drowned in the Catawba river, early on Saturday morning . . . while duck hunting, with his two young sons. He shot a duck on the opposite side of the river and plunging into the stream to secure his game, was carried down. . . ."[71]

CHAPTER EIGHT

# FRUITFUL YEARS

The trustees considered themselves most fortunate in securing as the fifth rector of St. Mary's the Reverend George William Lay, who had been for many years a master at St. Paul's, an Episcopal school for boys in Concord, New Hampshire. Bishops Cheshire and Strange had been most favorably impressed when they visited the Lays at St. Paul's in June, 1907, and Bishop Cheshire said that the fact that Lay was the son of Bishop Henry Champlin Lay and the grandnephew of Bishop Atkinson would "give him a strong hold upon the affections of our people."[1] Lay had hesitated to leave St. Paul's, but after consideration decided to go to St. Mary's regardless of the lower salary because of the challenge there. He wrote:

I shall have a great opening to do something worthwhile for the South among my own people. . . . the next ten years in Raleigh ought to be much more fruitful than the same years spent here . . . the South is the coming country . . . the tide is just beginning to rise. What is done now will tell far more than what is done later. . . . I shall deem it a high privilege to help . . . St. Mary's . . . to rise to greater prosperity and efficiency.

He knew that challenges involve risks, for his letter of acceptance continued, "There will be hardships . . . in doing what . . . must eventually be done, without offending good and worthy people . . . and in trying to perform with meager resources. . . ."[2]

The new rector was prescient. There were hardships; good and worthy people were offended and said so; resources remained comparatively meager; but the 11 years of his tenure were among the most fruitful of St. Mary's long history.

George W. Lay was born in 1860 in Huntsville, Alabama, the son of a

The Reverend George William Lay, D.D., rector, 1907–1918

Virginian who was successively missionary bishop of the Southwest, bishop of Arkansas, and bishop of the Diocese of Easton in Maryland. His mother was Elizabeth Withers Atkinson of Virginia.[3] George Lay was educated at St. Paul's before entering the junior class at Yale in 1880. He took his theological degree at the General Theological Seminary and was ordained deacon in 1885 and priest in 1886. He had served as assistant at St. Paul's Church, Erie, Pennsylvania, before going to St. Paul's School in 1887 as assistant minister. The next year he became a master, teaching Latin and Greek. He was active in the diocesan affairs of New Hampshire, serving for years as secretary of the mission board. In 1894 he married Anna Booth Balch, the daughter of Rear Admiral George Beall Balch, who had been commandant of the Naval Academy, and Mary Ellen Booth.[4]

The Lays arrived in Raleigh in late August. Because the furniture did not arrive on time, the seven Lay children temporarily occupied the infirmary; that turned out to be appropriate since all fell ill from excitement, fatigue, or maybe malaria. Their parents were appalled to discover that there were no window screens at St. Mary's. Lay, an expert ahead of his time on sanitary conditions, soon found money for screens. The children—George, Elizabeth, Ellen, Anna (called Nancey), Lucy, Henry, and Virginia, ranged in ages from 12 years to three months. The older children loved to march along the Civil War breastworks, still discernible on the edge of campus, singing a favorite song, "Marching Through Georgia," but they soon sensed that it was not a favorite in Carolina. St. Mary's, although that year included within the city's limits, was still like a farm, with cows, and pigs, and a horse called Rock to pull the buggy. Lay soon sold the cows and pigs, and Anna Lay planned new flower beds and someday a greenhouse.[5]

Lay wrote a long letter to his mother about the mosquitoes and the humid heat, noted that gentlemen smoked only at home, never in public, and rarely at business, and commented of the people, both black and white, "Such courtesy I have never seen." He wrote of the teachers:

They are a fine set. Some of them deserve to be canonized for the work they have done here in years past with so little comfort. They are willing to work for a quarter to one-third less here than they could get elsewhere. . . . Miss McKimmon has been here for 35 years and her home is a room in a dormitory of board partitions. . . . Her dormitory is the most popular one in the School. That tells what she is![6]

The 65th session of St. Mary's opened with more fanfare than Lay liked. Because the Convocation of Raleigh was in session, Bishop Cheshire arranged "somewhat of a function" with 15 clergy in the procession for the opening chapel service, a more elaborate than usual address from the bishop, and a welcome to Lay from the clergy of the

The Lay family, c.1917

diocese.[7] Enrollment was high, with the dormitories filled and several girls living at the home of the William E. Stones. The new rector immediately grasped the predominant fact of life for the administrator of St. Mary's, for he wrote to his mother, "It is hard to make ends meet here."[8]

## BREAKING NEW GROUND

Theories concerning education in general and the education of women in particular were in ferment again in 1907, as were theories concerning most of the fundamental social issues. By 1900, 80 percent of the colleges, universities, and professional schools would admit women.[9] The *Muse* of 1907 carried an advertisement that stated: "The University of North Carolina admits women to the higher classes. . . . Graduates of St. Mary's who wish to carry their studies further would do well to write for catalogue and information." Between 1890 and 1910 in the United States the number of women in coeducational colleges increased by 438 percent, and the number of women in colleges for women increased by 348 percent.[10] By 1910 there were 8,437 women with degrees.[11] The feeling that women should be free not only to study where they pleased but also to study and practice any profession they chose had definitely emerged by the 1890s, but doors did not open automatically to women. The 1910 census showed 142,117 men and 9,015 women practicing medicine. The federal commissioner of education reported 406 Ph.D. degrees granted during 1909–1910, 44 of them to women, and 1,637 master's degrees, 465 of them to women. Only 39 of the master's degrees granted to women were in science. Of the 8,009 studying theology in 1901 at 154 schools, 181 were women.[12]

Little of this struggle for equality in graduate professional training touched southern women, who were likely to be educated at their regional institutions for women. As late as 1915 only six of the 140 of those calling themselves "colleges for women" were recognized as standard colleges by the Southern Association of College Women.[13]

Career opportunities for college women everywhere in the years before the first world war still lay mostly in the various aspects of education, social work, church work, or journalism, and only the most venturesome southern women considered anything else. Emilie Watts McVea, who had been one of the organizers in 1903 of the Southern Association of College Women, returned to St. Mary's to speak in 1904. After making a strong plea for true professionalism in teaching, she urged St. Mary's women to consider "breaking new ground" professionally. She said, "even in these days of broadening opportunity the chance of an occupation is limited for a woman by timidity, by tradition, and by lack of preparation. This is especially true in the South." She advised her young listeners to think about careers in real estate, horticulture, architecture, photography, and insurance, to be "bold" and to seek work that they would love for its interest and challenge.[14]

When McVea returned to Raleigh in 1910 to speak at the centennial commemoration of the birth of Aldert Smedes, she declared that new conditions demanded new training for women. She made it plain that she meant "nothing faddish," just greater effort to acquire knowledge, stricter self-discipline, more devotion to the home, deeper religious devotion. She knew that most St. Mary's women thought of working as something to do to escape boredom or to support themselves until marriage. She added a plea that women should recognize the root causes of the social and economic ills of the day and should then use their time and talents to attack them through all means, direct and indirect, available to women.[15] By then she was crusading effectively for a dozen reform movements as a leading citizen of Cincinnati.

Inevitably there were critics of the new educational opportunities for women. They considered intellectual women at best "unfeminine" and at worst a downright danger to the preservation of the race. St. Mary's students were aware of the continuing discussion of what constituted a proper education for young women. As early as 1900 an editorial in the monthly *Muse*, apparently written by a student, had declared, "The higher education of women will soon be . . . a necessity for life. . . . A college education . . . brings the power for doing faithfully and well the work that lies nearest. . . . Learn the secret of life . . . the knowledge that brings power." [16]

George Lay did not go to St. Mary's fresh from the North eager to shake the place from its very foundations. He appreciated the foundations, perhaps because he had once spent a summer in the same house with Bennett Smedes. [17] He soon had, however, a "well-defined purpose": to make the school "one of the very best in the south." [18] At the Aldert Smedes centennial luncheon he said, "It should be the endeavor of all of us to reverence the past and to preserve all things in it that were true and noble, while having our eyes set towards the future. . . . We must try to do things . . . as we believe he [Aldert Smedes] would have done them, if he were living now." [19]

"Striving to become one of the very best" would consume large amounts of money. Lay, a man of vision, soon found himself racing just to stay even with the changing times. Basically, St. Mary's was an institution that worked and, therefore, an institution difficult to move except in times of crisis. Staying even seemed to most of the school's patrons and trustees all that could be expected. That did not seem enough to George Lay; it would not have seemed enough to Aldert Smedes.

The new rector took a strictly no-nonsense approach to academic life. He advised students, "Do not postpone your best endeavors." [20] It was evident from the first day of school in the fall of 1907 that there was to be what Eleanor Thomas later referred to as "a general stiffening of academic standards and discipline," a task that Lay accomplished "with courage and with unswerving honesty of purpose and integrity." [21] Some of the students and their parents grumbled, but the serious students—and there were beginning to be more of them at St. Mary's—welcomed the "stiffening." Lay went over each report card before signing it; a separate mark for "industry" was recorded.

Reporting the events of his first week of school to his mother, the rector had described it as "chaos" with half of the students, new to the school, requiring classification by examinations in several subjects. That was the traditional system at St. Mary's. Lay reported that one mother had announced that her daughter was to be a junior, but that of course her child could not take "those examinations," while another wrote that her daughter was not to be required to take mathematics and "other foolish things."[22] It was soon evident, however, that St. Mary's was in the hands of an experienced educator. Class attendance was made absolutely compulsory. All entering students were required by the English department to take a written grammar test and to write a composition; some, to their dismay, found themselves "conditioned" in English. By 1912 requirements for entrance to the freshman class (the third year of high school) had been raised: two years of composition, English and American literature (Longfellow, Irving, Hawthorne, Scott, and George Eliot), algebra through quadratic equations, the "essential facts of Greek, Roman, British, and American history," Latin through the first three books of Caesar, one year of either French or German, physical geography, and physiology.[23] During 1908–1909 Lay taught 12 hours of recitations weekly—about 100 girls—in order to get the feel of the place. He seemed to possess unbounded energy, and he was not a worrier.

Standards at St. Mary's were higher than at many of the institutions in the South calling themselves colleges, but that fact was not widely recognized even by the school's clientele. Lay certainly would not suddenly call St. Mary's a college and begin granting degrees because the work done there was not equal to that required for the baccalaureate in the good colleges for women in the North. He, therefore, agreed for the time being to continue calling St. Mary's simply a "school." He decided against naming the institution a junior college because that term was still in the process of definition.[24] However, he commented that he had found the requirements for diplomas and certificates at St. Mary's "most rigid" and that they had been granted to only a "select few" since 1879.[25]

The "college question" was at that time a matter of controversy among educators throughout the nation; to make the patrons of St. Mary's aware of that fact, Lay published excerpts from an address by Henry S. Pritchett, president of the Carnegie Foundation. Pritchett estimated that over half of the 1,000 institutions in the United States calling themselves colleges were colleges in name only, many of them actually doing secondary school work.[26] Soon the St. Mary's catalog began to set forth the institution's status more clearly:

The course . . . is of a type that has been given by many of the higher institutions for the education of women in the South, and is one suited to the needs of the large majority of students. It is therefore designed to be complete in itself.

At the same time those who desire to enter some higher institution . . . can be prepared to do so . . . ; their courses must be elected with a view to the requirements of the college to which they wish to go.[27]

The catalog explained that a graduate of St. Mary's should have no difficulty in entering the junior class of any good college and that a student who had completed the sophomore year should be able to enter the freshman class of her chosen college.

His quest for a precise understanding of educational standards in the South—standards that he had soon discovered to be incredibly imprecise—led Lay to attend as many professional meetings as possible. He soon became a well-known, respected, and sometimes controversial figure among his fellow educators. In an address to the 1913 meeting of the Association of Colleges and Secondary Schools of the Southern States in Knoxville, George Lay urged the continuation of the strict approach to accreditation and told the association that its "lack of popularity" was temporary because its work was not yet appreciated. Lay's paper, it was reported, "engendered considerable discussion."[28]

During the Lay administration the college curriculum at St. Mary's was reorganized to cover exactly the freshman and sophomore years as taught in most senior colleges. St. Mary's required 60 points (units) for graduation from the two-year college course. The usual course met four hours a week and was worth two units per semester. Electives were allowed within the specific limits of 12 points in English, 15 in foreign languages, 6 in history, 6 in philosophy, 5 in mathematics, and 4 in science. The remaining 12 points were free electives. Only 12 points of technical work in the fine arts could be counted for graduation. However, a student could elect to take a certificate in one or more of the arts instead of being graduated; even so, 35 points of academic work were obligatory. Lay had planned well, for no fundamental change in the system was necessary until the general confusion within academe during the 1960s resulted in few specific course requirements.

Under the Lay administration the curriculum at St. Mary's was enriched, but some courses were offered only in alternate years. The rector found himself seldom teaching his favorite subject, Greek. Spanish, Italian, and German were taught whenever demand warranted. Social service, "an elementary treatment with discussion of practical problems," was added as a philosophy course. The rector taught a two-hour course in pedagogy in addition to his classes in Bible and ethics. The catalog warned that no course in pedagogy could make a good teacher of one who had previously "lacked thorough scholarship" and expressed the hope that when St. Mary's women became teachers they would emulate their own best teachers.[29] Those studying pedagogy did some practice teaching in Kate McKimmon's department, and sometimes a bright senior would serve as a student assistant to one of the teachers.[30]

A full domestic science course counting toward graduation or a certificate in domestic science was added in 1911 when room for a kitchen and serving room became available in the main building with the opening of the new dining hall. A certificate could be earned in home economics by taking all of the courses in cooking and serving plus chemistry and the other required academic units. The business department suddenly burgeoned as a result of the war; during 1917–1918 Lizzie Lee and Juliet Sutton heroically managed to teach 37 students instead of the usual 25.

Physical training, always emphasized more at St. Mary's than at most schools for young ladies, was first placed under a full-time director in 1914–1915. Despite the fact that the new gymnasium had been in use for several years, the trustees had not provided funds to separate physical culture and elocution. One teacher had continued to handle both with other faculty members coaching the team sports during recreation hours. The first director of physical training was Mabel H. Barton, a graduate of Sargent Normal School of Physical Education. Daily exercise was still required of every student as a point of honor, but physical training classes took care of that requirement three days a week. Lessons in aesthetic dancing (at $10 for 20 lessons) could count as one physical education course. The St. Mary's catalog reminded students that the best of educations could become comparatively useless to one felled by poor health.[31]

Further enrichment of the college curriculum seemed unnecessary to meet the needs of the time and the place. Women everywhere still chose few science and mathematics courses beyond the minimal requirements. There was little consideration by St. Mary's women of careers except in teaching, in the fine arts, or in business offices. Lay demonstrated how he felt about permanent careers for women when he immediately discharged a music teacher who married.[32]

An editorial in the *Muse* expressed the prevailing opinion in 1911, an opinion that was not to change perceptibly until the World War I years. Entitled "The Call of the South for the College-Bred Woman" (and probably written by the rector as part of an address), the article deplored the backwardness of the South in educating its women and blamed the situation partly on the fear that higher education would "shatter the ideal of the woman of the South as she . . . has been so fondly cherished." The article made a case for college education as broadening a woman's horizons so that she could "best conduct the home, and indirectly lift the nation itself in exact proportion to her own greater development."[33] That was the educational philosophy of Aldert Smedes updated to 1911.

Lay found that the standards of the preparatory department at St. Mary's needed no revision. Girls who completed the sophomore year had earned two credits beyond those required for graduation from the public high schools; the extra credits normally were accepted as two college units if a student transferred from the sophomore class at St.

Mary's into the freshman year of a four-year college.[34] Local girls continued to attend St. Mary's for high school despite the fact that Raleigh had a public high school. Lay took great interest in North Carolina's secondary schools and advocated a high school diploma based upon a uniform examination serving as a statewide competency test.[35]

His contributions to the advancement of education and to the South in the several other fields in which he worked and published articles—public health, general science, social services, conservation, good roads, folklore—were recognized when in 1915 the University of the South conferred upon George William Lay the honorary degree of doctor of civil laws.

## THE STRONG TRIUMVIRATE

Lay was forceful and farsighted enough to have moved St. Mary's ahead under any circumstances. He was, however, fortunate to have with him during all of his years there Ernest Cruikshank, and during most of them Eleanor Thomas. Each secure enough to work with two other strong personalities, together they shaped those fruitful years.[36] They could count on the old guard—McKimmon, Dowd, Lee, Sutton, and Fenner—along with Stone and Florence Davis, who were to be the ones of the new guard to spend their lives at St. Mary's. Lay deplored the fact that the annual turnover rate of the faculty was about 25 percent,[37] but for the girls the St. Mary's traditions seemed forever safe, for the very walls of the place were permeated with them.

George Lay was a consistent man—consistently reasonable and realistic, consistently forthright and firm, and absolutely consistent in applying the stated rules of the school. He was also consistently businesslike and blunt. He gave the impression of being a larger man than he was because of his vitality. He talked in a booming preacher-teacher voice, and his presence seemed to fill a room. But he sometimes broke into original humorous verse, and he loved to sing. He was also, although few outside his immediate family realized it, an introspective man quite sensitive to criticism.[38]

Ernest Cruikshank, although as frail in appearance as Lay was robust, could keep up with him when it came to working hard and long. He had a remarkable ability to handle details efficiently. Lay gave Cruikshank the title of business manager and relieved him of some of his teaching duties. He continued to work with the seniors on the *Muse*, and he remained a popular counselor and confidant.

Lay, before taking the job of running St. Mary's, had asked the trustees to restore the position of lady principal. Lenora Walmsley Sheib served in that capacity and taught psychology during 1907–1908.[39]

The next lady principal was Eleanor Thomas, who had returned to

St. Mary's in 1905. She was the third member of the strong triumvirate that left a permanent imprint upon the school. She headed the English department and taught some courses as well as serving as lady principal, 1908–1917 (except for a leave of absence, 1912–1913). In the classroom and as lady principal at St. Mary's Eleanor Thomas was both stern and just, and her rare compliment upon exceptional work was "like an accolade." She was remembered for her "scholarship, integrity, and the magic gift of a glowing personality that illumined her every word and act." [40] A glimpse of her personality is revealed in the portrait of her in later life that hangs at St. Mary's, the gift of her grateful students. After leaving St. Mary's, she taught for 30 years at the Flora Stone Mather College for Women of Western Reserve University in Cleveland, Ohio. She earned her doctorate at Columbia University, and in 1931 that university's press published her book on Christina Georgina Rossetti. [41]

As life became less static everywhere during the first quarter of the twentieth century, more young and interesting teachers joined the faculty briefly, thus enriching the intellectual mix. In 1908, "fresh from Smith," Georgina Kellogg arrived to teach French; on warm Sundays, maverick that she was, she sat serenely in the grove (in full view of those attending divine services in the chapel) and sewed. Yanita Cribbs, with "her famous row of blonde curls surmounting her stylish pompadour," taught elocution and physical culture from 1905 until she married an A&M professor in 1909. [42] Helen Urquhart, who went in 1910 to teach Latin, was a graduate of Mount Holyoke. She taught at Winthrop College, 1913–1914, but returned to St. Mary's until she went into Red Cross service during the war.

At the end of Lay's first year at St. Mary's, a 22-year veteran, Martha Dowd, was appointed the first woman director of the music department. She insisted upon the academic integrity of the music certificate because the school stood, she said, "for thoroughness and breadth" and "would not permit the sacrifice of a well-rounded education." Furthermore, she warned students that the marks in music courses would indicate "the quality of work, not the quantity." [43] She developed a course equivalent to that of the normal schools, and teaching certificates could be earned at St. Mary's in piano, organ, violin, and voice. In 1916 there were seven teachers on the music faculty, and 150 of the school's 250 students were taking music lessons.

Handsome and effervescent R. Blinn Owen arrived on the St. Mary's scene in the fall of 1909 as instructor of voice and director of the orchestra and chorus. He had moved to Raleigh the year before as organist and choirmaster at Christ Church. His new glee club gained membership rapidly when it became known that he also was directing the glee club at A&M. Lay considered him a "useful and desirable" member of the faculty who had done "excellent work for very low pay," and he was happy when he could afford to engage him full time in the fall of 1914.[44] He was a native of Michigan with a master's degree from the Detroit School of Music, study in New York, and teaching experience, including his school of music in Greensboro. He founded and directed the St. Cecilia Choral Society of Raleigh, a women's chorale; and he and Martha Dowd encouraged the Peace–St. Mary's concert series that featured musicians of note each season. The St. Mary's orchestra of about 25 (14 of whom were men in 1910) with the St. Mary's choral groups presented a series of the Gilbert and Sullivan operas. Owen became director of music in 1917–1918 when Dowd decided to devote most of her time to her normal course for music teachers. In 1919 he moved to a church job in Savannah.[45] In 1920 Martha Dowd joined the faculty of Fassifern School.[46]

Under the Lay administration St. Mary's was more academically oriented than it had been since the days of Elizabeth Czarnomska in the 1880s. Among the top students there was tough competition for the prestigious Niles medal. The academic year was divided into two semesters of two quarters each, and under the grading system the final examination counted one third of the semester grade in a course. The catalog announced firmly, "Examinations are regarded by the school as of the utmost importance, not only as a test but as an essential part of education." The honor roll requirement was an average of 90; the passing grade was 75.

The *Muse* reported the successes of alumnae. For example, Mary Mitchell Chamberlain was in the Ph.D. program at the University of Pennsylvania and in 1915 was coauthor of an article in the *Journal of Experimental Zoology*.[47] St. Mary's was using a text, *The Physiology of Man and the Lower Animals*, written by Annie Moore (who had taken her Ph.D. at Cornell) of the class of 1895. Bessie Lewis Whitaker of the class of 1893 was teaching at Winthrop College, and her master's thesis had been published as one of the *James Sprunt Historical Monograph* series.[48] Margaret Busbee Shipp, whose earliest stories had been published in the *Muse* in the 1880s, was selling regularly to national magazines. Lucy Cobb was publishing folklore tales, poetry, and plays; Henrietta Smedes, valedictorian of 1887, musician and librarian, was publishing poetry. Anna M. Dunlop had studied with Whistler in Paris and then gone on to Dresden to learn "decorative art."[49] A New York art critic had mentioned the "delightful little landscape" by Mary B. Hanckel, who taught clay modeling at Teacher's College, Columbia University.[50] Emilie Rose Knox studied in New York and was in demand as a concert violinist.[51] In 1909, 11 of the 76 teachers in the Raleigh school system were St. Mary's alumnae.[52] When May F. Jones was appointed private secretary to Gov. Locke Craig in 1916, the *News and Observer* approved this "recognition of the ability of women to hold positions which have heretofore been held as exclusively appertaining to men."[53]

Historian Anne Firor Scott has suggested that "the attitudes and assumptions" of the college a woman attends have much to do with the shaping of her career expectations.[54] Expectations were slowly changing at St. Mary's, and interest in possible careers and in current affairs was stimulated by speakers at the school as the traditional lecture series was expanded under Lay.

The literary society debates remained the most exciting intellectual event of the school year, fully reported to the alumnae in the *Muse*. They were held in the new auditorium, and more townspeople attended than in past times. The panel of judges sometimes included a state supreme court justice. In the first 12 years of the societies' existence, Sigma Lambda won over Epsilon Alpha Pi eight years. A third society, named Alpha Rho for the southern poet Abram Ryan, was organized in 1913 because of the school's increased enrollment. That necessitated a series of three major debates; by 1917, however, the old societies had reabsorbed Alpha Rho. The question of woman suffrage, defeated in the 1908–1909 debates, won when debated again in 1912–1913. (The rector had been happier with the earlier decision; he thought women should be well educated but not allowed to vote.)[55] The closed shop lost in 1914, "the burden of the affirmative" on that question being too great for any North Carolina girl. The next query in the 1914 series concerned Greek letter fraternities, and the "air was tense with excitement" because the question was a sore one on the St. Mary's campus at the time. Not unexpectedly, fraternities were favored.

In 1916 the debates "were laid aside," and everyone participated in the Shakespearean tercentenary celebration. Eleanor Thomas was determined that almost no one this side of London would outdo St. Mary's in paying homage. Many events were held, including a festival in the grove on May 1. An audience of 500 saw all of St. Mary's in Elizabethan costume as a village festival attended by richly garbed Shakespearean characters was enacted. After the dances, Act V of *A Midsummer Night's Dream* was performed, with the ancient, moth-eaten wolf of Bennett Smedes's science classroom appearing as Moonshine's faithful dog.[56]

## "A TIME FOR DEVELOPMENT AND EXPANSION"

In 1907 when George Lay became St. Mary's rector, Bishop Cheshire said, "This is the beginning of a new stage in the progress of St. Mary's School . . . a stage of development and expansion."[57] The trustees made it clear that they contemplated no immediate changes in the basic

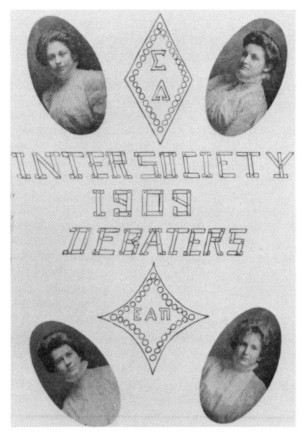

Inter-society debates, 1909: Mary Shuford, Janie
DuBose, Julia McIntyre, Ida Rogerson

character of the school; they recognized, however, the immediate need
for new buildings. At the last board meeting of the DuBose administration the trustees had authorized the executive committee to make any
alterations necessary to provide additional classroom space and to erect
a dining hall at once. The ways and means were left to the committee,
provided they placed no mortgage upon the property. Manna fell from
heaven when the remainder of the Clement estate was forwarded to St.
Mary's with the death in August, 1908, of Frances O'Connor. Eleanor
Clement died in 1904; her will provided an endowed scholarship as a
memorial to her mother. The residue of the estate was bequeathed to
St. Mary's upon the death of Frances O'Connor, who had continued to
live with Eleanor Clement after the death of Madame Clement and the

sale of their school. The Clement bequest, of about $30,000, provided much of the money for a dining hall and gymnasium and the wings to the main building.[58] Some trustees, particularly W. A. Erwin, felt that the Clement legacy, although unrestricted, should be regarded as an endowment.[59] Once the decision to build was made, the new rector set about learning all that he could about institutional kitchen equipment and other details. The building committee consisted of the executive committee,[60] and the architect was Charles E. Hartge.[61] Minor snags occurred: the new auditorium could not be used during the winter of 1907–1908 because the contract for the heating was not let until late autumn. Overloads caused by the new electric lights, installed in the buildings and in the grove during the DuBose administration, kept blowing fuses. Lay had wanted four comfortable suites for the supervising teachers, each to contain a small sitting room, a bedroom, and a bath. He lost when one trustee proclaimed, "Gentlemen, this bathing business is the ruination of the country!"[62]

The cornerstone of the wings to the main building was laid on April 3, 1909. Bishop Cheshire said the occasion marked "the conclusion of the first period of development of St. Mary's under Church ownership and the inauguration of the second period."[63] The wings, first occupied in the fall of 1909, accommodated 56 students, thus bringing the spaces for boarders to 175.[64] The lower floors contained eight new classrooms, four in each wing. To the girls, the closets in the rooms were the noteworthy feature. To the public, the remodeling of the front of the main building was "the most imposing part of the new work."[65]

In 1910 the remodeled main building was named Smedes Hall in honor of Aldert Smedes. Two years earlier Col. Bennehan Cameron had placed a tablet to the memory of his great-grandfather, the Reverend John Cameron, D.D., in the Old Blandford Church of Petersburg, Virginia. On it was the statement that Cameron was the father of Duncan Cameron, the founder of St. Mary's. Henrietta Smedes objected so strenuously to that claim that Cameron had it removed from the tablet. On May 26, 1909, the trustees "confirmed, endorsed, and reaffirmed" a 1908 resolution of the executive committee stating "that the Rev. Aldert Smedes, D.D., was the sole founder of St. Mary's School and that it cannot be truthfully claimed that anyone else has any part in that honor." Bishop Cheshire contended that Duncan Cameron had seen the school as investment property; Bennehan Cameron insisted that it was "by Judge Cameron's wish" that the campus had become a school for females.[66] It seems unfortunate that the trustees, while naming Aldert Smedes as founder, did not at the same time find a way to acknowledge the crucial part that Duncan Cameron played in making the school possible.

The other building completed in 1909 was Clement Hall, named for

Eleanor Clement and her mother. The large two-story building erected 150 feet to the rear of the main building served as the dining hall and gymnasium for over 60 years. The dining room was opened in December. After the dark, crowded room on the lower floor of the main building, that spacious and many-windowed room was "truly a delight." It could accommodate 300. Soon a covered walkway connected Clement and Smedes, making it possible to go about the school day completely protected from rain.[67]

Lay, in helping to plan Clement Hall, took every precaution to protect the health of the campus community. He constantly wrote articles and gave talks on sanitation, a matter he felt to be too much neglected in the South. Augustus W. Knox, husband of Eliza Smedes, was appointed school physician when Peter Hines, who for over 30 years attended the families of the rectors and the students when needed, died in 1908.[68]

The smallpox scare of 1913 was handled with admirable calmness. Within a few hours after the suspicion was confirmed that a student had that dreaded disease, the vaccination of everyone on campus was in progress, and letters to all parents were in the midnight mail. The Halloween party went on that night as scheduled except for the absence of the day pupils. The patient recovered quickly while her unhappy roommate remained in isolation for the incubation period. Only six boarders were called home temporarily.[69]

The fine new gymnasium that was such an important part of Lay's plan for the well-being of the college community was still without equipment of any kind by the 1910 commencement. Over $70,000 worth of buildings had been added during 1909 leaving the school with a $50,000 debt after the Clement legacy had been spent. (The estimated value of the St. Mary's campus was $200,000.) McNeely DuBose, an active trustee, was named chairman of a fund-raising committee.[70]

Meanwhile, Lay and his wife determined to beautify the grounds. Anna Lay restored the old flower beds on front campus after the builders departed. Elizabeth Lay Green, speaking to the alumnae in 1950, recalled her childhood memories:

I was a child of ten when we moved to St. Mary's. Therefore, my most vivid memories are those of a child—the sensations of smell, taste, and odor. . . . the odor of wistaria on West Rock, the magnolias, the musk roses on the old covered-way . . . , the taste of wild strawberries . . . , the lilac carpets of pansy violets, the purity of Mother's calla lilies brought from her greenhouse to the Chapel altar, the freshness of her pots and vases of blooms on the tables in the dining room.[71]

The rector was fully convinced that comparatively large returns could be gained from a modest investment in faculty salaries. Every year at the annual meeting of the full board, Lay disagreed with the policy of keeping faculty salaries "twenty-five to fifty percent below the salaries of teachers of like grade in institutions of like grade," saying that he felt quite "hampered" in his efforts to fill vacancies with suitable teachers.[72] Jeudwine, writing from England to Cheshire in 1912, said he had heard that some of the old guard were "depressed," adding, "It is so much the easiest way to save money to underpay the teachers and overwork them. . . . I think it tells against efficiency and always ends in reducing the standard of teaching."[73] Neither Jeudwine's advice nor Lay's pleas changed the salary situation appreciably because enrollment fluctuated with the uncertain times. Lay did succeed in 1917 in gaining a tenure policy of sorts. The executive committee accepted the policy that "any teacher engaged for the second year shall therefore understand that she is permanently employed with the privilege on the part of either party of terminating the engagement at the end of any year on three months' notice."[74]

Total enrollment in the school climbed to 242 in 1911–1912 and to 301 during "the banner year" of 1912–1913 when seven boarders were placed in faculty homes. However, total enrollment dropped to 279 the next year and to 234 during the war years of 1917–1918. There were good years when the dormitories were filled, but there were years when as many as 25 vacancies existed. The lean years devastated the budget, and Lay and Cruikshank urged, unsuccessfully, that the trustees launch a national advertising campaign compared to those that had built up Sweet Briar and Hollins.[75] The rector, William E. Stone, and Ernest Cruikshank continued their recruiting efforts in the Carolinas, and there were more girls from other sections of the country than in the past. The student body remained largely alumnae-connected and Episcopalian, only 29 boarders being reported in 1911 as "from families not of our communion."[76]

The faculty-student ratio remained quite favorable, about one to ten. The class of 1915 with 27 graduates was the largest ever. Only eight of the class had not taken their high school work at St. Mary's. Full graduates from 1879 through 1915 numbered 318.[77]

The regular charges at the school in 1911 were $281, about half the cost at northern schools, creating the feeling among some that the quality of education must be inferior. There were others who objected to the charges as too high in comparison with the state institutions.[78] By 1912 the regular charges for an academic year at St. Mary's were $300 for boarders and $53.50 for day students.

Despite the most careful management, the cost of operating the new buildings left only a few hundred dollars each year for debt retirement. Many summers Cruikshank had to borrow on short-term notes in order to make critical repairs; however, he was always able to pay the notes when the fall tuition came in, and some years he was able to make ends meet exactly. Nearly all of the scholarships were tied to funds that had been spent for buildings and could not, therefore, earn interest. In effect, the school was giving in free tuition and board annually about the equivalent of the interest on a $50,000 endowment, but no such endowment existed.[79]

Bishop Cheshire, in his address to the 1912 convention, confidently announced his intention of celebrating the 20th anniversary of his consecration by paying off the St. Mary's debt *and* raising a $100,000 endowment fund by October 15, 1913. The convention approved the idea and a committee was appointed, but no one had "cast great gifts into the treasury of God" by the appointed time. Perhaps it was the growing international tension. Perhaps it was, as the rector put it in the *Carolina Churchman*, that Episcopalians were just inclined to be that way.[80]

By 1916 it was plain that St. Mary's could not keep up standards while trying to operate on fees lower than those of comparable private schools. Either the trustees had to give up the policy followed since 1897 and raise charges to $500 immediately, or they had to provide operating income from other sources, Lay said at a meeting of the executive committee in February, 1916. The combination of low tuition, no operational funds from the dioceses, no income from endowment, and large interest payments and scholarships from operating funds was proving disastrous. Most of the $235,000 spent on the school since incorporation came from individual gifts, none of them large except the Pittman and Clement bequests. About $50,000 was raised through the efforts of Mary Iredell and the alumnae and of Alfred Pruden in earlier campaigns; slightly over half of that was given by women. Only $12,000 could be traced to the education funds of the Diocese of North Carolina, although most of the individual gifts from both Carolinas were from Episcopalians. Over $40,000 was still owed by the school; therefore, Lay felt that the time had come for more asking and greater giving.[81]

The trustees agreed with the rector. At a special meeting of the full board on March 16, 1916, it was decided to conduct a campaign for $250,000, with $100,000 designated for endowment, $100,000 for buildings and equipment, and $50,000 for debt retirement and campaign expenses. The drive was to be a part of the celebration of St. Mary's 75th anniversary. The 1916 convention of the Diocese of North Carolina approved the campaign,[82] and the trustees engaged the Reverend Francis M. Osborne as their full-time special agent. A committee of three trustees was put in charge of the drive and empowered to appoint committees "in the Carolinas and in various cities of the country."[83] The plan was to raise the quarter of a million dollars in two years in a popular canvass "like a YMCA campaign," with presentations at luncheons and dinners. Articles and leaflets reminded the 25,000 communicants in the Carolina dioceses that St. Mary's had been a good investment for the church and that "proportionately our Episcopalians have more money than any other body of Christians in this part of the country."[84]

The drive got off to a successful start in October, 1916, in Raleigh, where $20,000 was pledged.[85] After war was declared, some felt that the campaign should be halted immediately. However, the executive committee of the board issued a statement in September, 1917, emphasizing "the sacred duty" of training young women for more effective contributions to their country, and the trustees' committee on the endowment fund published a leaflet that virtually equated support of St. Mary's with saving the world for democracy.[86] The drive faltered. In addition to the many war funds, there had been campaigns among Episcopalians for Sewanee and for the church's pension fund. Lay and Osborne did not always agree, and Lay's insistence upon high standards and absolute obedience to the rules upset some patrons; but the trustees publicly endorsed the Lay administration in May, 1917. The endowment and building fund materialized slowly in a campaign that was carried over into the next administration at the school.

Wartime inflation hit St. Mary's particularly hard because there was no contingency fund. When the 1917–1918 charges of $325 proved inadequate, an "emergency fee" of $50 per student was added to cover part of the $80 to $100 loss the institution was incurring for each student.[87] The charges for 1918–1919 went up to $400. Financial problems were accelerated by the great freeze over Christmas in 1917 when water and steam pipes were severely damaged. Through it all, Cruikshank remained optimistic and efficient.

## "OF SWEET RECOLLECTIONS AND LOVE"

The philosophy governing daily life at the school was stated in the 1912 catalog: "The aim of St. Mary's is to make the daily life of the student that of a well-regulated Christian household. . . . to direct the physical, intellectual and moral development of the individual, with all the care that love for young people and wisdom in controlling them render possible."

Lay liked order with dignity, but he never quite succeeded in making St. Mary's fit his New England model. His catalogs stated the cardinal rules succinctly—the school could not accept responsibility for anyone whose sense of honor was not sufficiently developed that she could be trusted "not to endanger life and property by forbidden use of fire, not to go off the ample school grounds without permission," and not to be out of her proper place "when expected to be in bed." There was another cardinal rule; that one was that the rector's "nay" meant "nay." But Lay was not all business. One early fall, after three weeks of continuous rain and more than the usual measure of homesick tears, when the sun shone forth during breakfast Lay spontaneously declared a holiday.[88]

The school rules were obeyed by most students. Hardly anyone would have thought of leaving campus unchaperoned, and only the boldest ever smoked anywhere. Arrival at the dining room "after Sydney closed the doors" meant demerits. The punishment for minor infractions was "detention" in an extra study hall. An accumulation of demerits or a serious offense led to "restriction" on campus and the missing of the Monday trip to town. Almost worse than the punishment was the agony of sitting outside Eleanor Thomas's office to await sentencing.

Kate McKimmon's system of discipline in West Rock was posted in plain sight. After daily inspection, she wrote on her list the name of the culprit followed by initials indicating the offense. "S.O.F." meant "shoes on floor" instead of on the closet shelf. "H.I.B." was "hair in brush" and meant no Monday trip to town. "C.O.F." indicated "crumbs on floor," evidence that forbidden food had been taken into the dormitory. It was customary for the girls in West Rock to have their midnight pickles and crackers with mayonnaise on the stairway, for Kate McKimmon was a sound sleeper.[89] Kate McKimmon remained vigorous until a fall during Christmas vacation in 1914 left her dependent upon a crutch. She gave up the supervision of her dormitory but continued to live in a room on the first floor of West Rock. During the summer of 1916 "Miss Katie's dormitory" was converted into rooms, and the last alcoves disappeared.

The busy school day began with a 7:00 rising bell and breakfast at 7:30 followed by mail call and then chapel at 8:30. Classes met from 9:00 until the 1:30 lunch and again until 3:30. Everyone exercised for an hour in a scheduled physical culture class, walked, or played games, posting her "units" on a chart. Everyone dressed up a bit for dinner at 6:00 and chapel at 6:30. Another mail call was followed by an hour and a half of quiet study, then noisy chatter until lights out at 10:00. During the hours after dinner there were scheduled meetings of literary societies, the chorus, orchestra, and other organizations. Saturday was a school day, but Saturday night was a free evening.

The afternoon athletic activities generated intense excitement after the organization of the Sigmas and the Mus. The increased interest in athletics was due to the times, to the rector's natural bent, and to his

"Miss Katie's" primary group, 1909

interest in good health practices. The "match game" of basketball played in November, 1909, proved, according to the *Muse*, "that the two athletic clubs, Atalanta and Olympia, were too uneven to allow of any more good games." The societies were dissolved, and all boarders and the athletically inclined day students who volunteered were divided into two sides named for the Greek letter initials of the school. The old athletic association was retained as the supervising board over all athletic activities with a president and treasurer elected by the members of both clubs. The Sigmas and the Mus each elected a club president and captains of their basketball and tennis teams.[90] It soon became the custom to have pre-game pep rallies with rousing cheers and songs.

"Almost the whole school turned out" for the field day contests between the two athletic clubs. The tennis tournaments were quieter affairs; the games were described as "short and snappy" in 1915. The costume for tennis was a white skirt six inches above the ankle worn with a white middy blouse and a knotted tie. The required equipment for other sports and for gymnastics in 1917 was "one pair full, black bloomers, four all white middy blouses, one black kerchief tie, three pairs of black cotton stockings." The proper shoes would be fitted at school, the catalog advised.

The rector's "favorite scheme" was realized finally in September, 1914, when the new equipment for the gymnasium was installed—a double boom, saddles, a vaulting horse and stall, bars, scales, a spirometer to measure lung capacity, and a dynamometer to measure strength of grip. Lay and Mabel Barton were determined that St. Mary's girls would "gain in erectness, strength, and grace." [91] The rector was sure that fitness was the reason the infirmary stood empty most of the time. Students attributed the situation to the fact that upon admission each patient received "a whopping dose" of castor oil or Epsom salts, regardless of her original ailment. [92]

After a strenuous afternoon of basketball or tennis, some were content to sit after chapel on the wooden benches scattered near the circle. Often the group would sing. Strains of violin music on orchestra rehearsal nights or the sound of a piano as someone banged out the current hits for dancing could be heard in the half-hour before study hall. The dances that everybody was doing were the Turkey Trot, the Bunny Hug, and the Grizzly Bear. [93]

In the dormitories when the girls sat around in their boudoir caps chattering before bedtime, the talk was more likely to be of improbable dreams like seeing one's name on Broadway billboards than of men and marriage. Most of the school saw Maude Adams in *The Little Minister*, "the greatest theatrical event of some years in Raleigh." That same winter, 1916, the Russian Symphony Orchestra and then Paderewski played in Raleigh. Performances such as those added zest to daily life at school. Sometimes old girls stopped by en route home from the dances at Chapel Hill with stories of all the fun, but more of the old girls were teaching school than were "doing society." A few of the seniors got bids to the dances. [94] The catalog warned that an evening dress should not "approach any extreme of fashion that might necessitate the prohibition of its use."

Lay encouraged the Saturday visits of young men; the girls thought that he missed his St. Paul's School boys because he took so much of the one hour allowed chatting with each young man. There was not a great swarm of suitors because a letter from a girl's parent had to be presented, including not only the permission to call on a specific night but also a description of him. He was kept waiting a few minutes before being joined at a double desk in the schoolroom by his young lady. Peppery Juliet Sutton, often on Saturday night chaperone duty, discouraged or abetted romances according to her estimate of the young swain. Most girls were more likely to spend Saturday nights, except during Lent, in the parlor with the other girls learning the latest dance steps.[95]

It was possible to receive a telephone call from a beau; but the telephone was in Juliet Sutton's East Rock office.[96] Sometimes there were young men in the dining room. The rector asked a few boys from A&M to sing with him and the St. Mary's choir at Sunday evening chapel. They usually stayed for supper in the dining room and gazed about the room with great interest while conversing with Lay at his table. Young George Lay was home for holidays and sometimes on weekends from Chapel Hill. At least twice during his senior year, 1917–1918, his sophomore roommate, Tom Wolfe of Asheville, accompanied him. Ellen Lay wrote of 17-year-old Wolfe in her diary, "I like the way his hair curls in front."[97]

It was possible to glimpse an A&M man while doing the afternoon walking laps around campus, but demerits were given to anyone who dared communicate or even to go beyond "the deadline," as the path encircling the grove was called. It was legal, chaperoned of course, to view the ROTC dress parade on the field west of the St. Mary's campus. About 9:00 after an A&M football victory, a great crowd of college boys would appear in the grove carrying lighted torches made from tightly rolled newspapers. As the boys neared the circle, the girls spilled onto the porch and steps, flanked by the faculty. Lay gave a short congratulatory speech, and the girls were permitted to cheer loudly the departing group.[98]

About the wildest escapade that most St. Mary's students managed was "a chicken salad and two creams" at Brantley's drug store on Monday afternoons. Chattering away, they waited in the summer house for the special express streetcar to go downtown. On damp days the rector saw to it that everyone wore overshoes, thus spoiling somewhat the effect of a carefully chosen costume. The girls were forbidden to wear "beauty spots," but some of the bold ones applied crescents and stars en route before making an appearance on Capitol Square.[99]

Simplicity in dress was officially encouraged. The St. Mary's wardrobe of about 1912 was likely to include a "coat suit," a winter coat, a white coat for Easter and for concerts downtown at night, a church dress (often of taffeta), a hat or two for Sunday mornings, an evening dress, and some not-so-new dresses for dinner. Blue serge skirts and middies were essential; a blue middy over a skirt would do for dinner in the dining room, and everyone had plenty of white middies—almost a uniform. During the war skirts went up a few inches. Hair was worn in a loose Psyche knot, and a black ribbon across the forehead directly above the eyebrows was considered a smart touch.[100]

No matter how near Raleigh a student lived, there was no running back and forth in the family automobile, for "machines" were rare. An automobile trip to Durham in 1909 was described in detail in the *Muse*. Eleanor Thomas, Margaret Jones, Yanita Cribbs, Ernest Cruikshank, and Herbert Hodgson, determined to hear a lecture by Pres. Charles William Eliot of Harvard, set out despite a high March wind; they were "cheered and encouraged by the assembled school." Back in Raleigh, they reported a trip "almost devoid of the usual delays and mishaps that beset motor cars." [101]

Most of the sweet recollections of St. Mary's women of the era were of good times on campus. Every occasion called for a party; if nothing else were going on, Cornelia (Ducky) Allen, the tiny black waitress who worked at St. Mary's from 1903 to 1922, would go through her repertoire of recitations and dances in the dormitory halls. Her annual ice cream parties for the girls at her table were memorable. [102]

The biggest party of the fall had been for generations the Halloween grand march. It developed into a full-fledged masquerade ball with the faculty participating. Beginning in the fall, each of the chapters of the junior auxiliary gave a play or an entertainment.

Christmas brought the Christmas play, the elocution recital, the club parties, the big party in the gymnasium where a tall candlelit tree shimmered, the carol sing, and the last chapel service closed with the singing of "On Our Way Rejoicing." [103] Some years special "St. Mary's Pullmans" were made up in Raleigh, and the partying continued on the train.

After examination time there were club parties and sometimes a Mardi Gras ball. In 1910 the girls "who came as beaux were very gallant in knickerbockers." [104] Anna Lay's parties were usually described with great appreciation in terms of the food and flowers. She was a quiet but beautiful influence on the lives of the students. When Eleanor Thomas resigned in 1917 the board of trustees offered her the post of lady principal, but she declined because of other commitments. [105]

The marriage of Ernest Cruikshank and Margaret Jones brought another family in residence on campus. They were married in New York in 1911 after her year at Columbia and spent the summer honeymooning in Europe. In the fall they settled into the apartment on the first floor of senior hall. Their place soon became the scene of frequent merrymaking, for Ernest Cruikshank loved to plan a party. The Cruikshanks lived in those rooms until 1919 when a brick cottage was built on campus for them. The couple had three children—Ernest, Mary Pride, and Olive Echols.

By 1910 the senior parties given by the seniors in turn and by some of the faculty had become "quite a feature of life at St. Mary's." The class of 1910 boasted 18 members, called itself "the comet class," and took full credit for the reappearance of Halley's Comet. The round of parties for the class began with a feast at the home of the Stones (William Stone was their honorary member) and included a hayride and picnic and a long train ride given by the St. Mary's seniors as a party for the Peace and Meredith seniors.

The class functions enjoyed official encouragement, but by September, 1912, Lay had decided to abolish sororities. The decision was evidently accepted calmly, although a picture pamphlet was inserted in at least some copies of the 1913 annual *Muse*. The page was entitled "Men Without a Country" and showed girls dressed for traveling with the Greek letters of their sororities prominently displayed on their suitcases. Nell Battle Lewis, class of 1911, succinctly summed up the sorority experience when she wrote, "The sororities skimmed the social cream of the school. For the girls in these charmed circles, they were fun; for the girls outside they were not. They did St. Mary's no particular good—and no serious harm—and Mr. Lay had good grounds in democratic theory when he requested that they surrender their charters."[106]

For a time a number of ephemeral clubs arose as they do on campuses. During that era they were devoted to eating and were named "W.M.T.E." (We Meet To Eat) or "E.T.U.B." (Eat Till You Bust), "The Follies," and "The Merry-makers." It was soon decreed that such silly organizations could not be pictured in the yearbook, and they disappeared from the scene.

The literary clubs, although each held a formal reception annually in the parlor, expended most of their energy on the debates. The annual championship debate took on more than ever the air of an athletic contest when it was moved to the new auditorium. After the debate, the alma mater was sung with decorum, but when the decision was announced there was pandemonium as the winning club mobbed its victorious team. Celebrations continued over illicit midnight feasts.[107]

The most exciting and mysterious parties were those planned by Ernest Cruikshank for the Muse Club. The purpose of the club was to edit the monthly school magazine and the yearbook, both named the *Muse*. Cruikshank developed the leadership of the school in putting together the magazine. In 1908 the editor of the *University Magazine* said that among six magazines of "the female colleges," he found the *Muse* "the pick of the flock."[108] A surprising number of women who began writing as members of the Muse Club were published later— Elizabeth Lay, Nell Wilson, Martha Byrd Spruill, Jane Toy, Mary Yellott, Irma Deaton, and others. Nell Battle Lewis and Elizabeth Gold became professional journalists.

Many members of the Muse Club were among those selected to be listed in the "statistics" or "who's who" section of the yearbook. A number of the leaders in student activities later became influential members of the alumnae association. Cruikshank encouraged the club to foster an appreciation of the history of the school. For example, the 1910 yearbook edition of the *Muse*, edited by Mary Campbell Shuford, featured the commemoration of the centennial of the birth of Aldert Smedes.

Life at St. Mary's was barely disturbed by the outbreak of war in Europe during the summer of 1914. That fall Mademoiselle Rudnicka, a Parisian who had been in charge of the French department since 1912, made the war seem real when, in an article for the *Muse*, she described the "cruel parting scenes" at railway stations, the food shortages in Paris, and her harrowing 14–hour train trip from Paris to Le Havre with "travellers, soldiers, and prisoners all mingled together." [109] For Christmas that year, the St. Mary's students acted upon Eleanor Thomas's suggestion and contributed clothing and toys to the Christmas ship sent to the children of Belgium, France, Germany, England, and Russia. [110] Flags of all nations were popular decorations, and everyone learned the "Marseillaise." Instead of exchanging Christmas gifts in 1916, many gave to Belgian relief. However, the European war did not really touch life within the grove until the spring of 1917.

Three days before the United States declared war on Germany, Lay talked with the students in a special meeting. He spoke of his own conviction against war, of the patient forbearance of Woodrow Wilson, and of the great burdens laid upon the president. "What shall we do," he asked, "to show our sympathy and loyalty?" At a second meeting that night the assembly adopted a resolution addressed to Eleanor (Nell) Wilson McAdoo and signed by the class presidents, by Lay, and by Eleanor Thomas for the faculty. The resolution asked Eleanor McAdoo to extend the sympathy and to express the loyalty of the St. Mary's family to Wilson. Wilson, through Nell, sent his "deep appreciation," and she sent "my thanks and my love to my school." [111] From that day, patriotism at St. Mary's was unbounded. The senior class gave the school a larger United States flag. Kate McKimmon reluctantly accepted its presence and became almost "reconstructed" when she discovered that her young relatives serving in France were referred to as "Yanks" over there. [112]

Before leaving school in May, nearly every St. Mary's girl signed "the mobilization for war pledge" suggested by Lay and drawn up by him and a student committee. Each girl promised "to be economical in dress, ice cream, soft drinks, and toilet articles," to mend her clothes, to carry her own parcels, to help more at home, to plant a garden, to join the Red Cross or another service organization, to cheer up those at the front by sending packages and letters, "to take an interest in measures for local betterment," and "to interest others in woman's part in the war." [113]

The students returned in the fall with broadened horizons and more serious purpose. A few had left to take nurse's training, and more than ever signed up for the business courses. Others, after careful consideration, chose the college course as "the more patriotic thing in view of the future services to be rendered." [114] The war was reflected in every aspect of daily life at the school. Themes of the stories and poems published in the *Muse* related to the war. The girls sang "Over There," "Keep the Home Fires Burning," and their own patriotic song, "Hail to Our Boys in France!" with music by R. Blinn Owen and words by Aline E. Hughes, editor in chief of the monthly *Muse*. [115] The lecture series featured a Paris editor, a Canadian officer who had fought in Europe, and an American diplomat who explained the future League of Nations. [116]

The war gave impetus to Eleanor Thomas's desire to develop a greater sense of responsibility by giving the students some voice in decisions affecting their daily lives. Perhaps that was the reason that "the war sacrifices" were so successful that Bishop Cheshire praised the St. Mary's students in his address to the diocesan convention in 1918. In a student body meeting it was decided, "Since we could not go and fight ourselves, the next best thing was to send our wheat and meat," and wheatless and meatless days were accepted uncomplainingly. [117] As prices rose, the dining room fare became even plainer; "corn-bread fingers" were a popular substitute for cake. Cruikshank told the trustees that the fact that his many war economies were cheerfully accepted by the students, plus the $50 emergency fee, made it possible for him to keep the school solvent. [118]

In the spring of 1918 students decided to fill the manpower gap by taking responsibility for maintenance of the grove, tennis courts, playing field, and large vegetable garden. About 150 volunteers worked in squads in their assigned sectors, and the best pairs of workers were "decorated." Young Lucy Lay toiled all summer canning produce from the garden for use in the dining room. [119]

The money saved by self-discipline on the Monday trips to town and by such strategies as having shoes half-soled went into thrift stamps. The school in the fall of 1918 was divided into five competing sections, and everyone connected with the campus owned a thrift stamp card. Amid "high rivalry" the contest was won by the SOTKs (Stamp Out The Kaiser). "Much more important, however," the *Muse* noted, "is the fact that over a thousand dollars worth of stamps were sold between January and June. Meanwhile, the Liberty Loans claimed our patriotic attention, and . . . two bonds, amounting . . . to $350 . . . were turned over to the Endowment Fund." The four other stamp clubs were named Kaiser Killer, The Stamp Act, Hun Hunters, and Lick 'Em. [120]

The Red Cross also claimed the support of 100 percent of the boarders and faculty and of most of the day students with a membership of 224 at St. Mary's. Every Monday afternoon the *Muse* room became a Red Cross workroom under the direction of Lizzie Lee. A committee of students consulted with the Raleigh chapter and accepted an assignment to make layettes for Belgian babies, hospital gowns, and surgical dressings. And always everyone was knitting socks and mufflers. The students were justly proud of the $660 raised for the second Red Cross war fund; their goal had been $250. Eighty teachers and students took the first aid course, and the faculty volunteered for work outside the campus community with the local exemption board and other agencies.[121]

The list of leaders of volunteer services in any North Carolina town "read like the membership list of the St. Mary's Alumnae Association," the *Muse* declared. Fannie Neal Yarborough, the wife of North Carolina's wartime governor, Thomas W. Bickett, was at the same time (1918–1919) president of the association. Emilie McVea lectured for the YMCA and the YWCA and served as coordinator of Virginia's student volunteers for the Federal Food Administration. Nell Wilson, the wife of the secretary of the treasury, William G. McAdoo, was national head of the Women's Liberty Loan Committees and head of Washington's largest Red Cross auxiliary composed of 4,400 women of the treasury department.[122]

The younger St. Mary's alumnae flocked to Washington to take the government jobs then open to women. Several actually enlisted in the navy and as yeomen performed the office jobs assigned to women;[123] a few alumnae served overseas with the YMCA or the Red Cross. St. Mary's claimed "Sister Glory Hancock" (Madelon Battle), a Red Cross nurse who was four times decorated for bravery.[124]

## "THE FULL CIRCLE"

During the 12 years of the Lay administration, the St. Mary's Alumnae Association grew in strength and numbers. The rector's first open letter to the alumnae in the fall of 1907 revealed the appreciation of a professional educator of the importance to the institution of its alumnae. He wrote:

Each of you may feel that she can do very little; but if each of you will feel an obligation to do that . . . the result will be an incalculable force to help us on in the work which centers here . . . , but which must get its inspiration from the full round of the circle, if its influences for good are again to go out to those all about us.[125]

Ernest Cruikshank worked indefatigably to aid alumnae activities through the *Muse*. When in 1910 the alumnae association adopted the

*Muse* as its official organ, the alumnae section of the magazine was enlarged and two of the ten issues were designated as alumnae issues. In June, 1907, the alumnae association elected Martha Dowd treasurer to relieve Kate McKimmon, who had served as both secretary and treasurer since 1879. Mary Iredell remained the permanent president. The series of "Wednesday afternoons" instituted by the administration in the fall of 1907 encouraged the local alumnae, as well as the townspeople, the legislators, and friends of the students and faculty to take tea in the parlor. Founders' Day of 1907 saw "the first real observance of this day other than at St. Mary's" as many chapters of the alumnae association met to reorganize and to set priorities. [126] The alumnae initiated plans to raise $6,000 within two years to endow two scholarships honoring Kate McKimmon and Mary Johnson Iredell. The desire was to honor "these two much beloved ladies before their earthly course was ended." [127] The fund grew slowly despite the energetic direction of Emilie McVea. At commencement in 1916 the fund was closed at $5,000. It had been decided five years earlier to place the fund as it was raised into bonds with the 6 percent interest to be paid to Mary Iredell and Kate McKimmon for life because the school had no retirement policy. [128]

Because strengthening loyalty to St. Mary's was the first priority of the alumnae association, the direct descendants of alumnae then in attendance at the school were organized in 1909 by Kate McKimmon. The granddaughters club had as members 11 granddaughters, 27 daughters, and five students who were the third generation at St. Mary's. [129]

The 1910 commemoration of the centennial anniversary of Aldert Smedes's birth was the most ambitious affair ever undertaken by the alumnae. Although alumnae records were scanty, 1,000 of the 3,000 living alumnae outside of Raleigh were reached by mail, and over 50 attended and stayed at the school. The program for the Smedes centennial was impressive. Addresses by the Right Reverend Robert Strange, D.D., bishop of East Carolina, by Emilie McVea, and by Josephus Daniels, editor of the *News and Observer*, were complemented by parties and musical programs. [130]

At the annual meeting of the alumnae association on May 24, 1910, a new constitution was adopted vesting the general management of alumnae affairs in a council of ten members. Mary Iredell declined another term as president, saying that her work was "in a measure completed with the adoption of the constitution"; she was elected honorary president for life. Margaret Busbee Shipp was elected president, a drive for 1,000 members was planned, and the dues were set at $1. One of the most interested chapters was organized in 1909 in New York City where Florence Slater, chapter president, and several other alumnae

Tennis Team, 1908, with Pittman Auditorium in background

Faculty, 1913, including longtime faculty and staff members William Stone,
Ernest Cruikshank, Florence Davis, Kate McKimmon, Frances Bottum,
Martha Dowd, Blinn Owen, Clara Fenner, and Lizzie Lee

who also had taught at St. Mary's resided.[131] In 1910 the association elected Mary Ferrand Henderson as "a traveling secretary" to spend several weeks a year visiting local chapters to take the news of the school and explain its needs.[132]

The movement to secure the election of two women to the St. Mary's Board of Trustees originated in the New York chapter and was endorsed by the association at its annual meeting on May 13, 1912. The trustees replied, "The Board has no power to elect trustees except in case of the failure for one year of the conventions of the dioceses of North Carolina, South Carolina, East Carolina and the Jurisdiction of Asheville to make an election."[133] That answer, while true, did not satisfy the alumnae who had requested "that proper steps be taken" to make the election of women possible. Therefore, the alumnae sent a delegation to the board meeting of 1915. They received essentially the 1912 reply with the suggestion that if they wished to pursue the matter they should "present it to the councils interested."[134] The persistent New York chapter wrote in 1917 a circular letter urging all chapters to support the movement to put pressure upon the board to arrange for the alumnae association to elect a trustee. The men were not enthusiastic, but in 1925 the alumnae won representation when the Diocese of North Carolina elected Jennie Bingham and Fannie Neal Yarborough Bickett.

In its 1917 circular letter the New York chapter gave the Lay administration an unequivocal endorsement.[135] Lay, however, remained under fire from some alumnae and parents, and not all of the trustees were prepared to take the criticism accruing from changes that the rector advocated as necessary to make St. Mary's first-rate in all departments.

The celebration on May 12, 1917, of the 75th anniversary of the founding of St. Mary's School was alumnae oriented. Speakers were Dr. Emilie Watts McVea, president of Sweet Briar College, and Dr. W. S. Currell, president of the University of South Carolina. After chapel on Saturday morning, the literary societies gave a program; an afternoon pageant in the grove began with a grand march of the alumnae, with each class designated by a banner and dressed as schoolgirls of the appropriate period. The evening's entertainment was an operetta.[136]

Lay, although he had previously had no real connection with the school, grasped the essence of the place immediately upon becoming rector. In his open letter to the alumnae in 1907, the new rector wrote, "I am more and more impressed with the importance of the position that St. Mary's girls have taken in the community . . . . I am both humbled and inspired by the loftiness and beauty of the ideals which old St. Mary's girls have derived from their Alma Mater, and which they devoutly believe are inseparable from her very existence."[137]

The girls realized that the daily chapel services gave "a certain unity to the . . . varied activities of . . . school life."[138] The extent to which that was true was evidenced by the reaction of the students to the news of the sinking of the *Titanic*, April 14–15, 1912. All was quiet after lights out, but precisely at 11:00 the solemn strains of "Nearer My God to Thee" were heard across campus. The girls had quietly assembled in their dormitory halls and were singing in memory of the dead.[139] Music for Lay was an especially important aspect of worship. The Lays were a musical family; Anna Lay possessed a lovely alto voice and he a booming bass, and several of their daughters were talented in music. The rector took voice lessons at St. Mary's and performed in the student recitals. Lay and Stone also sang with the choir of 35, and often the organ was supplemented by strings. The organ was more reliable after Hodgson in 1909 installed a "kinetic blower" to replace human power; the St. Mary's congregation sang almost as well as the choir because everyone rehearsed the hymns for Sunday after chapel on Saturday.[140]

Even little four-year-old Thomas Lay knew all of the words of his favorite hymns. Tommy, the Lay child born in Raleigh, died of diphtheria in January, 1915. Bishop Cheshire said the private graveside service, and on Sunday morning the quarantined Lay family listened from the porch of the rectory as the students sang Tommy's favorite hymns.[141]

George W. Lay, dedicated educator, was first of all the dedicated priest; he considered preaching a major function of the rector of St. Mary's; and he returned to the parish upon leaving St. Mary's. He spent time preparing his sermons and filled them with practical theology. He preached one sermon to each new generation of students. Entitled "The Duty of Being Good Looking," it emphasized the Christian's duty to care for the God-given body.[142]

The required Sunday school classes then numbered six, and Stone and other faculty members helped with the teaching. Some years Lay's class for seniors met at the rectory on Sunday night. Always communicants' classes met during the winter as Palm Sunday was traditionally confirmation day. During those years slightly over 75 percent of the students were Episcopalians. Kate McKimmon continued her careful training of the altar guild composed of about 20 college students who were communicants. In the fall of 1917 an eighth chapter of the junior auxiliary was organized and named in her honor. Each chapter continued to have a faculty "directress" and student officers, but a new council made up of student representatives from each chapter supervised the varied activities. The chapters "sewed a great deal for the poor," gave entertainments to raise money for the Smedes scholarship at the Emma Jones School in Shanghai and for Thompson Orphanage, and had local projects such as carrying food to the elderly retired St.

Mary's servants. As much as $700 annually was contributed to church causes through the chapel. While working on their sewing projects, the girls were read to from the *Carolina Churchman* and told inspiring stories of missionaries.[143]

Because Lay was interested in serving the church at large as well as in training young Episcopalians, he inaugurated in 1910 his summer conferences. The trustees of the school invited about 100 clergymen and lay leaders to the school for a week in June. Lay planned each conference around a theme and secured speakers "from elsewhere." As chairman of the diocesan commission on social service, he was particularly interested in all aspects of that subject. The conferences proved "valuable in stimulating church work and life," and the men reported that the atmosphere at St. Mary's was "peculiarly rich in devotional and spiritual power." Women were invited for the first time in 1914, and a number of alumnae, being leaders in their churches, returned to the campus. Unfortunately, the war and inflation made it necessary to discontinue the conferences.[144]

Lay must have conveyed to his charges the depth of his feeling for the priesthood, else Nell Battle Lewis could not have written of the chapel as she did years later in her column for the *News and Observer*. She confessed that in doing a column on "the ten most beautiful things in North Carolina" she had omitted the scene that should have headed the list. She wrote:

I was sitting in the Chapel at St. Mary's. . . . There was in progress a Communion service. . . . As I watched a group . . . as they knelt before the altar . . . I thought, "Here is deep beauty that has true promise—the dedication of youth to this matchless ideal of love and service. . . . Yes—this is the most beautiful thing in North Carolina."[145]

The ten seniors of 1918 did not know that an era was ending both for St. Mary's and for the world. They did not know that the next school year would bring both a new administration at St. Mary's and the end of the Great War. It was no dramatic incident, no sudden failure, but a gradual erosion of relations between Lay and the board of trustees that resulted in his resignation in June, 1918. He did not feel that his work at St. Mary's was done. In fact, he not only hoped for the accreditation of St. Mary's as a junior college but thought that in the long run it should become a four-year college, perhaps retaining the preparatory department as an academy organized separately but using the same facilities.[146] He was, in fact, full of plans and hopes, none of which could be realized lacking the firm support of the board and the church. Lay was impatient with what he considered inertia on the part of the board regarding operational matters such as faculty salaries and general repairs. He felt that the board had failed to grasp the importance of making St. Mary's a truly excellent school and that the diocese really did not care.[147] On the other hand, there were those among the trustees who considered the rector's personality to be abrasive. Parents complained that Lay was absolutely rigid concerning concession to meet special circumstances. That was true; Lay refused exceptions to one and all, including the daughters of trustees.

The board was much influenced by William A. Erwin, textile magnate (and husband of Sarah Lyell [Sadie], daughter of Aldert Smedes), who had been a trustee since the school's incorporation. Although not a member of the executive committee at that time, he dominated board meetings through persuasion and influence. He did not support Lay's policies, an open fact that both men acknowledged courteously.[148] The more academically oriented members of the faculty continued to support the rector's philosophy of education.[149]

It was some time after Lay's resignation before his contributions were publicly acknowledged, but eventually many agreed that George Lay's departure from St. Mary's was a great loss to the cause of education in general.[150] Lay left St. Mary's stronger than ever before academically and with an enlarged enrollment. The school was solvent, an endowment campaign was in progress, and the value of the plant had been increased by $90,000. With perseverance and energy he had given to St. Mary's always his best.[151]

Lay served Christ Church in Springfield, Massachusetts, during 1918–1919 while its rector was in YMCA work and then returned to North Carolina, where for nine years he was the rector of St. Paul's Church in Beaufort. He established St. Andrew's mission in Morehead City.

He retired to Chapel Hill in 1928 but was acting rector for a few months in 1930 at the Church of the Good Shepherd in Raleigh. The Lays returned to St. Mary's for several ceremonial occasions, and Lay liked to say that his chief claim to fame was that his five daughters were St. Mary's graduates. George and Anna Lay stayed busy in Chapel Hill, she with her gardening and he writing articles and completing his unpublished *The Language of Scientists*, an exposition of the Greek and Latin derivations of scientific terms.

George W. Lay died on August 12, 1932, at 73.[152] The epitaph he chose for his gravestone in the Chapel Hill cemetery seems most fitting. It is simply the Greek for "Then Shall I Know."

## CHAPTER NINE

# "THE GOLDEN CHAIN"

The sixth head of St. Mary's School, the Reverend Warren Wade Way, was a man already favorably known to the board of trustees as the rector of St. Luke's in Salisbury. When he took office in the fall of 1918 he was aware of the strengths and weaknesses of St. Mary's because he was the close friend and confidant of his predecessor.[1] His wife was a cousin of George Lay and a grandniece of Bishop Atkinson. Warren Way, quite different in personality from George Lay, shared a dream with him—the dream that St. Mary's would become a four-year college. That dream was not to be realized; instead, Warren Way spent most of his 14-year tenure wrestling with the problems of the postwar inflation and then with those of the Great Depression. He did gain for St. Mary's accreditation as a junior college.

Dr. Lay (who was later referred to in the *Raleigh Times* as being "particularly known for his eleven years of creative work at St. Mary's"),[2] immediately upon hearing of Warren Way's selection in June of 1918, wrote to the secretary of the board, "I am delighted. . . . I cannot think of anyone who could have been chosen that I would consider better fitted for the duties of the office."[3]

Way, who was born in Irvington, Illinois, in 1869, was the son of Newton Edward Way and Lizzie Heaton Erwin. His father died when Wade (as his family called him) was 12. His mother managed to keep her family of two sons and two daughters together, and young Wade eventually went to work in the railway shops in Mt. Vernon, Illinois. When he decided to enter the ministry, he went to a preparatory school before entering Hobart College, where he was graduated in 1897. He entered the General Theological Seminary and was ordained priest in

The Reverend Warren Wade Way, D.D., rector, 1918–1932

1899. Way served as assistant rector at All Angels' Church in New York City and as a missionary in Illinois before going to Grace Church in Courtland, New York, where he was rector from 1901 until he accepted the call to Salisbury in 1914. In 1903 he married Louisa Atkinson Smith from Virginia. Their three children—Evelyn, Warren Wade, Jr., and Roger Atkinson—were 14, 12, and 10 when the family moved to the St. Mary's campus.[4]

Although he had no experience as an educator, Way had "always been deeply interested in educational matters." He indicated that in running the school he "would be very greatly influenced by the judgments and wishes of his Bishop" as the chairman of the board.[5] Some thought him a trifle pompous and vain, but even they found him perceptive, sympathetic, and always gracious.[6] The St. Mary's girls were so impressed that they dedicated the yearbook to him at the end of his first year.

Almost immediately after St. Mary's opened on September 19, 1918, with the largest enrollment in its history (202 boarders and 88 day pupils), the devastating Spanish influenza epidemic hit. On September 26 Dr. Knox reported 52 cases of flu, and the executive committee of the board of trustees authorized emergency measures. All healthy students were allowed to go home or to friends and relatives nearby if their parents so wished. Before the month-long siege was over, there had been 155 cases of flu, and one death at St. Mary's.[7] The west wing of Smedes was converted into an infirmary, and the teachers assisted Dr. Knox, Dr. Aldert Smedes Root, and Anne Alexander, the infirmary nurse. The day students, although not allowed to visit on campus, were pressed into service as runners to drop off medical supplies.[8] Way himself was a flu patient. The *Muse* reported alumnae deaths, among them Margaret Rosalie DuBose Avery.[9]

At St. Mary's, classes were canceled for two weeks, and attendance was spotty for three more weeks. The time was made up by schedule changes and by telescoping the course work. It was, as the rector put it, "a year of dislocations"; but everyone, including the student leaders, was "valiant."

The day students had not returned to classes, and the ban on public gatherings was still in effect in Raleigh when it became apparent that peace in Europe was imminent. Excitement ran high. At lunch on Thursday, November 8, Way announced the false news that an armistice had been signed, and a service of thanksgiving was held in the chapel. It was 3:00 A.M., November 11, when "all St. Mary's was awakened by the clamor of factory whistles, church bells and automobile horns." The scene was described in the *Muse*:

the lights in the hall are on, and everyone is throwing on sweaters and coats . . . . Everyone is yelling and beating on dust pans. . . . As we watch the Stars and Stripes rise against the pale skies a great solemnity comes over us—every hand goes up to salute. Someone starts "The Star-Spangled Banner," and how we sing![10]

The girls dressed and then danced in the parlor until breakfast time. When the State boys poured down Hillsborough Street in a "shirttail parade," each holding the shirttail of the man in front of him, a few St. Mary's girls joined the crowd. Several blocks away they came to their senses and ran back to campus. For that grievous infraction they were restricted until Christmas and had their grades lowered for skipping classes.[11] When North Carolina's 113th Regiment later returned home and marched down Hillsborough Street, St. Mary's students stood at the edge of the grove and sang "Dixie."

## TEACHERS, COUNSELORS, AND FRIENDS

Way found the academic program at the school well organized because Lay had carefully designed the curriculum to be complete in itself and to meet the anticipated standards for the future accreditation of the school as a junior college. With minor changes, the catalog of the Lay administration met the needs of students transferring to senior colleges for the next 40 years. Enough flexibility was built into the system to allow for granting advanced standing to qualified students upon examination. Students could specialize in the fine arts, earning certificates instead of, or in addition to, graduation diplomas. (For a number of years, beginning in 1921, the name of the institution was spelled "Saint Mary's," instead of the original abbreviation.)

Way's memorandum to the faculty at the opening of school in 1919 summed up what had always been the St. Mary's philosophy. He wrote, "Do the best you can to keep poor students up with the work, but if this is impossible, do not let the required work of the better suffer thereby." Frequent and detailed report cards went to parents, and much time was consumed in faculty meetings determining "the industry marks" for borderline students. Any student failing three subjects was "automatically excluded," sometimes at mid-year. The editor of the 1929 *Muse*, writing just before "the dreaded report card period," admonished, "Your report card is like a motor. You get about as much out of it as you put fuel in."[12]

Often the lady principal gave a dinner for "the honor roll girls." The grading system was changed from a numerical one to letters in 1926, but everyone knew the numerical equivalents: A (95) was excellent; B (85) was good; C (75) was fair; D (65) was poor, but passing. E meant not passing, and F was for flat failure. Quality points were not yet used. There were no class cuts; students were either in class or in the infirmary. A great boon was granted in 1927 when underclassmen with satisfactory academic records and a grade of at least B on conduct were released from nightly study hall. Earlier only juniors and seniors had studied in their rooms.

Student turnover remained a problem. Only seven of the class of 1920 had been at the school for four years or longer,[13] although the freshman class of 1916 had numbered 50. On the other hand, at least one of the 1920 graduates had been at St. Mary's for ten years, and a member of the class of 1923, Lucy Lay, had started school with Kate McKimmon 14 years before.

Way reorganized the administration of academic affairs making use of standing committees of the faculty to perform a number of tasks. In 1921 he created the position of academic head after Ernest Cruikshank resigned to head Columbia Institute, a small Episcopal school in Tennessee. Way felt that he needed a man whose sole function would be that of business manager. The departure of the Cruikshanks brought sorrow to the students, and it brought upon the rector a storm of criticism from the alumnae.

The first academic head remained for only a year, but she made a major contribution by encouraging more students to go on to senior colleges. She was Ophelia Stone Stone, younger sister of Imogen Stone. The girls found her so forbidding that they never succumbed to the temptation of referring to her as "double Stone."[14]

Sara Clarke Turner served as academic head from 1921 to 1926. She was capable and experienced,[15] with a bachelor's degree from Goucher and a master's degree from Columbia, and she was a strong and demanding teacher. She inspired the less ambitious students to register for the most dreaded subjects and to resolve to use their brains. She was also a kind friend to the students.[16]

Virginia Holt, academic head from 1926 to 1932, was a graduate of Smith College with a master's degree from the University of Virginia.[17] She was indefatigable and successful in her efforts to establish more solidly the academic reputation of the school. Both as consultant on matriculation problems and in her literature classes, Virginia Holt spent long hours encouraging the girls to make the most of their opportunities. The students appreciated her penetrating and humorous comments on the foibles of human nature, including her own, and they admired her. The faculty enjoyed her talents as a mimic and raconteur.[18] When she left St. Mary's, Virginia Holt continued graduate work and later became academic head and dean of students at Chatham Hall in Virginia.

The rector's invaluable assistant in many areas of the life of the institution and the girls' teacher, counselor, and friend was William Enos

Stone, who by the beginning of the Way administration had been at St. Mary's for 15 years. Stone was born in 1859 near Boston and was educated at the Boston Latin School and in Switzerland and Germany. He was a Harvard graduate. He went south to engage in the textile business and married Sue Dick of Greensboro. Forsaking business, William Stone taught school in Edenton and in Charleston, South Carolina, before accepting the St. Mary's position.[19] He had been interested in the school from the 1880s when he had heard Mary Iredell talk at his church.[20] He was a devout churchman, the lay reader, and the treasurer for the St. Mary's Chapel. Over the years Stone taught a number of subjects—literature, German, economics, sociology, political science— but history was his specialty. He was a master teacher of concepts and attitudes, for he had a way of putting things into perspective.[21] One of his contributions was to increase for the whole student body awareness of current events.

For generations of students Stone was the first St. Mary's person they knew because he met the trains the first days of school. The cane he swung as he walked, the close-cropped mustache, the twinkling blue eyes, and the rose from his garden worn in his lapel presented such a debonair effect that the girls of the 1920s never realized that William Stone was in his sixties by then. They called him "Sweet William," and the song of that title written for the 1919 senior party became a school classic. On most Sunday afternoons Stone roamed Cameron field and the woods beyond, giving informal lectures to any who wished to join him. Sometimes the group explored a section of Raleigh as he narrated its history. On the return trip, the group was often followed by boys from town and from State College who slowed their cars to a creep in order to talk to the stragglers. Stone would allow this for a few minutes before sending someone back with a message.

He died in January, 1928, after a brief illness. The editor of the *Muse* wrote, "No girl knew him, but was the better woman for it."[22]

By the late 1920s the old guard among the faculty was dwindling. By then only Lizzie Lee, Juliet Sutton, and Kate McKimmon remained of those who had gone to St. Mary's before the turn of the century.

In 1919 Kate McKimmon had voluntarily retired from teaching, and the primary department was discontinued for financial reasons.[23] At the trustees' request she remained at the school on a small salary supervising the altar guild and performing such other duties as her strength would allow. Her room in West Rock was a popular place. Young girls need heroines, and about Miss Katie more than about anyone else they knew there clung the aura of the Old South. They called her "the oldest and dearest St. Mary's belle";[24] she was the last link to Aldert Smedes.

By the summer of 1928, Kate McKimmon was too ill to be cared for any longer at the school. Appropriately enough, she went to the Home for Confederate Women in Fayetteville. She thought that she was there only for the summer and assured visitors, "I shall be back at St. Mary's on September 15th." On September 15, 1928, the chapel at St. Mary's was filled to overflowing, for that was the day of her funeral.[25]

Clara Fenner (she called herself "C. F.") remained her inimitably breezy self. She continued to tour Europe's art museums in the summers, and she presided over the art department adding new courses— textile design, costume design, stained glass window design, pottery— as the times demanded. When Clara Fenner died on June 30, 1926, from the effects of an earlier traffic accident, some of the zest went out of life at St. Mary's. She had been the art department for 28 years, 1892–1896, 1902–1926.[26]

Susan Reavis Cooke, whose degree was from the University of Chicago, taught English and sometimes history or Bible, 1921–1928. Of an indeterminate age, she was small and fragile with an extremely pallid complexion. Her head, however, was large, and she bore a striking resemblance both in physiognomy and expression to the great stone face. That, of course, was what the girls dubbed her. Nonetheless, Susan Cooke was known as a good teacher and a kind dormitory supervisor.[27]

A succession of young teachers passed through briefly; they added interest and vitality, but the academic head and some of the students felt a degree of instability developing by the mid-twenties. That was not to be serious, for each of the three strongest younger additions to the faculty—Mabel Morrison, Elizabeth Bason, and Ruth Lineberry— was to serve St. Mary's for about 40 years. And so was Florence Davis, who went to the school in 1911.

The new generation of teachers carried on. The girls realized that kind, precise Elizabeth Bason taught, along with cooking and the handtucking of petticoats, "the general art of living."[28] Florence Davis, while insisting upon Shakespeare so that her girls would carry away something of lasting value in return for their hours spent memorizing lines, experimented with the workshop method of preparing plays. Ruth Lineberry handled the mathematics courses with quiet competence. Mabel Margaret Morrison, the only Ph.D. on the faculty, arrived in 1929 from Canada. Her Latin classes were rigorous. The music department was headed by William H. Jones from 1919 until 1940. He kept his department academically sound, and in 1927 he reorganized the St. Mary's orchestra. A number of piano teachers assisted Jones over the years. During the 1920s Sue Kyle Southwick, who went to St. Mary's in 1918, was well known for her recitals and as an excellent teacher. The science classes were taught, 1912–1925, by Frances

Ranney Bottum, graduate of St. Mary's and Peabody. She drew illustrations for the yearbook, and she enjoyed helping to plan the elaborate literary club programs.

William C. Guess, who remained on the faculty until 1967, taught economics and sociology; the students enjoyed bachelor Bill Guess. In his sociology classes he carefully avoided discussions of subjects that could be considered "of a delicate nature."[29]

Way taught most of the Bible classes. Everyone was required to take Bible one hour a week; the two-year course was designed to cover both the testaments and Bible history. Way's reputation was recognized when he was invited to give a series of lectures at the University of the South in the summer of 1925. In 1924 he had received the master's degree in religion from the University of Chicago. In 1929 the University of the South conferred upon him the degree of doctor of divinity.

Rivalry between the two literary clubs remained an important facet of campus life. All year Sigma Lambda and Epsilon Alpha Pi vied for points and for possession of the year's cup. A model club meeting was a part of the contest. It was a dignified proceeding with the presidents in academic gowns and a panel of townspeople to judge the business meetings and the papers. The climax of the year continued to be the annual debate. Interest in the literary societies declined after a 1931 reorganization dropped the practice of compulsory schoolwide participation and made scholarship and writing ability the criteria for membership.

At times editing the *Muse* was shared by the literary clubs and became a part of the contest for the literary club cup. The class of 1920 produced magazines rivaling those editions of the days of Elizabeth Czarnomska in the 1880s. After Ernest Cruikshank's departure, the Muse Club was no more. The *Muse* changed its name to the *Bulletin* and back again and its form to a tabloid-size paper, but by the latter part of the Way administration the format was again the familiar small magazine. It was called the *St. Mary's School Bulletin*, and there were four issues each year—the catalog, the school-life number, the alumnae number, and the commencement number.

Students attended, sometimes voluntarily, sometimes by requirement, lectures and cultural events in Raleigh. Peace and St. Mary's continued to sponsor a series of concerts given in the St. Mary's auditorium. Of great interest was Florence Slater's return in 1927 with her lecture and a University of California film on "How Life Begins."[30] The English clubs of St. Mary's, Meredith, and State held regular joint meetings.

Sports became increasingly popular, and some girls spent all afternoon after gym class was over playing team games. The costume for gym was still a pair of full, black bloomers and a white middy blouse worn with black stockings. Way was adamant about the stockings. The rector attended the track meets and kept sending word to the participants to pull their bloomers down over their knees, thus making the high jump, for instance, a doubly difficult feat.[31] By 1929 pictures in the *Stagecoach* revealed the knees, albeit stockinged, of members of the athletic teams, and the tank suits worn by the swimming team were rather modish. The "natatorium" was added to the gymnasium in 1927. Measuring 20 by 50 feet, it was heated, was "purified by the violet ray," and cost a little over $16,500.[32]

Two new tennis courts were built on front campus during the summer of 1923. In 1928 Caroline Tucker was runner-up for the state women's singles tennis championship, and at the school she won the tennis championship for the Sigmas, thus giving them enough points to win the trophy. A silver shield trophy had replaced the traditional banner in 1925.[33] Rivalry between the Sigmas and the Mus had been building to a fever pitch since 1919–1920 when Mary (Moke) Hoke and Rainsford (Rene) Glass had led the two athletic clubs to scores of 67 and 66 for the year with the Sigmas winning the banner.

All boarding students and those day students who wished to join belonged to either the Sigmas or the Mus. Each year the new girls waited anxiously to be chosen, and then everyone celebrated with a snake dance through the grove and a bloomer party in the gym with Dixie cups and lollipops for refreshments. Basketball was the most popular team sport but was always intramural until 1923 when St. Mary's played Peace Institute and won both games. By 1931 intramural basketball was so popular that there were three St. Mary's teams, and ten frenetic games were played.

The letter club was organized in May, 1927, with a mysterious night "walk" and a not-too-grueling initiation ordeal. The club was made up of those who over a period of two years had compiled 300 points in athletic events to earn a monogram.[34] Grace Houchen, physical director, 1923–1928, was responsible for reorganizing the athletics program. She was attuned to the times, for both in England and in the United States there was then an increased interest in the proper physical education for women and in women's sports.

ST. MARY'S SCHOOL AND JUNIOR COLLEGE

As soon as he assumed the rectorship of St. Mary's, Warren Way began to prepare himself to make decisions regarding educational policy by becoming active in professional societies. He was convinced that Lay had read the times aright when he had organized a curriculum that favored the humanities and that was easily transferable to a senior college. There remained, however, the nagging question of how soon accreditation would become essential to the school's survival. In 1923 the high school department was accredited by the Association of Colleges and Secondary Schools of the Southern States. The high school diploma, known as "the college entrance certificate," was granted for 15 standardized units; it was given only to students who had been at St. Mary's for two years.

The library, some had thought, would present accreditation problems for the college because its 3,000 volumes were uncataloged. However, because the library more than met the association's 2,500-volume requirement for a junior college and cataloging was in progress, the situation was acceptable. There was no qualified librarian, but until 1927 a succession of women worked part time in the library while teaching or helping with chaperonage. That fall Ann Strudwick Nash went to St. Mary's as the first professionally trained librarian. A graduate of the Library Training School of the Carnegie Library of Atlanta, she had been the only assistant librarian at the University of North Carolina for a decade, 1907–1917. She had also been librarian at Sweet Briar College. By the spring of 1929 she had reorganized the library, and 4,500 volumes were cataloged.[35] The library facilities, located in half of the first floor of the art building, were inadequate; but the hope for a new library did not materialize until four decades later.

As early as 1921 Way began his campaign to secure junior college accreditation. Although the junior college movement was still "in a formative state," in 1924 there were 233 institutions in the country calling themselves junior colleges; 12 of those were in North Carolina. The American Association of Junior Colleges had 79 members.[36]

To secure accreditation, improvement in the science program was necessary. Therefore, "a modest biological laboratory" was equipped during 1923–1924. The rector also recognized the need to upgrade faculty salaries. It was time, he told the trustees, to rescue the faculty from "their condition of threadbare respectability."[37] The major snag in the accreditation process was St. Mary's lack of the required $10,000 in annual income from sources other than student fees. The school had $5,000 annually from endowment and $3,000 from the Diocese of North Carolina. The southern association accepted the trustees' plan to ask the other dioceses for the remaining $2,000 annually. Finally, in December, 1927, St. Mary's was accredited as a junior college by the Association of Secondary Schools and Colleges of the Southern States, making it one of only 13 junior colleges then fully accredited by that body.[38]

While awaiting the junior college accreditation, the rector took soundings on his idea that St. Mary's should become the only four-year Episcopal college for women in the nation. "It is," he told the trustees, "a reproach to ourselves that in the length and breadth of this immense

America, the Episcopal Church has not one college where a daughter of the Church can get a bachelor's degree. . . ."[39] Bishop Bratton warned, "The church cannot afford to offer second rate college equipment on the plea that it offers the best in religion. Her best in religion must in addition be the best in education."[40]

In the spring of 1926 Way asked for an immediate campaign to raise $600,000 to make St. Mary's into a four-year college, but the board wished to study the matter further. In November of that year the Synod of the Province of Sewanee, representing 15 dioceses in nine states, unanimously endorsed the idea of a four-year college at St. Mary's.[41] However, Way had to report in 1928 that "not much progress" had been made in mustering support from the alumnae and the church. At a special meeting of the board on October 31, 1929, the rector reported "a growing interest" in the college work at St. Mary's with 52 percent of the student body enrolled in the college program as opposed to 42 percent three years before. There was prolonged discussion, and Fannie Yarborough Bickett, one of the first alumnae trustees and a member of the board's executive committee, "spoke very strongly against any change from what St. Mary's had been in the past."[42] The date of that meeting—two days after the stock market crash—explains in part the board's reluctance to make a decision.

At the meeting of June 3, 1930, the board voted nine to eight, with Bishop Edwin Anderson Penick, then chairman, casting the deciding vote that "the immediate educational objective shall be the development and improvement of St. Mary's as a Junior College." A second resolution passed by the same vote with Bishop Cheshire presiding (after Bishop Penick had been called away) and with Cheshire's the deciding vote. That second resolution read:

Resolved: That the further educational objective of such effort shall be the development of St. Mary's into a four-year liberal arts college of the type required by the standards of the Southern Association of Colleges and Secondary Schools; provided that this be commenced if and only when solid and sufficient financial support seems assured.[43]

Soon desperate measures were required to survive the Great Depression; St. Mary's remained unchanged, which was probably what most of the alumnae had hoped would be the case.

## PROGRESS TOWARD "EQUALITY OF PERSONALITY"

In the twenties St. Mary's became a feeder institution for the University of North Carolina. The relationship worked well for both institutions until the university in the 1960s opened its freshman class to women and siphoned off a portion of the St. Mary's clientele.

There were only 15 women students at the University of North Carolina in the fall of 1917 when Elizabeth Lay went there; by 1921 there were 61 coeds.[44] Frank Porter Graham, then in the history department, said, "I believe education in a University is not a sex right but a human right. . . . Woman has advanced from chattel to person, to equality of personality."[45] The handful of Carolina coeds organized the woman's association in 1906 with St. Mary's graduate Minna Bynum as secretary. In 1921 under the presidency of Ellen Lay they organized a basketball team. St. Mary's graduates were prominent in the woman's association and in the sororities because they had been trained to leadership on the small St. Mary's campus.[46] Six of the 25 members of the class of 1920 went to Chapel Hill together, and they actively recruited others to follow them, creating the strong St. Mary's-to-Chapel Hill tradition.[47]

St. Mary's girls at the university became active in writing and dramatics. Elizabeth Lay, in 1918, was the first woman on the *Tar Heel* staff. (Tom Wolfe wrote most of the paper in those days.)[48] In April, 1918, the University Dramatic Club presented *The Man of the Hour* at St. Mary's, and Elizabeth Lay played the heroine.[49] Her play *When Witches Ride* was one of those chosen for production by the Carolina Playmakers in the spring of 1919. All three plays selected for production in the spring of 1922 were written by St. Mary's alumnae who had written for the *Muse*. The authors were Jane Toy, Elizabeth Lay, and Mary Yellott.[50] In 1922 Elizabeth Lay and Paul Green wrote for the Playmakers *Blackbeard, Pirate of the Carolinas*. Theirs was to become a lifelong partnership. The volume of plays entitled *Carolina Folk-Comedies* published in 1932 contained plays by St. Mary's alumnae Jane Toy and Helen Dortch.

St. Mary's women were distinguishing themselves in scholarship, too; the only junior who made a grade of one [A] on all subjects at midyear of 1921 was Mary Yellott.[51] In 1923 Jane Toy had the next-to-highest average of any Chapel Hill student.[52] The honor roll regularly contained a fair share of St. Mary's names. In 1930 the only coed elected to Phi Beta Kappa was St. Mary's Sarah Falkener.[53] The president of the university wrote to Way in 1926 that the university's experience with St. Mary's graduates had been "unusually delightful" and that their records bore "ample testimony to the thoroughness of their training."[54] Not everyone went to Carolina. The *Muse* reported that members of the class of 1923 scattered—three to Chapel Hill, two to Sweet Briar, two to Converse, one to William and Mary, and one to New York. Seven had gone directly into teaching, and one was in Europe. Eleven were at home,[55] some awaiting already-set wedding dates.

The prominent men who went to lecture at St. Mary's in the years immediately following the war invariably spoke about the irrevocable changes the war had wrought in the status of women. All noted that new freedoms always carried with them new responsibilities. Most St. Mary's women of the twenties chose the demands of the family as a career but spent tremendous amounts of energy and time in volunteer service. Only a few chose a career outside the home combined with marriage, but by the early 1930s the Great Depression had sent young women job hunting. Finding openings almost nonexistent, many took business courses and relied upon friends of their fathers to find work for them. Weddings often were postponed; the good life suddenly seemed dislocated in general.

Those women who during the 1920s chose careers over marriage could look to their St. Mary's teachers as women who had successfully denied the southern notion that an unmarried woman was a failure. While the number of women in the professions had increased by 226 percent between 1890 and 1920,[56] and women's share of the baccalaureate degrees granted in the United States had jumped from 17 percent in 1900 to 34 percent by 1920 and to 40 percent by 1930,[57] the overwhelming majority of educated women still became teachers. Even in the teaching profession, women gained few of the top positions either as supervisors in public education or as professors in the colleges and universities that were not exclusively institutions for women. In 1921 only 53 percent of the coeducational institutions gave women equal pay for equal rank. At the colleges for women not quite 75 percent of all faculty members were women; about three fourths of those institutions for women paid equal salaries for men and women of the same rank.[58] At St. Mary's Way frequently reminded the trustees that he needed more money for salaries in order to employ more than the usual three men on a faculty of 25 to 30. Men were paid more, partly because of the fact that they lived off campus.

Glimpses of St. Mary's career women appear in the alumnae news of the 1920s and early 1930s. Nannie Lee Williamson, after a career in the public schools, in 1937 founded Ravenscroft School in Raleigh where she served as principal for 20 years.[59] Susan Iden began her 25-year career with the *Raleigh Times* in 1908, serving as its first society editor and later as city editor.[60] Isabella Perry was a surgical pathologist on the faculty of the University of California and for three years was executive secretary of the National Research Council. As chairman of the international Cancer Congress she organized and wrote much of a multivolume work on tumor pathology.[61]

News of the younger alumnae revealed that Daisy Cooper in 1926 became the first woman to receive the new doctorate under the five-year law program at the University of North Carolina.[62] Sociologist

Margaret H. Bottum summarized her interviews with West Virginia miners in a pamphlet illustrated by Frances Bottum, and it was published by the American Constitutional Association.[63] Nancey Lay taught music and then went to New York to study and to try show business. She was in the chorus line of *Poppy*, starring Madge Kennedy and W. C. Fields. Nancey had plans made to study opera in Europe when she decided to marry instead, a decision she "never regretted for one moment."[64] Most St. Mary's women of that era would have made the same decision with no hesitation.

## "THE FEVERISH FOLLY"

The drastic changes that occurred in the way that Americans went about their daily lives in the 14 years from 1918 to 1932 were unsettling. Way tried desperately to hold the line against what he called "the feverish folly of these trying times,"[65] and he did remarkably well considering the pressures upon him. The 1924–1925 catalog stated the school's position clearly: "One of the first lessons . . . learned by the new students is that there are certain things a St. Mary's girl may not do." St. Mary's girls did not go to moving pictures (except on a rare school party), did not paint their faces, did not contract bills in Raleigh, did not sit in windows or on fire escapes, and did not receive boxes from home except at Thanksgiving and Christmas. Smoking, leaving campus without permission, and "being out of one's bed when supposed to be there" were shipping offenses, and a few girls actually were expelled.

Over the years of the Way administration the rules were relaxed somewhat, and daily life at the school changed in many ways. Everyone agreed, however, that the underlying philosophy of the place never fell victim to the "trying times." Somehow it was transmitted—in the chapel services, by the longtime teachers—from student to student. The rector liked to call it "the golden chain" binding the St. Mary's generations to one another and to God. The traditions of the school were deliberately nourished each November 1 at the Founders' Day programs presented by the literary clubs. During the commencement festivities of 1925 the name change of the yearbook from the *Muse* to the *Stagecoach* was marked by the appearance in the grove of an authentic stagecoach of 1840s vintage. Katie McKimmon and Ophelia Crawford of Goldsboro, who had "finished" at St. Mary's in 1858, were escorted ceremoniously to "the ancient vehicle" by a student in costume.[66] The very buildings on the campus exuded tradition—the Rocks, Smedes, the chapel. Smedes was by 1919 so well worn that William A. Erwin gave generously to renovate that building. The new spiral stairway added greatly to the beauty of the reception area. Portraits of Aldert and Sarah Smedes were presented by their daughters, Sadie Erwin and Bessie Leake. The bedrooms in Smedes were replastered and painted and "luxurious" tiled baths installed.[67]

Daily life at St. Mary's was supervised by a succession of lady principals. Lucy Graham Hester, a Raleigh alumna who served during Lay's last year, did not return.[68] Alice Edwards Jones, former Latin teacher at the school, stayed only during 1918–1919. After several years in Chapel Hill, she went to Dallas as principal of St. Mary's College there.[69] Carolina Virginia Perkins was lady principal during 1919–1920. The widowed daughter of the Reverend Israel Harding, she was well known to St. Mary's patrons. She had been for a number of years at the National Cathedral School in Washington.[70]

Bertha Adele Morgan, the lady principal 1921–1925, "was known as 'BAM'; and to the school 'BAM' became the symbol of discipline with a big D." With a degree from Boston University and 15 years teaching experience, she took command with crisp northern assurance. The students liked and respected Bertha Morgan, who also taught Latin. She as lady principal and Sara Turner as academic head formed a strong administrative team.[71]

Way, despite Bertha Morgan's aid, found himself nonplused by the irresponsibility of some of the students. Because his only daughter Evelyn behaved exactly as he wished her to and was also an excellent student, the rector had supposed that most girls were dutiful and happy. Disillusioned, he once remarked at a meeting of the board, "Alas, letters of recommendation, like tombstones, are not always models of veracity." Nonetheless, he had praise each year for "the large number of young ladies" who had exhibited "force of character" and "superior qualities of leadership."[72]

The title "lady principal" was changed to the modern "dean of students" when Catherine Seyton Albertson assumed the position in 1925. As a girl she had attended St. Mary's for four years when Bennett Smedes was rector. She had been principal of the high school at Elizabeth City and had studied at the Universities of North Carolina and Virginia and at Columbia and at Harvard. Catherine Albertson projected a faintly Victorian image despite her modern title. The girls felt that their lives would have been easier had the disciplinary matters been left entirely to her, but the Ways were inclined to take part in the details of daily life. When the job of dean of students was abolished in 1932, Kate Albertson went to Greensboro as a housemother. She continued her life-long interest in the history of the North Carolina coastal regions, and several of her short works were published.[73]

Student government made considerable progress under the Way administration. Eleanor Thomas, during the last years of the Lay administration, had reduced chaperonage in order to "develop greater independence and sense of responsibility in girls who were really young women in their late teens and early twenties . . . and to encourage the esprit de corps which had always been resident in St. Mary's."[74] As early as 1910 there were student hall monitors. Under Sara Turner a council composed of the class presidents and the heads of all student organizations was designed to strengthen student leadership. In September, 1919, Way established the school council composed of three members of the faculty, the lady principal, and nine student representatives elected by the classes; the rector served as chairman. Later a tenth student was added to give the freshman class representation. The council's purpose was "to get a fine feeling of loyalty among the students and better cooperation in securing high and happy standards of Christian living in our family household."[75] The 1923 catalog stated that the council functioned "as an honor committee and judicial body" and called it "a first step toward student government." The first president of the student body, Mary Elizabeth Powell, was elected for 1923–1924.

The senior class in 1923 unanimously adopted a simple system of self-government in senior hall. They elected two representatives from downstairs and two from upstairs as a committee to work with Bertha Morgan in drawing up a set of rules and punishments to be approved by the class. Every week each senior reported any "misdemeanors" in writing and "explained her reasons" to the student committee that imposed punishments. The lady principal reviewed each senior's record every two weeks. Also that year an "honor study hall" of 23 members studied together with no supervision, and hall proctors were appointed to enforce lights out and Sunday quiet hour rules.[76] The dormitory teachers, of course, still held authority to see that all ran smoothly. The second semester of 1925–1926 brought the privilege of studying in her room to every student with satisfactory grades. By December, 1926, the school council was described as consisting of an executive committee composed of faculty and staff and an honor committee composed of 12 students,[77] a system with the inherent problem of reversals of student decisions by the executive committee. Way informed the trustees in 1927 that "a notable and significant event" of that spring was the decision to establish a real honor system. It did not happen without a struggle, for a minority of the students tried to bargain for new privileges as the condition for accepting an honor system. The honor pledge, written by the student committee, required the student "to be truthful, to be honorable in all school affairs, to be in her room at night, not to use any form of fire in the school buildings, and not to leave campus

School Council, 1921, forerunner of Student Government Association

without permission." In addition, the student was "expected, when off campus as well as when on, to behave in such a way as will not bring discredit upon her school."[78] Student leaders realized that their honor pledge simply made formal declaration of the responsibility that the school had laid upon its students since 1842. Now that the system was defined, only time could tell how well it would operate. Kate Albertson was able to report at the alumnae luncheon in 1928 that not one student was expelled during the first year under the system.

By the second semester of 1928–1929, there was need for a precise definition of cheating, and a committee drew up a specific statement. Cheating included, in addition to the obvious examples, copying another's homework (with or without the owner's permission with guilt upon the willing lender as well), deriving ideas from another's original work, and writing translations between the lines in preparation for class recitation in a foreign language. Studying together and discussions were approved so long as one did not "appropriate another's original idea." Teachers were asked not to proctor tests. Final examinations were held in the study hall (the large schoolroom across from the parlor) with one teacher present to answer questions. The pledge to be signed at the end of all written work read, "I pledge that I have neither given nor received help on this paper."[79] It was evident that young women were learning responsibility and leadership skills. Jane Toy wrote over a half a century later of her three years at St. Mary's: "Besides providing sound teaching, they bridged the gap between an extremely sheltered childhood and a more realistic adult world."[80]

The daily life of the almost all-feminine community at St. Mary's between 1918 and 1932, when viewed through the veil of time, does not seem so "feverish" as the rector considered it to be. There was the same 7:00 rising bell, the same rush to breakfast, the "dire reckoning of misdeeds" in assembly, the "respite of chapel," classes, music practice, evening chapel, and a short recreation time before study period.[81] During recreation hour the parlor was the scene of dancing, as always. But Aldert Smedes would hardly have considered the Charleston to be dancing or "Strut, Miss Lizzie" to be music. (Way seems to have forbidden the Charleston in 1927.) A sizable portion of allowance money went for sheet music of the current hits. It was 1930 before one radio appeared in the dormitories; after that, music in the parlor was not so important in campus life.

Strolling around the grove was still the most pleasant way for the less athletic to get the required daily exercise that was a part of the honor system. It was still the fashion in the 1920s to have "a crush"—a senior to admire extravagantly as a role model. The seniors felt that it was a status symbol to have several admirers. As more freedom to see boys was allowed, "crushes" became less important as a phase of the growing-up process.[82]

The freshmen and sophomores of the 1920s and 1930s engaged in as much horseplay as they could get by with in their West Rock quarters. There was a brief flirtation with the ouija board, as there had been in the 1860s and, probably, in every generation since. Way, as had Smedes, forbade that excitement.[83]

There was more excitement than anyone would have wished for in January, 1927, when Way called a special assembly to announce that there was a case of smallpox on the campus. An assembly line was set up, and 250 vaccinations were administered; no one fainted. There was no other case, although the one case was severe.[84] The school was not put under quarantine for smallpox as it had been for over six weeks during the flu scare of the winter of 1920. There was not a single case of flu on campus during the 1920 flu scare, but the day students lost a month of classes. When the quarantine was lifted in mid-March, everyone was given a "spring weekend," and the campus emptied. Influenza was frightening to every community after the 1918 epidemic, and a third flu scare in 1928 sent everyone home early at Christmas.[85]

Dr. Knox, who had been the school physician and an interested member of the campus community since 1908, resigned in March, 1927. The board elected as his successor Dr. Hubert Benbury Haywood, Jr., who also had strong alumnae ties to the school.

Way was strict about food boxes from home; he said they caused too many trips to the infirmary. Boxes were allowed at Thanksgiving and Easter because students did not go home then. Each student was also allowed a birthday cake from home. A "little store" located in lower Smedes in the area under the steps and porch was operated several afternoons a week by various groups over the years. Sales of candy, crackers, popsicles, and class pins brought in enough profit during 1931–1932 to buy a baby bed for the children's ward at Rex Hospital. Eagerly anticipated were the Wednesday afternoon trips to the drugstore on Hillsborough Street, where groups could spend 20 minutes. Some girls wore their fanciest hats, for they knew that the college boys would be riding by.[86]

Daily life on campus was luxurious for the seniors of 1928–1929, for they were the first to occupy Holt Hall. The class of 1923 had contributed $600 to a dormitory fund and had added $100 the next year when 14 members returned for their first reunion. In 1927 William A. Erwin made the new dormitory possible by a gift in memory of his sister, Margaret Locke Erwin Holt. The infirmary was moved slightly westward to make room for the three-story brick veneer building. Neoclassical in style, it was designed to house 50 students and three teachers. There were tiled baths, a kitchen on each floor, and "even sockets for the curling irons" that were forbidden in the old buildings. The rector insisted that a rocking chair be placed in each room. The parlor in Holt immediately became a popular spot for bridge games.[87]

Social life remained campus centered. Every Sunday night the Ways held open house at the rectory. On winter evenings the girls munched popcorn and listened to Louisa Way's ghost stories. She was a gracious hostess both in her home and at the rector's table in the college dining room. Although she had many duties at St. Mary's, she was active in church work and was elected president of the auxiliaries of both Christ Church and the diocese. The students enjoyed being in the Way home. The Way sons eventually went off to school, Warren to Sewanee and Harvard Business School and Roger to medical school. Warren married a St. Mary's girl, Ann Lawrence of the class of 1926. Evelyn Way was educated at St. Mary's from the age of 14. She began her long teaching career at the University of Mississippi during which time she earned the master's and Ph.D. degrees in Latin from the University of North Carolina.[88]

In the 1920s and 1930s student parties on campus were still the main source of excitement, for rarely was permission granted for off-campus functions. The holiday dinners in the dining room were provided by Nannie H. Marriott, the school dietitian, who enjoyed planning the special feasts and party refreshments. Parties were enlivened by various musical groups. The old–girl-new-girl party of 1926 featured dancing to jazz played by one pianist, three violinists, "two on the uke," and "one gazootist."

The Halloween party of 1929 included as very special guests the members of the new day students' club. Day students were included in the school parties, but the Way administration discouraged visits by the boarders to the homes of day students for fear the boarders would meet boys secretly. The day students felt so left out of things that Florence Davis took the lead in organizing their club. Its aims were "to work up interest among day students and resident students and to get the day students to take a larger part in the school activities."[89]

Christmas traditions remained unchanged. There was the "royal feast" and the carol singing in the candlelit dining room, the senior play, the Nativity play, the Christmas tree in the gym, and the choral vesper service. The final "jubilation" was the traditional predawn caroling by the seniors in a candlelight procession around campus on the morning of the start of vacation.[90]

The colonial ball celebrating George Washington's birthday remained a highlight. For days there was much scurrying about to get together costumes (for there were prizes for the best) and much rehearsing of the minuet. After a festive banquet, the grand march, and the minuet performed by the seniors, there was general dancing in the parlor until the blinking of the lights signaled the end of the party at 9:45.[91]

The last social events of each school year were the parties for the seniors. Catherine Albertson usually planned a hayride, and students gathered in the circle to watch the loading and "to see Mr. Way in sport clothes."[92] The junior-senior banquet by the late twenties was a real gala held at the Sir Walter Hotel with an orchestra for dancing. The juniors presented the seniors with corsages, gave them favors such as monogrammed silver bracelets, and served as escorts.[93]

Emily (Pank) Badham Coxe, 1929 graduate, described in her book the off-campus fun when, with parental permission, she escaped Way's surveillance:

In old Smedes Hall I had the same room as my grandmother and my great-grandmother before me. . . . the year that followed: rolled stockings, knee-high dresses, lavendar face powder, open roadsters, the portable vic, Gene Austin singing "Sleepytime Gal," debutante parties . . . academy hops, proms at Chapel Hill, midnight necking, fraternity pins. . . .[94]

The North Carolina debutante ball, which became a tradition for

Colonial Ball, 1923

many St. Mary's families, began in 1925 when the Raleigh Merchants Association presented 30 young women as a part of its fall festival. In 1928 the Terpsichorean Club, a private club for young men, assumed sponsorship of the debutante ball and made it a social event of first importance statewide.[95]

Clothes by the late twenties had assumed greater importance than in many years. In the mid-twenties skirts went up, waistlines came down, and "flesh-colored" silk stockings were popular. Boyish bobs, marcelled and spit-curled, were hidden under chic cloches. The school catalog of 1925–1926 warned, "Dresses of extreme style may not be worn." Articles of clothing prohibited were sleeveless dresses for day or evening wear, fur coats, expensive jewelry, and "mules" for bedroom slippers.

Monday was still the day for the trip to town as classes were held on Saturdays, instead of Mondays, to discourage studying on the Sabbath. The school catalog in 1922 advised parents that $2 a month was a "sufficient" allowance; girls often were heard to complain, "I'm so hungry, I could croak!" Even so, everything was "grand" or "simply marve." Stu-

The Sigmas, 1924

dents went to town in groups of five accompanied always by a teacher or a senior. They could shop on Fayetteville Street only and were on their honor not to meet boys. Beginning in 1925 they could attend movies with parents, and in 1926 seniors were given movie privileges in chaperoned groups, not to include dates. *Ben Hur* and *The Hunchback of Notre Dame* were on the list of approved movies; *Don Juan* was not.[96]

The approach to dating at St. Mary's was still definitely Victorian. Way stated proudly, "We do not introduce young men to girls here."[97] Written permission from a young lady's parents still was necessary before she could receive a male caller. Dating hour was still actually an hour, from 8:00 to 9:00 on Saturday nights, and the girls knew perfectly well that most of their callers had later dates arranged in Raleigh. The line of dressed-up young men, patent-leather slick hair parted in the middle, formed outside the rector's office in East Rock long before 8:00, for Way liked to chat with each one in order to determine his "suitability." It was good to be able to present the date card early enough to get one of the double desks partially hidden by the heavy door of the study hall. Only quiet conversation was allowed, hand holding never. Even so, a surprising number of successful courtships and one elopement were managed. Later, the parlor was used for dating, and couples sat stiffly about the room as the teacher who was "keeping the night" walked in and out.[98]

Attending football games at State and Carolina was a great excitement even in the required chaperoned groups. The *Muse* reported that at the game in Raleigh between the two arch rivals in 1923 St. Mary's was given a special cheer by Carolina and that State's band played "Hail St. Mary's." Serenading St. Mary's was still the custom of the winning team after the State-Carolina classic. The rector, who was a great sports fan, always stood out front "to draw the deadline" between the male and female cheering groups and made a congratulatory speech.[99]

The height of status in St. Mary's female world was to be the recipient of Easter corsages from more than one admirer. Recipients were generous in lending the extras to friends to wear to church. The Easter morning procession to the chapel was filmed by the Kiwanis Club in 1927 as a part of its "moving pictures" to boost Raleigh.[100] There were a few memorable occasions when groups of young men were on campus, as for concerts by the University of North Carolina Glee Club, when "St. Maryites could gaze unrebuked at the forbidden species." The most memorable social event of the 1920s, "perhaps the most enjoyable in the entire history of St. Mary's" according to the *Bulletin*, was the visit of the Sewanee Glee Club in 1926.[101]

And so the girls of the years between 1918 and 1932 considered the school rules to be mid-Victorian, and the rector considered some of his charges to be quite frenzied in their pursuit of pleasure. The truth lay somewhere in between. A student writing in the 1928 *Bulletin* observed that the new freedom permitted genuine friendships between boys and girls, friendships often prevented by rigid convention in the past.[102]

## "DOWN THROUGH THE GENERATIONS"

Higher education had lost its religious orientation except in the denominational institutions. St. Mary's stated its orientation as firmly as ever in the 1932 catalog: "The Chapel is the soul of St. Mary's, and daily teachers and students gather there on a common footing." Way expressed his philosophy in a message to the alumnae. He wrote, "Our aim is to understand our time . . . , yet never to surrender the changeless principles of Christ's religion . . . to the feverish folly of these trying times."[103] The burden of the times lay heavily upon the rector. Bishop Cheshire was more sanguine than the rector in his opinion of the state of the world. On his 80th birthday, March 27, 1930, he observed, "The world is a much better place today than it was when I was young. Young people today have more personal religion than they did then."[104]

The Episcopal service was particularly inspiring under Warren Way's rectorship, for he read the service beautifully and his sermons were thoughtful. The Easter services were, as they had been for generations, particularly impressive, and Evensong at St. Mary's was so lovely that townspeople attended regularly. Way introduced more formality with a robed choir and chapel caps. The choir wore white dresses and for some years white shoulder-length veils.[105] The veiled choir was changed later, but for the next half century students were required to wear chapel caps.

The beauty of the chapel services was enhanced by a new organ given by the alumnae and dedicated to the memory of Bennett Smedes on October 3, 1926. The class of 1920 had established the organ fund in 1925 with a gift of $500. The alumnae association raised more money and then borrowed the remainder of the needed $8,000.[106]

On October 3, 1922, "the Chapel was thronged with sorrowing friends, many of the school's servants occupying the seats in the east transept," for on that day funeral services were held for Ernest Cruikshank. He became ill after only a year as head of Columbia Institute. The trustees of St. Mary's passed a resolution expressing gratitude for "the pervasive influence" in the life of the school of "this noble Christian man."[107] Mary Iredell died on January 7, 1919, and Martha Dowd on July 27, 1925. Within a few years, six of the stalwarts died—Iredell, Cruikshank, Dowd, Fenner, Stone, McKimmon—all of them links in the golden chain of lives spent for St. Mary's.

Way spoke more than once in his reports to the trustees of the responsibility he felt as their priest to lead his charges toward a commitment to service. When the Episcopal church replaced the junior auxiliaries with the Church School Service League, the entire student body was organized into chapters. The league studied missions and sent contributions to various fields, including the usual scholarship to Shanghai. The students of the Way rectorship caught the vision, for one valedictorian said, "We realize that now it is our turn to go out into the world and serve, and it is with heartfelt gratitude that we turn to St. Mary's and thank her that we are in part fitted to do this."[108] The women of the Way era, flighty and silly though they may have seemed during their flapper stage, did serve. Twenty-five years later, in any gathering of the leaders of the women's work in the Diocese of North Carolina, over half of those present would be St. Mary's alumnae. Bishop Cheshire said that many a parish could not have functioned without those women.[109] Women, however, did not run their churches officially. In 1913 the 97th convention of the Diocese of North Carolina, after "a lively discussion," voted against extending to women the vote in parish elections, partly because in their auxiliary convention the women voted by a majority of 24 against suffrage.[110] In 1924 the *Muse* reported the election to the Virginia Board of Missions of its first woman, a St. Mary's alumna, calling it "truly a step forward for St. Mary's and for Southern women."[111]

New avenues of influence and opportunities for service other than church work were opened to women through the woman's club movement. Exercise of influence, both by direct effort and through influence with the men who hold the seats of power, can be viewed as a definition of leadership when the ideas espoused are ahead of the times. By this definition, women were becoming leaders in social reform by the 1920s. They had learned at boarding school and college that forming a club was a good way to accomplish tasks and to enjoy friendships at the same time.

In 1921 the Southern Association of College Women merged with the Association of Collegiate Alumnae to form the American Association of University Women. Over the years St. Mary's faculty women were active in the AAUW, and at least five of them were presidents of the Raleigh branch.[112] The first president of the Chapel Hill branch was Louise Venable Coker.

The patriotic societies appealed to women from old families. The National Society of the Daughters of the American Revolution [113] and the Colonial Dames drew a number of St. Mary's alumnae. The North Carolina division of the United Daughters of the Confederacy was organized in April, 1897, with Kate McKimmon as recording secretary. Most of the women's clubs were not so specialized as the educational and patriotic organizations. The General Federation of Women's Clubs was formed in 1890; St. Mary's alumna Laura Montgomery Henderson was president of the Alabama federation.

St. Mary's women were active in the Raleigh Woman's Club. Anna Lay was in the midst of her term as president of the club when her husband resigned the rectorship of St. Mary's in 1918. Susan Moses Graham, who had taught French, German, and Greek at St. Mary's during the Bratton regime, was among others active in the state federation. A founder of the Chapel Hill club was Jennie Bingham Toy, the only St. Mary's graduate of 1886.

The same pattern of service was being repeated by St. Mary's women all over North Carolina or wherever they lived. Often their memberships included a church organization, at least two of the patriotic organizations, a cultural club or two, and a service club or two.

An organization with the sole purpose of service was the Association of the Junior Leagues of America founded in 1924 to demonstrate the effectiveness of trained volunteers. A group of Raleigh women, a number of whom were St. Mary's alumnae, formed in 1927 the Raleigh Junior Guild with the idea of affiliating with the association, which they did in 1929.[114]

In the 1920s all kinds of women's clubs everywhere, in addition to promoting self-improvement and the arts, were tackling problems related to the public schools, public libraries, and public health. The reforms women sought at first were, historian Thomas Woody concluded in 1929, nearly always "an extension of woman's nurturing function."[115] Most men approved of that interpretation. Furthermore, such reforms had become a matter of public policy during the Progressive Era. When some of the women turned radical and demanded full participation in the political process, most of the men were extremely disapproving.

A report made in 1912 to the tenth convention of the North Carolina Federation of Women's Clubs on the legal status of women showed how much work remained to be done before women could exercise basic legal rights.[116] The federation waited until 1918 to endorse the woman suffrage amendment because women were so deeply divided on that issue with leaders on both sides active in the federation. The speaker at the St. Mary's commencement exercises in 1911 had not only summarized the immediate past but had predicted the future more accurately than he could have realized. Edwin Mims of the University of North Carolina said:

Women . . . are playing an increasing part in education and literature and science and music and social welfare; while at the same time they have not left out of consideration the true interests of the home. . . . The test of a college like this may be found particularly in the contribution its graduates make to the communities. . . . you should . . . attempt to make conditions of . . . life more satisfactory. . . . you will do so without losing any of the womanly qualities that have been particular characteristics of Southern women. In this era of remaking our civilization, you may have a commanding post.[117]

The fight over the ratification of the woman suffrage amendment in North Carolina did find St. Mary's women in commanding posts on both sides. Probably more alumnae of the school agreed with the anti-suffrage leaders, Mary Hilliard Hinton and Minnie Fitch Tucker Baker, than with suffragists like Barbara Bynum Henderson and Nell Battle Lewis. Barbara Henderson managed to remain the southern lady, but some of her St. Mary's classmates had their doubts about hard-hitting journalist Nell Battle Lewis. At the height of the fight, a friend sighed and remarked sadly, "Anyway, Nell, you were *born* a lady!"[118]

The woman who called herself "the first suffragist in North Carolina" attended St. Mary's during 1844–1845. She was Sarah Jane Bailey

Cain. While still quite young she read about a case involving property rights that was settled, amid a flurry of publicity, against the woman involved. She asked her father to explain the laws regarding property, marriage, and inheritance, and from that day she was an advocate of woman suffrage; she lived long enough to be able to vote.[119]

The North Carolina Equal Suffrage Association grew out of a meeting called on November 21, 1894, by Helen Morris Lewis, who had attended St. Mary's School under Aldert Smedes. Lewis was elected the first president of the organization. The association's first attempt to get a bill through the North Carolina legislature failed in 1897; the senate referred the bill to its committee on insane asylums.[120] The woman suffrage movement then collapsed in North Carolina until the summer of 1913 when several St. Mary's women were among those who revitalized it. Most of the girls at St. Mary's in the 1890s would have been more in harmony with the legislators than with alumna Helen Morris Lewis.

In 1913 the Equal Suffrage League of North Carolina was organized by Minna Bynum Henderson, who was elected its first president and unanimously reelected in 1915. (As strong-minded as she was intelligent, she changed her given name to one she preferred, and it was as Barbara Bynum Henderson that she led the suffrage struggle.) In her presentation to the joint hearing before the North Carolina Senate Committee on Elections and the House Committee on Constitutional Amendments in February, 1915, she began by noting that the question most frequently put to her was, "Why are you, one of the most fortunate of women, working for woman suffrage? What can the vote do for *you*?" She answered:

all women are sisters. . . . Surely it is the happy wives and mothers who must feel most urgently their duty to those less fortunate. When I come to render an account of my stewardship, should I say to the God who gave me the greatest gifts in his giving that I was content to enjoy them while my sister women suffer? Nay, more when my little daughters grow to womanhood, could I face them with a sense of duty done if they are denied the power to bring about the reforms to which I have trained their social conscience?[121]

Archibald Henderson, thoroughly in sympathy with his wife's cause, often made speeches for the league; his sister, Mary Ferrand Henderson, a 1903 graduate, was the league's manager for the 1915 legislative hearings. Other St. Mary's women who were leaders in the Equal Suffrage League included Lida Tunstall Rodman, state treasurer; Mary Shuford, state corresponding secretary; and Suzanne Bynum, president of the Charlotte league.

Successive bills to give North Carolina's women the vote failed. In 1919 Congress finally acted and approved the Nineteenth Amendment, but it was added to the federal Constitution without North Carolina's consent.[122] Mary Hinton, chairman of the North Carolina chapter of the Southern Women's Rejection League, announced that since the vote had been forced upon women through no fault of their own, they should face "stern reality" and vote.[123] Probably the majority of people in the state, male and female, agreed with Bishop Cheshire when he wrote in 1919, "I am strongly opposed in sentiment and in judgement to woman suffrage in both civil and ecclesiastical matters. It seems to be opposed to the very fundamental conception of the very important and sacred function of women in the scheme of human life."[124] Women did vote, but it became apparent immediately that there was no women's bloc, for women expressed as many shades of political opinion as did men.

Meanwhile, the serious women reformers continued to work for other causes—the secret ballot, penal reform, equal job opportunities for women. Emilie Watts McVea and Nell Battle Lewis became nationally known. Both the University of Cincinnati and the University of North Carolina conferred honorary doctorates upon McVea in recognition of her scholarship and her public service.

Nell Battle Lewis became a real power in North Carolina through her column, "Incidentally," which ran in the Sunday *News and Observer* for 35 years beginning in 1921. She practiced law briefly and became a crusader for improved conditions in the penal institutions. She never minced words, and she never hesitated to expose injustice wherever she saw it. When she went to St. Mary's to teach in the mid-1930s, she stirred the placid waters there considerably.

Alumnae of both persuasions, the conservatives and the feminists, worked for St. Mary's side by side even as they differed sharply on the suffrage question and other issues of the day. The school was, as the rector said in his 1923 message to the alumnae, "rich in the possession of a large body [about 4,000] of living alumnae" who cherished for their alma mater "a peculiarly strong and tender attachment." The rector assured them that his only desire in making improvements was "to keep, not to break faith, with the fine heritage" of the school.[125] By the 1920s there were some strong chapters of the alumnae association. The Raleigh chapter reported "upwards of 200 active members" in 1923. Active chapters outside the Carolinas included those in Norfolk, Baltimore, Washington, and New York. Alumnae representation on the board of trustees continued through the conventions. In 1932 Easdale Shaw was elected by the Diocese of North Carolina; the first woman trustee from the Diocese of East Carolina was Annie Gray Nash Sprunt, elected in 1935.

Organized reunions at the alumnae meeting during commencement

Granddaughters Club, 1930

Alumnae group, class of 1904, gives sun dial to school, 1927: Virgie Eldridge, Susan Iden, Esther Means, Margaret Stedman, Kitty Coleman, Carrie Helen Moore, May Montague, Daisy Green, Minnie Burgwyn

week strengthened "the peculiarly tender attachment." In 1920 over half the class of 1910 returned. There was a special celebration of the 80th anniversary of the school's founding on alumnae day in 1922. The class of 1904, holding its first reunion since graduation, presented in 1926 the sundial that stands beside East Rock. In 1929 Elizabeth Czarnomska returned for the 50th reunion of the first class to receive diplomas. Four of the five 1879 graduates were present.[126]

St. Mary's lost within the decade Annie Smedes Root and Emilie McVea. Annie Smedes Root had been a faithful and enthusiastic worker in the alumnae association until her death in 1923. Emilie Watts McVea, who spent 22 years of her life at St. Mary's as student, teacher, and lady principal, always said that the school was her real home. Illness forced her retirement in 1925 from the presidency of Sweet Briar College; she died in 1928.[127]

Although the old guard, both among the faculty and alumnae, was decimated by deaths during the 1920s, memories were preserved through the publication in 1932 by Lizzie Wilson Montgomery of her memoirs of her student days at St. Mary's, 1863–1867. The booklet entitled *The Saint Mary's of Olden Days* was written at the urging of Way. Always active in the alumnae association, Lizzie Montgomery assigned to the organ fund the proceeds from the sale of the booklet. The publication of her account and the 90th anniversary of the founding of St. Mary's were celebrated on alumnae day with the presentation by the students of a pageant depicting scenes from daily life at the school from 1842 to 1932.[128]

Alumnae efforts during the Way administration were concentrated upon fund raising and the organization of new association chapters. The national campaign for $300,000 for an endowment and building fund, which had been begun under the Lay administration and had been slowed by the war, was reorganized. Its director, Francis M. Osborne, had resigned in 1920 to accept the chair of theology at the Theological School of the University of the South. Way was eager to add at least $40,000 to the school's meager endowment fund and $60,000 worth of buildings in order to strengthen the application for accreditation as a junior college. Accordingly, the trustees made plans to raise at least $100,000 outside the Carolinas. Although the campaign was under the direction of a three-man committee of trustees aided by a professional fund-raising organization, it was the alumnae who headed local committees. Eleanor Wilson McAdoo served as national chairman of the advisory committee. Way took an active part in the campaign, traveling to speak to a number of groups. Under a campaign device labeled "the 2–6–0," each alumna outside the Carolinas was asked to obligate herself "to get or to give, preferably to get" for St. Mary's $1 each week over a five-year period—a total of $260.[129]

Commencement marshals, 1919: Marian Drane, Maude Valentine, Carrie Louise Toler, Nina Hine Burke, Mildred Elizabeth Kirtland

The most spectacular of the fund-raising events was a pageant entitled *The Cross Triumphant* produced by the Washington area alumnae in May, 1922. Presented in the National Cathedral Close, it depicted in 17 scenes the history of the Christian church. The climax was the illumination of a cross, at the foot of which clustered the cast of almost 1,000.[130]

In addition to their efforts on behalf of the endowment fund, the alumnae were slowly paying off the debt on the organ. Another project, under the chairmanship of Katherine Batts and sponsored by the class of 1920, was the Ernest Cruikshank Memorial Fund—a trust with his widow for the education of the three children.

In December, 1924, the *Muse* became a newspaper. It combined both student and alumnae news but printed few literary features besides those winning awards in the annual literary club contests. The rector explained that the new format provided news from the school for alumnae chapter meetings.[131]

Way agreed with the officers of the alumnae association that the need for an alumnae secretary was acute. Such a person as he envisioned—one who was "intelligent, constructive, and sympathetic"—could, he said, "stir things up," organize new chapters, and complete the files. After being approached a number of times, the trustees finally in 1929 appropriated the salary for the position. Mela Royall, a 1927 honors graduate and president of the student body, was selected. She had just received her degree from the University of North Carolina. She began work in late June and by December had organized 19 new chapters of the alumnae association.[132]

## "SLIPPING BACK"

When Warren Way went to St. Mary's as rector in 1918, the trustees believed that he was the man to complete the fund drive started in 1916. Everyone felt sure that the money was in the hands of Episcopalians and that it would be forthcoming as soon as the war was over. No one, however, realized how serious the postwar inflation would become, and certainly no one expected a deep depression.

Inflation was causing problems in the operation of the school as early as October, 1919, when Ernest Cruikshank reported the necessity for raising the charges for resident students above $450 in order to meet expenses; the budget could be pared no further. "We are providing better board," he said, "than $450 pays for."[133] Charges were raised to $550 for the 1920–1921 session. The auditor's report at the end of the 1923–1924 academic year revealed that the actual cost to the institution of each resident student had increased from $584.90 for 1920–1921 to $684.38 for 1922–1923 while the charges remained at $550. Finally, charges were raised to $600 for the 1925–1926 session. The increased extra fees for music ranged from $80 to $100, for art from $50 to $75, and for domestic science from $20 to $30; the fee for private expression lessons was $60. The new business manager, A. W. Tucker, who took office in the summer of 1921, had been a member of Way's church in Salisbury. A graduate of Massachusetts Institute of Technology, he went south to work as a mining engineer. The Tucker family lived on campus in "the cottage" built for the Cruikshanks.

The lower preparatory department was suspended in 1919 because it needed, as the rector told the trustees, three teachers "to do the work well." The fees, since all were day students, would support only two.[134]

The upkeep of the buildings was a constantly escalating expense. During the summer of 1928 the art building, the study hall, and the parlor were refurbished. The frame house known as senior hall had never seemed to the rector "a proper place for young ladies to live." He said that St. Mary's was "steadily and not slowly slipping back" while other schools in the vicinity were moving forward. He felt that the enrollment could be increased by 100 when a modern dormitory was built.[135] Although Holt Hall was erected in 1928, enrollment remained about the same until it plummeted in 1931–1932.

The campaign in the Carolinas provided $185,000, and several generous donors gave most of the remaining $15,000 of the North Carolina quota. The Diocese of South Carolina placed in its budget $30,000 for the St. Mary's fund.[136] Thus, in November, 1922, the trustees were able to liquidate the $40,000 debt incurred in the major building program of 1909 when the wings were added to Smedes Hall. That was a great relief to the rector, who declared, "The perpetual motto at St. Mary's had been 'the debt must be paid!'"[137] The drive to raise the remaining $100,000 shifted into high gear the next month with all the trappings of a professional canvass. Alumnae and friends worked faithfully; the senior class of 1923 earned $600 to contribute. Then came what Bishop Cheshire called "the magnificent gift" of $25,000 by B. N. Duke, who wrote that he made the gift of 250 shares of Duke Power Company stock out of friendship for W. A. Erwin.[138]

By June, 1926, only $42,000 of the $100,000 had been raised, including the Duke gift. (The fact that the seven-year nationwide campaign of the Protestant Episcopal church occurred simultaneously may have affected adversely the St. Mary's campaign.) By June, 1927, the trustees of the school were unhappy with the responses of the five controlling dioceses. The rector remarked at the board meeting that Episcopalians seemed to expect St. Mary's to offer "a very superior brand of education in a superior environment and to do it below cost." Over 70 percent of the student body continued to be Episcopalians. The trustees passed unanimously a resolution "that the five dioceses be formally petitioned to make some appropriation annually towards the payment of the current expenses of the school."[139] Appropriations were made; the Diocese of North Carolina pledged the substantial sum of $3,000 annually in addition to its gifts to the endowment. However, by December, 1930, the dioceses were $6,860 in arrears in their pledges since 1928. When the Diocese of North Carolina asked the executive committee of the St. Mary's board if its pledge were "absolutely necessary" to the school, the answer was a resounding "Yes!" By then every dollar was "absolutely necessary."[140]

Bishop Cheshire was deeply disappointed by the turn of economic events. He had repeatedly said that keeping St. Mary's in operation had been "his most important work." Although he rightly insisted that he had "no authority whatsoever" in the internal discipline of the school, his influence was felt in the daily life, for he "counted it a privilege to live within sight and sound of the school."[141] In 1922 Cheshire asked for assistance in administering his diocese, and the convention elected as bishop coadjutor the Reverend Edwin Anderson Penick, then rector of St. Peter's Church, Charlotte. Bishop Penick was consecrated on October 15, 1922, which was the 29th anniversary of Bishop Cheshire's consecration. The two men worked well together in mutual respect and affection, although they did not always find themselves in mutual agreement on policy.[142] Gradually Cheshire gave more and more responsibility to his assistant. At the opening chapel service of the 1927–1928 academic year at St. Mary's Bishop Cheshire reviewed the school's history and then announced that he was turning over the chairmanship of the board of trustees to Bishop Penick. Cheshire had been chairman of the board since the school's incorporation in 1897.[143]

On Bishop Cheshire's 80th birthday (March 27, 1930), St. Mary's honored him with a reception attended by over 400 persons from all over North Carolina, and a year later, on April 9, 1931, he was honored again at the presentation of the life-size portrait, a striking likeness, that hangs in the college parlor.[144] He died on December 27, 1932, having served longer than any other bishop of the Diocese of North Carolina. The science building on the St. Mary's campus was named in his honor.

During the Way administration the board of trustees lost by death several faithful members of long service—R. H. Battle in 1922, Charles E. Johnson in 1923, W. A. Hoke in 1925, and W. A. Erwin in 1932.

By the winter of 1930–1931 the rector realized that the school was in crisis. Operating expenses ran high, but the board feared the consequences of raising tuition above $650. For several years the business manager had borrowed for operating expenses and summer repairs more than could be repaid from current revenues, and Tucker estimated that it would be necessary to borrow $36,000 in order to operate until the collection of registration fees in the fall of 1931.[145] New buildings and improvements—the swimming pool, the enlarged infirmary, and Holt Hall—had added substantially to operating expenses. The permanent scholarships, whose endowments had long been spent for buildings, continued to cost the school about $2,400 per annum. Payments on pledges to the fund drive fell behind as economic conditions worsened. The number of boarders passed the 200 mark for the first time in 1919, then dropped to 183 and 190 for the next two years.

The banner year of 1926–1927 saw 215 boarders enrolled, but after that resident enrollment stayed below 190. When only 173 boarders and 52 day students enrolled for 1930–1931, it became obvious that the situation was critical. Furthermore, the instability was accentuated, as it had been for several years, by a number of withdrawals at the end of first semester. A few students were helped by two new loan funds.[146]

At the meeting of the trustees in October, 1931, the business manager predicted an operating deficit of $20,000 for 1931–1932; a loan of almost $35,000 had already been spent to operate during the previous year. The trustees finally resolved that if "the dangerous deficit" were "still anticipated" after expenses had been "cut to the bone," the executive committee of the board should call together the officers and teachers of the school, explain the precarious situation, and "ask them to accept such a cut in salary as may be necessary, not however to exceed fifteen percent of the present cash salary." [147]

The executive committee delayed taking such drastic action. Way felt that the majority of the faculty would acquiesce but that morale would suffer. He entertained grave misgivings regarding that solution to the financial crisis, for he regarded the salary agreements for that year as a moral commitment, and he disliked the pressure for voluntary reductions. Finally, on November 5, 1931, the executive committee met with the faculty and staff and asked each to take a voluntary salary cut of 15 percent; each one was to give a confidential response in writing. Fourteen persons accepted the cut and 13 did not. Most of those who refused explained that they did so not from lack of loyalty to the institution, but for their own rather desperate personal financial reasons. Furthermore, many felt that the board's treatment of the faculty had habitually been "parsimonious" at best. [148]

The obvious alternatives were a drastic cutback in faculty and staff in view of the low enrollment or more borrowing against the college property. Erwin, who was not in favor of a mortgage, estimated that the property was worth "about a million in ordinary times." [149] The executive committee failed in its effort to raise $50,000 "in a quiet way before Christmas." When in January, 1932, Tucker estimated that $45,000 more than was "in sight" would be needed in order to operate until June, the trustees authorized an $80,000 loan that was arranged in New York. [150]

The rector had submitted his resignation to Bishop Penick immediately after the salary crisis of November, 1931, to take effect at the end of the academic year, but he was persuaded to reconsider. Penick in a long letter to Cheshire wrote that he considered Way more competent to meet the crisis than anyone else he knew and that as a respected educator, Way lent strength to St. Mary's. Also, Penick feared (and rightly so) that the hope of making St. Mary's a four-year college would end if Way left. On the other hand, he was aware of "considerable adverse feeling" against the rector. But since it seemed to stem from Way's arbitrary enforcement of the rules, Penick was inclined to defend him because he felt that lax enforcement would have been detrimental to the school. [151]

When the trustees ordered for 1932–1933 a balanced budget based on a projected enrollment of 125 students, Way requested again that his resignation be accepted. The announcement of his leaving was made in March after Margaret Jones Cruikshank had been elected to head her alma mater.

Way went from Raleigh to the parish of St. James in Atlantic City, New Jersey, where he served as rector for ten years. He and his wife left behind many friends in North Carolina, for both had been active in wider circles than the college, she in Episcopal women's work and he as chairman of the board of examining chaplains and as a member of the board of religious education of the Diocese of North Carolina. Way was well known also among professional educators, having served as president of the Southern Federation of Episcopal Educational Institutions and as vice-president of the American Association of Junior Colleges.

Warren Wade Way was rector of St. Mary's for 14 years, making his the longest administration since that of Bennett Smedes. In June, 1932, Hobart College honored him by bestowing his second honorary degree, the LL.D. The Ways retired in Tryon, where he died a year later on June 11, 1943, at the age of 73.[152]

# "A VERY GREAT LADY"

Margaret Jones Cruikshank, one of the institutions's most devoted daughters, went to St. Mary's to head the school with the full knowledge that she was to take charge of a school in crisis. The nominating committee appointed by the trustees had been instructed by the executive committee of the board to consider a woman.[1] But it was not they who showed courage in selecting Margaret Cruikshank. It was she who displayed courage in accepting. For St. Mary's had a projected enrollment for 1932–1933 of only 125 and a deeply slashed budget; a new administration would be enforcing controversial decisions already made. The nation was in economic crisis, also. It was not a good year to become a college administrator.

Margaret Cruikshank was not, however, a woman afraid to face hard decisions. After the death of her husband, she ran Columbia Institute and taught several subjects while rearing her three children. Ernest Cruikshank had hoped to enlarge and strengthen Columbia when he went there as president a year before his death. His wife saw it fall victim to the Depression.[2]

Margaret Mordecai Jones and her fraternal twin sister, Mary Pride, were born in October, 1878, in Hillsborough, the daughters of Halcott Pride and Olive Echols Jones, both of whom had numerous connections with prominent North Carolina families.[3] The sisters attended the excellent school in Hillsborough run by the Misses Nash and Miss Kollock. Their mother died when they were 13 and their father soon thereafter. In 1893 they were sent to St. Mary's,[4] where Margaret was to spend more years of her life than at any other place.

After graduation Margaret spent a year in Alabama with an older

Margaret Jones Cruikshank, president, 1932–1946

brother and then returned at 18 to teach mathematics at her alma mater. During 1901–1902 Margaret, on leave of absence, was one of those early coeds at Chapel Hill. She later had two additional leaves of absence to study at Columbia University, where she earned her B.S. degree. During her last leave she also taught at a girls' school and spent some months in Europe. Between the time of her marriage in 1911 and 1921 she did not teach regularly but could be counted on "to fill in" whenever necessary no matter how busy she was with the babies.[5]

Just after Margaret Cruikshank was elected to head St. Mary's, Bishop Cheshire wrote her a letter that reveals why she was such an excellent choice for the formidable task ahead. The fact that the letter is marked "unsent" indicates that the bishop must have remembered that he was no longer chairman of the board of trustees, albeit still a member. He wrote:

My Dear Margaret,

The Board of Trustees . . . today elected you as head of the School to have the same authority and function, except the duties of Chaplain and Pastor, which the Rector has exercised. . . .

The trustees were so engrossed with the important matter of choosing a head for the School that no one thought of the question of salary which I really think is creditable both to *you* and to us. . . . I can only say that we determined upon a general reduction of fifteen percent in all salaries. . . .

Hereafter the teachers will be appointed by the Board upon your nomination. You may depend upon a cordial and sympathetic . . . support should you come to us. We have no conceit of our own wisdom . . . in managing a school.

Dr. Way commanded our very high regard and his resignation has no kind of ill feeling connected with it. It was really that we might have a free hand in making necessary readjustments in providing for somewhat reduced expenses.[6]

Alumnae, especially those who had adored Ernest Cruikshank, rejoiced that Margaret Cruikshank had returned. Somehow everything fell into place under her; everyone accepted her decisions because everyone knew that her devotion to St. Mary's was complete. To the credit of the trustees, they paid a woman the salary Way would have received. The board had made the "necessary readjustments" in personnel by dropping the equivalent of five or six full-time positions, thus saving over $11,000. Furthermore, the positions of academic head and dean of students were merged. Margaret Cruikshank elected to take upon herself both jobs because there would be the expense of a chaplain-teacher under the first lay head of the institution. At first she was called the "principal," but in 1936 the title of "president" became official, making her the first to bear that title.

Margaret Cruikshank decided that the assistance she most needed in her triple role was that of Elizabeth Tucker, who for seven years had been her secretary and had also taught in the business department at

Columbia Institute. The board agreed, and so Elizabeth Gordon Tucker, a St. Mary's graduate of 1921, also joined the staff in 1932.[7] She remained 36 years, rendering invaluable assistance throughout almost the entire span of two administrations.

Margaret Cruikshank's method of administration was unobtrusive, and she was a very private person who seems to have wrestled alone with administrative problems. Her decision, once made, was usually impartial and always enforced; but her manner of speaking seemed inconclusive. There was a hesitancy in her speech, a slight pause for breath between phrases, and her sentences seemed to end with question marks.[8] Margaret Cruikshank was a decisive administrator without creating a great deal of opposition because she understood thoroughly the constituent groups with which she dealt—parents, alumnae, faculty, students.

One of "the necessary readjustments" resulted in a smaller and more intimate campus community. For several years West Rock was not used as a dormitory, and the top floor of each of the other buildings, except Holt, was closed. For several reasons the institution was able to stay open with a total enrollment of only 164 in 1932–1933 and of approximately 170 the next year. All of the school's debts were consolidated under the $80,000 loan, which, with frugal management, was being carried successfully. Furthermore, a $20,000 legacy was received after the death of William Allen Erwin. Erwin was a trustee from the incorporation of the school and a faithful and hardworking member of the executive committee of the board for 25 years.[9]

## "NOT A FINISHING SCHOOL"

Margaret Cruikshank was determined that there should be no lowering of academic standards. She met the problem of enlarging the enrollment without endangering standards by employing the best teachers who could be persuaded to join the faculty for the salaries offered; and, as usual, some were found who were willing to take a cut. Dedicated teachers spent time giving additional help to students who were willing to work to overcome deficiencies in their educational backgrounds. As academic head of the school, the president kept up with each student's progress. She signed every report card, sometimes adding a comment like, "Good report." Being as forthright in her appraisal of students' capabilities as she was forthright in other matters, she sometimes wrote to parents, "I would advise you not to send your daughter here next year. Furthermore, it would be a waste of money to send her anywhere." When the problem was what she called "an appalling lack of knowledge" because of poor training elsewhere, Margaret Cruikshank was willing to spend hours tutoring. She would say to a weak student, "Come by my office, and I will help you."[10] In her 1941 report to the board of trustees she said, "Preparation of students seems increasingly poor, with the result that many girls are able to make mediocre records only for their first year here. They usually make notable improvement their next year, and are able to graduate creditably."

Margaret Cruikshank kept an eye upon faculty performance, too. Although she refrained from forcing her opinion in small matters upon teachers, she handled major problems with dispatch. Sometimes, after due warning in writing, faculty contracts were not renewed. She did not supervise classroom teaching, for her philosophy was that there was room for all approaches so long as the students learned. She was quick to uphold the faculty, except in that rare case where she found upon investigation that a student had grounds for claiming unjust treatment. In such cases, she talked with everyone concerned and arranged a solution. When parents complained that teachers were "too hard," the president of St. Mary's always defended academic standards. After a session with her, parents were more likely to depart with expressions of appreciation than in anger.[11]

Margaret Cruikshank's own commitment to scholarship was lifelong; at 59 she completed a master's degree in history at Duke University. During her administration the St. Mary's catalog carried the following statement of educational policy: "St. Mary's is not 'a finishing school.' It expects the student to learn to think independently, to discriminate, and to reason clearly. Learning any or all of these involves hard work."[12] The students realized that their diplomas would not automatically be forthcoming. Sage advice from upperclassmates with regard to good study habits often went unheeded, especially during the first semester, and cramming for tests became frantic. Yet, as Margaret Cruikshank told the board, the majority of the students eventually did learn to study and made creditable records at the institutions to which they transferred.

More St. Mary's graduates were continuing their education at universities and colleges for women outside the South than in earlier years. During 1932–1933 St. Mary's women were continuing their work at North Carolina State, at Duke, at the Universities of Florida, Georgia, and Delaware, at Northwestern, and at Rice Institute. The majority, however, chose Woman's College in Greensboro (now the University of North Carolina at Greensboro), Chapel Hill, or one of the small southern colleges for women. Woman's College was more popular than Chapel Hill in the late 1930s, but during the war years one third to one half of each St. Mary's graduating class moved en masse to Chapel Hill. The trend continued after the war, despite the return of veterans clamoring for places, because St. Mary's graduates were known to be well prepared for the university.[13]

Few major revisions in the curriculum were made during the Cruikshank administration. Margaret Cruikshank was not a great innovator; besides, neither the times nor St. Mary's situation as a junior college called for innovation. Therefore, the curriculum was broadened and enriched just enough to keep it in proper alignment with the required courses of the freshman and sophomore years at senior colleges. Geography and American government were added as electives, and a second semester of psychology replaced the course in logic. Economics and sociology had been included in the curriculum during the Way administration. The social sciences, not generally accepted as academic disciplines until the twentieth century,[14] appealed to the idealists who hoped to find solutions to society's problems.

Other curriculum changes of the Cruikshank years included the addition of a course in physics. In 1936 the Southern Association of Colleges and Secondary Schools had warned St. Mary's that the science laboratory equipment was "insufficient."[15] That situation was remedied when the science department received in 1941 a legacy of $4,000 from the estate of Florence Slater, former science teacher. Also added to the curriculum were advanced courses in Spanish. A rigorous Latin course was pursued in the college. However, the most advanced course offered in mathematics was analytical geometry.

The trustees voted in 1933 to grant a high school diploma (in place of the traditional certification that a student was ready for admission to the freshman class of college) to those students who had satisfactorily completed 16 units of college preparatory work, who were considered by the faculty "to be properly qualified in general," and who had been at St. Mary's for at least one full academic year. Students were strongly encouraged to stay for four years; the catalog suggested that advanced high school seniors could "occupy their spare time profitably in one or more classes of the college." Also there were many choices in the fine arts. By the 1930s the trustees wished to drop the ninth and tenth grades; they reconsidered, however, when the Raleigh alumnae objected. The ninth grade was eliminated in 1937–1938, but a small tenth-grade class, called the sub-freshmen, was retained throughout the Cruikshank administration.

Class attendance rules were still strict, and beginning in 1934–1935 college classes met on Saturday mornings despite the fact that Saturday, not Monday, was the "day off." Holidays were not extensive—one day at Thanksgiving, two weeks at Christmas, one week in March. As had been the tradition since the founding of the school, everyone remained over Easter for the beautiful special services. A few weekends away from campus were allowed with written permission from parents and written invitations from hostesses. "Extended weekends" involving class cuts were possible under a complicated system that took into account the student's grades. Many weekends, especially those before examination periods, were "closed," and all students remained in Raleigh. A student who "overstayed" her absence permission risked being asked "to terminate her connection with the school." About 1940 a strong academic standards committee was added to the standing committees of the faculty.[16] With faculty approval that committee instituted plans for broadening the educational background of the graduates with a program of required "summer reading" for rising seniors. The requirement remained in effect for over 25 years.

Strengthening of the academic background of the faculty continued. By the 1930s most of the faculty held master's degrees, a number had taken work toward the doctorate, and one had a Ph.D. The trustees were always willing to grant leave (without pay) for further study.

A major accomplishment of the Cruikshank administration was the improvement of the library, which remained located on the first floor of the art building. The cataloging begun by Ernest Cruikshank during the summer of 1906 often was not completely up to date because until 1927 the various librarians were part time and untrained. Basic books in each field were available, although often tattered; but the library budget, which was only $330 as late as 1933, never provided enough recent books to meet the needs of the serious students.[17] It was a joy to Margaret Cruikshank to have Ann Strudwick Nash continue her work as librarian at St. Mary's during five years of her presidency, for they had been childhood friends.

The St. Mary's library collection was augmented by four major gifts during the Cruikshank administration. At commencement in 1934 a gift of $500 for the purchase of books was presented as a memorial to Emilie Watts McVea by her classmates of 1884 and others.[18] Over 1,200 books arrived in November of 1934, left to the school by Louise Floyd Wickham. She had known St. Mary's through Mrs. Bancker Smedes, an assistant in the school she operated in New York City. She also knew Florence Slater and Elizabeth Dancy Battle and often visited St. Mary's, where she was confirmed in the chapel. The Wickham collection was given in memory of Elizabeth Dancy Battle, St. Mary's alumna, teacher, and assistant to Bennett Smedes.[19] By June, 1935, the Wickham books were cataloged; the total number of volumes in the St. Mary's library then numbered 6,150, and the facilities and staff were sorely overtaxed. A few books were placed in reading rooms in dormitories and in the infirmary, and on warm days the open air reading room under the trees south of the library building was popular. Library fines provided the lawn furniture.[20]

In June, 1937, St. Mary's was awarded a grant of $4,500 from the Carnegie Corporation to be used for the purchase of library books. Gaps in the collection were filled, and valuable reference sets were acquired. It was gratifying to be recognized as one of only four junior colleges in North Carolina to merit one of the 92 grants awarded that year. The grant was also a recognition of the valiant service of Ann Nash as librarian.[21] A fourth gift went to the St. Mary's library in 1940 upon the death of William H. Jones. Most of the 700 volumes received from his estate were works on music or travel.

Ann Nash retired to Chapel Hill in 1938. The year before her retirement, she announced that her new assistant, Helen Abel Brown, who had moved south because her librarian husband had joined the staff at North Carolina State, was "a real treasure." And Helen Brown proved to be just that as head librarian at St. Mary's for the next 33 years. The library had burst its seams by the spring of 1938. More than 1,600 volumes were housed elsewhere on campus, and the seating capacity of the library could accommodate only 13 percent of the students. The trustees voted to make the erection of a new library the first project to be financed by the centennial fund; the building was to be a memorial to Bishop Cheshire.[22] The centennial fund became a reality, but there was never enough money to build the library; the 1939 remodeling, which everyone hoped would be a temporary expedient, served for a quarter of a century. Walls were removed to incorporate two classrooms, thus more than doubling the floor space and expanding the seating capacity from 38 to 70.[23]

From the first years of her presidency Margaret Cruikshank favored dropping the traditional extra fees for courses in the fine arts. The board was divided on "the new plan" because it would mean the loss of about $8,000 in fees,[24] but in 1937 Cruikshank persuaded the trustees to try her plan. Enrollment in fine arts tripled, necessitating the employment of part-time teachers. Students and parents were pleased with the policy. The policy remained in effect until the 1970s when the financial exigencies caused it to be abandoned.

A music building, the low clapboard structure in use over 40 years later, was built during the summer of 1937 on the site of the old hockey field. Into his new studio the chairman of the music department, William H. Jones, moved his music, his books, and his World War posters brought from France. Jones had gone to St. Mary's in 1919 directly from a YMCA assignment overseas. Educated at Trinity College (Duke) and in Berlin, he had spent nearly 20 years in Norfolk as organist and choirmaster in three different churches. A North Carolinian, he was born in Warrenton but grew up in Greensboro, where his father, the Reverend Turner M. Jones, was president of Greensboro Female College.[25] William H. Jones was known in Raleigh for his organ recitals. He directed Raleigh's Saint Cecilia Choral Society, and he founded and directed the Raleigh Male Chorus. The men rehearsed at St. Mary's and sometimes gave their concerts in the school auditorium. Jones also was organist and choirmaster at Christ Church in Raleigh.

For 21 years Will Jones was very much a part of the daily life of the school. An affable and witty bachelor, he spent his summers in Europe. Because he was an inveterate smoker, the girls tried to enlist his aid in their drive to obtain smoking privileges on campus. His reply was, "Putting a cigarette in a woman's mouth is like putting mud on a lily."[26] On the other hand, it was Jones who during his first years at St. Mary's had managed to get permission for the girls to wear trousers—under certain conditions. When the students chose H.M.S. Pinafore as the annual operetta, Jones refused to have the Pinafore's crew in skirts. One of the cast saved the day by managing to secure an authentic navy uniform to be used as a pattern.[27] Jones was still teaching at St. Mary's when he died at 69 in February, 1940, of a heart attack.[28]

The Cruikshank policy of not charging extra fees increased interest in music. Some years, over one third of the students were taking music lessons. Attendance at concerts on campus was required, and evening dresses were worn. There was grumbling because study hours had to be made up in the afternoon, but mostly the girls were appreciative, especially of the faculty recitals. They thought that Mary Ruth Haig, who arrived in 1937 to teach piano, "should be on the concert stage."[29] The St. Mary's students felt the same way about her playing when she retired 41 years later. Russell Broughton, a Fellow of the American Guild of Organists and a composer, arrived in 1940 to head the music department. That same year Geraldine Spinks Cate joined the music faculty to teach voice and to direct the choral groups. In 1944 Donald Peery, who had taught piano at St. Mary's 1940–1941, rejoined the department following a period of military service. That strong group worked together for 35 years, contributing immeasurably to the school and to the community.

St. Mary's students attended many cultural events available in Raleigh. The school held a block of tickets to the Civic Music Association's concerts, and the students were required to attend. They were given a lecture-demonstration in assembly to enhance their appreciation before they heard the artists—Flagstad, Rubinstein, Pons, Lehmann, Melchior, Rachmaninoff. No one complained about having to go to hear Nelson Eddy in 1937. Enterprising reporters for the Belles joined the rest of the press and obtained interviews with celebrities, sometimes being photographed with them.

Interest in dramatics had been high ever since Florence C. Davis began teaching "elocution and physical culture." The removal of the extra

Music faculty: Russell Broughton, Mary Ruth Haig, Donald Peery, and Geraldine Cate, with Beverly Gilliam at the piano

fees increased enrollment to the point that some of her lectures had to be delivered to all sections at once, sometimes at night, in the auditorium. President Cruikshank backed Davis in her determination to teach academically sound, full-credit courses. Requirements for the certificate in speech and theatre arts were stiff and were in addition to the required courses in English, history, mathematics, and a foreign language. All students in the school were required to take a noncredit speech course for as many weeks as were necessary for each to acquire a certain facility in public speaking and reading.

The commencement play was always a Shakespearean production attended by many visitors. Early in her career at St. Mary's the director solved the problem of the "no trousers for women" custom by presenting only Shakespeare at commencement. High boots worn over tights gave a proper Elizabethan effect without offending anyone. The Dramatic Club's 1934 production of *Little Women* had the student audience in tears, despite the fact that the male parts were played by St. Mary's girls.[30] That was the year that Florence Davis began to take her plays to the Carolina Dramatic Association's state tournament at Chapel Hill. The St. Mary's production of Moliere's *Les precieuses ridicules* won the plaque for the best presentation of a one-act play by a junior college. The exuberant cast upon their return to the campus went straight to Margaret Cruikshank's house, although it was long past midnight, and awakened her to share the news.[31] Nine times St. Mary's won in the tournament.[32]

"Stardom" was not in Davis's vocabulary. Everyone who was interested enough to try out for the dramatic club made it, and each participated in some phase of the production of a play. Although she taught at St. Mary's for 46 years, she never let herself grow stale. Many summers were spent in studying and seeing plays, and she would return in the fall "erupting with new ideas."[33]

Florence Davis wanted her drama students to see as many plays as possible. For years they had season tickets to the productions of the Carolina Playmakers, and they saw productions of professional companies that visited Raleigh. When, in 1933, 40 girls saw the original cast in *The Green Pastures*, they reported that they were "impressed and moved" by the play.[34] It was Florence Davis, too, who saw to it that someone presented on the St. Mary's concert-lecture series each year was of especial interest to her students. The whole town was interested in Edna St. Vincent Millay's appearance to read her own poems in 1938, and people were turned away from the overflowing auditorium.[35] During the Cruikshank regime Davis performed many of the duties of a dean of students, and she was strict in the enforcement of the letter of the law. The girls who did not work with her in dramatics were apt to refer to her as "Flossie" and to consider her idiosyncrasies fascinating, but they knew she had their best interests at heart.[36]

The number of art students in Caroline Harris's art classes jumped from 18 the year before to 47 in 1937–1938 as a result of the abolition of the extra fees. A graduate of H. Sophie Newcomb Memorial College, she had taught with Margaret Cruikshank at Columbia Institute and then at Huntington College before moving to St. Mary's in 1934. Four of her students won awards in 1939 in the North Carolina School Art Exhibition.[37]

The faculty under Margaret Cruikshank's presidency consisted (as had been the case throughout St. Mary's history) of a mixture of well-trained, but quite individualistic, persons. There were those whose major contribution was excellent teaching, those whose influence was most felt in extracurricular activities, and those known as "characters," who added a dash of spice.[38]

For 22 years (1935–1957), Charles Albert Petigru Moore *was* senior English at St. Mary's. The reading assignments were horrendous (if one read all of them), but the class hours were fascinating. Moore held forth from an easy chair surrounded by hundreds of books in his west wing classroom-office that had been Will Jones's studio before the music building was erected. Moore's lectures were unstructured and strewn with stimulating ideas. He urged the girls to read, read, read— for the sake of learning, not just for grades. The grades were usually weeks late in forthcoming, for Moore was inclined to take on responsibility for too many extracurricular activities. He was undeniably charismatic; a slight limp, the result of a childhood bout with polio, only made him the more interesting to the girls, as did his courtly manner. His two daughters attended St. Mary's when they were older. C. A. P. Moore had taught at The Citadel and was head of the English department at Rutherford College before heading the St. Mary's department. His bachelor's and master's degrees were from the University of North Carolina. During his tenure at St. Mary's he studied at Yale while on a leave of absence.[39]

The high school students were held as spellbound by Nell Battle Lewis as were the college students by Al Moore. During most semesters from 1937 through 1944 she taught high school sections of English or Bible or history. A solidly built woman, she would stride briskly into the classroom, briefcase in hand, and arrange her papers. Then leaning back in her chair, she would say, "Now girls, catch these pearls from my lips. You can think what you want to think, but on tests you had better give back to me what I tell you."[40] Strange words from the lips of that firebrand crusader who, by then, was so conservative that in 1939 Josephus Daniels wrote to her: "Once I gave you advice not to be too radical. Now I give you the advice not to be too conservative."[41] By the late 1930s she was crusading for a return to the old virtues. She had planned to teach at her alma mater temporarily, being much involved with her many other interests—peace movements, the State Historical Commission, the League of Women Voters. She was intrigued by psychic phenomena and by folklore; she painted; she built model ships; she read detective stories. All the while she was producing her weekly column, writing for national magazines, working on two novels and on a book about the parables of Jesus.[42] Nell Battle Lewis found that she loved the position of "old maid school marm," although she had thought it would be "the last on earth" for her and although she called it "the hardest sort of work because you have to put out so much."[43] She once remarked, "How I wish Mama and Daddy could see me now, a *teacher* at St. Mary's!"[44] Her students, nonetheless, considered her quite avant-garde, probably because she was so forthright. They recognized a deep spirituality within their unconventional Bible teacher and remembered her lectures as "an exciting approach to the word of God."[45] Lewis could be difficult to live with. She absolutely refused to teach grammar in her English course, thereby causing that department to hold its meetings at times when she could not be present. After she left St. Mary's in 1944, she continued to write her *News and Observer* column and to work for her many causes. She died suddenly; her newsboy discovered her early one November morning in 1956 fallen outside her home on St. Mary's Street, the victim of an apparent heart attack the night before.[46]

Mary Helen Dodd, who taught physics, chemistry, and German, 1932–1944, was also considered a "character." She had completed the resident work for the Ph.D. degree at Columbia and had taught at the Emma Willard School. Some days she decided that the science class was caught up but that the German class was behind and used the chemistry lecture hour to teach German to some who were not taking German. She organized an active German club; the Deutscher Verein studied German music and ate authentic German cakes at the Sunday night meetings. She was in her mid-thirties when she went to St. Mary's, but the girls thought that she was years older because her clothes and hairstyle were of a bygone era. She ruled her dormitory with an iron hand, leaving a trail of little notes reprimanding the girls for minor inadequacies. Helen Dodd died unexpectedly during the summer of 1944.[47]

Marjorie J. Lalor, the Goucher graduate who taught biology and hygiene, 1929–1945, was considered a bit of a free thinker because she regularly voted for Norman Thomas. She felt it her duty to educate the faculty by reading aloud certain items from the newspaper to those gathered in the faculty sitting room on the first floor of East Rock. In class she was methodical and concise. She tended a wildflower garden near the recreation hut on back campus.[48]

There were the less unconventional pedagogues, several of whom stayed long enough to leave permanent imprints upon the institution. In 1937 Martha Dabney Jones, St. Mary's graduate of 1926, returned to teach English. After being graduated from Sweet Briar she had taken her master's degree at the University of North Carolina and further work at the University of Virginia. Her keen intelligence and lively sense of humor made her an interesting as well as a strong teacher.

For 20 years, 1936–1956, Watson Kasey Partrick taught Latin and Bible. She had headed the mathematics department and taught Latin at Salem College after being graduated from the University of North Carolina. Her husband, the Reverend Theodore Partrick, Jr., was rector of the Church of the Good Shepherd in Raleigh, and she remained active in church work after she was widowed and resumed her teaching career. Her Bible course was considered difficult but stimulating. Her students, 20 years after their St. Mary's days, found that the best approach to leading a Bible study for the Episcopal Church Women was "to dig out Mrs. Partrick's notes."[49]

In 1936 Lizzie Lee retired as head of the business department,[50] and four years later Juliet Sutton retired. Both had been "institutions" at St. Mary's and the last direct links to Bennett Smedes's administration.[51]

Just as the music department generated interest in concerts and recording, so other classes spawned academically oriented extracurricular activities. The literary societies, although still active, were not so important a part of student life as they had been in past years. In 1933 E. A. P. studied the modern novelists—Galsworthy, Glasgow, Cather, Conrad. Sigma Lambda that year studied the Little Theater movement, attended the state dramatic festival, and presented a one-act play at St. Mary's. The next year Sigma Lambda studied the cinema, and E. A. P. studied contemporary poetry. By 1937 the literary societies were engaging in creative writing and criticizing one another's work as they had in earlier years. The competition for the literary society cup was renewed, and the year ended with a formal banquet at the Sir Walter Hotel where the winning poems, essays, and short stories were read. Al Moore's poetry reading half hour on Sunday nights was a popular feature of campus life.[52]

The first issue of the campus newspaper, the *Belles of St. Mary's*, made its appearance on September 30, 1937, under the editorship of Louise Jordan. A staff of 18 advised by Moore got out a semimonthly so creditable that St. Mary's was accepted immediately for membership in the North Carolina Collegiate Press Association. At first the *Belles* was notebook size and printed in two wide columns; two years later it was enlarged to a four-column tabloid. The paper during its first five years of existence missed its publication date only three times.[53]

Under Moore's editorial direction the *Muse* became the *Saint Mary's School Bulletin*. The spelling of the school's name, "Saint Mary's," which had come into general use under the Way administration, was retained. In 1938 the *Stagecoach* won first place in its classification (schools with an enrollment under 1,000) at the North Carolina Collegiate Press Association meeting. The three school publications, although diverse in content, all sought "to mirror a picture of the school for the students of yesterday, today, and tomorrow."[54] The traditional name, the *Muse*, disappeared until the next administration separated the literary magazine from the alumnae publication.

William C. Guess of the social science department was adviser to an active political science club. Affectionately known as Willie, Guess enjoyed participating in school activities. St. Mary's sent a contingent of eight to the first N.C. Student Legislature, November 12–13, 1937.[55]

The columns of the *Belles* during the late 1930s reveal an increasing interest in world affairs and an increasing apprehension concerning the future on the part of the student writers. Doubtless that was the result to a great degree of the radio news broadcasts. Margaret Cruikshank managed to budget funds to provide annual lectures on world affairs. The most intriguing of a series of speakers on the USSR was Countess Tolstoi, daughter of the author of *War and Peace*.[56] The editorial in the *Belles* of September 30, 1938, was headed "Men on the March" and concluded, "And our hands are tied. We can but pray for the Munich Conference!" Passing references in the college publications show that there was discussion of world affairs in almost every class. "Credo, A.D. 1940," written by two students and published in the *Bulletin* of November, 1940, began, "We feel that our lives in many ways parallel those of the girls of 1916." It continued:

We look into uncertainty. . . . . We have emerged as young citizens in the greatest democracy in the world, only to find that our responsibility is to keep it from crumbling about our ears. . . . We believe that democracy can and should work better. We believe in a patriotism of quiet endeavor and self-sacrifice. . . . If we have to face a war, we believe that we shall be prepared to win it. . . . women today are free to enter any field of endeavor. Before us is a new way of life.[57]

Most St. Mary's girls did not think such thoughts. As late as the week of Pearl Harbor, one wrote of her typical schoolmate that she read the paper by first checking "Terry and the Pirates" and then "the big headlines," that she listened to the news only "if the radio happened to be on," and that she listened more or less attentively to the current events programs in assembly.[58] Life changed quite suddenly on that Sunday afternoon of December 7, 1941, when at vespers Chaplain Henry Felix Kloman quietly announced the Pearl Harbor attack. As the students realized that brothers and sweethearts in uniform would be in a war instead of training for a possible war, the tears flowed. The Young People's Service League had scheduled for that evening a speaker known to be a pacifist, and the girls found themselves actually booing and then were shocked that they could have done such a thing.[59] Margaret Cruikshank took the position that the best way students could serve their country was by doing their best at their presently assigned job, which was school, thus preparing themselves for greater service in the future. In that spirit, the editors of the *Belles* in the issue of December 12, 1941, wrote:

We are engaged in a war that can have but one outcome—victory for the United States and her allies. All our efforts must be directed toward that end. Without hysteria, without complaint, and without loss of time, each must find his place and take it. No matter how small the task seems now, in the end it will have counted toward the final victory.

President Cruikshank reported to the trustees at the beginning of the 1942–1943 session that the students exhibited "a somewhat more serious attitude toward work in general and a readiness to get down to routine promptly," and by 1945 she observed the best academic work she had seen during her tenure.[60]

## "WE HAVE LOTS OF FUN"

Until World War II, the daily life of the campus community followed the usual St. Mary's pattern. The rules were strict for the times, and the girls grumbled about "being in jail"; but they admitted, "We have lots of fun." The sports program provided daily recreation. Physical education on two days a week was required of all. On the other days, each student was honor bound, as students had been since the opening of the school in 1842, to take an hour of exercise. Consequently, there was much late afternoon sports activity on campus. The Sigmas and the Mus organized teams in the major sports—basketball, volleyball, field hockey, tennis, and swimming—and kept records for the cup competition and for individual letters. A new playing field was made on the unworked old garden area north of Clement Hall in the summer of 1937 when the music building was constructed on the former playing field. Basketball was so popular that in 1934 there were ten organized teams. In addition, there was the quite disorganized faculty basketall team whose game against a student team was a highlight of the year. Girls who were less athletically inclined could earn their points in the minor sports like ping-pong, badminton, darts, and shuffleboard. Everyone was required to take ten hours of swimming, and the pool, known as "the bathtub," was popular for recreational swimming. Bowling at the nearby alleys under supervision was accepted for physical education credit beginning in 1941. Horseback riding and golf could be arranged. Margaret Cruikshank was interested in sports; as a young teacher at St. Mary's she had sometimes coached the younger girls in basketball. Although the required hours of physical education did not carry academic credit, Cruikshank asked Rebecca Harvey, head of the physical education department, 1937–1943, to insist upon "a stiffening of the girls' attitude toward gym work."[61]

Posture week, probably originated in 1933 by Olga Dodds of the physical education department, was a feature of school life for over 30 years. A "graceful and ladylike bearing" had been one of Aldert Smedes's requisites of a St. Mary's girl, so the principle was not new. The Sigmas and the Mus competed all week with team captains and policemen who gave slouchers actual black marks on their identification tags.[62] The week ended with an assembly program on good health

Dancing in the parlor, c.1935

practices followed by the awarding of prizes; some years a posture queen was crowned. The physical education department gave remedial classes to those with posture faults.

All students took creative dancing once a week for physical education. Jane Goss went in 1938 to teach the dance and was director of the physical education department, 1943–1951. She was educated at Cortland State Normal and at the University of Wisconsin. At St. Mary's she immediately organized Orchesis, a dance club composed of her advanced students. Each year those students, under her direction, took the lead in planning, writing, costuming, and choreographing the May

Day pageant. Enthusiastic and friendly, Jane Goss was a campus favorite.[63] She married William Guess in 1941.

Cruikshank approached the supervision of the daily life of the school as she would have that of a smaller family. Her philosophy was that crises could be avoided if everyone understood that the rules had been "drawn up in the fairest manner possible" and that "within reasonable limits" individual requests would be granted.[64] She changed few of the rules immediately, but she instinctively knew how to handle the problems of daily life. Furthermore, there were always on campus students whose mothers had known Margaret Jones Cruikshank and whose grandmothers had loved St. Mary's. In 1938, 53 of the 218 students were the daughters, granddaughters, or great-granddaughters of alumnae. The ties made it easier for Margaret Cruikshank to determine precisely where "the reasonable limits" lay than it had been for rectors of the past.

Margaret Cruikshank was held in great respect by the students, but most of them considered her "distant," even "formidable." She was thoughtful in many small ways. Whenever one of Raleigh's rare snowfalls came, she would announce in assembly, "Anyone who wants to, may use my sled." The fortunate students who worked with her in student government or who were tutored by her found her approachable, and some of them became deeply devoted to her.[65]

Margaret Cruikshank always kept her own home and family life from being engulfed by her official life. She never let her children see her worried about the school's problems.[66] Once, State College boys dating Mary Pride and Olive Echols at their home asked the president, "And what do you teach here at St. Mary's?" Her quick reply was, "Oh, I don't teach; I work in the office."[67] Both daughters were leaders at St. Mary's and were graduated from the University of North Carolina. Ernest Cruikshank, Jr., took degrees at Duke and Harvard.[68]

New girls at St. Mary's in their first letters home wrote of the long registration lines, of the dashing about to the ringing of bells, of the surprisingly good meals, and of the friendly seniors to whom newcomers were assigned as "little sisters."[69] Sally Digges, who taught French and Spanish, was a guest columnist for "The Faculty Corner" in the *Belles* in the spring of 1940. Writing what she called "a pre-Easter bouquet" to the students, she commented:

You have a rather rare distinction to be able . . . to impress casual observers. . . . It seems to me that what sets you apart is genuine kindness. . . . All civilized groups are polite to newcomers, but your reception of the incoming girls each fall is so hospitable that within a very few days the new girls, too, have "that St. Mary's air." Like guests in an informal, but dignified household, they find themselves living up to the standards, without conscious effort. . . .[70]

Faculty and officers, 1936. Front row, left to right: Susan Cooke, Pressley Walsh, Lizzie Lee, Lora Simbolotti, Henry Kloman, Mabel Morrison (with Chaps), Mary Weise, Bessie Brown, Elizabeth Tucker. Back row, left to right: Juliet Sutton, Nannie Marriott, Florence Davis, William Guess, Caroline Harris, Alice Alexander, Elizabeth Bason, Louise Egleston, Lola Naylor, Sally Digges, C.A.P. Moore

Senior dance in the old gymnasium, 1942

Some of the teachers who lived on halls in a supervisory capacity felt that a good deal of effort was required during the settling down process. Rooms were subject to daily inspection. A well-organized new girl soon slipped into the school's routine; a disorganized one soon fell behind with "the mountain of work." After nearly everyone got a radio, it became necessary for a while to have a "radio contract" signed by the owner in order to control the noise level during the hours that radios and victrolas could be played. Violations meant "storage" of the radio and the risk of missing the "Hit Parade" on a dateless Saturday night.

Too much wasted time meant the old flashlight-in-the-closet method of cramming for tests. Sometimes a bolder girl, who feared not the ghost of Aldert Smedes that was rumored to walk the creaking hallways of Smedes, would sneak up into the attic spaces under the eaves with books, blanket, flashlight, and food. Also, the blanket cupboards over the closets in some dormitories were perfect for after-lights studying. Penalties for minor infractions like failure to be in one's own room at exactly 10:10 at night or washing out stockings during study hall were minor; one punishment was two nights in study hall for a girl who normally merited room study; another was walking an assigned number of laps around the hockey field.[71]

Smoking on campus at St. Mary's was considered a serious offense during the Cruikshank regime. Until the 1938–1939 *Handbook*, the only acknowledgment made by St. Mary's that some women smoked was one sentence prohibiting smoking on campus by day students. The *Handbook* still carried its traditional statement forbidding "the use of fire." The 1938–1939 *Handbook* made a plain statement of policy:

As we consider smoking detrimental to adolescent girls . . . we expect every St. Mary's girl to refrain from smoking so long as she is under our regulations. . . . If any girl in our group is unwilling or unable to conform to our point of view, we do not expel her, but we ask her to change to some school where smoking is permitted.

Smoking was permitted in the home or automobile of an approved hostess and even in public when a student was with her own parents. By the late 1940s a student could smoke in public when accompanied by an approved chaperone. Probably few students were habitual smokers, but the clandestine smokers created a fire hazard and weakened student government.

Student government at St. Mary's reached maturity under the Cruikshank presidency. In 1920 Way had made a beginning with the school council of faculty and students whose function was largely advisory.[72] Student government with faculty participating as advisers to, and sometimes members of, the component organizations, came in 1938–1939 upon petition of the students and with the encouragement of the president and faculty. A vocal minority of students had opposed the 1937 extension of the honor system to matters outside the classroom, and the student officers and the *Belles* had to fight hard for student government.[73]

The constitution of the Student Government Association approved in 1938 by Margaret Cruikshank and a committee of the faculty served well for a quarter of a century with only a few fundamental changes. An honor council composed of the student government officers, class presidents, and class representatives served as a judicial body; day student representatives were included. Action on major offenses was reviewed by the faculty executive committee, and a small faculty committee advised the honor council but did not sit with it. Protection of the rights of the accused was spelled out in the constitution.

The legislative body was made up of students and faculty and empowered to act upon student petitions and to initiate legislation on social and dormitory regulations. All measures required a two-thirds majority of the legislative body and the approval of the president of the college.[74] It was difficult for the student members of the legislative body to resist peer pressure to push for new privileges,[75] for the students considered the rules at St. Mary's to be "very, very strict." Some long overdue revisions of rules did pass, but those not considered right for St. Mary's were firmly vetoed by Margaret Cruikshank; the students said that she "ruled with an iron hand." In 1939 the hall committee was reorganized as the hall council and the SGA constitution amended so that the responsibility for enforcement of dormitory regulations was placed more upon a hall's officers than upon its resident teacher.

Student government always places tremendous pressures upon the student leaders. Students and faculty agreed that more than ever the happiness of the campus community depended upon the cooperation of everyone. By 1945 the editor of the *Handbook* could write:

Years of student government have made the whole student body jealous of this privilege of governing themselves; consequently, they regard any violation of the honor code . . . as dangerous to student government. . . . but more significant is the attitude that has developed within the whole student body. . . . Here a girl's word is her bond.[76]

It was Margaret Cruikshank's idea that morale would be strengthened if a small group of campus leaders felt a special responsibility for fostering the St. Mary's spirit on campus. In the late fall of 1938 she invited several students to her home one night. They went in fear and trembling but learned that they were charter members of "a very high sounding organization." The students decided upon the name and by-laws of the new honorary organization.[77] They decided to call it the Circle because

Longtime staff members: Julia Jordan, Frances Vann, Elizabeth Tucker, Mary Lewis Sasser, Bessie Brown, with Sarah Vann, center

Student Government Association, 1946. This organization became very strong during the Cruikshank years.

as the circle symbolizes unity, so the purpose of this organization shall be to promote a spirit of cooperation among the students by the cultivation of high ideals of fellowship, service, citizenship, and scholarship and to assist new students in finding their places in school life and activities.

The first group planned the secret initiation ceremony and the torchlit late night walk around campus that became traditional.[78] Membership in the Circle was regarded as a high honor.

Student life was not all serious responsibility. There was a round of all-girl parties on campus from the formal old-girl-new-girl reception of orientation week to the romping school party in May. During the Depression the student social committee was instructed to keep "the number and expenses of parties low." Most of the Christmas traditions remained—the school party with Santa, the gaily decorated dormitories, the concerts, the Christmas dinner, the play, the Nativity pageant presented by the seniors in the chapel, and caroling by the seniors at dawn on the day vacation started. Scattered through the year were special treats like Al Moore's Sunday night ghost story sessions held in his classroom eerily lighted by a single green bulb. Student fellow conspirators provided the clanging chains and the glimpses of sheeted figures flitting past the windows.[79] Some years the faculty gave an original stage presentation; and for years a senior vaudeville was presented. The scene was always laid in "an unusual boarding school" run by an extremely eccentric faculty harassed by students who exploited every opportunity.

William H. Jones gave an annual feast for his choir, and Margaret Cruikshank's "spreads" were said to be memorable; sometimes after supper in her home the girls danced to Wayne King's music on the radio. Occasionally the girls danced in the parlor, but not nightly as of old. The most exciting evening of the winter of 1938 was that of the formal dinner, followed by a concert by the University of North Carolina Glee Club with a reception and dancing in the parlor afterward.

In the 1930s the school party, which since about 1911 had been held on the Saturday night before the May examinations, was both a play time and a serious time. There was a class costume or an insignia using the class colors for all members of each class, and there were stunts and songs. That was also the night when results of elections for the next year's student body officers were announced.[80] Picnics and weiner roasts at "the hut" were popular after a log cabin was built behind the president's home in the spring of 1940. The class of 1939 began the project with the gift of an outdoor fireplace, and the faculty and some friends of the college gave the funds for a small building with an indoor fireplace.[81] Besides the round of annual social events, there was the special pleasure each girl experienced when "sung to" at dinner in the dining room on her birthday. Excursions off campus, except for trips to "the little store" and downtown, were infrequent during the 1930s for most students.

By 1934–1935 two college students could go to town and even to a matinee unchaperoned. Night movies always required a chaperone. All dates were entertained on the campus until the spring of 1941, so it was the chaperone's duty to keep her movie group within sight. All St. Mary's was agog when in the fall of 1936 a freshman received a telephone call from Gene Raymond for her winning letter on "The Movie I Liked Best." She generously shared the time with everyone who could crowd into the office.[82] Elizabeth Bason's students, who usually won prizes at State College's style shows for the clothes they made from fabrics designed and woven by the students in the textile school, were always delighted when the prize was a supply of movie passes. Everyone, including Bason, "wept copiously" through *Gone with the Wind* at least once. Students were allowed to cut classes one afternoon to see that epic.[83]

It was possible to spend Saturday afternoon or most of Sunday in a Raleigh home, but the strictest rules still surrounded the privilege. Invitations went directly to school authorities from the hostess, who was supposed to chaperone the guest during the visit. Even after smoking off campus was legal with the permission of one's hostess, Juliet Sutton felt it her duty to deliver her lecture against the use of tobacco. St. Mary's students did not spend the night off campus in Raleigh except with their mothers on very special occasions. The president told the trustees in 1941 that new privileges were being granted gradually and that the girls were "assimilating" them responsibly. "But," she sighed, "we seem unable to live down the reputation of being a jail!"[84]

The accusation that rules for dating at St. Mary's were not much changed from those of the turn of the century was true until the late 1930s. Dates could be entertained only on campus and only on Saturday evenings from 8:00 to 10:00 and Sunday afternoons from 3:30 to 5:00. The boys gathered on the porch ready to sign the date book when the doors were opened. That date book, because each caller recorded the name of the young lady he had come to see, made fascinating reading for some other young ladies who were "just checking." Until the late 1930s dates were entertained either at the double desks in the study hall or in the parlor under the observant eye of a chaperone. On Sunday afternoons the benches on campus could be used provided "the deadline" was not crossed. When dating hours were over, the bell on the porch of Smedes—actually an old streetcar bell mounted in a box that worked with a foot pedal—rang loudly.[85] By 1937–1938 dating was allowed in the recreation room in lower Smedes. The room, entirely in the charge of the student social committee and its chosen faculty adviser, was equipped with bridge tables, a ping-pong table, and "an electric victrola for dancing."[86] Dating at St. Mary's was never quite the same after Juliet Sutton retired at 79 in May, 1940.[87] She had "kept the night" hundreds of times over 42 years.

Margaret Cruikshank decided early in her first year as head of the school that boys should attend dances at St. Mary's. And so the senior dance of December, 1932, was "marvelous, amazing, delightful" with "throngs of boys and a real jazz band," according to the *Belles*. The band was Jimmy Poyner's famous State Collegians.[88] All dances were chaperoned with a proper receiving line and no pass-outs except to the fenced-in area (known as "the bull-pen") beside the gymnasium, where couples could get a breath of air and talk to friends. A girl's "main date" was expected to send flowers. The two other friends to whom she sent bids were expected to be enthusiastic stags. After the dance, five-minute good-byes were said at the gymnasium, and the girls went back to their rooms.[89]

Decorations for the dances were creative, and their gowns became increasingly important to the girls until the war years. Then flowers were omitted, and the music was provided on records. The stag lines, however, were long because of the presence of so many servicemen in the area. The high school students were likely to do their swinging and swaying in the parlor because the freshman and sophomore classes were small. The *Belles* reported that their 1943 dance was a phenomenal success, the ratio of boys to girls being 127 to 37 because of the presence of the naval preflight cadets. Margaret Cruikshank instituted the popular informal Saturday night girl-break dances. Each girl paid 25 cents to admit herself and her date to an evening of dancing to records in the gymnasium.

The more sophisticated girls "prom-trotted," but not often. During the 1930s only one weekend away from school each semester was permitted; honor students had more. During the next decade the rules were less stringent, but classes could not be missed except on the few "extended weekends." In college towns those girls attending dances stayed only with approved hostesses who were responsible to St. Mary's for enforcing the curfew. Football was so important that Saturday classes began an hour early on big game weekends so that the students could make the chartered bus. Until the late 1940s St. Mary's girls could not ride in cars with dates; in fact, they only rode in cars legally with special permission.

With their increased social freedom and the beginnings of recovery from the Depression, the students became as clothes-conscious as those of the early 1920s. For the big dances in the late 1930s the ulti-

Casper Lilly announcing mealtime for the students of the 1940s

mate in sophistication was "a slinky flame crepe" with rhinestone straps or "a black velvet strapless." The less slinky types wore very full net skirts caught with velvet bows. For class the students wore sloppy saddle shoes and ankle socks, skirts and sweaters, and pearls. It was all right for the pearls to be from Woolworth's, according to the *Belles*. Inch-long, blood-red nails and vivid lipstick were much in evidence. Jangling silver "slave bracelets" were popular, and earrings had "swept the campus." Hair was worn longish and very curly.[90]

The war brought simpler styles requiring less material. The "perfect picture" of the winter of 1942 was "a Lady Chesterfield coat, white scarf and string gloves, black derby, and black suede pumps." For class a few girls sported authentic field jackets complete with the loved one's insignia.[91] Loafers replaced saddle shoes. When silk hose disappeared and nylon hose all but disappeared, women made do with leg makeup and rayon stockings.

### "CONTINUING AS USUAL"

St. Mary's entered her second century in the midst of the fourth war of her existence. Margaret Cruikshank approached the problems of running a school during wartime the same way in which she had approached life always—with equanimity. Immediately after the girls returned to school in January, 1942, she set the tone for the war years in her speech in assembly. "We shall," she said, "disrupt as little as possible by continuing the usual program, adding conservation drives."[92] The year before, the Circle had raised the large sum of $1,100 for British war relief besides sending boxes of clothing to Bundles for Britain, and the student body had adopted several children through the Save the Children Federation.[93]

In January, 1942, the school was organized for black-out and air-raid drills with student wardens and faculty supervisors, and drills were carried out regularly "with speed and almost no confusion."[94] During 1943–1944 as part of the physical fitness program St. Mary's students were organized into 12 platoons under the cadet squad leaders from North Carolina State.[95] Because the college was classified as "an essential war industry," more emphasis than ever before was placed upon the science, mathematics, history, and geography courses. "Maps for Miss Morrison" could then be considered doing one's bit for the war effort. Each weeknight everyone remained at the tables after dinner to listen in silence to a broadcast of world news. There were regular news summaries and special speakers in assembly, and a large bulletin board carried the headlines of each day.

There was a brief excitement when Mabel Morrison was questioned as a possible spy. She had spent the summer at her home, the busy port of Halifax, Nova Scotia. During her last week there, her father had been searching the house for his copy of Carlyle's *French Revolution*. At the same time, the storm door could not be located. A few days later her sister and a friend in Halifax, who was an amateur radio operator, decided to send a message to Raleigh. The message, "We found the storm door, but we lost the French revolution," sounded to Washington like coded information on port activities, and the St. Mary's teacher had some explaining to do.[96]

In the mock election held on campus in 1944 President Roosevelt won by 79.5 percent, and the headline in the *Belles* read, "As St. Mary's Goes, So Goes the Nation." Only three faculty members and 63 students did not vote the Democratic ticket.[97] The student newspaper was edged in black in April, 1945, when it carried the headline, "Nation Mourns Loss of Franklin D. Roosevelt." On May 8 everyone gathered in the school auditorium to hear the broadcast of Pres. Harry S Truman's official announcement of victory in Europe. Then students, faculty, staff, and servants attended a prayer service in the chapel. Before the girls returned to school in the fall, Japan had surrendered.

The war years were busy ones at the college. Students through their campus organizations conserved and collected everything that could be salvaged; for instance, the thread from 444 stockings could be made into one parachute.[98] A number of students and teachers took Red Cross classes. A group of faculty women sewed one night a week for the Red Cross, and all over campus knitting needles clicked. The teachers in the business department taught extra classes so that more students could learn to type. The *Handbook* urged every student to put at least 10 percent of her allowance into war savings stamps, noting that a "wise" girl could manage on an allowance of less than $10 a month. The *Belles* staff handled the stamps, and the school's goal was $1,100 (the price of one jeep) in each drive as the halls competed for the Treasury Department's citations. Also, St. Mary's annually gave about $800 to the Red Cross, always exceeding the quota.[99]

Despite all of this, the material privations were relatively minor. For some girls the war years brought one round of parties after another, especially at home during the summer and over Christmas, for "entertaining the servicemen" was a recognized patriotic duty. The United Services Organization's dances and canteen duty and parties at officers' clubs and hospitals provided endless opportunities to meet men from all over the country.

There were those who had a father, a brother, or a fiancé overseas. For them the twice-daily trip to the post office in lower Smedes was often a disappointment, for awaiting a letter from "somewhere in Europe" or from the China-Burma-India Theater was an agonizing business. The first issue of the 1944–1945 school newspaper showed that some students understood the times. Editor Maria Gregory wrote:

Rome has fallen, and Paris has been liberated. Some American soldiers will march into Berlin. But as we near our goals, our advances become more and more costly in human life, and America as well as Britain and Russia must pay this price. It is they [the men] who suffer the physical agonies of war. But, we, the women must sit and wait—wait—wait. We are called upon to put up the front of normal existence, when all the time our minds are far distant—if—if—if.[100]

For those who were engaged (a minority in so young a student body), there was the hard decision of whether to marry or to continue work toward a degree. A few young women chose to marry and to continue their educations at four-year institutions. The wartime wives kept busy and wrote cheerful letters, but for some the long wait became forever.

After Pearl Harbor, career decisions suddenly became important for St. Mary's students. Some decided to go directly into the good office jobs available. A number chose nursing because of the active recruiters in that field, and the serious shortage of teachers made that profession more attractive than it had been in years. To most women, however, their work was still a job to fill the time before marriage, not a lifetime commitment to a career.

St. Mary's lost four feminine members of the faculty to the armed services in 1943—Martha Dabney Jones of the English department, Rebecca Harvey, the director of physical education, and Rachel Johnson and Margaret Bailey of foreign languages. Herbert A. Bird of the music department had gone into the army the year before and reported that because he was a trained musician it somehow had seemed logical to his interviewer to place him in a cavalry unit.[101] Martha Dabney Jones was a member of a company of WAACs landed in Normandy in July, 1945, the first American women other than nurses to be sent to Europe.[102] The catalog for 1944–1945 proudly noted that "many" St. Mary's graduates had enlisted in the WAAC and WAVES. Caro Bayley, a graduate of 1941 who took flying lessons while at St. Mary's, joined the WASP where she flew target planes for gunnery practice. She became an officer in the Air Force Reserve.[103] Women served exceedingly well, releasing 200,000 men for other duties, and by their efforts, as in World War I, laid the foundation for greater political and economic recognition.

## "WE'VE GOT SOMETHING HERE"

An added strength during the war was a chaplain who did not carry also the burden of serving as head of St. Mary's and who had time to be pastor and counselor to the girls. Margaret Cruikshank, steeped as she was in the traditional spirit of the school, understood the mystique of the St. Mary's Chapel, and she did not minimize in any way the importance of the chaplaincy. Nell Battle Lewis told the alumnae:

We've got something here. . . . The influence which a church school has on a student is so subtle that for years it may be imperceptible. . . . It is natural for young people to think chapel is simply a nuisance or a bore. . . . But the leaven is working on you . . . , and it works, I find, for years.[104]

It was true that some students of the 1930s and 1940s resented being lined up in the study hall and then led by the marshals in a double line down the steps of Smedes and around West Rock into the chapel. It was true that some giggled and whispered through the repetition week after week of the noble cadences of the prayer book. Several times each year the *Belles* published editorials on chapel behavior.

But most St. Mary's women remember the chapel services as "a set time and place to pray every day" that became a "sustaining factor in our lives." One of them wrote of the evening prayer at 5:00 on Sundays: "After prayer . . . Mr. Broughton played something magnificent on the organ, with only the candles on the altar burning. This was the time that any turmoil within us came out, for there was always someone quietly crying. It seemed that afterwards a peace and quiet settled over us all, and we were ready to begin another week of our life . . . at St. Mary's."[105]

The question of a chaplain for St. Mary's arose for the first time in May, 1932. For exactly 90 years the head of the school had been a clergyman. The trustees agreed that the chaplain should be elected by the board, to serve at its pleasure, a policy that presented no conflict with church authorities because bishops of the controlling dioceses were members of the St. Mary's Board of Trustees. St. Mary's remained officially an unorganized mission. Until a chaplain was found, Bishop Cheshire went from his home on campus to conduct chapel, and the girls walked downtown to church on Sundays. Margaret Cruikshank, in her practical fashion, solved the problem of activating the Young People's Service League in the fall of 1932 simply by calling a meeting of the student body. The decision was made to divide the students into groups, each of which would be responsible for certain meetings and activities.[106]

In November, 1932, the Reverend Joseph Fletcher and his wife arrived on campus. They lived in Smedes among the students until senior hall, which had been closed during the worst of the Depression, was renovated and reopened in the summer of 1934. "Father Joe" was an exciting conversationalist, a powerful preacher, a challenging teacher. He and his wife Forrest, a poet, added sparkle to the daily life during their brief stay at St. Mary's.[107] The class of 1934 dedicated the *Stagecoach* to him.

Joseph Fletcher was ahead of his colleagues—always speaking and writing about whatever was to become the next burning social issue. He soon proved much too avant-garde for St. Mary's. A graduate of the University of West Virginia, Fletcher received his divinity degree from Berkeley and then spent several years in research at Yale and at the University of London's School of Economics. While in London he for two years served a parish in a working men's district and became much interested in democratic socialism as the best route to economic justice. He was coauthor of a book entitled *The Church and Industry*.

Activist Fletcher, arriving in North Carolina in a day when the textile industry was resisting unionization, became involved in seeking justice for workers accused of violence. The trustees by the winter of 1935 felt that the chaplain's activities were much too public for the good of the school. The executive committee of the board in February, 1935, wrote Fletcher that although it had "no statement to make with reference to the personal opinions or attitudes of an individual citizen," it wished "to record as its considered judgement that the association of the Chaplain with the Defense Committee in the Burlington case is detrimental to the welfare of St. Mary's School." The committee then "affectionately urged" the chaplain "to limit his activities" in defense of those accused of dynamiting a Burlington textile mill. The executive committee sincerely meant that "affectionately," for at least one member supported Fletcher. The chaplain replied with a statement on the Christian imperatives as he saw them and his letter of resignation.[108] The Fletchers left at the end of the school year. He became director for nine years of the new School of Applied Religion in Cincinnati, professor of Christian ethics for 25 years at the Episcopal Theological School in Cambridge, Massachusetts, and then visiting professor of medical ethics at the University of Virginia. When he returned in the 1960s to conduct a series of seminars at St. Mary's, Joseph Fletcher was a world-famous author and the foremost exponent of "situation ethics," which was the current controversial moral issue.

The second chaplain to serve at St. Mary's was the Reverend Henry Felix Kloman. He and his wife moved into senior hall in November of 1935. The Sunday night "bull sessions" at their apartment were as likely to be discussions of marriage as of religion, and annually the Klomans planned a series of small parties so that they would know each student.[109] A native of Virginia, the chaplain received his divinity degree from Virginia Theological Seminary, served a number of parishes in Virginia and Maryland, and was the dean of the cathedral in Fargo, North Dakota, before moving to Raleigh. At St. Mary's he car-

ried a heavy load of teaching and services—241 services during 1942.[110]
The Young People's Service League remained active. In 1939 an impressive pageant was presented in the chapel to commemorate the 150th anniversary of the adoption of the prayer book. By the late 1930s the St. Mary's congregation was giving annually well over $600 to diocesan and national church funds.[111]

Henry Kloman retired at the end of the school year in 1942, and he died that summer. His wife had died unexpectedly on Christmas day of 1941.[112]

The Reverend Israel Harding Hughes, who became chaplain in the fall of 1942, had known the school all of his life, and he claimed that he could count 18 relatives plus his grandmother, mother, and two sisters who were alumnae. His wife, Josephine Bowen, was one of five sisters attending St. Mary's. Born at Chocowinity, he was the son of the Reverend Nicholas Collin Hughes, Jr., and Elizabeth Harding Hughes. A graduate of the University of North Carolina and the Episcopal Theological School, he taught at preparatory schools and served for four years as rector of Holy Trinity Church in Greensboro and for 14 years at All Saints in Concord. He edited the *North Carolina Churchman* both before and during his St. Mary's tenure.[113] Hughes had been a trustee of the college since May, 1939, and had served on the executive committee of the board.

Harding Hughes was to be very happy at St. Mary's for 15 years. He loved people; he enjoyed the faculty, his table in the dining room with its regular changes of occupants, and the parties. As effervescent as a boy, he simply refused to grow old. One of his students recalled a favorite memory—the sight of the chaplain and his wife hand in hand, skipping merrily down the covered way en route to the Christmas party. Hughes was as good a pastor and counselor as he was a playmate, and he could be counted on in times of trouble. The presence of Harding and Josephine Hughes on campus was a stabilizing factor during the war years.[114]

Soon after Hughes arrived, Margaret Cruikshank suggested that the chapel services be reduced to four a week; some years before Bishop Cheshire had advised that action. Chapel was thereafter held for everyone before classes on Mondays, Wednesdays, and Fridays and for the residents on Tuesday nights. The schedule freed Tuesday and Thursday mornings for required assemblies. The majority of the students, according to the *Belles*, approved compulsory chapel because they felt that otherwise they "would neglect praise altogether." A minority thought that "each one should worship at her own time and place." [115] Hughes's sermons emphasized good will and loving-kindness.

Hughes saw the training of future leaders of the Episcopal church as an important part of his function. In his first report to the board as chaplain he said, "One has only to listen to graduates to learn of the remarkable effect the Chapel has had through the years in maintaining a lasting influence upon the girls who have gone from St. Mary's." During his tenure he made several changes that emphasized leadership training. In the fall of 1943 the service group took the name of the Episcopal organization in colleges and became the Canterbury Club. The next fall half of the 130 Episcopal students were organized into the woman's auxiliary with four guilds.[116] The non-Episcopalians organized a YWCA, and the two groups cooperated in planning meetings and projects. Each year students from St. Mary's attended intercollegiate conferences. The every-member canvass of 1945 resulted in 100 percent student participation and pledges from the students and faculty of over $1,200.[117]

By the late 1930s the campus facilities were being used again, as they had been during the Lay administration, for church conferences. In St. Mary's centennial year the convention of the Diocese of North Carolina met at the college.

## "THE MOST CAREFUL MANAGEMENT"

Bishop Penick and his family became a part of St. Mary's in 1933 when they moved from Charlotte to Ravenscroft on the campus. The girls enjoyed the bishop's presence, the parties his wife gave, and his showing of movies of church activities. In those they saw their home churches and themselves and their friends on the St. Mary's campus or at summer conferences.[118]

Bishop Penick administered the diocese with a firm hand, but he was wise enough to allow the competent to make most of the decisions within their own realms. He understood that Margaret Cruikshank knew what she was doing, a fact acknowledged by the trustees when they gave her "a rising vote of commendation" at the end of her first year.[119] Although the term *junior college* had been in use as part of the name since accreditation under the Way administration, the charter was not amended until November 15, 1945, to make the institution's official name Saint Mary's School and Junior College, Inc.[120]

Bishop Penick in 1933 organized the board of trustees into ten committees in addition to the executive committee. The four women trustees served that year on the executive and long-range planning committees, as well as on the buildings and grounds and library committees. The minutes show that over the years the women members spoke up and presented motions at board meetings. A board of 29 members was, however, unwieldy; even before wartime gas rationing, one of the two meetings was canceled some years for lack of a quorum. Margaret Cruikshank remarked, "I hope this may be interpreted as a feeling of confidence and not lack of interest."[121]

Although President Cruikshank had said when appointed that she wished to leave financial matters in the hands of A. W. Tucker, who had remained as business manager, she realized that the school could not long survive with a total enrollment of only 162. During her first year she drove throughout the Carolinas recruiting students. The next year 60 prospective students visited the campus for a weekend, and the *Bulletin* reported that "by departure time a good many had decided on a future room at St. Mary's."[122] After much discussion, Cruikshank persuaded the trustees to spend $2,500 during 1934–1935 on advertisements in *Vogue, Cosmopolitan, American, Good Housekeeping*; at least eight new students were directly traceable to those advertisements.[123]

Recruiting efforts, the confidence of the alumnae in Margaret Cruikshank, and the improved economic outlook had brought the enrollment up to slightly over 200 by 1935–1936. By then the dormitories in East Rock and West Rock had been reopened. Two years later the school was filled to its capacity of 220 boarders, and it remained filled with a waiting list for the rest of the Cruikshank administration. The total enrollment, despite increased fees, was up to 290 by 1938–1939, and it held there. Margaret Cruikshank felt that her plan to offer the fine arts courses with no extra fees attached had been vindicated. Some of the clergy and some trustees felt that the charges, which were raised from $650 to $750 for 1939–1940, were too high. The president of the college made clear her opinion in a report to the trustees in May, 1939: "The students we want and should have here would not want to be here and would not come unless they had the standards and advantages which can be supplied to them only with the fees now in effect." By 1945–1946 the charges were $800 for boarders and $200 for day students. Day student enrollment during the 1930s and 1940s fluctuated between 50 and 85. The dropping of the ninth grade in 1936 had changed the composition of the student body slightly. In 1941, 62 percent of the students were in the college courses, 25 percent in the high school, and 13 percent in the business course. As had been the case for years, about 20 different states were represented in each student body. The president liked that "broadening influence and the rubbing off of our provincialism," but she admitted that the student body was still "perhaps too homogeneous."[124] Invariably, over half the resident students were North Carolinians. Always between 50 and 60 percent of the student body were Episcopalians, with Methodists, Presbyterians, and Baptists the only other denominations represented in appreciable numbers.

Margaret Cruikshank always insisted that she took no part in the business affairs of the institution, but she expressed opinions regarding priorities. By the fall of 1933 the business manager was able to keep within the operating budget and also to pay the interest on the $80,000 debt; patrons were paying their bills when due. The $20,000 Erwin legacy was spent to liquidate the debt on Holt Hall as William A. Erwin had directed in his will. It was July, 1936, before the operating budget showed a surplus of as much as $1,000. The perennial problem of imperative repairs to well-worn buildings was met by borrowing scholarship endowment money and paying interest on that note back into the scholarship fund. By 1939 over $21,000 had been replaced. Two years earlier the major loan, then down to $60,000, had been renegotiated and the interest fixed at 4.5 percent.[125] Support from the controlling dioceses lagged during the Depression years. The anticipated total revenues for 1936 were about $153,000; of that amount, $2,000 was to come from the Diocese of North Carolina.[126]

As president of St. Mary's Margaret Cruikshank felt keenly the responsibility for keeping the institution "above the criticism of the Southern Association." Faculty salaries and the science department's equipment were areas of vulnerability. Both Way and Penick had considered salary cuts a last possible resort during the early years of the Depression. The trustees finally settled upon a plan to meet the uncertainties of the 1933–1934 session. There would be a 10 percent cut in all salaries—administrative, faculty, and staff—unless resident enrollment reached the optimistic figure of 140. Also, Tucker was authorized to borrow up to $12,000 for operating expenses. The enrollment of boarders was only 101, and in October the salary cuts went into effect with a promise of restoration when resident enrollment reached 130. The executive committee expressed "a desire to increase" faculty salaries but felt it "necessary to be conservative in the matter of school finances due to the present debt of the school coupled with business uncertainty." When recruitment efforts brought enrollment up to 153 boarders by 1934–1935, salaries were restored. Pay for resident women faculty ranged from $800 to $1,200 plus room and board (with attendant dormitory duties). That year Margaret Cruikshank was seeking a man for a vacancy in the English department at a beginning salary of $1,600. In 1937 the 14 teachers who had remained at the school throughout the lean years received a 15 percent raise. The next year each of the 38 teachers and officers received a bonus; the teachers got $50.[127]

During the late 1930s and early 1940s the board authorized from one to two thousand dollars annually to cover all salary increases for the faculty. By February, 1941, Margaret Cruikshank was indignant. She had just attended a meeting of the southern association and learned that the approved minimum salary for instructors in four-year colleges was $1,200. (It was $2,700 for professors.) She wrote to the executive committee of the board, "It is not a matter of mere opinion to state that our teachers are poorly paid. We have had the matter more than once called to our attention by our accrediting body." That year St. Mary's was paying a faculty member with a master's degree and 30 years' service to the school $1,200 and subsistence.[128] The next year $3,000 was allocated for faculty raises for 1944–1945, and the college began to pay on a 12–month basis.

Although she did not succeed in raising faculty salaries as much as she had hoped, the president did succeed, with strong support from Bishop Penick, in securing approval of a retirement plan. It had been the custom for some years to grant to certain teachers who had given exceptionally long service a pension of about $300 a year. To a few others retirement gifts of $300 had been granted by vote of the board. The retirement question languished in the executive committee from May, 1935, until October, 1942, when another committee was appointed to investigate various annuity plans. Penick, Cruikshank, Guess, and Tucker had already made such extensive investigation that within the month the executive committee accepted a plan. The full board gave official approval in July, 1943.[129] The faculty in a formal letter of appreciation to the board wrote:

Such a plan will give us confidence in facing the readjustment of a post-war world, and this confidence is bound to be reflected in the quality of our work. We are proud that St. Mary's has kept pace with the national sense of social responsibility and that among schools of her own type she has led the way.[130]

Margaret Cruikshank then began to think in terms of sabbaticals and funds for professional enrichment, but those remained unrealized hopes.

At the end of her first decade as president of St. Mary's, Cruikshank was able to report to the board a full school operating under a strong student government and a debt reduced to less than $32,000, despite the fact that some $40,000 had been spent for remodeling Smedes Hall and installing a sprinkler system, remodeling the library, and constructing the music building and a warehouse.

Plans for a fitting commemoration of the centennial of the school were initiated in June, 1936, when the trustees voted to hold a formal celebration. In the spring of 1938 the *Saint Mary's School Bulletin* began publishing articles that summarized all of the history of the school that could be documented at that time. Librarian Helen A. Brown published a plea for old photographs, letters, scrapbooks, and back issues of St. Mary's publications. Alumnae response enabled her to bind an almost-complete file of all the school publications from 1879. Her efforts resulted in the establishment of the college archives to which she added materials throughout her long tenure.[131]

The alumnae association voted in May, 1939, to redecorate the school parlor in time for the centennial festivities and to cooperate fully in whatever plans were made by the trustees for a fund drive.[132] Because of the war, by the time final plans were being laid for the centennial celebration the trustees experienced difficulty in reaching a decision concerning the centennial fund. On August 29, 1941, the trustees voted unanimously to set a goal of $150,000 to be raised between February, 1942, and commencement week and to contract with a New York fund-raising firm. A new science-home economics building and long-delayed renovations and furniture purchases were planned. It was hoped that enough money could be raised to build a modern dormitory, thus freeing East Rock and West Rock for administrative offices and an alumnae house. A new home for the chaplain was needed, and scholarship funds were inadequate. After Pearl Harbor, the executive committee recommended that "a campaign of our own . . . without professional advice be put on to accept Government Securities and Bonds under a plan to hold them to maturity, unless in case of an emergency it becomes necessary to use them as collateral." When the called meeting of the full board lacked a quorum, the executive committee decided to proceed and authorized Penick, after consultation with Cruikshank, to appoint a campaign committee. Expenses were to be paid from the school's operating fund so that all contributors would be assured that their gifts would be invested immediately in defense bonds.[133]

The *North Carolina Churchman* reminded Episcopalians that the woman's auxiliaries in many parishes of the Carolinas were "almost alumnae units of St. Mary's girls," that the summer conferences were "brightened and strengthened by that subtle but very real influence that St. Mary's has sent forth year after year," and that "husbands, children, and grandchildren" had been "blessed by the influences which had their early beginnings under the care of the Church at St. Mary's."[134] By the 1942 commencement approximately $7,000 had been contributed.[135] Eventually, substantial gifts were received.

A special 1941 summer issue of the *Belles* announced the early opening of school so that the St. Mary's centennial commencement could be scheduled without conflict with commencement exercises at nearby institutions. Soon everyone on campus and the alumnae became involved, and the results were rather spectacular—a centennial cantata, a historical pageant, and a book.

*Life at Saint Mary's*, the centennial volume, grew out of the desire of the class of 1920 to memorialize Ernest Cruikshank. (The class of 1920 had organized itself permanently before graduation.) When Katherine Batts Salley, who had been active in the Muse Club, went to Margaret Cruikshank with her plan to write a pamphlet memorializing Ernest Cruikshank's life, the president suggested that her husband's contribution was only part of the St. Mary's story, that all of the story should be told. Together the two women planned the volume,[136] and Katherine Salley undertook the exacting task of editing it. She also wrote the biographical sketch of Ernest Cruikshank with which the book ended. Elizabeth Warren Thompson, who attended St. Mary's 1906–1912, was art editor. *Life at Saint Mary's* was dedicated simply "To Ernest Cruikshank."

Chapters were written by Katharine Drane Perry, 1842–1860; Emilie Smedes Holmes, 1860–1885; Alice Dugger Grimes, 1885–1900; Nell Battle Lewis, 1900–1915; Jane Toy Coolidge, 1915–1930; and Anna Brooke Allan, 1930–1942. All authors were alumnae; Alice Dugger Grimes and Anna Brooke Allan, as well as Nell Battle Lewis, had been or were faculty members. The University of North Carolina Press published an 800-copy edition of *Life at Saint Mary's*,[137] an interesting account which was well received.

As the centennial date approached, the alumnae planned the largest reunion ever. Alumnae secretary Sarah Vann located most of the 5,000 alumnae listed in the files. The faculty committee, all alumnae—Martha Dabney Jones, Nell Battle Lewis, Elizabeth Tucker, and Letty Lassiter— had been appointed by Margaret Cruikshank in 1940. They undertook a historical pageant, written by Martha Dabney Jones, that would emphasize "the continuity in daily Christian life at St. Mary's."[138] Sadie Root Robards, granddaughter of Aldert and Sarah Smedes, wrote articles on the early history of the school that were published in the Sunday papers throughout the state.

By Saturday, May 16, 1942, all was in readiness; the festivities began with the usual high school and college class day programs. The *Stagecoach* was dedicated "to the memory of Dr. Aldert Smedes and to Mrs. Ernest Cruikshank." Editor Carol Cobb and her art staff carried the historical theme throughout the yearbook. Editor Kathryn (Jonny) Norman made each issue of the *Bulletin* that year a contribution to the story of "life behind these walls" where for 100 years "St. Mary's girls have studied, played, laughed and cried just as we have."[139] Editor Mary-Gene Kelly of the *Belles* kept everyone up to date on the yearlong preparations for the centennial.

Early Sunday morning, the 44 seniors knelt in the chapel for their last Communion service as a class, and at 11:00 they marched into the chapel in cap and gown. Chaplain Kloman's service was "even more

*Centennial Cantata, 1942*

beautiful than usual," and Bishop Penick preached an eloquent sermon. At the alumnae vesper service an overflow crowd heard the *Centennial Cantata*, Russell Broughton's lasting gift to all St. Mary's women. The cantata ended with his St. Mary's hymn, "We Build Our School on Thee, O Lord." [140] The Ernest Cruikshank memorial window and other gifts were dedicated. [141] At Monday's alumnae association meeting the first copy of *Life at Saint Mary's* was presented to Bishop Penick; a resolution was passed paying tribute to Juliet Bisco Sutton; and plans were adopted to place a memorial plaque to Aldert and Bennett Smedes. [142] In her talk to the alumnae, Mary Yellott Denny predicted correctly:

It is a new world into which we are moving, one in which we women will have greater opportunities. . . . We must insist upon our right to rear and have a voice in the education of the children we bear; we must establish not only our right to work at paid jobs if we please, . . . we must maintain respect for "home-making" as a job, in which, also, the laborer is worthy of her hire. We must shoulder our share of the burden and privilege of self-government. . . .[143]

Monday night's pageant was presented on the steps and in front of Smedes Hall. Martha Dabney Jones's narrative was both terse and rich in interpretive detail. Students in drama, music, and the dance took part, and many of the costumes were lent by the granddaughters of the St. Mary's girls who had worn them. An authentic coach deposited Mabel Morrison in an 1840s bonnet and her "daughter" at the door of Aldert Smedes's new school. Several Smedes descendants were in the tableaux; Aldert Smedes Root played the grandfather for whom he was named. Kate McKimmon was portrayed by her great-niece and namesake.

Guests viewed with admiration the pageant and an exhibit that the library staff arranged. Each exhibit section was planned around a chapter in *Life at Saint Mary's.* Alumnae had lent costumes, letters written from St. Mary's in the 1840s and 1860s, the gold medal for scholarship awarded one of "the original thirteen," and other family treasures.[144]

The academic procession for the Tuesday morning commencement exercises included representatives from 23 educational institutions. The ceremonies began near Ravenscroft, then usually just called "the bishop's house." Margaret Cruikshank traced the development of education for women in the South and noted that the decade from 1832 to 1842 seemed "to mark the high tide in the Southern religious education movement." Dean Virginia G. Gildersleeve of Barnard College delivered the centennial commencement address entitled "Tools for Victory." She urged St. Mary's graduates "to prepare to take the places of men in all fields," and suggested that more women should major in mathematics.[145]

In one of its stories about the centennial the *News and Observer* described what it called "the St. Mary's paradoxes":

It is unmistakably a church school, . . . a parish in itself where all girls are required to attend the Episcopal Church, yet girls of every denomination attend and are free to maintain their own beliefs. It is frankly a Southern school with a predominance of Southern girls, yet students from every state and some foreign countries continue to enroll and feel at home. . . . It is by no means a showy place. . . . Yet the dignity of the school is at once apparent and the atmosphere . . . is one that large endowments might exhibit to better advantage, but could never buy.[146]

The centennial celebration strengthened alumnae ties to the school. The fact that during the Cruikshank administration there were sometimes as many as nine alumnae on the faculty and staff further strengthened the ties. Easdale Shaw served as president of the St. Mary's Alumnae Association, 1931–1937. Always mindful of the accomplishments of the earliest officers of the association, she embarked upon a program that she called "reorganization and rebuilding." In 1934 the presidents of all local chapters became associate members of the executive council and the loyalty fund replaced annual dues. The custom of an annual memorial service for alumnae who had died during the year was begun in 1933.[147]

Because of Easdale Shaw's special desire for an alumnae house on campus, the association for a few years had the use of West Rock. Much work went into the chapter projects for West Rock, resulting by the fall of 1933 in "five daintily furnished bedrooms" to be used for guests. When in 1936–1937 the school reached full enrollment again, the administration had to reclaim all of the building except a small office. The alumnae were gratified when the trustees, in recognition of the time and money spent on the renovation of West Rock, assumed the unpaid balance on the organ debt that the association had struggled since 1926 to repay.[148] Alumnae fund raising continued, and in 1937 chapter projects were augmented by the sale of the St. Mary's Wedgwood plate. An etching of Smedes Hall was commissioned in 1936 as a gift from the school to St. Mary's brides. Ruth Doris Swett, who after finishing her studies at St. Mary's in 1922 had become a recognized artist, executed the etching.[149]

The alumnae association found itself unable to assume the full cost of an alumnae secretary in 1932, as had been the plan; the trustees agreed to provide room and board in return for the performance of various other duties.[150] The position of alumnae secretary soon had the reputation of being a passport to matrimony. When Mela Royall left to be married, Katherine Duff took the position, which she held from February, 1933, until the next November. Mildred Waddell assumed the post for most of 1935. She was succeeded by Alice Alexander, who served for two years. Kate Spruill filled the position for two years beginning in November, 1937. Then the work was taken on by Elizabeth Tucker with the assistance of alumnae Frances Vann and Letty Lassiter. Frances Vann had remained at the college as a secretary after graduation, and Letty Lassiter, a Smith College graduate, was teaching English at St. Mary's. In 1940 Sarah Vann became the full-time alumnae secretary. She served for two years and was succeeded by Margaret D. Hopkins, who served through the remainder of the Cruikshank administration.[151] During those years there were about 30 active chapters of the alumnae association, including a New York chapter.

At the general business meeting of May, 1938, the association accepted several changes in procedure. The council was to consist of nine members with three rotating off each year; they were to be elected by mail ballot. Association presidents were to serve for three years and to remain on the council in an advisory capacity the following year. There were to be two vice-presidents, "one from the east and one from the west." The automatic succession to the presidency was changed to nomination by a committee elected at the annual meeting of the association.[152]

Great alumnae effort went into the centennial fund campaign. In 1938 the alumnae returned the McKimmon-Iredell fund, which was started in 1907 and reached its goal of $5,000 in 1916, to the original purpose of a memorial scholarship. Elizabeth Czarmonska, to whom the interest from the fund had gone for some years as a gift of gratitude for her service as teacher and lady principal, had died.[153]

Achievements of St. Mary's women prominent in the 1930s in community and church activities and, later, in wartime volunteer work were featured in the *Bulletin*. Among them were Cantey Venable Sutton for her painting and her work with the Raleigh Little Theatre; Emilie Smedes Holmes for her work for world peace; Lucy Worth London Anderson for her work as historian-general of the United Daughters of the Confederacy; Fannie Yarborough Bickett for receiving a law degree at age 60; Mary Yellott Denny for her speech on radio's "Town Meeting of the Air."[154]

Throughout the Cruikshank administration, the trustees and the business manager struggled continuously to make ends meet. No sooner had the Depression been weathered than wartime inflation hit. During the Depression years only the most urgent repairs were made, and little equipment was purchased. Beginning in the summer of 1936 with yet another remodeling of the third floor of Smedes and the wings, catch-up work was done until by the opening of school in 1938 "everything was newly painted and shone like a new penny." Pittman Auditorium, which had been judged unsafe for capacity use, was reinforced and redecorated.[155] The frame music building was erected during the summer of 1937. The auditor's report of July, 1937, showed a total investment in land and buildings of $346,243 and an equipment investment of $89,664.77. The auditor considered his figures "a very low estimate."[156]

By 1938 the loans on the chapel organ and the swimming pool had been liquidated, and the trustees turned their attention to the acute need for more library space. They reversed their earlier decision to extend the first floor of the 1887 building and voted instead to give the library the use of the entire first floor of the building. Also in 1939 a large studio for the head of the music department was added to the music building, and a warehouse was built. The next year the sprinkler system was installed in Smedes and the wings, and a grand piano was purchased.[157] The post office was moved that year from East Rock to lower Smedes, where it remained for over 30 years. The grove required attention; several of the trees removed in 1940 were estimated to be 130 years old. In a replacement program 75 young trees—oaks, maples, and dogwoods—were set out.[158]

In addition to those improvements, the administration by 1942 had paid over $50,000 on the loan taken out in 1932; however, Albert Tucker reported that borrowing for necessary repairs over the summer of 1942 would be required unless the centennial fund campaign gained momentum. At the end of June, 1943, Tucker resigned as business manager after 22 years at the college. He wrote to Penick, "The detailed duties of my position, due largely to war conditions, are increasing to such an extent that I do not have the strength to handle them to my satisfaction."[159] He served part time for several years as secretary-treasurer of the board of trustees, as trustee of the annuity plan fund, and as a fund-raiser. Those who worked with him closely over the years considered him "a splendid business manager."[160] He had worked harmoniously with Margaret Cruikshank, and it is difficult to assess how much credit for the improved economic condition of St. Mary's can be attributed to his management, how much to her quiet authority, and how much to the end of the Depression with the outbreak of war.

The new business manager was Eliot F. Stoughton, a native of New Hampshire who held a master's degree from the Dartmouth School of Finance. He had moved to Raleigh several years earlier as assistant treasurer of the Carolina Coach Company.[161] Unaccustomed to the St. Mary's habit of living in "genteel poverty," Stoughton found the place deplorably run down. He informed the trustees in 1944 that immediate needs included a new power plant, a new laundry, refurbishing of most of the dormitories, modernization of the kitchen, additional classroom space, and complete landscaping of the campus. He found the day-to-day operation of the institution increasingly difficult because of the labor shortage; the trustees opposed employing students. Stoughton and Nannie Marriott managed to keep the dining room fare up to par despite shortages and inflation, but it became very difficult to meet the government requirements of a 20 percent decrease in fuel consumption—equivalent to 200 tons of coal each school year.[162]

Both Stoughton and Cruikshank urged the trustees to revitalize the centennial fund effort. The president noted, "Much of our equipment is antiquated and entirely unsuitable for a school of the standing of St. Mary's."[163] A special meeting of the board in February, 1944, authorized a major drive and left the details to its executive committee. The New York firm whose contract had been postponed in 1942 was reengaged, and the fund's goal was set at $350,000. Bishop Penick and former governor J. C. B. Ehringhaus served as cochairmen. Cantey Venable Sutton chaired the alumnae campaign committee.

By October, 1944, pledges totaled $152,045. St. Mary's women gave generously—$7,952 from the Raleigh alumnae and $47,444 from other alumnae. Raleigh businesses and citizens pledged over $57,000 and parishes and parents over $47,000. By June, 1945, only $157,247 had been pledged, and the board of trustees voted that each diocese be asked to accept a quota of $30,000 to be met before June, 1948. By December, 1946, the centennial fund stood at $203,202. There had been several generous gifts. St. Paul's Church in Winston-Salem pledged $18,000, and a "magnificent gift" of $42,000 was made by Roger Gant, a member of the Church of the Holy Comforter, Burlington, in the name of his alumnae daughters.[164]

## "A GREAT LADY"

Margaret Cruikshank assessed the situation at St. Mary's during 1945 and found the financial outlook brighter, the caliber of the student body encouraging with a long waiting list "clamoring to get in," the faculty strong, and herself at 67 ready to plan her retirement. Characteristically, she made the decision quietly; she simply wrote to Bishop Penick in August, 1945, that she wished to retire at the end of the 1945–1946 academic year, her 14th as head of the school. The bishop decided to wait until November to inform the trustees so that the academic year would be well under way before that unsettling news was made public.[165] At the November meeting, President Cruikshank thanked the trustees for their support and said that she was "particularly happy" that the $80,000 mortgage placed on the school the year before she came had been paid off on October 1, 1945. She said, "I am sure that you will agree that St. Mary's is ready for new blood, so as to face with strong leadership the era that is ahead, and with that motive I have offered my resignation." The trustees accepted the resignation with "deep regret and sincere appreciation of her outstanding contribution to the School." When the news reached the faculty, there was profound regret.[166]

The 50 seniors of 1946 enjoyed the usual whirl of legitimate parties during commencement week and the usual illegitimate midnight snacks provided by State boys and pulled up to dorm windows in baskets attached to long ropes. There was the not-so-old tradition of stepsinging,[167] the very old tradition of receiving diplomas in the chapel, and the tradition of the dropping of the handkerchief by the chief marshal to signify the ending of the school year.[168] And then, "buckets of tears," also traditional. The graduates of 1946 brought the total of college graduates since diplomas were first conferred in 1879 to 1,050.[169]

After her retirement, Margaret Cruikshank lived in Raleigh with her widowed twin, Mary Pride Castleman,[170] who had moved to the city from New York in 1934 to be near her sister. Although the house that the sisters bought together was in nearby Cameron Village, Margaret Cruikshank busied herself with interests outside St. Mary's. She taught mathematics briefly at the local high school, and she was active in St. Saviour's (later St. Timothy's) because she "was needed there more."[171] She enjoyed her home and her grandchildren, and from a distance "she took a quiet satisfaction in watching others build on the foundations she had reinforced."[172]

Margaret Jones Cruikshank died unexpectedly of a heart attack on December 26, 1955, while on a Christmas visit in Fayetteville with the family of her daughter Mary Pride Clark. The *Bulletin* reported, "She left life as serenely as she had lived it."[173] The alumnae association immediately planned a scholarship fund as a tribute "to our beloved former president and sister alumna." Under the chairmanship of Elizabeth Montgomery, 1901 graduate, the goal of $10,000 was reached by alumnae day, 1958. Cruikshank Hall, a three-story dormitory located on the back campus and named in honor of Margaret Cruikshank, was dedicated in October, 1966.

Only a few persons were privileged to know Margaret Cruikshank well, for she was unusually reserved. But those who did know her well, without exception, knew her to be what Richard Gabriel Stone called her—"a very great lady."[174]

## CHAPTER ELEVEN

# "A NEW ERA"

Richard Gabriel Stone was to serve as head of St. Mary's for 23 years—longer than any of his predecessors except the school's founder. The president-elect, a 42-year-old man still in military uniform, was introduced during commencement of 1946. He did not make a speech, for he considered that to be Margaret Cruikshank's day; he had appeared only at the insistence of the trustees.[1]

The search committee settled upon Stone because of his academic and administrative experience.[2] His name was given to the committee by Joseph Blount Cheshire IV, who had served under him in the military and whose father, the son of the late bishop, was a member of the search committee. The names of several women were suggested, and the committee to select a candidate included one woman, Mary Wilson Stoney, a trustee.

Richard Stone's qualifications were excellent. He held a Ph.D. degree in economics from the Johns Hopkins University, and the university had published in 1933 his dissertation on economist Hezekiah Niles.[3] Stone's undergraduate degree was from Western Maryland College. He had taught history and economics at Wofford College before going to Converse College, where he had remained for a decade. Lillian Adele Kibler wrote of him in her History of Converse College, 1889–1971: "He was a productive scholar and stimulating teacher, with high standards and rigid requirements in his courses. Before being granted a leave of absence in January 1943 to enter the armed forces, he had established an excellent economics department at Converse."[4] Captain Stone had been stationed in Atlanta in charge of the Investigative Branch of the Security and Intelligence Division of the Fourth Service Command. He retired as a major with the Army Commendation Ribbon.[5]

Richard Gabriel Stone, president, 1946–1969

The candidate did not fit trustee requirements in one particular—he was not an Episcopalian. The Right Reverend Thomas H. Wright, D.D., bishop of the Diocese of East Carolina, said that he "was humiliated that a suitable Episcopalian apparently could not be found."[6] Stone, the son of the Reverend Daniel Stone of the Methodist Protestant church, was a member of that denomination, but at Converse he habitually attended the Episcopal church with his wife and young son. The trustees unanimously elected him president of St. Mary's. Stone joined the Episcopal church after he moved to Raleigh, a decision not difficult to make because his mother, Katie Hunt Stone, had been reared a devout Episcopalian.[7]

The Stone family arrived at the school in late summer to find the landscaping of the front campus in progress. Eventually, the brick entrance, the paved circular driveway, and the brick walks were complete. The area in front of Smedes was paved with Pennsylvania flagstones, and boxwoods and tulip magnolias were planted. Six boxwoods were planted on either side of the walk to the chapel to symbolize the twelve Apostles.[8] The Stones had been promised a new house but had decided that the ten-room frame rectory built for the Bratton family "would do."[9]

Marye Stone (her name, pronounced "Marie," was a family surname) had married her history professor a year after her graduation from Converse in 1934. A Virginian, she was the daughter of Burnam Grove, a dentist of Roanoke, and Elizabeth Garner Grove. Her husband's ancestors were Virginians, also, having moved after the Civil War from Fredericksburg to Baltimore where Richard G. Stone (called Dick) was born. Nine-year-old Richard G. Stone, Jr., was destined to become a history professor and an author.[10]

The Stones made a conscious decision not to subordinate their family life to that of the school as completely as had all of the former heads of the institution. That first year they had lunch daily in the dining room, but after that, they usually ate only Sunday dinner at the school. They joined the Church of the Good Shepherd in town, instead of worshiping always in the St. Mary's Chapel, so as to have a family life independent of the school and in order to enter into the life of the city. Marye Stone enjoyed her two book clubs, was active in her church, and served as president of the woman's auxiliary. Stone, in addition to the offices he held in the church and in educational organizations, served as president of the Raleigh Rotary Club (1955–1956).

The new president had expected to spend much of his time performing the duties of the academic head of St. Mary's. However, three days after his arrival on campus, he found himself the acting business manager for the college when E. F. Stoughton went into the hospital.

Stoughton died in February, and Stone decided to continue managing the business affairs of the institution. He did not want to perform the duties of the dean of students as Margaret Cruikshank had, and he needed to find the funds for a dean's salary.[11] The trustees were so pleased to have secured a president who could supervise the major repairs being made with the proceeds from the centennial campaign that they passed a resolution in appreciation.[12] The students dedicated the 1947 *Stagecoach* to the new president and foresaw "a new era."[13]

The Stone administration built upon the past, for there was no fundamental disagreement with the foundations already laid. The stronger members of the faculty simply carried on as before, instilling the traditions. Stone had gone to St. Mary's because he knew the reputation of the school and that its graduates were accepted at the senior colleges and universities of their choice. Bishop Penick told him that he was elected because of his background and experience as an educator and that the board wished to emphasize academics.[14] The new president discovered immediately that he could leave the daily details of academic administration in the capable hands of Elizabeth Tucker. It was not until 1962–1963 that she was given the title to match her duties, that of registrar.

As academic head, Stone suggested few changes in the curriculum. He found the college curriculum finely adjusted to the basic freshman and sophomore courses in any liberal arts college—composition; history of the English novel; the Shakespeare comedies and tragedies; survey courses in American and English literature; directed readings in world literature; French courses through advanced composition and conversation and a survey of French literature; Latin through Plautus and Terence (as had been the case since 1842); beginning and intermediate German; Spanish through intermediate composition and conversation with a literature survey; American history, English history, and the history of western civilization; the basic courses in government, economics, sociology, and psychology; mathematics through differential calculus (Stone added calculus); biology; hygiene; organic and inorganic chemistry; speech and theatre arts; home economics. The basic theory and survey courses were offered in music and art, and a talented pupil could receive advanced training in those departments. Certificates were awarded to those who specialized in art, music, the theatre, or home economics in addition to taking the courses required for graduation. Everyone was required to take Bible and physical education. The business department served about 25 students, and a number of special students took only music or art courses each year. Over the years advanced courses in Spanish, mathematics, and biology along with Christian ethics, physics, and several courses in government, anthropology, and sociology were added.

The commercial education department, established in 1897, was discontinued after the retirement of Ernestine Boineau in June, 1965. A graduate of Winthrop College with further study at Southern Business University and Appalachian, she taught at St. Mary's for 15 years.[15]

No serious thought was given to making St. Mary's a four-year college after the discussions of the 1920s during the Way administration. Stone told the board that he felt that there were already too many weak four-year institutions and that an endowment of at least $10 million would be required to transform St. Mary's into a senior college. His goal was to make it one of the very best junior colleges.[16] The official name was changed in 1954 to St. Mary's Junior College. The original spelling was used again, although the amendment to the charter did not abbreviate the name.[17]

The in-between institution known as the junior college was an American invention. After the legislation of 1957, community colleges burgeoned all over North Carolina. Because those institutions had purposes different from those of St. Mary's, Stone was not active in the American Association of Junior Colleges. He was, however, a regular participant in the North Carolina College Conference, which included junior and senior colleges, and he served as its president for 1951–1952. He was also active on committees for the Southern Association of Colleges and Secondary Schools. When he returned to Western Maryland College in 1951 for the 25th reunion of his class, he made the commencement address, taking as his topic "Liberal Arts in a Church-Related College." At that commencement his alma mater awarded him the honorary degree of doctor of humane letters.

It was not necessary to make fundamental changes at St. Mary's during the 1950s because the nation was in the throes of a conservative reaction that placed women about where they had been 100 years before—in their homes as the guardians of the moral values. World War II had left women with a heightened sense of commitment. Postwar rhetoric was making women responsible for the preservation of the democracy that the men had fought to save. Eleanor Wilson McAdoo emphasized the redemptive role of women in her address to the 1954 graduates. She said:

Young women today face two important tasks, to re-create family life in a Christian home and to work for peace on home, community, national and world levels. . . . You cannot change the world overnight. Start with the family. This is the heart and core of America.[18]

Most St. Mary's women fully expected to be wives and mothers, but educated women had to make a conscious choice during the postwar years. On the one hand, the broadened opportunities resulting from the war were still open. On the other, the joys of the perfect mother

The Order of the Circle marker, placed in front of Holt Dormitory, 1947

ensconced in the perfect house in perfect suburbia were extolled end-
lessly in the women's magazines and on radio and television. The result was that over 60 percent of the women in the United States who
had earned bachelor's degrees in 1958 were full-time housewives five
years later.[19]

Early marriages took their toll of college women. In the 1950s one
half of all the women in the country were married by the age of 20.
The percentage of women attending college in comparison with men
dropped from 47 percent in 1920 to 35 percent in 1958. Worse yet, 60
percent of the women students dropped out, many of them because
they already had found a mate at college. Consequently, as early as
1958, five of the colleges for women had closed and 21 had gone
coeducational.[20]

Those women who continued to work after marriage and children
and the unmarried career women found themselves concentrated

in the traditionally feminized professions—teaching, nursing, social work, accounting, auditing, library work. Indeed, women, despite their increased numbers in the work force, lost ground professionally after 1930; they then held 50 percent of the professional and semi-professional jobs. By the 1960s less than 35 percent of those jobs were held by women.[21] In 1930 two out of five bachelor's and master's degrees were awarded to women; in 1962 the figures were one in three for bachelor's degrees and one in ten for master's degrees.[22] Historians have noted that women's history reveals "a cyclical pattern of development" with "shifting patterns" resulting from "the interaction of social, political, and economic forces."[23] They have seen the need to open jobs to returning veterans after World War II as a powerful economic and political factor influencing society's view of women.[24]

By the late 1950s an occasional nontraditional note was being sounded at St. Mary's. North Carolina author Frances Gray Patton spoke at the alumnae luncheon of 1957 on "The Position of Women in the World Today." She concluded her talk by saying, "But now that we have this freedom and have this power, I trust we shall use them like gentlemen."[25] In 1960 the *Belles* reprinted an article by the editor of the *Red and Black* of Georgia Tech that warned: "There is a danger in the world today far more critical than the threats of the most ominous world power. . . . It is the Revolution of Women. . . ."[26]


## "STUDY, STUDY, AND STUDY SOME MORE"

"A good college administrator respects his faculty. It is his job to help them do their jobs because teaching is the most important function of an educational institution."[27] Thus Richard G. Stone practiced his philosophy during the 23 years of his presidency. Those who worked with him, when asked to characterize his administration, most often replied, "integrity, respect for the faculty, high academic standards."

While he found the curriculum basically sound, Stone did suggest immediately certain changes to bring academic procedures in line with those of other colleges. Over the years the process continued under the direction of strong faculty committees on academic standards. The meticulous minutes of faculty meetings kept by Librarian Helen Brown for 25 years show long discussions of matters academic. Stone presided over faculty meetings, expressing his opinions but not giving the impression of directing the vote. He freely admitted his occasional errors in judgment. Elizabeth Tucker kept up with practices at other institutions and often reported to the faculty on the need for considering a change in a procedure.[28]

At his first working faculty meeting in the fall of 1946 Richard Stone appointed a catalogue committee chaired by Mabel Morrison and instructed the committee "to make a thorough study of other catalogues and re-write the St. Mary's catalogue with a view to our students' needs." He recommended that the "conditional" grade be dropped and that the faculty adopt "a true quality point system."[29] All of those changes were made. The faculty set 64 units with 60 quality points as graduate requirements, meaning that a student had to make a grade of C (then 70–79) on all academic subjects and had to take four units (then ungraded) of physical education in order to receive the junior college diploma.

Class schedules for new college students were made out during orientation week by a faculty committee working together in a large classroom, where in a marathon session they negotiated switches in sections for students with scheduling conflicts. All academic advising was handled by President Stone and Elizabeth Tucker during the 1950s, and she checked all matriculation slips against the requirements at St. Mary's and those at the senior college to which a girl planned to transfer. The system was laborious, but it worked for a student body of about 300 during those years when few electives were offered anywhere to college underclassmen. High school electives were sparse at St. Mary's, but all state requirements were met. Stone successfully resisted local pressure and eliminated the tenth grade beginning in 1947–1948.

In his first report to the trustees Stone said that the institution's "antiquated and below standard science equipment" could endanger accreditation. Three badly overcrowded rooms in the library building were used for 660 student-periods in science each week; one chemistry laboratory section met at night.[30] A science building became the primary goal of the new president.

In that same report Stone also spoke of the library's overcrowded conditions. The library included about 11,000 volumes, far above the minimum required for junior college accreditation; but the president believed that a really good library should have 25,000 volumes. Lack of space restricted purchases. Magazine subscriptions by 1949 were increased to 74, including French and Spanish magazines.

During the 1950s there was much discussion in faculty meetings of the academic level of the student body as revealed each year by the results of the achievement tests taken during orientation week. Most years Mabel Morrison reported that the St. Mary's scores were slightly above the national average for college freshmen, but some years she stated flatly that "the entire school scored too low on mathematics" or that a particular class "made a very poor showing."

There were lengthy faculty deliberations over class attendance policy. The system was a strict one and under the control of the faculty; Stone had set up an absence committee during his first year to deal with exceptions to the policy. Students were expected to be in class unless they were in the infirmary. (Repairing to the infirmary "because of fatigue" on Mondays was discouraged by giving a zero for each class missed.) A complicated system of excused weekend absences was finally established.

Weekends and dating were synonymous for most St. Mary's girls, but during the week *study* was the operative word. The *Student Handbook* each year of the 1950s advised:

STUDY, STUDY, AND STUDY some more. . . . Don't waste time *talking* about work—*do it*! Work hard. Afternoon studying is necessary. . . . Begin your outside reading the day it is assigned. . . . Work when you work, and play when you play. Talk to instructors outside of class if you're worried; they'll help you.

Martha Dabney Jones gave an annual pep talk in assembly on study habits. She liked to remark, "The one thing that people are willing to pay for and not get is a college education."[31] Actually, achievement scores rose steadily, reaching a peak in the mid-1960s.

Continued education remained the expectation of most St. Mary's women, although in the 1950s the proportion of those going on to further study dropped as low as 87 percent some years as wedding plans for seniors were announced in the *Belles*. "The Hill is the place to go" was still the St. Mary's slogan.[32] Twenty-two of the 53 graduates of 1952 transferred to Chapel Hill; but the annual lists of college destinations included not only the women's colleges in North Carolina and Virginia and the Universities of Georgia and South Carolina, but also Vassar, Wellesley, and the Universities of Chicago, Southern California, and Wyoming. St. Mary's best students continued to do well wherever they transferred. In 1951 Sonoko Yamamoto wrote from New York:

I do not think that Barnard is any more difficult than St. Mary's. Now I realize the high standards which St. Mary's has. I was excused from English for foreign students. . . . When I entered St. Mary's, . . . I could not understand a thing in the classes. . . . Miss Jones and Miss Morrison used to speak to me very slowly so that I could keep up with the conversation. . . . I feel that I can never be grateful enough to them. . . . I miss my beautiful St. Mary's so very much.[33]

Richard Stone felt enough confidence in the program at St. Mary's to volunteer to be one of the four pioneer junior colleges to do a self-study in 1959 for the Southern Association of Colleges and Secondary Schools. Beginning in 1960 the association required every member institution to make a self-study and to be evaluated every ten years by a visiting committee of educators as a part of the reaccreditation process. The purpose of a self-study, Stone explained, was that a college should "reassess its objectives, measure its success in attaining them, and explore ways and means by which it can improve its educational effectiveness." [34] Because no guidelines had been developed, St. Mary's had the task of structuring such a report; the visiting committee later commended highly the result.

For many months, beginning in February, 1958, subcommittees of the faculty working under a steering committee studied every facet of campus life. [35] Chairman Carl Cannon wrote a statement concerning the objectives of the institution that reflected the educational philosophy of the 1950s as well as an understanding of the history of St. Mary's:

In the effort to make our contribution we are constantly aware of our complex situation. We must recognize 1) that our students must be prepared to transfer to other institutions with constantly rising standards, 2) that our students today, as well as those in the past, properly have as their highest ambition marriage and the establishing of families and homes, 3) that they have the potentiality and willingness to become leaders in church, civic, cultural, and educational activities in their communities, 4) that they have chosen to attend a church-affiliated junior college. [36]

The report of the visiting committee found the curriculum well established and a workable means of changing it through recommendations from the academic standards committee to the faculty. [37] The committee agreed with the self-study that more audiovisual equipment should be acquired by the departments and that a language laboratory was needed. It found the facilities for physical education "insufficient" and "overcrowded" and the library space inadequate, but its services, under trying circumstances, "excellent."

The faculty, then consisting of 24 full-time and four part-time instructors, was characterized as "excellent, and loyal with an active interest in the intellectual and social welfare of the students" that led to "a close relationship with the students." The report noted, "The status of the faculty . . . seems high, and individual members have ready access to the president." However, it emphasized the need for a clear program of faculty development with provision for sabbatical leaves. The visiting committee recommended that the probationary period before tenure be changed from one year to three years and that the retirement age be lowered from 72 to 68.

The administrative organization of St. Mary's, being virtually a one-man operation, was characterized in the report as "unusual and unfamiliar." The committee found Stone "unusually well-equipped to serve as the leader of the faculty" but thought that the administrative duties assigned to various faculty and staff members had produced a situation "not particularly conducive to a good creative administration or good faculty and student morale." The recommendations, designed to alleviate the situation as much as was possible in the absence of both an academic head and a director of admissions, were that department chairmen be appointed and given departmental budgets, that the faculty be involved in academic counseling, that an admissions committee be formed, and that more attention be given to recruiting students.[38]

Academic policy during the 1960s was directed toward enrichment of the curriculum and toward carrying out the recommendations of the 1959 visiting committee. A faculty committee produced a comprehensive statement of the purpose and objectives of the institution that was adopted by both the faculty and the trustees and published in the college catalog. The statement seemed to be the objectives of Aldert Smedes stated in contemporary language; the eternal verities did not change.

PURPOSE: St. Mary's, today as in the past, has as its ultimate purpose to provide opportunities, under the influence of the church, for young women to lay the foundation for developing both their individual potentialities and a sense of obligation to society.

The statement continued with emphases placed upon character development, upon general academic excellence as preparation for further education, and upon appreciation of the arts and sports as lifetime assets.

Gradually the president appointed department chairmen, beginning with John U. Tate, Jr., whose appointment as chairman of the English department was announced in April, 1960. Two years later Mabel Morrison became chairman of the social studies department and Robert Lee Green Connelly of the foreign languages department. (The music department had had a director since the school's founding.) In 1967 Mary Oliver Ellington became chairman of the biological sciences. The departments consisting of one or two persons remained unorganized, despite the visiting committee's suggestion that area division chairmen be appointed.

The southern association's suggestion that "a clear definition of the meaning of a letter grade" be formulated led to long discussions of grading philosophy during faculty meetings. In 1961–1962 a system based on a ten-point spread, except for the D that was 65–69, went into effect. But by the winter of 1964 some of the teachers thought that a grade of 80 should not be designated as "good" and that 65 was too low a passing grade. The system adopted was A, 94–100; B, 86–93; C, 78–85; D, 70–77. In 1962–1963 the quality point system was changed to the 4–3–2–1 system used by most of the area colleges although many of the faculty were reluctant to grant a quality point for a D.[39] Academic counseling was strengthened when for 1961–1962 each student was assigned to a faculty adviser and expected to meet regular conference dates.

The library staff was able to offer increased services after completion of a new building in 1966. In 1952 Mary Johnson Browne became assistant librarian. The wife of Owens Hand Browne of the chemistry department and a chemistry teacher herself, Mary Browne fell into library work when her daughter was unable to complete a summer job and volunteered her mother's services. The ever-increasing library collection opened new horizons to the serious students and provided sources for term papers that were more than superficial surveys; one of the papers was published.[40]

Concerts and lectures still were considered an essential part of the St. Mary's educational program. For many years the entire school continued to attend the concerts sponsored by the Civic Concert Music Association. During the same week in February, 1949, the students heard Artur Rubinstein and watched bobby soxers mob young Leonard Bernstein. For well over a decade pianist William Masselos played at St. Mary's almost every year, and he composed music for the St. Mary's Glee Club concerts. His close friendship with the music faculty and Mabel Morrison brought him back year after year even though he was in demand on the most prestigious of concert circuits.[41]

The annual lecture series at the college was planned by Mabel Morrison and her committee that included students. The objectives always were to stimulate campus-wide interest in a broad range of subjects and to expose the students to interesting and vital people. Usually, in addition to the post-lecture informal discussion, the speakers consented to meet with one or more classes. The topic of the year emphasized in turn the various facets of the educational program—foreign policy, religion, science, literature, art, athletics. The twice-weekly required assemblies in the auditorium often featured local speakers. During the early years of his administration President Stone sometimes spoke on current events topics.

There is evidence in the pages of the college newspaper that the students were interested in the world around them during the late 1940s and the 1950s. In a hard-hitting editorial in February, 1948, criticizing the University of Oklahoma's refusal to admit a black woman to law school, the *Belles* came out against segregation: "Deep-rooted ideas which warp our minds against our fellow citizens must be pushed away, and we must begin to survey the situation free from prejudice. To advocate racial segregation is to corrupt the very core of our democratic government." A poll taken the next week revealed that most of the students disagreed; they insisted that "separate, but *really* equal" was the solution to America's racial problem.[42] President Truman went to Raleigh during his tough battle for reelection in the fall of 1948. The *Belles* reported that the president ended his speech with a plea to the voters to exercise the franchise.

St. Mary's students were aware of the developing cold war. In the fall of 1946 an editorial in their paper entitled "Rumors Are Flying" deplored the "dangerous, hysterical talk that war with Russia is inevitable." The autumn of 1948 found the United Nations stalemated over Berlin and over the control of atomic energy. A front-page article in the *Belles* declared firmly, "The United States and Britain have been putting up with Russian stubbornness long enough." The student writer of a current events column wondered in 1954, "Will the Russians beat us to the moon?" and predicted that the trip would be made "in our generation."[43] Usually there were several international students on campus who could speak about conditions in other countries, and the mixture of nationalities always characteristic of the faculty helped to correct the native tendency to provincialism.

The college publications of the era reported more interest in public issues and politics than might have been expected in the fifties. As early as 1953 a film on the dangers of water pollution was shown in assembly. The year before, a busload from St. Mary's went to Chapel Hill to hear Eleanor Roosevelt. The day that Adlai Stevenson visited St. Mary's in March, 1954, was remembered as "a great day." C. A. P. Moore, adviser to the Young Democrats, persuaded the caravan to stop en route to the airport, and classes were dismissed.[44] The Republican minority decided to organize and in November 25 students formed a Young Republicans Club.

Moore managed another coup in February, 1955, when presidential hopeful G. Mennen Williams spoke at the college. As the 1956 election approached, a mock election was held; the Eisenhower-Nixon ticket won by two to one, with 271 persons voting.[45] A graduate of St. Mary's and of the University of North Carolina, Mary Laurens Withers Richardson, vice-chairman of the State Democratic Executive Committee, spoke to the college assembly in 1957. She urged St. Mary's students to become politically active as "the duty of an educated woman."[46] In 1959 the visiting lecturer in December was a "Mr. Henry Kissinger of Washington, D. C., who spoke on foreign policy."

The 1960s were not turbulent at St. Mary's. Interest in current affairs continued, and most years the college newspaper ran a good column on world affairs. United Nations Day was observed each October. Mabel Morrison was adviser to the campus chapter of the Collegiate Council for the United Nations, organized in the fall of 1961. Each year the St. Mary's chapter was assigned to be a particular "nation" at the state

Mock General Assembly of the United Nations, and the delegates had to learn enough to be able to speak and vote as that nation would in the General Assembly meeting in New York.

Foreign affairs continued to dominate the news in the eyes of the students; their newspaper ran a regular column called "World News for Busy Students." The *Belles* interviewed the teacher of American history and government, Martha Stoops, who said, "I feel that we shall live in this atmosphere of crisis for many years to come. It is very important for us to become well informed. Our worst enemy, however, is fear, and this we must overcome."[47] Then came November 22, 1963. At lunchtime word spread that Pres. John F. Kennedy had been shot. The first reaction was utter disbelief. Then, as a radio was brought into history class, disbelief turned to dismay and then to anguish. A memorial service that night filled the chapel. In the faculty meeting a few days later, Stone said, "The loss of a strong, able, dedicated president possessing such qualities as Mr. Kennedy's gift of oratory, his keen sense of humor, his appreciation of the arts, and his profound knowledge of history is irreparable. . . . We owe his successor, President Johnson, our greatest support and loyalty."[48]

In general, Pres. Lyndon B. Johnson received the support of the campus community. Later, a few St. Mary's students spoke out against the U.S. involvement in Vietnam, and a few protesters wore black arm bands. More students spoke out against the new civil rights laws. One student, however, urged St. Mary's women to join the call of the student body president at the university in Chapel Hill for a boycott of segregated business. She saw this as a way for a student "to stand up for [her] beliefs without breaking the law."[49]

In 1967 as the Far East became a topic in the daily news, the committee on the lecture series decided to follow Mabel Morrison's suggestion that for three years experts on China, India, and Japan be invited to the campus. The most fascinating of a number of interesting lecturers was Han Suyin, whose book was the basis for the movie *Love Is A Many Splendored Thing*.

One of the visiting lecturers on literature put St. Mary's in a book. The British author T. H. White spoke at St. Mary's in October, 1963, just a few weeks before his death. His journal of the tour, *America at Last*, was published posthumously.[50]

The Stone administration, in the process of widening educational opportunities, strengthened the physical education curriculum. In 1948 the faculty voted to give four hours of credit, but no quality points, for physical education that was required of everyone. By 1969 the department was offering a health course and 28 different semester courses in physical education. Jane Goss Guess directed the department until she resigned in 1951 to take her master's degree in sociology at North Carolina State. She continued to teach dance and to direct the May Day pageants, and she returned in 1955 to teach part time while completing her graduate work. She began the library's collection of vocational guidance materials. After 1951, a succession of instructors filled the two positions in the physical education department for several years.

In 1957 Doris Simpson Bailey went to St. Mary's to teach dance. A native San Antonian, she was a graduate of Texas Woman's University and had studied at Jacob's Pillow University of Dance in Massachusetts. She had worked with Nancy Stamey (who also joined the college faculty in 1957) as a volunteer choreographer and director of dance in the Raleigh Children's Theatre. Doris Bailey, the mother of three young sons, was one of the first of a new breed of teachers at the college—the wives of men whose careers had taken them to Raleigh and who were sufficiently broadminded to want their wives to pursue their own careers. Stone soon realized that those women made good faculty members and were more likely to remain than were the young women working only until marriage.[51] Doris Bailey stayed for 16 years, and during those years many outstanding performances were presented by her students.

Two new dance groups were organized—in 1962 the Caperettes, who performed tap dance routines, and in 1969–1970 the Scottish Dancers, later known as the Gillie Callum. Orchesis remained the honorary modern dance club made up of the best dancers and choreographers. New members were tapped into the dance groups by "paired, silent figures" in black leotards who carried candles as they ran through the dormitories at night. The induction ceremony was held in the gymnasium. Doris Bailey arranged master classes whenever well-known teachers of the dance were in the area, and her students were invited to take part in fine arts festivals on other campuses. St. Mary's was, in fact, one of the first institutions in the state to teach modern dance.[52]

The May Day pageant was enjoyed by large crowds each year. Students who wished to participate were placed in dance classes for physical education. Each year a theme was chosen, and their director worked with students to write, choreograph, and costume a program built around that theme. May Day was celebrated intermittently at St. Mary's from the early years of the school, but the celebration did not become a regular custom until the 1920s. The festival was suspended during the depths of the Depression and resumed in 1935 with the queen and her court in Grecian costumes. After 1937 members of the May Court wore the traditional long dresses in pastels and the queen was gowned in white.[53]

Tennis had been popular at St. Mary's since the turn of the century. In 1948 Alice Marble was on campus, and the *Belles* reported that "the greatest of all women tennis players" emphasized "the will to win" and the importance of physical fitness.[54] Mary Louise Jones, tennis coach at Myers Park High School in Charlotte, went to St. Mary's in the fall of 1961 and was made head of the physical education department in 1963. Stone was prescient, for Lou Jones was to be the number-one player in the South in women's doubles by 1972 and at the peak of her career to be included in the North Carolina Tennis Hall of Fame. Her bachelor's and master's degrees were from the University of North Carolina. When she arrived at St. Mary's, she found two tennis courts on front campus and two behind the library, all in poor shape and "watered only by God." By the fall of 1965 there were still four courts, but they were new, all-weather grasstex courts built on back campus at a cost of nearly $27,000.[55] In 1965 St. Mary's participated for the first time in the state intercollegiate tennis tournament and reached the semifinals in doubles before being defeated by Duke. The next year St. Mary's reached the finals and lost the state championship to Duke. When the girls played mixed doubles with the North Carolina State University team, they also competed "very successfully."[56] Tennis for fun became so popular at St. Mary's that in 1966 three fourths of the students elected tennis for physical education class. That pleased Lou Jones, for she believed that everyone should become sufficiently skilled at several sports to enjoy playing for recreation and physical fitness throughout a lifetime.[57]

Swimming, despite the handicap of "the bathtub size" pool, was a popular choice for physical education credit. In fact, every student was required to pass an elementary test in swimming before being graduated. The most proficient swimmers had for some years formed the swimming club. The name was changed to Sea Saints in 1962. The group presented beautiful programs of synchronized swimming. Both Orchesis and the Sea Saints appeared in a 1963 film on education and culture in North Carolina made to be shown to civic clubs around the state.[58] The Sea Saints worked under several coaches during the 1960s. Margaret C. Duncan remained for five years, 1967–1974. An excellent teacher, she was a strong faculty committee worker as well.

## "NOT LIGHTLY CONSIDERED"

Because of the affluence of the fifties and sixties and the stability of the administration at St. Mary's, there were so many student applications that it was possible to tighten admission policies. By 1960 all applicants to the college, even graduates of St. Mary's high school, were required to submit scores on the Scholastic Aptitude Test of the College Entrance Examination Board, and applicants for admission as freshmen were required to take the Secondary School Admission tests. Stone assured the alumnae that St. Mary's would continue to follow "the well-defined policy" of years' standing of considering several factors when weighing applications. He explained that the standardized tests were necessary because academic standards, and thus, grades, varied greatly from school to school. Senior colleges, he said, were raising standards, and it was important that St. Mary's graduates continue to do well wherever they transferred.[59] The pool of applicants was large and strong enough that the average total score on college boards for juniors at the college was raised by 69 points between 1960 and 1965, placing the St. Mary's average just between the national average for first year junior college students and the national average for freshmen at senior colleges. The average total score for juniors at St. Mary's rose seven points for 1966–1967 and held there the next year.[60] That was considered to be high among junior colleges and proof of academic soundness. The waiting list was often closed in mid-spring. In 1966 there were three applicants for each available space; the new Cruikshank Dormitory had made possible increased enrollment.

The teachers were delighted; some of the alumnae were not. President Stone held firm because experience, he believed, had proven him to be right. It had always been the policy to give preference to alumnae-connected applicants, other factors being equal. He told the trustees that he had yielded to alumnae pressure and admitted for 1964–1965 ten alumnae-connected students whose preparation was weak. Half failed. "We believe it unwise," he said, "to admit a student whose . . . success is doubtful. We think the ultimate separation of this student does more harm than the failure to admit in the first place." In 1965–1966, 35 percent of the student body was alumnae-connected.[61]

Adverse criticism continued. At the general meeting of the alumnae association on May 7, 1966, a resolution was passed recommending that an admissions board consisting of the president, the registrar, the dean of students, and a teaching faculty member be established. Also, the resolution recommended "that the Admissions Board be ever aware of a practical need to give fair consideration first to the applications of daughters of alumnae and members of the Episcopal Church— the keystone support to the future growth of St. Mary's." The resolution ended with "the earnest hope that this request . . . not be lightly considered."

At the meeting of the board of trustees a few days later, at which the resolution was discussed, President Stone noted, "The Southern Association is very specific concerning pressure of any sort on admissions policies." He felt that the trustees "should make it clear that admissions policies are the responsibility of the Board." The trustees thanked the alumnae association for its interest, promised to keep alumnae informed, and appointed a committee to study admissions policy.[62] In the fall of 1966 Stone appointed an admissions committee, composed of three faculty members, to review borderline cases; its recommendations usually were accepted by the administration. Richard Stone and Elizabeth Tucker continued to handle the applications of students who obviously were qualified. The fact that a committee decision could be cited when an applicant was refused and the fact that the extremely positive admissions picture began to change when the University of North Carolina opened its freshman class to women quieted the clamor over admissions policies.

By the spring of 1966 the alumnae were disturbed also by rumors that the two years of high school at St. Mary's were to be dropped. The alumnae council passed a resolution on May 7, 1966, "opposing any future plans to discontinue" the high school. Actually, an ad hoc committee appointed by the board to study the high school question had reported in October, 1965, that, after considerable research, its members "found no compelling reason" for any change in the organization of the institution. Requests for information about the high school were increasing as other junior colleges dropped their high school divisions. That committee also explored the feasibility of making St. Mary's a four-year college; it recommended against such expansion because it would necessitate a great increase in the endowment. The report concluded by suggesting that the question be studied again in five years.[63] In 1969 the self-study report showed that St. Mary's unique four-year combination still worked. That decision proved to be an important one, for the high school enrollment doubled after 1965.

The alumnae were not the only ones passing resolutions. For years the students regularly petitioned for and the *Belles* crusaded for a cut system similar to the one prevalent in the senior colleges, rather than the complicated system of weekends, "extended weekends," and overnights in effect at St. Mary's. Periodically, the faculty decided that "the girls are not studying enough *now*." Finally, in the spring of 1966, the faculty adopted a system of one legal absence per credit hour in each class with restrictions placed on students on academic probation and extra cuts for those on the honor roll. The penalty for overcutting was a lowered grade.[64] The high school operated under the rules in effect in the public schools, and no class cuts were allowed. However, a minimal number of excused absences could be arranged under certain conditions.

Another student grievance aired almost annually was the tight examination schedule. A free "reading day" for study between the last day of classes and the first day of examinations was instituted by the faculty in January, 1965. The next year the "summer reading" was modified and the reading list changed to novels on which a critical paper was to be written during the academic year.[65] Thus arose generations of students who knew not Homer.

The abolition of Saturday classes became the next target. Students and teachers alike were weary of that burden. After the student petition of the fall of 1968, a faculty committee worked out a schedule that shifted to 90-minute periods for Tuesday-Thursday classes, and Saturday classes were no more.

As the decade drew near to its close, the idea of placing students on all faculty committees was broached; but Richard Stone thought that "needed study," being "a little drastic."[66] He did not intend that students were to be denied freedom of expression. Everyone at St. Mary's could express an opinion on anything. The southern association insisted upon a formal statement as a part of the reaccreditation process, and the trustees reaffirmed the accepted policy in a statement: "The Board of Trustees of St. Mary's Junior College hereby reaffirms its traditional policy of granting the members of the faculty, staff, and student body of St. Mary's Junior College the right of freedom of expression."[67]

The emphasis placed on academic standards during the Stone administration meant that, as in the past, over 90 percent of the institution's graduates earned bachelor's degrees. Only 20 of the 579 graduates between 1962 and 1967 did not continue their studies.[68] It was still "traditional" to transfer to Chapel Hill, and at least 40 percent of each senior class did so. A few selected North Carolina State and majors nontraditional for women; a few chose a year in Europe; a few went directly into business school or nurse's training. The alumnae news reported a fair share of Phi Beta Kappa keys earned at other institutions by St. Mary's graduates, and St. Mary's small high school class often boasted a National Merit finalist. There was an Angier B. Duke Scholarship winner in 1961.[69] As St. Mary's women became more aware of the feminist movement, more of them began to take graduate degrees.

St. Mary's was reaccredited by the Southern Association of Colleges and Schools in 1969. The second self-study was directed by Mabel Morrison; for months nearly everyone on the faculty and staff and a number of students worked diligently on the various committees. The result was a report of which President Stone said, "Nowhere have I seen a better study in depth to seek the truth."[70] The president knew whereof he spoke, for he was serving then a second term of six years on the college commission of the southern association and had evaluated the report of many a visiting committee.[71]

After the committee's inspection visit of March 16–19, 1969, Morrison reported to the faculty: "The six members of the visiting committee[72] toured every nook and cranny of the campus, interviewed all but three faculty members, and about 130 students. . . . No weakness or deficiencies were discovered of which we were not aware."[73] The general tone of the visiting committee's report was that there was nothing wrong at St. Mary's that money could not cure.

## "FOR THE INFLUENCE OF A TEACHER NEVER ENDS"

Upon assuming his duties as president, Dick Stone found that the teachers were "surprisingly good," but that their salaries were "entirely too low." During his 23 years as president, he tried to maintain a high level of faculty competence and to improve the salary situation.[74] He understood the importance of good teaching, which he once defined as "simply the stimulation and guidance of learning,"[75] and he agreed with a statement made in the 1966 *Stagecoach*, "The influence of a teacher never ends." In his first report to the board of trustees Stone noted that many teachers "had contributed much for love of the school and the Church." St. Mary's could not, he said, "continue to depend upon those who are willing to make such sacrifices." Furthermore, he asked for a better balance between men and women, and that, he said, would cost money.[76] There were six men on the faculty then—Guess, Moore, Broughton, Peery, Hughes, and Eugene Fred Parker, who had just arrived. There were four of those women who "had contributed much, indeed"—Davis, Lineberry, Bason, and Morrison.

For 46 years Florence Davis retained her zest for life at St. Mary's. Each year she admonished the girls "to stand up straight," taught them to walk to center stage and speak extemporaneously on a topic announced only that moment, taught them to speak Shakespeare's lines in the commencement play, and above all, to behave "like a St. Mary's girl." In her farewell speech in 1959 she said that daily life at the school in her time had changed from stately waltzes in the parlor with no boys allowed to Saturday night picnics in Bermuda shorts, boys, cars, and "late returns," but that "the St. Mary's girl remained the same with her charm, personality, high ideals, and love of the chapel."[77] Her portrait hangs in Pittman Auditorium, the gift of several alumnae.[78] Florence Davis returned to Raleigh in 1960 and lived there until her death on September 21, 1966. Her funeral was held in the St. Mary's Chapel.[79]

Elizabeth Bason went to the school in 1924 and was for 37 years the arbiter of ladylike behavior and the guardian of the chapel. A native of Burlington, she took her undergraduate work at Flora Macdonald College and her master's degree at Columbia University. She was the

Mabel Morrison

Jane Rabon

Martha Stoops

Mary Oliver Ellington

Mary Browne and Helen Brown

home economics department at St. Mary's. She was one of those quiet people who worked efficiently behind the scenes to make daily life run smoothly. She could walk through the dining room and tell exactly who was missing and at the same time observe table manners. At Bason's table a sandwich was never eaten until it was cut precisely into four pieces. Casper Lilly, whose service to St. Mary's in many capacities on the custodial staff spanned well over half a century, remarked in 1979, "*This* generation would kill Miss Bason dead!"[80]

Yet behind that prim and proper facade was one whose kindness was "infinite," one who knew instinctively how to help in a crisis.[81] The 1962 *Stagecoach* was dedicated to her. She was adviser to the altar guild and to the marshals. She said upon her retirement, "The girls and the Chapel have been my primary interest . . . and my principal concern has been to improve the conduct of the girls."[82] The home economics department was discontinued upon her retirement in 1962. She planned to "sit in peace and quiet" with her three sisters and then to travel. Elizabeth Lampkin Bason died on August 7, 1967.

Another quiet one who contributed much to St. Mary's was Ruth Lineberry, who taught mathematics for 40 years (1927 to 1967). Because her family lived in Raleigh, she was not so well known to all of the girls as were the teachers who lived on the halls. She worked with student government as adviser to the legislative body. A graduate of Meredith College, she took her master's degree at Columbia University and had taught in high school and college before returning to Raleigh. In the classroom she explained each problem methodically and thoroughly. She encouraged those who feared mathematics, and she pushed her best students to do independent work. By the time she retired, more women than in earlier years were considering mathematics as a major because they recognized a number of career possibilities. The president depended upon Ruth Lineberry to carry a heavy load of committee work; he said that he could always trust her judgment and that she usually solved any problems that arose.[83] She continued to live with her sister in the family home after retirement. Ruth Lineberry died on October 16, 1980.

During the 1950s St. Mary's lost four others of the veteran teachers besides Florence Davis—Watson Partrick, Al Moore, Katherine Morris, and Jane Guess. Watson Partrick retired in 1956.[84] Charles Albert Petigru Moore, who was involved in everything from 1935 to 1957, was in wretched health by the end of his teaching career. He left St. Mary's in the spring of 1957 and died unexpectedly at his home on June 5 at age 52.[85]

Katherine Currin Morris of the art department was a native of Henderson. She studied art at St. Mary's under Clara Fenner and stayed on after graduation to help in the art and physical education departments. After Clara Fenner's death, she continued her study of art at other institutions, including the University of North Carolina and the New York School of Fine and Applied Art. She taught, did free-lance work, and held positions in the Works Progress Administration and the North Carolina Art Society before returning to St. Mary's in 1945. The girls admired Katherine Morris greatly; she was a striking brunette, a good teacher, and an interested friend. Her valiant battle against cancer was an inspiration to all who knew her, and while ill at her apartment across from the college she was still very much a part of the St. Mary's family. She died on December 20, 1958.[86]

The art department was taken over by Margaret Click Williams, who had joined the faculty in 1956 to assist Katherine Morris. She held both the bachelor's and master's degrees in fine arts from the Woman's College of the University of North Carolina and had studied further at the University of California at Berkeley and at Burnsville School of Fine Arts. Before going to St. Mary's, she was director of fine arts for the North Carolina State College student union. She was in Raleigh because her husband was with the North Carolina Museum of Art.

In the summer of 1959 Jane Guess lost her battle against cancer. She, too, was valiant in the face of the inevitable. Her colleagues wrote of Jane Guess, "Her greetings and her smile made sunshine. . . ."[87]

William C. Guess went to St. Mary's in 1928. A native of Moore County, he was educated at the University of North Carolina and at the Johns Hopkins University. Before going to Raleigh, he had taught at the college level in several locations. His major contribution to St. Mary's was the successful management of the institution's investments, with the advice and consent of the finance committee of the board. He was trustee of the pension fund and from 1947 secretary-treasurer of the board of trustees, duties he continued to perform after his retirement from teaching in 1962. Also, he was treasurer of the chapel and for 18 years secretary of the faculty. William Guess died just two years after his retirement. He bequeathed to the college one half of his estate to be designated as the Jane Guess Endowment Fund with "the income only to be used for the general purposes of the school."[88]

Richard Stone taught the economics classes for two years after Guess's retirement. He enjoyed the students but found the schedule too confining because of his other duties. A succession of part-time faculty members handled the course for several years thereafter.

Throughout the Stone administration the music department remained strong. Russell Broughton, Mary Ruth Haig, Geraldine Cate, and Donald Peery agreed on the fundamentals of teaching music, on the importance of the study of theory. Broughton directed the music department for 25 years. Born in Indiana, he grew up in Grand Rapids, Michigan. After taking his bachelor's degree in music at Oberlin College, he enlisted in the armed services during World War I and was assigned to a hospital in Paris. After the war, he went to Burlington, Iowa, as organist and choirmaster at the Episcopal church. He was married to Janet Louise Robinson of Burlington in 1925, and soon they departed for France because Russell had won the prestigious Estey scholarship to study at the Conservatoire Americain in Fontainebleau. When the Broughtons returned to Oberlin, he completed his master's degree and taught while she took her master's degree in mathematics.[89]

At St. Mary's Russell Broughton taught organ, theory, and music composition. He had over 30 published compositions to his credit when he moved to Raleigh. The St. Mary's choir, which he directed, and the other choral groups directed by Geraldine Cate often sang his music; his *Centennial Cantata* was repeated on several special occasions. The students dedicated the 1944 *Stagecoach* to Russell Broughton "for the songs he wrote especially for us, for his clever wit, . . . patience, and for his chapel music."

The chapel organ, St. Mary's second since the 1870s, needed replacing. Some rearrangements of the interior of the chapel were necessary when the new Reuter organ was installed in 1954; a new screen hid the organ console and robing room.[90] To commemorate Russell Broughton's 25th year at St. Mary's, in April, 1961, Chaplain Moultrie Guerry and the choir planned a special chapel service.[91] Broughton was an organizer of the Raleigh Chamber Music Guild in 1941 and served as the first president.[92] He retired in 1965; Russell Broughton died February 7, 1969.

Janet Broughton joined the staff in 1940 as library assistant. The fact that Margaret Cruikshank employed a married woman, and a faculty wife at that, caused considerable comment.[93] Soon Janet Broughton was teaching French and mathematics at St. Mary's. She would spend endless time helping a floundering student; at the same time, she saw to it that the bright students learned to think analytically.[94] The next hour would find her engaging a class in animated conversation in French.

The Broughtons and Elizabeth Tucker were such avid and accomplished bridge players that they traveled as far as California to play in national tournaments. After Russell Broughton's death, Elizabeth Tucker visited in Raleigh (by then, she had retired to her Hertford home) to look after Janet Broughton, who was in failing health and who died on January 9, 1981. Her funeral was held in the St. Mary's Chapel.

After Russell Broughton's retirement, Mary Ruth Haig was named chairman of the music department. A succession of teachers took the organ pupils, and Donald Peery played for some of the chapel services. His bachelor's degree was from Oberlin College, and he took a leave of absence during 1947–1948 to earn a master's degree at Columbia University. Born in Kansas on the campus of Midland College where his father was the president, he moved to Raleigh when his father became pastor of Holy Trinity Lutheran Church. A fine pianist, for 15 years he was a judge and faculty member of the National Guild of Piano Teachers, and for nine years he conducted his own summer workshop for piano teachers. He taught classes at St. Mary's in theory, music history, and music appreciation, as well as giving individual piano lessons.[95]

During Broughton's chairmanship the choral groups were under the direction of Geraldine Spinks Cate, who also taught the voice students. A native of Columbia, South Carolina, she was graduated from the University of South Carolina with a degree in foreign languages, and received the bachelor of music degree from Westminster Choir College. In 1933 Gerry Cate went to the Philippines to organize a music department at Silliman University, a Presbyterian mission school. She returned to New York for further study, earning a master's degree in music from Teachers College, Columbia University. She taught at St. Mary's for 36 years.

Geraldine Cate demanded and received from students their best. She followed with excitement the careers of two of her students, Marilyn Zschau and Jeanne Smith, who were members of opera companies.[96] Cate was active in the National Association of Teachers of Singing, serving as regional governor and then as national vice-president, 1975–1979. She was appointed visiting instructor in voice at the North Carolina School of the Arts (1968–1973). For a number of years she directed the St. Cecilia Choral Society, and later the Raleigh Oratorio Society. She worked for the racial integration of both groups.

The only member of the faculty besides the three musicians—Mary Ruth Haig, Gerry Cate, and Don Peery—and the librarian, Helen Brown, to serve through the entire Stone administration was Mabel Margaret Morrison. Although she was for many years the only Ph.D. on the faculty, she was known as "Miss Morrison" until Camilla Hoy of the foreign languages department received her doctorate from Bryn Mawr in 1954. Thereafter, the faculty minutes always referred to "Dr. Hoy" and sometimes to "Dr. Morrison." Camilla Hoy left the next year to go to Birmingham Southern College.

The academic degrees with which Mabel Morrison arrived in 1929 were the bachelor's and master's degrees from Dalhousie University in Nova Scotia and the Ph.D. degree from the University of Toronto. Her master's degree was in psychology and history and her doctorate in philosophy. She studied further at the London School of Economics, 1933–1934. She taught at various times logic, psychology, Latin, En-

New library given to the college

glish history, geography, and western civilization. Mabel Morrison was a formidable force in the classroom as she delivered scholarly lectures, pausing occasionally to ask the questions to ferret out the one or two girls who were not prepared. Her lectures were enriched and her outlook on life broadened because she traveled extensively. Her students appreciated more fully what Mabel Morrison meant to them years later when they had begun the process of evaluating their own lives in terms of what it means to be an educated woman.[97] She meant to stay at St. Mary's for no more than a few years and never relinquished her Canadian citizenship. Over 50 years later, though retired, she remained a vital part of the college.

Although a goodly number of the faculty remained for years, every year some few left. President Stone was able to fill such vacancies with competent and experienced persons already living in the area. In the twentieth century, as in the nineteenth, the location of St. Mary's contributed in a number of ways to its survival.

A longtime faculty member who was not from the area was Sara Esther Jones; she arrived in the second year of the Stone administration and was for 19 years a strong member of the English department and an indefatigable laborer on faculty committees. The daughter of a physician, she grew up in Berea, Kentucky. She received her bachelor's degree from Asheville College. She taught in the public schools and was affiliated for five years with Georgia Teachers' College.[98]

Sara Esther Jones went about the campus with an air of majestic calm. However, chatter in chapel or undue noise on her hall in Holt aroused her wrath. A student wrote of her, "She prides herself on being 'a slave driver,' but to her classes she reveals a humorous, kind-hearted personality." The residents on her hall found "S.E." "stern, but kind."[99] The seniors chose her as their sponsor for four years straight, 1956–1960, and the 1955 *Stagecoach* was dedicated to her. She was adviser to the *Muse* and to the *Bulletin* and was a member of the college publicity committee. In 1966 she tendered her resignation.[100] She had recently undergone a not entirely successful eye operation, and she retired to live in Lexington, Kentucky, with her sister. Sara Esther Jones died on November 17, 1981.

When Owens Hand Browne went from Lenoir-Rhyne College in 1950 to teach chemistry at St. Mary's he was returning home. His family moved to Raleigh in 1908 when his father joined the faculty at A&M. As a small boy, he spent many a summer afternoon playing with the Lay children in the empty St. Mary's buildings. He took his undergraduate work at North Carolina State and his Ph.D. at the Johns Hopkins University. He married a Meredith College teacher, Mary Martin Johnson, who was a Raleigh native and a professor's daughter. By then he was teaching at Virginia Military Institute, and she had given up the idea of completing study at Cornell for her doctorate. Later, Owens Browne taught at Cherokee Indian Normal School (now Pembroke State University) and served for two years as interim president there. When the Brownes moved to Lenoir Rhyne, both taught chemistry.[101]

At St. Mary's Browne made do with the crowded classroom-laboratory in the library building until his fine new quarters in Cheshire Hall were completed in 1953. He saw to it that his students knew their chemistry; he could always be counted on for a little extra help. A photography buff from his youth, Owens Browne took many reels of movie film of campus life that he showed in assembly and to alumnae groups. Each spring he spent hours taping the music for May Day. When Browne left St. Mary's in 1968, the college lost its last husband-wife team. There had been the Guesses, the Broughtons, and, before them, the Cruikshanks. For a time after leaving the college, Owens Browne managed the American Opinion Bookstore in Raleigh.

Stone felt "especially fortunate" to find Eugene Fred Parker already in Raleigh when in 1947 he needed a teacher of Spanish and German. After a long career in education, Parker had gone to Raleigh as the broker for a mutual fund. He was persuaded to return to teaching part time at St. Mary's, and he stayed for nearly 14 years. A native of North Dakota, he held the master's and Ph.D. degrees from Harvard, and had studied at the Sorbonne and at the University of Madrid. He was an experienced college teacher when he joined the St. Mary's faculty. He and his wife took a great interest in student activities and enjoyed entertaining the faculty. After his retirement in June, 1960, the Parkers toured Europe. Then he returned to St. Mary's to fill an unexpected vacancy during the second semester of 1960–1961. After that he continued to be available as a tutor. He died in January, 1963.[102]

The Latin classes were taught for some years by another professor already in the city, Lawrence E. Hinkle, who had retired from North Carolina State. Raleigh was home also to Ann Eliza Brewer who taught French from 1963 to 1968 and was respected at St. Mary's as she had been when she taught at Meredith and at Brenau.[103]

In addition to educators already living in Raleigh, Stone found during the last years of his administration two retired military persons who had prepared for a second career. In 1967 August R. Lawrence, who had retired from the United States Air Force with the rank of lieutenant colonel and had just completed his master's degree at Duke University, went to teach mathematics and acted as chairman of that department. Lawrence seemed to the St. Mary's students more a friend and a father figure than a military type. In 1968 Patricia E. Connelly, who had retired from the United States Air Force with the rank of captain, joined the English department. A native of Raleigh, she held degrees from the University of North Carolina and St. Mary's University in Texas. When she doffed her uniform, Pat Connelly also left behind her military manner, except for commencement time when it was her duty to see that the procession was lined up correctly and moved on time. She said that life at St. Mary's after 21 years in the military was "a rebirth into a new world."[104]

Already pursuing careers in Raleigh before they joined the St. Mary's faculty were two other competent women, in addition to Margaret Williams of the art department. Mary Oliver Ellington, a native of Raleigh, left the public school system in 1947 to teach biology and hygiene at the college. She left St. Mary's in 1952 but returned five years later to spend 22 more years as one of those who helped to preserve the character of the place. In 1957 Stone persuaded Nancy Stamey to take the dramatics department after Florence Davis retired. She had for nine years directed the Children's Theatre in the city. For the next 20 years Nancy Stamey worked miracles on the St. Mary's stage and reaped sheaves of rave reviews from the local press.

By the 1950s it had become apparent to Stone that a number of well-educated and experienced wives and mothers were in the area because their husbands were with either the state government or one of the universities. He began to receive applications from women who were ready to resume their careers. Some had finished their full-time mothering and were helping then to educate several children. Others boldly resumed their careers the first year that the children were in school all day. The fact that inexpensive domestic help was available in the 1950s and 1960s made their lot considerably easier than that of their younger colleagues of the 1970s and 1980s. Furthermore, a master's degree from a good institution was considered sufficient, and those women already held that degree. During the Stone administration a few working mothers joined the staff. Stone made it quite clear in his letter offering a position that no one, faculty included, could expect the St. Mary's schedule to be tailored to fit the family schedule of an employee.[105]

Louise Keith Cell was the first of the mothers resuming her career at St. Mary's. She taught a section of English during the second semester of 1951–1952, became a full-time member of the faculty the next fall, and remained until her retirement in 1966. A native of Texas, Louise Cell held degrees from Texas Woman's University and Southern Methodist University and had taught at Southern Methodist and North Carolina State. She was in Raleigh because her husband was on the faculty at North Carolina State. An excellent teacher, Louise Cell was dedicated to upholding academic standards at St. Mary's and worked toward that end as a member of the academic standards committee. Her sound judgment and judicious approach to crises made her the perfect sponsor for the honor council under a difficult system that did not permit the faculty member responsible for advising the council to be present at its deliberations. After 15 years at St. Mary's she retired to read and to travel with her husband.[106] John Cell died soon thereafter; Louise Cell continued to live in their home in Raleigh until her death in June, 1977.

Carolyn Peacock Poole was the mother of three older sons and a young daughter when she began in 1953 to teach English (and sometimes American history) to the high school students at St. Mary's. Her bachelor's degree was from Meredith College and her master's was from Oberlin College. She taught for six years at Meredith before her marriage to Gordon Poole, a Baptist minister. They returned to Raleigh when he went into hospital administration. She was deeply involved in church and community activities; during her term as president of the local branch of the American Association of University Women the group was racially integrated. She rejoined the Meredith faculty in 1965. In the summer of 1967 she discovered that she had terminal cancer; she died that November.[107]

Mothers using their degrees for the first time or returning to the teaching profession joined the St. Mary's faculty almost every year, for President Stone depended upon that source of experience and talent. Catherine W. Fish went to teach biology (and sometimes hygiene) in 1960 and stayed for 11 years. She had taught at Needham Broughton High School and an accelerated biology class for high school students at North Carolina State. Her credentials were impeccable—a bachelor's degree from Vassar and a master's degree from the Johns Hopkins University. She had married a fellow biologist and was in Raleigh because of his career. For a number of years she worked with the students who planned the weekly assembly programs.[108] After her husband's death she continued to live in Raleigh.

In 1960 Martha Sprouse Stoops began what was to be a long career at St. Mary's. She was in Raleigh because her husband had returned to North Carolina State, his alma mater, as a professor and administrator. She held a bachelor's degree from Mary Baldwin College and a master's degree from the University of Wisconsin, where she was a teaching assistant in a day when few women received such appointments. She taught all of the history courses at Peace College in Raleigh, 1945–1949. After 11 years at home with two children, she went to St. Mary's to teach American history and government. An active Presbyterian, she became so involved with St. Mary's that she spent a decade of her life trying to get on paper the story of that Episcopal school.

Jessie Gardner Zepp, who also was in the city because of her husband's career, went to St. Mary's in 1964 as the Latin teacher. Helen Hayes Smith joined the faculty two years later. She was called "Bible Smith" by the students in the early years to distinguish her from "Madam Smith," "Math Smith," "Infirmary Smith," and "Switchboard Smith." Her husband, a Presbyterian minister, called her one day with this message, "You have an appointment with Dr. Stone in an hour. He needs a Bible teacher."[109]

From 1842 interesting people from many other countries enriched the intellectual mix at St. Mary's. A succession of young instructors of foreign languages passed through the department, but for 27 years under three administrations Madame Julienne Smith (the students always called her "Madam Smith") presided over some of the classes in French. Julienne Mongin arrived in the United States in the early 1920s, after studying at the Sorbonne, to attend Winthrop College. She received a teaching fellowship at the University of South Carolina where she completed the bachelor's and master's degrees. She taught at Queens College in Charlotte before marrying a University of North Carolina faculty member. Her husband died a few years after she went to St. Mary's. The students held Madame Smith in great affection, for she

Dedication of Penick Hall, 1957. Dr. Stone, the Reverend James Dick, Bishop
Penick, Mrs. Penick, Bishop Baker

was kind. A serious student of French could learn much from her.
After retirement, she continued to live in Raleigh until her death, August 15, 1977.[110]

In 1966 Renate Hoffmann Haddon joined the faculty to teach German. A native of Offenbach, she "grew up in Hitler Germany." When
she went to St. Mary's, she held a master's degree in economics and
business from Goethe University in Frankfurt and was working on a
master's degree in German literature, which she later received, at the
University of North Carolina at Chapel Hill. She had returned to
graduate school so soon as all of her five children were "more or less
out of diapers."[111] Most years she taught part time at St. Mary's and
part time elsewhere. In 1975 she married a local physician, Everett
Thompson.

The chairman of the foreign languages department, 1969–1970, was Joelle Brun de Pontet Gatling, a native of France, who had taught at East Carolina University and at Meredith College. She and Doreen Saxe were instrumental in reactivating the Alliance Française in Raleigh.[112] After her divorce, she returned to France.

Richard Stone was able to employ a few promising young men, but often they left the region after completing degrees at the nearby universities. One who gave the St. Mary's students a valuable new point of view was Walter George, who taught German, economics, and government from 1962 to 1966. His boyhood memories of Nazi Germany were so vivid that he said over and over again, "The one thing I can do for my students is to make them see how lucky they are." After graduate work at Chapel Hill, he went to Nebraska to teach and then served as a state senator before going into business.[113]

Stone grew to depend upon Carl F. Cannon, Jr., during his three years, 1957–1960, as the teacher of the American history and government classes. A Virginian, he was a graduate of Duke University and was working toward his doctorate there when he went to St. Mary's. He was "an excellent and stimulating teacher," popular with students and faculty alike. Everyone, including Cannon himself, regretted that he found it necessary to leave teaching for a museum appointment. Subsequently, he took a position in business.[114]

In 1966 another young man, Donald R. Roberts, went to teach political science and some of the American history classes. A former member of the faculty at Needham Broughton High School in Raleigh, he added zest to life at St. Mary's for the next 14 years. He contributed to campus life as the perpetrator of mock political conventions, as singer and actor in many campus productions. He served under Stone as secretary to the board of trustees and was active on faculty committees.

Another of the president's promising young men was Robert Lee Green Connelly, who joined the St. Mary's faculty in 1960. Dick Stone depended on him for many of the difficult committee chores and also enjoyed his friendship. A native of the Raleigh area, Connelly received the bachelor's and master's degrees from the University of North Carolina at Chapel Hill. After a year as a Fulbright scholar in Paris, he returned to Chapel Hill for further graduate work. Upon his appointment in 1962 as chairman of the St. Mary's foreign languages department, he expanded the offerings until it was the largest department in the school.

Connelly was popular with the students as teacher, mentor, class adviser, and participant in extracurricular activities. He played in seven major productions of the St. Mary's Dramatic Club and was elected a member of St. Genesius, the honorary drama society. The St. Mary's community was stunned on Saturday morning, October 14, 1967, to learn that a few hours earlier Bob Connelly had died as the result of an automobile accident. He was in his 35th year. The students dedicated the next issue of the *Muse* to him and published a commemorative poem.[115]

The language laboratory, the installation of which Connelly had supervised, was dedicated in his memory on October 15, 1968. It was made possible by a gift from Mr. and Mrs. L. I. Swindell and their daughter, Patricia Swindell Searcy, a 1954 St. Mary's high school graduate.[116] In 1980, just before her retirement after 12 years on the English faculty at St. Mary's, Patricia Connelly established a scholarship fund as a memorial to her younger brother.

John U. Tate, Jr., who joined the English department in 1957, became invaluable to the institution in many ways and a favorite teacher and friend of generations of students. He took his undergraduate work at Louisiana State University in two installments because military service intervened. While at Chapel Hill working toward his master's degree, he taught freshman English; and he met his future wife, Brita Moberg, who had left her native Sweden to help with research in virology at the University of North Carolina Medical School. The Tates immediately became a part of campus life at St. Mary's, always on hand for extracurricular activities even after three children arrived. The Circle traditionally held its party with John Tate costumed as Santa, often with one of his children on his knee, reading *The Night Before Christmas*. Parties at the Tate home always were quite special.

John Tate introduced hundreds of St. Mary's students to the cultural delights of Washington, New York, and the great cities of Europe. Tate and librarian Helen Brown built for the St. Mary's library one of the strongest Shakespeare collections in the area. He served on the library committee for many years and chaired it for several years. He was chairman of the English department from 1960 until his resignation from that position in 1980. Over the years Tate performed innumerable committee tasks, edited the *Faculty Handbook*, and was adviser to the *Belles*.[117]

The academic climate at St. Mary's was described by one of the more serious students of 1960–1964, Susan H. Ehringhaus, who became assistant and general counsel to the chancellor at the University of North Carolina at Chapel Hill:

There was among some of the faculty a tolerance for the deviation from the norm that I have seen nowhere else. They comforted in a very special way those at *both* ends of the academic spectrum. I happened to be one who took great pleasure in academic achievement, and John Tate would let me know (not by praising me before the class, but subtly) that he also took great pleasure in my achievement. . . . There was no dishonor in being a non-conformist. . . . it was all right to express one's own ideas in class discussion, in a paper, on a test. St. Mary's let me find my way, my own self- definition.[118]

The faculty recognized academic achievement by the conferring of three medals at each commencement. The Niles medal continued to recognize the student in the junior college making the highest average for the year, and the Cooper medal recognized the high school student making the highest average for the year. The latter was established in 1944 by Fannie Closs Cooper Gilliam in memory of her brother, Hill Parham Cooper. An award for the outstanding piano student of each year was established in 1967 in memory of Eleanor Mann Connor by her son.

The faculty during the Stone administration exhibited a spirit of openness and of concern toward one another as well as toward the students. Mabel Morrison recalled, "The faculty kept up a continuous griping about minor matters, as faculties do, and there were good, clean fights—according to Queensberry rules to be sure. But in time of need one could always count on one's colleagues."[119]

## CHAPTER TWELVE

# STRENGTHENING THE FOUNDATION

<hr>

Daily life at St. Mary's under Richard Stone's administration was supervised by two deans, Martha Dabney Jones from 1947 to 1955 and Edith A. Richardson from 1955 until into the next administration. Although quite different in personality and operating style, both kept campus life on an even keel. Under both, changes were made gradually and only when the demands of changing times became insistent, for the president disliked change for change's sake.

During his first year on the campus Stone found that "the reins of authority needed to be tightened." Florence Davis, continuing to perform the various functions she had been assigned under Margaret Cruikshank, was in fact acting as dean of students in addition to her teaching load. The other women on the faculty took turns handling much of the work normally assigned to a dean.[1] In February, 1947, the executive committee of the board authorized the president to appoint a dean of students. Stone hesitated to take Martha Dabney Jones from the classroom because she was a strong teacher—demanding, yet fair. On the other hand, her characteristics were exactly those most needed in a dean of students. She insisted upon continuing to teach at least one section of English and asked for Elizabeth Bason as her assistant. They were an effective team.

Martha Dabney Jones was a 1926 St. Mary's graduate whose grandmother had attended the school. She was a member of the faculty under the Cruikshank presidency. Thus, she became a link in "the golden chain," knowing what a St. Mary's girl did and what she did not do.

There were those who thought she was too strict. She had "rules, rules, rules." Maybe, they said, she thought she was still in the WAAC. The current students knew of the dean's army experience because her Croix de Guerre arrived in the mail in May, 1947. It was awarded for her efficiency from September, 1944, until the following September in screening civilian personnel to work in and around Paris at a time when the French government was in chaos.[2]

Martha Dabney Jones ran a tight school. Daily a list was posted of those who were to report to the dean's office, located at first in East Rock and later in faculty house. Sometimes a student searched her conscience all morning, only to discover that the dean wished to congratulate her upon an honor received or work particularly well done. Although they considered her strict, the students admired Dean Jones. In the 1948 and 1952 editions of the *Stagecoach* they expressed gratitude for her warm friendship, for her unflagging interest in them, and for her understanding, helpfulness, and guidance. The dean provided guidance, not only in those private talks in her office but also in her talks to the entire student body during assembly.[3]

One major rule was changed by President Stone during the first months of his tenure. It was almost too good to be true; St. Mary's students could smoke! Students accepted the "conditions": they were to smoke only in their rooms, never in public, even on campus, and never downtown in Raleigh. The faculty decreed that there would be no smoking in classrooms at any time.[4] The new privilege seemed a very adult one; therefore, one *had* to smoke or be labeled "square." By 1953 the *Student Handbook* noted that "Students may smoke . . . in Raleigh but must use discretion as to time and place." Day students could smoke in the day student room in lower Smedes.

The removal of the no-smoking rule actually strengthened student government; smoking had become so common that the rule was unenforceable.[5] The prohibition against drinking, being still enforceable, was still plainly stated in the *Student Handbook*.[6] There was to be no drinking "while on campus or under the jurisdiction of the school" at all times when school was in session, except when a student was "away from the vicinity of Raleigh in the charge of her parents." The penalty for drinking was possible expulsion, and enforcement of the rule was exceedingly strict.

Stone was a strong supporter of student government. At his first faculty meeting he said that the purpose of an honor system was "to build the character of the students" and suggested that the faculty should consider "a complete honor system" with no proctoring of tests.[7] The Student Government Association constitution as formulated in 1937 was changed in 1941 to reduce the size of the honor council and in 1945 to strengthen the hall council. For some years the *Student Handbook* had carried the statement that "adoption of complete student government based on the Honor Code was motivated by the students' belief that self-government guided by rigid honesty is the most intelligent and pleasant method of administering a well ordered society."

Richard Stone, reporting to the faculty on the 1951 meeting of the North Carolina College Conference over which he had presided, noted that 13 percent of the institutions saw cheating as their most serious discipline problem while about 7 percent saw drinking as their most serious problem.[8] He believed that the honor council at St. Mary's usually made just and reasonable decisions. An editorial in the college newspaper caught the essence of the system: "St. Mary's is a little world within itself. If a student can live successfully in this society, she can live in the outside world too."[9] There were, inevitably, those who could not live in that "little world," and they were sent home, sometimes temporarily, sometimes permanently. Cheating, lying, stealing, and remaining off campus without permission were very serious matters.

The Circle and the Beacon assumed special responsibility for fostering support for the honor system and school spirit. The Beacon was organized in December, 1948, at the request of a group of high school students who thought that a society comparable to the Circle would bolster morale among the high school students.[10] Not knowing exactly how to go about organizing, they petitioned the honor council. The council and Stone approved, and the charter members chosen for all-around excellence were named by a committee of students and faculty.[11] Beacon members chose the lantern as symbolic of their desire "to help others find the way" and designed the pin worn by members. Elizabeth Bason was the first sponsor.

Petitions from students for changes in the rules governing daily living passed the legislative body frequently during the early years of the Stone administration, but the new president was not so lenient as the students had hoped he would be. He refused some petitions and withdrew a few privileges that were abused. Permission to stay with approved hostesses over Saturday night in Raleigh, granted for 1947–1948, was rescinded. The *Belles* explained the reason: "Last year the school got numerous reports about the ill-considered behavior of S. M. C. girls, usually after dances. They would be seen at late hours, perhaps in a public place, without the proper chaperonage. . . ."[12] By 1951, however, the stringent rules were relaxed considerably for the college students.

St. Mary's women of any vintage when reminiscing about their days on the campus always talk about how hard they studied, and of their favorite teachers, and of the eccentricities of the faculty in general. They describe "the strict rules" and how their particular dean enforced them. Then they talk of the intimate life on the halls, of the hours spent just helping one another with personal problems, of lifelong friendships formed. Friendship is a part of life on any campus, but because the student body numbered only 400 and because so many new students had a network of cousins and hometown friends already attending, St. Mary's circle of friends was a wide one for many. Sounding a positive note for the year, the *Belles* in October, 1948, declared, "At the end of the first three weeks a new girl knows or knows of every girl on campus. The friendly spirit that prevails around the halls, in the classroom, and on the athletic field *is* St. Mary's." [13]

To be selected by the dean and her committee of student officers as a hall counselor was a great honor for a senior, but it was a greater responsibility, for the maintenance of hall discipline was placed almost entirely in the hands of the students. The hall council handled all offenses not considered infractions of the honor code. The senior counselors on the high school halls spent a great deal of time as surrogate mothers. By 1948 only one teacher resided in each building. Most of the faculty women settled into apartments nearby but continued to be on campus for all special events.

There is no denying that dormitory life *was* intimate. In the oldest buildings where one or two bathtubs served as many as 16 there was a nightly 9:30 race for a tub. One of the boons granted in 1951 was the privilege of taking a bath during class hours, provided the bathroom was not situated directly above a classroom. The 1909 plumbing ran through the classrooms in the wings of Smedes Hall, and the sound of rushing water combined with the clatter of the antiquated heating system broke the fragile thread of concentration at frequent intervals.

Promptness for meals was an imperative. A few organized students were dressed for class before breakfast, but many arrived with uncombed pincurls wearing raincoats to cover rolled-up pajama legs. [14] If a pajama leg escaped, "points" were accumulated, and they added up to campus slips. The *Student Handbook* of the era advised, "To dinner, we wear tailored dresses and suits, not the skirt and sweater we've worn all day." That meant heels, stockings, and often pearls and earrings. A food protest, "not without some reason," Martha Dabney Jones recalled, was organized during her first year as dean of students. When the students arose soon after grace to leave the dining room, she said, "Return to your seats. That is an order." And return they did. That evening they went to dinner dressed in black. Each student with a polite "No, thank you" declined to be served and was handed an empty plate. The faculty simply ignored the situation, carrying on a conversation while enjoying the especially good meal. President Stone took the students' dissatisfaction seriously, though he did not condone their way of expressing it, and the meals improved.[15]

Until 1951 when the college students were given permission to use their own discretion about bedtime (but not about noise after 10:00), "lights out" time was 10:30 for underclassmen and 11:00 for upperclassmen, with a half-hour extension on Saturday nights. Quiet hour for study was observed from 7:30 until 9:30. At 9:30 bedlam reigned for half an hour. Popular recreational activities were "table lifting," canasta, and bridge. Sunbathing was allowed only on the sun porch, located on the roof of Smedes porch and reached through a third-floor dormitory room. It operated under strict rules—no radios, food, or drink, and no standing on the railing.

On-campus social life was important in the 1950s. There was the traditional series of entertainments and parties, beginning with the talent show and the formal old-girl-new-girl reception of orientation week. Halloween remained a big night. The Christmas season brought parties and programs galore. In addition to the hall parties, and the Christmas tree party in the parlor, and the glee club concert, and the caroling, there was the formal dinner. Nannie H. Marriott's last one was Christmas, 1948, for she retired the next June after 32 years as dietitian. She had scrounged and skimped through two wars, always a careful manager. She loved good food, and above all, she loved the bustle and excitement of a party or special dinner. She kept fresh flowers or plants from her garden and greenhouse on the tables.[16]

Integration of the day students into the social activities on campus was discussed periodically by the faculty, and periodically the day students aired their complaints in the columns of the *Belles*. Day students were elected to offices and even tapped into the Circle, and they worked on the publications. However, when not in class, they were relegated to a dingy, shabbily furnished room tucked under the stairs in lower Smedes. The air in the day students' lounge was always blue with cigarette smoke, and a perpetual bridge game progressed with different players as classes changed. The day students possessed one grand privilege. They could have cars; also they could leave campus for 45 minutes to eat lunch. They made a point of driving the three blocks down Hillsborough Street to the Blue Tower.[17]

During the 1950s and 1960s competition between the Sigmas and the Mus took on new life. The old literary clubs disappeared, leaving

Student publications: The *Belles*

The *Stagecoach*

sports as the only area of extracurricular competition. Everyone, including day students, was required to belong to one or the other of the athletic clubs. In an exciting "tapping in" ceremony each fall, old members ran through the dormitories delivering the news to those chosen. Cheerleaders kept the crowds frenzied during all athletic events. Sigmas and Mus battled it out in no less than 15 tournaments annually—tournaments in everything from basketball to bridge. The stars made the prestigious letter club by earning points and making teams. Posture week continued under the sponsorship of the two athletic clubs, and some years a "slump queen" was chosen as well as the "posture queen."

After all of this athletic activity, frequent trips to "the little store" were popular. More exciting, however, were the expeditions to the downtown movie theaters. Popular music was a major interest. A radio might barely suffice at school if one's roommate had a record player. It was absolutely necessary to have access to a supply of long-playing albums. Several times a year big name bands gave concerts at Memorial Auditorium in Raleigh, and everyone scrambled for tickets. On Saturday nights, after their dates, the high school girls danced in the wide halls of Smedes until bedtime. Almost everyone listened to "Our Best to You" over radio WPTF. Each girl lay in her bed, an ear glued to her radio turned low in hopes that a boy had dedicated a song to her; sometimes she sent in a dedication to a boy. The times were good, and life was thrilling.[18]

Because the times were good, there was more interest in clothes than during the Depression and the subsequent war years. The "new look" of 1947 meant a new wardrobe. The skirts were bouffant worn over crinolines; the length was middie, the necklines plunging, the shoulders sloping, the waistline defined. Shoes were elaborate and hats even more so. The "new look" was luxurious, but, as historian Lois Banner noted, "Not since the Victorian era had women's fashions been so confining."[19] New arrivals of 1950 on the St. Mary's campus were pictured in the *Belles* dressed mostly in fall suits, high-heeled pumps, hats, and carrying gloves as well as suitcases. For classes the look was a good wool skirt hovering a few inches above white bobby socks worn with loafers or saddles, a long pullover sweater, and the inevitable pearls. A round-collared white blouse worn under a long cardigan also was popular. A St. Mary's sweat shirt and jeans or pedal pushers was the outfit for study, but pants could not be worn in public, not even on front campus. By the early fifties hats were no longer required for off-campus shopping, but hats and gloves were worn for the Sunday church service on campus. Young ladies did not appear in public without lipstick although excessive makeup also was considered unladylike.[20] By 1954 ponytails were disappearing in favor of the short, curly look.

During the eight years that Martha Dabney Jones was dean of students, there was a gradual relaxation of the social restrictions in keeping with the trend of the times. By the early fifties the date list of ten boys approved by parents was abolished. Even if a student's list of eligible young men were long, the telephone situation would have discouraged all but the most ardent. From 1946 when the switchboard was installed, there was only one telephone on each hall; for years there were only five outside lines and only 40 minutes a night and few times during the day when three-minute calls could be taken. The switchboard was in the charge of Martha Ebie Simpson from 1940 until her death in September, 1949. Many years of her life were spent at St. Mary's. She was a business student, 1901–1903, then taught music and was chapel organist from 1913 until her marriage in 1921. In 1940 she returned to the college as assistant housekeeper and later took over the switchboard. Ebie Simpson was cherished by the faculty, staff, and students alike for her cheerful and sympathetic nature.[21]

Once the arrangements for a date had been made, the young man presented himself to Mary Jane Hornback, who was hostess for eight years (1948–1956). She entertained the young men while they "signed for" and awaited their dates, and she enjoyed her job. She kept in the drawers of her little desk a supply of men's ties to lend to tieless dates. Any man who had been drinking was packed off immediately. High school students could not single date at night. Especially reliable high school students were approved as chaperones; therefore, the date had to provide an escort for that student. Girls who had parental permission could ride in cars. A movie and then a cheeseburger, or perhaps an approved fraternity party at State, where St. Mary's girls had to be "cool" while not drinking with the others, was the usual plan.[22] Parties at apartments were off limits. A date for a football game in Chapel Hill was "the greatest." It was possible, by using two permissions, to stay away from school from 11:00 A.M. until 10:30 P.M. In 1946 two of Carolina's majorettes were St. Mary's alumnae.[23]

Dating the same boy (they were referred to as "boys," not "men," in the *Handbook*) three times on one weekend required special permission from the dean. Presumably that rule was designed to keep young people from getting too serious. Nonetheless, the first issue of the *Belles* in January, 1951, announced that over Christmas two students had married and were not returning to school; one of the brides was the student body president. For the great majority of St. Mary's women not seriously considering marriage, there was the excitement of bids to the big college dances. The rules concerning approved hostesses were strict. The dances on campus at St. Mary's, after a few years of wartime austerity, were once more formal affairs with a band. The biggest thrill of all was to be a debutante. In 1949 over one third of the "debs" were St. Mary's girls. Those who were not "debs" always took the matter in stride.

Spring madness among college boys takes different forms in different decades. In the 1950s "panty raids" were the game. One night in the spring of 1952, word was received somehow that hordes of boys from surrounding colleges were about to hit Raleigh. Dean Jones made a fast tour of the halls. "Arm yourselves!" she cried, holding a Coca-Cola bottle aloft. The girls barricaded the stairs and ran to the windows planning "to enjoy every fabulous moment." By the time the raiders arrived, the police were ready for them. The crowd pushed on to Meredith, much to the disappointment of the St. Mary's students.[24]

The "fabulous fifties" were good years to be young. They were good years at St. Mary's with Richard Stone and Martha Dabney Jones in control and Mary Jane Hornback as monitor. Hornback continued her interest in St. Mary's affairs after her retirement. She died on August 29, 1970.[25]

By 1955 Martha Dabney Jones had spent 20 years within the grove—as student, teacher, and dean. She left in June of that year to become headmistress of another Episcopal school, Stuart Hall, in Staunton, Virginia. She filled that position with distinction until her retirement in 1972, after which she continued to live in Staunton.

## THE "MISS R." ERA

She had barely heard of St. Mary's before 1955, and yet Edith Ann Richardson typified St. Mary's to hundreds of young women during her 18 years as dean of students. She was an experienced educator and administrator who had spent a successful career in New England schools. She heard of Martha Dabney Jones's resignation through a Raleigh friend.

Edith Richardson (often called Pat) was born in Carlisle, England, and remained there at preparatory school when her father, a professor of Greek, took the family to the University of Edinburgh. In her late teens she went to school at Dana Hall in Massachusetts and later received her bachelor's degree from Wellesley with a major in English; still later, she studied at Harvard during a number of summers. She moved to St. Mary's from Lasell Junior College where she was assistant dean of students. She had also had administrative and teaching experience in two Boston private schools.[26] At St. Mary's she taught freshman English for several years while serving as dean.

Basketball, 1951 style

Her approach to the duties of dean of students was "to try to do everything possible to make the girls happy," and almost immediately she became known as "Miss R." She knew that problems at home or with boyfriends affected a student's relationship with her roommate and her academic work. Often her light was seen at 2:00 in the morning because everyone knew that she felt that it was "necessary to talk with a girl whenever she needs to talk."[27] During those years the honor council met in great secrecy late at night in Miss R.'s office-sitting room to avoid unsettling the whole campus with rumors while a case was in progress. The dean worked closely with the faculty adviser to the council. Alumnae of the period say that affection for Miss R. and the strength of student government kept the St. Mary's family spirit intact.

The visiting committee for the 1959 reaccreditation said of her: "That she is liked and respected by those who work with her does much to sustain the generally good tone of the campus." That committee agreed with the recommendation of the faculty's self-study that "full consideration should be given to additional ways in which the Dean's work load can be lightened" and noted, "Her responsibilities now continue throughout every waking hour during the weeks that the college is in session."[28] Ten years later, the visiting committee for the 1969 reaccreditation, despite the fact that some help had been given, noted that the dean continued to be overworked. That was Miss R.'s nature. She did slip away for a few hours each week to the apartment she kept nearby, and she kept in communication with a host of friends.

After "Miss I. T." went in 1960 to live in Penick Hall as an adult counselor, Miss R. had her closest confidante on campus, for Miss I. T. was her sister. It was Elizabeth Bason's idea that perhaps Isamay Turnbull Richardson would be willing to leave Chapel Hill where she was engaged in research. Miss I. T.'s field was English history. A graduate of Wellesley, she was for many years assistant to the headmistress at Abbott Academy in Massachusetts. She took her graduate work at Simmons College. During World War II she returned to Bermuda to care for her parents and there aided the war effort as a censor of the mails. She was a worthy successor to Elizabeth Bason in the care she took of the chapel furnishings and as adviser to the marshals. She died suddenly in January, 1970.[29]

Dean Richardson found upon her arrival a successful system of student government in operation, but it was more successful some years than others. The tone of a particular school year was set by the student government association officers, especially the president, and by the attitude of the members of the Circle and the Beacon.[30] Most students dutifully memorized long sections of the *Student Handbook* because it was easier to get it over with by passing the handbook test the first time it was taken. Each January, honor week was observed with a number of special activities—articles in the college newspaper, group discussions on the halls, and appropriate quotations posted at strategic locations. The report of the 1959 visiting committee from the Southern Association of Colleges and Secondary Schools noted, "The girls themselves place value on . . . spiritual growth, academic excellence, and moral integrity." The committee felt, however, that "a full consensus as to the responsibilities" of student government was needed on the part of all constituencies of the college community.[31] The constitution of the Student Government Association was revised in 1958. In 1960 it underwent a complete overhauling that improved the electoral process by requiring a runoff whenever a candidate did not receive a simple majority of votes cast; a preferential ballot had been the practice. Major offices were to be filled separately through spaced elections, thus allowing a strong leader who lost one office to be nominated for another. The required grade average for holders of major offices was raised to B minus; for other officers it was C. All names placed in nomination, even those from the floor, had to have had prior approval from the president of the college; he habitually approved the students' choices unless a nominee's grades were unacceptable.[32] The constitutional revisions were worked out by a committee composed of four students, Edith Richardson, and Louise Cell; they were approved by the legislative body.[33]

Student government was maturing. By 1961, however, it showed definite signs of breaking down over the drinking question. Students, when away from the campus, often considered themselves under their parents' jurisdiction, and family attitudes on that social question differed. Stone, himself a nondrinker, realized that the situation posed a real threat to the whole concept of student government. Therefore, he asked the SGA officers, the dean, and Louise Cell to recommend a solution to the problem. The resulting statement was discussed at length by President Stone and Bishop Richard Henry Baker, who was then chairman of the board of trustees. When the bishop consulted the executive committee of the board, that committee expressed confidence in the administration and moved that the policy on alcoholic beverages "be determined by the usual authorities on campus."[34]

The new policy, announced just before spring vacation in 1961, kept the strict prohibition against any alcoholic beverages on campus and at any St. Mary's function off campus. No student could drink any alcoholic beverages while officially representing the school. The policy on drinking off campus under other circumstances placed the burden of decision upon the student. It read:

St. Mary's does not approve of the use of any alcoholic beverages. A St. Mary's girl must conduct herself as a lady at all times. She must assume this responsibility for herself; and as a member of Student Government she is also bound to require any fellow student whose conduct is such as to bring discredit upon the student body, to report herself. If she is not willing to accept this dual responsibility, she does not belong at St. Mary's and may be expelled by the Student Government.[35]

The St. Mary's Alumnae Council in May, 1961, "voted unanimously to uphold the position of the school and its authorities." Because there had been such wide discussion of the policy, the council at its fall meeting directed the publication in the Bulletin of the exact wording of the rule. In an article describing the reasons for the change in policy and the method of arriving at the new rule, President Stone wrote, "We do not know if this change will be successful, but we have hopes that the reasonableness of the approach will bring very general support by the student body and the families from which they come."[36] The alumnae council did not reverse its support of the administration's policy despite the fact that it received in the spring of 1962 a resolution from the Fayetteville alumnae chapter opposing the use of alcohol by any student at St. Mary's.[37]

Meanwhile, the honor council was struggling with the tricky problem of defining "unladylike conduct" and was trying, very hard but not always successfully, to maintain consistency of definitions and penalties from year to year. There was also the new and difficult problem of "the apartment rule." By the mid-sixties students at other colleges often had their own apartments, and they were the favorite partying places. St. Mary's girls, however, were allowed to attend in Raleigh and vicinity only parties approved by the dean. They could not even enter a hotel unchaperoned. By 1964 it was evident that faculty members should be sitting on the honor council. The traditional system whereby the students met alone, emerging now and again to seek the advice of the faculty adviser or the dean, was not working. The executive committee, six members of the faculty and administration, whose task it was to review the written reports of serious disciplinary cases, often disagreed with student decisions. If persuasion failed to convince the executive committee, honor council decisions were reversed. The result was general frustration.

The 1963–1964 honor council, working with Dean Richardson and the council's faculty adviser, devised a new system in time for constitutional changes to be approved by the students and the administration in April. A newly instituted group, called the honor board, consisted of seven students—the three SGA officers, a senior class representative, two junior class representatives, and a sophomore elected by both high school classes—and three faculty members appointed by the president of the college to three-year nonconsecutive terms. All decisions required a two-thirds vote, with at least one faculty member present and voting. The new system worked well, but it was not equal to solving the alcohol problem; that was to become by the 1970s a major problem on most college campuses and for society in general.

The hall council system of self-government in the dormitories was functioning successfully when Edith Richardson became dean of students; it continued to do so, despite the greater burdens that changing social conditions placed upon the counselors. The members of the 1959 visiting committee noted, "The weight of responsibility which the hall counselors carry seems to be extremely heavy relative to the youth, inexperience, and full schedules of the seniors. Having several living units in which there is no adult resident makes this problem even more acute. . . . the seniors must cope with many major problems or else carry them to the dean of students."[38]

The fact that Miss R. was accessible at all hours was a primary reason for the success of the student hall counselor system. Her suite, which included a large and comfortable office and her living quarters, was located in the heart of Smedes Hall. The old study hall area across from the parlor was remodeled during the summer of 1955 to provide the dean's quarters and three dating parlors. Edith Richardson was assisted by the heads of house; they were women of refinement and experience who lived in the dormitories, replacing the women faculty as they moved to their own apartments. Although they worked closely with the dean, they were not responsible for hall discipline, which was in the hands of the student hall counselors. They in some cases exerted a great deal of indirect influence as counselors and confidantes, just as the teachers living in the dorms had done over the years. Ruth P. Pendergraph, 1960–1973, and Christine Dodd Johnson, 1965–1973, were among the resident counselors upon whom Dean Richardson depended.

An alumna experienced in student government returned for 1964–1965 as assistant dean of students. She was Margaret Elizabeth (Betsy) Nichols, valedictorian of the class of 1962. She took her bachelor's degree at Smith College. After one year back at St. Mary's, she decided to take a position teaching English in public high school. Later she became an engineer with Pacific Telephone and by 1981 was a district manager.[39]

One of Miss R.'s goals as dean of all the students was to make the day students happier. She initiated a plan whereby each hall "adopted" some day students and invited them to hall parties. The remodeling in 1956 of the dismal day student quarters in lower Smedes raised morale among the town girls. In 1967 the day students were given the brick house built during Lay's administration for Ernest and Margaret Cruikshank. When the new library was built, the little house was moved from its original position to the north side of Cheshire Hall and enlarged for the chaplain's family. The erection of the Alice McKenzie Classroom Building made a second move necessary, and the house was located just behind Cheshire.

Life at St. Mary's changed considerably between 1955 and 1969; but the changes were so gradual that life at the school seemed placid compared to the turmoil on other campuses during the 1960s.

The daily life of the school changed in 1963 when, upon the retirement of the dietitian, the management of the dining room was contracted to a food service company. During the 11 years, 1952– 1963, that Della B. Truitt was the school dietitian, meals still were served family style with grace said by the chaplain, the dean of students, or a member of the faculty. Meals were times for fellowship and the enjoyment of Della Truitt's special recipes. The students continued the tradition of singing a welcome to guests and congratulations to fellow students on special days of celebration.

During the first year of the food service, only breakfast was served cafeteria style; and breakfast was made voluntary. By 1964–1965 classroom space was at such a premium that lunch was scheduled across two hours so that classes could meet at both noon and 1:00, and by 1967–1968 all meals were served cafeteria style. Most of the food service directors, after several successful years at St. Mary's, moved to larger institutions. Each one made special efforts to please student appetites and to produce memorable holiday parties.

One person still on campus in 1965 who remembered the days when the dining room in Clement Hall was almost new was John Hill, who went in 1915 to work in the kitchen. He soon was made a waiter and later rang the heavy handbell to announce meals. Fifty years and many changes later John Hill still worked on campus. His wife Floyd worked in the infirmary. They were only two of a number of loyal workers on the custodial staff who spent almost their entire working lives at the school. John Hill retired in August, 1970, after 56 years at St. Mary's. He died in November of that year.[40]

Lola Brodie Naylor, fondly known as "Nursie Naylor," was in command of the infirmary from 1928 until she resigned in 1952. At that time the trustees praised her as "a vigorous advocate of preventive medicine."[41] In the fall of 1953 Hubert B. Haywood resigned after 26 years as the college physician. He had taken special precautions during the polio epidemics.[42]

With the opening of Penick Hall in 1957 and the air-conditioned Margaret Jones Cruikshank Dormitory in 1966, daily life became much more comfortable for some of the students. Each summer Richard Stone spent as much money as could be found to modernize and redecorate the oldest dormitories. Even so, the rooms in Smedes and West Rock were not much different from the days when the grandmothers of some of the occupants had lived there. No one ever apologized for the differences in living quarters, and the administration never thought of different charges for some of the quarters. For 18 years, 1946–1964, Evie Callahan presided over the housekeeping chores "with a cheery smile and a jingle of keys." She liked the hustle and bustle of the opening and closing of each school year, and knowing the girls and seeing to their comfort was a real joy for her. A native of Raleigh, she lived near the school.[43]

With the addition of new dormitories the boarding population was up to just under 400 by the last years of the Stone administration. That made the student body large enough to overcrowd many campus facilities but not large enough to endanger the friendly atmosphere. The minority of students who were not North Carolinians sometimes felt isolated during the first days, but a surprising number of them became campus leaders.

From the late 1950s the change in daily life that was most noticed—and most deplored—by the adults on campus was the increase in the noise level. To the students, loud music seemed a natural and necessary accompaniment to daily living. When rock and roll became predominant, the *Belles* explained that its "elements" were "pop, gospel, hillbilly and blues" and commented that although such music was "a wholesome outlet for the teenager's energy," there was the danger that "parents with delicate musical perception may go insane." In the winter of 1964 the school paper announced that 'Beatlemania" had struck St. Mary's.[44]

At almost every faculty meeting during the 1950s and 1960s someone declared, "The girls are not working hard enough." In 1968 the academic standards committee reported that fully one third of those students on the academic probation list had achievement test scores indicating that they "could do the work at St. Mary's if they would."[45] The students thought that the teachers were "too hard" and that there was not enough time for extracurricular activities. Duringthe 1950s, social activities on campus were manageable, but by the end of the decade there were signs that the times were changing. For years the senior follies was a highlight of the year. Until the late fifties the follies consisted of fairly innocent, but hilarious, skits lampooning all facets of campus life. Prim Elizabeth Bason even lent her clothes to the senior "doing" her.[46] By 1959, however, the faculty had become so critical of "the tone" of the performances that there was discussion of limiting the audience to the college community,[47] whereupon the seniors canceled the follies that year and the skits became an annual assembly program somewhat less questionable in "tone."

The seniors' Christmas dance was no longer black tie, but the traditional programs and parties became more elaborate as groups proliferated. December also brought "peanut week." During the last week before Christmas vacation the residents on each hall drew names, and each "shell" kept the name of her "peanut" secret. A little gift was slipped nightly into the stocking hung on the peanut's decorated door. On the last day "a nice gift" was bestowed and identities revealed.[48] The junior dance was held each spring. In 1962 the Embers played, and the old gymnasium was decorated with abstract paintings and "nebbishes, some personifying the faculty." Owens Browne, as usual, helped with the lighting and sound equipment; he had purchased ear plugs for such occasions. The *Belles* admitted that the music was "blaring." [49]

In the fall of 1959 St. Mary's own combo, the Cold Cuts, became a recognized campus organization with a constitution and sociology teacher Herbert Shellans, a guitarist who was interested in folk music, as adviser. The combo developed more or less by accident the year before when a group of juniors fell into the habit of "just messing around in the room in the bottom of Holt where there was an old piano." Whatever the Cold Cuts played was unique. Their "instruments" included, besides the piano and the bongo drums, the washboard played with thimbles, the washtub, castanets, sandblocks, spoons, and sticks. In 1960 new numbers were "Handyman," "Cherry Pie," "You Talk Too Much," and "When the Saints Go Marching In." The lyrics were sometimes original and, in later years, often bawdy. The early uniforms consisted of real farmers' overalls worn with madras shirts and straw hats of various sizes and shapes. The group pictured in the 1960 *Stagecoach* numbered 14. [50] The Cold Cuts gave programs for civic groups and performed at fraternity parties.

Frequent trips to the campus post office in lower Smedes remained an important part of daily campus life. Hope ran especially high if one had kicked "the kicking post" several times that week when en route to Hillsborough Street's "little store." That post was the last one on the path across campus, and kicking it was supposed to bring a letter. [51] For 22 years Bessie Burkehead Brown presided over the post office, bank, and bookstore that had so long been Juliet Sutton's domain. A native of Raleigh, she had gone to St. Mary's in 1934 as assistant to the dietitian. "B" Brown, as the old guard of the faculty called her, ran a tight ship, but there was often a twinkle in her eye. She declared that she got personal credit for letters, that the recipient would stop her on campus to thank her for that long-awaited letter from a male friend. Actually, the student probably just wished to talk with Bessie Brown, for she was always interested to hear the details. She retired in 1962 and died in March, 1976, at the age of 87. [52]

The dress code did not change drastically until the 1970s. Edith Richardson was every inch a lady; white gloves remained de rigeur. A tweed suit was the proper attire for a St. Mary's student at football games. As late as 1968–1969 the *Student Handbook*, in describing the "necessities," listed gloves, hats, heels, and "conservative dresses or suits for church and Sunday dinner," gloves and "appropriate dresses" for concerts, and loafers, skirts, sweaters, and blouses for class. Sports clothes were only "for picnics and study hours." Sometimes when the

Granddaughters Club, 1967

May Day, 1957. Coleman Jenkins, Queen of May

occasion seemed to demand pants, a pantsuit (never slacks or jeans) could be worn under a coat to an off-campus function. If Miss R. had ruled that pants could be worn, they were rolled up out of sight under the coat until the destination was reached. During the "Camelot era," St. Mary's students happily followed the styles set by Jacqueline Kennedy—the pill-box hats, the just-below-the-knee hemlines, the shoes with the pointed toes and the spike heels. For classes they wore loafers and knee socks or hose with their shorter skirts; later they began to go barelegged summer and winter. They gave up hats, but some for parties piled their hair into "the beehive" style which was a bit reminiscent of their grandmothers' pompadours. As skirts went up, hair came down until the shining, long, straight tresses of a St. Mary's girl often seemed about to meet the hemline of her mini.

Although Edith Richardson fell in love with St. Mary's the moment she saw the place, she was not willing to commit herself to the task of keeping several hundreds of young women happy until she knew the answer to the essential question. Therefore, one of the first questions she put to Richard Stone was, "Are there boys nearby for the girls to date?" He replied, "Thousands." [53] In the spring of 1956 the college students were given the privilege of dating until 11:00 on Friday nights, provided the two hours of closed study were made up on Thursday or Friday afternoon. Curfew was at midnight on Saturdays for the college students. Dating rules were liberalized by 1968–1969. However, all parties still had to be approved and properly chaperoned, and 12:30 was the curfew, even after a formal dance. The rules were observed by most of the students, and the honor system worked surprisingly well. The honor board was inclined to view blatant disregard of major rules by a few as a threat to the reputations of all St. Mary's students. Punishments were severe—often more severe than the adult authorities would have meted out. [54]

The social rules were no great deterrent to romance. It was a matter of community interest when a student was "spoken for." The *Belles* reported in January, 1956, that 56 St. Mary's women were "tied down" (which meant any status from married to "charmed," with engaged and "lavaliered" somewhere in between). Miss R. was a great aider and abettor of romance. She knew that the graceful Italian Renaissance gazebo had become a trysting place as soon as it had been moved in 1964 to the campus from the garden of the late Minnie Tucker Baker. [55] Thus, when Pryor N. Hicks, the kind and gentlemanly night watchman who went to St. Mary's in 1958, knocked on her door one moonlit night with a very embarrassed young couple in tow, Miss R. was not surprised to learn that they had been caught in the gazebo. The young man, greatly agitated, asked to speak with the dean privately. "I was just about to give her the ring," he whispered. "What do I do now?" Miss R. replied, "Go back out there, and do it right!"[56]

Besides Hicks, who made his rounds turning out lights, locking doors, and chasing girls in robes and slippers from telephone booths late at night, there was Robert Randolph, the off-duty policeman who directed traffic in the circle on weekend nights. The combined efforts of all the campus guardians could not protect St. Mary's from the panty raid of 1964. A crowd of college men, estimated to number about 2,000, roared onto the campus, and some actually got into West Rock before the city police arrived. The residents of West Rock, who had armed themselves with Coca-Cola bottles, took refuge in one room, shouted, "Here we are!" and then attacked the intruders. After that, the authorities at the universities took appropriate steps to prevent recurrences. The day of the panty raid had passed.[57] During 1968–1969 increased campus security was provided by a private agency and the addition of a number of outside lights.

The daytime activities of everyone on campus were supervised for 14 years, 1953–1967, by Stella Todd Smith. Referred to as "Switchboard Smith" after several other Smiths joined the staff and faculty, she knew where everyone was at a given time and why. It was her custom to arrange bouquets from her flower garden for her cubbyhole and for the business office.[58]

## "THE GRACE OF CONNECTION"

St. Mary's women always have felt for one another what novelist Marilyn French called "the grace of connection."[59] The students recognized (usually unerringly) those among the group possessing the gift of leadership by electing them to office. Others, whose special gift was that of caring, were recognized by their peers and the faculty when certain special awards were presented at commencement.

Two awards were established in the 1960s to recognize members of the senior class making special contributions to the community life. The King award was established in 1964 by Mr. and Mrs. Madding King of Florence, Alabama, in gratitude for the happiness her time at St. Mary's brought to their daughter, Harriet Susan King. The medal is given annually to the senior who, in the opinion of a faculty committee, has "most consistently practiced good citizenship at St. Mary's and inconspicuously served as an example to others."[60] In 1968 a fund of $2,000 was established by friends, family, and alumnae as a memorial to Marian Drane Graham of the class of 1919. The first award, consisting of the annual income from the fund, was made in 1969 on the 50th anniversary of her graduation from the college. The Marian Drane

Graham award is given to a member of the senior class who, in the opinion of a committee representing faculty, students, and alumnae, best "exemplifies Marian's reverence and humility of spirit, scholarship without pride of excellence, zest for life, fun and friendship, faith and fortitude, and all-around development in the course of her radiant and nobly useful life."[61] The tribute was written by her husband, Frank Porter Graham, longtime president of the University of North Carolina. The member of each year's high school graduating class "who best exemplifies the Christian idea of helpfulness to others motivated by her genuine love for all members of the St. Mary's family" receives the Margaret and Ann Highsmith medal. Established in 1969 by Mr. and Mrs. Seavy Highsmith of Fayetteville, the award was named for their daughters, who were high school graduates of 1967 and 1970.[62]

Not everyone, even on a small campus, assimilates into the family group. Every campus has its loners, and they, too, make a contribution by causing the reexamination of long-held group values. There is always, also, that small group that defies the common values for the sake of defiance. During the Stone administration, such a group was almost nonexistent at St. Mary's.

It was the enduring friendships and the love for St. Mary's that most impressed Dick and Marye Stone when they first visited alumnae chapters. The new president "had not expected to find so much love." He had, however, expected to find much greater financial support from the alumnae than was forthcoming.[63] A succession of young alumnae struggled valiantly to strengthen the alumnae work despite the handicap of a stringent office budget. Margaret (Peggy) Hopkins continued to serve as alumnae secretary through June, 1946. She left to take a position in the hospital at the Johns Hopkins University and soon married. She worked to improve the *Bulletin* because she understood the desire to read news of friends. Recalling "the serious and perennial money problem" at the college, she said, "Old families are prone to hold on to their money."[64]

Alice P. Bell succeeded Peggy Hopkins and stayed a year. Jane Kistler Bell, during 1947–1948, moved the office from West Rock to East Rock and tried to reactivate chapters of the alumnae association. At the beginning of her tenure there were only eight chapters active; at the end, there were 30. Under Dora Winters, who held the job for about two years, the loyalty fund was set up. Logan Vaught was the secretary for part of 1951, and Jane Peete took the position in September, 1951. When she resigned in the winter of 1953, Luck C. Flanders filled in until June and marriage plans. Despite "strenuous efforts," no one was found for the position until the fall of 1954 when Mary Jo Paul took over the post. She stressed chapter work until her resignation in 1956.

Betty Debnam, who was alumnae secretary for the two years follow-ing, stressed alumnae giving. Barbara Hauser served from the fall of 1958 until January, 1960. Upon her resignation, Mary Elva Winston, who had been assisting in the alumnae office intermittently for seven years, "held things together" until September when Robin Fuller ar-rived. The new secretary had a degree in philosophy from the Univer-sity of North Carolina at Chapel Hill and had been working in New York City. In her first message to the alumnae she diagnosed the prob-lem accurately: "It is time for us to cease to take St. Mary's for granted." In the year and a half before marriage claimed her, she established an Addressograph system and worked to increase contributions to the loyalty fund.[65] She and Mary Elva Winston were an efficient team.

During those years of frequent changes and vacancies in the alum-nae office, Martha Dabney Jones, Elizabeth Tucker, and Frances Vann took on the extra work necessary to keep the alumnae association afloat. It was St. Mary's good fortune that the next alumnae secretary continued her career after marriage. Jane Lawrence (Chip) Augustine remained at the college for 19 years, working to build a strong part-nership between the institution and its alumnae. Salutatorian of the St. Mary's class of 1959, she earned a degree in French at Chapel Hill and then worked for both Raleigh newspapers. At first everyone, in-cluding the new alumnae secretary herself, entertained doubts about how that Ohioan would be received by the so-southern St. Mary's alum-nae. Before long she was admired by the alumnae and her colleagues alike for her dedication to St. Mary's. Mary Elva Winston, who con-tinued to work in the office part time, was "a walking encyclopedia" of information concerning the alumnae. The association in 1957 elected her an honorary alumna. She retired in 1969, but for years she reap-peared in the alumnae office in times of need.

The alumnae association was fortunate in having a number of ca-pable and dedicated presidents during the Stone administration. (See appendix C.) Alumnae projects were directed toward improving the appearance of the campus. The alumnae contributed toward the new brick entrance to the campus and paving of the circle, which were com-pleted in the fall of 1947. There had been talk of building a replica of the summer house where earlier generations waited for the streetcar, but that nostalgic gesture proved to be too expensive. Next, the alum-nae redecorated the dining room in Clement Hall, and students arriv-ing in the fall of 1949 found the room much improved by the lowered and soundproofed ceiling and several gifts of handsome furniture.[66]

The continuity that Jane Augustine provided proved to be an invalu-able asset. Soon she became enmeshed with information about the 6,000 alumnae in the active files. However, the clerical details always diverted too much time and energy from "the real issue, the utilization of alumnae potential to the fullest degree," she said.[67] The alumnae office was funded from the general college budget, and expenses had to be kept at a minimum. Not until 1968 when Rosalie Hanley, a St. Mary's graduate of 1965 and a graduate of the University of North Carolina at Chapel Hill, joined the staff was there a full-time associate who could assume some of the writing and editing responsibilities. By then the alumnae office was located in spacious quarters in Ravenscroft, the Diocese of North Carolina having moved its operations to its new building in Raleigh. In 1966 the Ravenscroft property reverted to the college for $1,000—its purchase price at the turn of the century.[68]

Jane Augustine sought to improve the quality and appearance of the alumnae magazine. She felt that it should be more than a newsletter—that it should interpret the institution to its alumnae. The *Muse* and the *Bulletin* had been divorced in December of 1956. The 1968 decision to send alumnae publications to all alumnae on file, instead of sending news of the college only to those who had made financial contributions, proved to be a wise one.[69]

Over the years the loyalty fund, set up in June, 1950, claimed much of the time and efforts of the alumnae secretaries. The average gift that first year, according to Dora Winters's annual report, was $6.50. Being more than double the average gift of the year before, that represented the first step away from the long-prevalent idea that annual dues of about $2 constituted sufficient support of one's alma mater.[70] Proceeds from the loyalty fund went into the general fund. Richard Stone liked to save as much as possible of the fund for increases in faculty salaries. In 1957–1958 the alumnae association reached its goal of 1,000 contributors when 1,093 contributors gave over $6,000. Class agents had made effective appeals, and the senior class had contributed. Robin Fuller had concentrated her efforts on the fund, and 1,500 contributors gave $9,200 in 1960.[71] Jane Augustine was an indefatigable fund raiser. In 1962 the fund went over $10,000 and by 1969 it reached $21,972 from 1,701 contributors. That seemed exciting news until it was revealed that the average gift was $13 compared to alumnae gifts ranging from $20 to $92 at the neighboring colleges for women. President Stone, in his last message to the alumnae association in May, 1969, said, "Our present giving has not kept up with the devastating effect of inflation. We have not extended ourselves much. . . ."[72]

Class reunions became important during the 1960s with about 300 usually in attendance. Finally, order was brought to the confused class lists. The alumnae office personnel had, over a period of seven years, checked 20,000 individual records.[73] The presentation of the May Day pageant on alumnae day, a practice that began in 1961, added to the air of festivity. By the 1960s the 50th reunions were attended by a surprising number of women. On their 50th anniversary the class of 1920 gave $1,000 for the library.[74]

Alumnae day was more than a day for renewing old friendships. At the association meeting or at the luncheon, reports of the year's work were received and outstanding achievements recognized. One of the most ambitious projects, the $10,000 Margaret Jones Cruikshank Memorial Scholarship fund, was completed in 1958. Elizabeth Montgomery, graduate of 1901, was honored for her untiring efforts as chairman of that project.[75]

Constitutional changes made in 1957 during Betty Debnam's tenure as alumnae secretary increased the effectiveness of the alumnae council. North Carolina was divided into five regions, each with a regional vice-president who served on the council. The first vice-president of the association was made the chairman of annual loyalty fund drives, and the treasurer was chairman of class agents.[76] In 1968 the alumnae association was at last given representation on the board of trustees. The first two trustees, elected by the association by secret ballot, began their three-year terms in October, 1968. Peggy Holmes Stevens, 1938 graduate, and Katherine Duff Powell, graduate of 1928, met the requirement that the association's representatives should be active and interested graduates of St. Mary's Junior College of ten years' standing.[77]

Outstanding alumnae and other prominent figures were invited to speak at the annual luncheon. In 1964 North Carolina's Vermont Royster, then editor of the *Wall Street Journal*, said, "St. Mary's is a school that is not afraid to recognize that we are all children of God . . . a place where virtues are handed from one generation to another."[78] This he knew firsthand from relatives and from his wife, Frances Claypool, a 1933 graduate. An alumna who attracted considerable attention from the press when in 1954 she was the speaker for the alumnae luncheon and the commencement exercises was Eleanor Wilson McAdoo. At the luncheon she reminisced about her St. Mary's years, 1907–1909, retelling that favorite story about being written off as a Yankee by Kate McKimmon, who apologized profusely upon learning that Nell Wilson's parents were a Virginian and a Georgian.[79] In 1953 Eleanor Thomas, dean emeritus of Flora Stone Mather College, Western Reserve University, returned as speaker and was greeted by "a large number of her girls" of 1900–1917. The 1957 alumnae day speaker was Anna Clark Gordon, who was North Carolina's "mother of the year" and a church leader. Four of her six daughters were St. Mary's graduates. Emily (Pank) Badham Coxe, the first woman to represent the Diocese of South Carolina on the St. Mary's Board of Trustees and a civic leader, was chosen to speak in 1962.

Volunteerism was still a way of life for many St. Mary's women in the 1950s and 1960s. The *Bulletin* over the years published vignettes of some of those who made major contributions to their communities through their varied volunteer activities. Examples included May Vivian Johnson, a founder of the Raleigh YWCA; Mary Lyde Hicks Williams, who served for 20 years on the Board of Directors of Dorothea Dix Hospital, as state president of the UDC, and as state regent of the DAR; Catherine Miller Thomas, who was president of the Episcopal Churchwomen of the Diocese of North Carolina.[80]

Among the St. Mary's women active in political affairs was Elizabeth Henderson Cotten, who in 1901 had helped to win the passage of a bill to increase pensions for Confederate veterans by her address to the North Carolina General Assembly. She was named vice-chairman of the Democratic party in the Eighth Congressional District in 1928 and 1930. The St. Mary's *Bulletin* in 1954 cited also her work with the League of Women Voters, her war work in both world wars, and her long service to the Episcopal church, as well as her contributions as curator of the Southern Historical Collection at Chapel Hill.[81] Also politically active as members of the state committee of the Democratic party were Martha Gold Winstead Borden and Mary Cross Dent.[82] An alumna who was a political wife in the 1960s was Marie Tyler, wife of James C. Gardner, who in 1966 was elected to Congress. Another was Ann Cooper Broughton, whose husband, J. Melville Broughton, Jr., was one of the candidates in the 1968 Democratic gubernatorial primary.

Many St. Mary's women, married and unmarried, were choosing careers. The *Bulletin* featured a number of them. One career woman of the class of 1910 was Ila Rountree Pridgen, who performed much of the laboratory work for her husband, Claude L. Pridgen, on the Rockefeller project to eradicate hookworm in North Carolina. In 1943 she received a law degree with honors, remaining at the University of Florida as law librarian, sometimes teaching law, until her retirement in 1955.[83]

Laura Owens was one of the organizers of the Charlotte Children's Nature Museum and its second director.[84] Frances Yarborough Bickett, of the class of 1947, was the first woman judge of the Wake County Domestic Relations Court.[85] Lillian Lucas Cole, director of a division of the New Jersey Neuro-Psychiatric Institute, published a number of articles and wrote a section of a medical school text.[86] Elizabeth L. Lawrence was a lecturer, consultant, and the author of several books on gardening.[87] Also known as an authority on gardening and as an artist was Isabelle Bowen Henderson;[88] Isabel B. Busbee was a landscape architect and civic leader;[89] and for many years Blanche Blake Manor wrote for the *News and Observer* a Sunday column called "Chatter."

It is evident that students of the post-World War II years did not lack for different kinds of role models among St. Mary's women of all ages. The dominant feminine image, however, remained that projected by women's magazines—the image of the ideal housewife-mother-volunteer. Some of that generation of St. Mary's students accepted the perfect wife stereotype; others were achieving success in various fields. Many women were beginning to gain new perceptions of themselves. Two of the independent ones made it to Broadway. The 1969 *Bulletin* reported that 1961 graduate Pamela Payton-Wright was playing opposite Dustin Hoffman in *Jimmy Shine*. Penelope (Penny) Fuller, 1955–1956, also was a recognized actress.[90] One alumna who became nationally known for her extreme independence was Barbara Dearing Howar, who in 1969 was hosting a daily television talk show from the nation's capital. The *Bulletin* quoted her on women in television in the late sixties:

A woman in television must be better read and more articulate than a man, for there is tremendous prejudice against women in the industry. It is difficult to break into the field and highly competitive to remain. . . .[91]

## "THAT INDEFINABLE SPIRIT"

A St. Mary's graduate of 1960, Lynda Sanderfoot, writing in 1965 from Guatemala where she was with the Peace Corps, said, "You seek out the problems of a community and set about to help the *people* solve them. The main factor . . . is people."[92] Concern for others, first learned by most St. Mary's women at home, was reinforced during their years at the school. A new chaplain of the 1960s observed after a few months on campus:

The two things that have impressed me most . . . are the high regard the girls have for their Chapel and Chaplain, and the St. Mary's spirit. The Chapel is the center of campus life and the students look to the Chaplain for guidance, understanding, and instruction. I am sure the alumnae understood this relationship, for it is traditional at St. Mary's.

The St. Mary's spirit is indefinable; the girls have a real love and concern for one another. This spirit would be difficult to duplicate anywhere. The best way I can interpret it is to say that it is the reflection of the love of Christ for us all.[93]

During the first decade of Stone's administration, I. Harding Hughes continued to serve as chaplain. In his classes he sought to train future church school teachers. Upon his retirement in 1957 the *Bulletin* noted, "For fifteen years . . . Mr. and Mrs. Hughes have held open house and open hearts for the faculty and students. . . ."[94] When Josephine Bowen Hughes (St. Mary's, class of 1904) died in 1961, her husband set up a memorial scholarship at the college. Harding Hughes died on March 16, 1970, at the age of 86.[95] He was survived by several years by his second wife, Marguerite Ghent Smith, whom he married in 1966.

St. Mary's fourth chaplain was Moultrie Guerry. It was the college's good fortune that Dr. and Mrs. Guerry were persuaded to leave Old St. Paul's in Norfolk, Virginia, where he had been rector for nearly 20 years. By the fall of 1957 he and "Precious," as he always called his wife, were settled into the little brick cottage near the library.

Moultrie Guerry was born in Lincolnton on Lincoln's birthday, 1899, but he grew up in Sewanee, Tennessee, and in Charleston. His father, William Alexander Guerry, was the bishop of South Carolina, 1907–1928. Moultrie Guerry was educated at the University of the South and at Virginia Theological Seminary; his honorary doctorate of divinity was bestowed by the seminary. He taught English at the College of Charleston before going into the ministry, and he served as chaplain and professor of religious literature at the University of the South for nine years.[96] Moultrie Guerry took delight in the daily events of campus life at St. Mary's. He and "Mrs. Precious," as the students often called his wife, appeared at every event. Elizabeth Parker Guerry, a Charlestonian educated at Ashley Hall, understood St. Mary's, and she enjoyed her years at the school. She often read on the screened-in side porch of their home, keeping an eye out for a lonely student in need of an invitation to stop in for a glass of orange juice. Moultrie Guerry was especially interested in sports and drama. He played softball with the students, and he taught them how to throw his homemade boomerangs. His sermons were sprinkled with illustrations drawn from campus life, and he always devoted a sermon to a Biblical interpretation of the play then in production in the college auditorium. It was a tradition that the sun always shone on the bride when he performed the ceremony.[97]

Chaplain Guerry always spoke of the chapel service as "our corporate worship." He insisted, "Religion is not a department of the College, for St. Mary's is a family where religion and learning can be woven together in the natural fabric of daily life."[98] The student body continued to be about 50 percent Episcopalian. Guerry taught nearly half of the student body each semester. The freshmen hour was designed to give the young people "a firmer grasp upon their faith." The sophomore hour was based upon his own mimeographed textbook, *The Vine, Education According to Christ*. The juniors took a full academic course in the Old Testament. The New Testament was approached as a stirring drama of Christ's life.[99]

Moultrie Guerry once wrote that he thoroughly agreed with Aldert Smedes's philosophy that St. Mary's women should be educated "to be blessed and a blessing."[100] The YWCA and the Canterbury Club normally consisted of about 50 members each who spent many hours in Raleigh institutions such as the Methodist Home for Children. In dedicating the 1963 *Stagecoach* to Guerry, the students wrote of him, "His faith in the students as individuals provides a challenge for the perfection of character."

Noted outside speakers also challenged students; Mabel Morrison as chairman of the lectures and concerts committee saw to that. In 1959, John Baille, a president of the World Council of Churches and dean of the faculty of divinity at Edinburgh University, spent two days on campus lecturing on "What It Means to be a Christian." In 1963 George F. McCleod, founder and leader of the Iona Community, was the Danforth visiting lecturer.

In his 1960 address to the students, the Right Reverend Richard Henry Baker, bishop of the Diocese of North Carolina, delineated the challenge. He said, "We must take going to St. Mary's as a responsibility. . . . People will look [to St. Mary's women] for standards—all sorts of standards . . . . [for] a leadership that will discern the true values and nurture them with relentless courage."[101] The traditional St. Mary's network of friendship and service remained operative. Of the 1,200 alumnae who answered a detailed questionnaire sent out in the midsixties by the college's development office, 50 percent held leadership positions in volunteer community work and 57 percent were church leaders.

In his first report to the trustees, Richard Stone said, "It is my opinion that religious training and religious emphasis are very important in the education of young people. The religious aspects of the program at St. Mary's have always been important and will continue to be so in the future." His personal commitment was clear: 12 years on the vestry of the Church of the Good Shepherd, 3 years on the executive council of the Diocese of North Carolina, 2 years as president of the laymen's association of the diocese, frequent parish delegate to the diocesan convention, 4 times representative of the diocese at the provincial synod, 4 times deputy to the general convention, member of the committee that nominated Arthur Carl Lichtenberger as bishop, and 6 years on the national council. Richard Stone was the first representative from his diocese to be elected to the national council, the highest honor any layman could receive. While a member of the council he was a trustee of the Seminary of the Caribbean and a member of the Joint Commission on Holy Orders.[102]

Thus, Stone realized the importance of the chaplaincy at St. Mary's. At the end of the 1964–1965 session Moultrie Guerry retired, and he and his wife moved back to Norfolk where he spent his time writing articles and corresponding with former students.[103] The chaplaincy was filled during the next academic year by the Reverend Grant O. Folmsbee. He held a degree from the Berkeley Divinity School of New Haven, Connecticut, and a master's degree in guidance and counseling. The chaplain's home was moved to the far side of Cheshire Hall and enlarged. During the first semester of 1966–1967 the Reverend E. F. Moseley served as acting chaplain. An Oxford graduate, he was a firm, fair, and well-liked teacher.

St. Mary's next chaplain was familiar with life at St. Mary's as a trustee of the college from the Diocese of South Carolina. He was the Reverend Robert C. Baird, who arrived during the winter of 1967 and stayed through the remainder of the Stone administration. Born in Alabama and reared in Charlotte, he held degrees from Davidson College and the Virginia Theological Seminary and the master of sacred theology degree from the University of the South. He was ordained in the Diocese of North Carolina and served St. Thomas' Episcopal Church in Sanford. He moved to Raleigh from St. Paul's in Bennettsville, South Carolina, where he had been rector since 1949. He went to the college because he was interested in young people and in counseling. One of the conditions of his acceptance of the position was that the Bairds could live off campus. Richard Stone agreed reluctantly. The Bairds soon found a house in town, and Bob Baird settled into his duties as pastor, professor, and kind and caring friend to students and faculty alike.

## "MAKING ENDS MEET"

President Stone realized very soon after he went to St. Mary's that making ends meet was to be his perpetual problem. The plant was deteriorating, and the need for new buildings was acute; the real problem was the inadequacy of the institutional endowment.

There was no enrollment problem. Although applications were down slightly during the 1950s, as they were at neighboring institutions,[104] the school remained filled with a waiting list. The trustees in 1959 decided to limit the St. Mary's student body to about 500.[105] Throughout the 1960s there were enough applicants to ensure a student body that was strong academically. Longtime faculty members remember those as "the good years" when serious students were well prepared and worked diligently. Normally, about two thirds of the students were North Carolinians and about half of the students were alumnae-connected. The granddaughters club of 1959–1960 boasted 19 great-granddaughters and four great-great-granddaughters. Almost a decade passed before the full impact of the admission of freshman women at Chapel Hill and the granting of the liberal arts degree (1963) by North Carolina State University was felt at St. Mary's. An enrollment of 452, with 396 in residence, filled every room, including those in the new Margaret Jones Cruikshank Dormitory, in 1968–1969. Applications were down only slightly from the peak year of 1966–1967.[106] The high school enrollment increased only gradually during the Stone administration; the graduating high school class (St. Mary's sophomores) numbered 47 for 1965–1966 and 52 for 1968–1969.

In the summer of 1968 Elizabeth Gordon Tucker retired as registrar after 36 years.[107] When her retirement plans were announced, a young faculty member inquired anxiously, "Do you think that St. Mary's will fall to pieces when Elizabeth retires?" Characteristically, Elizabeth Tucker spent weeks working with her successor, Alice Anne Horne.

Despite the tight financial situation, President Stone managed not only to make ends meet but also to make major renovations, to buy two lots facing Hillsborough Street to add to the campus, and to build new buildings—the heating plant, the laundry, the science building, two dormitories, and the library. He always placed primary emphasis upon academic matters, thinking that bricks and mortar could wait "until the money was in sight." He knew that he was faulted by some for his fiscal conservatism, but it was a deeply held conviction. He had been well aware of the college's financial condition before he decided to take the presidency, and he told Bishop Penick that he "had no talent for fund raising." The bishop replied, "It will get done."[108]

St. Mary's was managed by Richard Stone without an official budget. There was an unofficial budget in the minds of Stone and Julia Jordan, the purchasing officer. It was a generally accepted fact that no one was to spend much money and that Julia Jordan would question every penny of that. When queried by a trustee about the system, the president explained that the school "operated on the basis of judgments about previous annual expenditures and current funds available."[109] The system worked for Stone because everyone understood it. He inherited able assistance in operating the institution. The financial secretary, Mary Lewis Sasser, had worked with business managers Tucker and Stoughton for almost 38 years. Stone said of her, "I had great confidence in any report that she completed and all records were in perfect order at all times." She continued this faithful performance of her duties throughout two years of seriously declining health. Mary Lewis Sasser died on November 18, 1961.[110]

Another competent and tireless aide inherited by Stone was Julia Jordan. With her titian hair confined by a green eyeshade, she presided over a desk piled high with purchase orders and bills. A 1915 graduate of the St. Mary's business department, she had worked for a while with Ernest Cruikshank when he was business manager. It was 1937 when she ran into A. W. Tucker, who asked if she could "help out a little" at St. Mary's.[111] She stayed for 32 years. Mary Lewis Sasser was her first cousin. They were an efficient pair although their disagreements over details were never private. When Jordan retired in 1969, she continued to live in Raleigh.

Another experienced person in administration when Stone assumed office was Frances Vann, who then was the college bursar. She returned to St. Mary's immediately after her student days to work for Margaret Cruikshank and gave over 45 years of devoted service to the college. She was interested in every aspect of campus life, particularly the lives and careers of alumnae.

The purse strings had to be kept tightly drawn because during all of the Stone administration over 90 percent of the institution's income was derived from the students; the figure was 94 percent in 1958–1959.[112] At the end of his first year Stone asked the board to raise resident charges from $860 to $950 and those for day students from $200 to $250 for 1947–1948. Food costs for that year proved to be surprisingly high—$3.17 per person per day.[113] By 1952–1953 instructional costs (not including the library) were $281 per student while day students still paid $250.[114] The board reluctantly raised charges to $1,175 for boarders and to $325 for day students. As the president explained in a letter to parents, most educational institutions had raised fees several years earlier. In the 1952 fund-raising brochure the trustees made a great point of "the moderate charges," giving figures to prove that St. Mary's charged from $200 to $600 "less than private and church-related schools of comparable standing." Stone felt that the board never agreed to charge enough.[115] By the last year of his administration, inflation had forced charges up to $2,020 for residents and $745 for day students.

When asked what had been his greatest problems as president, Stone replied, "The selection and retention of a really good faculty. The problem was always money. The good teachers usually had several offers, and we had to sell St. Mary's to them."[116] Salaries had to be raised for Stone's first year because, as Margaret Cruikshank had predicted, the southern association sent a letter of warning during the spring of 1946.[117] By the fall of 1948 faculty salaries met minimum standards, but Stone was still at a disadvantage when recruiting faculty. He found the best answer to his recruitment problems when in the late 1950s he discovered the qualified married women already living in the area.

For 1949–1950 Stone suggested a 10 percent raise for faculty and staff, except for himself. The board accepted his recommendation and included him. He managed to squeeze increases from the budget until by 1960 faculty salaries ranged from $4,000 to $5,500. The self-study of 1969 showed that during the previous year the median faculty salary at St. Mary's ($6,500) was $365 lower than the median at private junior colleges in the Southeast. In reporting those figures to the alumnae, Jane Rabon wrote:

If St. Mary's were producing an inferior product, discrepancies in salaries would be justified. But the record of . . . students at senior colleges and univer-

John Tate in *The Heiress*, 1958

sities indicates that the quality of instruction they received at St. Mary's was superior.

[The College] has been fortunate . . . for years in having several instructors and administrators who not only were excellent in their field, but who have dedicated their lives to St. Mary's without great salary demands. Great sacrifices have been made. But this old guard has been rapidly changing, and in a few short years this kind of teacher will have disappeared from the college scene altogether.[118]

From the beginning of his administration, Stone asked for adequate retirement and health benefits for all employees. A voluntary retirement annuity plan had been set up in 1942. When Social Security coverage was extended in 1951, everyone working at St. Mary's became eligible. The required two thirds enrolled, meaning that retirement benefits for most would be about doubled.[119] The retirement age policy set by the trustees to become effective in 1957 made retirement voluntary at 68 and mandatory at 72. However, employment after 68 was on a year-to-year basis. There was no set policy for leaves of absence because of illness; but Richard Stone's attitude toward such situations was generous, and the finance committee accepted his recommendations. By 1958 a major medical insurance plan was available.

By the end of the Stone administration, the faculty numbered about 40, including several who taught part time, and the staff and administration numbered about 28. The president still worried because he could not afford more men teachers, and he was concerned about faculty salaries in general. His last budget request was for $28,000 for faculty and staff salary increases; he got $35,000.[120]

Each year Stone faced the problem of the deteriorating buildings. "Venerable" buildings required care. Stone followed the traditional and necessary practice of making repairs and improvements bit by bit each summer, often borrowing against the fall's tuition payments. For many years Clifford Goolsby and Lewis Hatley carried out improvement projects and gave faithful attention during the school year to the physical plant.

Stone's reports to the trustees show that during 1946 almost $75,000 of the centennial fund raised during Margaret Cruikshank's administration was spent, as planned, for landscaping the front campus, a new heating plant, an all-electric kitchen, renovation of the president's house, and the new organ. Between 1947 and 1954 all dormitory rooms were refurnished. The wooden floor in lower Smedes was cemented in 1949, and the next year the walk and roads on back campus were paved.

There was the perpetual problem of what Stone called "the distractingly noisy heating system." Part of the campus was forever being dug up as steam issued from unlikely spots. The plumbing was just as unreliable. Over the years some of the antiquated bathrooms were modernized, and during the summer of 1950 all of the water pipes in the wings were replaced, but the pipes in Smedes remained unreliable. Only a year after the parlor had been redone in 1954,[121] pipes above that room broke. Fortunately, a senior class meeting was in progress there, and rugs and furniture were rescued. Five years later, pipes broke over the fourth of July, and considerable damage was done. The paintings and the chandeliers escaped, but the room had to be redecorated ahead of schedule.

Major damage to the grove occurred when Hurricane Hazel swept through it on October 15, 1954. Forty trees, 30 of them the oldest oaks, fell. There were no injuries and little other damage, except to roofs.[122]

Other renovation of existing buildings included new chairs for the main floor of the auditorium in 1956,[123] and replacement of the termite-ridden floor of the gymnasium in 1957. The next year the president's home and office were renovated. The modern lighting system with dimmer panel and the shutters were installed in the auditorium in 1960. The parlor in Holt Hall was refurbished by the Holt family in 1956; a portrait of Margaret Locke Erwin Holt was unveiled on January 5, 1957.[124]

It became apparent by 1951–1952 that the renovation of old buildings was not enough. Enrollment was down a little, and expenses had risen a great deal (from $185,000 in 1945 to $262,000 in 1950) with student charges up only 25 percent.[125] The lack of a modern science building and the need for a new dormitory were factors in what the president called an "alarming" situation. Everyone—the president, the trustees, the faculty—agreed that a building-fund campaign had to be organized. Stone insisted that "people do not like to pay for buildings after they are built; a college should never build until the money is in sight. Buildings should never be placed ahead of academic excellence."[126] The science building had become, however, an academic necessity.

The St. Mary's Development Fund was approved by a special meeting of the board of trustees on May 2, 1951, and launched on January 7, 1952. Directed by a professional fund-raising organization,[127] it was to end on July 5, 1952. The goal was to obtain $300,000 in gifts and pledges payable over a two-year period, half to be used for a science and general classroom building and half to be added to the unrestricted endowment. The endowment then stood at $212,000, of which $102,000 was in trust funds not controlled by the college administration. It was proposed that $50,000 of the new endowment be added to the $52,898 scholarship fund.

A well-executed brochure entitled *Saint Mary's and the Challenge of Our Times* not only explained the needs of the school but also made a strong case for St. Mary's as "a permanent . . . commercial asset" that had "managed to stay open without interruption for 110 years, through the Civil War and five other wars, through panics, epidemics and inflations." Episcopalians were told that $300,000 was "a relatively moderate asking" for this "ward and responsibility of the Church . . . an historic asset of immeasurable value to the Church. . . ." The statistics of the constituency were quoted—49,609 communicants in the five owning dioceses in 180 parishes, 169 organized missions, and 51 unorganized missions served by 146 active and canonically resident clergymen.[128]

Penick as chairman of the board of trustees of St. Mary's wrote of the role of church-related schools in keeping young people within the church and added:

Strong and characterful leadership is urgently needed today in every phase of our complex society. Women are . . . a vital part in providing this leadership. They know better than all others how to create and maintain a moral and spiritual climate. The progress of civilization is largely due to the influence of the family.[129]

It was decided that the development campaign would be directed "mainly toward individuals in the five owning dioceses" but that the parishes would be expected to give "strong aid." The expectation was that "generous aid" would be forthcoming from others because of the institution's "service to the whole community."[130] A host of volunteers gave untold hours working under three diocesan general chairmen,[131] 19 district lay chairmen, and the 11 clergymen designated as associate district chairmen. The alumnae were organized under Mary Richardson Davis. The faculty contributed, and the students pledged to give $500 through their self-denial boxes. By September, 1952, the amount "in sight" was $165,000 and the science building was assured. More than 15 parishes had exceeded their quotas while others had fallen woefully short. The extended campaign closed in late October, 1953, having reached 61.4 percent of the $300,000 goal (almost $185,000). About $126,000 was used to build and equip the science building and to bring the endowment up to somewhat over $286,000. By June of the next year, the endowment with some additions from the old centennial fund had climbed to over $313,000, but Richard Stone told the trustees that $1 million was needed for an adequate endowment.[132] Stone took satisfaction in the knowledge that during his administration "not one dime" was taken from the corpus of the endowment for operational expenses and that he paid back the money borrowed from the endowment by the Cruikshank administration.[133]

Ground was broken for the new science building on February 2, 1953, and the building was ready for occupancy in the fall of that year.[134] It was named in honor of the Right Reverend Joseph Blount Cheshire. With its quiet classrooms (no noisy steam pipes), laboratories, storage closets, and faculty offices, the two-story building seemed luxurious. The science department shared the space with the social studies department until the 1970s.

The next building project was the construction in 1956 of a warehouse-laundry building on the north edge of the campus so that the old facility could be razed to make room for the new dormitory. The residence hall was built with a 40-year loan of $190,000 (at 2.75 percent interest) from the federal government's House and Home Finance Agency.[135] Dedicated on May 4, 1957, the building was named in honor of the Right Reverend Edwin A. Penick. The facility housed 56; however, only 35 new students were enrolled because some students were to be moved from overcrowded dormitories.[136]

By 1965 well-qualified applicants were being turned away for want of dormitory space; also, the overcrowded condition of the library had become critical. A new dormitory could be financed by a federal loan, and grants of $132,987 from the Sarah Graham Kenan Foundation and $25,000 from the Mary Reynolds Babcock Foundation were promised.

With that much "visible money," the trustees authorized both buildings. The dormitory, costing $440,300, was financed almost entirely by a 40-year federal loan at 3 percent. The library, of a contemporary and somewhat controversial design, provided space for about 35,000 volumes on the first floor and on the second floor study rooms, storage space, and a large meeting room. The $310,000 cost of the building was covered by the two grants and accumulated endowment income. Class gifts, alumnae gifts, and the library fund were used over a period of several years to complete the furnishing and equipping of the carpeted, air-conditioned building.[137]

October 11, 1966, was a great day at St. Mary's. Both new buildings were dedicated. The library was named in honor of Sarah Graham Kenan of Wilmington, who attended the school 1892–1893. Trustee Charles M. Shaffer in expressing appreciation said, "Mrs. Kenan upholds the philanthropic tradition of her family and the future of her alma mater."[138] The dormitory was named to honor Margaret Jones Cruikshank. President Stone paid tribute to her as "a very great lady."[139]

Returning students in the fall of 1966 saw changes in the physical appearance of the campus in addition to the two new buildings. The old library became the language-art building. The art department occupied the top floor, as it had since 1887, but the first floor was converted into classrooms and a language laboratory. The frame house, known as senior hall in the 1920s and later as faculty house, was gone, and in its place was a grassy open spot.

By the middle sixties there was talk of another campaign for funds. Sources outside student charges were providing only 10 percent of income while inflation and the addition of two large buildings had raised operational costs. About 2 percent of the outside money came from the North Carolina Foundation of Church-Related Colleges, a source of some income since 1953. St. Mary's was a charter member of that foundation organized to solicit funds from the business community, and Stone was a trustee.[140] Occasional bequests[141] and the gifts from individuals made up about 2 percent of each year's income, alumnae gifts about 1.7 percent, and church support about 2.9 percent.[142] A development director, H. M. Bitler, was employed in March, 1965, to prepare for a campaign; and all seemed well until the special meeting of the trustees in November.

The minutes of that meeting of November 10 show that a motion for a campaign to raise just over $1 million for capital improvements failed because the festering problem of the college's relationship to the Episcopal church had reached the point where it had to be resolved. At that meeting, the Right Reverend Thomas A. Fraser, bishop coadjutor of the Diocese of North Carolina, reported that the council of his diocese

Cold Cuts, 1960

was "not enthusiastic" and supported the idea advanced by another trustee that "the church was a handicap to diocesan schools." The bishop then proposed a board of trustees made up of lay persons. He felt that the school needed federal funds to survive and that some of the bishops would be unhappy over the prospect of "government interference." Whereupon a lay trustee proposed, "If we believe in St. Mary's, let's say we are going to support this campaign. Then we can determine whether to break with the Church." So much of the ensuing discussion was negative that Stone proposed that consideration of a campaign be "put aside." He thought that "lack of unified support would damage the image of the college." The Right Reverend Gray Temple, bishop of the Diocese of South Carolina, felt that the bishops should give "personal enthusiastic approval" and return home to get the support of their dioceses. Finally, by a unanimous voice vote that idea was accepted, and in January the executive committee of the board endorsed plans to proceed with the campaign. Those plans, however, remained in limbo during a reorganization of the board.

When Stone retired in July, 1969, he left a quarter of a million dollars that he had saved (perhaps for a fine arts building). He made a fervent plea that the money be placed in the endowment; the board, however, decreed that the new president should decide how the funds should be used.[143]

Richard Stone's relationship with the trustees of the college was from the beginning one of mutual trust. In his first report to the board in November, 1946, he pledged that he would "in every possible way attempt to administer the affairs of St. Mary's in the best interest of the school and the owning Church." He made it clear, however, that he expected administration to be "centralized in the president." Stone said of Bishop Penick, "He always gave me both the support and the freedom that I needed."[144] In turn, President Stone always prepared specific information for the board meetings. The faculty had almost no contact with the trustees; no one considered it necessary. Because Richard Stone placed the same confidence in the faculty and staff as Margaret Cruikshank had, those persons continued to perform effectively the many quasi-administrative duties assigned to faculty committees. After the 1959 self-study, the visiting committee from the southern association reported that Stone's relationship with the board was "pleasant" and "not affected by outside influences." The trustees on October 18, 1955, in voting a salary increase for the president, expressed "a comfortable feeling among the trustees that the school is in safe hands," praise for Richard Stone as "an outstanding Episcopal layman and civic leader," and appreciation of his encouragement of the alumnae association.

Bishop Penick had been chairman of the board of trustees for 19 years when Richard G. Stone became president of the college. Edwin Anderson Penick (1887–1959) was born in Frankfort, Kentucky, the son of the Reverend Edwin Anderson Penick and Mary Shipman Penick. He held a bachelor's degree from the University of the South, a master's degree from Harvard, the bachelor of divinity degree from Virginia Theological Seminary, and three honorary degrees—the D.D. from Virgina Theological Seminary (1922) and from the University of the South (1923) and the LL.D. from the University of North Carolina (1948). He was ordained to the priesthood in 1913 by Bishop Guerry and served churches in South Carolina. In 1917 he married Caroline Dial of Columbia. After service as an army chaplain, he became rector of St. Peter's Episcopal Church in Charlotte and in 1922 was elected bishop coadjutor of the Diocese of North Carolina.[145] He supported St. Mary's faithfully for 32 years as chairman of the board, 1927–1959. He became the sixth bishop of the Diocese of North Carolina in 1932. The *Belles* wrote of Penick, "residing . . . on the corner of the campus, [he] became a vital part of the spirit that is St. Mary's."[146]

Penick and Stone were disappointed and worried when the 1952 financial campaign failed to reach the goal. During the meeting of the trustees in the fall of 1952, Stone asked if "the question of ownership should be reviewed." He said, "A number of the members of the Board lacked interest in the campaign and regarded it as secondary to all diocesan or parochial projects." The South Carolina bishops acknowledged that there had been "a lessening of interest" in their dioceses. Bishop M. George Henry of the Diocese of Western North Carolina offered a resolution, which passed, asking each diocese to increase its budgeted amount by $1,000 as the Diocese of North Carolina had just done. The discussion ended with a rising vote of thanks to President Stone for his "candid presentation" and "the highly beneficial" exchange it had engendered.[147]

The candid discussion had brought into the open the two problems: the board of trustees was overloaded with the clergy, and the church was giving the school insufficient financial support. That year 14 of the 30 members of the board were clergymen. Financial support in 1953 from what were always referred to as "the five owning dioceses" was budgeted by them at $5,500.[148]

There were then, as there always had been, interested and active board members among both the clergy and the laity. The devotion of Mrs. C. C. Dawson as a representative of the Diocese of Western North Carolina was such that she was made an honorary alumna in 1950. In an effort to increase the number of lay persons on the board, Stone in 1954 proposed "a full discussion of the method of selecting trustees." Penick appointed a study committee, which included only one clergyman, and the changes proposed were made in the charter in 1959. The bishops were made members of the board ex officio. Twenty-three members—eight from the Diocese of North Carolina, four each from the dioceses of East Carolina, Western North Carolina, and South Carolina, and three from the Diocese of Upper South Carolina were to be elected for four-year terms. The term had been six years for the elected diocesan representatives. Twelve, instead of six, members constituted a quorum if as many as three dioceses were represented.[149]

Restructuring of the board resulted in little change in policy and did not solve the problems of defining the exact nature of the relationship of the Carolina dioceses to their educational institutions. The old Diocese of North Carolina had not in the 1830s supported the Episcopal

School of North Carolina; Episcopalians did not send their sons to Aldert Smedes's Trinity School; the Diocese of North Carolina had no financial responsibility for St. Mary's during the years from 1842 to 1897. It was an acknowledged fact that most Episcopalians habitually took their educational institutions for granted. In 1914 the *Carolina Churchman* put it plainly enough:

Whatever may be the cause, it is the universal testimony all over the country that our Church people do not support their own Church institutions, especially those for education, as they themselves support educational institutions with no connection with the Church, and as the members of other religious bodies do certainly efficiently and generously support their own institutions. . . .[150]

Perhaps the explanation lay in the long experience in England and in the colonies with an established church and the consequent absence of the strong sense of stewardship that the dissenting denominations had to develop in order to survive.

During the 1950s and 1960s the Diocese of North Carolina steadily increased its support of St. Mary's until it amounted to $11,000 annually by 1966. The other four dioceses were budgeting by then from $500 to $1,500 annually for the school. In 1968 total support from the Episcopal church was just under $20,000; that amount included moneys from the diocesan budgets, from the Episcopal Churchwomen, and from parishes.[151] Few Episcopalians were aware of the fact that some of that money was being returned each year through the scholarships at St. Mary's for daughters of the Episcopal clergy.

The Right Reverend Richard H. Baker, D.D., succeeded to the bishopric in 1959 and was elected chairman of the Board of Trustees of St. Mary's Junior College. He had served as bishop coadjutor for nine years and thus had been a trustee. A native of Norfolk, Virginia, he was educated at the University of Virginia and Virginia Theological Seminary. His honorary degree was conferred by the seminary in 1950. He had taught and served as chaplain at the Virginia Episcopal School and had served parishes in Louisiana and Virginia. He moved to North Carolina from the Church of the Redeemer in Baltimore. His fellow trustees wrote of him, "He was never too busy to give unstintingly of his time and talents . . . to the service of St. Mary's."[152] He did not live on the campus, as had Bishops Cheshire and Penick, because Ravenscroft was then the diocesan headquarters. Continuing the traditional commencement practice, Bishop Baker presented their diplomas to the seniors in the chapel. Upon his retirement, the bishop and Mrs. Baker moved to Baltimore, where he kept busy as a volunteer hospital chaplain. He died on April 13, 1981, at the age of 81.[153]

Bishop Baker's successor was Thomas A. Fraser, who had been bishop coadjutor since May, 1960. A native of Atlanta, Georgia, he was educated at Hobart College, the University of Jena, and Virginia Theological Seminary. Ordained to the priesthood in 1942, he held honorary degrees from Virginia Theological Seminary, the University of the South, Wake Forest, and Hobart. He had served St. Paul's in Alexandria, Virginia, and St. Paul's in Winston-Salem.

Bishop Baker on January 20, 1965, told the trustees of St. Mary's that he planned to retire in July of that year. After making that announcement, he asked Bishop Wright of East Carolina to preside over the remainder of the board meeting, and he left so as to give the trustees full freedom to discuss future plans. Bishop Temple proposed that a vice-chairman, who would succeed to the chairmanship, be elected immediately. The minutes of that meeting record that "Bishop Temple further stated that Bishops have many responsibilities and that it was often burdensome to add additional responsibilities and expressed an opinion that it should be possible to elect any member of the Board of Trustees [to the chairmanship], be that person a Bishop, Presbyter, or Lay Person." Temple then moved that the position of vice-chairman be created and that Arthur L. Tyler fill it. That motion was approved unanimously. The election was unquestionably legal under the terms of the institution's incorporation; it was only by custom that the trustees had elected the bishop of North Carolina as their chairman.

Arthur Lynwood Tyler had served as a trustee of St. Mary's since 1956, giving much time to his duties as chairman of both the executive and finance committees and conferring often with Dick Stone. He served as chairman of the board until 1968 when he resigned because of declining health. A self-made man, he was vice-president of the Belk-Tyler stores. In 1973 St. Mary's conferred the first honorary degree ever given by the college, the associate degree in humane letters, upon Arthur Tyler for his long service to several institutions of higher education in North Carolina.[154] The lounge in the student union at St. Mary's was named to honor Arthur Tyler and his wife, Elizabeth May Tyler. Arthur Tyler died on May 6, 1978.

The question of the relationship of St. Mary's to the five dioceses became the main subject of the board meeting of October, 1966, under Tyler's chairmanship. Confusion, frustration, and some dissension were evident. Finally, the trustees adopted a resolution prepared by Bishop Wright:

*Whereas,* there is considerable confusion and difference of opinion within the five owning Dioceses as to the future of St. Mary's School;

*And, whereas,* there is the opinion of some persons that the time has come for the Church to relinquish the ownership and operation of St. Mary's;

*And, whereas,* there is the opinion of others that the Church should continue ownership and operation of the School but that this should be given to *one Diocese only;*

*And, whereas,* there is the feeling within some of the five Dioceses that the administrative set-up of St. Mary's should be clarified, as to such things as Tenure of Office, Admissions Policy for New Students, etc;

*And, whereas,* it is the conviction of this Board that nothing further of a constructive nature can be accomplished by this Board until *the Dioceses themselves* have individually declared themselves—stating by way of their Conventions and otherwise *where they stand* in regard to St. Mary's and *what their intention* is regarding St. Mary's;

*Be it Resolved, therefore,* that the Chairman appoint a committee of two lay persons from each Diocese—one to be a member of this Board and one to be an Alumna of St. Mary's—to facilitate this matter—the two representatives from each Diocese being asked *to obtain from their respective Diocesan Conventions (and otherwise)* a written statement as recorded above—these written *"Statements of Belief and Intention"* to be consolidated by the Committee into one report and given to the Chairman of the Board to be reported back to this Board.[155]

Eventually, all five dioceses replied favorably, indicating intent to support St. Mary's.

Meanwhile, the trustees still felt that St. Mary's was not moving ahead fast enough in many areas despite the new buildings. Tyler was succeeded as chairman of the board in October, 1968, by the Reverend Thomas J. C. Smyth, who had been a trustee since 1964. Deeply committed to the church and to education, he was both Episcopal chaplain and dean of students at the University of North Carolina at Greensboro. He was born in Belfast, Northern Ireland, where his parents were stranded during World War I. He was educated at Elon College and the University of the South and ordained to the priesthood in 1945 by Bishop Penick. Smyth was a trustee of the University of the South, which conferred upon him in 1970 the doctor of divinity degree.[156]

One of Smyth's first acts as chairman of the Board of Trustees of St. Mary's was to appoint a special committee of trustees to study the structure of the board, the admissions policy, and tenure for administrative personnel. As a result of that committee's report, the trustees voted on January 9, 1968, to amend the charter of the college to reduce the board from 31 to 15 members, at least two thirds of whom had to be communicants in good standing of the Protestant Episcopal church.

New bylaws written by the board restructured it to include eight members-at-large elected by the board for ten-year terms, one member elected by each diocese for five years, and two alumnae elected by the alumnae association for three years. The trustees were required to meet quarterly instead of annually, and a majority constituted a quorum. The executive committee was abolished. Since a 1947 amendment to the college's charter it had exercised powers such as those of "the directors of a commercial or business corporation" between annual meetings of the full board.[157]

A board of visitors was the new feature: "A Board of Visitors, not to exceed thirty in number, shall be composed of all the Bishops of the

Closing the school year, 1960

Protestant Episcopal Church exercising jurisdiction within the States of North Carolina and South Carolina and, by appointment of the Board of Trustees, such other persons, clerical and lay, who manifest an abiding interest in the continuing advancement of St. Mary's Junior College." [158] Admissions policies were declared to be a matter for board decision, and administrative personnel were required to retire at 65. Those sweeping changes were designed to bring interested businessmen and educators onto the board, to place control of school policy back into the hands of the full board, to placate the alumnae, and to give the bishops and influential lay persons some input through the board of visitors.

The reorganization provided the apparatus for St. Mary's to move in new directions. It did not solve the problem of the college's relationship to the owning dioceses, and the financial position of the school remained precarious. A preliminary study looking toward another fund drive proved inconclusive.

Unfortunately, the relationship between St. Mary's and her home diocese became complicated during the sixties over the most painful question of the decade—race. In June, 1963, the executive council of the Diocese of North Carolina wrote to the college administration asking for a specific admissions statement from the board. Baker wrote to Stone concerning that inquiry, "It is my strong opinion that the intent of the letter is simply to make plain to the Board of Trustees the conviction of the Executive Council that we should let it be known that St. Mary's is ready and willing to accept qualified students irrespective of race." [159] The board of trustees discussed its position on admissions at the meeting of October 16, 1963. The motion was made and seconded that "as there are no restrictions outlined in the charter of St. Mary's Junior College relative to the admission of female students on the basis of race alone, it is the policy of this school to consider all properly qualified students on an equitable basis." A lengthy discussion ensued in which Bishop Fraser took a prominent part. The motion was lost. The board finally agreed to answer the council's query by restating the school's admissions policy:

The current admissions policy is based upon five important factors: the applicant's previous High School record, the recommendations from school officials, class rank, test scores, and the time of application. The early applicant is given first consideration providing other factors are equal, and preference is given to daughters of alumnae and members of the Episcopal Church. [160]

The executive council considered that an equivocal statement as it was known that Stone held conservative views on desegregation. Soon after he became bishop of the Diocese of North Carolina, Fraser clarified his position on race and the church in a statement to the 1967 convention:

God created all that exists and He said, "It is good." No Christian church can act in a manner that would be contrary to God's will, which would be to set apart, to segregate, or grant inferior membership to any creation of God. . . . This is the law of God. . . There can be no exclusion of race from any area of the Church's life. [161]

The admissions office at St. Mary's processed the few applications received from blacks in the routine manner. It was 1972, however, before a black student was enrolled. Almost no black women pursued the application beyond the first inquiry. The college offered no full scholarships; major scholarships were available during those years to qualified blacks at most institutions. Several Asians attended during the Stone administration. Persons who branded St. Mary's "a snob school" at that time felt justified because it was a school to which blacks did not apply for admission.

The resolution of the question of the relationship of St. Mary's to the Episcopal church was a matter of priority to Smyth when he assumed the chairmanship of the board. In his hard-hitting speech at the 1968 commencement exercises, Smyth explained that the reduction of the number of trustees by half was designed "to provide greater involvement of the Church without challenging the administration's responsibility or academic freedom." He continued:

There is today great competition for able faculty and staff personnel, and the church institutions cannot and should not settle for less than the ablest. We have depended for years upon the loyalty and the commitment and devotion of gifted teachers and this in the final analysis has been the source of our success at this campus. . . It seems to me immoral for a church institution to penalize talented people because of their devotion. . . .

Let me say quite candidly that the only way we can continue this kind of institution is by the support of the church and church people . . . we must put forth our best efforts on behalf of education unless you are willing to give it all over to the secular forces.[162]

There was prolonged applause from an overflow audience.

Stone announced in February, 1968, his plans to retire in June, 1969. He told the faculty that administration of the school was becoming to him "a heavy burden."[163] It looked as though the next years would be very busy ones with 15 new trustees who were asking many questions and demanding "vigorous leadership." In his last message to the alumnae he said, "There is no virtue in standing still. We change in order to achieve."[164]

In July, 1968, the Stones moved to the home in Raleigh that had been purchased by the college for their use. (The president's home on campus was used as a dormitory that year.) In the spring of 1969 there were parties and gifts for the Stones. And there were tributes on all sides—tributes in appreciation of Richard Stone's integrity, of his respect for the faculty, of his insistence upon high academic standards, of his prudent fiscal management while making major additions to the value of the campus, of his 23 years of service.

In his last report to the trustees, Richard Stone sounded his eternal theme when he said, "There is very little wrong here that could not be strengthened with a sizeable increase in capital money."[165] The trustees accepted President Stone's resignation "with great appreciation and gratitude to God for this servant of God who has so tirelessly served to the benefit of St. Mary's."[166]

## CHAPTER THIRTEEN

# "A MANDATE FOR CHANGE"

Frank Warren Pisani, who became the ninth head of St. Mary's in July, 1969, believed that the trustees of the college had given him "a mandate for change."[1] Dynamic, charismatic, optimistic, volatile, impulsive, unsystematic—he was a man to be viewed always in the extreme. There were those who believed that Frank Pisani saved St. Mary's from closing; others thought that he almost caused the demise of the institution. Some persons held both views of the Pisani years. To some, his administration was exciting and challenging; to others, it was threatening, even traumatic. He himself said, "I dragged St. Mary's, kicking and screaming, into the twentieth century."[2] Within seven years' time almost every facet of life on campus was changed; there were new buildings, new social and academic rules, and a greatly expanded administration.

The trustees chose the Reverend Frank Warren Pisani from among the some 70 persons who expressed interest in the position. He had been assistant dean at Virginia Theological Seminary, 1963–1964, and then associate dean. He had directed the seminary's second century fund development program, which with an original goal of $5 million had reached $7.85 million. Born in 1922 in San Francisco, he was the son of Gioacchino Pisani, who at 14 landed in America as a stowaway on a boat from Italy, and within a few years owned a business and brought eight members of his family to this country. Gioacchino Pisani married Zillah Brown, a granddaughter of a governor of Maine. Frank Pisani received a bachelor's degree in political science from the University of California at Berkeley, served in the army as a first lieutenant during World War II, and then engaged in various enterprises before

The Reverend Frank Warren Pisani, D.D., president, 1969–1976

beginning graduate work in religion at the University of Florida in Gainesville. He taught in the continuing education department there. Having decided to enter the Episcopal ministry, he received his degree from Virginia Theological Seminary in 1955 and was ordained deacon in 1955 and priest in 1956. He was rector at the Church of the Holy Comforter, Tallahassee, Florida, for eight years before joining the seminary administration. In May, 1970, the degree of doctor of divinity was conferred on him by Virginia Theological Seminary. In 1946 he married Harriet Hazard of Augusta, Georgia. Their children, Sara Alice (Sally) and John Franklin (Jack) were 16 and 10 when they moved to St. Mary's.[3]

Immediately after his election to the presidency, Pisani told the trustees that because his administration would be "student oriented," a new president's home with more space for official functions was a necessity. He also asked for a management study, a fund-raising consultant, and that the position of academic dean, already approved by the board, be filled. In the meantime, Mary Lou Eaton, who was the first woman to receive the master's degree from Virginia Theological Seminary, was academic counselor as well as a member of the religion department. President Pisani was inaugurated on November 14, 1969. After the service of Holy Communion in the chapel, there was luncheon on the grounds. Then buses transported everyone downtown to Memorial Auditorium where Gordon W. Blackwell, president of Furman University, spoke. He observed that St. Mary's had "been characterized by continuity, steadfastness of purpose, and strong leadership," and that its future held "promises of new opportunities."[4] In his inaugural address Pisani declared, "Change we must—change we will! Some ancient ways are not valid any longer. But unchanging are the basic values. . . ."[5]

## "A MORE FLEXIBLE LIFE"

No one on the faculty in the 1970s thought that change was unnecessary. Everyone agreed that new buildings were essential, and it was exciting to see them rising all over campus. The question for the faculty was, "How much academic change is necessary or wise?" The faculty approved at once a number of changes such as liberalizing the rules for dropping and adding courses. An impasse developed, however, when the president succumbed to student demands for optional class attendance for college students. The plan was to give unlimited class cuts to all college students, except first semester juniors and those on academic probation. Most of the faculty were aghast. Pisani announced that absence policy had become an administrative matter, and optional class attendance went into effect by presidential order on March 23,

1970, with all grades lowered for overcuts after September, 1969, restored.[6] By the next year, a pattern of nonchalance concerning classes was set despite some tightening of the policy from time to time by the administration. Eventually the catalog carried a provision that a student had to attend 75 percent of the meetings of a course to receive credit.

At the same time that classes were made a matter of freedom of choice, increased emphasis was placed upon extracurricular activities. Students, in the habit of participating in almost everything when there were few clubs, continued that pattern, and many fell into academic difficulties. Pisani said that the students were frustrated because of "the unrealistic academic standards of some of the faculty here."[7] The students admitted that their lack of self-discipline was part of the problem.

Soon both the curriculum and the faculty were expanded. President Pisani said, "My mandate was to change, improve, enrich and make more flexible the academic life."[8] Students demanded an increased number of electives, and the faculty curriculum and academic standards committees agreed that some courses should be added. However, they did not expect the addition of 69 new semester courses and 8 faculty members by 1972–1973. By 1975 the 53-member faculty, including the president and chaplain, offered 200 courses. Faculty concerns about financing the new programs were answered by presidential statements making it clear that finances were not within the province of the faculty. Small classes of college freshmen and sophomores studied such subjects as existentialism in literature, contemporary French thought, the geopolitics of Latin-America, and opera.

After much discussion, curriculum requirements were adjusted in 1971 to match those of the University of North Carolina at Chapel Hill. The English and foreign language requirements for graduation were reduced from 12 to 9 hours, and a foreign language-mathematics option was allowed. Soon financial exigency caused a number of the new courses to be dropped. By then students who needed courses not offered were taking them at one of the other colleges or universities in Raleigh through the Cooperating Raleigh Colleges, organized in 1968. Each year about a dozen St. Mary's students enrolled for a class at another institution within the CRC. By 1976 the St. Mary's curriculum, devoid of frills, occupied a solid middle ground.

The liberal arts program was strengthened in 1975 by requiring for graduation two courses in history and at least one other course within the social studies department. That department carried the largest student load after the physical education department; the English department was next in size. The academic departments made a conscious decision not to add a number of women's studies. The usual method was to integrate the achievements of women into the courses and to use textbooks and films that took that approach.

The college was behind the times in conferring the associate in arts degree, a degree recommended by the American Association of Junior Colleges as early as 1942.[9] Beginning in 1970 that degree was conferred on all who met the college graduation requirements with a quality point ratio of 2.0 or better. The board of trustees offered the degree retroactively to all qualified alumnae upon request.[10]

Tribute was paid to two alumnae in 1975 when they were awarded honorary associate in humane letters degrees. Mary Sherwood Smedes Poyner, daughter of Bennett Smedes, was honored. Alice McKenzie Ragland was recognized for her leadership in St. Mary's renewal program; the classroom building given by the Ragland family was named for her. In 1974 the same honor went to Elizabeth Gold Swindell for her distinguished service to St. Mary's, to her community, to her state, and to the profession of journalism.

The Chi Beta Chapter of Phi Theta Kappa National Honor Fraternity of American Junior Colleges was organized at St. Mary's in 1970 with ten charter members. That fraternity had been approved in 1929 by the American Association of Junior Colleges.[11] The St. Mary's High School Honor Society was organized also in 1970 with 11 charter members.[12]

Despite all efforts, it seemed to many of the teachers that the academic climate continued to deteriorate. By April, 1975, extreme concern over academics, governance, and financial matters led the faculty to request "a candid discussion" with the trustees on the day before their scheduled meeting. The purpose was not to fix blame but for "the renewal of our community." President Pisani was informed of the faculty discussion and had a copy of the planned presentation. Helen Smith, the intrepid first faculty representative to the board of trustees, speaking for the majority of the faculty, said that academics were not given "the basic priority which characterizes a college . . . but placed on a par with social and recreational aspects of college life." She concluded, "The question of jurisdiction and responsibility is clearly (and urgently) at stake. . . . We do not have functioning channels for shared decision making in areas affecting academic affairs."[13] An impassioned defense of President Pisani was given by faculty member Demetrios F. Nixon.

Pisani noted in his report to the trustees the next day that he considered the St. Mary's girl of the 1970s as "mature, as intelligent, and of as good caliber as ever," and that he was impatient with "the rigid attitudes that sometimes characterize the academic world." He said, "I see education as a total experience, not just a classroom experience." He added that he saw "no use in debating the issue." Some trustees praised his academic changes.[14]

While the definition of "academic atmosphere" remained an unresolved issue, faculty and administration agreed that the student of the seventies was not the student of the sixties. Pisani said, "The St. Mary's girl of the seventies . . . is not as well prepared academically since she is the product of a deteriorating public school system and of, in some cases, new and less than effective private academies."[15] And there was the national phenomenon of declining scores on the Scholastic Achievement Test (SAT). From the 1940s through the mid-1960s, the SAT scores increased steadily. Then came the decline in measurable achievement,[16] a fact that the St. Mary's faculty found hard to accept. Although the mean score of the St. Mary's college students remained somewhat above the national mean for all college-bound students, the faculty wondered if the admissions process were as selective as it could be. By 1975 the prevailing attitude of the faculty was one of resigned realism. An increased workload was inevitable if standards were to be held at an acceptable level despite the fact that many entering students were deficient in the basic skills.

Mabel Morrison provided some sense of stability on the academic scene during the early years of the Pisani regime. Her appointment as dean of academic affairs in January, 1970, was hailed by her colleagues as a stroke of genius. The president agreed.[17] She was in 1970 a veritable legend on campus and was also a staunch supporter of President Pisani. She had been a member of the selection committee, and her faith in him was as strong as his faith in her. She conceded that he was not the most efficient of administrators, and she told him so.

Dean Morrison was interested in a 1970 study called *16–20: The Liberal Education of an Age Group*, funded by the Carnegie Corporation and published by the College Entrance Examination Board. Its thesis was that "the division of the formal education of adolescents into its two present established parts (secondary school through grade 12, college starting with grade 13) does not seem related to any basic, human need." The members of the 16 to 20 group were treated, the study committee wrote, "too much like children while in school and too much like adults at college." The document proposed a return to an idea of the 1920s, that of an "intermediate college."[18] And so St. Mary's began to call itself an intermediate college—a new term but not a new direction. There was increased emphasis on placing advanced high school students in college classes for college credit, and a few accelerated tenth graders were first accepted as day students in 1976–1977. There was never a differentiation between high school and college instructors.

Another Pisani appointment, besides that of Dean Morrison, proved to be a source of strength. In the summer of 1971 Thomas H. Johnson became registrar. He had been director of admissions and registrar at Peace College, 1965–1971, and also director and founder of the drama department at Peace. Before moving to Raleigh, he was associate professor of English at St. Andrews Presbyterian College. His degrees were from Wake Forest University and George Peabody College for Teachers.[19] In addition to his other duties at St. Mary's, he organized the first summer school in 1973. Tom Johnson played a quiet, but effective, part in the preservation of community spirit during difficult years.

The festivities surrounding Dean Morrison's retirement in the spring of 1972 were entirely fitting—her portrait by Sarah Blakeslee Speight presented to the college by the alumnae on alumnae day (when she was made an honorary alumna), a recital by pianist William Masselos in her honor, a Hogarth print from the faculty, a trip to the Soviet Union from the trustees, and a gala formal dinner. Many tributes poured in. In retirement, Mabel Morrison remained a visible and often-consulted member of the college community, and she continued her many community activities.

On an interim basis, academic guidance was provided by Tom Johnson; the director of guidance also was involved in academic and vocational counseling. The first director of guidance was alumna Martha Barber Dosher, who was appointed in 1970. She began teaching mathematics at the college in 1966 and took a master's degree in guidance and personnel services. Upon Dosher's resignation in 1971, Barbara Rice Bunch was named to the position, and a guidance center was established in lower Smedes. Bunch was in Raleigh because of her husband's career. She had previously taught English and had been a high school director of guidance. Her degrees were from Meredith College and the University of North Carolina at Chapel Hill. Her first task at St. Mary's was the reorganization of the system of advising students on academic matters.

In the time between deans, the faculty in 1972 reorganized academic affairs under an academic council that absorbed the functions of the old academic standards and curriculum committees. The new council was composed of certain administrative officials, a faculty member from each department, and several students. The bylaws provided that the chairman should be a faculty member elected annually by the council, that all recommendations made by the council should be presented at a faculty meeting, but that a vote of the faculty was unnecessary for acceptance of the recommendations except when a vote was requested. The system worked well. During the early seventies the faculty accepted some student requests but refused self-scheduled examinations and kept the passing grade at 70 while giving more leeway in grading to the academic departments.

Robert James Miller II was named dean of academic affairs on July 1, 1973. Miller went to St. Mary's from Radford College (University) in Virginia where he was vice-president for academic affairs. He held three degrees from Yale University—master's degrees in forestry and science and the Ph.D. A native of Dunn, he was a graduate of North Carolina State University.[20]

By the 1970s the Ph.D. degree had become "the union card" for college academicians. Miller added to the St. Mary's faculty a number of people with doctorates who were already living in the area. At first some of them soon departed to earn higher salaries, but faculty turnover minimized as economic conditions tightened. Dean Miller was from the beginning a strong advocate of the liberal arts curriculum and of academic excellence.

During the early seventies a number of different kinds of learning experiences were offered on campus and in Raleigh. St. Mary's continued to bring to the campus well-known lecturers and performers—persons as diverse as scientist Ralph Lapp, black activist James Farmer, and Japanese mime Yass Hakoshima.

Some of the faculty and some of the students took up causes. An environmental concern organization worked diligently, and the St. Mary's environmental group, along with others, petitioned successfully for a marked bicycle route through Raleigh. (In the early 1970s bicycles were everywhere on campus.) The *Belles* was particularly activist under the editorship of Betti Click, 1971–1972. There was an awareness among the students of the developing national trauma over Vietnam. In the spring of 1970 some St. Mary's women were among the 4,500 students who marched 20 abreast down Hillsborough Street chanting "Peace Now." A poll of over 150 St. Mary's students revealed that an overwhelming majority favored a gradual withdrawal from Southeast Asia, that a majority rejected the death penalty, even for murder, and that only 7 percent admitted to having tried illegal drugs. On balance, the students seemed to consider themselves to be "moderate conservatives."[21]

The social studies department encouraged students to become involved in the community. The sociology and psychology classes helped with several surveys that proved to be of real value to the community, and much activity was generated through Don Roberts's political science and history classes. He was one of a rare breed—a liberal Mississippi-born Baptist. His degrees were from Baylor University and the University of Connecticut. His students participated in the North Carolina Student Legislature, did precinct work, and visited local courts. Presidential election years meant a semester of frenzied activity on the part of political science and other interested students, who prepared for the mock conventions in the spring. Roberts always managed to secure as speakers persons of importance on the North Carolina political scene. The conventions were great fun, but their real purpose was to demonstrate to students that they could be direct decision makers, that women no longer needed to wield political power only indirectly as the daughters and wives of the powerful. The social studies department invited women politicians to speak on the campus—Representatives Ruth Cook and Marie Watters Colton and Betty Ray McCain. Colton and McCain were St. Mary's alumnae.

The celebration of the national bicentennial generated a number of special events at the college. President Pisani asked Mabel Morrison, then dean emeritus, to serve as coordinator. St. Mary's was the first official bicentennial site to be designated in Raleigh and the fourth in the state.[22] A flag pole was installed on front campus, and on January 12,

1976, a flag that had been flown over the national Capitol was raised with proper ceremony. In the spring a bicentennial oak and 76 Japanese cherry trees were planted on campus.

The bicentennial forum on "The Continuing Revolution in Women's Education" was the major event. The forum, which was funded by the North Carolina Humanities Committee, featured five prominent women educators: Mary Atwell of the history department at Hollins College, Katherine Hobbie, former dean of professional studies at New York State University; Anne Gary Taylor, president emeritus of Sweet Briar College; Jane Mathews of the history department of the University of North Carolina at Greensboro; and Elizabeth Tidball, professor of physiology at George Washington University Medical Center. All encouraged women to prepare themselves for their roles in a society that offered more to women and expected more of women than in times past.[23]

By the 1970s there were several different types of role models among the women on the St. Mary's faculty for students to choose from as professors, advisers, or friends. There was the old guard composed of married women who had returned to teaching. The new guard was composed of women who had entered graduate school after some years of full-time mothering and the very young women, some married and some single. College women still flocked to teaching; 84 percent of all elementary school teachers in 1960 were women. High school faculties, on the other hand, were normally over 50 percent male. Only 20 percent of the teachers in higher education were women; and in private colleges, including those for women, only 14 percent of the teachers were female—a figure lower than 25 years earlier. Women's colleges were appointing men as deans of student affairs. Women with more than five years of higher education were usually career oriented, and 70 percent of them were employed.[24]

In the early 1960s those women who did not work outside the home still appeared to be content, even proud. In 1963 Betty Friedan in *The Feminine Mystique* named the vague, unexpressed yearnings of the American housewife the problem of "the forfeited self." She called for the education of women for "a life purpose," urging institutions of higher learning wishing "to encourage women to take education seriously to recruit for their faculties all the women they can find who have combined marriage and motherhood with the life of the mind. . . ." She wrote, "It has barely begun, the search of women for themselves."[25]

By 1970 feminism had taken its place alongside Vietnam, inflation, and student unrest as a national issue. The Equal Pay Act of 1963 and the inclusion of the word "sex" in the omnibus Civil Rights Act of the following year laid the necessary legal groundwork, but the rights of women were largely ignored until the National Organization for Women was founded in 1966. NOW was concerned with gaining economic and political equality within the system. The women's groups split, as they had during the fight for suffrage, and the media gave full coverage to "women's lib" in all its manifestations. St. Mary's students in the 1970s were questioning everything. They identified, however, more with the idea of student power than with women's lib.

Faculty-student relations, sometimes strained during the early Pisani years, were almost as happy as usual by 1974. That year the yearbook declared, "Teachers are down to earth . . . neat people." Three of the staunchest of the old guard retired in 1971—Madame Julienne Smith, who had taught French for 27 years, and Mary Browne, who for 18 years had worked in the library with Helen A. Brown. Helen Brown retired in the summer of 1971 after 34 years at St. Mary's.

Helen Abel Brown's bachelor's and master's degrees from Middleburg College were in Spanish, as was her graduate study at the University of Mexico. After teaching in a mission school in Mexico, she took a graduate degree in library science at the University of Michigan. She was head librarian at Russell Sage College before her husband's career took her to Raleigh. Helen Brown, always working with a slim budget and a small staff, built the St. Mary's collection to 21,000 books. Now and again she taught a class in Spanish, and she served as faculty secretary for 23 years. She was prominent in professional circles. The Helen A. Brown Library Endowment Fund was established in recognition of her outstanding service to St. Mary's.[26]

Linda Paez, St. Mary's next librarian, left after a year when her husband's career took them from Raleigh. Sara Gardner Seagle, who had been assistant librarian and cataloger since 1970, became acting librarian. She had worked in college libraries and as a civilian librarian for the U.S. armed forces. She was a member of the St. Mary's library staff for 13 years. In July, 1974, Andrea Plummer Brown, who had assisted Helen Brown before entering graduate school, was named librarian.

Another retiree was Donald Peery, who left in 1976 after 31 years on the music faculty. The title of professor emeritus was conferred upon him by the board of trustees in 1978.[27] The music department also lost Geraldine Cate in 1976. She retired after 36 years at St. Mary's during which she had taught over 1,000 voice students.[28] In January, 1976, William Masselos played at St. Mary's in her honor. The trustees established the Geraldine Cate Collection of Recorded Music at the listening center in the Sarah Graham Kenan Library, and in 1978 they named her professor emeritus.

Several competent members of the faculty resigned during the early seventies. For most of them the academic and administrative problems played a part in the decision. In 1971 Catherine Fish of the science department decided to stop teaching. Two years later Doris Bailey, the dance instructor, resigned after 16 years at St. Mary's. The next year three other members of the faculty, each of whom had served seven years, resigned. Margaret Duncan of the physical education department bought Camp Robinhood in Pennsylvania, where she had been the assistant director for 15 years. Ann [Noe] Brown of the English department told a reporter for the *Belles* that, in part, "the changing policy of the administration toward academics" prompted her resignation. Active in the American Association of University Professors, she was instrumental in the organization of a chapter at St. Mary's. She went to teach at North Carolina State University. The chairman of the mathematics department, August (Gus) Lawrence left "with deep regret";[29] he, too, had disagreed with administrative decisions on academic matters. He rejoined the faculty of Duke University.

Two of the strong, longtime members of the faculty still teaching were Mary Oliver Ellington, who was appointed chairman of the sciences, thus including chemistry and physics under her supervision, and Margaret Williams, who was named the chairman of the enlarged art department. Both remained throughout the Pisani administration.

Mary Louise Jones, as chairman of the physical education department, made tennis an important factor in attracting students to St. Mary's. Her tennis teams, which were undefeated for eight consecutive seasons (1961–1969), continued to compile victories and went undefeated in 1975. In the summer, beginning in 1975, she operated the Mary Lou Jones Tennis Camp at St. Mary's. Jones and Pisani brought nationally known golfer Peggy Kirk Bell to the campus to conduct golf clinics.[30] The students expressed their admiration of Lou Jones when they dedicated the 1973 *Stagecoach* to her.

Helen Smith was appointed chairman of the department of religion in 1971, and during her nine-year tenure she enlarged the faculty and curriculum to make the department a strong and respected one academically. There was no formal department of religion when she joined the faculty in 1966; the chaplains always had taught the Bible classes. Before going to St. Mary's, Smith taught in the continuing education program at Tennessee Wesleyan College. A graduate of Geneva College, she had a master's degree from the Presbyterian School of Christian Education in Richmond, Virginia. In addition to her teaching and administrative duties, Helen Smith did more than her share of work on faculty committees because whenever a difficult job needed to be done with thoroughness and tact everyone seemed to think of her.

Another strong member of the faculty appointed during the Stone administration was Rebekah McBane, who joined the English department in 1966. With degrees from the University of North Carolina at Greensboro and Tulane University, she had taught at H. Sophie Newcomb College and had been assistant director of admissions at her alma mater in Greensboro.[31] She and John Tate formed the nucleus of a demanding department. When she married Robert Gunn and moved to her native Pittsboro, she continued teaching. After a leave of absence for full-time mothering, she returned to St. Mary's when her daughter was of school age.

In 1969 Catherine Gregory Barnhart and Ann Culley joined the English department. They had been teaching at Georgia State College. Barnhart's degrees were from Salem College and the University of North Carolina at Chapel Hill, and she had taught at North Carolina State. An experienced editor, she worked with student publications at St. Mary's. Ann Culley, a native of Atlanta, held degrees from Georgia State. She, too, was much interested in her students and worked with student organizations. Both resigned in 1979 planning to devote their time to writing.[32]

Hannah Scoggin, who joined the social studies department in the second year of the Pisani administration, had always been a career woman. A native of Charleston, South Carolina, she received her bachelor's and master's degrees in sociology and anthropology from the University of Louisville. Hannah and her husband, Elmo, spent five years in Israel as representatives of the Southern Baptist Convention. During that time, they became experienced archaeologists. Later, grants and consortium arrangements enabled them to introduce students to archaeological fieldwork. Hannah Scoggin was available to teach at Campbell College and later at St. Mary's when her husband joined the faculty at Southeastern Baptist Theological Seminary in Wake Forest.[33]

Dolores Lado, who joined the foreign language department in 1970, was in the area because her husband was on the faculty at North Carolina State. A native of Spain, Lado received her degrees from the University of Madrid and from the University of Florida, where she earned a master's degree in American history and a doctorate in Spanish literature. The mother of three young children, she taught Spanish at the University of Florida before moving to Raleigh.[34] At St. Mary's she taught classes in Spanish and a course in twentieth century Europe as seen by writers. In 1972 she was appointed head of the foreign language department. She became a leader of the middle guard of the faculty by the next administration.

In 1974 another working mother already in the area, Betty Eichenberger, joined the art department. Her degrees were from Pratt Institute and the University of North Carolina at Chapel Hill. She continued to teach after marrying state legislator Allen Adams and remained to become a valued member of the faculty.

By the 1970s a number of interesting and competent women were more or less transient members of the faculty, leaving when a husband's career or children's needs demanded. Their students will remember something special about each—Joan Fleming Cremin, Judith Ann Oslack, Marguerite Cressman, Joan Phillips [Samson] Plummer, Olivann Hobbie, and others. During those years a group of bright, ambitious, and energetic mothers who were completing doctorates began teaching at St. Mary's. Five of them—Georgette Campbell, Marjolijn Werman, Doreen Saxe, Elgiva Watson, and Marcia Jones—remained into the next administration and emerged as leaders.

St. Mary's alumnae did not return to teach as often as alumnae had in earlier years, but several returned briefly. Elizabeth Harris Skinner taught dance, Ann Hoover Smith taught psychology, and Chan Poyner Pike, who had studied with Geraldine Cate, assisted her. Alumna Dianne Ricks returned to teach psychology when Mabel Morrison relinquished her classes to become dean. After earning bachelor's and master's degrees at Chapel Hill, she taught at Virginia Commonwealth University. In Raleigh, she taught and had a private practice as a psychologist. "Ricks" was a great favorite of the students. She resigned in 1975, studied theology, and then took a doctorate in clinical psychology.

Another perceptive young woman who joined the faculty early in the Pisani administration was Beth Mackie, who was a member of the department of religion, 1971–1979. A native of Gastonia and a graduate of Agnes Scott College, she understood St. Mary's and the inherent possibilities of the school, possibilities that did not seem to her to be fully realized. She earned a doctorate at Duke University and continued her career elsewhere. Four other young women who joined the faculty were Margaret Underwood, who taught art and physical education for several years, and Alice Zawadski Greiner, Mary Lida Alexander, and Ellen Birch, who remained into the next administration. A number of the women on the faculty, among both the Stone and Pisani appointees, were members of Phi Beta Kappa or Phi Kappa Phi and held other scholastic honors.

During the Pisani years a number of young alumnae worked on the administrative staff. Susan Carroll, an admissions counselor, became associate director of admissions and then director of admissions in 1976. Minta Aycock was publicity director and then associate alumnae director. Alumnae worked as recruiters and in secretarial positions.[35]

The men on the faculty, although they never comprised over one fourth of the total number, added talent and interest. There was

Demetrios F. Nixon, usually called "Jimmy," who carried memories of his wartime boyhood in Greece. He taught at several colleges before going to St. Mary's in 1970 to teach courses in the social studies department and serve as assistant to the president. He left after six years for an administrative career with Hardbarger Junior College of Business in Raleigh.[36] James M. Appleton, a native of New Jersey and a Rutgers graduate who taught physics, 1969–1979, was a popular teacher. He had moved to Raleigh for graduate work at North Carolina State. Michael C. Bulley, a native of Spokane, Washington, joined the faculty in 1967. An accomplished organist, he was chairman of the music department, 1973–1976. He had moved east to take a master's degree at the College of Church Musicians in Washington, D.C. He left St. Mary's to return to his native state.[37]

Three of the men who went to the college during the Pisani administration—Arthur McRae, Harry R. Callahan, and Hamilton W. Fish, remained into the next administration. They were joined by a number of males as the employment situation in academe changed. The faculty mix was international (at one time in the 1970s there were natives of six different European nations), ecumenical, liberal, and conservative. Always, however, a sense of community prevailed.

## "THE SIGNS OF THE TIMES"

The turbulence of the sixties had little effect on daily life at St. Mary's. During the Stone administration there had been the suggestion that students serve with faculty on decision-making committees, and editorials in the *Belles* protested compulsory chapel; but the proposals were ignored. Perhaps the confusion of the sixties would have overtaken St. Mary's in the seventies no matter who was at the helm, for that generation of students had made a rough passage through elementary and high school. Drastic change, however, was inevitable under President Pisani, for he believed that "St. Mary's had operated quaintly." Early in his administration he told the students that every tradition should be challenged. "Those that are valid will withstand the challenge," he said.[38] Although the unrest at St. Mary's was nothing like the riots on many campuses, the experience was traumatic for the whole college community and for the alumnae.

During the first months of his administration, the new president approved petitions as fast as the legislative body passed them. He believed that the discarded rules had been "too restrictive and outdated,"[39] as many of them were. Soon the student attitude was, "If they won't give it to us, we'll take it."[40]

Life within the grove changed drastically. The visible evidence of change was the dress code. In November, 1970, the *Belles* announced that slacks could be worn to class and to meals, except Sunday meals. Dresses were required for chapel services and on days designated as "special days" when guests would be on campus. Instead of pantsuits, many girls began wearing army fatigues or frayed and faded, or cut-off jeans; other students wore miniskirts. The *Handbook* noted that pantsuits, but "not shorts, slacks, or dungarees," could be worn on dates. For classes anything went. The faculty ignored the whole matter except to require shoes. Hand-crafted leather sandals, hiking boots, and topsiders became common. The president decreed that the women of the staff were not to wear slacks to work, but some of the faculty women began wearing pantsuits.

The real revolution was in dating habits, a revolution that had taken place a few years earlier on most campuses. The students became casual in their relationships with men as well as in their dress. By 1971 seniors had unlimited "overnights," and everyone else had a generous quota. Seniors and second semester juniors could go into men's residences under a modification of the "apartment rule" adopted near the end of Richard Stone's administration; parental permission was required and a girl had to be accompanied by at least one other couple. Seniors could date any night of the week, and second quarter juniors could date on one school night each week. Curfews were from 11:30 to 1:30 A.M., depending upon the night and status of the student. Seniors with a C average were allowed to have cars.

For all that coming and going security guards were hired; they were always referred to by the students as "the Pinkertons." Also for security, so many lights were installed that dates began to call the front campus "the airport." The penalty for late signing-in was one that worked—a half hour subtracted from the dating limit for a number of weeks and the embarrassment of appearing before one of the student disciplinary groups. Lying was an honor board offense, a serious matter. Dating regulations were stricter for underclassmen than for juniors and seniors.

By 1975 the school authorities had given up acting in loco parentis to college students whose parents were willing to give their daughters "blanket permission." The *Handbook* for 1974–1975 read, "Blanket hostess and parental permission is available for Seniors and Juniors provided their parents have signed the written blanket permission form . . . [which] allows a student to take overnights from St. Mary's at the places she designates on her overnight absence card without hostess invitations." Some parents were quite permissive. Others were dismayed to find parenting so different in the 1970s.

It was easy for St. Mary's students to meet men at any of the popular hangouts on Hillsborough Street. The trustees took note of the new mores by suggesting in 1973 "that the SGA president ask the girls to be more discreet about where they entertained their boyfriends and demonstrated their affection."[41]

In a 1970 editorial the *Belles* reported:

St. Mary's has finally made public acknowledgement of the "now" problem of today's youth.

The school has not taken a stand on sex, but it has made available through the guidance department sex information booklets which objectively and frankly discuss anatomy, contraceptives, and venereal disease. This booklet, while being extremely helpful does not attempt to moralize or sermonize about premarital sex, but yet says nothing to condone it.[42]

In 1972 the trustees discussed a communication from the Wake County Health Department that offered to set up a family planning program in the college infirmary because their clinics were overcrowded with clients, including St. Mary's students. The trustees decided not to authorize the program on campus because they considered her sex life to be the individual's concern. The minutes read, "She is free to consult the proper agency."[43]

The dilemma faced by the young woman possessed of this new social freedom was described in 1975 in an article in the *Belles*. Written in the form of a letter to a younger sister and entitled "You Asked Me What College Life Was Like," it read:

There are fraternites, blind dates, mixers and bars. Some are great but some are downright lousy. You will have to decide for yourself . . . what your limits are. Here you become aware of your own set of morals from all that . . . parents have taught. . . . Remember, though, that you will never be totally alone, for there is God. . . .[44]

The first major confrontation between President Pisani and the students came over compulsory chapel. There had been forewarnings during the last months of the Stone administration—misbehavior in chapel and articles in the *Belles* decrying the lack of participation in worship. At the beginning of the Pisani administration attendance at chapel was required twice a week and at one service on Sunday. (Chapel caps were no longer worn.) The intensity of the controversy surprised everyone. There had been quite a flurry in January and February, 1971, as the result of an article in the college newspaper. It was written by two students who explained: "We are not opposed to God; we realize that many, many girls really dig the services, [but] we feel that religion here consists solely of meaningless, stifling ritual."[45] The article spawned five pages of letters in the next issue. They were from teachers as well as students; most were reasonable, and many contained positive suggestions for improving the services. In the same is-

Sea Saints, 1974

Lou Jones's tennis team, 1975

sue the authors of the original impetus explained that they were not attacking the chaplain but were seeking positive solutions.[46] When only 166 students completed a questionnaire for the *Belles*, the matter was dropped for that year. However, a committee for noncompulsory chapel was formed.

In November, 1971, the chapel committee published in the *Belles* a position paper signed by 15 students, including the SGA president. Insisting that their aim was to strengthen rather than to undermine the religious atmosphere on campus, the students presented a petition for a voluntary chapel attendance policy. They argued that compulsory attendance further alienated from the church those who went involuntarily, that those who wished to worship were disturbed by those who did not want to be in chapel, and that "a freedom of choice" class attendance policy was inconsistent with compulsory chapel. The legislative body ruled that the question was outside its jurisdiction and sent the petition to Pisani. He denied it but gave the students permission to take the matter to the board of trustees at the January meeting.[47]

Meanwhile, a group of students favoring compulsory chapel prepared a position paper making a plea for "the spirit of unity among us," which they saw as centered in the chapel.[48] Both position papers were distributed to the trustees. During their consideration of the petition on January 27, the trustees heard four students who presented varying points of view. Pisani noted that theologically he agreed that Jesus would not have coerced worship, but that as a realist he knew that few students would worship voluntarily. Therefore, he asked the trustees to support him. He said, "The worship . . . in the Chapel is where the community of St. Mary's finds strength for tasks, forgiveness for mistakes, and hope for the future. St. Mary's is not a secular institution; it is a church institution, and every church says its prayers." The trustees voted 13 to 1 to keep the chapel attendance requirement.[49]

At that meeting Frank Pisani told the trustees that he "had passed 40 or 50 petitions out of 70" and still the students were unhappy. "The student climate," he said, "is one of deterioration."[50] An alumna says of that year, "It was the worst of my four. We were anti-everything."[51] The showdown over authority culminated in February, 1972, and the story, including the names of those involved, was printed on the front page of the *Raleigh Times*.[52] The honor board by a vote of seven to two meted out a long suspension to a student whose date was seen in her dormitory room after 2:00 A.M. Everyone knew that the strict rule against men in the dormitories was inviolable, but some said that the man just walked into the building followed almost immediately by "the Pinkerton."[53] Because the student told conflicting stories and because she already was on social probation, Pisani remanded the case, asking for expulsion. When the honor board refused to change its verdict, Pisani expelled the student. The Student Government Association constitution plainly gave the president of the college final authority when such an impasse occurred, but nearly always a compromise was worked out. That was, in fact, the first expulsion of the Pisani regime.

A stormy meeting with some 300 students was reported by the *Times* as "emotional." Both the expelled student and her friend were there, and he asked Pisani not "to ruin her life."[54] A statement signed by the majority of the student body was presented to Pisani. It read:

Our interpretation of Dr. Pisani's action is that he supports student government at St. Mary's only under the conditions that our decisions regarding peer group government agree with his. One solution to closing the gap between students and administration is to abolish student government . . . and recognize the President of the school as sole disciplinarian and authority. In our opinion such an action would destroy every ideal St. Mary's is built upon and would result in complete dissolution of the school. Another solution is to recognize student government as a powerful and dynamic force, giving the students the opportunity to truly participate in democratic community living.[55]

When the students realized that Pisani would not change his mind, they, as he put it, "carried on the balance of the week with campus demonstrations, obscene phone calls and assemblies to the accompaniment of the press, radio, and T.V. The issue was really one of authority."[56] The night march on Pisani's home and his hanging in effigy were covered by television. Not all students marched, for they were divided. The faculty, in a called meeting, unanimously endorsed President Pisani's action. He reported to the trustees that he had received over 200 telegrams, letters, and calls; all but six supported his action.[57]

After having dealt with that crisis, Pisani sent a letter to all returning students reiterating the policies of the college. He wrote, "If you think you'll be happy here, come back." Fifteen did not return; over 300 parents sent favorable letters.[58] The confrontation left its scars. Some said that President Pisani had tried to divide the students; others said that he needed to realize that St. Mary's was too small for power structures. Lane Turner, who later became a strong SGA president, wrote of 1971–1972, which was her freshman year:

The students demanded the freedom of a university world, and when they lost . . . the walls grew higher. . . . The blame for this period can rest on no one in particular. . . . St. Mary's simply began to reflect the signs of the times. . . . We were all a bit guilty. I personally stood and watched. . . . I was miserable like so many of my classmates. I admired the demonstrators for the strength to strive for what they thought was right, and deep down, I admired the administration for holding fast to its decision.[59]

Rebellion for rebellion's sake had run its course by 1972–1973. The student government officers under Margaret (Margie) Worthington were able, with a great deal of wise counsel from Edith Richardson, to keep daily life on a fairly even keel. The serious problem of that session was the use of illegal drugs, mostly marijuana, on campus. In January, 1973, Pisani called a special student body meeting. He laid out the new ground rules, to which SGA officers and the faculty had given prior approval. All illegal drugs were to be removed from campus immediately, and those on his list of known users were to be given a second chance. Pisani made it clear that the penalty for the use of illegal drugs on campus thereafter would be expulsion. The *Belles* expressed approval of the administration's approach, including the use of room searches if necessary.[60]

Student government at that time was composed of the honor board, the social board, the minor offense committee, and the hall council. The honor board dealt with offenses involving lying, cheating, stealing, and "extreme misconduct" and could impose penalties from "a severe warning" to expulsion. The social board, composed of elected student members and two appointed from the faculty, dealt mostly with "leaving and remaining" (being off campus without permission or being excessively late in returning). The penalty most frequently imposed was "a strict campus." The minor offense committee, made up of some members of the social board, dealt mostly with late arrivals and those who repeatedly broke hall regulations. Its strongest penalty was to campus. The hall council, composed of the chairman and the secretary of the social board, two counselors from each hall, and three day student counselors, had jurisdiction over "routine matters." There were provisions for appeals from early curfews and campuses, and the whole procedure involved much time and paperwork. The system was operating fairly smoothly again by 1973.

The members of the Circle and the Beacon worked to restore the St. Mary's spirit. By 1974 the student leaders were "as straight as arrows," as one of them put it, or had "grown up," as another put it. More of the high school graduates were staying for college; the student mood was upbeat, pro-St. Mary's, pro-Pisani. Frank Pisani told the trustees at their spring meeting that the class of 1974 had restored "the spirit, tradition and loveliness of St. Mary's."

Dean Edith Richardson deserved much credit for the restoration of the St. Mary's spirit. But by the fall of 1972 she was tired and ill, and Elizabeth Booth Jones was appointed associate dean. It was fortunate that she was experienced, having served five years as assistant dean at Meredith College, for soon Edith Richardson was hospitalized. Elizabeth Jones became acting dean and then was appointed dean of students when Dean Richardson retired in the summer. There were tributes, and gifts, and a dinner to honor Edith Richardson. President

Emeritus Stone, who had worked with her for 13 of her 18 years at St. Mary's, said of her, "She leaves the imprint of a gracious lady."[61]

## "THE ESSENCE MUST REMAIN"

Life on a small campus is people oriented. The 1972 *Stagecoach*, done in psychedelic colors, carried this statement: "St. Mary's must alter her face, but her essence must remain." And that essence did remain, through all the temporary disturbances and the physical changes as the new buildings were completed. Life on campus outside the classroom during the week consisted of people-oriented activities—clubs, SGA meetings, athletic contests, the Cold Cuts, hall parties and other eating binges followed by dieting binges, the wild initiations of the underground clubs. The post office remained a popular gathering place. The immediate successor in 1962 to "B" Brown in the post office and bookstore was Kennon Taylor Beam. She managed the move from lower Smedes to spacious quarters in the new student union. The students dedicated a *Stagecoach* to her for her interest in their needs. Upon Beam's retirement in 1974, the bookstore and post office were managed by Rebecca Jordan until she resigned to devote full time to her child. Doris Barwick Parker, who went to the college in 1967 as the friendly guardian of the switchboard, took over the post office and bookstore in 1979.

Young people had not changed as much as they thought they had. When Don Roberts and Company "rendered" in assembly *The Grasshopper Cantata*, they did not realize that it had been hilariously successful on several occasions, beginning in 1905. Faculty-student athletic contests were popular again; with an increased number of men on the faculty, the teachers usually won. The Christmas party was still special; the *Belles* declared in 1970, "The REAL Santa Claus lives in Raleigh and teaches English at St. Mary's." May Day was called the spring festival and came earlier in the year because graduation was scheduled for early May. Really special was father-daughter day, arranged for the first time in 1970 at the request of the students. The fathers, 250 of them, accepted the invitation. For several years father-daughter day was in the autumn and mother-daughter day was planned to coincide with the spring festival and alumnae day.

Life at St. Mary's had begun to return to normal, and in 1976 Pisani said, "Amazingly, when the turbulence of 1972 abated, a kind of renewal began. . . . there was more openness, more love. . . . the students, increasingly 'doing their own thing' began more and more to put their religious convictions to work."[62] The student vestry played a large part in that regeneration, working each year with the chaplain to plan special and "relevant" services and programs. The vestry had been organized by Chaplain Baird in 1969 to supplement the altar guild.[63] With the department of religion it planned seminars, lectures, and discussions each year. Several Ingmar Bergman films were the basis of one series of faculty-student discussions, and a lecture-concert presenting religious music in America before 1850 was a part of the bicentennial celebration.

The vestry, along with Guidance Director Bunch, encouraged volunteerism. Among other projects, the vestry gave a Christmas party for children from the Governor Morehead School, helped with the tutoring program at Catholic Children's Home, and sponsored blood drives. Each year about $1,000 was available from the chapel offerings to be distributed by the vestry to various church and community causes.

The chapel was renovated and air conditioned during the summer of 1970, a $20,000 project. Carpeting in a rich blue replaced the familiar red carpet, and the kneelers and cushions were covered in blue velvet. The class of 1970 presented a specially designed St. Mary's flag. When it became apparent that the exterior of the chapel needed considerable preservation work and repainting, the vestry undertook the project. Students of 1974–1975 contributed $1,500, and alumnae and parents contributed about $2,000. Memorial gifts added to the beauty of the chapel.[64]

The evidences of a renewed spirit on campus were tangible. At a candlelight service in October, 1974, each young woman went forward, signed her pledge to live by the honor code before the SGA officers, lighted a candle from an officer's candle, and returned with it to her seat. It took a long while, and quite spontaneously the congregation began singing, concluding with, "We are in the Spirit. We are in the Lord. . . . And they will know we are Christian by our love, by our love."

Several men served as chaplain during the Pisani years. The Reverend Robert C. Baird left the chaplaincy in the spring of 1970 to join the staff of St. Timothy's Episcopal Church in Raleigh and to be the guidance counselor at Hale High School. One of Baird's reasons for going to Raleigh had been to be near North Carolina State University so that he could take a master's degree in guidance and counseling.[65]

The Reverend Robert Bryan Hobgood was college chaplain, 1970–1973. He had known Frank Pisani when a student at Virginia Theological Seminary. He went to Raleigh from St. Marks Episcopal Church in Jacksonville, Florida, his native city, where he had served as deacon and then as assistant rector. Pisani, who always considered himself to be one of the chaplains at St. Mary's, told the trustees that he needed 27-year-old Hobgood "to provide a balance to the ministry."[66] The students knew that Bob and Nancy Hobgood welcomed their visits to the new chaplain's residence just west of the chapel. Hobgood returned to Florida pastorates.

Both Baird and Hobgood taught, as well as being responsible for the chapel services and doing a great deal of counseling. Pisani taught one class each semester and was sought out frequently by students in need of counseling. He was an outstanding preacher, and he enjoyed his role as priest.

The Reverend John W. S. Davis began his work as the college chaplain in the fall of 1973. His wife, Sarah Dawson Davis, was an active alumna. Davis had served as a St. Mary's trustee from 1966 to 1968 and was the son of alumna Mary Shuford Davis. A native of Henderson, he held a degree in business administration and had been in business before entering the ministry. He received the bachelor of divinity degree from Virginia Theological Seminary. He was ordained to the priesthood in 1955 and served several North Carolina churches before becoming the founding rector at St. Stephen's in Durham, where he was rector for 14 years.

The new chaplain supported compulsory chapel, but by then the only required services were Wednesday night and Sunday morning, and excuses were granted upon request. Johnny Davis regarded services as "an opportunity for thanksgiving to God."[67] His low-key sermons appealed to young people. He set about making the Wednesday evening services varied, and the students responded with their highest praise— "open-minded and relevant."[68] An altar was built on back campus from stones brought by the students from their home towns. The sophomore class of 1974 gave the necessary money.[69] Davis took great joy in his teaching, and his door was always open to any girl in need of counsel. Sarah Davis enriched life at St. Mary's in many ways— working with the altar guild, the alumnae association, and wherever else a helping hand was needed. A call from his home church took the Davises back to Henderson, where he became the rector of the Church of the Holy Innocents in June, 1975.

A WORKING BOARD

The board of trustees began to play a more important role during the Pisani administration than ever before in the institution's history. The 1968 reorganization had brought 12 new members to the board. Pisani began his administration with an able group, but the trustees had not been together for many meetings. By tacit consent, they had postponed long-range planning until after the 1969 self-study. The new chairman, Thomas J. C. Smyth, had been elected to a five-year term on the board. The new vice-chairman, Dr. George D. Penick, was a son of the late bishop. He had been chairman of the committee that nominated Frank Pisani as president, and both he and Smyth had great plans for St. Mary's in the 1970s. Unfortunately, St. Mary's was destined to lose both men. Dr. Smyth died in November, 1970, having resigned the chairmanship in October because of precarious health. Penick resigned in July, 1970, to take a position at the College of Medicine of the University of Iowa. Southern Pines attorney, R. F. Hoke Pollock served as vice-chairman until 1976.

James M. Poyner, great-grandson of Aldert Smedes, was elected chairman of the board in October, 1970. Rollie Tillman, Jr., professor of business administration and director of the executive program at the University of North Carolina at Chapel Hill, was chairman of the St. Mary's trustees, 1973–1975. Thomas Willis Alexander, retired insurance executive, succeeded Tillman, serving from July, 1975, until January, 1981.

In 1973 the college charter was amended to add to the board three members-at-large to be nominated by a committee of trustees and to stipulate that at least two thirds of the 18 members should at all times be communicants in good standing of the Protestant Episcopal church. Early in his administration Frank Pisani realized that the relationship of St. Mary's to the Episcopal church was both confused and strained. The new board of visitors, on which the bishops served, seldom met. The uneasy relationship between the college and the Episcopal church was exacerbated during the early 1970s by the financial problems of the college, by the question of the ownership of St. Mary's, and by the question of the admission of blacks.

In discussing the race question again at the July, 1970, meeting, trustees lamented the lack of funds for full scholarships for minorities, adding, "Discrimination has not been practiced since no applicant has ever been turned down for this reason."[70] Ethiopian Senait Hidara, the first black student, enrolled for the spring term of 1971. Pisani addressed the racial issue in a statement published in the *North Carolina Churchman* in 1971. He wrote:

St. Mary's shares with all Christians deep social concern in those areas which have divided so much of the church today. . . . We conform to the law of the land and the law of our conscience in critical social areas.

St. Mary's, however, is not going to try to force an artificial or contrived situation in this community in the name of "better race relations." Applicants to St. Mary's are processed without regard to race. This policy will continue.[71]

The convention of the Diocese of North Carolina in January, 1971, elected a black educator to fill Smyth's unexpired term. He was Cecil L. Patterson, dean of the undergraduate school at North Carolina Central

University. In his report to the convention the next year Patterson praised "the dynamic optimism" of President Pisani and said that "the stresses and strains" at the college appeared "to result from the straining after new goals rather than from a desire to maintain the status quo."[72]

The relationship of the St. Mary's chaplain to the Diocese of North Carolina was a complicated and controversial question. The diocese viewed the St. Mary's Chapel as an unorganized mission and the chaplain as under the jurisdiction of Bishop Fraser. The college thought of the chaplain as both a member of the faculty and of the administration under the jurisdiction of the college trustees. Bishop Fraser instituted a policy of "not accepting any clergy in this diocese unless the Bishop had something to say about their hiring or their firing." That policy applied to all of the institutions, for the bishop considered it a necessary protection of the clergy in his diocese.[73] Therefore, Chaplains Baird, Hobgood, and Davis, and Frank Pisani were canonically resident in other dioceses. The problem was resolved when the next administration recognized that, according to the 1897 charter of incorporation of St. Mary's, the chapel belonged to the diocese rather than to the trustees. The college chaplain became once again canonically resident in the Diocese of North Carolina, and the bishop was consulted regarding appointments.

The question of "the ownership of St. Mary's" became a topic of conversation among Episcopalians after the board's reorganization. The trustees clarified the matter by explaining that, according to the charter of incorporation, the trustees held title to all college property except the chapel. The five dioceses of the Carolinas held a residual right to the property should the trustees determine "to abandon the trust imposed upon them."[74]

The question resulted in such increased tension between the school and the church that at their July meeting in 1975 the trustees discussed seriously the possibility of "no representation from the dioceses because they do not claim ownership." Finally, they agreed that "since St. Mary's was a church-related school . . . and since the bank [Wachovia Bank and Trust Company] particularly requested a closer relationship with the dioceses, the diocesan representatives to the Board of Trustees were vitally important."[75] The bylaws of the board were changed to provide three-year terms in lieu of the five-year terms for the five diocesan representatives and to provide that those representatives be appointed by their respective bishops rather than elected by the conventions; the ten members-at-large were to serve six-year terms. The alumnae representation remained at two members elected for three years.

President Pisani asked for an executive committee "to bring matters to the attention of the Board," and one was created in May, 1975; but it could not have the authority of the original executive committee under the amended charter. The Pisani boards had more knowledge of internal governance problems than previous trustees. There was almost no faculty communication with trustees until the joint committees of the 1969 self-study. By January, 1971, Pisani was exasperated enough with the faculty to ask the board to clarify the question of authority. The proposed change in requirements for junior college graduation was at issue. Educators Rollie Tillman and W. E. Highsmith replied that such matters were usually resolved by asking a faculty, through its committee system, to present a plan for presidential approval. The actual outcome at St. Mary's was that the faculty (with some misgivings) approved the president's plan. Pisani at the next board meeting said that some persons were exhibiting "an inability to deal with authority" because the faculty had "in the past made key decisions which were administrative in nature," and that some faculty members were finding it "difficult to adjust to the policy of this administration."[76] By then, faculty resentment was running high over the academic effects of the "freedom of choice" class attendance policy decreed by the administration.

In January, 1972, the faculty met with the finance committee and the chairman of the board over the salary misunderstanding. A change in bookkeeping resulted in overlapping contracts for two months of that year and the loss of two months' salary on the old contract—a fact that escaped everyone's attention for a time. The matter was settled without animosity, but the college's operating budget suffered a substantial blow.[77]

At their January, 1973, meeting the trustees voted to accede to the faculty's request and "to invite a member of the faculty, elected annually by the faculty, to attend the Board meetings as a non-voting observer, except at such times as the Board is in executive session."[78] The president of the Student Government Association had been given that privilege, at Pisani's request, "with overwhelming approval" in April, 1971. The faculty decided that only tenured faculty should be eligible and that a representative could be reelected twice. Helen Smith was elected in March, 1973.

In September, 1974, a letter signed by 46 of the 48 members of the faculty was sent to President Pisani and through Helen Smith to the trustees. With expressions of regret for "having to speak of salaries" during the economic crisis faced by the college and with a reaffirmation of loyalty to the college, the letter presented the facts of the situation. Most members of the faculty had received only a small increase in salary over several years. The added cost of instruction with the enlargement of the faculty was one cause of the problem. By 1974 not one of the faculty was the sole support of a family on the St. Mary's salary, and even the single persons were taking part-time jobs. The trustees voted salary increases of about 5 percent for each of the next two years. Teachers could not agree with the priorities set. They said that too much was being spent on bricks and mortar and on administrative expenses. The trustees, especially the businessmen among them, were inclined whenever the salary question was broached, to say, "If we do not have adequate buildings and equipment, we will not have the students; and if we do not have the students, we will not need any teachers."

Another cause of faculty concern was the new tenure policy, which lengthened the prerequisite service for tenure from three to seven years. A feature of the new policy, included at the suggestion of the faculty, was a tenure committee composed of three tenured faculty. That committee, after hearing a case in the summer of 1974, found the instructor to have been incompetent even when granted a four-year contract, but that insufficient written evidence and warning had been given him before his termination at midyear. (The case was eventually settled out of court.) Besides the tenure policy, a much improved faculty benefits policy, including maternity leave, was instituted during the Pisani administration.

A faculty appeal to the board of trustees in April, 1975, was over governance. The board consented to meet with faculty on the afternoon before the regular board meeting. Helen Smith presented the faculty position paper (to which there were several dissents). She said, "There does not exist at St. Mary's a functional or functioning system for orderly, informed, participatory decision making." Other concerns were the "erosion" of academic standards and the "blurred" responsibility for the business management of the institution. The report suggested administrative reorganization to clarify jobs and responsibilities, giving administrators "the normal authority" within their areas of expertise. Businessmen on the board continued to feel that "management makes decisions," and an organizational chart was adopted at the July meeting.[79] At the October meeting, Helen Smith reported "continued inconsistent decisions" and "considerable internal academic confusion." There was also concern over the size of the administrative staff in comparison to the size of the faculty in view of the budget problems. The president insisted that the expanded administrative apparatus was necessary to process students and to raise funds.

The major problems faced by the trustees were not governance, but were finances. Inclined to give Frank Pisani free rein to carry out his "mandate for change," the board authorized a professional survey preparatory to the largest fund drive in St. Mary's history. Dorothy Dodge, in October, 1969, became the college's first business manager since 1947. She had worked with Pisani at the Virginia Theological Seminary where she was an accountant. Dodge had the St. Mary's payroll computerized by the bank, had the insurance on the college property increased, and then turned her attention to people. She arranged for improved health insurance coverage; hourly employees had no insurance of any kind through the college up to that time. Hourly wages were raised to $1.60, soon to become the legal requirement. Then she began work on a budgeting system that received the approval of the management consultants. On December 8, 1970, Dorothy Dodge died suddenly, only a few hours after making a detailed report to the faculty meeting.

On October 8, 1970, the decade of renewal fund-raising campaign was launched with a goal of $7.5 million over a ten-year period. Of that amount, $3.5 million was designated for endowment and $435,000 for scholarship funds. The remainder was "for campus renewal, carefully phased." The plan included residences on campus for the president and chaplain, a classroom building, a physical education center, a dining room and student center, a dormitory to house 200 students, and a fine arts center (neither built because of lack of funds). Plans to tear down Pittman Auditorium were abolished, and that building was renovated in 1976. The front campus was to be restored to almost its original appearance by razing the wings of Smedes. The upper floors of Smedes were to be converted into administrative and faculty offices. East and West Rock were to be renovated for offices, a day student center, and an alumnae guest house. Those plans did not seem impossibly optimistic given the times, Pisani's infectious enthusiasm, and the advance pledges. The campaign steering committee included five trustees and a number of prominent businessmen.[80]

By December, 1970, just over $1 million had been pledged, and excitement ran high. A gift from Mr. and Mrs. N. K. Dickerson established in the English department an endowment fund named for their daughter, Ann Dickerson Whitehurst, and one for the social studies department in honor of Sara Craig Dickerson's mother, Annie Welsh Craig. All three women were St. Mary's alumnae.

The new home for the college president was ready for occupancy before the campaign began. It was situated slightly west of the site of the former rectory and president's home; that house was razed. The campaign for funds proceeded with the aid of John Bondeson, a professional fund raiser with Ketchum, Inc., who was engaged early in 1970. Bondeson told the trustees that a campaign for $7.5 million would not be easy, adding that there was "money in the two Carolinas," but that competition for that money was "strong."[81] The trustees in January,

1970, authorized the position of development director, and Henry Witten was employed. His title soon was changed to that of director of development and college relations. A native of Ohio, he held the master of divinity degree from Virginia Theological Seminary and had been ordained deacon. He was ordained priest in April, 1971, by the Right Reverend Thomas H. Wright, D.D., bishop of East Carolina. For the first time since it was built in 1856, the St. Mary's Chapel was the setting for the rite of ordination.

The trustees in July, 1970, gave Pisani authority "to rearrange priorities as funds came in and to designate unrestricted and undesignated funds."[82] In April, 1971, the trustees accepted the offer of Wachovia Bank and Trust Company to lend funds to the college against the decade of renewal pledges. The indebtedness was not to exceed $1.2 million, and the college was not to begin new buildings until their cost was covered fully by cash or pledges. The full $1.2 million was borrowed.[83] By the October board meeting the consensus was, "The development program is not going as well as we had hoped it would." The trustees then ordered the cessation of any new construction, other than the completion of the $520,000 dining room-student union and the $750,000 gymnasium-natatorium then under way.

The physical education department moved into the traditional, brick, columned gymnasium-natatorium located behind Holt Hall that fall. It boasted sophisticated equipment, including bowling lanes with automatic pin setters and an Olympic-size pool with an underwater sound system for the synchronized swimming performances of the Sea Saints. The dance studio was named in honor of Mary Smedes Poyner York, a gift from her family because of her interest in the dance and drama.[84] Also that fall, on November 22, the English, social studies, mathematics, and religion departments moved into the new Alice McKenzie Ragland Classroom Building. The $425,000 building was made possible by gifts from members of the Ragland family. The faculty lounge and a classroom were furnished as memorials.[85] The board authorized the expenditures necessary to raze Clement Hall when the student union building was completed.

Alumnae thought the new image they saw when returning to the campus was "fabulous"—the spacious new president's home, the comfortable, air-conditioned classrooms, the pool, the Nancy O'Herron Rankin terrace off the dining room. And yet, the traditional image remained almost intact because the new buildings were placed behind the early ones.

At the October, 1971, meeting of the trustees, the new business manager, John M. Biggs, reported that he was working to complete "the difficult to understand but excellent system" of records keeping that Dorothy Dodge was organizing before her death. Because he spent so much time supervising the new building projects, his records were not yet up to date. He expressed concern because unrestricted funds previously used for operation were being diverted to new building. Biggs, a native of Raleigh, held a degree in business administration from the University of New Mexico and had previous business experience.

By the end of 1971 the financial position of the college was precarious. There was a deficit of $377,500 in the operating fund, and the administration was committed to $2.5 million in construction bills. To generate operating funds, student fees were raised. The housekeeping functions had been contracted to a professional company after the death in January, 1971, of Katherine P. Adams, who had been in charge of housekeeping since 1964. As operating and construction deficits mounted, Wachovia agreed to extend an earlier loan and to make an additional loan to be secured by the college's "unencumbered property." The entire amount was to be paid out by April 1, 1975; however, it was generally agreed that long-term financing could be arranged for any balance remaining.[86]

Although several North Carolina foundations gave substantial gifts,[87] the decade of renewal campaign was not producing the necessary funds. Pisani told the trustees that he had "extended" beyond the funds received because he was "both aggressive and optimistic."[88] When Bondeson left with the expiration of his contract at the end of 1972, approximately $2 million had been raised. Although that was a "tremendous" record in view of St. Mary's past campaigns, the problem remained; about $4 million had been spent.

The change of the official name of the institution to "Saint Mary's College," approved by the trustees in July, 1972, was made primarily "to fight the junior college image," for Pisani said many foundations had strict rules against giving to two-year colleges.[89] Therefore, the new St. Mary's image, that of a four-year intermediate institution, was emphasized.

HEROIC EFFORTS

The problem of paying the immediate costs of the new buildings remained a critical one. In September, 1972, Bernard W. Conrad became business manager of the college. (Jack Biggs remained for some months as director of campus planning to supervise completion of new buildings.) Conrad had 30 years of industrial experience. He had been vice-president and general manager of several modular building corporations, two of which he founded, and an administrative troubleshooter for Studebaker Corporation. A native of Boston, he was educated at Purdue and Indiania Universities with special training in corporate management methods, which he prophetically called "the key to St. Mary's future." [90]

Both Pisani and Witten continued to blame "the lack of national leadership" for the lag in the financial campaign. Consequently, there was jubilation when in March, 1973, James C. Gardner, Rocky Mount businessman and former congressman, agreed to be the national chairman of the decade of renewal campaign. By the July board meeting he was able to report $170,000 in new pledges. Unfortunately, he resigned the chairmanship in January, 1974. In the meantime, Henry Witten had resigned to take a parish; therefore, for a time, Frank Pisani acted as development director. He commented that in the sixties he could "have easily found millions for the school." He did raise over $200,000 in less than six months.[91] By 1974 there was a national economic crunch with steep inflation and unemployment.

At St. Mary's the economic crunch arrived somewhat earlier than on the national level. By April, 1973, Conrad had set the tangled financial records in order and had prepared a balanced operating budget for 1973–1974. "We must live within the budget," he declared as he decreed a long list of belt-tightening measures that included limited salary raises for anyone on campus. The trustees ruled that no deviation from the budget could be made without approval of the board's finance committee.[92]

It became imperative that the St. Mary's story be taken to the individual Episcopal congregations. In his first report to the trustees of the college Pisani had stated flatly that he found the lack of diocesan support "appalling." In 1969 the five dioceses of the Carolinas budgeted a total of about $14,000, and the Diocese of North Carolina, which had since the early sixties budgeted about $10,000 annually for St. Mary's, eliminated all educational institutions from its next budget. That exclusion of the Episcopal educational institutions was a part of the plan to place responsibility for program upon each parish in the hope that each congregation would give generously and would find creative ways to meet many kinds of needs.[93]

Beginning in July, 1973, the congregations of the five dioceses were asked to contribute to "the Christian education of a young woman" program. Smaller parishes were asked to underwrite the education of from one to three students by contributing from $800 to $2,400. By then the actual cost of educating a student at St. Mary's was $3,800; charges were $2,800, and an additional $200 for each North Carolina student was paid by state aid. Therefore, the college had to find about $800 per student. The Diocese of Western North Carolina responded to pleas for help with a $5,000 grant from the Episcopal Fund. Communicating with large groups was Frank Pisani's great talent. He and a group of bright and enthusiastic students participated in "St. Mary's Sundays" at many churches. By July, 1974, Pisani could report that 67 churches had contributed $17,580.[94]

At the October, 1973, board meeting, Conrad had delineated the college's financial situation: "The cash deficit will become a serious matter in the first half of 1974 . . . and the availability of borrowing power is uncertain." There was a $300,000 cash deficit in operating funds caused by earlier transfers to the building program, and funds were not available to pay the over $200,000 in interest due annually on the money borrowed for the buildings.

Even the students were aware of the financial crisis because increased enrollment resulted in overcrowded dormitories and the mixing of classes on residence halls. The faculty questioned priorities in the letter of February, 1974, to the board regarding faculty salaries. The faculty understood the need for new buildings; 100 percent of the faculty had contributed to the decade of renewal fund. However, they felt that the educational program bore more than its share of the stringent economies.

Alumnae, too, sought funds for St. Mary's. Annual giving was designated each year to a particular project. The 1970–1971 annual giving, which totaled $37,893 from 1,387 donors, was used to renovate Holt Hall.[95] In 1971–1972 gifts of $26,092 went to increase the corpus of the Smedes Scholarship. The decade of renewal report showed that of the $2 million raised by December of that year, slightly over $900,000 was pledged by alumnae; however, several large gifts accounted for much of that sum.[96] The next year's annual giving of $31,789 made the Smedes Scholarship a full one and raised the corpus of the Cruikshank Scholarship to $14,000. Only 15 percent of the 7,000 persons solicited actually contributed, and the average gift was $28 compared to a national average for women's colleges of $50.[97]

The alumnae council had voted on April 18, 1973, to allocate the annual giving again to scholarships. On April 25 at a called meeting, the executive committee of the council was told by the president and business manager of the immediate crisis caused by the deficit in the college operating fund. When asked "to recycle the 1972–1973 alumnae scholarship fund to the operating fund of the college," the committee voted to do so with the understanding (that was later honored) that the money would be returned to the scholarship fund whenever possible.[98]

It was obvious that the alumnae would have to make heroic efforts to raise operating funds. In the fall of 1973 trustees and other friends of the college established a substantial challenge fund to match new and

Graduation day c.1976

increased alumnae gifts. The resulting alumnae gifts amounted to $67,559, and the total with matching gifts was $131,827 from 1861 persons. By July, 1974, the operational deficit was reduced to $102,000. The 1973–1974 St. Mary's annual alumnae giving program ranked third in the nation in the junior college division in both total alumnae gifts and total number of donors.[99]

That success challenged the alumnae to attempt a national telethon the next year. Smedes parlor was equipped with telephones, and during three weeks in January and February over 200 volunteers talked to 6,220 alumnae and parents of students; 40 percent of those called contributed a total of $95,000.[100]

Funds from chapter projects were given in 1976 for the badly needed restoration of the James Hart confirmation painting. The St. Mary's history became an alumnae association project in 1976. Alumnae association projects were many and varied during those years.[101]

In April, 1974, Conrad reported that the operating budget for the year was in the black, that deficits were being reduced, and that the projected operating budget for 1974–1975 was a balanced one. However, he expressed grave concern over the ability of the college to meet the schedule set by the bank for repayment of loans amounting to over $2 million. The board authorized short-term borrowing of up to $150,000 over the summer, and President Pisani's habitual optimism deserted him.[102] Student fees had been increased again. Nearly all academic departments had been shrunk by not rehiring some untenured faculty whose contracts had expired, and strict economizing continued everywhere. Additional money was given by the Episcopal churches; total church support continued to amount to approximately 1 percent of the college's educational and general expenses. The college still shared in the support given by the business community of the state to the North Carolina Foundation of Church Related Colleges. St. Mary's share of the foundation's 1973 distribution was slightly over $23,000.[103]

But the sources of additional income were insufficient to meet college needs. On June 5, 1975, a called meeting of the board of trustees heard Eugene Hardin, senior vice-president of Wachovia Bank, and Dodge Geoghegan, vice-president, explain that the loan of $1 million made in March, 1972, to be paid out on April 1, 1975, was in default. (Interest was paid up to March 31 and $50,000 had been paid on the principal.) Furthermore, the college had violated the terms of the 1971 loans by committing on building contracts about $1 million "beyond the cash and pledges on hand for such purposes," thus necessitating the 1972 loan. Then the bank presented a plan that called not only for a quick response, but "for personal involvement and dedicated leadership" on the part of the trustees. Wachovia's proposal was that St. Mary's borrow from college endowment, mount a campaign to raise $500,000 by September 30, 1975, and take out a 15-year loan for the remaining debt. After discussion, it was agreed that the unrestricted endowment funds would go as a loan to help pay off the debt and that with the donors' consent, the Dickerson endowment would be used and replaced later.[104]

The discussion of the progress of the development campaign revealed that there was at that time neither a volunteer national chairman nor a Raleigh chairman. However, the campaign was in the hands of professional fund raiser, Mike C. Dunne, who had arrived on campus in February and planned to raise $2 million in about eight months. Dunne had asked Chairman Tillman to insist that the board record its intention that no more financial commitments be made for construction "until the present debt is effectively eliminated or controlled."[105]

Pisani outlined his "priorities for the next eighteen months" in his April, 1975, report to the trustees. Students, fund raising, and admissions were his priorities, in that order. He said that he would be "dele-gating more authority to the other administrative officials." [106] The in-stitution's financial problems did not stem from enrollment problems, although the total number of applicants declined after 1967. A vigorous recruiting program, the enlargement of the high school, and the change to a system of admitting qualified students as soon as their applications were processed kept the enrollment at around 500 with a record high of 518 in 1973–1974.

On July 17, 1975, the trustees heard a report on negotiations with the bank given by Thad Eure, Jr., who had been elected the previous year to a ten-year term on the St. Mary's board. He presented a plan that he, Tillman, Pisani, and Conrad had worked out with the bank's officials. The college would, through the sale and borrowing of certain endow-ments, meet its current obligations and reduce the debt to $1.37 million by September 1, 1976. A general campaign would begin in September and would be completed by the end of November. The college would hire a full-time director of development by January, 1976. By the begin-ning of the 1976–1977 academic year, the college would have reduced the faculty-to-student ratio, which had been at about 10 to 1 since the enlarged curriculum, to 14 to 1. The board would fill its three vacancies "with strong, financially capable and/or business-oriented men after consultation, advice, and assistance from Wachovia Bank." Further-more, the college would "begin a program to substantially improve the relationship between St. Mary's and the Episcopal Diocese." Everyone anticipated the liquidation of the college's debt "within the next five to seven years." [107]

Conrad gave a detailed report that showed that the carried-forward operating deficit had been eliminated and that the college could service the $1.37 million debt. Dunne reported that his goal of $100,000 from the trustees had been exceeded by $1,450 and that the steering commit-tee, including alumnae, was functioning effectively. [108] By October, 1975, the financial picture had brightened considerably, and the board expressed appreciation to Conrad for "remarkable results" and to the faculty and staff "who helped him make these figures possible." After some discussion, the trustees approved fees for boarding students at $3,850, still "considerably lower than many Eastern schools." The col-lege had arranged a 15–year loan at 10 percent interest with Wachovia and Durham Life Insurance Company for the long-term debt of $1.38 million. [109] Development director Clifton W. Beggs had arrived on cam-pus with 25 years experience in industrial management and a record of successful development fund raising to his credit. Thad Eure, Jr., ac-cepted the chairmanship of the campaign and was off to a good start toward the goal of $750,000 in three-to-five-year pledges. Trustees, alumnae, and businessmen organized citywide campaigns.

At that October meeting alumna Eve Hargrave Smith was elected secretary-treasurer of the board, and another alumna, June Bourne Long, was nominated for the chairmanship of the board. That was the first nomination of a woman to that position in the history of the board, but Long declined the nomination.[110]

Difficulties continued to face the board. Inflation had escalated costs, and the college had borrowed heavily from its endowment fund. However, by the spring of 1976 the capital campaign to raise $750,000 was drawing to a successful close—a success due in large measure to Eure's indefatigable efforts.

Alumnae took a lively interest in the eventful Pisani years. The alumnae magazine published full and objective accounts of the academic and social changes, the controversies over student government authority and compulsory chapel, the restructuring of the board of trustees and the college's relationship to the Episcopal church, and the financial situation. By 1973 budget cuts made it necessary to change the magazine for some years to a tabloid called *St. Mary's College*.

The alumnae secretary changed both her name and her title in 1969 when Jane Augustine married newspaperman Roy H. Rabon, Jr. Her decision to remain at St. Mary's provided needed stability, for there was considerable turnover in the administrative offices. The reorganization of administration, as recommended by a management consultant firm, gave her the title of executive secretary of the alumnae association (changed to alumnae director in 1974) and placed the alumnae office under the director of development and college relations. That year Jane Rabon was made Chairman of Women's Colleges for District III (nine southeastern states) of the American Alumni Council.

The St. Mary's alumnae council had attempted to forestall reorganization of the association's office by sending resolutions to the board of trustees. The council noted that the alumnae association had existed since 1879 and that its purpose was much broader than fund raising. The council requested that the president of the alumnae association serve on the board ex officio and that the alumnae secretary be appointed to policymaking committees so that she could "represent the college's point of view as well as the alumnae point of view" in speaking to alumnae groups and as editor of the magazine. Included also in the resolutions were requests for adequate staffing and budget and a recommendation that gifts from alumnae to any fund be credited to the alumnae office.[111]

Alumnae news followed a predictable pattern—reports of weddings and jobs, children, and volunteer work, travel, clubs, grandchildren and a few great-grandchildren. On campus in 1974 were four students who could claim St. Mary's women unto the fourth, fifth, and sixth generations, and 113 other students whose mothers or grandmothers were alumnae.[112] Alumnae also reported achievements in various fields. News of graduates of the 1920s included career diplomat Sara Falkener's stint as United States consul in Vienna, Patti Sherwood Smith's book on Joseph Pulitzer, Frances Scott Sewall's book on decoupage, and Helen Badham House's one-woman show of paintings at the Morehead Planetarium. Some graduates of the 1930s and 1940s had returned to universities, sometimes studying along with their children there. Elizabeth Nicoll Felton had prepared 37 original maps for *Silent Warfare*, a book on submarine warfare in the Pacific. Pilot Page Shamburger was editor of *Air Progress* and the author of five books, and Sarah Sawyer Allison's first novel, *Ginger Hill*, had been published. Betty Debnam Hunt had originated in 1969 a weekly children's *Mini Page* that was to become syndicated in some 450 newspapers.[113]

The news of the graduates of the sixties and seventies included Barbara Knight's auto racing, Martha Hardee's assignment in Australia for *Reader's Digest*, and Meg Christian's Olivia Records, a company run by women producing music "about what it really means to be a woman." Lelia White had been responsible for a program that relocated 600 Laotians, and Elisabeth Keller Savitz was a pediatrician.[114]

Some alumnae of earlier years were involved in nontraditional causes. Beth Yarborough Brooks edited a weekly, the *Old Saybrook Pictorial*, and was active in NOW. Jane Hurt Yarn was named Georgia's 1969 "conservationist of the year" for her part in getting protective legislation for coastal areas.[115]

Working women in many fields, but especially in education, needed master's degrees. A questionnaire sent to all alumnae in 1971 was answered by enough of them to present "a fairly accurate picture," according to Jane Rabon. Eleven percent of those responding had taken some graduate work, and two thirds of those held graduate degrees. The percentage of St. Mary's women taking graduate work rose from 6 percent in the 1920s to 15 percent for alumnae of the classes of the 1960s.[116]

On the St. Mary's campus, increased support from the alumnae and other sources gradually began to brighten the picture. Frank Pisani was beginning by 1976 to see the end of the long financial crisis. But, problems remained—administrative problems and personal problems.

## "A NEW BEGINNING"

It was in September, 1975, that a memorandum addressed "To the St. Mary's Family" was received by the trustees, faculty, staff, and the Student Government Association president. Signed by Harriet and Frank Pisani, it read:

We need to share with you distressing news. At the same time we trust the action we are taking will prove beneficial to all concerned.

After much prayerful thought we are, with great sadness, ending our marriage. We do this with continued concern for each other, without rancor, and with no outside factors affecting our decision. . . .

The St. Mary's community received that news with regret and with a feeling of sadness for all of the Pisani family. That school year the pressures of the various crises at St. Mary's seemed to weigh heavily on Frank Pisani. It was just after the Christmas holiday that he stood in the hallway near his office bantering with the young alumnae who recruited for the admissions office. As usual, they complained of their dateless nights when on the road. That time he rejoined, "Let's form the Singles Club. We shall have lunch together tomorrow as our first club meeting." [117]

Soon Sara Frances Walters and Frank Pisani were often seen together. She had returned to St. Mary's in the fall of 1974, one of nine young alumnae on the staff and faculty in 1975. In early February at a private party at the president's house, they announced their engagement to be married. Pisani failed to take into account the dismay that the announcement would create among some of the trustees and alumnae—dismay because his divorce was not final. Believing that he had acted in "the most honest and above board manner possible," he was surprised when Chairman Alexander of the board of trustees reprimanded him, and he offered to resign.[118] His offer was accepted.

On February 18, 1976, Sara Frances Walters, who had been reared a Methodist, was confirmed along with several St. Mary's students by the Right Reverend Hunley Agee Elebash, D.D., bishop of the Diocese of East Carolina. After the solemn service in the college chapel, Pisani spoke to the students and faculty gathered there. He said:

This is a time to reflect upon where St. Mary's is and upon my own life. If this sounds theological, it is. . . . I was called to do a job. . . . I grew to love the students, as I do now. I hope I have made a contribution to your life; you have to mine.

Buildings have been torn down, and buildings have been built. The faculty has been expanded and then contracted. A large debt was incurred to save this institution. Then a way was found to manage it. My style often resembles that of a bulldozer. I have made friends and have estranged others. Maybe that is the lot of a college president. Maybe it is just me.

But lives shift and values change. As you know, this has been a difficult year for me personally. Then it all came together these last few weeks with the greatest gift God can give a man, the love of a sensitive, caring young woman.

Then, Pisani announced his resignation as president of the college, effective at commencement, "with a sense of sadness, but also with a sense of joy in the new beginning for us all—a new beginning for St. Mary's, and a new beginning for Sara Frances and me."[119]

The sound of quiet weeping filled the little chapel, for many there loved Frank Pisani. On the other hand, many of the students were furious—angry because their priest, father image, and friend was marrying someone so near their own age and was also leaving St. Mary's.

The remainder of the school year was not easy. To some, in retrospect, the events of the past seven years seemed to have been leading almost inevitably to a conclusion of Pisani's presidency. To others, it seemed that the man who had saved St. Mary's was being thanklessly and needlessly dismissed. One who knew him well called him "the Saul who *had* to precede a David—the necessary catalyst."

Of St. Mary's, Pisani said, as he left, that the college was "teetering" in the midst of an identity crisis. "In ten years," he said, "St. Mary's will either be an outstanding school or dead." Of his experience at St. Mary's, he said, "It was always theologically oriented . . . a very intensive Christian humanism." In his prepared public statement, he said, "I am resigning for both personal and professional reasons. I feel my work here has, for the most part, been completed."[120]

Sara Frances Walters and Frank Warren Pisani were married on May 22, 1976, in her hometown of La Grange. They moved to San Francisco where he was a public relations and fund-raising consultant. By the spring of 1981 they had returned to Raleigh, and he had launched a handsome, but short-lived, magazine called *Carolina Arts*. In 1982 the Pisanis and their young daughter Caroline moved to South Carolina where he had accepted the rectorship of the Church of the Resurrection at Surfside Beach.

# SUCH AN INHERITANCE

I t was apparent from the day he arrived on campus in the summer of 1976 that John Thomas Rice would understand St. Mary's. The tenth head of the institution was equipped both by experience and background to view the long history of St. Mary's as a valuable heritage. At the end of the first year of his administration he said, "I see myself as the inheritor of the tradition—a tradition which is an inspiration to enable us to build on our strengths."[1]

John Rice always considered himself a Virginian, although he was born in Delaware, for he grew up in Richmond.[2] He enrolled in the engineering curriculum at Virginia Polytechnic Institute but soon changed to sociology. "I realized," he said, "that I am a people person."[3] His peers agreed, for he was elected president of the class of 1961, was cadet major, and attained membership in national scholarship and leadership fraternities. After military service, he took a master's degree in sociology at the University of Tennessee.[4]

He was guidance director and the wrestling coach at Fork Union Military Academy and the first dean of men at Madison College (now James Madison University) in Harrisonburg, Virginia. His grandmother, Althea Loose Johnston, who was for over 40 years on the faculty of that institution, was a major influence in John Rice's life. Going to Madison was like going home for his wife, Grace Arendall, whom he married in 1960, for she was a Madison College graduate. Following terms in administrative positions at Florida Junior College and St. Anne's School in Charlottesville, Rice assumed the position of assistant to the president of Sweet Briar College in 1972. In 1974 he was made dean of student affairs there.

John Thomas Rice, president, 1976–

John Rice decided to accept the presidency of St. Mary's because he saw "even greater opportunities" for the entire family—for him, the chance to put into practice all of his philosophy concerning the education of young women; for his family, the wide cultural and social opportunities available in Raleigh. The four young Rices—William Thomas II (Tom), Sarah Cunningham, Anne Carrington, and Robert Coleman (Bobby)—ranged in age from 15 to 5 years. (In due course Sarah and Anne became St. Mary's graduates.) Grace Rice, who majored in history in college, said later, "I was not sure that we were making the right decision. But when we had visited the campus and I had read the early history of the school, I knew that I wanted to be a part of this very special place."[5]

The duties of the president of St. Mary's delineated in the bylaws of the board of trustees directed the president to see that the college administration was properly organized to maintain and enhance good relations with faculty, students, alumnae, and the Episcopal church, as well as to maintain a full enrollment of qualified students, a sound fiscal basis, and a successful development program. In addition, the college's relationship to the Raleigh community was to be an expanding one. Rice told the members of the search committee that he was willing to accept the challenge if the board agreed to "a long term arrangement, for a minimum of five years and much longer if the Board were satisfied."[6] The faculty found the new president to be enthusiastic, student-oriented, but also committed to academic excellence.

The inauguration of John Rice was set for April 17, 1977. He requested that the ceremonies be held on the campus at a time when Bishop Fraser could participate and that the focus should be on the college instead of on the president. Pres. Harold B. Whiteman, Jr., of Sweet Briar College, was the principal speaker at the inauguration held in front of the Sarah Graham Kenan Library. The day's events included services in the chapel and a luncheon for official guests, among whom were representatives from 60 colleges, members of families of former heads of the school, and President Emeritus Stone. During the investiture, Board Chairman Thomas W. Alexander presented the college's first inaugural commemorative medallion.[7]

The speakers emphasized the long service of the institution. Elgiva Dundas Watson, faculty representative to the board of trustees, said, "John Rice is capable of both honoring the traditions of this college and leading it into the future." Rice said, "We talk much about the sense of family at St. Mary's because it is so. This is . . . our chance to do together something that will stand as significant in the long history of this school."[8]

John Rice was aware of the serious problems facing the school when he took the presidency, and for awhile the challenge seemed almost overwhelming. By the fall of 1979 he had found a new sense of direction. "Now," he told the faculty at their first meeting, "we shall begin to build."[9] He did not mean new bricks and mortar; for the modern buildings Rice often expressed gratitude. By "building" he meant a strong academic program, emphasizing the traditional reputation of the school. It was a propitious time for redefining the mission of the institution because its third self-study for reaccreditation by the Southern Association of Colleges and Schools was scheduled for 1979. Marjolijn de Jager Werman directed the study, and reaccreditation was granted with the recommendations of the visiting committee concerning mostly problems already in the process of being addressed. Two years later, at the insistence of President Rice, the board of trustees ordered an internal long-range planning report. By then the institution had defined its role once more. That 1981 statement of mission read:

St. Mary's is an intermediate college, historically associated with the church, which combines the last two years of high school and the first two years of college in a traditional liberal arts curriculum. Its primary mission is to prepare young women of ability for continued study and scholarly attainments in a baccalaureate program. In addition, St. Mary's seeks to provide an opportunity for women of all ages to develop their individual potentialities and thus prepare themselves for future careers.

Since its inception in 1842, St. Mary's has considered itself a community where caring, responsibility, and discipline combine to foster intellectual, spiritual, artistic, and physical development. It is the goal of the College that each student gain a deeper knowledge of and respect for herself, understand and take pride in her cultural heritage, and appreciate and feel a responsibility for her community and the world around her.[10]

Rice said that in the early 1970s he had realized that "the way we educate women would be the real challenge of the eighties."[11] Furthermore, a renewed respect for the liberal arts curriculum became apparent by the 1980s. The conjunction of the two movements found St. Mary's in the process of making the adjustments necessary to meet the needs of the time and place. "We must," Rice told the faculty, "find the proper path for us."[12] For the first time, St. Mary's students faced the fact that 90 percent of them would be working women. They began to realize that a standard of living even approaching that of the families in which they grew up would require two incomes. Furthermore, most said that they wanted a few years of independence before marriage. However, John Rice told them that "to equate learning exclusively with economic return" was not only dangerous, but also weak and wrong. He said:

A true college education must also be evaluated in terms of the ability to live, to communicate with others, and to contribute to the growth of societal life. . . . In time, those in charge of our system will once again understand the importance of a corps of women who have a strong liberal arts background and also a strong sense of identity and purpose. . . . Women must have the strength and diversity to meet whatever demands they choose for themselves—from motherhood to corporate president.[13]

Those words from a man who admitted that he had "no patience" with the radical feminist movement encompassed a program that seemed to fit the needs of the majority of St. Mary's students of the 1980s while, at the same time, encouraging them to set higher goals for themselves.

The dean of the college also described himself as "a strong educational conservative" who saw the liberal arts courses as providing "far more than mere vocational skills." Bob Miller noted, however, that in a dynamic society changes and modifications in curriculum became necessary from time to time.[14] There was general agreement at St. Mary's that no change should be made in the fundamental precept that the liberal education of young women could best be accomplished in a small, single-sex college with a Christian orientation. There was also general agreement within the organization in the 1980s that the unique St. Mary's concept of a four-year institution educating young women between the approximate ages of 16 and 20 within a single administrative unit was a valid and practical concept. During 1981–1982 almost 55 percent of the freshman class (62 students) enrolled in 172 college courses, thus earning transferable college credits. The administration continued to resist local pressure to include a tenth grade, but the few accelerated tenth graders accepted each year were usually able to complete most of the work of the first year of college while technically high school seniors.

The back-to-basics movement of the 1980s required few changes in the St. Mary's curriculum because peripheral courses had been dropped during the financial crisis of the mid-seventies. The academic council continued to function effectively under a reorganization that removed all administrative officials except the dean of the college, leaving eight faculty members elected by the academic departments and five student members. The entire faculty still reserved the right to review all decisions of the council. The associate in arts degree requisites reverted to the pre-1970 requirement of both a foreign language and mathematics.

The internal long-range planning report of 1982 showed "a remarkable unanimity of opinion" throughout the St. Mary's community on the mission of the college and "an extraordinary," though not a total, degree of consensus on how that mission should be fulfilled.[15] There was general agreement among the faculty that a liberal education involved analysis, synthesis, and values transmission. There was agree-

The John Rice family, 1982

ment, too, that a St. Mary's grade and course should represent at least its equivalent at any institution to which a student transferred.

During the early years of the Rice administration various official steps were taken to encourage academic achievement. Beginning in 1979 an annual honors convocation with a procession of the faculty in academic regalia recognized St. Mary's best students. A chapter of the Société Honoraire de Français was organized in the high school, and both the high school and college honor societies established awards for the greatest scholastic improvement.[16] New competitive scholarships were offered to local high school graduates. In 1982 a St. Mary's student placed first in the state on the standardized French examination,[17] and the year before a prestigious John Motley Morehead scholarship to Chapel Hill was awarded a high school senior.[18]

Experience continued to prove that those holding the associate degree from St. Mary's succeeded in gaining admittance to the institutions of their first or second choice. Members of the class of 1981 were accepted at 40 colleges and universities, including a number outside the Southeast. Following tradition, 61 of the class of 107 members went to Chapel Hill, as did 10 of the high school graduates. Also following tradition, nearly every graduate, whether of the high school or college, continued her education.

Several St. Mary's graduates traveled from Chapel Hill to offer advice during an assembly in the fall of 1981. Their advice went like this:

> When you get to Carolina you have to have your head on straight . . . I would have been lost over there at 18 . . . It's run like a business. . . . You don't know who is grading your papers. . . . You soon learn that you have to make for yourself rules about like those here. Prepare yourself for the university at St. Mary's where people have time for you. . . . You are the first women in history to have such job opportunities. Take them seriously.[19]

Every effort was made at St. Mary's to guide students in the early choice of majors and possible careers, keeping in mind the flexibility provided by the liberal arts education. The guidance director supervised an internship program that gave experience to volunteers wishing to learn more about a career preference before making a choice. Even the male members of the faculty said, "A woman still has to be more highly motivated than a man in order to achieve."[20]

The library played an important role in the effort to keep academic standards high. First an English teacher, head librarian Andrea Plummer Brown thought of the library as an integral part of the learning process. After completing a library degree at Chapel Hill and establishing a library at a private academy, she returned to St. Mary's as librarian in 1974. Typical of so many young academic couples, the Browns managed graduate work for two, two careers, and parenting. Also, Andrea Brown became active in professional circles, as well as in committee work at St. Mary's which included eight years on the academic council.[21]

The library collection numbered over 36,000 volumes in 1982, and its growth rate of around 5 percent annually soon filled the shelving area, keeping longtime library assistants Jean C. Plummer and Mary T. Pearson very busy. A growing collection of periodicals on microfilm increased research material. A listening center provided facilities for use of records and cassettes.[22] (Many audiovisuals were housed outside the library in the academic departments owning them, and moneys from the Dickerson Fund made possible in 1982 a video recording system for the college.)

The Friends of the Library of St. Mary's College was established in 1982, a dream long held by John Tate, who for many years was active on the library committee and served as chairman. Mabel Morrison was elected first president of the organization.

The library played an important role in another approach to academic excellence, that of enriching the cultural offerings available on campus. From the beginning of the Rice administration, there was a return to the emphasis on concerts and lectures on campus. They met another of President Rice's goals, that of a closer relationship between town and gown. The Thomas Wolfe Fest, sponsored by the library, not only served that purpose but also brought national attention to the college.

One of the four major institutional collections of materials concerning North Carolina novelist Thomas Wolfe developed at St. Mary's because in 1975 the father of a new student was impressed with the library. John O. Fulenwider, Jr., a physician from Pageland, South Carolina, who had collected Wolfe materials for some 15 years, wanted his collection to be accessible to young people who could discover Wolfe during their college days. When he offered his collection to St. Mary's along with funds to enlarge it, President Pisani accepted with gratitude.[23] Through Dr. Fulenwider's generosity, the Thomas Wolfe Room was constructed in the Sarah Graham Kenan Library. After Fulenwider's death in 1979, the collection continued to grow through gifts and institutional support.[24] The first town and gown event of the Rice administration was the dedication of the Thomas Wolfe Room, October 21, 1976, with Fred Wolfe, brother of the novelist, making his second visit to the college.[25] The banquet speaker was Wolfe scholar Richard Walser.[26]

The Wolfe Fest, a two-day symposium, became an annual event providing a new kind of educational experience for the students and bringing to the campus nationally known speakers. Each year students entered the Thomas Wolfe essay contest.[27] The Thomas Wolfe Society was organized in 1979 at St. Mary's. Andrea Brown was made a trustee of the society, which within a year had over 250 members internationally.

Musicales in the parlor became the custom again after a new grand piano was given by Mary Collett Wilson Stoney, 1919 graduate and longtime trustee. It was almost like a soiree of 1844 on the night of December 1, 1977, when Michael Zenge played a recital honoring Mary Stoney—except that the arrival of guests was heralded by the slamming of automobile doors rather than the crunch of carriage wheels, and the program included Debussy as well as Mozart. The room was exactly right for the annual Smedes Parlor Concert Series. Visitors, upon entering the wide hallway, saw the new portraits of Aldert and Bennett Smedes presented by Mr. and Mrs. James Poyner on behalf of the Smedes family, and in the parlor some of the orginal Smedes furniture was in use.[28]

Definitely twentieth century was the career emphasis of the 1981–

1982 forum series. A committee, headed by Terry Thompson of the performing arts department, invited 18 outstanding career women to give candid descriptions of their work. The lectures were open to the public. Speakers included a legislator, a physician, a stockbroker, an Episcopal priest, a newscaster, a designer, and Jane Goodall, the internationally known primatologist. That series reinforced the 1979 series of classroom visits by career-oriented alumnae which the alumnae association sponsored.

The 1980–1981 forum series celebrated the diversity of the arts in North Carolina; musicians, painters, writers, dancers, and an opera company visited the campus. An earlier series presented films about women. Thompson also took the major responsibility for the Smedes Parlor Concert Series. With degrees from Chapel Hill and study in Europe, she was known as a fine pianist.

A new cultural offering of 1981–1982 was *Muse* Week in January. Conceived and planned by Anna Wooten-Hawkins, adviser to the literary magazine, and its staff, the week brought to the campus successful writers in the area. The *Muse* continued to sponsor an annual writing contest and to publish student literary and art work.

The *Belles* made valiant efforts to increase student awareness of life beyond the halls of St. Mary's and fraternity parties at Chapel Hill. The college newspaper ran articles deploring low college board scores and student apathy regarding questions of public policy, and articles on abortion, the Equal Rights Amendment, environmental protection, and the importance of volunteerism. Intellectual horizons were broadened for dozens of St. Mary's students over the years through trips to New York and Europe with English professor John Tate. In the summer of 1979 Tate began his Shakespeare in London course. Other professors arranged tours abroad periodically.

## "TO OPEN A DOOR"

President Rice, speaking to students at the opening assembly in 1980, said, "We are here to give you a key to open a door for you later. You must assume responsibility. You must adapt to our standards." He meant academic as well as social standards, for Rice thought of himself as a teacher. "I still teach as I work through problems with student leaders," he said. "I have never lost sight of the fact that teaching is the central enterprise. . . . No one on campus can forget that." [29]

During the first two years of his presidency, Rice did not propose important academic changes—a decision that was validated when the visiting committee's report for the 1979 reaccreditation labeled "the outstanding faculty as a major strength." [30] Rice told the trustees that the faculty "had not succumbed to the runaway grade inflation" but rather had given the extra effort to make students "do solid work."[31]

By the spring of 1978 Rice was ready to establish a faculty ranking system. "We need to let people know who we are," he said.[32] The system established by the administration provided for consideration of experience and degrees with the rank of full professor reserved for those whose performance had been "characterized by the highest academic and professional achievement and by distinguished service to St. Mary's College for a minimum of twelve years." Tenure and rank were not interdependent. Inevitably, there were divergencies of opinion, but two thirds of the faculty expressed satisfaction with their assigned rank.[33] No one disagreed with the ranking of Mary Oliver Ellington, John Tate, and Mary Louise Jones as the first full professors. The students continued to refer to all faculty as "the teachers." In the long run, faculty ranking proved to be a good and necessary move. Rice told the trustees in January, 1980, that the change, which required "both diplomacy and firmness," resulted in "opportunity and growth potential" both for individuals and for the overall academic program.[34] Rice dropped his plan to rotate department heads on a three-year schedule when the rank and file of the faculty objected.[35] By 1982 the majority of the faculty had been engaged after Dean Miller's arrival in 1973. The mix was interesting. Listed in the catalog were more Ph.D.s but fewer years of experience than under previous administrations. The mix, although less international than in some periods, included natives of several other countries and degrees from European universities.

By 1982 the balance of control within the faculty had shifted away from a dwindling old guard. A strong middle guard of those who had been at the college for a decade carried a heavy burden of committee work. A vocal young guard, working hard to gain recognition, added zest. Tenured faculty numbered almost 32 percent, and earned doctorates in their fields were held by 36 percent of the faculty. Eight of the 26 women held doctorates. That year 11 of the faculty were pursuing research for publication.[36]

Diverse as they were in personality and background, most held in common a firm belief in the fundamental importance of good teaching. Those with doubts did not stay long, for the demands made on the St. Mary's faculty always were great. President Rice recognized that fact when he said at a faculty meeting, "This is an emotionally demanding environment."[37] The "golden chain"—that link to the long history of the place among the faculty—was not broken as late as the 1980s. Some doubted, however, that such devotion could possibly survive for another generation.

The first member of the old guard to retire under the Rice administration was Nancy White Stamey, who for 20 years and 40 plays delighted Raleigh audiences and enhanced the reputation of the college. She was the entire drama department from 1957 until Harry Callahan joined her in 1971. Nancy Stamey possessed an incredible ability to draw out talent. Her goal was not to prepare her students for Broadway, although at least two made it there, but to introduce young people to the joy of creative drama. Although she chose a variety of difficult plays, she never once received a bad review.[38] Stagestruck since her debut in a Christmas pageant at the age of six, Stamey studied drama and then traveled the old Chautauqua circuit. In Raleigh she organized the Children's Theatre. Nancy Stamey was a great favorite with the St. Mary's students, who dedicated a *Stagecoach* to her and presented her portrait to the college.[39] In 1977 the trustees conferred on her the title of professor emeritus, the first to be given.

In 1978 Mary Ruth Haig retired after 41 years on the music faculty. Haig told her students that music suggested colors to her. "The key of C is white," she said. "B flat is red." Possessing perfect pitch, she began teaching piano when she was 12, and as a young girl in Bloomfield, Indiana, she also played the piano for silent movies. Her master's degree was from the Julliard School of Music, and she had studied at Fontainbleu. She was a fine cellist, and she liked to paint with her artist mother. A brilliant pianist, Mary Ruth Haig served as chairman of the music department, 1965–1973, and as professor emeritus she continued to teach part time. She died August 31, 1979; her funeral service was held in the St. Mary's Chapel.[40]

In 1979 Mary Oliver Ellington retired, although no one thought of her as being that age. Hundreds of St. Mary's women remembered her crisp, well-organized lectures laced with whimsical humor. A native of Raleigh, she held a master's degree in entomology from North Carolina State, where she also completed course work for the doctorate and worked for several years executing drawings for publications. In addition to her years at St. Mary's, 1947–1952 and 1957–1979, she taught 20 years in public schools and was for three years dean of girls at Needham Broughton High School in Raleigh. Her calm, friendly manner and her quiet devotion to her church and to St. Mary's led students to seek her advice, and she served on both the honor board and the social board. She was appointed professor emeritus.[41]

Mary Oliver Ellington was the last of the faculty to have served as long as 25 years. The old guard then consisted of Margaret Williams, John Tate, Martha Stoops, and Lou Jones. Margaret Williams, with her usual good judgment, decided to keep abreast of the times and earned a doctorate in industrial arts education at North Carolina State University while teaching full time and making little to-do about the whole process. She was made a full professor in January, 1980. Hers was a one-woman art department until 1970, when a fine arts requirement was added for graduation from St. Mary's. Williams said, "I think all students have potential. Our goal is to educate both those who will be artists and those who will be art consumers."[42]

In 1982 she attended the opening at the National Portrait Gallery of an exhibition entitled "American Portraiture in the Grand Manner" that included the college's portrait of Bishop John Stark Ravenscroft. The full-length portrait painted in Philadelphia in 1830 by Jacob Eichholtz (1776–1842) was commissioned by Charles Peter Mallett of Fayetteville, from whom Aldert Smedes obtained it.[43]

The first members of the stalwart middle guard of the faculty to retire were Jessie Zepp, Patricia Connelly, and Helen Smith, all of whom left in 1980. An avid sailor, Patricia Connelly retired to New Bern.

Jessie Gardner Zepp taught Latin for 16 years. Hardly anyone remembered her part-time status because she was always available when needed; she worked so closely with the dean of students that Miss R. called her "my right hand." Her devotion to the college and to her students was as great as her love of "the beautiful precision of the Latin language." Zepp had taught at Enloe High School in Raleigh. She was acting chairman of the St. Mary's foreign language department, 1971–1972.[44]

Helen Smith decided during the summer of 1980 to take early retirement to the mountainside home in Montreat where she and her husband continued their classical bookbinding business. Upon leaving she said, "St. Mary's taught me who Helen Smith is. Before, I had seen myself as daughter, then as a minister's wife and mother."[45]

The women who joined the faculty during the Pisani and Rice administrations continued to provide for their students a variety of role models. Marjolijn de Jager Werman, who joined the foreign language department in 1970, spoke six languages, had been a fashion model, and was completing her doctorate in Chapel Hill. Born in Borneo of Dutch parents, she spent four years with her family in a Japanese prison camp during World War II. She completed her undergraduate work in the United States while mothering two children. Of women and careers, she said, "I cannot conceive of not being a part of 'the workforce' now."[46] After a leave in 1980, she decided not to return to Raleigh.

Elgiva Dundas Watson joined the faculty part time in 1971 while completing the doctorate in history in Chapel Hill. The daughter of a British naval officer and an American mother, she was educated in English boarding schools and at Duke University, where she earned a degree in mathematics. Her husband's business took her to Raleigh, and with all three children in school, she decided to take graduate work. "My friends thought me quite strange," she said. At St. Mary's, Giva Watson's forthright certitude soon made her a leader, and she was appointed head of the social studies department in 1973.[47]

Doreen Saxe went to Raleigh in 1964 for what was to be a one-year assignment at North Carolina State University for her husband, a nuclear scientist. Born in Northumberland, England, she was educated in England and France. She taught in France and then made her career doing parliamentary work in the British government service. She earned a doctorate at the University of North Carolina at Chapel Hill while teaching first at Meredith, and then at St. Mary's, and rearing two sons. In 1976–1977 she was on leave in France studying linguistics at the University of Aix-Marseille. She became head of the foreign language department in 1980, and her colleagues elected her their third representative to the board of trustees, 1979–1982.[48]

Mary Holden McNeill, also in Raleigh because her husband was on the faculty at State, also earned a doctorate while teaching at St. Mary's and mothering two children. McNeill believed in learning by experience, and in the spring of 1978 some 40 of her psychology students were doing supervised volunteer community work as class projects. Torn between teaching and mental health work, she did both for a while before leaving the college.[49]

Among the 13 new faculty appointed by the Pisani administration in 1971 were several women who were to remain for a number of years. Georgette Jeries Campbell, a Christian Arab born in Nazareth, Israel, was studying at Hebrew University and teaching Hebrew and Arabic when the president of Georgetown College in Kentucky offered her a scholarship. After graduate work, marriage, and two children, she was in Raleigh because of her husband's career. Before joining the science department, she had taught at four other colleges. When the children were older, Georgette Campbell resumed work on her doctorate and also taught a computer course in St. Mary's continuing education program. She was adviser to the international students at the college; she said, "I know how it feels to be in a strange land."[50]

Alice Zawadski Greiner, a transplanted northerner with degrees from Douglas College and Rutgers University, taught in the Raleigh public schools before she joined the science department. She said: "At St. Mary's I have the opportunity to teach the fundamentals of science to future professionals and to help them grow as informed, caring world citizens."[51] Her organizational skills made her a valuable member of faculty committees.

Two young career women who joined the faculty in 1972, Mary Lida Alexander and Ellen Anthe Birch, remained to become a part of the middle guard. Alexander completed her master's degree at Chapel Hill while teaching at St. Mary's. An all-around athlete who enjoyed teaching, she taught several sports and coached the basketball and golf teams. Ellen Birch, within three years and while still in her twenties, became the head of the mathematics department. A native of Raleigh, she completed her master's degree at North Carolina State University while teaching there and at St. Mary's and continued to teach at both institutions. Said Birch, often winner of the "super teacher" award, "I see no reason why a rigorous course cannot be taught so that students can understand it."[52]

By the 1980s the faculty always included mothers of young children and mothers-to-be. They made a variety of arrangements. Some, like Charlotte Koontz Jones of the English department, had children in nearby schools. Some, like Sandra Lynn Sappenfield, who became the swimming coach in 1976, took short maternity leaves. Some, like Candis Boyer Coxe, who taught French 1969–1971, took a few years out. She returned in 1980 and subsequently taught as a single parent. Some, like Ellen Anderson of the art department, taught part time. Some, like Karen Johnson Hillman of the foreign language department, planned to manage it all—mothering, full-time teaching, and graduate school. Always there were several young marrieds like Susan DeWalt Brown, who taught dance, and Catherine Williams Peacock and Dana Holton Jenkins of the mathematics department. The young wives and mothers had good rapport with students, and they added an important dimension to the faculty mix.

The students liked having alumnae as teachers. Suzanne Ishee, 1971 graduate, taught voice before pursuing a stage career. Karen Rose, 1974 graduate, taught drama while completing her master's degree. By the 1980s there were usually several highly motivated divorcees with doctorates who continued their research and writing while teaching. Therefore, any St. Mary's student could find a mentor among the diversity of the small faculty.

Students took an interest in the professional activities of the faculty. They knew that Karen Kalmar, who joined the social studies department in 1981 while completing her doctorate at Chapel Hill, was finishing her biography of Richard B. Russell and that Anna Wooten-Hawkins of the English department was a published poet. They were fascinated by the travels of Janice Carlton Coffey, the taxonomic botanist who was chairman of the science department. Her career took her to the USSR three times, and she had lectured in India, Australia, and Egypt.[53] Students also recognized Sharon Reed's musicianship.

The students enjoyed their male professors, and the feeling was mutual. By the fall of 1982 only John Tate among the men had been on the

Room presented by Dr. and Mrs. John O. Fulenwider, Jr. to house the
Thomas Wolfe Collection, 1976

faculty for more than ten years. Hamilton W. Fish, who joined the
mathematics department in 1972, retired in May, 1982, after a second
career at St. Mary's following retirement from the military. To the students, he was a wise counselor, to his department chairman, one "willing to disagree and often right."[54] Fish was appointed professor emeritus, the first person serving less than 20 years on the faculty to be thus
honored. In 1982 Paul Oehler Hudson also retired. After a long career
at several institutions, he taught psychology for four years as a visiting
professor.

Henry Richard Callahan became chairman of the drama department
in 1975 and in 1979 chairman of the new department of the performing
arts, including drama, dance, and music. With degrees from Rutgers
and Chapel Hill, he was in the city with the Raleigh Little Theatre.
Callahan viewed the St. Mary's theater (renamed Applause, Inc.) as "a
way to expand the horizons of a small college . . . involving the school
and community in a mutually beneficial way." He used townspeople

for the mature feminine roles as well as for the male roles to give his students the opportunity to work with experienced actors.[55] Nearly half of the students at the college became involved in some aspect of the dramatics program. The mime group, started by Karen Rose and later directed by Sandra Petersen Stallings, always had a full schedule of performances in local schools.

Another of the young men who became part of the strong middle guard was Wylie Savanas Quinn III, who joined the St. Mary's faculty in 1973 while completing a doctorate in religion at Duke University. He taught religion and philosophy and was appointed chairman of the department in 1979. Quinn's philosophy students found him either the most stimulating teacher they had encountered, or they found him incomprehensible. (He considered either opinion a compliment.) An accomplished organist, he was chairman of the music department, 1976–1979. He restructured that department, helped to institute the Smedes Parlor Concert Series, and to design a new organ for the chapel.[56]

The other males who joined the faculty also were already in the area. James Arthur McRae, a native of Red Springs who held degrees from the state universities in Chapel Hill and Raleigh, went to the mathematics department in 1974. With years of teaching experience on the junior college level, he was considered particularly patient and helpful. In 1977 John Chandler Hume, Jr., after completing a doctorate at Duke University, went to St. Mary's to teach world and European history. His years in India and Pakistan, where his father directed United States medical programs, brought him naturally to his interest in Asian and medical history. Steven William Esthimer joined the religion and philosophy department in 1979 while completing a doctorate at Duke. James Thaniel Faucette went to the same department the next year while working toward a doctorate at Duke.

The English department found four men already in the area. Charles Douglas Murray completed his doctorate at Chapel Hill while teaching at St. Mary's. James Barton Rollins, whose degrees were from Brigham Young and Duke universities, became a member of the English department in 1981 and served as chairman for two years. Thomas Michael Bauso, whose degrees were from Rutgers University, taught at St. Augustine's College in Raleigh before going to St. Mary's. Alfred Robert (Jack) Kraemer, a native of New York with degrees from Beloit College and the University of North Carolina at Chapel Hill, went from the faculty of the Patterson School in North Carolina to the St. Mary's library staff and then to the English department. Soon the male recruits were prominent on faculty committees.

Emmett White Windham and his musician wife chose to move to

Raleigh when they left the Boston area because they "wanted to live in a place active in the arts." They founded the Johnston County Choral Society. With degrees from the Cincinnati and New England conservatories of music, he went to St. Mary's in 1978.[57]

By the 1980s there were visible signs of the reversal of traditional roles. More than one faculty male admitted that his wife's career was a big factor in keeping him in the area. And often faculty men were seen escorting their children to the nearby public school and tending them after school.

## "A SPECIAL PLACE"

If the era of the 1970s and 1980s was an exciting time to be a young woman, it was also a difficult time to be young, and female, and vulnerable. The Rices knew that when they decided to move to Raleigh from another college for young women. John Rice once said, "I never take administrative problems home, but if I say to Grace that the freshmen in Smedes seem unhappy, she will reply, 'Let's have them to dinner and see what they need.'" She said, "But, it is the students who have given me so much."[58] They showed their appreciation of Grace Rice by inducting her into the Circle.

Those who know, say that the St. Mary's spirit emanates from the unchanging factors. They say that those are the close student-faculty relationship, the devotion of the students to one another, and the chapel.

The young women attested to their relationship to one another; the 1982 valedictorian spoke of "that special caring for one another—my mother says it was here when she was a student, and she can still feel it here."[59] Not everyone felt that way. That same year a student wrote in the *Muse*, "I feel sorry for [my classmates] as I feel sorry for everything stagnant."[60] In 1981–1982 students were from 22 states, and 15 international students were from 7 foreign countries. Despite the language difficulties, the international students assimilated into dormitory life. They found their American roommates extremely friendly, noisy, and untidy; the Americans were impressed by the ability and perseverance of the international students.

The young women at St. Mary's did not see themselves as grouped by class or race, but by personality type. As late as 1982 the majority group was labeled "the party type, always on the go and very preppy." However, those considered wild soon found themselves condemned by their peers. The nonsocializers usually, but not always, were serious students. The group of serious students was, in fact, much larger than most people realized because often serious students were socializers who simply had their priorities straight. There were enough subgroups for each one to find her place, and there was universal agreement that "St. Mary's girls stick together in times of crisis."[61]

The current wisdom of the 1980s said that women needed to develop a strong sense of identity apart from their men. Most St. Mary's students seemed to feel instinctively the importance of sharing the experience of being female. They knew that they had what Rhoda M. Dorsey, president of Goucher College, called "the best of both worlds—the supportive atmosphere of a woman's college situated near the social opportunities offered by the universities and the colleges for men."[62]

Because there were no prospective dates in the classrooms and because there was no dress code (except that shoes were required and curlers prohibited) student dress was casual. By 1982 the preppy look —pink and green all-cotton and monogrammed everything—was on the decline. By then sports outfits, mostly gym shorts even in unsuitable weather, were the costume for class. Doris Parker transformed the college bookstore into a veritable department store, and the students began to look as though they were in uniform. On a dressy weekend, the costume was reminiscent of the 1940s, including pearls.

The successful student government was a St. Mary's strength that John Rice recognized immediately. Soon, however, both he and Dean Elizabeth Jones agreed with student leaders that the system needed reorganization. The changes in student government, approved in the spring of 1978, set up a judicial board to handle the most serious cases and replaced the minor offense board with the dorm council. Essentially, that was a return to the system devised under the Stone administration because it placed all major offenses within the province of one board composed of ten elected students and three faculty members appointed by the president of the college. The dorm council, run by students with a faculty adviser, handled late returns and minor infractions. However, lying under any circumstances was a "J-board" offense, and the use of alcohol on campus remained a major offense. Jack Hume said of his service as a faculty member of J-board, "The students are very mature. They see the offender as having hurt the whole community, and, at the same time, they are very concerned about the individual."[63] A new hall council became a liaison group. Also, the house mothers, known as resident counselors, were given more authority; those women who befriended "their girls" were an important stabilizing force.[64] Some parents and alumnae felt that the younger students, although under much stricter rules than those in the college dormitories, had too much freedom. After discussing "the rules" at several board meetings, the trustees were reminded by one of their number, "The board chose the administration to run the daily life."[65]

In the second year of the Rice administration changes in the social rules encouraged mature decision making. Self-determining hours on weekends were instituted for those college students whose parents gave permission for such freedom. The number of "overnights" was no longer limited and, with parental permission, could be taken wherever the sign-out card indicated. Rules for signing in and out were strictly enforced as a means of keeping track of everyone.

Growing concern for the quality of student life outside the classroom led to the student development program initiated in the spring of 1981. Designed "not to tell the students what to do, but to let them see the choices," the program was an attempt to change the value neutrality so prevalent among young people to a commitment to individual integrity. The program included outside speakers and small group discussions, which were often led by members of the faculty and staff. The program, suggested by business manager Bernard W. Conrad, who chaired the first committee, was later directed by Deborah Shelley, who went to the college in 1977 as secretary to Elizabeth Jones and then became housing director until 1982, when her husband's career took her from Raleigh.

When Elizabeth Jones left St. Mary's in the summer of 1981 to pursue other interests, President Rice wrote, "The role of Dean of Students grew under her leadership."[66] Students said of her, "Dean Jones has been a personal friend to every student. . . . She has yet to be 'too busy,' and her office has been a retreat for many."[67]

Marcia Bell Jones of the faculty became the next dean of students. In announcing her appointment, Rice said, "She is an academician . . . with a full appreciation of the need for faculty involvement in student life."[68] Marcia Jones once said, "From the moment I came on campus, I knew I wanted to be at St. Mary's. There's something about the place— the trees, the buildings, the sense of all those women out there, those thousands of women educated within the grove."[69] A native of Pittsburgh, she was a graduate of Mount Holyoke College. As a student volunteer in Alaska she met W. Burns Jones, a medical missionary. Eventually his career in public health took them to Raleigh, where, while mothering three children, she took the master's degree at North Carolina State and the doctorate at Chapel Hill. She taught English at St. Mary's, 1973–1975, while in graduate school, taught at State, and then returned to St. Mary's in 1977. She succeeded John Tate as chairman of the English department, serving for two years.

Marcia Jones approached her new position "with a belief that the best environment for young women between the ages of 16 and 20 is one balanced between freedom and discipline." She admitted that "the balance is sometimes precarious." Although an ambitious and strong-minded woman herself, Jones said, "The feminist movement polarized women; that was a mistake. I want our women to be perfectly comfortable with their feeling that men are okay and with their love for little children. We cannot take that away from them."[70] To that end she encouraged the campus clubs to undertake volunteer projects working with children.

The college administration struggled with the difficulty of establishing the parameters of freedom and responsibility. During his first year as president sociologist Rice had said, "The traditional role of women is now shattered, but society has not yet decided what the new role is."[71] By 1981 he was ready to declare, "The times have created an illusion of greater maturity than exists among our students."[72] At the same time, he was ready to commit the institution to what had been all along a primary goal of the feminist movement—to help women develop self-knowledge and its end product, self-confidence. In assembly talks he told the students, "Your task from now on is to make your own decisions about your morals, your friends, your goals. Discover who you are. . . . Seek help. We will love you whether you succeed or fail. . . . but you must face your mistakes yourself."[73]

College life in the eighties placed unprecedented pressures upon young women. With some 50,000 college students in the Raleigh area, social life was fast paced and relationships often casual. A "real relationship" meant early sexual pressure that was hard for "the truly liberated" young woman to resist. Coping with peer pressure regarding the use of tobacco, alcohol, and other drugs required maturity. Smoking was popular, but it was permissible to refrain on the grounds of health. "Doing drugs" was not a major problem among St. Mary's students.

Alcohol was the universal collegiate problem in America by 1979. The Raleigh *News and Observer*, giving results of surveys at universities in the area, reported that 77 percent of students of both sexes drank (mostly beer and wine). The alarming statistics were that 26 percent of the students called themselves "heavy drinkers" (compared to 10 percent in the overall population) and that 15 percent said that they had "a drinking problem."[74] Dropping by Zack's up Hillsborough Street for "happy hour" late Friday afternoon was a relatively harmless pastime, but the beer was plentiful and the music earsplitting. Chapel Hill was still the place to be on football weekends. Students admitted, "We depend too much upon alcohol for our social life."[75]

St. Mary's authorities faced the problem squarely through the student development program, which was continued with a student-faculty committee headed by the chaplain. The new director of housing and student development was Pia Price. A native of Italy with degrees from Duke and North Carolina State, she was experienced in working with young people. The response of the students to Mercedes McCambridge, the actress and author who spoke on campus during alcohol awareness week, revealed their anxieties. By 1982 signs of maturity regarding the use of alcohol were emerging.

Chief guardian of the health of the students was Chauncey Royster, who took the appointment as college physician in 1954 as a "temporary" assignment and stayed through 1978. He and his alumna wife, Phoebe Harding, were very much a part of the St. Mary's community.[76] Life in the infirmary, located on the first floor of the old bishop's house, was supervised during the Rice administration by head nurse Gladys M. Jones with the assistance of nurse Betsy Wicker and others.

Whatever changes each year wrought in the institution, the memories of their own special years remain forever with St. Mary's women: long talks with best friends . . . "pigging out at hall parties" . . . jogging around Cameron park . . . the Beach Boys or Earth, Wind, and Fire blaring from 101 stereos . . . *General Hospital* (an afternoon class was "the pits") . . . the Cold Cuts . . . the Christmas party in the parlor . . . flowers on Valentine's Day . . . "catchin' a few rays" between classes in April . . . the giant tulip trees in bloom . . . parents' weekend . . . spring festival . . . the Sea Saints . . . chapel outside . . . the Circle and Beacon walks . . . SGA induction . . . graduation.

A "new tradition" was the first lighting o' the green in December, 1981. Bright bulbs, as big as balloons, festooned the tall pine near the chapel, and gifts of food for the needy were piled beneath the tree. The granddaughters club placed 492 luminaries (lighted candles glowing through paper bags) around the circle—one for each member of the student body. Apart in the grove shone two more placed there in memory of Georgia Kinsey, class of 1981, and Elizabeth Marlowe, class of 1982.[77] The scene was described as "breathtakingly beautiful from Hillsborough Street"; it was a gift to the community.

The old traditions were kept at graduation. The marshals wore long, white dresses, and at the close of graduation ceremonies the newly elected chief marshal dropped the traditional handkerchief. One who had been a member of the campus community for longer than anyone else came from retirement in 1982 to perform a rite that became "a new tradition" in the 1970s. After the dropping of the handkerchief, Casper Lilly ceremoniously closed the front doors of Smedes Hall to signify the end of another academic year. Across 51 years Lilly was, as the students wrote in dedicating to him the 1974 *Stagecoach*, "a living part of the true St. Mary's spirit."

The chapel remained a special part of the heritage treasured by each generation. The bell tower erected in 1982 near the west entrance added authenticity, for it was an adaptation of a tower designed by

Granddaughters Club, 1977

Honors Convocation, 1982

Richard Upjohn in the 1850s. The tower, given as a memorial to Ann Renee Smith Ehrgott by her family and friends, was dedicated on alumnae day.[78] Although they loved the chapel, many students admitted to being "not very religious." A 1980 survey showed only about 18 percent of the students as perceiving that chapel services changed their lives in any way. Those saw the chapel as "a refuge that brought me closer to God," or as "a symbol of the togetherness that changed me." In her paper reporting that research, a student wrote: "The chapel is not fully appreciated until after one's graduation when it becomes a symbol of the unity and close friendship so characteristic of our St. Mary's society."[79]

The question of required chapel attendance was debated once again in the winter of 1982, but with considerably less rancor than in 1971. The vestry met the issue early on by presenting a panel discussion in assembly; the tone of the meeting was calm and reasonable. President Rice explained that students did not make chapel attendance policy but indicated his willingness to take the matter to the trustees "for careful consideration." Over the years Rice had expressed his belief that required chapel was one of the strengths of St. Mary's. And over the years the Reverend Starke S. Dillard, Jr., who had become college chaplain in January, 1977, had expressed his wish that attendance could be voluntary. However, neither gave an opinion at the meeting. Of 339 students polled by secret ballot "a surprising 56.5 percent" voted to continue requiring attendance under the honor system at the Tuesday night service and on Sunday mornings for those on campus.[80]

Dillard, known to the students as "Mr. D.," went to the college from pastorates in Texas and Ohio. The son of alumna Alice Walker Dillard, he grew up in Greensboro and was a graduate of the University of North Carolina at Chapel Hill and the Virginia Theological Seminary. He had served several parishes in North Carolina.[81] He and his wife Angela lived on campus, and he taught in the religion department. In the fall of 1982 Dillard became the school's first full-time chaplain. Dillard said:

My work here is so basic. It is beginning to dawn on these young women that they do not necessarily have to be an appendage to a man. . . . [They] find the future both exciting and frightening . . . I am here to help them sort out their problems. I like being with them because they are so honest. . . . This is my parish. We share the happy times and the sad times.[82]

The St. Mary's College Chapel in the early 1970s began to operate like a parish of 500 members with a vestry of some 20 young women elected by the outgoing vestry. Election was considered an honor; each of the four classes was represented. Student government leaders served as crucifers, and the vestry elected the cupbearers. A volunteer altar guild and a projects committee brought to over 60 the number of young women willing to give the time required to operate the chapel program and community projects. Thus, the school continued the tradition of training future leaders of the Episcopal church. Furthermore, 1980 statistics showed that about 20 percent of the St. Mary's graduates not originally Episcopalians eventually changed to that denomination.[83]

When he went to the presidency of St. Mary's, John Rice, a lifelong Episcopalian, saw as an immediate priority the revitalizing of the college's relationship to the church. During his first year he attended the conventions of the five Carolina dioceses, and he visited the national headquarters of the church. In December, 1977, the bishops of the Carolinas went to the college for "a very fruitful meeting."[84] Bishop Fraser was the 1982 commencement speaker, and by the time of his retirement, the relationship between the college and the church was revitalized. The St. Mary's acolytes and marshals were invited to serve at his investiture by the Right Reverend Robert Whitridge Estill, D.D., who succeeded Fraser as Bishop of North Carolina.

Strengthening ties with the Episcopal church was a priority with Henry Read, who became director of college development in February, 1977. For two years, 1980–1982, Emma Jane McDermott held the new position of director of annual funds and the church relations program. For "E. J.," the wife of an Episcopal clergyman and a woman whose varied experience included a term in the South Carolina legislature, visiting the dioceses was just renewing old friendships.

The individual churches did begin to invest more in St. Mary's, as Fraser had predicted they would once they became program-oriented. Total church support of 1981–1982 was just under $61,000. Although that was double the support received for 1977–1978, it amounted to not quite 2 percent of the college's operating budget. St. John's, Fayetteville, and St. Paul's, Winston-Salem, gave special gifts. St. John's, a longtime supporter of the college, gave matching funds for capital indebtedness reduction and funds for an endowed scholarship,[85] and St. Paul's generously supported the Smedes Hall restoration and the general scholarship fund.[86] The Diocese of North Carolina Scholarship Fund was established with over $52,000 raised by the venture in mission program, and Bishop Fraser added $25,000 from his contingency fund.

By the 1980s the future of private church-related educational institutions seemed both more uncertain and brighter than in many years—uncertain because of the economic outlook and brighter because of the signs of a return to the eternal verities. There was a renewed appreciation of the importance of the diversity supplied by the some 800 church-related institutions of higher education. These, most of them with less than 1,000 students, comprised 40 percent of the private colleges and universities and 20 percent of the total number, and they enrolled 10 percent of the nation's students.[87] There was also a renewed appreciation of the value of the liberal arts education in a scientific age. Van Quinn, who became the fourth faculty representative to the St. Mary's board of trustees, said:

Our task . . . is not simply, or even primarily, to prepare the student for a vocation, but . . . to join with the student in her own search for truth, and to help her confront truth in her own life. A liberal arts college is by definition a community which seeks with all the power and clarity it can command to embody the Good, the True, and the Beautiful. . . . A community which seeks truth through all avenues of human inquiry and activity acknowledges both the unity and the diversity of truth.[88]

## "PEAKS AND VALLEYS"

John Rice once promised to write a book about the joy and the pain of life as a college president; his title would be *Peaks and Valleys*. "Every president," he said, "has four constituencies—the students, the faculty, the alumnae, and the board of trustees. Each exerts different pressures."[89]

It was not Rice's administrative style to make drastic immediate personnel changes. In April, 1977, he changed Dean Miller's title to dean of the college to indicate that he was to be in command when the president was out of town.[90] Faculty committees were reorganized to emphasize long-range planning, and the department heads met weekly with the dean. Administrative relations with the faculty were strengthened as Rice insisted that the trustees address the problems resulting from the fact that "the St. Mary's salary scale was quite seriously out of line with virtually all other comparable private schools."[91] By 1982 progress was evident. Also, the Peggy Crevensten Dukes Memorial Fund was established in 1977 by trustee William W. Dukes, Jr., and his wife in memory of their daughter Margaret (1943–1974), a member of the class of 1963. Designated for faculty programs and activities enhancing the quality of instruction, it met a real need and raised faculty morale.

In 1980 Rice tightened the administrative organization with the appointment of Faye Barkley Fussell as his full-time assistant. She coordinated the growing number of special events on campus and the continuing education program, served as liaison with a number of groups, and on the president's advisory council composed of the major administrators. She had been secretary to Dean Morrison and then to the president of the college.

When Rice went to St. Mary's, he found Registrar Thomas H. Johnson and his small staff working to complete the safeguarding of the permanent student records through microfilming. On March 18, 1980, Johnson succumbed to heart disease. He was 53. Betty Mulder Petway, who had worked with him for nine years, was appointed registrar. She continued to give sound advice to students and directed the computerization of the records.

Another Rice appointee was Robert T. Simpson, who became director of admissions in August, 1979, upon Susan Carroll Alexander's resignation. He had been associate director of undergraduate admissions at Duke University. That summer the admissions office moved into spacious quarters in Smedes Hall across the hallway from the parlor.[92] The move gave prospective students and their parents a first impression that conveyed at the same time the history of the place and the vitality of present campus life. The admissions office added an assistant director, a position first held by alumna Lou White. Upon her resignation, Barbara Williams Craig, a graduate of Mary Baldwin College and a former teacher, was appointed in August, 1980. By 1980 the long-predicted enrollment crunch was a reality, and the admissions directors and a succession of young alumnae working as recruiters began to travel extensively, both out of state and in North Carolina.[93] Conferences on campus for out-of-state school guidance counselors and Simpson's activities on the southern association's college admissions council broadened recognition of St. Mary's. Intensive recruiting produced a larger number of applications, despite the declining number of young people in the population, and despite inflation.

The college was then engaged in a determined effort not to sacrifice quality for quantity. The quantitative factor was reduced somewhat when remodeling left Smedes Hall with fewer beds. By 1980 the business manager was budgeting for about 490 students, 415 of them boarders, no less than 60 percent of them college students. Such careful management meant that acceptable standards could be maintained. The continued acceptance of St. Mary's graduates into over 50 recognized baccalaureate institutions attested to that fact and to the successful supervision of the transfer process by the guidance office.

John Rice inherited as business manager of the college B. W. Conrad, who understood that despite his planned economies the financial position of the institution remained precarious. Survival was the immediate objective of many colleges for women then; of the 281 in 1968 only 122 existed in 1978.[94] Cause for rejoicing was the successful completion in the fall of 1976 of the capital funds campaign under the chairmanship of trustee Thad Eure, Jr. The $750,000 goal was exceeded, leaving the college with a manageable long-term indebtedness of $1.2 million.

In May, 1980, the 1975 pay discrimination suit was decided in favor of the college. The U.S. Equal Employment Opportunity Commission contended that the institution practiced sexual discrimination against 18 women custodial workers and 10 (past and present) female heads of academic departments and asked back pay and damages of about $300,000. Federal Judge Franklin T. Dupree, Jr., upheld the college's claim that the male custodial employees performed different and heavier work from that assigned the females and that factors other than sex determined the salaries of all academic department heads.[95] The ranking system and salary scale instituted by the Rice administration were in operation by the time of the trial.

By 1979 the financial position of the college was pronounced "sound" by Board Chairman Eugene B. Hardin, Jr.[96] Conrad had, as John Rice noted, "consistently provided the glue which holds St. Mary's together and in a positive operating posture."[97] The annual budget had been balanced for eight years and the capital debt reduced from $2.2 million in 1972 to $530,000 in 1979. Tuition and fees were kept below inflation rates. As the debt was reduced, operating funds became available for campus improvements such as the renovation of Pittman Auditorium and the music building and the sandblasting of the language-art building. In 1978 the college bought a small piece of property adjacent to the campus. The computer center, to be installed in Ragland during the summer of 1983, was financed from accumulated operating funds.

By 1982 funds were becoming available for the beautification of the grounds. Landscaping of the quadrangle in front of the library was funded by special gifts,[98] and long-range plans were designed "to accentuate the beauty of this historic campus."[99] In 1977 Lewis Hatley, superintendent of buildings and grounds, retired. For 30 years he made life on campus more comfortable for everyone, for he always found a way to build or repair whatever was needed. After Hatley's retirement, maintenance of the grounds was contracted to the firm already maintaining the buildings and campus security. Windel Crawley, retired from the U.S. Navy and living in the area, became manager of buildings and grounds. Several of the longtime custodial staff remained. Two of those, Josephine Williams and Roscoe Pettiford, had seen many years of changes in daily life at St. Mary's.

Astute business management and an expanded development program that produced new endowments enabled the college to plan to pay in full the bank mortgage by June, 1983, seven years ahead of schedule, and also to repay money borrowed from the endowment funds in 1975 and 1978. The policy of returning to principal 20 percent of the annual earnings on new endowments helped to bring the endowment to almost $3 million by the end of 1982. Only the long-term government loans on Penick, Cruikshank, and Smedes were outstanding. The campus was valued at over $11 million.[100]

Fund raising was expanded after Henry M. Read became director of college development. A native of Warrenton, he was a graduate of Hampden–Sydney College. His experience included administrative positions at his alma mater and at the University of North Carolina at Chapel Hill, The Citadel, and Sullins College. All fund raising and college publicity were handled through Read's office with the aid of Jane Rabon. The first full-time director of college relations was Susan Cranford Ross, 1977–1982, who laid an excellent foundation for her successors, Linda Howell Weiner and Marian Green.

The 1981 report of consultants labeled Read "a true professional" whose job was complicated by the fact that "St. Mary's may not be viewed by the majority of its constituents as needing considerable gift support."[101] By 1981–1982 total gift support from all sources was up to $670,215. But it had been, Read said, "an agonizingly slow" process.[102]

A new source of support, both financial and moral, was the St. Mary's Parents Association organized during parents weekend in 1977. John Rice told parents that the college needed their general input and their help in recruitment as well as their financial support, that they were "a vital part of the well being of St. Mary's."[103] Each autumn nearly 500 parents gathered in Raleigh for a weekend of social activities and to attend classes with their daughters and talk with the faculty. An active council governed the association and planned an annual phonathon. In 1981–1982 parental participation was 62 percent and nonalumnae parental gifts amounted to $46,000. The goal for the next year was $70,000 because of a special challenge gift. Even before organization of the association, interested parents helped to make possible in 1977 the desperately needed renovation of West Rock.[104]

The first big financial project of the Rice administration was the $1.085 million renovation of Smedes Hall accomplished during 1979–1980 under the terms of a $636,000 long-term, low-interest federal loan for energy conservation. No major renovation of the 1835 building had been undertaken after the facade and wings were added in 1909. The parlor had been handsomely redecorated in 1978 by the trustees' building and grounds committee. All high school boarders lived in Smedes. While they considered it great fun to be there, they found it uncomfortable because of the antiquated heating and plumbing systems. The business manager had lent contingency funds for the complete rewiring of the building during the summer of 1979. The development office, with a selective approach to some 40 good friends of the college who were asked to give $10,000 or more,[105] raised the funds for a complete renovation designed to produce substantial savings in the annual budget for energy despite the new air conditioning. A $10,000 grant was received because Smedes Hall was entered in the National Register of Historic Places.[106]

## "WITH CONFIDENCE AND EXCITEMENT"

The Rice administration realized early that a major capital funds campaign would be necessary. It was "highly dangerous," said Rice, to be so dependent on student fees.[107] By the January, 1980, meeting of the trustees, the president was convinced that the time was right for long-range planning. Furthermore, the visiting committee for the 1979 reaccreditation had made such a recommendation. Rice said to the board:

We are now ready for a new decade of service. By all acceptable standards—outside evaluation, student evaluation, admissions applications, alumnae support, community awareness, and fiscal soundness—we are alive, strong, and well.[108]

A development consulting firm advised a period of careful preparation for the campaign, and by the spring of 1981 an internal committee composed of administrators and faculty and a committee of trustees were setting goals and determining needs.[109] The basic planning document was accepted by the board in May, 1982, and a capital campaign steering committee chaired by trustee Smedes York was appointed.[110] The campaign of the 1980s was seen by the trustees as one to provide a permanent endowment large enough to strengthen the operating budget and, thus, the academic program, and it was hoped that a fine arts center could be the major capital improvement.

Board Chairman Eugene B. Hardin, Jr., agreed with President Rice that the trustees should concentrate on policy, financial soundness, and future planning, leaving internal matters to those on campus.[111] The board committees, which at Rice's suggestion included faculty and students, prepared reports for the three meetings each year.

Greater commitment from the alumnae was an imperative, as John Rice soon discovered. The round of visits to alumnae clubs made by the Rices during their first year did much to increase alumnae interest. The revised constitution adopted by the alumnae association on April 22, 1977, established new areas of alumnae involvement, such as recruitment, and created new association leadership positions. Led by an acquisitions committee, alumnae clubs became active once again in refurbishing public areas of the buildings, and a number of valuable gifts were received.

Alumnae reunions became weekend affairs with activities both on and off campus. President Emeritus and Mrs. Stone always attended.

The 50th reunions had grown; the class of 1929 remained intact until 1979. In 1980 Anna Clark Gordon returned to observe her 75th anniversary. The oldest alumna was Lizzie Ashe Flint, who died at 99 in 1977; Elizabeth Montgomery died at that age in 1981. The young alumnae attended their class reunions in greater numbers than ever before. The graduates of the sixties said, "St. Mary's is really much the same with so many good things added."[112]

Intergenerational ties remained strong. The 1976–1977 granddaughters club listed 30 granddaughters, 11 great-granddaughters, and 5 great-great-granddaughters. In 1980 an alumna saw two granddaughters, the fourth generation at St. Mary's, graduate; and a commencement marshal could count 15 relatives at St. Mary's over six generations.[113]

The St. Mary's Alumnae Association celebrated its 100th anniversary on alumnae day, April 21, 1979. The association's objectives remained those announced by the 50 women who founded the association June 19, 1879. They wrote:

Our object is not only to maintain a friendly interest in each other's welfare, and to preserve a cordial affection for our alma mater, but also to give tangible expression to these sentiments.[114]

In celebration of the centennial the association sponsored lectures and published an alumnae directory. Also, a college motto was selected, and three gift societies were organized.

The series of lectures and classroom discussions was designed to expose students to career possibilities. The alumnae lecturers were: Nancy Correll Roberts, author of over 20 books; Jacquelin Nash Jenkins, painter and sculptor; Marie Watters Colton, the first St. Mary's alumna to serve in the North Carolina legislature; Jane Hurt Yarn, a member of the three-member presidential Council on Environmental Quality; Elizabeth Gordon Taylor, who delivered the chapel sermon; and Roberta Blue, a statistician.

The alumnae association conducted a search for a motto "to represent the unchanging strengths of St. Mary's." The selection, made by a committee from the 20 final entries, was *Scientia Fides Amicitia* (Knowledge, Honor, Friendship), which was suggested by Mary Lawrence Hicks, 1978 graduate. The alumnae directory of the some 8,000 known living women was made possible by years of past work on records by Jane Rabon's office. Three gift societies, established "to honor those alumnae and friends who cherish the special qualities St. Mary's offers," were named The Smedes Associates, The Order of the Grove, and The 1842 Society.[115]

The annual fund continued to be an essential source of operating

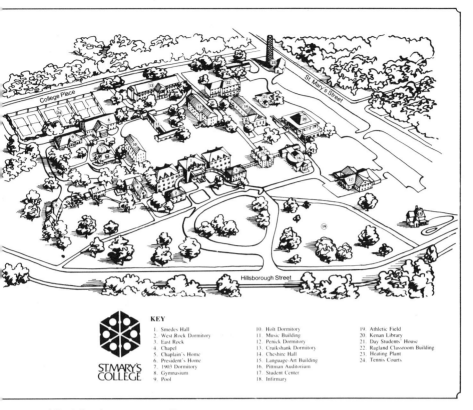

Map of St. Mary's campus, 1982

funds. The 1977–1978 challenge to excellence fund of $70,000, made possible by a small group of donors,[116] encouraged new and increased gifts and brought that year's alumnae annual giving to $107,483. By 1981–1982 total alumnae gifts to all funds was $242,609; and alumnae participation was 38.6 percent, a figure that placed the college in the top 1 percent of two-year colleges in the nation.

Jane Rabon left St. Mary's in February, 1981, to become assistant director of the annual giving program at the University of North Carolina at Chapel Hill. With a high degree of professionalism and what John Rice called "a special and rare love for St. Mary's" she served under three college presidents and with nine presidents of the alumnae association. Recognizing her work as editor of alumnae publications, the college established the Jane Augustine Rabon *Belles* Award to go to the student member of the *Belles* staff who each year contributed most to the excellence of the paper.[117]

Sterling H. Remer, who had worked with Rabon for three years, became alumnae director in May, 1981, and served until the next summer when her husband was called to be rector of Calvary Church, Tarboro. She worked to interest the younger alumnae and to educate current students "to understand what they could mean to St. Mary's."[118] The annual alumnae phonathon involved nearly everyone on campus as well as many alumnae. Each night excitement mounted as goals were reached and then surpassed amid cheers and the awarding of prizes to the most successful callers. Also, alumnae bequests were made to the college.[119]

In 1982 there were some 40 alumnae clubs. The New York club was reactivated, and there were several in South Carolina and one in Atlanta, Georgia. When Margaret E. Burgwyn, a graduate of the St. Mary's high school and college, became alumnae director in December, 1982, the new job description placed great emphasis on the development of alumnae relations.[120]

Volunteerism was still strong, even among the younger alumnae. A student of the eighties said, "I'll do some volunteer work even if I have a career. I grew up with the idea that every educated woman does it." Alumna Reba White Williams, Wall Street executive turned freelance writer, told the students, "I will not accept the feminist pressure against volunteerism, this depreciation of all the work for which women have not been paid, except in the most important coin of all— satisfaction, the joy of contribution. . . ."[121] St. Mary's in 1979 awarded an honorary associate in arts degree to Jane Bourne Long in recognition of her volunteer services to St. Mary's and the Diocese of North Carolina. Organizations made the necessary adjustments to the new woman. The Raleigh junior league in 1981 had its "day-actives" and its "professionals"; 52 percent of the 389 active members held full-time jobs.[122] St. Mary's alumnae of all ages continued to be cited for their volunteer work with news of their contributions appearing in the alumnae magazine. Caroline Whitehead Cobb was chosen 1978 woman of the year by the Goldsboro Jaycees and Jaycettes. Josephine Ehringhaus Ayers's volunteer job with the Alabama Shakespeare Festival became a career as the festival gained national attention. She traced her love of Shakespeare to classes under John Tate and Louise Cell.[123]

Graduates of the forties and fifties reported the usual grandchildren, but by then they often reported graduate degrees and all kinds of new careers for themselves. Josephine Gaither Jones had sold her first novel to *Good Housekeeping* and owned a publishing company. Attorney Nelson Blount Crisp was the first woman to serve as a commissioner on the state Board of Corrections, 1973–1977.

A 1960 graduate and an alumna trustee, Judith Metcalfe von Seldeneck, was the 1982 commencement speaker. She had been executive assistant to Sen. Walter F. Mondale before starting in Philadelphia a successful employment agency for professional women. To the graduating class and in an earlier article she summed up the feminine dilemma:

Right now is the most exciting time to be a career woman. . . . [But] the tough question still remains to be answered. That is, how do you have it all? How do you successfully combine a meaningful career, marriage, family and outside interests? [124]

Susan Ehringhaus, 1964 graduate, said, "Women still pay an extra price for excellence." After graduating first in her law class at Carolina, private practice, and work with the antitrust division of the federal Department of Justice, she returned to Chapel Hill as assistant to the chancellor of the university. [125] An alumna trustee, Susan was the third generation of her family to serve on the St. Mary's board.

Other young alumnae held top-level jobs. The speaker for alumnae day, 1980, was Lockhart Follin-Mace, 1962 graduate, who despite an accident that left her with paraplegia, completed graduate work and became director of the Governor's Advocacy Council for Persons with Disabilities. The 1978 baccalaureate was delivered by Elizabeth (Ibba) Peden, a 1971 graduate and the first St. Mary's woman to be ordained to the Episcopal priesthood. She said that the long talks about theology with Frank Pisani and Bob Hobgood were instrumental in her decision to enter the priesthood. [126]

Alumna Lee Henessee spoke at the college in 1981 and was billed by the local paper as "a Wall Street whiz" earning at 28 about $140,000. [127] A 1971 graduate, Lucy Hancock Bode, was appointed in 1982 deputy secretary of the Department of Human Resources, making her at 30 responsible for the daily operation of the largest department in state government. [128] A 1972 graduate, Dianne Cates-Cantrell won her third Emmy in 1980 for her television camera work. She said, "I had to set higher goals than the men because I had to prove a few things before anyone would take me seriously." [129] Terry Bennett, 1980 high school graduate, proved her mettle when she became the only woman member of the premiere competition team of the army's famed Golden Knights skydivers. [130]

## MANY DIFFERENT PATHS

St. Mary's women were following many different paths by the eighties. As they listened to the alumnae speakers, some of the students began to realize that they were to be the transitional generation—the women who would seek the new middle ground for their sex. Others were sure that they "could have it all" and on their own terms. Some faced the future with confidence and excitement, some with trepidation. In essays written in the early 1980s on "How I Feel About Being A Woman Today," the students revealed their hopes and their fears. For nearly every young woman, marriage sometime was an accepted fact. A very few said that marriage would be enough. They wrote:

Raising children properly will be challenge enough for me. The most important aspect of our future is who will be in charge of it. How our children are raised is important!

I just love being a woman. People say that we are the weaker sex, but we can control our men. . . . Men cannot do without us, and we cannot do without them. So we are already equal in some respects!

Many of the young women wrote of their mixed feelings:

Sure, it's complicated and chances are it will become worse, but I would rather have a complex, interesting life than a dull, boring life. But, I would like to go back to some old-fashioned ideas about dating.

I feel caught in the middle. . . . The problem for me is that I want men to open doors for me, but I want my rights, too. I suppose if it came right down to it, I would choose my rights over my femininity.

Sometimes it is frightening to think that I have to take care of myself, but I would much rather not find myself at 40 hunched over a cup of coffee, wearing a flannel bathrobe and curlers, wondering where life passed me by.

It scares me no end. . . . I'm 20 and I don't even know what I am going to do with my life. Years ago women just conformed to society, got married and raised children. That has been what I have wanted to do also, but in today's world you are looked down upon for dreams like I have (or had). . . . The doors have opened for women. The only problem for me is finding the open door. I think being a woman today is too demanding. I hate being a woman today. I just want a big family.

A surprising number of the writers put careers first; marriage was to be postponed, maybe decided against. They agreed, "It is wonderful to be a woman today!"

My career is the most important factor in my life. . . . Being a successful person right now is most important. . . . I realize that no one is going to do it for me. Women must be willing to work harder than ever before. . . . It is exciting.

Women can go as far as their determination and intelligence will take them. . . . Maybe soon there will be a woman president. . . . I am grateful to the women of past generations who fought so that my life could be like this.

The majority saw themselves as "doing it all" and reaping great satisfaction. They took a realistic view of some of the difficulties ahead.

However, they had little conception of the problems involved in finding good day care for children. Nor did they understand the career damage sustained by women who "take a few years out" to care for their small children. They wrote:

The only way an educated woman can be "truly fulfilled" is to have both a career and a family. . . . I am not afraid of men as competitors, but of the forces against all of us.

My mother has encouraged me to be "whatever I want to be." I think that along with wishing me success and happiness, she is dreaming of what she could have been.

A woman has to have the children, feed them, get them off to school, send the husband off to work with his cup of coffee in hand, and she has to be at work by 9:00 herself.

Women are free . . . but the role of men must change along with the changing role of women. This is already beginning to happen, but it will be a long, slow road as with the road to equal rights.

I am my own person. I can be an ambitious go-getter and still be feminine. I think I have struck that balance. Being a woman today is a challenge I gladly accept.

They would choose many different paths—the new St. Mary's generations. Nearly every one of them, however, would agree with the one who, upon leaving to accept a prestigious scholarship, wrote, "No matter what, I'll always be a St. Mary's girl."

And when they returned to visit St. Mary's, they would hope to find an institution still with a sense of mission, and a pride in tradition, and with the ability to change enough to meet the needs of succeeding generations of young women.

# APPENDIX A

*Memorial Windows, St. Mary's College Chapel*

The Angel of Annunciation window above the altar was given in memory of her mother by Sarah Smedes Erwin. The inscription reads: "In loving memory of Sarah Lyell Smedes, beloved wife of Aldert Smedes, D.D., and daughter of Thomas Lyell, D.D. 'For all Thy Saints, who from their Labors Rest.' March 27, 1813–April 11, 1889."

The side windows in the chancel are memorials to Fannie Dumas Hazard and Gioacchino Pisani given by Harriet Hazard Pisani and Frank Warren Pisani.

The triple window in the west transept is a memorial to Ernest Cruikshank, August 19, 1879–October 1, 1922, faculty member and business manager. At the request of St. Mary's alumnae it was moved from the chapel of the closed Columbia Institute in Tennessee.

The east transept window is in memory of Thomas Atkinson Lay, October 28, 1910–January 27, 1915, son of the rector of St. Mary's. Given by the Lay family, the window was executed in England. On each side of the east transept entrance are memorial windows to faculty members. One is to both William Conrad Guess, September 5, 1889–April 17, 1964, and his wife Evadna Jane Guess, April 11, 1912–July 4, 1959. The other is a memorial to Russell Broughton, July 5, 1894–February 7, 1969.

The window above the east entrance is a memorial to Laura Placida Clark given by friends and her classmates of 1914. The lotus, the child angels, and the ship symbolize her years as a missionary to China, where she died in 1948.

The first window on the west wall of the nave (on the right when leaving the chancel) is in memory of Stella Shaw, alumna, teacher, and organist during the Smedes administrations. Next are the window for alumna Jean Graham Ellis Rossell, October 9, 1860–May 25, 1897, and the window in memory of Mary Johnson Iredell, 1838–1919, alumna, teacher, and lady principal. The other window on the west wall was inscribed in memory of Anne Saunders, April 26, 1837–May 29, 1906, who was the infirmary matron and parlor hostess. Described when installed as "of Tiffany glass," it was executed by two New York women, M. Y. Stone and Julia P. Wickham.

East windows in the nave memorialize three alumnae who taught at St. Mary's: Elizabeth Dancy Battle, November 12, 1865–November 9, 1899; Nannie Belvin, April 3, 1882–December 15, 1904; and Martha Austin Dowd, November 1, 1866–July 27, 1925. The other east window is a memorial to Gertrude Sullivan, January 20, 1888–August 6, 1909, a student of 1903–1906. The Battle and Sullivan windows also were executed in Tiffany glass by Stone and Wickham.

# APPENDIX B

*Members of the St. Mary's Board of Trustees with dates of first election as listed in the college catalogs*

1897–

Right Reverend J. B. Cheshire, D.D.
Col. T. F. Davidson
Reverend McNeely DuBose
W. A. Erwin
Col. Wharton Green
Charles E. Johnson
Reverend Julian E. Ingle, D.D.
Reverend F. J. Murdock, D.D.
Reverend Robert Strange, D.D.
Right Reverend A. A. Watson, D.D.

1900–05

Right Reverend Ellison Capers, D.D.
Right Reverend Junius M. Horner, D.D.
Reverend M. M. Marshall, D.D.
Reverend T. M. N. George
Reverend E. N. Joyner
Reverend Churchill Satterlee
Dr. R. H. Lewis
W. A. Erwin
Richard H. Battle
Col. John W. Atkinson
Dr. F. L. Frost
John R. London
Silas McBee
Reverend Robert B. Drane

K. P. Battle, Jr.
Reverend W. P. Witsell
Reverend H. J. Mikell
Reverend T. C. Wetmore
David Y. Cooper
Frank Wood
H. P. Duval
P. T. Hayne

1906–07

Reverend Richard W. Hogue
Reverend Walter Hughson
George C. Royall
F. A. Clinard

1908

Right Reverend W. Alexander Guerry
Reverend A. P. Noe
T. W. Bacot

1909–11

Reverend M. A. Barber
Reverend T. T. Walsh
Reverend L. G. Wood
Reverend W. H. Hardin
Hon. W. A. Hoke

1912–13

Reverend Harris Mallinckrodt
Reverend R. R. Swope, D.D.
Reverend W. R. Dye
Reverend J. W. Areson

1914

Reverend Isaac W. Hughes
Reverend H. N. Bowne
Graham Andrews

1915

Right Reverend Thomas C. Darst, D.D.
Reverend R. N. Willcox

1918

Ven. J. H. Griffith
Reverend F. P. Lobdell
W. D. Anderson

1919–22

Reverend G. F. Hill

1923

Right Reverend Kirkman G. Finlay
Right Reverend Edwin A. Penick, D.D.
Reverend G. F. Hill
Reverend S. Cary Beckwith
Reverend W. E. McCord
Thomas H. Battle
W. D. McMillan, Jr.
W. S. M. Manning
David G. Ellison

1924

Reverend W. S. Poyner
Reverend William Way
Reverend J. W. Cantey Johnson
Reverend John H. Griffin
Reverend W. E. McCord
George H. Holmes
Addison G. Mangum
Reverend W. S. Poyner
Dr. W. Egleston

1925

Reverend J. B. Gibble
Mrs. W. D. Toy
Mrs. T. W. Bickett

1926

G. H. Green
Reverend Malcolm S. Taylor

1927–29

Richard H. Lewis
Thomas E. Myers
J. Nelson Frierson
Edmund R. Heyward
Reverend William Johnson

1930

Right Reverend Albert S. Thomas
Reverend J. Preston Burke

1931–32

J. Cheshire Webb
Mrs. J. W. C. Johnson
Reverend B. M. Lackey
Reverend T. T. Walsh, D.D.

1933

Miss Easdale Shaw
Joseph B. Cheshire, Jr.
Reverend Robert E. Gribbin, Jr.
Hon. J. J. Parker
Mrs. Frank S. Spruill
B. Allston Moore
L. A. Emerson
W. B. Moore, Sr.

1934

Judge George W. Conner

1935

Reverend George S. Gresham
Mrs. Laurence Sprunt
Reverend W. C. Cravner
Dr. F. R. Lucas

1937

Reverend Thomas P. Noe

1938

Dr. S. R. Lucas
Mrs. A. B. Stoney
Reverend Maurice Clarke

1940

Right Reverend John J. Gravatt, D.D.
Reverend Worth Wicker
E. O. Rehm

1941

Reverend W. Tate Young
Reverend E. F. Moseley
Reverend Allen B. Clarkson

1942

Reverend I. Harding Hughes
Reverend I. Wayne Hughes
Stephen E. Burroughs
Mrs. J. Cheshire Webb
Reverend G. Mark Jenkins

1944

Right Reverend Thomas N.
  Carruthers, D.D.
Reverend John A. Wright
Reverend John A. Pinckney

1946

Reverend James McDowell Dick
Hon. J. C. B. Ehringhaus
W. H. Ruffin
Reverend James F. Ferneybough
Reverend Richard Patton
J. E. Powe

1947

Right Reverend Thomas H. Wright, D.D.
Mrs. C. C. Dawson

1948

J. W. Harrelson
Reverend John C. Grainger
N. C. Green
J. S. Stevens
Reverend Alfred P. Chambliss
L. A. Emerson
E. M. Gwathmey

1950

Pembroke Nash
Mrs. Henry C. Bourne
Right Reverend M. George Henry, D.D.

1951

Charles A. Tucker
Reverend Mortimer W. Glover, Jr.
Reverend Homer L. Hoover

1952

Right Reverend Richard H. Baker, D.D.
Col. John W. Moore
E. M. Jones
Reverend John Q. Beckwith
Reverend Stiles B. Lines

1953

Hyman Battle
Col. Gordon Smith
Charles Tucker
Mrs. H. Fitzhugh Lee
Mrs. Fred Outland

1955

David T. Oats
Reverend Robert C. Baird
Right Reverend C. Alfred Cole
W. W. McEachern
H. Bland Hammond, Jr.
Reverend E. Hopkins Weston

1956

Hon. Francis O. Clarkson
Haywood Duke
Reverend Gordon Bennett
John G. Dunn, Jr.
Arthur L. Tyler
Miss Elizabeth Smith
Reverend Moultrie McIntosh
Mrs. Thomas C. Coxe, Jr.

1957

Earl Mobley
Reverend Thomas L. Hastings
Mrs. John W. Tuton
Reverend Robert B. Campbell
Hugh L. Willcox
Reverend John M. Barr
C. Dwight Cathcart

1958

R. Lee Covington
Sam Peirson
T. C. Heyward

Mrs. William T. Cheatham
Reverend William A. Thompson

1959

Dr. Charles H. Ashford
Reverend Roscoe C. Hauser, Jr.

1960

Richard G. Stone
Erskine Duff
Reverend Joseph A. DiRaddo
Reverend Winfield Smith
Harry Stephenson, Jr.
Stephen D. Mitchell
Reverend Gray Temple

1961

Right Reverend Thomas A.
    Fraser, Jr., D.D.
Alva M. Lumpkin
Reverend Edward M. Spruill

1962

Reverend Howard M. Hickey

1963

Reverend Henry Johnston, Jr.
Thurman Williams, Jr.
Mrs. Frank B. Rankin
Reverend Walter Roberts
W. W. Dukes, Jr.
Reverend Richard C. Fell
Reverend John W. Hardy
Mrs. Gray Temple
Charles E. Thomas

1964

Charles M. Shaffer

1965

Dr. George D. Penick
Mrs. E. D. Powe
Reverend Thomas J. C. Smyth
Reverend Edwin B. Jeffress, Jr.
Mrs. Grady Stevens
Reverend Claude E. Guthrie

1966

Mrs. Laurence Rankin, Jr.

1967

Reverend John W. S. Davis
Reverend C. Edward Sharp
Mrs. Edward Bullock
Dr. Samuel O. Cantey
Reverend Samuel T. Cobb
Reverend P. G. Porcher, Jr.
C. Poinsett Exum
Reverend Charles Cannon
Charles H. Wickenberg

1968

Reverend W. Moultrie Moore
H. Hyman Philips, Jr.
R. E. Hoke Pollock
John L. Simmons

1969

R. Mayne Albright
C. H. Robinson
William E. Highsmith
John S. Hill
Rollie Tillman
Mrs. R. L. Woodruff
James H. Ellison
Mrs. Thomas C. Powell, Jr.

1971

James M. Poyner
Norvin K. Dickerson
Cecil L. Patterson
ex officio: Laura Dell Parker

1972

Mrs. Harry G. Walker, Jr.
Mrs. Seavy Highsmith
ex officio: Margaret Rascoe Worthington

1973

Mrs. Wiley J. Long, Jr.
Helen Barnes
Albert N. Shew
ex officio: Helen H. Smith
          Lane Turner

1974

Mason G. Alexander
James C. Gardner
Douglas Van Ness Parsons
Mrs. David Rankin
ex officio: Margaret Lucas McAlister

1975

Mrs. Sherwood H. Smith, Jr.
Thad A. Eure, Jr.
Edwin Pate
Mrs. William J. Armfield
ex officio: Barksdale Spencer

1976

Thomas W. Alexander
Eugene B. Hardin, Jr.
Mrs. Colin Montgomery
ex officio: Llewellyn Faircloth
        Elgiva D. Watson

1977

Mrs. Mary Pride Cruikshank
Thomas C. Coxe
Mrs. John W. S. Davis
Mrs. Robert James Page
ex officio: Frances Schultz

1978

William G. Clark III
Elizabeth Gold Swindell
Reba White Williams

Peter Brown Ruffin
ex officio: Marian Green

1979

Jesse S. Capel
Peter V. Daniel
Frank A. Daniels
Margery Scott Johnson
R. Peyton Woodson III
Nancy Hamel Clark
Roy W. Davis, Jr.
Reverend Philip H. Whitehead
ex officio: Doreen Saxe
        Lanier Brown

1980

Susan Haughton Ehringhaus
Judith Metcalfe von Seldeneck
ex officio: Margaret Ellen McGlohon

1981

G. Smedes York
Elizabeth W. Tyler
ex officio: Nancy Lee Wilkinson

1982

Thomas Fanjoy
John N. Landi
James G. Peden
ex officio: Wylie Savanas Quinn III
        Helen Millice Rogers

# APPENDIX C

*Presidents of the St. Mary's Alumnae Association*

Anna Frank Strosnider DuBose, '50: 1981–1984
June Bourne Long, '43: 1978–1981
Sallie Lee Walker, '46: 1975–1978
Luke Hill Page, '50: 1972–1975
Lila Spilman Rankin, '48: 1970–1972
Janet James Lindsey, '40: 1968–1970
Peggy Holmes Stevens, '38: 1966–1968
Elizabeth Ferguson Anderson, '34: 1964–1966
Katherine Duff Powell, '28: 1962–1964
Margaret Darst Smith, '35: 1959–1962
Jane Purrington Maddison, '31: 1957–1959
Barbara Henderson Webb, '30: 1955–1957
Elizabeth Smith Wolff, '28: 1953–1955
Emma Bouknight Miller, '14: 1951–1953
Martha Gold Winstead Stroud, '14: 1949–1951
Mary Richardson Davis, '36: 1947–1949
Betsy London Cordon, '06: 1945–1947
Ida Rogerson Cheshire, '10: 1943–1945
Minnie Burgwyn Long, '04: 1940–1943
Ellen Faucette Cooper, '96: 1937–1940
Easdale Shaw, '82: 1930–1937
Maude Amyette Bragaw: 1929–1930
May Hill Davis Higham, '92: 1928–1929
Pattie Carroll Whichard, '02: 1927–1928
Laura Newsom O'Neill, '94: 1925–1927
Rena Hoyt Clark, '05: 1924–1925
Lottie Sharp Lewis, '06: 1923–1924
Cantey Venable Sutton, '05: 1922–1923
Sadie Root Robards, '98: 1921–1922
Rebe Hill Shields, '10: 1920–1921
Fannie Yarborough Bickett, '87: 1919–1920

Emilie Smedes Holmes, '84: 1918–1919
Minnie Tucker Baker, '89: 1917–1918
Ella Tew Lindsay, '79: 1916–1917
Alice Dugger Grimes, '89: 1915–1916
Annie Philips Jackson, '84: 1914–1915
Anna Nash Buxton Beck, c. '00: 1913–1914
Sophronia Horner Winston: 1912–1913
Eliza Smedes Knox, '79: 1911–1912
Margaret Busbee Shipp, '89: 1910–1911
Mary Johnson Iredell, '55: 1900–1910, made lifetime honorary president
*Annie Patterson Harris, '76: 1896–
Mrs. Edward Trapier: 1892–
Kate DeRosset Meares, '47: 1881–1882
Penelope Bradford Cox: 1880
Mary Kinsey Boylan, '46: 1879
*Early alumnae association records are incomplete.

# APPENDIX D

*Named Scholarships*

Minnie Tucker Baker Endowed Scholarship
The Frank and Sallie Borden Foundation Scholarship
Coles Burroughs Scholarship Fund
Mary Cain Endowed Memorial
Capehart-Tucker Memorial
Mary E. Chapeau Endowed Memorial
D. Russell Clark Scholarship Fund
The Madame Clement Endowed Memorial
Robert Lee Green Connelly Memorial Scholarship
Margaret Jones Cruikshank Endowed Memorial
Mary Shuford Davis Endowed Memorial
Roberta Phillips Davis Scholarship Fund
The Alice Walker Dillard Scholarship Fund
Diocese of North Carolina Scholarship Fund
Episcopal Churchwomen, Diocese of North Carolina, Scholarship
Emma Barnwell Heyward Endowed Scholarship
Josephine Bowen Hughes Endowed Memorial
Mary Johnson Iredell-Kate McKimmon Endowed Memorial
Henrietta Perkins Martin Endowed Memorial
Kathreen Tucker Massie Memorial
Nancy Elizabeth Marlowe Scholarship Fund
Lizzie Wilson Montgomery Scholarship
David R. Murchison Endowed Scholarship
Eugene F. Parker Memorial Scholarship Fund
Eliza Battle Pittman Memorial
Catherine Ruth Procter Endowed Memorial
Smedes Endowed Memorial
Mary Ruffin Smith Endowed Memorial
Esther Stearn Whitehurst Endowed Memorial

# APPENDIX E

*Student Government Association Presidents*

| | | | |
|---|---|---|---|
| 1923–1924 | Mary Elizabeth Powell | 1954–1955 | Harriet Little Mardre |
| 1924–1925 | Ellen Camden Melick | 1955–1956 | Elizabeth Carol Kemper |
| 1925–1926 | Ruth Loring Clark | 1956–1957 | Margaret Barrington Bowen |
| 1926–1927 | Mela Allen Royall | 1957–1958 | Caroline Collier Cobb |
| 1927–1928 | Elizabeth Platt | 1958–1959 | Jeannette Gilkey Cross |
| 1928–1929 | Margaret Duncan Cameron | 1959–1960 | Nancy Pauline Fulkerson |
| 1929–1930 | Roxana Williams Eaton | 1960–1961 | Edith Eugenia Alston |
| 1930–1931 | Nancy Gatewood Jones | 1961–1962 | Cornelia Elliot Hines; |
| 1931–1932 | Caroline Winder Dunn | | Margaret Elizabeth Nichols |
| 1932–1933 | Melba Brown Chamblee | 1962–1963 | Merrie Haynes Walker |
| 1933–1934 | Katherine Blount Harding | 1963–1964 | Rose Patterson Watson |
| 1934–1935 | Katherine Wimberly Spruill | 1964–1965 | Susan Dianne Ricks |
| 1935–1936 | Ann Palmer Scoggin | 1965–1966 | Roslyn Anne Bowers |
| 1936–1937 | Virginia Etheridge Worth | 1966–1967 | Margaret Stevens |
| 1937–1938 | Mary Louise Riddick | 1967–1968 | Mary Holden Harrell |
| 1938–1939 | Helen Rutledge Montgomery | 1968–1969 | Mary Morrison Pennington |
| 1939–1940 | Mary Helen Rodman | 1969–1970 | Katharine Curtis Harrison |
| 1940–1941 | Adelaide Rodman Curtis | 1970–1971 | Pamela Erskine DeVere |
| 1941–1942 | Charlotte Ann Mahan | 1971–1972 | Laura Dell Parker |
| 1942–1943 | Anne Talbot Dickson | 1972–1973 | Margaret Rascoe Worthington |
| 1943–1944 | Elizabeth Liles Edwards | 1973–1974 | Lane Turner |
| 1944–1945 | Kate Broadfoot | 1974–1975 | Margaret Lucas McAlister |
| 1945–1946 | Nancy Kathryn Fulton | 1975–1976 | Betty Barksdale Spencer |
| 1946–1947 | Margaret Mann Swindell | 1976–1977 | Mary Llewellyn Faircloth |
| 1947–1948 | Elinore Page Parrish | 1977–1978 | Frances Myrick Schultz |
| 1948–1949 | Frances Wood Drane | 1978–1979 | Marian Green |
| 1949–1950 | Barbara Kathryn Wooten | 1979–1980 | Sujette Lanier Brown |
| 1950–1951 | Betty Ann Williamson | 1980–1981 | Margaret Ellen McGlohon |
| 1951–1952 | Mary Alice Hicks | 1981–1982 | Jean Huske Schaefer |
| 1952–1953 | Nell Deans Eley | | |
| 1953–1954 | Marie Hollingsworth Timmons | | |

# NOTES

| | |
|---|---|
| DU | Manuscript Department, William R. Perkins Library, Duke Univ., Durham, N.C. |
| EBC | Elizabeth (Bessie) Brownrigg Cain |
| EJW | Edward Jenner Warren |
| EK | Emma Kimberly |
| FM | St. Mary's College faculty minutes |
| FP | Frank W. Pisani |
| GL | George W. Lay |
| IJ | Isaac Jarratt |
| J Papers | Daniel W. Jordan Papers, Manuscript Department, William R. Perkins Library, Duke University, Durham, N.C. |
| JBC | Joseph Blount Cheshire, bishop of North Carolina |
| JBC Papers | Joseph Blount Cheshire Papers, Division of Archives and History, North Carolina Department of Cultural Resources, Raleigh |
| JBC-SHC | Joseph Blount Cheshire Papers, Southern Historical Collection, Wilson Library, Univ. of North Carolina at Chapel Hill |
| JDNC | *Journal, Diocese of North Carolina* |
| JHC | John Henry Curtis |
| JK | John Kimberly |
| JLB Papers | John Lancaster Bailey Papers, Southern Historical Collection, Wilson Library, Univ. of North Carolina at Chapel Hill |
| J-PF Papers | Jarratt-Puryear Family Papers, Manuscript Department, William R. Perkins Library, Duke Univ., Durham, N.C. |
| JR | John Thomas Rice |
| JSH | John Steele Henderson |
| K Papers | John Kimberly Papers, Southern Historical Collection, Wilson Library, Univ. of North Carolina at Chapel Hill |
| KC | Kate Curtis |
| KDeR | Kate DeRosset |
| KDeRM | Kate DeRosset Meares |
| KMcK | Kate McKimmon |
| KPB | Kemp P. Battle |
| LK | Lizzie Kimberly |
| LS | Lou Sullivan |
| LSI | Levi Silliman Ives |
| LW | Lucy Warren |
| M-D Papers | Meares-DeRosset Papers, Southern Historical Collection, Wilson Library, Univ. of North Carolina at Chapel Hill |
| MFH | Mary Ferrand Henderson |
| MJC | Margaret Jones Cruikshank |
| MJI | Mary Johnson Iredell |
| MJJ | Mary Jane Jarratt |
| MMM | Mabel M. Morrison |
| MS | Marye Stone (Mrs. Richard G. Stone) |
| MSL'E | Madeleine Saunders L'Engle |
| MSP | Mary Sherwood Smedes Poyner |
| NCC | North Carolina Collection, Wilson Library, Univ. of North Carolina at Chapel Hill |

## CHAPTER ONE

1. *RR*, 12 May 1842. A copy of the 1842 brochure is in the Willie P. Mangum Papers, Library of Congress, Washington, D.C.

2. Sadie Root Robards, "St. Mary's 100 Years Old," *Observer* (Charlotte), 17 May 1942. Robards was the granddaughter of AS.

3. M. E. A. Jones (?) to Mildred Cameron, 14 May 1842, CF Papers.

4. Annie Haywood Ruffin, "First Day of School—May 1842," *SMM*, Apr. 1906, 5. Six generations of *direct* descendants starting in 1842 with Mary Kinsey (Kincey) of New Bern attended St. Mary's.

5. Mary Pearson Davis, "Reminiscences of St. Mary's, 1855–'56," *SMM*, June 1908, 10.

6. Montgomery, *Olden Days*, 15.

7. William Hooper Haigh diary, 18 Aug. 1844, William Hooper Haigh Papers.

8. *RR*, 10 May 1842.

9. Hofstadter, Miller, and Aaron, *United States*, 290.

10. *JDNC*, 1836, 11.

11. Ibid., 1833, 45.

12. Michael T. Malone, "Episcopal School of North Carolina, 1832–1842," *North Carolina Historical Review*, XLIX (Apr. 1972), 180n–81n. Bishop George Washington Doane of N.J. wrote, "To the Church of North Carolina belongs the honour of establishing the first truly Episcopal School."

13. *JDNC*, 1833, 51; *JDNC*, 1836, 55.

14. George W. Freeman to DC, 21 Oct. 1833, CF Papers.

15. The note was signed by Bishop Ives, George W. Freeman, DC, Thomas Devereux, and George Badger. Copy, 3 Dec. 1833, CF Papers.

16. Proceedings of school committee, Episcopal School of North Carolina, 3 Apr. 1834, JBC-SHC.

17. *JDNC*, 1835, 47.

18. Proceedings of school committee, Episcopal School of North Carolina, 17 June 1834, JBC-SHC.

19. Proceedings of building committee, 12 Feb. 1835, Episcopal School of North Carolina Papers, A&H; *JDNC*, 1835, 38–40.
20. Included were Thomas Ruffin, N.C. chief justice; George E. Badger, congressman and later secretary of the navy and U.S. senator; Charles Manly, N.C. governor; William H. Haywood, Jr., later U.S. senator; William M. Green, later bishop of Miss.; George W. Freeman, later missionary bishop of Ark. and the Southwest.
21. Malone, "Episcopal School," 182; Waugh, *North Carolina's Capital*, 9, 60–61.
22. Richard H. Battle, *Memorial Address*, 4.
23. *JDNC*, 1832, 34–35.
24. Bancroft became the first national historian, Polk's secretary of the navy, and founder of the Naval Academy.
25. See McLachlan, *American Boarding Schools*, 63, 80–81, 97–100, on Round Hill.
26. Ibid., 105–7; *JDNC*, 1834, 9.
27. Thomas B. Bailey to his mother, 9 Apr. 1838; Thomas B. Bailey to his father, 28 Feb. 1836, JLB Papers.
28. Malone, "Episcopal School," 182, 188.
29. *JDNC*, 1835, 40.
30. Ticknor, *Cogswell*, 202–3.
31. Ibid., 190–91, 199.
32. Ibid., 206.
33. *JDNC*, 1836, 20, 45–46.
34. Ibid., 1839, 30–33.
35. Ibid., 1839, 31; proceedings of school committee, Episcopal School of North Carolina, notes dated Jan. 1841, JBC-SHC.
36. Curtis (1808–72) was also a musician. He composed an anthem, "How Beautiful Upon the Mountains," for his ordination as deacon.
37. *JDNC*, 1840, 24.
38. Richard H. Battle, *Memorial Address*, 5.
39. *RR*, 9 June, 22 Dec. 1840.
40. *JDNC*, 1840, 28.
41. Ibid., 1841, 23–24, 29.
42. Ibid., 1842, 13.
43. BC to Alfred A. Berkley, 1 Sept. 1910, BC Papers.
44. BC to JBC, 22 Dec. 1910, BC Papers.
45. Receipt, 1 Jan. 1842, CF Papers.
46. For later land development of Cameron Park and Cameron Village see *NO*, 15 Dec. 1974.
47. Dawley, *General Theological Seminary*, 76.
48. "Old-field" schools were often built on worn-out cleared land.
49. Johnson, *Ante-bellum North Carolina*, 283–85; Sizer, *Age of Academies*, 12.
50. *RR*, 2 Apr. 1853.
51. Coon, *North Carolina Schools*, xxxv.
52. Woody, *Women's Education*, I, 381.
53. Scott, *Southern Lady*, 4–79, passim.
54. *RR*, 13 May 1842.
55. Sklar, *Catherine Beecher*, 82–86; Catherine Beecher, "An Essay on the Education of Female Teachers," in Goodsell, ed., *Pioneers of Women's Education*, 167–87.
56. Stern, *Margaret Fuller*, 331.
57. Lutz, *Emma Willard*, 64–65, 100–01.
58. Drake, *Higher Education in North Carolina*, 248.
59. Ibid., 253; Powell, *Higher Education*, 1–84, passim.
60. Raper, *Schools of North Carolina*, 202.
61. Taylor and Haight, *Vassar*, 70.
62. Ibid., 5–6.
63. Coates, *By Her Own Bootstraps*, 45.
64. Lizzie Wilson Montgomery, untitled ms., n.d. SMCA.
65. AS, "St. Mary's School," *Our Living and Our Dead*, III (July 1875), 113.

66. MSP interview, 3 Mar. 1972. MSP (1883–1976) was the granddaughter of AS and SS. Roeloff Jans (Jansen) and Anneke (Annetje) Webber were married in Holland in 1626 and emigrated to New Amsterdam (New York). The father of the founder of St. Mary's was Abraham Kiersted Smedes (1780–1835), one of the seven children of Aldert Smedes (1750–1844) and Elizabeth Mancious (1749–1824). See Beach, *Descendants of Jacob Sebor*, 76–78; letter from Sarah Erwin Bellamy, granddaughter of AS and SS, to Martha Stoops, 15 Oct. 1971, SMCA.

67. Beach, *Descendants of Jacob Sebor*, 7–12.

68. Abraham K. Smedes was an importer and commission merchant. See Beach, *Descendants of Jacob Sebor*, 25–30.

69. Beach, *Descendants of Jacob Sebor*, 16.

70. *Observer* (Raleigh), 26 Apr. 1877.

71. Original certificates of ordination are in AS Papers.

72. Thomas Lyell (1755–1848) was a Methodist minister during his early career. In 1801 he was chaplain to the U.S. House of Representatives. Sarah's maternal grandfather, the Rev. Abraham Beach, D.D., was among the organizers of the Episcopal church in the U.S. and was three times president of the House of Deputies. Beach (1740–1828) was for 29 years associated with Trinity Church in N.Y.C.; Beach Street is named for him. See Sprague, *Annals of the Pulpit*, V, 255, 495, and Sadie Root Robards, notes, n.d., SMCA.

73. Hanson, *St. George's Church*, I, 133–39. Hanson refers to Smedes's ministry as "eminently successful."

74. Aldert, the firstborn of AS and SS, died in infancy.

75. AS journals, 1837–38, AS Papers and AS-SMCA.

76. KPB, "The Rev. Aldert Smedes, D.D., Founder of St. Mary's School, Raleigh," *North Carolina University Magazine*, new series XIII (Nov. 1893), 77.

77. LW to Mrs. EJW, 23 Aug. 1867, EJW Papers.

78. Eliza Smedes educated her children by operating a boarding house in N.Y.C. See *SMM*, Apr. 1883, 168.

79. *SMM*, yearbook, 1910, 73.

CHAPTER TWO

1. AS, "St. Mary's School," *Our Living and Our Dead*, III (July 1875), 113.

2. AS, *She Hath Done What She Could*, 13. Copy is in S Papers.

3. Ibid., 14–15.

4. As to AJDeR, Feb. 1847, DeRF Papers.

5. AS, *She Hath Done What She Could*, 6–7.

6. AS, "St. Mary's School," 113. In the early days the school was sometimes referred to as "St. Mary's Hall."

7. *Banner of the Cross*, IV (3 Sept. 1842), 284.

8. AS, "St. Mary's School," 114.

9. AS, *Manual of St. Mary's School*, 11–15.

10. CC to Mrs. IJ, 3 Oct. 1846, J-PF Papers.

11. AS to Daniel W. Jordan, 10 May 1855, J Papers.

12. Avirett, *Old Plantation*, 158, 160–61.

13. KPB, "The Rev. Aldert Smedes, D.D., Founder of St. Mary's School, Raleigh," *North Carolina University Magazine*, new series XIII (Nov. 1893), 80.

14. MJI, "Madame Clement: An Appreciation," *SMM*, Dec. 1906, 7.

15. Beck Haigh to KDeR, 27 July 1848, DeRF Papers.

16. MSL'E, "Thoughts of My School Days," *SMM*, Dec. 1906, 13; Ellen Brownlow, "St. Mary's in the Forties," *SMM*, June 1908, 106.

17. AS to KDeR, 21 Oct. 1848, DeRF Papers.

18. MJI, "Miss O'Connor, 1820–1908," *SMM*, Nov. 1908, 106.

19. LW to Mrs. EJW, 6 Apr. 1867, EJW Papers.

20. Mary Pearson Davis, "Reminiscences of St. Mary's, 1855–'56," *SMM*, June 1908, 11.

21. Published by F. D. Benteen (Co.), Baltimore, 1845. See Lucy Williams music scorebook, Manuscript Dept., William R. Perkins Library, Duke University.

22. Tempe Neal to Mrs. C. C. Neal, 5 Sept. 1844, SMCA.

23. Brownlow, "St. Mary's in the Forties," 15–16.

24. Fannie Bryan Aiken, "Recollections of 1848–'52," *SMM*, Dec. 1906, 10–11.

25. Murray, *Wake: Capital County*, I, 340. Solomons's "The Young Ladies' Polka Gallopade" was "composed for and respectfully dedicated to the young ladies of St. Mary's School" and published in Maryland in 1846. SMCA.

26. Montgomery, *Olden Days*, 22; Mary Wheat Shober, "Reminiscences of My School Days," *SMM*, Nov. 1910, 95; MSP interviews, 1972–75.

27. Mason had been president of Geneva College (later Hobart) in N.Y. and of Delaware College in Newark, Del. He had served Christ Church in New Bern. He was a High Churchman of the school of Bishops Hobart and Ravenscroft. See the *National Cyclopaedia of American Biography*, XII, 516.

28. Brownlow, "St. Mary's," 14.

29. Nannie Lane Devereux, "St. Mary's in the Later Fifties," *SMM*, Dec. 1906, 19; Lizzie Wilson Montgomery ms., n.d., 9, SMCA.

30. Arrietta Hutton Sherwood to Mrs. A. H. Sherwood, 3 Nov. 1858, SMCA.

31. LK to JK, 18 Sept. 1858, K Papers.

32. MJI, "The Founder of St. Mary's—The Rev. Aldert Smedes, D.D.," *SMM*, Nov. 1905, 4.

33. The contemporary grading system at Chapel Hill was "Honors, first, second, or third, Respectable, Tolerable, Bad and Very Bad." See KPB, *Old-Time Tar Heel*, 80.

34. AS, *Manual of St. Mary's School*, 13–14.

35. Robert Strange, "Founders' Day Address," *SMM*, Nov. 1910, 78.

36. Montgomery ms., 3.

37. Raper, *Schools of North Carolina*, 114–27.

38. MSP interview, 23 Mar. 1972.

39. RR, 17 May 1842.

40. Only two of AS's account books survive. Those for 1863–65 and 1873–74 are in SMCA.

41. MSP interview, 23 Mar. 1972.

42. Richard H. Battle, *Memorial Address*, 8.

43. Ibid., 12; Montgomery, *Olden Days*, 9; AS to KPB, 18 Feb. 1856, BF Papers.

44. BC to JBC, 22 Dec. 1910, BC Papers.

45. AS to DC, 2 Nov. 1842, CF Papers.

46. See list of assets of Margaret Cameron Mordecai, July 1859, and 18 June 1856, George W. Mordecai Papers.

47. AS to DC, 13 July 1849, CF Papers.

48. *JDNC*, 1859, 46.

49. AS, "St. Mary's School," 116.

50. Avirett, *Old Plantation*, 98.

51. AS, "St. Mary's School," 113.

52. *SMM*, Apr. 1910, 139–40.

53. *JDNC*, 1844, 25.

54. The chapel was built by DC's daughters, Mildred Cameron and Margaret Cameron Mordecai (Mrs. George W.), who had inherited the property and who lived across Hillsborough Street from St. Mary's. Mildred, a semi-invalid, often was wheeled over for services. AS donated the protecting entrance hood and the stone steps. The baptismal font was given by Mary Virginia Proctor, a student of 1846–47. The communion service, contributed by students, had been used in the East Rock chapel.

55. *JDNC*, 1858, 22.

56. Lawrence Wodehouse, "Upjohn's Rural Architecture in North Carolina," *North Carolina Architect*, XV (Nov. 1968), 15.

57. AS to Richard Upjohn, 1, 5, 9, 15 May, 9 June, 7 July, 7 Oct. 1856, Richard Upjohn Papers. Copies are in SMCA.

58. In 1971 the St. Mary's Chapel was entered in the National Register of Historic Places.

59. Emilie McVea, "St. Mary's of a By-Gone Day," *SMM*, Apr. 1906,24–25.

60. AS, *She Hath Done What She Could*, 15–16.

61. Ibid., passim.

62. Ibid., 6, 12.

63. EK to JK, 3 Aug. 1861, K Papers.

64. Annie Moore Parker, "Personal Recollections of St. Mary's," *SMM*, Dec. 1906, 24–35.

65. Anna Brooke Allan, "A Sore Throat, A Saint, And A Centennial," *SMCB*, Mar. 1938, 7.

66. LS, essay, Nov. 1864, papers in private collection.

67. Lena Smith, "Thoughts of Dear Saint Mary's Suggested by the Postcard," *SMCB*, Mar. 1938, 40.

68. Richard H. Battle, *Memorial Address*, 9–10.

69. BS, "The Rector's Farewell Address," *SMM*, June 1879, 33.

70. MJI, "Madame Clement," 8.

71. MSL'E, "My School Days," 17.

72. Strange, "Founder's Day Address," 80.

73. JDNC, 1842, 39. The communicants numbered 1,421.

74. JDNC, 1844, 19.

75. LSI to Mrs. Martin, Feb. 1842, quoted in *SMM*, Apr. 1910, 150. See French, "Recollections of Valle Crucis," typescript, 34–35, William Glenney French Recollections, SHC.

76. JDNC, 1842, 9.

77. Ibid., 1845, 19.

78. SS to KDeR, 10 Mar. 1849, DeRF Papers.

79. MSL'E, "My School Days," 16. Madeleine, the daughter of Judge Romulus M. Saunders, lived at Elmwood. Soon after her St. Mary's days, she lived at court in Spain where her father was ambassador. Eugénie Montijo, later wife of Napoleon III and Empress of France, was her dearest friend.

80. Brownlow, "St. Mary's," 17; Ruffin, "First Day of School," *SMM*, Apr. 1906, 6. In notes made in 1890, JBC added Sue Hart, sister of the artist, to those in the painting. He identified the other students as Eugenia Hinton, Laura Washington, and Sarah Crawford (the bishop's hands resting on her head). He wrote, "I have this from my aunt, Miss Arabella C. Parker, who was in the school at the time." JBC Papers.

81. KPB, "Aldert Smedes," 79.

82. Haywood, *Lives of the Bishops*, 112.

83. JDNC, 1853, 56. The bishop's resignation was uncanonical; he wrote to his diocese instead of to the House of Bishops. See Albright, *Protestant Episcopal Church*, 244.

84. RR, 12 Feb. 1853. Some of the resentment among Episcopalians against LSI stemmed from the fact that he had received in advance six month's salary ($912) before his departure. To return the unearned salary, LSI asked AS to sell his property. To prevent its seizure by others, AS attached the LSI property before he received the official papers giving him power of attorney. He was severely criticized by some Catholics. See *JDNC*, 1853, 13; BS's letterbook, 1895, SMCA.

85. MJJ to Mrs. IJ, 12 Feb. 1852, J-PF Papers.

86. LSI to AS, 16 Apr. 1853, Carson Collection.

87. John O'Grady called LSI and Mother Seaton "The two most prominent converts of the Catholic Church in the United States." LSI was known, not only for his administrative ability, but also for his "simplicity and devotion," and for his "heroic self-sacrifice" on behalf of the Society of St. Vincent de Paul and the Society for the Protection of Destitute Catholic Children. See O'Grady, *Levi Silliman Ives*, vii, 4, 67.

88. JDNC, 1853, 12–14.

89. AS to KDeR, 26 Feb. 1850, DeRF Papers.

90. RR, 4 May 1847.

91. AS to AJDeR, n.d., 1851, DeRF Papers.

92. Devereux, "St. Mary's," 20.

93. Sebastian W. Meyer (words) and Russell Broughton (music).

94. KDeR to AJDeR, 1 Dec. 1844; 16 July 1846; 3 May 1851, DeRF Papers.

95. SS to KDeR, 10 Mar. 1849, DeRF Papers.

96. *Observer* (Raleigh), 7 May 1877.

97. *RR*, 13 Nov. 1846.

98. Ibid., 5 Sept. 1851.

99. Francis T. Bryan to William Shepard Bryan, 22 Nov. 1853, William Shepard Bryan Papers.

100. Mary Jones Withers to Francis John Levert, 12 Aug., 3 Nov. 1854, Levert Family Papers.

101. Robert Treat Paine to his wife, 19 Nov., 22 Dec. 1844, Robert Treat Paine Papers, quoted by permission of Robert N. Miller, Santa Marguerita, Calif.

102. *RR*, 21 Oct. 1845.

103. "Discipline of St. Mary's School," Apr. 1853, J-PF Papers.

104. KDeR to AJDeR, 10 July 1846, DeRF Papers.

105. Eliza Howerton to Philip Howerton, 1 Feb. 1845, Philip H. Howerton Papers.

106. AS, *Manual of St. Mary's School*, 12–13.

107. CC to Mrs. IJ, 9 Jan. 1847, J-PF Papers.

108. EK to JK, 25 July 1857; 19 Feb. 1859, K Papers.

109. Woody, *Women's Education*, I, 405.

110. KDeR to AJDeR, 8 Mar. 1846, DeRF Papers.

111. William H. Battle to his wife, 3 Jan. 1855, BF Papers.

112. William Hooper Haigh diary, 172.

113. MJJ to Mrs. IJ, 22 Apr. 1854, J-PF Papers.

114. Brownlow, "St. Mary's," 17–18.

115. LK to JK, 9 Aug. 1857, K Papers.

116. MJJ to IJ, 31 July 1852; CC to Mrs. IJ, 11 Aug. 1846, J-PF Papers; EK to JK, 4 June 1859, K Papers.

117. CC to Mrs. IJ, 11 Aug. 1846; MJJ to IJ, 31 July 1852, J-PF Papers.

118. AS to DC, 10 July 1845, 30 Nov 1846, CF Papers.

119. Devereux, "St. Mary's," 18.

120. SS to Edward Smedes, March n.y., SMCA.

121. Shober, "Reminiscences," 96.

122. MSP interview, 10 Oct. 1971.

123. MJJ to her brother, 16 Dec. 1852, J-PF Papers.

124. Charles Graham Smedes died in 1840, aged one year.

125. CC to Mrs. IJ, 3 Oct. 1846; MJJ to Mrs. IJ, 19 Aug., 4 Nov. 1854, J-PF Papers.

126. Montgomery, *Olden Days*, 15–16.

127. Ibid.

128. Ibid.

129. MJJ to Mrs. IJ, 5 Nov. 1854, J-PF Papers.

130. Shober, "Reminiscences," 92–95.

131. MJJ to her brother, 1 Apr. 1853, J-PF Papers.

132. MJJ to Mrs. IJ, 22 Apr. 1854; MJJ to her brother, 2 Dec. 1852, J-PF Papers.

133. MJJ to Mrs. IJ, 6 May 1856, J-PF Papers.

134. KDeR to AJDeR, 10 July 1846, DeRF Papers; MSL'E, "My School Days," 16.

135. *RR*, 6 June 1843.

136. KPB, *Old-Time Tar Heel*, 81.

137. Matthew Howerton to Judy Howerton, 23 Aug. 1844, Philip H. Howerton Papers.

138. MJJ to her brother, 19 Feb. 1853, J-PF Papers.

139. Arrietta Hutton Sherwood to her mother, 3 Nov. 1858, SMCA.

140. William E. Anderson to MCM, 10 Dec. 1855, CF Papers.

141. MJJ to Mrs. IJ, 20 Oct. 1854, J-PF Papers.

142. Eliza Howerton to Mrs. Philip Howerton, 5 July 1844, Philip H. Howerton Papers.

143. MJJ to her brother, 30 Oct. 1852, J-PF Papers.

144. *Observer* (Raleigh), 8 May 1877.

145. Haigh diary, 134, 259–60.

146. *RR*, 25 Sept. 1845.

147. Judy Howerton to Mrs. Philip Howerton, 1 Feb. 1845, Philip H. Howerton Papers.

148. Arrietta Hutton Sherwood to her mother, 3 Nov. 1858, SMCA.

149. Young, *Cycles of Fashion*, 81–84.

150. KDeR to her aunt, 4 Apr. 1845, DeRF Papers.

151. CC to Mrs. IJ, 8 Mar. 1847, J-PF Papers.

152. MJJ to Mrs. IJ, 16 Apr., 19 Aug. 1854; MJJ to her brother, n.d., J-PF Papers.

153. CC to Mrs. IJ, Aug. and n.d. 1846, J-PF Papers.

154. Emily Taylor Brower interview, 2 July 1976.

155. Lucy Catharine Moore Capehart, "My Impressions, 1853–58," *SMM*, Apr. 1906, 7.

156. Charlotte L. Daly to KDeR, 10 Feb. 1847, DeRF Papers.

157. Leslie, *Behaviour Book*, 94–95.

## CHAPTER THREE

1. *RR*, 19 Apr. 1844.

2. William Hooper Haigh diary, 13 Apr. 1844, William Hooper Haigh Papers.

3. *RR*, 1 Jun 1847.

4. EK to JK, 28 May 1859; LK to JK, 1 June 1859, K Papers.

5. *RR*, 2 Sept. 1860.

6. EK to JK, 6 Nov 1860, K Papers.

7. Lefler and Newsome, *North Carolina*, 448.

8. Lefler, *North Carolina History*, 285–86.

9. Louise (no surname) to "Dear Carrie," 30 Apr. 1861, John Thomas Wheat Papers.

10. *RR*, 15 June 1861. Gov. Ellis's wife was St. Mary's alumna Mary Daves.

11. KC to JHC, 22 Apr. 1861, C Papers.

12. Copy of AS's letter to Andrew Johnson requesting an executive pardon, undated, 1864–65 account book, AS-SMCA.

13. AS to "My Dear Old Friend," 13 May 1861, S Papers.

14. AS's brother, William Crosby, Vicksburg attorney and railroad president, was a member of the Miss. secession convention. His brother George lived in nearby Raymond. A third, Bancker, lived on a La. plantation. SS's father was born in Va. See Beach, *Descendants of Jacob Sebor*, 27, 16.

15. *NO*, 21 Apr. 1910.

16. Sadie Root Robards, "100 Years at St. Mary's," *NO*, 20 May 1942.

17. MSP interview, Oct. 1972; Montgomery, *Olden Days*, 26.

18. AS, *She Hath Done What She Could*, 7. See "An Act to Prevent All Persons from Teaching Slaves to Read or Write, the Use of Figures Excepted," *Acts Passed by the General Assembly of the State of North Carolina at the Session of 1830–31*, 6.

19. KC to JHC, 27 Apr. 1861(?), C Papers.

20. Ibid.; unknown author to Mrs. Frank Shober, n.d., John Thomas Wheat Papers.

21. Mary Bond Thompson to unknown person, 27 June 1861, letter in possession of Richard Urquhart, Raleigh.

22. Aldert Smedes, "The Hand of God," sermon, July 1861, AS Papers.

23. EK to JK, 3 Aug. 1861, K Papers.

24. RBCr to AS, 31 Aug. 1861, Cr Papers.

25. Montgomery, *Olden Days*, 12.

26. MSL'E To Edward M. L'Engle, 18 Mar. 1862, Edward McCrady L'Engle Papers.

27. Josie MacRae to John MacRae, 16 Mar. 1862, copy, SMCA.

28. RBCr to BCr, 13, 19, 23 Feb. 1862, Cr Papers.

29. Hattie Harold to Rev. Edward M. Forbes, n.d., Cr Papers.

30. George W. Mordecai to Mildred Cameron, 2 Apr. 1862, CF Papers.

31. After the war, the Freedmen's Bureau Agency occupied the Peace building. Thus, although founded in 1857, Peace Institute did not open until 1872. See Wilson, *Peace College*, 6. The Wake Forest College building became a hospital in June, 1864. The college was "suspended" after May, 1862, when the new conscription law took all but five of the students. See Paschal, *Wake Forest College*, I, 442–43.

32. Jane Meares to KDeRM, 28 Oct. 1862. John W. and Augustus Williams Papers.

33. *State Journal* (Raleigh), 18, 25 June 1862.

34. Ross, *Mrs. Jefferson Davis*, 4, 71, 119, 130, 314; Annie Moore Parker, "Personal Recollections of St. Mary's," *SMM*, Dec. 1906, 22.

35. Varina Davis to James A. Briggs, 1 June 1895, Jefferson Davis Papers. Her good friend in Raleigh was Nancy Haywood Blount Branch, wife of Gen. Branch.

36. Lucy Walke Cruikshank, "A Few Recollections, 1863–64," *SMM*, Apr. 1906, 13.

37. KMcK, "Some Notes of Happenings at St. Mary's During Her School Days, by the Oldest Inhabitant," *SMM*, Apr. 1906, 10.

38. Lizzie Wilson Montgomery, ms., n.d., SMCA.

39. Parker, "Personal Recollections," 23; Arrietta Hutton Sherwood to her mother, 31 Jan. 1860, SMCA.

40. Frances Marriner, "Miss Katie," *SMCB*, June 1927, 10.

41. Nannie Brodnax to William Cain, 1 Dec. 1863, JLB Papers.

42. LS, "Saturday at St. Mary's," an assigned composition, 1863, LS Papers.

43. *RR*, 19, 23 Apr. 1862.

44. E. B. Long and Barbara Long, *The Civil War*, 720.

45. LS to Mr. and Mrs. Calvin Jernigan, 17 Feb. 1863, LS Papers. No official lists of students exist before 1879; Montgomery listed students of the 1860s in *Olden Days*.

46. Nancy Haywood Branch's autograph book is in the possession of Nancy Branch Maupin Neely, Raleigh.

47. Katherine Polk Gale, "Recollections of Life in the Southern Confederacy, 1861–65," ms., Gale and Polk Family Papers.

48. Parker, "Personal Recollections," 23.

49. Lee, *General Lee*, 50. Lee suggested to his wife in the fall of 1861 that she consider settling in Raleigh, but Mildred went to Mrs. Powell's school in Winchester, Va. In the summer of 1862 Mrs. Lee and her daughters accepted the invitation of a relative, William Duke Jones, to stay at his White Sulphur Springs resort in Warren County, N.C. Anne Carter Lee died there at 23 of typhoid fever.

50. R. E. Lee to Mrs. Lee, 18 Nov. 1862, Lee Papers. Quoted in ms. of book on the Lee children by Mary P. Coulling, Lexington, Va., and used with her permission.

51. R. E. Lee to Mrs. Lee, 27 Mar. 1863, quoted by Coulling referring to Clifford Dowdey and Louis H. Manarin, *The Wartime Papers of R. E. Lee* (Boston: Little, Brown, and Co., 1961), 498–99.

52. Lee, *General Lee*, 247–48.

53. Ibid., 133, 139, 304.

54. Lena Smith, "Thoughts of Dear St. Mary's Suggested by the Postcard," *SMCB*, Mar. 1938, 39–40.

55. Irene McNeal to Patti Thompson, 27 Dec. 1861, letter in possession of Richard Urquhart, Raleigh, N.C.

56. St. Mary's School circular, 2 Jan. 1865, LS Papers.

57. Nannie Brodnax to DC, 5 Apr. 1864, CF Papers.

58. Mary Louisa Curtis to M. A. Curtis, 26 Aug. 1864, C Papers.

59. EK to JK, 3 Aug. 1861, K Papers.

60. BCr to KC, 5 Feb. 1862, C Papers.

61. RBCr to BCr, 1 Dec. 1861, 11 Mar., 23 Feb. 1862, Cr Papers.

62. Nannie Lane Devereux, "St. Mary's in the Later Fifties," *SMM*, Dec. 1906, 19; Montgomery, *Olden Days*, 24. After the war, Madame Gouyé returned to her home in Mobile where she died.

63. Eliza Evertson to KDeRM, 30 Mar. 1854, DeRF Papers.

64. Montgomery, *Olden Days*, 15–16.

65. M., "Mrs. Mary Iredell: A Tribute," *SMM*, May 1905, 21.

66. *RR*, 31 Oct. 1860.

67. Montgomery, *Olden Days*, 22–23.

68. Ibid., 24–25.

69. Margaret Walker Weber, "Reminiscences," 12 Mar. 1904, typescript in possession of Sallie MacNider Shadrach, Wilmington. After the war, the Webers had a school for girls in East Nashville, Tenn.

70. MSP interview, 3 Mar. 1972.

71. Montgomery, *Olden Days*, 21. Wheat served as rector of the Chapel of the Cross, Chapel Hill, 1853–56 and 1858–60.

72. LS to Mrs. Calvin Jernigan, 17 May 1864; LS to Mr. and Mrs. Calvin Jernigan, 30 Nov. 1864, LS Papers.

73. Susan Dabney Smedes, *Southern Planter*, 187–89.

74. AS to KDeR, 15 Feb. 1861, DeRF Papers.

75. Ibid.

76. EK to JK, 17 May 1861, K Papers.

77. KC to JHC, 22 Apr. 1861, C Papers.

78. Susan Dabney Smedes wrote *Memorials of a Southern Planter* (1887), which drew upon 50 years of detailed family letters. Reissued, it became a classic often quoted by scholars.

79. E. A. Evertson to KDeRM, 13 May 1863, DeRF Papers.

80. Ibid.

81. Montgomery, *Olden Days*, 20.

82. AS to Mrs. John Thomas Wheat, 23 Mar. 1863, John Thomas Wheat Papers.

83. KC's notebook after JHC was killed in Mar. 1865, C Papers.

84. Frank Shober to his wife, 5 June 1863, John Thomas Wheat Papers.

85. Montgomery, *Olden Days*, 20.

86. E. B. Long and Barbara Long, *Civil War*, 718; Lefler and Newsome, *North Carolina*, 457.

87. *RR*, 12 July 1863.

88. Fannie Aiken, "Recollections of 1848–'52," *SMM*, Dec. 1906, 10; Collier, *Women of the South*, II, 257–58. In 1862 Helen Johnstone married the Rev. George Carroll Harris.

89. LS to Mr. and Mrs. Calvin Jernigan, 13 Apr. 1864, LS Papers.

90. AS's account book, SMCA; *NCS*, 3 Jan. 1865. Some prices quoted are from Wilmington.

91. Montgomery, *Olden Days*, 10.

92. LS to Mr. and Mrs. Calvin Jernigan, 9 Aug. 1864, LS Papers.

93. *NCS*, 6 Jan. 1865.

94. *Daily Progress*, 3 Mar. 1865.

95. *RR*, 21 June 1862; *NCS*, 6 Jan 1863. Tuition at Chapel Hill was $30 and dormitory space $5 a session.

96. *NCS*, 9 June 1863.

97. AS to John H. Peebles, June 1863, Wait and Leone Hines Collection.

98. Fragment of AS letter, SMCA.

99. *NCS*, 20 Dec. 1863, 1 Feb. 1865.

100. Ibid., 5 Jan. 1864.

101. *JDNC*, 1864, 51.

102. Richard H. Battle, *Memorial Address*, 7.

103. St. Mary's School circular, 2 Jan. 1865, LS Papers; Salley, *Life*, illus. opp. 150.

104. Augusta (no surname) to KMcK, 31 Jan. 1865, KMcK Papers.

105. AS's account book, SMCA; Salley, *Life*, 40.

106. Montgomery, *Olden Days*, 22.

107. Mrs. RBCr to BCr, Nov. 1861, Cr Papers.

108. LS to Calvin Jernigan, 7 Mar. 1864, LS Papers.

109. Parker, "Personal Recollections," 21.

110. Anna Brooke Allan, "A Sore Throat, a Saint, and a Centennial," *SMCB*, Mar. 1938, 12.

111. Ibid.

112. Enrollment at the university was about 50, with 8 graduates in 1864. See *NCS*, 31 May 1864.

113. Montgomery, *Olden Days*, 19.

114. Nannie Brodnax to DC, 14 May 1864, CF Papers.

115. Montgomery, *Olden Days*, 19–20.

116. *JDNC*, 1863, 11.

117. Haywood, *Bishops of North Carolina*, 166.

118. Clark, *Regiments*, IV, 606.
119. KC to BCr, 15 Aug. 1863, Cr Papers.
120. Confederate States *JDNC*, 1863, 11, 17–18.
121. Clark, *Regiments*, IV, 606.
122. Montgomery, *Olden Days*, 21.
123. KC to BCr, 15 Aug. 1863, Cr Papers.
124. Frank Shober to his wife, June 1863, John Thomas Wheat Papers.
125. Some sermons of BS are in the AS Papers.
126. Montgomery, *Olden Days*, 18–19.
127. Salley, *Life*, 41.
128. Confederate States *JDNC*, 1865, 13.
129. Cruikshank, "A Few Recollections," 14.
130. E. A. Evertson to KDeRM, 26 May 1864, DeRF Papers.
131. Montgomery, *Olden Days*, 12.
132. Frank Shober to his wife, 23 May 1864, John Thomas Wheat Papers.
133. Ibid., 18 May 1864.
134. *Daily Progress*, 12, 21, 23 Jan. 1865.
135. Ibid., 23 Feb. 1865.
136. Amis, *Historical Raleigh*, 133.
137. *Daily Progress*, 20 Feb. 1865.
138. Catton, *This Hallowed Ground*, 377.
139. Barrett, *Sherman's March*, 183–84.
140. E. B. Long and Barbara Long, *Civil War*, 654.
141. A mother to her sons, 20 Mar. 1865, Edward Vernon Howell Papers.
142. Ridley, *Battles and Sketches*, 456.
143. Barrett, *Sherman's March*, 201.
144. Harriet Cobb Lane (Mrs. William Penn Lane), "For My Children," typescript in possession of John Collier Cobb of Goldsboro by whose permission it is quoted.
145. Arbuckle, *Civil War Experiences*, 145.
146. Susan Elizabeth Collier (1847–1935) diary, 11 Apr. 1865. Original is in possession of Caroline Cobb Whitehead of Goldsboro by whose permission it is quoted.
147. Lane, "For My Children;" Mary Bayard Devereux Clarke, "General Sherman in Raleigh," *The Old Guard*, IV (Apr. 1866), 226.
148. Collier diary, 11 Apr. 1865.
149. Ibid., 12 Apr. 1865.
150. Ridley, *Battles and Sketches*, 457.
151. Clark, *Regiments*, IV, 59–60.
152. Johnston, *Military Operations*, 397–400.
153. Accompanying Governors Swain and Graham were Dr. Edward Warren, surgeon general of N.C., Maj. John Devereux of Gov. Vance's staff, and Col. James G. Burr of the State Guards.
154. Barrett, *Sherman's March*, 215–16.
155. Amis, *Historical Raleigh*, 143.
156. Collier diary, 13 Apr. 1865.
157. Ibid.; Mongomery, *Olden Days*, 21.
158. Collier diary, 13 Apr. 1865.
159. Howard, *Autobiography*, II, 159.
160. EBC to SJBC, 16 Apr. 1865, AH Papers.
161. Sherman, *Memoirs*, II, 348–49; Howard, *Autobiography*, II, 155–56; Barrett, *Sherman's March*, 230–33.
162. Collier diary, 17 Apr. 1865.
163. Amis, *Historical Raleigh*, 145–46; Hitchcock, *Marching with Sherman*, 307.
164. EBC to SJBC, 18 Apr. 1865, AH Papers.
165. Collier diary, 17 Apr. 1865; EBC to SJBC, 18 Apr. 1865, AH Papers.
166. Sherman, *Memoirs*, II, 359–61.
167. Ridley, *Battles and Sketches*, 460.
168. KPB to William H. Battle, 21–30 Apr. 1865, Daniel Harvey Hill, Jr., Papers; KPB, *Old-Time Tar Heel*, 193–94.

169. KPB to William H. Battle, 21–30 Apr. 1865, Daniel Harvey Hill, Jr., Papers.

170. Clarke, "General Sherman in Raleigh," 304.

171. Ibid., 230–31.

172. Ibid., 231. Mary Bayard Clarke, daughter of Thomas Pollock Devereux of Raleigh, wrote under the pseudonym "Stuart-Leigh" and poetry under that of "Tenella."

173. EBC to SJBC, 29 Apr. 1865, AH Papers; Collier diary, 28 Apr. 1865.

174. *Daily Standard*, 1 May 1865; Collier diary, 24 Apr. 1865.

175. Walter S. Clemence diary, 29 Apr. 1865, NCC.

176. Aldert Smedes, untitled sermon, AS Papers.


## CHAPTER FOUR

1. Susan Elizabeth Collier diary, 11 May 1865.

2. Ibid., 3, 4 May 1865.

3. AS, "St. Mary's School," *Our Living and Our Dead*, III (July 1875), 115.

4. Collier diary, 11 May 1865.

5. Harriet Cobb Lane, "For My Children," typescript in possession of John Collier Cobb of Goldsboro by whose permission it is quoted.

6. Mary Bayard Devereux Clarke, "General Sherman's Officers," *Old Guard*, June 1866, 351.

7. Putnam, *The Lady*, 322–23.

8. Massey, *Bonnet Brigades*, 130.

9. Noble, *Public Schools of North Carolina*, 245.

10. Massey, *Bonnet Brigades*, 121.

11. Lena H. Smith, who finished at St. Mary's in 1872, is included in *Some Pioneer Women Teachers of North Carolina* (Delta Gamma Society, 1955). She was principal of Vine Hill Female Academy and established the Cottage Home School.

12. James McKimmon to KMcK, 11 May 1868, KMcK Papers.

13. Becker, *Biography of Christian Reid*, 23.

14. Massey, *Bonnet Brigades*, 45.

15. JDNC, 1864, 51; list of 1865 students written by Kate Clements Ellis, SMCA.

16. JDNC, 1876, 130.

17. Peter Evans Smith to Lena Smith, 15 Feb. 1871, Peter Evans Smith Papers.

18. Circular, 7 June 1867, SMCA.

19. Amis, *Historical Raleigh*, 109

20. KPB, "The Rev. Aldert Smedes, D.D., Founder of St. Mary's School, Raleigh," *North Carolina University Magazine*, new series, XIII (Nov. 1893), 80–81.

21. AS to KPB, 7 July 1876, BF Papers.

22. MJI, "The Founder of St. Mary's—The Rev. Aldert Smedes, D.D.," *SMM*, Nov. 1905, 5.

23. Montgomery, *Olden Days*, 26.

24. KPB, "Aldert Smedes," 81.

25. Proclamation of Amnesty, 29 May 1865.

26. Penciled draft of Smedes's letter to President Johnson is in his account book for 1864–65, SMCA. Copies dated 30 June 1865, and his petition for pardon are in the Civil War Collection, Petitions for Pardon, 1865–1868, A&H.

27. Mary Devereux Clarke to Willie Clarke, 1868 or 1869. Letter is in possession of Mary Moulton Barden, New Bern.

28. MFH to Mrs. AH, 1 Feb. 1874, AH Papers.

29. Nellie Jackson Mason, "Pleasant Recollections, 1869–'70—Smedesborough," *SMM*, Apr. 1906, 15.

30. Richard H. Battle, *Memorial Address*, 10.

31. MSP interview, Oct. 1972.

32. MFH to Mrs. AH, 11 Feb. 1874, AH Papers.

33. Ibid., 26 Sept. 1873, AH Papers.

34. LW to Mrs. EJW, 5 May 1866; 10 Aug. 1867, Edward Jenner Warren Papers.

35. Lena Smith, "Thoughts of Dear St. Mary's Suggested by the Postcard," *SMCB*, Mar. 1938, 39.

36. BS to JBC, 17 Sept. 1898, JBC Papers; *SMM*, Apr 1882, 188.

37. Nora Devereux Cannon to Willie Clarke, 11 Feb. 1873, letter in possession of Mary Moulton Barden, New Bern; notes from Barden to Martha Stoops, 1 Feb. 1979. In 1881 Nora Cannon was elected a county superintendent of public instruction, the first woman elected to public office in Tenn.

38. Monthly report of St. Mary's School for Bessie Cain, Nov. 1867, AH Papers.

39. Lizzie Jones to Mollie Nixon, 30 Jan. 1872, 2 Apr. 1873, letters in possession of Dorothy Nixon Horton, Hertford, N.C.

40. MFH to Mrs. AH, 11 Feb. 1874, AH Papers.

41. Josie Myers to Louis Meares, 22 Oct. 1876, M-D Papers.

42. Ibid.

43. LW to Mrs. EJW, 20 Oct. 1867, EJW Papers.

44. Ibid., 2 Feb. 1867.

45. Ibid., 9 Mar. 1867.

46. Ibid., 24 Feb. 1866.

47. Mason, "Pleasant Recollections," 15–16.

48. Smith, "Dear St. Mary's," 39.

49. LW to Mrs. EJW, 7 Apr. 1866, 10 Nov. 1867, EJW Papers.

50. MFH to Mrs. AH, 4, 11 Oct. 1873, AH Papers.

51. Kate Meares to Louis Meares, 25 Dec. 1876, M-D Papers.

52. Bessie Cain to Mrs. JLB, 28 Nov. 1867, JLB Papers.

53. LW to Mrs. EJW, 12, 29 Oct., 5 Nov. 1867, EJW Papers.

54. Ibid., 5 May 1867.

55. MFH to Mrs. AH, 7 Nov. 1873, AH Papers.

56. Ibid., 11 Feb. 1874.

57. "Viator," "Visit to St. Mary's," *Daily Sentinel*, 16 May 1871, reprinted from the *Maryland Church Record*.

58. Haywood, *Bishops of North Carolina*, 172–75.

59. Halliburton, *St. Augustine's College*, 1, 8; *JDNC*, 1873, 87; *JDNC*, 1877, 174. During the tenure of Dr. J. E. C. Smedes (the D.D. degree was conferred upon him by UNC in 1833), St. Augustine's student body grew from 17 to over 100. By 1882, 160 alumni were teaching in the public schools and 9 had been ordained to the ministry.

60. *JDNC*, 1874, 56.

61. Ibid., 1873, 22.

62. Richard H. Battle, *Memorial Address*, 10.

63. Annie Bitting to KDeRM, 12 May 1877, M-D Papers.

64. MJI to KDeRM, 1 June 1877, M-D Papers.

65. Richard H. Battle, *Memorial Address*, 10.

66. Annie Bitting to KDeRM, 12 May 1877, M-D Papers.

67. Ibid.

68. AJDeR to KDeRM, 2 May 1877, M-D Papers.

69. "Viator," "Visit to St. Mary's"; KPB, "Aldert Smedes," 77.

70. Emilie W. McVea, "The Professional Woman as Teacher," *NO*, 24 Nov. 1904.

71. *Observer* (Raleigh), 22 Apr. 1877.

72. Resolutions, Convocation of Raleigh, Diocese of N.C., 26 Apr. 1877, JBC-SHC.

73. Richard H. Battle, *Memorial Address*, 9.

74. *JDNC*, 1877, 47.


CHAPTER FIVE

1. *Observer* (Raleigh), 22 Apr. 1877.

2. MJI to KDeRM, 1 June 1877, M-D Papers.

3. BS to KDeRM, 3 July 1877, M-D Papers.

4. Ibid.

5. KMcK, "A Tribute to the Smedes Rectors," *SMCB*, Dec. 1921, 7.

6. BS to KDeRM, 25 June 1877, M-D Papers.

7. KDeRM to Louis Meares, 10 Oct. 1877, M-D Papers.

8. MSP interview, 20 Nov. 1974.

9. Salley, *Life*, 46–47.

10. Henrietta Harvey Smedes's grandfather was Matthew Harvey (1781–1866), U.S. congressman, governor of New Hampshire, and federal judge.

11. Bishop Lyman to unknown man, 26 Dec. 1879, SMCA.

12. Woody, *Women's Education*, II, 183.

13. BS sermon, BS Papers, SMCA.

14. *Observer* (Raleigh), 22 Apr. 1877.

15. BS to Ellen Tew, 19 July 1879, SMCA.

16. *SMM*, Apr. 1882, 205.

17. Salley, *Life*, 60; *St. Mary's School Catalogue*, 1896–97.

18. Unidentified clipping, Smedes Papers, GTS.

19. Emilie McVea, centennial address, *SMCB*, Apr. 1910, 8.

20. Murray, *Wake: Capital County*, I, 601.

21. Kate Cannon to Willie Clarke, 17 Sept. 1869. A copy of letter is in possession of Mary Moulton Barden. Letter is included in Beth G. Crabtree and James W. Patton, eds., *"Journal of a Secesh Lady": The Diary of Catherine Ann Devereux Edmondston, 1860–1866* (Raleigh: Division of Archives and History, Department of Cultural Resources, 1979), 730.

22. *St. Mary's School Catalogue*, 1880–81.

23. Carrie Freer to SJBC, 16 Sept. 1883, JLB Papers.

24. *St. Mary's School Catalogue*, 1893–94.

25. Paul C. Cameron to his sisters, 30 June 1877, CF Papers.

26. AS to KDeRM, 31 May 1876, M-D Papers.

27. BS to KDeRM, 12 July 1877, M-D Papers.

28. Ibid., 29 June 1881.

29. Salley, *Life*, 44. Czarnomska's deaconess aunt, Sister Eliza Coakley, lived with her at the school and kept the infirmary.

30. Fragment of letter probably from KMcK, M-D Papers.

31. Rebecca Collins to her mother, 24 Apr. 1879(?), Collins Papers.

32. *SMM*, June 1884, 204.

33. Czarnomska taught Hebrew language and literature and served as dean of women at the University of Cincinnati and taught Biblical literature at Sweet Briar. Macmillan, N.Y., published v. I, *The Authentic Literature of Israel* in 1924, v. II in 1928. Czarnomska died in 1938 at 88. Her portrait is at St. Mary's. See *SMM*, Sept. 1904, 15; *SMM*, Dec. 1918, 13; *SMCB*, June 1938, 54, Marie Elizabeth Josephine Czarnomska Papers.

34. Emilie McVea, "St. Mary's of a By-Gone Day," *SMM*, Apr. 1906, 22; *St. Mary's School Catalogue*, 1880–81.

35. *St. Mary's School Catalogue*, 1894–95.

36. Carrie Freer to Mrs. JSH, 27 Jan. 1884, JSH Papers.

37. *SMM*, June 1905, 10–11.

38. Ibid., Nov. 1881, 38.

39. Ibid., June 1882, 284.

40. Salley, *Life*, 52; Jessie Degen, "When McKimmonsville Flourished," *SMM*, Apr. 1906, 32; *SMM*, Oct. 1896, 53; *SMM*, Apr. 1906, 32–33; MSP interview, Oct. 1972.

41. Degen, "When McKimmonsville Flourished," 32.

42. McVea, "By-Gone Day," 24.

43. BS, "Exhortation to Faculty in Preparation for the First Communion of the School Year," 30 Aug. 1878, AS Papers.

44. Emilie McVea's mother, widow of a La. judge, Charles McVea, moved her family to Raleigh.

45. Salley, *Life*, 65–66; *SMM*, Oct. 1896, 51; *SMM*, Apr. 1906, 31–32; *SMCB*, Apr. 1922, 37–38; *Sweet Briar College Bulletin*, Apr. 1928, 16–23; Agatha Knox Chipley interviews, 2 Oct. 1977, 28 Mar. 1978; Elizabeth Montgomery interview, 23 July 1977.

46. Campion, *Look To This Day*, 110; Annie Hinsdale Joslin interview, 8 Nov. 1974; Montgomery interview, 23 Aug. 1977.

47. Salley, *Life*, 81.

48. MSP interview, Oct. 1972; Susan Linehan Steele interview, 19 Apr. 1978.

49. Salley, *Life*, 66–67; *SMM*, June 1905, 17; *SMM*, Feb. 1908, 19; Montgomery interview, 29 Mar. 1972; *SMCB*, Apr. 1941, 4–7. Florence Slater died in Winston-Salem, 22 Jan. 1941.

50. Montgomery interview, 29 Mar. 1972; Lizzie Ashe Flint, undated ms. of 1957 talk to St. Mary's students, SMCA.

51. *SMM*, June 1885, 189; *SMM*, Oct. 1896, 43–44.

52. Annie Moore, 1890 valedictorian, graduated from Vassar and made Phi Beta Kappa. Jessie Degen, 1894 graduate, took her degree at Wellesley and became principal of the May School in Boston. See *SMM*, Oct. 1896, 50; *SMCB*, Oct. 1934, 19.

53. *SMM*, Nov. 1882, 41.

54. KDeRM to Louise M. Meares, 14 Mar. 1878, M-D Papers.

55. Salley, *Life*, 44–45, 55, 62.

56. It is impossible to determine exact dates for Kursteiner's tenure because files of both the *SMM* and the *St. Mary's School Catalogue* are incomplete for the 1880s.

57. Salley, *Life*, 77, 62; *SMM*, Nov. 1882, 50.

58. Salley, *Life*, 77.

59. *St. Mary's School Catalogue*, 1893–94.

60. *SMM*, Jan. 1908, 23.

61. Salley, *Life*, 80; *SMM*, Oct. 1896, 43.

62. Salley, *Life*, 60; *SMM*, Nov. 1881, 52; *SMM*, June 1885, 189–94.

63. *SMCB*, Dec. 1955, 38. Mary Lyde Hicks married Marshall Williams.

64. *NO*, 14 Jan. 1885.

65. *SMM*, June 1885, 190, 177; BS to Paul C. Cameron, 7 Jan. 1885, Smedes letterbook, AS-SMCA; MSP interview, 21 Sept. 1971.

66. *NO*, 7 June 1887.

67. *St. Mary's School Catalogue*, 1893–94.

68. Salley, *Life*, 48; Frances Marriner, "Miss Katie," *SMCB*, June 1927, 10.

69. Mary Hoke Slaughter interview, 9 July 1977.

70. Degen, "When McKimmonsville Flourished," 27–28.

71. Salley, *Life*, 71–73; MSP interview 29 Oct. 1971.

72. MSP interview, 13 Dec. 1972.

73. Ibid., 27 Aug. 1971.

74. Ibid.; Mary Fowle Stearns interview, 6 Aug. 1971; *SMM*, Oct. 1896, 53.

75. MSP interview, 27 Aug. 1971.

76. Ibid.; Stearns interview, 6 Aug. 1971.

77. Salley, *Life* 74–75; MSP interview, 27 Aug. 1971.

78. Abraham died in 1884 in Goldsboro where he had practiced law; he was 39. George died at 35. Neither had married. George won distinction in Latin at the University of Virginia and taught the classics at St. Mary's and at a boys' school in Maryland before returning home to live with his mother and to practice law. In 1880 he was elected to the state House of Representatives. He founded the Raleigh SPCA.

79. Carrie Freer to Mrs. JSH, 12 Sept. 1883, JSH Papers.

80. Ibid., 11 Feb. 1884; MSP interview, 13 Oct. 1972; Stearns interview, 6 Aug. 1971; Carrie Freer to Mrs. JSH, 11 Feb 1884, JSH Papers.

81. McVea, "By-Gone Day," 21.

82. Salley, *Life*, 73; *SMM*, Feb. 1883, 90.

83. *SMM*, Oct. 1896, 52.

84. Salley, *Life*, 74; MSP interview, 11 Oct. 1971.

85. BS to JBC, 11 Sept. 1898, JBC Papers.

86. *SMM*, Apr. 1882, 208.

87. BS to Mrs. Devereux, n.d., 1884 letterbook, SMCA.

88. Salley, *Life*, 71–72.

89. McVea, "By-Gone Day," 21.

90. Ibid., 20; Salley, *Life*, 73.

91. *SMM*, Apr. 1882, 209; McVea, "By-Gone Day," 19.

92. *SMM*, Nov. 1881, 39; *SMM*, June 1885, 183.

93. Salley, *Life*, 75; *SMM*, Jan. 1907, 8–9. Anne Saunders was the daughter of Rev. Joseph Saunders who had taught at the Episcopal School.

94. Riley, *Carolina Power and Light Company*, 10, 19–20.

95. *SMM*, Nov. 1882, 42.

96. Salley, *Life*, 68–69.

97. *SMM*, Oct. 1896, 45.

98. Ibid., Jan. 1881, 150.

99. Salley, *Life*, 55.

100. MSP interview, 11 Oct. 1971.

101. For accounts of switchback accident, see Salley, *Life*, 90–92; *Daily State Chronicle*, 5 Apr. 1893. The Fairgrounds were located near A&M College on the later site of the Raleigh Little Theatre.

102. MSP interview, 21 Sept. 1971.

103. Richard Meares to Louis Meares, 6 Dec. 1878, M-D Papers.

104. Excerpts from diary of Charlotte Allston, 1891–92, *SMCB*, Mar. 1942, 28; Carrie Freer to SJBC, 21 Oct. 1883, JLB Papers.

105. KDeRM to one of her sons, 20 Oct. 1879, M-D Papers.

106. *SMM*, May 1879, 2.

107. Salley, *Life*, 84. Christine Sanders married Edward Rembert.

108. *St. Mary's School Catalogue*, 1880–81.

109. BS to A. L. DeRosset, n.d. 1880, M-D Papers.

110. Henrietta Collins to her mother, 5 Oct. 1887, 23 Sept. 1888, Anne Cameron Collins Papers.

111. Rebecca Collins to her mother, 9 Apr. 1880, Anne Cameron Collins Papers.

112. Carrie Freer to Mrs. JSH, 6 Apr. 1884, JSH Papers.

113. Henrietta Collins to her mother, 6 Nov. 1887, Anne Cameron Collins Papers.

114. *SMCB*, Mar. 1942, 11.

115. Annie M. Dughi, "Fashions and Follies," *SMM*, June 1899, 46.

116. Carrie Freer to SJBC, 21 Oct. 1883, JLB Papers.

117. Bessie Henderson to her mother, 4 June 1893, JSH Papers; *Daily State Chronicle*, 31 May 1893; Marie D. Moore, "The Last Ride of Jefferson Davis," *NO*, 29 May 1977.

118. *SMM*, June 1884, 197.

119. *SMCB*, June 1929, 2.

120. Story related by Mary L. Withers Richardson. Pescud was the granddaughter of Jane Constance Miller of the original 13 students.

121. *SMCB*, June 1929, 2; Flint, ms.

122. Degen, "When McKimmonsville Flourished," 33.

123. *St. Mary's School Catalogue*, 1880–81.

124. Salley, *Life*, 63.

125. BS sermons, AS Papers.

126. KDeRM to Louis Meares, 14 Mar. 1878, M-D Papers.

127. *SMM*, Oct. 1880, 19–20; *SMM*, Nov. 1880, 66–67; *SMM*, Dec. 1880, 104–11.

128. *Observer* (Raleigh), 28 Apr. 1877.

129. *CCh* (later *NCCh*), III (Nov. 1911), 4.

130. *JDNC*, 1881, 84.

131. *SMM*, June 1884, 215. Bishop Ives confirmed 21 in 1850.

132. *SMM*, Dec. 1880, 125.

133. *JDNC*, 1892, 77.

134. *NO*, 7, 8 June 1892; *Semi-Centennial Celebration of St. Mary's School*, pamphlet, n.d., n.p. The six graduates were Charlotte Allston, M. Elise Carwile, Jennie H. Pescud, May H. Davis, Janet W. Dugger, and Frances Tunstall.

135. *Observer* (Raleigh), 25 Apr. 1877.

136. BS to KDeRM, 3 July 1877, M-D Papers.

137. Annie Collins to Anne Cameron Collins, 3 Feb., 20 Sept. 1878, Anne Cameron Collins Papers.

138. *St. Mary's School Catalogue*, 1880–81.

139. School catalogs for a few years of BS's administration are extant; they list the students.

140. Salley, *Life*, 47.
141. Joslin interview, 11 Nov. 1974.
142. *JDNC*, 1879, 226–27.
143. BS to Bishop Lyman, 28 July 1888, penciled draft of letter in account book, SMCA.
144. Inventory of Executors and Administrators, Wake County, N.C., 497–504, A&H.
145. Richard H. Battle, *Memorial Address*, 13.
146. BS to Paul C. Cameron, 28 May 1885, draft of letter in account book, SMCA; *SMM*, Oct. 1880, 30.
147. *NO*, 6 Jan. 1885.
148. Kate Meares to her father, Richard Meares, 4 Apr. 1897, M-D Papers.
149. BS to KDeRM, 12 July 1877, M-D Papers.
150. Kate Meares to Richard Meares, 4 Apr. 1897, M-D Papers; *SMM*, Nov. 1910, 91.
151. *JDNC*, 1895, 64.
152. Cheshire, *Sketches*, 302.
153. *SMM*, Apr. 1909, 245–46.
154. *JDNC*, 1896, 21.
155. Ibid., 43.
156. Ibid., 64–65.
157. Members of the committee, besides Cheshire, were: Dr. M. M. Marshall, Rev. B. S. Bronson, Rev. F. J. Murdock, Rev. Junius M. Horner, Lawrence S. Holt, D. Y. Cooper, Charles E. Johnson.
158. "An Act to Incorporate the Trustees of Saint Mary's School," *Private Laws of the State of North Carolina, 1897,* c. 86. Note that both spellings are used.
159. The St. Mary's property had gone to Paul C. Cameron, the last surviving child of Duncan Cameron, and at his death in 1891 to his daughters and a granddaughter. Paul C. Cameron's will directed that "the grove of 25 acres in which the St. Mary's School buildings now stand is not to be sold but held and owned as it is now—a Female School of high grade unless improper and unreasonable taxes shall be imposed on it." See will dated 28 Feb. 1890, CF Papers.
160. The scholarships, the Mary E. Chapeau Endowed Memorial and the Mary Ruffin Smith Endowed Memorial, were still offered in 1982.
161. *JDNC*, 1901, 24.
162. *SMM*, June 1898, 73.
163. For the Saluda Conference, 23 Aug. 1898, see London, *Bishop Joseph Blount Cheshire,* 66; *JDNC*, 1899, 32, 73–77. The Diocese of Upper Carolina automatically became, upon its creation, a participant in the control of the school.
164. "An Act to Amend the Charter of St. Mary's School," *Private Laws of the State of North Carolina, 1899,* c. 3.
165. *Journal, Diocese of East Carolina,* 1899, 19.
166. *SMM*, June 1897, 77.
167. Charles Root to Margaret Mordecai Jones, 15 Apr. 1897, Root's letterbook, SMCA.
168. Reid, *From Raleigh's Past,* 37.
169. KDeRM to Richard A. Meares, 19 Feb. 1899, M-D Papers.
170. MSP interview, 29 Oct. 1971.
171. *Morning Post* (Raleigh), 23 Feb. 1899.
172. *NO*, 24 Feb. 1899.
173. Ibid., 25 Feb. 1899.
174. *SMM*, June 1885, 106; *SMM*, Mar. 1924, 9; *SMM*, Apr. 1906, 31.

CHAPTER SIX

1. The trustees paid $3,000 to Henrietta Smedes for furniture and equipment.
2. Margaret Harvey married John Irving Rose. Helen Lyell married Albert Whitehead Latta. Mary Sherwood married James M. Poyner. After his death she returned to Raleigh where her descendants became business and civic leaders.
3. Richard H. Battle, *Memorial Address,* 15.
4. Typescript, "Mississippi, Heart of the South," n.d., SMCA; *News and Herald* (Winns-

boro, S.C.), 6 Sept. 1978; MacDowell, *DuBose Genealogy*, 6. Bratton's mother was a descendant of Huguenots; her grandmother was the niece of Gen. Francis Marion.

5. Typescript, "Mississippi, Heart of the South," n.d., SMCA; Mrs. John Bratton, Sr., interview, 20 Sept. 1978.

6. Typescript, "Mississippi, Heart of the South"; *SMM*, June 1905, 12.

7. Kibler, *History of Converse College*, 51.

8. TM, 30 May 1900.

9. Ibid.

10. *JDNC*, 1901, 23.

11. *SMM*, Mar. 1914, 69; *SMCB*, Mar. 1935, 17; Annie Gray Nash Sprunt interview, 15 May 1973; Elizabeth Montgomery interview, 9 Aug. 1971; Annie Hinton Joslin interview, 11 Nov. 1974; Louise Venable Coker, "The Annals of My College Life," diary written at St. Mary's, 1902, lent to Martha Stoops by Mrs. Coker; Kate Herndon interview, 5 Sept. 1978; *SMC*, June 1978, 12.

12. *SMM* (yearbook), 1902, 21; *SMM* (yearbook), 1903, 28. 1902 graduates were Marie Bascot Brunson, Louise Manning Venable, Jennie Trapier, and Mary Spruill Weeks.

13. *JDNC*, 1901, 24.

14. Coates, *By Her Own Bootstraps*, 43–47.

15. *The Twig* (Meredith College), 22 Oct. 1964.

16. Elizabeth Lay Green interview, 2 Aug. 1975; Montgomery interview, 7 Jan. 1975.

17. Mary Hoke Slaughter interview, 9 July 1977.

18. TM, 30 May 1900.

19. Porter, *Straight Down a Crooked Lane*, 61–62; Wood, *Once Apunce a Time*, 168; Susan Linehan Steele interview, 3 Dec. 1974.

20. TM, 30 May 1900.

21. Ibid., Jan. 1902.

22. J. W. Jeudwine to JBC, 15 Mar. 1901, JBC Papers; *SMM*, Sept. 1904, 16; *SMM*, Feb. 1905, 14–15. After leaving Raleigh, Jeudwine was director of music in Miss Bristol's School, Washington, D.C. He was president of the Southern Music Teachers' Association, 1902–04. After he suffered a stroke in 1905, the Jeudwines returned to England.

23. By 1908 the Sanborns were teaching at Southern Seminary, Buena Vista, Va.

24. *St. Mary's School Catalogue*, 1908, 52.

25. Banner, *Women in Modern America*, 11–12.

26. TM, 30 May 1900.

27. Ibid., 30 May 1901, 25 May 1903.

28. *SMM*, Nov. 1905, 9–10; *SMM*, Oct.-Nov. 1917, 39.

29. *NO*, 14 May 1899.

30. The members of the executive committee of the board were Charles E. Johnson (brother of Mary Iredell), William A. Erwin (husband of Sadie Smedes), Richard H. Lewis, K. P. Battle, Jr., and F. J. Murdock.

31. *JDNC*, 1899, 33; *JDNC*, 1902, 34; TM, 30 May 1900, 27 May 1902.

32. *JDNC*, 1901, 24.

33. *SMM*, June 1905, 35; TM, May 1903. The corpus of the David R. Murchison fund was $5,000.

34. *JDNC*, 1901, 26–27.

35. TM, 25 May 1903.

36. Annie Shepard to Mrs. Paul C. Cameron, 2 Oct. 1896, CF Papers.

37. TM, 30 May 1900, 30 May 1901, 25 May 1903.

38. Coker, "Annals of My College Life."

39. *SMM*, Jan. 1905, 13.

40. Theodore DuBose Bratton to Richard A. Meares, 5 Feb. 1900, M-D Papers.

41. J. W. Jeudwine to JBC, 9 Oct. 1905, JBC Papers.

42. *SMC*, June 1978, 12.

43. *SMM* (yearbook), 1901, advertisement.

44. Sprunt interview, 15 May 1973; Salley, *Life*, 107; *SMM*, Dec. 1904, 7.

45. *SMM* (yearbook), 1901, advertisement.

46. *SMM* (yearbooks), 1900, 1901, 1902, advertisements.

47. TM, 25 May 1903.

48. *SMM*, Oct. 1904, 4. There were 5 sororities at Converse during Bratton's tenure. They were abolished about 1900. See letter from James G. Harrison, Jr., librarian, Converse College to Martha Stoops, 26 Sept. 1978, SMCA.

49. Beta Chapter, Edgewood School, Baltimore; Gamma Chapter, Columbia Institute, Columbia, Tenn.; Delta Chapter, Miss Stuart's, Washington, D.C. See *SMM*, Oct. 1904, 4.

50. *SMM*, Oct. 1904, 4. Kappa Delta, founded earlier at the Virginia State Normal School, was chartered in 1902. Phi Mu was founded at Wesleyan College, 1852.

51. Salley, *Life*, 105–06; *SMM*, Oct. 1904, 5.

52. Coker, "Annals of My College Life."

53. TM, 27 May 1902.

54. Ibid., 30 May 1901.

55. SMCB, Dec. 1928, 3.

56. TM, 27 May 1902.

57. Salley, *Life*, 99.

58. *SMM*, Nov. 1915, 68.

59. The address was republished in the *SMM*, Sept. 1906, 1–23, and also in pamphlet form.

60. Walter B. Capers, "A Personal Tribute to Bishop Bratton," *Bulletin*, St. Andrews Episcopal Church, Jackson, Miss., July 1944, 4.

61. Theodore DuBose Bratton was the third bishop of Mississippi. The first (1850–87) was the Rev. William Mercer Green from the Diocese of North Carolina.

62. Bishop Bratton later married Mrs. Ivy P. Gass.

63. *SMM*, Mar. 1914, 61–62. All Saints' is now a college preparatory boarding and day school for boys and girls, grades seven through twelve and is owned by the Episcopal dioceses of Ark., La., and Miss. The LL.D. degree was conferred upon Bishop Bratton in 1911 by the Univ. of Mississippi. His portrait was placed in the Mississippi Hall of Fame, and the chapel at All Saints' was consecrated to his memory.

64. *Who's Who in America*, 1944–45, 226. Bratton was the author of *Christian Education: The Church's Duty* (New Orleans: n.p., 1904?), *Wanted—Leaders! A Study of Negro Development* (New York: n.p., 1922), *An Apostle of Reality: The Life and Thought of the Reverend William Porcher DuBose, S.T.D., D.C.L.* (New York: Longmans, Green and Co., 1936), and *Sermons and Essays* (no publ. information found).

65. Capers, "Bishop Bratton," 2–3.


CHAPTER SEVEN

1. Salley, *Life*, 111.

2. McNeely DuBose to Bishop Capers, 11 July 1903, JBC Papers.

3. Dr. Anderson died suddenly at the rectory in 1905. Mrs. Anderson moved with the DuBose family to Morganton where she died in 1911. *SMM*, June 1905, 9; *SMM*, Feb. 1911, 189; *Highland Churchman*, XXII (Mar. 1953), 9.

4. For DuBose family see MacDowell, *DuBose Genealogy*.

5. SMCB, Sept. 1906, 5.

6. *SMM*, Mar. 1907, 16.

7. TM, 20 May 1904.

8. JDNC, 1904, 2.

9. Scott, *Two Forays Into Women's History*, 7.

10. *SMM*, Feb. 1908, 4–6. The article was written for the *SMM* by Margaret DuBose after she moved to Morganton with her family.

11. Woody, *Women's Education*, II, 220.

12. *SMM*, June 1904, 18; SMCB, Sept. 1906, 18–19.

13. *SMM* (yearbook), 1905, 29; *SMM*, Dec. 1906, 11.

14. *SMM*, June 1905, 14–15.

15. Ibid., 3.

16. *SMM*, Oct. 1904, 1.

17. Sherrill, *Annals of Lincoln County, N.C.*, 405.

18. See Fassifern catalogs, NCC. After Anna McBee died, Kate Shipp sold Fassifern. Kate Shipp died in Lincolnton, Nov. 16, 1932.

19. *SMM*, June 1904, 11.

20. Eliza H. Knox, "In Appreciation of Our Martha," typescript, SMCA; *SMM*, Dec. 1925, 6–8; MSP interview, 20 Jan. 1974.

21. She was Lucy Walke Cruikshank, St. Mary's 1863–64.

22. The last chapter of Salley's *Life*, 259–72, is a biographical sketch of Ernest Cruikshank by Katherine Batts Salley.

23. Anna Barrow Clark Gordon interview, 19 Apr. 1975.

24. *SMM*, Nov. 1905, 16.

25. Ibid., Dec. 1905, 10.

26. Ibid., Mar. 1905, 3–4; Florence Slater, tribute to Miss McKimmon, *SMCB*, Dec. 1928, 2.

27. *SMM*, Nov. 1904, 10; Florence Stone Hough, interview, 17 May 1976. Roosevelt's mother had gone to school in Georgia with Rosalie DuBose's mother.

28. *SMCB*, Mar. 1939, 5–6.

29. Isabel Clark James interview, 15 May 1973; Martha Dabney Jones interview, 12 Aug. 1975; *SMCB*, June 1940, 43–44.

30. *SMM*, Dec. 1905, 9; *SMM*, June 1904, 7; *SMCB*, Mar. 1939, 6.

31. *SMM*, Nov. 1905, 20; *SMM*, Apr. 1907, 20.

32. Salley, *Life*, 115.

33. *SMM*, 5 Oct. 1914, 12; *SMM*, Dec. 1925, 6–7.

34. *SMM*, June 1905, 7–9, 14–15; *SMM*, June 1906, 15–16; Salley, *Life*, 96.

35. Dorothy May Hughson diary, 1905, SMCA.

36. By 1910 Alpha Kappa Psi had a chapter at Fairmont School in Tennessee organized by St. Mary's alumna Jennie Trapier. Chapters were at Wesleyan College, Macon, Ga., Woman's College, Tallahassee, Fla., and Stetson University. Sororities were abolished at Stuart Hall in 1909. See *SMM* (yearbook), 1910.

37. Elleneen Checkley to Alpha Chapter, Alpha Kappa Psi, n.d., SMCA.

38. *SMM*, Mar. 1905, 19.

39. Unsigned, undated letter, SMCA.

40. George Howe III, son of Woodrow Wilson's sister Annie, was on the UNC faculty.

41. Eleanor Randolph Wilson to Jessie Woodrow Wilson, 21 Oct., 4 Dec. 1906, 29 Apr., 6 May, 13 May 1907, 6 Apr. 1908. Letters from Nell Wilson, 1906–08, to her sister Jessie Woodrow Wilson, a student at the Woman's College of Baltimore (Goucher College), are in the possession of The Very Rev. Francis B. Sayre, Jr., by whose permission they are quoted. Copies were given to SMCA by Frances White Saunders, biographer of Ellen Axson Wilson. Saunders generously shared her research. *SMM*, Mar. 1908, 4–9; *RT*, 27 May 1954; Salley, *Life*, 121; McAdoo, *The Woodrow Wilsons*, 91.

42. *SMM*, May 1905, 11.

43. *SMCB*, June 1940, 43.

44. Salley, *Life*, 120–121.

45. *SMM*, Dec. 1904, 9.

46. TM, 20 May 1904.

47. Ravenscroft was designed by Charles W. Barrett and built by W. B. Barrow, both of Raleigh, at a cost of about $9,000. *JDNC*, 1904, 23–24. (Cheshire's father had roamed that area when a student at the Episcopal School.)

48. London, *Bishop Joseph Blount Cheshire*, 75.

49. *SMM*, Sept. 1904, 3.

50. Ibid., 18.

51. Ibid., June 1905, 18, 13–14.

52. The holder of the Eliza Battle Pittman Scholarship must be an Episcopalian resident of Edgecombe County nominated by the vestry of Calvary Church, Tarboro.

53. Pittman Auditorium and its furnishings cost $16,000. *SMM*, Oct. 1905, 2; *SMM*, June 1907, 10; *SMCB*, Feb. 1908, 14.

54. JBC to trustees, 8 Dec. 1905, SMCA.

55. *JDNC*, 1906, 69; *SMM*, June-July 1907, 14. Because TM for most of the period are missing, it is impossible to give an accurate account of the gifts.

56. *JDNC*, 1906, 24–25, 30–31.

57. TM, 30 May 1906, 20 Feb. 1907, from printed pamphlet, SMCA.

58. *SMM*, Mar. 1905, 19; *SMM*, May 1905, 23.

59. Ibid., Apr. 1907, 22–23.

60. DuBose to trustees, 20 May 1904, SMCA; *SMM*, June 1904, 14. Winner of the competitive examinations was Lillian Farmer, who graduated in 1907 with an average of 97.45.

61. *SMM*, Sept. 1904, 5; *SMM*, June 1905, 9; *SMM*, Nov. 1905, 21, 25–26.

62. Ibid., June-July 1907, 14.

63. Ibid., Apr. 1907, 28.

64. Ibid., Mar. 1907, 15.

65. *NO*, 8 Jan. 1909.

66. *SMM*, May 1880, 32–33.

67. Ibid., Jan. 1909, 8.

68. Ibid., June-July 1907, 42.

69. GL to board of trustees, May 1911, SMCA.

70. *SMM*, Feb. 1908, 17.

71. *CCh*, II (May 1911), 5.


CHAPTER EIGHT

1. TM, 18 June 1907.

2. GL to Bishops Cheshire and Darst, 13 June 1907, SMCA.

3. *SMCB*, Mar. 1937, 14. The Lays lived in Little Rock where Bishop Lay served as rector until he was translated in 1869 to the Diocese of Easton.

4. *NO*, 18 June 1907; *RT*, 12 Aug. 1945.

5. Elizabeth Lay Green interview, 2 Aug. 1975; Salley, *Life*, 120.

6. GL to his mother, 24–28 Sept. 1907, GL Papers.

7. Ibid.

8. Ibid.

9. Banner, *Women in Modern America*, 6.

10. Knight, *Education in the United States*, 403.

11. Millstein and Bodin, *American Women*, 148.

12. Woody, *Women's Education*, II, 337–38, 360, 369.

13. The standard colleges were Agnes Scott, Converse, Goucher, Randolph-Macon, Sophie Newcomb, and Westhampton. Elizabeth Avery Colton, head of the English department at Baptist University for Women (Meredith College), made the studies of standards of women's colleges.

14. *NO*, 24 Nov. 1904.

15. *SMCB*, Apr. 1910, 5–14.

16. *SMM*, Dec. 1900, 113–114.

17. Ibid., Nov. 1907, 22. It is not known when or where BS and GL knew one another.

18. *SMM*, June 1909, 13.

19. Ibid., Nov. 1910, 84.

20. Ibid., Oct. 1915, 3.

21. Salley, *Life*, 129.

22. GL to his mother, Sept. 24–28, 1907, GL Papers.

23. *SMCB*, Feb. 1909, 11–14; *CCh*, II (Sept. 1911), 6.

24. Typescript of statement sent by GL to the officers of the Association of Colleges and Preparatory Schools of the Southern States, 20 Nov. 1912, SMCA.

25. *SMCB*, Feb. 1909, 10–14.

26. Ibid., 8–10.

27. Ibid., Aug. 1915, 28; *CCh*, II (Sept. 1911), 6.

28. *SMM*, Nov. 1913, 40–41; typescript, GL Papers.

29. *SMCB*, Aug. 1912, 53–54.

30. Mary Hoke Slaughter to Martha Stoops, 19 Sept. 1977, SMCA.
31. *SMCB*, May 1917, 20–21.
32. Nancey Lay White interview, 10 Feb. 1974.
33. *SMM*, Dec. 1910–Jan. 1911, 159–60.
34. *SMCB*, Sept. 1913, 26.
35. Ibid., 5–6.
36. Salley, *Life*, 143–207, passim.
37. *SMM*, June-July 1908, 24.
38. Salley, *Life*, 102–03, 128–29, 145, 167–68; White interviews, 10 Feb. 1974, 23 Aug. 1978; Green interviews, 28 Jan. 1974, 18 Feb. 1974, 7 Sept. 1976, 23 Aug. 1978; Irma Deaton interview, 7 Oct 1976.
39. Lenora Sheib, widow of a Tulane philosophy professor, took her degree at Columbia after his death.
40. Salley, *Life*, 129, 161–63; Deaton interview, 7 Oct. 1976; Annie Gray Nash Sprunt interview, 12 May 1974; Cantey Venable Sutton interview, 29 Oct. 1975; Arabella Thomas Rogers to Martha Stoops, 7 Aug. 1975, SMCA.
41. Eleanor Thomas died 13 July 1969, in Cleveland, O., at the age of 88. In 1936 Mather College awarded her the honorary LL.D. degree. Her portrait at St. Mary's, done by Nancy Bunch Sheridan, is a copy of one by Rolf Stoll commissioned by a Mather student. A committee composed of Elizabeth Gold Swindell, Arabella Thomas Rogers, Emma Boughtnight Miller, Agnes Barton Dysart, and Eleanor Relyea Johnston raised the funds.
42. Salley, *Life*, 130, 119; Porter, *Straight Down a Crooked Lane*, 57. Cribbs married C. L. Mann.
43. *SMCB*, Aug. 1909, 11.
44. TECM, 2 Mar. 1910.
45. *SMM*, May 1916, 216. Owen died 25 Feb. 1941, in Chattanooga where he taught at the university. See *SMCB*, Apr. 1941, 45.
46. Martha Dowd died 25 July 1925.
47. *SMM*, Apr. 1916, 179. Chamberlain's article with Jacques Loeb entitled "An Attempt at Physico-Chemical Explanation of Certain Groups of Fluctuating Variations" was published in Nov. 1915.
48. *SMM*, Apr. 1909, 252. See Whitaker, *Committees of Safety*.
49. *SMM*, Oct. 1904, 15; Elizabeth Cheek interview, July 1979. One of Anna Dunlop's paintings is owned by the Metropolitan Museum of Art, NYC. A number of her paintings are in the Anna Mercer Dunlop Gallery in the public library, Petersburg, Va.
50. *SMM*, Feb. 1910, 76.
51. Ibid., Aug. 1916, 15; *SMM*, Apr. 1917, 138; Agatha Knox Chipley interview, 15 Aug. 1978. Later, Emilie Rose Knox was heard regularly on radio with "The Velvet Violins."
52. *SMM*, Apr. 1909, 244.
53. Ibid., Aug. 1916, 16.
54. Scott, *Women's History*, 7–8.
55. Green interview, 7 Sept. 1976.
56. Salley, *Life*, 151–52; *SMM*, 1916 (yearbook).
57. *SMM*, June-July 1907, 45.
58. Eleanor Clement, soon after St. Mary's was incorporated, wrote a friend, "You will know how glad I am when I tell you that it has long been my wish to make some provision for St. Mary's in my will, and I could not do this while it was a private school. Now I can carry out my intention." See *SMM*, Jan. 1905, 10.
59. TM, 24 Nov. 1908.
60. JBC, GL, R. H. Lewis, Charles E. Johnson, and W. A. Erwin composed the executive committee.
61. Raleigh architect Charles E. Hartge also designed the Church of the Good Shepherd in Raleigh. He died in the great flu epidemic, Oct. 1918.
62. GW to his mother, 24–28 Sept. 1907, GL Papers.
63. *SMM*, April 1909, 242–43. The contents of the cornerstone are the Bible, the Book

of Common Prayer, a hymnal, copies of *SMCB*, the annual *SMM*, 1905–08, copies of the monthly *SMM*, and a copy of the last will and testament of Eleanor Clement.

64. *SMM*, Mar. 1909, 209.

65. The cost of remodeling Smedes and building the wings and covered ways was $64,794.27. See 1915 audit, 21, SMCA.

66. BC to Rev. Alfred A. Berkley, 1 Sept. 1910; BC to JBC, 22 Dec. 1910; JBC to BC, 26 Dec. 1910, BC Papers.

67. *SMM*, Dec. 1908, 130–31; *SMM*, Nov.-Dec. 1909, 95; *CCh*, I (Jan. 1910), 5; *TECM*, 3 Dec. 1909.

68. *SMM*, June-July 1907, 37; *SMM*, Nov. 1908, 105; *SMCB*, June 1918, 20.

69. *SMM*, Nov. 1913, 36–38.

70. *JDNC*, 1910, 27–28; *CCh*, I (Oct. 1909), 17; *CCh*, I (Jan. 1910), 5.

71. *SMCB*, June 1950, 43–45.

72. TM, 24 May 1915.

73. J. W. Jeudwine to JBC, 20 Dec. 1912, JBC-SHC.

74. TECM, 15 Mar. 1917.

75. Ibid., 7 Apr. 1911; *SMM*, Oct. 1912, 1; *CCh*, V (Aug. 1914), 7; TECM, 22 Sept. 1916; TM, 25 May 1918.

76. *JDNC*, 1911, 23.

77. TM, 24 May 1915; *SMM*, Oct. 1915, 24.

78. *CCh*, II (Aug. 1911), 12.

79. Ibid., 13. From 1897 to 1916 the school administration provided from operating funds scholarships worth $24,954. See TM, 11 Mar. 1916.

80. *CCh*, V (Aug. 1914), 8.

81. TECM, 23 Feb. 1916.

82. *JDNC*, 1916, 21–23, 38–39.

83. TM, 16 Mar. 1916. The trustees' committee on the endowment fund consisted of the Reverend Isaac W. Hughes, Graham Andrews, and George C. Royall. Osborne was then serving the Church of the Holy Comforter in Charlotte.

84. *CCh*, VII (June-July 1916), 4; *SMM*, Aug. 1916, 1, 5; *SMM*, Apr. 1917, 135.

85. *SMM*, Nov.-Dec. 1916, 76–77.

86. Ibid., Oct.-Nov. 1917, 45–49.

87. Ibid., Aug. 1917, 209–10.

88. Ibid.

89. Porter, *Straight Down a Crooked Lane*, 48–51. Porter's mother, Alice Capehart Winston, attended St. Mary's. Porter also wrote *Tomorrow Is Another Day, A Comedy of Manners* (New York: Exposition Press, 1952).

90. *SMM*, Jan. 1910, 43–44.

91. Ibid., Sept. 1914, 2.

92. Porter, *Straight Down A Crooked Lane*, 52.

93. Salley, *Life*, 130, 134; *SMM*, May 1913, 148–49.

94. *SMM*, Nov.-Dec. 1916, 69; Porter, *Straight Down a Crooked Lane*, 62–63. Mary Hoke Slaughter to Martha Stoops, Oct. 1979, SMCA.

95. *SMM*, Feb. 1911, 200–01; *SMM*, Nov. 1912, 27–28; Susan Porter Rawlings, "Saturday Evening at St. Mary's," *SMCB*, June 1940, 43–44; Porter, *Straight Down a Crooked Lane*, 56.

96. Salley, *Life*, 148.

97. Walser, *Wolfe Family in Raleigh*, 25. Only 100 signed and numbered copies were printed of this paper read on 21 Oct. 1976, upon the occasion of the dedication of the Thomas Wolfe Room in the Sarah Kenan Library, St. Mary's College. Green interviews, 28 Jan. 1974, 19 July 1976, 14 Aug. 1978.

98. White interview, 2 Feb. 1974.

99. Salley, *Life*, 137; Frances Cheatham Cooper interview, 1 Nov. 1977; Etta Burt Warren interview, 13 May 1974.

100. Porter, *Straight Down a Crooked Lane*, 49–50; Salley, *Life*, 139, 148; *SMCB*, Mar. 1935, 45; Cooper interview, 1 Nov. 1977.

101. *SMM* April 1909, 236.

102. Salley, *Life*, 123, 190; *SMM*, Nov.-Dec. 1909, 80; *SMM*, Jan. 1913, 85; Green interview, 2 Aug. 1975.

103. Annie C. Cameron, "The Christmas Tree," *SMM*, Mar. 1916, 17–18.

104. *SMM*, Feb. 1910, 57.

105. Ibid., Oct. 1911, 65–66; *SMM*, Dec. 1915, 94–95; *SMM*, Nov. 1914, 39; TM, 20 May 1917.

106. Salley, *Life*, 105–06. Gamma Beta Sigma was absorbed by Alpha Sigma Alpha. The records of Alpha Chapter of Alpha Kappa Psi remain in SMCA.

107. Coolidge, *Chapel Hill*, 94; Annie S. Cameron, "The Debate," *SMM*, Mar. 1916, 25–26.

108. *SMM*, Feb. 1908, 12.

109. Ibid., Oct. 1914, 17–19.

110. Ibid., Dec. 1914, 55–56.

111. Salley, *Life*, 158–59; *SMM*, Apr. 1917, 126–27.

112. Green interview, 14 Aug. 1978.

113. *SMM*, Aug. 1917, 207–08.

114. Jane Toy, "After High School What?" *SMM*, Mar. 1918, 2–4.

115. For complete text of "Hail to Our Boys in France," see *SMM*, May 1918, 36.

116. *SMM*, Oct.-Nov. 1917, 22; *SMM*, Dec. 1917, 15; *SMM*, Mar. 1918, 16–18.

117. Ibid., Dec. 1918, 17; *JDNC*, 1918, 32; Mary Yellott McNitt interview, 9 July 1977.

118. *SMM*, Oct.-Nov. 1917, 20; *SMM*, Jan.-Feb. 1918, 2; TM, 4 June 1918.

119. *SMM*, Mar. 1918, 1; *SMM*, Apr.-May, 1918, 2; *SMM*, Dec. 1918, 18–19; *SMCB*, Nov. 1939, 6; Slaughter interview, 9 July 1977; McNitt interview, 9 July 1977; *SMM*, Dec. 1918, 19; Green interview, 23 Aug. 1978.

120. *SMM*, Dec. 1918, 18; *SMM*, Jan.-Feb. 1918, 2–3; *SMM* yearbook, 1918; McNitt interview, 9 July 1977.

121. *SMM*, May 1918, 32–33; *SMM*, Dec. 1918, 18; *SMM*, May 1917, 157.

122. *SMM*, Dec. 1918, 49.

123. Ibid., 35–38, lists many "St. Mary's Girls in War Work."

124. *SMM*, Nov. 1915, 55–56; *SMM*, Aug. 1917, 211; *SMM*, Dec. 1918, 35–36.

125. *SMM*, Nov. 1907, 22.

126. Ibid., 19.

127. Ibid., June-July 1907, 49.

128. Ibid., 49–50; *SMM*, Oct. 1912, 23; *SMM*, Aug. 1916, 19–20.

129. *SMM* (yearbook), 1909, (yearbook), 1910.

130. Ibid., 71–85, 69. The daughters of AS presented to the chapel an alms basin.

131. *SMM*, Apr. 1910, 133, 161; *SMCB*, Sept. 1910, 5–6. The committee to draft the constitution consisted of Sadie Smedes Root, Eliza Smedes Knox, and Kate McKimmon.

132. *SMCB*, Sept. 1910, 8. Anna N. Buxton served as traveling secretary for 1911–12; the next year she and Annie Root divided the territory.

133. TM, 28 May 1912.

134. Ibid., 25 May 1915. The members of the delegation were Lizzie Wilson Montgomery, Alice Dugger Grimes, Annie Gales Vass, and Ellen Dortch Shore.

135. *SMM*, July 1917, 37.

136. Ibid., 11–14.

137. Ibid., Nov. 1907, 22.

138. Ibid., Oct. 1911, 51.

139. Laura Hoppe Alfriend interview, 21 Apr. 1979.

140. *SMM*, Apr. 1909, 235; *SMM*, Feb. 1910, 66; Green interviews, 28 Jan. 1974, 2 Aug. 1975, 17 Sept. 1976.

141. GL to his mother and other family members, 28 Jan. 1915, GL Papers; Green interview, 28 Jan. 1974.

142. Green interview, 17 Sept. 1976. Other students of the era corroborate the opinion that GL was first the priest.

143. *SMM*, Feb. 1910, 65; *SMM*, Feb. 1913, 100–01; *SMM*, Apr. 1913, 15; *SMM*, Mar. 1914, 57–58; *SMM*, Oct.-Nov. 1917, 38. Alumna Annie Webb Cheshire and Dr. A. S. Tucker, both missionaries to China, were married in the chapel, Easter week, 1914. Their fathers, the bishops of S.C. and Southern Virginia, officiated.

144. *SMM*, Jan. 1910, 44–45; *SMM*, Oct. 1915, 8; *SMCB*, May 1912, 24; *SMBC*, June 1914, 23–24.

145. Nell Battle Lewis, "Incidentally," *NO*, 17 May 1942.

146. Lay, *Some Additions to the Report*, passim.

147. See GL's reports to board of trustees, SMCA.

148. Kate Herndon interview, 5 Sept. 1978; William A. Erwin to GL, 2 June 1917, GL Papers.

149. Emilie McVea to JBC, 24 May 1917, JBC-SHC.

150. KPB to GL, 4 July 1918; Edward K. Graham to GL, July 1918, GL Papers.

151. Salley, *Life*, 167–68; *SMCB*, Dec. 1922, 11.

152. GL died at Duke Hospital where he had been taken only two days before, although he had known for several months that he had cancer. Anna Lay died 17 Nov. 1956.


CHAPTER NINE

1. Elizabeth Lay Green interview, 19 July 1976.

2. *RT*, 12 Aug. 1945.

3. GL to KPB, Jr., 26 June 1918, SMCA.

4. *Who's Who in America*, 1930–31, 2299; Evelyn Way notes, Aug. 1979, SMCA.

5. Report of William A. Hoke and JBC, TM, 25 June 1918. Bishop Darst, third member of the nominating committee, did not visit Way with the others on 15 June; he had said previously that he was "distinctly favorable" to Way.

6. Interviews with students and faculty of the period.

7. TECM, 26 Sept., 7 Nov. 1918; TM, 27 May 1919. The name of the flu victim is not recorded.

8. Frances Venable Gardiner interviews, 5 Aug. 1975, 31 Oct. 1978; Nancy Lay White interview, 23 Aug. 1978.

9. *SMM*, Apr.-May 1919, 36.

10. Jane Toy, "How the Armistice Was Celebrated at St. Mary's," *SMM*, Nov. 1919, 12–13; Salley, *Life*, 170–72.

11. Elizabeth G. Tucker interview, 28 Mar. 1977; FM, 18 Nov. 1918.

12. *SMM*, Dec. 1929, 2.

13. The seven, according to Mary Hoke Slaughter, who spent 10 years at the school, were Katherine Batts, Sarah Lorton Davis, Rainsford Glass, Mary Hoke, Nancey Lay, Jane Reynolds Ruffin, and Eleanor Sublett.

14. Mary Hoke Slaughter notes, Aug. 1979, SMCA; Helen Delamar Crockford telephone interview, 20 May 1980.

15. Sara Turner (1881–1952) taught at Miss Sayward's School, Philadelphia, at Ward-Belmont, and at the Comstock School, N.Y.C. She went to the Beard School, Orange, N.J., where she was headmistress for many years.

16. Eugenia Trexler Smith, trubute to Sara Turner, *SMCB*, Mar. 1953, 7; Martha Dabney Jones interview, 15 Apr. 1979.

17. Virginia Holt taught at Fairfax Hall in Va. and at St. Mary's Hall, Burlington, N.J. before coming to Raleigh.

18. *SMCB*, Oct. 1932, 4; Virginia Holt interview, 14 June 1974; MMM interview, 14 June 1974; Katherine Duff Powell interview, 21 Apr. 1979; Jones interview, 15 Apr. 1979; Elizabeth Thomas to Martha Stoops, 14 Feb. 1979, SMCA.

19. *SMCB*, Apr. 1928, 1; Florence Stone Hough interview, 7 May 1976.

20. *SMM*, Dec. 1926, 6.

21. Jones interview, 14 Apr. 1979; Mary Hoke Slaughter to Martha Stoops, Aug. 1979, SMCA.

22. Helen Andrews Scharrer, reminiscences, *SMCB*, Dec. 1960, 33. A portrait of William E. Stone by Clement Strudwick was presented to St. Mary's by the Greensboro alumnae.

23. The last two college graduates to attend primary school under KMcK were members of the class of 1926—Sylbert Pendleton who began at St. Mary's in 1913 and Ann Lawrence who entered in 1917. *SMCB*, June 1926, 8.

24. *SMCB*, Dec. 1921, 12.
25. Ibid., Dec. 1928, 1.
26. Eliza Smedes Knox, tribute, *SMCB*, Dec. 1926, 2.
27. Jones interviews, 12 Aug. 1975, 15 Mar. 1979; MMM interview, 14 June 1974.
28. TB, 10 Mar. 1939.
29. Elizabeth Thomas to Martha Stoops, 14 Feb. 1979, SMCA.
30. *SMCB*, Dec. 1927, 2.
31. Mary Hoke Slaughter interview, 9 July 1977; Frances Venable Gardiner notes, 19 Aug. 1979, SMCA; Elizabeth Thomas to Martha Stoops, 14 Feb. 1979, SMCA.
32. TECM, 30 Mar. 1927.
33. *SMCB*, Apr. 1928, 14; *SMM*, Mar. 1925, 5.
34. *SMCB*, Dec. 1927, 10; Salley, *Life*, 198–99.
35. Helen A. Brown, "Saint Mary's School Library—A Century of Progress," *SMCB*, June 1938, 25.
36. W. W. Way to board of trustees, 29 May 1923, SMCA.
37. Ibid., 24 May 1921.
38. *SMCB*, Dec. 1927, 1.
39. W. W. Way to board of trustees, May 1925, SMCA.
40. Theodore Bratton to W. W. Way, 8 Apr. 1926, SMCA; TM, May 1926.
41. *SMCB*, Dec. 1926, 1. Bishops Darst and Penick favored the four-year college.
42. TM, 31 Oct. 1929.
43. Ibid., 3 June 1930.
44. Green interview, 19 July 1976; Nell Battle Lewis, "Sixty-One Women Students Are Now Seeking Higher Education at the University," *NO*, 20 Mar. 1921.
45. Lewis, "Sixty-One Women Students."
46. Jane Toy, Ellen Lay, Frances Venable, Ellen Melick, Kitty Lee Frazier, and Mela Royall were presidents of the association.
47. The six were Katherine Batts, Catherine Boyd, Nina Cooper, Annie Duncan, Jane Toy, and Mary Yellott.
48. Green interview, 2 Aug. 1975.
49. *SMM*, May 1918, 18.
50. Ibid., May 1919, 31; *NO*, 26 Mar. 1922; *SMCB*, Apr. 1922, 14; *New York Times Magazine*, 31 Dec. 1922, 13.
51. *NO*, 20 Mar. 1921.
52. *SMM*, Dec. 1923, 15.
53. *SMCB*, June 1930, 10.
54. H. W. Chase to W. W. Way, 5 Jan. 1926, SMCA; TM, May 1926.
55. *SMM*, Dec. 1923, 13–14.
56. Woody, *Women's Education*, II, 381.
57. Stock, *Better Than Rubies*, 223.
58. Woody, *Women's Education*, II, 329–31.
59. *SMC*, Dec. 1977, 11.
60. Ibid., June 1977, 10.
61. Ibid.
62. *SMCB*, Dec. 1926, 4.
63. *SMM*, Dec. 1923, 16–17.
64. Nancy Lay White interview, 23 Aug. 1978.
65. Salley, *Life*, 185; TM, 25 May 1920.
66. *SMM*, June 1925, 1.
67. Ibid., Sept.-Oct. 1919, 10–11; Salley, *Life*, 174–75. The total cost of the project seems to have been $20,000.
68. Salley, *Life*, 165.
69. *SMCB*, Apr. 1922, 31. Alice Edwards Jones died 8 Nov. 1964.
70. Salley, *Life*, 176, 181.
71. Ibid., 187–88, 192–94; Jones interview, 12 Aug. 1975; *SMM*, Dec. 1924, 1.
72. TM, May 1924.
73. Delta Kappa Gamma Society, *Some Pioneer Women Teachers*, 15–17; Salley, *Life*, 195, 212; *SMCB*, July 1932, 25; *SMM*, June 1925, 10. Albertson died 7 Oct. 1954.

74. Salley, *Life*, 128.

75. FM, 15 Sept. 1919. The members of the first council were W. W. Way, Ophelia Stone, Florence Davis, KMcK, Martha Dowd, Nancey Lay, Eleanor Sublett, Jane Toy, Mary Yellott, Dorothy Kirtland, Betty Bonner, Susan Collier, Frances Venable, and Jane MacMillan.

76. *SMM*, Mar. 1923, 15; *SMM*, Dec. 1923, 34.

77. *SMCB*, Dec. 1926, 7.

78. Ibid., Apr. 1927, 2.

79. Ibid., Apr. 1929, 1.

80. Coolidge, *Chapel Hill*, 97–98.

81. *SMM*, May 1919, 33–35; *SMM*, Mar. 1923, 6–7.

82. Gardiner interview, 31 Oct. 1978; Mary Yellott McNitt interview, 9 July 1977.

83. *SMCB*, Apr. 1927, 7.

84. TM, 31 May 1927; *SMCB*, Apr. 1927, 10; Jones interview, 12 Aug. 1975; Holt interview, 14 June 1974; Powell interview, 23 Apr. 1979.

85. *SMM*, Mar. 1920, 41; *SMM*, Mar. 1923, 42; *SMCB*, Apr. 1929, 5; TM, 25 May 1920. During the 1922 Christmas vacation, a preparatory student, Agnes Davis, died at home of influenza.

86. Elizabeth Thomas to Martha Stoops, 14 Feb. 1979, SMCA.

87. Salley, *Life*, 202–03; *SMCB*, June 1924, 10–11; *SMCB*, Dec. 1927, 1; Elizabeth Thomas to Martha Stoops, 14 Feb. 1979, SMCA. Holt Hall cost about $50,000. The architects were Northrup and O'Brien of Winston-Salem and George Watts Carr of Durham.

88. Evelyn Way notes, Aug. 1979.

89. *SMCB*, Dec. 1929, 17. The first day students' club officers were: Mary Tucker, Margaret Harrington, Charlotte Houston, and Caroline Ashe.

90. *SMCB*, Apr. 1927, 5.

91. Ibid., 6; Gardiner interview, 15 Aug. 1975; Elizabeth Thomas to Martha Stoops, 14 Feb. 1979, SMCA.

92. *SMCB*, June 1929, 7.

93. Ibid., June 1927, 5; Elizabeth Thomas to Martha Stoops, 14 Feb. 1979, SMCA.

94. Coxe and Warfield, *Mother of the Maid*, 14.

95. *NO*, June 27, 1976; Adelaide Boyston White telephone interview, 20 May 1979. She led the 1925 ball.

96. *SMCB*, Apr. 1926, 8; *SMCB*, Apr. 1928, 2.

97. FM, 18 Nov. 1919.

98. Gardiner interview, 5 Aug. 1975; Tucker interview, 28 Mar. 1977; Jones interview, 14 Apr. 1979; Powell interview, 21 Apr. 1979.

99. Powell interview, 21 Apr. 1979.

100. *SMCB*, July 1931, 11; *SMCB*, June 1927, 14.

101. *SMM*, Nov. 1920, 32; *SMCB*, Apr. 1926, 7; Jones interview, 15 Apr. 1979; Elizabeth Thomas to Martha Stoops, 14 Feb. 1979, SMCA.

102. *SMCB*, June 1928, 2.

103. *SMM*, Dec. 1923, 32.

104. *NO*, Mar. 28, 1930.

105. *SMM*, Mar. 1920, 30–31; *SMM*, Dec. 1920, 37; Slaughter interview, 9 July 1977; McNitt interview, 9 July 1977; Salley, *Life*, 172; Irma Deaton interview, 22 May 1979.

106. *SMCB*, Dec. 1926, 1; *SMCB*, Apr. 1927, 2; *SMCB*, Apr. 1932, 10. The organ was a three-manual Hall organ.

107. *SMCB*, Dec. 1922, 9; *SMM*, June 1923, 54. See Salley, *Life*, 259–72, for biographical sketch of Ernest Cruikshank.

108. *SMM*, Sept.-Oct. 1919, 30.

109. Jones interview, 15 Apr. 1979.

110. *CCh*, IV (June 1913), 6.

111. *SMM*, Dec. 1924, 5. She was Pattie Carroll Whichard.

112. MJC, 1914–15; Eleanor Thomas, 1916–17; Mabel Shapcott, 1927–28; Marjorie Lalor, 1929–30; Carolyn Peacock Poole, 1959–61.

113. *SMCB*, Dec. 1955, 34, reported that Mary Weeks Spruill Lambeth had been elected DAR national vice-president for life.

114. "Junior League of Raleigh Annual Report, June 1929–June 1930," 8.

115. Woody, *Women's Education*, II, 466.

116. Cotten, *Federation of Women's Clubs*, 118. Leslie W. Syron contributed valuable suggestions for this section.

117. *SMM*, June 1911, 11–13.

118. Nell Battle Lewis, "The Woman Movement," *NO*, 10 May 1925.

119. Elizabeth Henderson Cotten, typescript, AH Papers (Bailey-Cain series).

120. A. Elizabeth Taylor, "The Woman Suffrage Movement in North Carolina," Pt. I, *North Carolina Historical Review*, XXXVIII (Jan. 1961), 46–48; A. Elizabeth Taylor to Martha Stoops, 13 Jan. 1977, SMCA.

121. *NO*, 3 Feb. 1915; Carolyn Happer, "Barbara Bynum Henderson," ms. written for *North Carolina Biographical Dictionary* and lent to Martha Stoops prior to publication. Henderson's father was William Shipp Bynum, an Episcopal clergyman; her grandfather was Moses Ashley Curtis.

122. The N.C. legislature ratified the 19th amendment in 1971.

123. Taylor, "Woman Suffrage Movement," 189.

124. Draft of reply to the committee on canons, Diocese of California, regarding status of women in Diocese of N.C., 5 Mar. 1919, JBC Papers.

125. *SMM*, June 1923, 37; *SMM*, Dec. 1923, 32.

126. *SMCB*, June 1926, 5–6; *SMM*, June 1929, 2. Czarnomska presented a portrait of herself done in pastel.

127. Emilie Watts McVea was buried in Oakwood Cemetery, Raleigh.

128. *SMCB*, July 1932, 16.

129. *SMM*, Jan.-Feb. 1921, 36–37; *SMM*, Dec. 1922, 18–19. The fund-raising committee for the trustees consisted of Isaac W. Hughes, chairman, Graham H. Andrews, and George C. Royall. The New York firm of Tamblyn and Brown directed the campaign.

130. *SMCB*, Apr. 1922, 10, 33; *SMCB*, June 1922, 65–66; *SMM*, Dec. 1924, 3. The pageant was written by Marietta Minnergerode Andrews.

131. *SMM*, June 1925, 2.

132. *SMCB*, June 1929, 1; *SMCB*, Dec. 1929, 3. The salary was $1200 plus $800 for expenses.

133. E. C. Cruikshank, report to the rector, 2 Oct. 1919, SMCA.

134. TM, 27 May 1919.

135. Ibid., 31 May 1927, 25 May 1920.

136. *SMM*, Jan.-Feb., 1921, 36–37.

137. TM, 25 May 1920.

138. Alexander H. Sands, Jr., to W. A. Erwin, 13 Aug. 1925, quoting from a letter written by B. N. Duke to Sands, JBC Papers.

139. TM, May 31, 1927.

140. A. W. Tucker, "Report on Finances to Dr. Way," 10 Dec. 1930, SMCA; TECM, 11 Apr. 1929.

141. TM, 18 May 1933; Nell Battle Lewis, "Incidentally," *NO*, 6 Oct. 1946.

142. London, *Bishop Cheshire*, 119–20.

143. *SMCB*, Dec. 1927, 1.

144. Ibid., Apr. 1930, 1; *SMCB*, July 1931, 7–8. The Cheshire portrait, commissioned by a group of trustees and friends of the college, was painted by Clement Read Strudwick (1900–58). The background depicts the altar and reredos in the St. Mary's chapel.

145. TECM, 29 Dec. 1930; TM, 25 Apr. 1931.

146. They were the Julia Johnson Andrews Student Loan Fund of $2,250, and the Masonic Fund of $500.

147. TM, 21 Oct. 1931.

148. TECM, 3 Nov. 1931, 28 Nov. 1931; MMM interview, 14 June 1974.

149. W. A. Erwin to trustees' executive committee, 12 Nov. 1931, SMCA.

150. TECM, 17 Nov. 1931, 5 Jan. 1932; TM, 30 Mar. 1932.

151. W. W. Way to Bishop Penick, 5 Nov. 1931, SMCA; Bishop Penick to JBC, 9 and 12 Nov. 1931, SMCA.

152. *SMCB*, July 1932, 1, 3–4. Warren W. Way is listed in *Who's Who in America*, 1928–1929, 2168. Louisa Way died 1 Apr. 1947.

## CHAPTER TEN

1. TECM, 24 Feb. 1932.
2. Elizabeth Tucker interview, 28 Mar. 1977. Columbia Institute was established in 1838 by Bishop James H. Otey as Columbia Female Institute. At the time of its closing it was an academy and junior college with a student body of 100 boarders and a number of day students.
3. MJC was a direct descendant of Willie Jones, delegate to the Continental Congress.
4. Nash, *Ladies in the Making*, 104; Salley, *Life*, 252; Mary Pride Jones Castleman interview, 14 June 1974; Mary Pride Cruikshank Clark notes, Aug. 1980, SMCA.
5. Salley, *Life*, 252–53; *SMM*, June 1905, 28; *SMM*, Oct. 1906, 20; *SMM*, Feb., 1908, 19; *SMM*, June 1911, 36; Tucker interview, 18 Dec. 1978.
6. JBC to MJC, 30 Mar. 1932, marked "unsent," SMCA.
7. Elizabeth Tucker's connections with St. Mary's went back to her grandmother, Isa Benedicta Gordon Granberry, educated under AS.
8. Tucker interview, 18 Dec. 1978; MMM interview, 6 July 1977; Cantey Venable Sutton interview, 27 Oct. 1975.
9. *SMCB*, Apr. 1932, 3–4; *SMCB*, July 1932, 3, 24. William Allen Erwin (15 July 1856–28 Feb. 1932) married Sarah Lyell (Sadie) Smedes (8 Oct. 1859–27 Nov. 1938) on 23 Oct. 1889.
10. MMM interview, 11 Apr. 1979; Tucker interview, 18 Dec. 1978; Letty Lassiter Wilder interview, 19 May 1976.
11. Salley, *Life*, 255; MMM interview, 11 Mar. 1979.
12. *SMCB*, Mar. 1944, 18.
13. Ibid., Oct 1932, 25; research conducted by Thomas H. Johnson, Registrar, St. Mary's College, July 1979.
14. Martha Stennis Sprouse [Stoops], "The Development Of Research In The Social Sciences As An Academic Function," 8–9, master's thesis, University of Wisconsin, 1944.
15. TECM, 27 Jan. 1936.
16. For many years the academic standards committee was composed of MMM, Ruth Lineberry, and C. A. P. Moore.
17. Helen A. Brown, "Saint Mary's School Library—A Century of Progress," *SMCB*, June 1938, 26–27.
18. *SMCB*, Mar. 1934, 30; *SMCB*, June 1934, 35; *SMCB*, Mar. 1935, 10.
19. *NO*, 9 Dec. 1934; *SMCB*, June 1938, 27; Salley, *Life*, 219.
20. *SMCB*, June 1938, 27.
21. Ibid.
22. TM, 31 May 1938.
23. *TB*, 9 Feb. 1940.
24. TM, 8 Oct. 1936.
25. *TB*, 23 Feb. 1940.
26. Salley, *Life*, 221.
27. Mary Hoke Slaughter to Martha Stoops, 2 July 1979, SMCA.
28. *TB*, 24 Feb. 1940. William H. Jones was buried in Oakwood Cemetery, Raleigh.
29. *TB*, 24 Feb. 1940.
30. *SMCB*, Mar. 1934, 19–21.
31. Salley, *Life*, 226–27; *SMCB*, June 1934, 21–22.
32. *SMCB*, June 1957, 9. In 1937 the plaque was won with an original play written by Phoebe Bashore, who directed the play and acted in it.
33. *SMCB*, Oct. 1932, 26; Salley, *Life*, 225–26.
34. *SMCB*, Oct. 1933, 6.
35. Ibid., Nov. 1938, 2.
36. Ibid., June 1957, 10; *SMCB*, June 1966, 9; FM, 5 Dec. 1966; Mary Ann Dixon Hogue interview, 19 Apr. 1975; Sarah Dawson Davis interview, 7 July 1979; Anna Brooke Allan interview, 11 July 1979.
37. Salley, *Life*, 220; *TB*, 25 Nov. 1938, 14 Apr. 1939, 31 Oct. 1941; *SMCB*, Dec. 1954, 35. Caroline Harris Edwards was listed in *Who's Who in American Art* (1941). She died in 1954.

38. MMM interview, 11 Apr. 1979.

39. Martha Dabney Jones interview, 12 Aug. 1975; Wilder interview, 19 May 1976; Davis interview, 7 July 1979; Mary Ann Cooper Broughton interview, 17 Feb. 1981; *SMCB*, June 1957, 13.

40. *SMCB*, Mar. 1938, 7; Broughton interview, 29 Apr. 1975.

41. Josephus Daniels to Nell Battle Lewis, 15 Nov. 1938, written from the American embassy, Mexico City, Nell Battle Lewis Papers.

42. The novels and the work on the parables of Jesus were never published. Some manuscripts are in the Nell Battle Lewis Papers.

43. Nell Battle Lewis, "Pedagogy in Retrospect," *SMCB*, Oct. 1937, 24; *SMCB*, Mar. 1939, 7.

44. Allan interview, 10 July 1979.

45. Hogue interview, 19 Apr. 1975; Broughton interview, 29 Apr. 1975; Wilder interview, 9 May 1976. See Lewis, *The Power of Prayer*.

46. *NO*, 27 Nov. 1956.

47. *SMCB*, June 1944, 67–68; Etta Burt Warren Marshall interview, 13 May 1974; MMM interview, 29 May 1979; Allan interview, 10 July 1979. Dodd's students gave the college her portrait painted by Clement Strudwick.

48. *SMCB*, June 1938, 15; Salley, *Life*, 248–49; Tucker interview, 18 Dec. 1978; MMM interview, 6 July 1979; Allan interview, 10 July 1979.

49. *TB*, 15 Dec. 1939; *SMCB*, June 1956, 52; MMM interviews, 6 July 1979, 8 Mar. 1981; Louise Partrick Newton telephone interview, 8 Mar. 1981.

50. *SMCB*, Oct. 1936, 6.

51. Juliet Biscoe Sutton was born in Pittsboro on 28 Mar. 1861, the daughter of Julia Anne Biscoe and the Reverend Robert Dean Sutton, rector of St. Bartholomew's Church, Pittsboro. See *SMCB*, June 1942, 36. Lizzie Lee died 3 July, 1947.

52. *SMCB*, June 1933, 22; *SMCB*, Oct. 1934, 8; *SMCB*, Mar. 1936, 10; *TB*, 30 Sept. 1937, 29 Nov. 1939, 16 Dec. 1938.

53. *SMCB*, Mar. 1942, 16.

54. *SMCB*, Oct. 1937, 7.

55. *TB*, 29 Nov. 1937.

56. *SMCB*, Mar. 1937, 5.

57. Ann Seeley and Nancy McKinley, "Credo, A.D., 1940," *SMCB*, Nov. 1940, 18–20.

58. *SMCB*, Dec. 1941, 18–19.

59. Davis, Broughton, Betty Michaux Graham, Ann Geoghegan White interview, 29 Apr. 1975; June Bourne Long notes, Aug. 1980, SMCA.

60. TM, 6 Oct. 1942, 15 Nov. 1945.

61. Florence Stone Hough interview, 7 May 1976; MJC to Rebecca Harvey, 22 Mar. 1939, SMCA. Rebecca Harvey died 23 Apr. 1958, at her home in Appomattox, Va. See *SMCB*, June 1958, 52.

62. *SMCB*, Mar. 1936, 13.

63. *TB*, 30 Sept., 28 Oct. 1938; Salley, *Life*, 228–29.

64. *SMCB*, Oct. 1935, 51.

65. Salley, *Life*, 255–56.

66. Mary Pride Cruikshank Clark interview, 17 Apr. 1977.

67. Jones interview, 12 Aug. 1975.

68. Ernest Cruikshank, Jr., died in 1969. Olive Echols Cruikshank Foss died in 1976.

69. *SMCB*, Oct. 1932, 8; Mary Martha Cobb to Mrs. W. B. Cobb, 12 Sept. 1939, Collier Cobb Papers.

70. *TB*, 8 Mar. 1940.

71. *SMCB*, Apr. 1941, 15.

72. Johnson, *Meredith College*, 132. Baptist University for Women (Meredith College) organized student government in 1905; Radcliffe did so in 1907.

73. *TB*, 29 Nov. 1937.

74. See 1938 constitution of the SGA in the *Student Handbook*, 1938–39.

75. Martha Dabney Jones notes, Feb. 1980, SMCA.

76. *Student Handbook*, 1945–46, 78.

77. Louise Jordan Smith to Perry Grimes, 24 Sept. 1964, SMCA; Eileen Brent Beckman to Perry Grimes, 15 Apr. 1965, SMCA.

78. Members of the Circle its first year were Louise Jordan, Eileen Brent, Sue Clapp, Anne Dawson, Sallie Fell, Anne Flowe, Erwin Gant, Mary Gault, Merrie Haynes, Elizabeth Hunter, Helen Kendrick, Jean Miller, Mary Elizabeth Neff, Rebecca Norman, Mary Louise Riddick, Sarah Sawyer, Lossie Taylor, Hallie Townes, and Mary Jane Yeatman.

79. *TB*, 11 Nov. 1938.

80. *SMCB*, June 1933, 19; *SMCB*, June 1934, 26.

81. TECM, 2 Apr. 1940. The hut was razed to make way for the gymnasium-natatorium.

82. *SMCB*, Oct. 1936, 15–16; *NO*, 30 Oct. 1936. The student was Dorothy Balsey.

83. *TB*, 23 Feb. 1940.

84. TM, 24 May 1941.

85. Casper Lilly interview, 26 June 1979.

86. *Student Handbook*, 1937–38, 22–23.

87. Because there was no pension fund, the trustees voted Sutton $25 a month for life. She lived with her sister in Raleigh until her death 30 Mar. 1942. She was buried in Oakwood Cemetery, Raleigh.

88. Salley, *Life*, 241–42. James M. Poyner is the great-grandson of AS.

89. Mary Martha Cobb to Mrs. Collier Cobb, 20 Apr. 1941, Collier Cobb Papers; Jones notes, Feb. 1980; Long notes, Aug. 1980.

90. *TB*, 17 Nov., 15 Dec., 21 Sept., 12 May 1939, 20 Sept. 1940; *SMCB*, Dec. 1941, 21.

91. *TB*, 6 Nov. 1942, 15 Dec. 1944.

92. Ibid., 16 Jan. 1942.

93. Ibid., 12 Dec. 1941; TM, 27 May 1941.

94. *SMCB*, Mar. 1942, 35.

95. Ibid., catalog issue, 1944–45, 23.

96. MMM interview, 27 July 1979.

97. *TB*, 3 Nov. 1944.

98. Ibid., 16 Jan. 1942, 12 Feb. 1943.

99. *Student Handbook*, 1945–46, 13; *TB*, 12 Mar. 1943, 19 Jan. 1945.

100. *TB*, 22 Sept. 1944.

101. Ibid., 25 Sept. 1942.

102. Jones was awarded the Croix de Guerre with bronze star.

103. Caro Bayley Bosca Sinatt received in 1952 the Bleriot medal from the Federation Aeronautique Internationale for the world record flight in a light plane. *SMCB*, Mar. 1951, 30; notes in Nell Battle Lewis Papers.

104. *SMCB*, June 1939, 46–48; *SMCB*, Oct. 1937, 25.

105. Nancy Travis Hunt Taylor to Martha Stoops, 2 June 1973, SMCA.

106. *SMCB*, Oct. 1932, 26.

107. Salley, *Life*, 214, 151–52; Wilder interview, 19 May 1976; MMM interview, 29 July 1979.

108. TECM, 27 Feb., 28 May 1935; Joseph Fletcher to Martha Stoops, 12 Mar. 1980, SMCA.

109. TM, 30 May 1938.

110. Ibid., 3 June 1942.

111. *SMCB*, Nov. 1979, 3; *NCCh*, XXVIII (15 Feb. 1938), 9; *NCCh*, XXVI (15 Feb. 1936), 7; *NCCh*, XXIX (1 Feb. 1939), 9.

112. *TB*, 16 Jan., 25 Sept. 1942; *NCCh*, XXXI (15 Sept. 1942), 2.

113. *NCCh*, XXXI (15 Sept. 1942), 3, 12; *TB*, 25 Sept. 1942.

114. *SMCB*, June 1957, 12; MMM interview, 29 July 1979; Olivia Lynch Hardin interview, 19 July 1979.

115. *SMCB*, Dec. 1941, 24.

116. TM, 15 June 1943, 4 Oct. 1944.

117. *TB*, 24 Oct. 1945.

118. *SMCB*, Mar. 1936, 10.

119. TM, 18 Oct. 1933.

120. The executive committee of the board of trustees, which had "like powers of the

directors of a commercial or business corporation," passed the resolution for changing the corporation's name on 28 Nov. 1944. The certificate of amendment was signed on 15 Nov. 1945.

121. TM, 31 May 1938.

122. Tucker interview, 18 Dec. 1978; SMCB, June 1934, 17–18.

123. TM, 23 Jan., 29 May 1934.

124. Ibid., 27 May 1941, 28 May 1940.

125. Ibid., 19 Oct. 1932; TECM, 30 July, 22 Dec. 1936, 9 Feb. 1939; TM, 3 Feb. 1937.

126. Copy of 1936–37 budget, Diocese of North Carolina, TM.

127. TECM, 26 Apr. 1933, 6 Apr. 1934, 22 Dec. 1936, 26 May 1938.

128. Ibid., 17 Feb. 1941; TM, 6 Oct. 1942.

129. TECM, 6 Oct., 27 Oct. 1942. The annuity plan was to cost the college $5,000, and no raises were given for 1942–43. The school and the employee paid equal amounts—4% of salary.

130. Letter of 1 Dec. 1942, is signed by Florence Davis, Martha Dabney Jones, and MMM, SMCA.

131. The first issues of the literary magazine, the Muse, were never located; V. I. N. 8, May 1879, is the earliest issue in the collection.

132. See SMCB, Mar. 1940, 54, and SMCB, Nov. 1940, 24, for list of gifts for the parlor.

133. TECM, 29 May, 27 June 1941, 11 Feb. 1942.

134. NCCh, XXXI (15 Mar. 1942), 1.

135. SMCB, June 1942, 91.

136. Katherine Batts Salley telephone interview, 3 Nov. 1979.

137. SMCB, Dec. 1941, 27; TB, 28 Nov. 1941. The UNC Press pronounced the book "an admirable piece of work . . . good without qualification." It sold for $2.50.

138. TB, 17 Apr. 1942.

139. Stagecoach, 1942, prologue.

140. Broughton composed the anthem hymn (copyrighted 1934) with an ornamental accompaniment on a plainsong melody and dedicated it to Leslie P. Spelman, chairman of the music department at Meredith College, where the hymn was used. The words are from Sebastian W. Meyer, an early 20th-century poet, and may be found in Milton S. Littlefield, ed., Hymns of the Christian Life (A. S. Barnes & Co., 1908). Broughton substituted "school" for "church." Beatrice Donley telephone interview, 1 July 1982.

141. See SMCB, June 1942, 16.

142. Ibid., 36; NO, 18 May 1942.

143. Mary Yellott Denny, "Tomorrow Follows Today," SMCB, June 1942, 28–36.

144. Helen A. Brown notes, Apr. 1980.

145. SMCB, June 1942, 55, 58–59; NO, 20 May 1942.

146. NO, 26 Apr. 1942.

147. SMCB, June 1934, 35–36.

148. Ibid., Oct. 1933, 14; SMCB, Mar. 1938, 30; TM, 3 June 1937. The alumnae spent $900 on West Rock. See TECM, 27 Apr. 1937.

149. SMCB, Mar. 1937, 26–27; SMCB, Oct. 1936, 25.

150. TECM, 7 Apr. 1932.

151. Approximate dates were gleaned from the brief annual reports of alumnae secretaries published in SMCB. Alumnae association records are incomplete for the period.

152. SMCB, June 1938, 49.

153. Ibid., 48.

154. Ibid., Mar 1935, 46; SMCB, Apr. 1943, 33.

155. Ibid., Nov. 1938, 2; TECM, 15 Feb. 1938. The cost of new floor supports for the auditorium, a maple floor, and painting was $3,000.

156. Report of K. W. Parham, CPA, 12 July 1937, SMCA.

157. TECM, 23 Feb. 1939; building committee minutes, 4 Mar. 1939, 3 June 1942, SMCA. The sprinkler system cost $17,000.

158. On Arbor Day, 1935, 6 willow oaks, a memorial to Bishop Cheshire, were planted by his 4 granddaughters, then St. Mary's students. See SMCB, June 1935, 15.

159. Albert W. Tucker to Bishop Penick, 9 Mar. 1943, SMCA.

160. Julia Jordan interview, 12 June 1979. Tucker retired to Florida where he died on 17 July 1956, at 79.

161. *TB*, 24 Sept. 1943.

162. TECM, 3 Feb. 1944, 11 July 1945.

163. TM, 3 Feb. 1944.

164. Ibid., 4 Oct. 1944; *NCCh*, XXXIV (Dec. 1944), 14; *TB*, 18 Jan. 1946. Erwin Gant was graduated from the college and Catherine from the high school in 1940.

165. Bishop Penick to MJC, 27 Aug. 1945, SMCA.

166. TM, 15 Nov. 1945; MMM notes, Apr. 1980, SMCA.

167. *SMCB*, June 1938, 14. Erwin Gant organized step singing in the spring of 1938 "in the hope that it will become an established tradition, as at many schools in the country." However, alumnae remember step-singing from the early 1930s.

168. The custom of dropping the handkerchief seems to have originated during the Way administration. Alumnae prior to that time do not recall the practice.

169. Estimates of graduates were compiled by Helen A. Brown from early lists in the *SMM* and college records. She counted 229 college graduates during the period 1879–1909, and a total of 1,119 through June, 1947.

170. Mary Pride Castleman died on 12 Dec. 1978 at the age of 100.

171. Clark interview, 21 Apr. 1979.

172. *SMCB*, Mar. 1956, 5.

173. Ibid. MJC was buried in Oakwood Cemetery, Raleigh.

174. *SMCB*, Dec. 1966, 11.

CHAPTER ELEVEN

1. RS interview, 11 Feb. 1977.

2. The search committee, representing the 5 owning dioceses, consisted of Bishop Penick, chairman; Bishop Wright, Rev. James McDowell Dick, Raleigh; Rev. Maurice Clarke, D.D., Camden, S.C.; Joseph B. Cheshire III; B. Allston Moore, Charleston, S.C.; Mary Wilson Stoney, Morganton. See *NCCh*, XXXV (Dec. 1945), 15.

3. RS, *Hezekiah Niles as an Economist*, The Johns Hopkins University Studies in Historical and Political Science, Series 51 (Baltimore: The Johns Hopkins Press, 1933).

4. Kibler, *Converse College, 1889–1971*, 349.

5. *TB*, 6 Sept. 1946, 4.

6. Trustees' special committee minutes, 23 Apr. 1946, SMCA.

7. RS interview, 13 June 1980.

8. Maria Gregory, "Relandscaping Saint Mary's," *NCCh*, XXXVI (Dec. 1946), 10.

9. MS interview, 13 June 1980.

10. *TB*, 4 Oct. 1946; MS and RS interviews, 13 June 1980. Richard G. Stone, Jr., is married to Elizabeth Clark; they have a daughter, Marye Elizabeth, born 1969.

11. RS interview, 11 Feb. 1977.

12. TM, 4 Feb. 1947.

13. *TB*, 31 May 1946.

14. RS interview, 13 June 1980.

15. Ernestine Boineau died at her home in Orangeburg, S.C., 22 May 1979.

16. RS interview, 13 June 1980.

17. The trustees voted on 27 Oct. 1953, to change the institution's name. A certificate of amendment to the charter filed on 19 Oct. 1954, repealed the amendment of 19 Nov. 1945. See certificate no. 73211, office of the Secretary of State of N.C.

18. *SMCB*, June 1954, 24–25.

19. Smith, *Promised Land*, 298.

20. Millstein and Bodin, *American Women*, 254.

21. Ethel J. Alpenfels, "Women in the Professional World," Cassara, ed., *Changing Image*, 73.

22. Smith, *Promised Land*, 295.

23. Conable, *Women at Cornell*, 11.

24. A. Elizabeth Taylor telephone interview, 12 Nov. 1979.

25. *SMCB*, June 1957, 6.

26. *TB*, 2 Dec. 1960.

27. RS interview, 13 June 1980.

28. The description of faculty meetings is based upon interviews with faculty, a reading of the faculty minutes, 1946–69, and the author's attendance at all faculty meetings, 1960–69.

29. FM, 7 Oct. 1946.

30. TM, 20 Nov. 1946; *Saint Mary's and the Challenge of Our Time*, fund-raising brochure, 1952, SMCA.

31. *SMCB*, Mar. 1950, 5.

32. *TB*, 30 May 1958.

33. *SMCB*, Dec. 1951, 23.

34. TM, 28 Oct. 1959.

35. The steering committee was composed of Carl Cannon, Moultrie Guerry, Sara Esther Jones, MMM, and Louise Cell. See *TB*, 30 Oct. 1959.

36. *SMCB*, Mar. 1959, 4.

37. The visiting committee was composed of Dean Cecil Abernethy of Birmingham-Southern College, Dean F. T. Lenfesty of Pensacola Junior College, and Dean Harriet Hudson of Randolph-Macon Woman's College. *TB*, 30 Oct. 1959.

38. "A Summary of the Report of the Visiting Committee to St. Mary's Junior College, October 19–21, 1959," SMCA.

39. FM, 28 Nov. 1960, 7 Dec. 1964, 2 Apr. 1962.

40. Barbara Craig's paper resulted in a pamphlet, *The Wright Brothers and Their Development of the Airplane*, published in 1960 by the N.C. Department of Archives and History and often reprinted.

41. *TB*, 25 Apr. 1952; Geraldine Cate telephone interview, 7 July 1980.

42. *TB*, 13 Feb., 21 Feb. 1948. Jane Gower was editor.

43. *TB*, 2 Oct. 1946, 22 Oct. 1948, 3 Dec. 1954.

44. Ibid., 26 Mar. 1954.

45. Ibid., 9 Nov. 1956.

46. *SMCB*, June 1950, 65–66; *SMCB*, June 1955, 33; *SMCB*, June 1958, 7. *TB*, 11 Jan. 1957; Mary Laurens Withers Richardson telephone interview, 11 June 1980. She served as chief clerk of the state utilities commission, 1953–1966.

47. *TB*, 10 Nov. 1961.

48. FM, 2 Dec. 1963.

49. Letter to editor from Alexa Draxler, *TB*, 2 Feb. 1964.

50. White, *America at Last*, 19, 69–73.

51. RS interview, 13 June 1980; Doris Bailey telephone interview, 8 July 1980.

52. *TB*, 14 Oct. 1960; Bailey interview, 19 Dec. 1981. Bailey served as chairman of the dance section of the state Health and Recreation Association.

53. *TB*, 1 May 1959.

54. Ibid., 7 May 1948.

55. TM, 13 Oct. 1965.

56. *TB*, 7 May 1965, 22 Apr. 1966, 12 May 1967, 15 Mar. 1963.

57. Lou Jones notes, Nov. 1981, SMCA; Lou Jones interview, 6 Jan. 1982.

58. *SMCB*, Dec. 1963, 6.

59. Ibid., June 1960, 12–13.

60. Profiles of the junior classes 1960–61 through 1967–68 prepared by the academic standards committee show the average combined score to have been 949 in 1960–61, 1018 in 1965–66, and 1025 in 1966–67 and 1967–68.

61. TM, 13 Oct. 1965.

62. Ibid., 18 May 1966.

63. Report of Ad Hoc Committee on Curriculum Study, 13 Oct. 1965, 2, SMCA. The members of this committee, appointed by Bishop Baker, were Rev. Claude E. Guthrie, Sibyl Goerch Powe, Dr. George D. Penick, and Robert Connelly. Peace College discontinued its high school in 1968.

64. FM, 5 Apr. 1965; *TB*, 12 Feb. 1965.

65. FM, 3 Oct. 1966.

66. Ibid., 1 Apr. 1968.

67. Approved by trustees by mail ballot, Jan. 1969.

68. Report of the Visiting Committee, Southern Association of Colleges and Schools, Mar. 1969, 4, SMCA.

69. Sophomore Kathryn Ann Vale won the Angier B. Duke Scholarship, St. Mary's first. See SMCB, June 1961, 15.

70. FM, 14 Apr. 1969.

71. RS served on the college commission of the Southern Association of Colleges and Schools, 1964–70. He submitted his resignation in December of 1968 as he had announced his approaching retirement. The resignation was not accepted, and he served the last year of his term.

72. Members of the 1969 visiting team were Dean Hamby Barton, Southwestern College; Dean Marguerite Chiles, Furman University; Mrs. Leslie Jones, head librarian, Young Harris College; W. T. Ingram, business manager and treasurer, Auburn University; Shirley Strickland, associate professor of sociology and anthropology, Randolph-Macon Woman's College; and Fred Lenfesty, chairman. David Kelly, control officer, SASC, was with the committee on Mar. 17 and 18.

73. FM, 14 Apr. 1969.

74. RS interview, 13 June 1980.

75. FM, 2 Feb. 1956. RS shared with the faculty an article from the Queens College Bulletin and made this statement.

76. TM, 20 Nov. 1946.

77. SMCB, June 1957, 10–11.

78. The portrait, by Isabelle Bowen, was the gift of Mary Ausley Allison, Martha Best Yorke, and Elizabeth Smith. See SMCB, June 1957, 9; TM, 18 Mar. 1957.

79. Florence Davis (20 Dec. 1879–21 Dec. 1966) was buried in her family plot in Elmira, N.Y.

80 Casper Lilley interview, 23 Oct. 1979.

81. Eve Hargrave Smith notes, 17 Nov. 1981; Olivia Lynch Hardin interview, 19 July 1979; MMM interview, 27 July 1979.

82. SMCB, Mar. 1962, 5.

83. Ibid., June 1967, 3; Foy Lineberry interview, 13 July 1982; RS interview, 13 June 1980.

84. SMCB, Mar. 1961, 5. Partrick died 4 Nov. 1961.

85. Ibid., June 1954, 13.

86. Ibid., Mar. 1959, 9–10; TB, 20 Feb. 1959; Hardin interview, 12 June 1980.

87. SMCB, Dec. 1959, 7; faculty resolutions, n.d., SMCA. Jane Guess died 4 July 1959.

88. SMCB, June 1937, 34; SMCB, June 1964, 24; TB, 31 Mar. 1939; TM, 28 Oct. 1964. The corpus of the Jane Guess Endowment Fund was $40,000.

89. TB, 1 Nov. 1940; Janet R. Broughton interview, 27 June 1980.

90. SMCB, Mar. 1954, 1–2; SMCB, Dec. 1956, 9; SMCB, Dec. 1953, 22; FM, 11 Jan. 1954. The three-manual Reuter organ cost about $17,000. Mr. and Mrs. James Osborne Moore gave the organ screen in appreciation of what the chapel meant to their daughters, Allison and Jane.

91. TB, 28 Apr. 1961.

92. Geraldine Cate, Donald Peery, Margaret Williams, and MMM served as officers or directors of the guild. Harlan and Helen Brown also were active. See Ellen Winston, "A Brief History of the Raleigh Chamber Music Guild, 1941–1973," mimeographed pamphlet.

93. MMM interview, 19 July 1980.

94. Susan Ehringhaus interview, 23 June 1980.

95. Donald L. Peery telephone interviews, 19 June 1980, 17 Jan. 1982; SMC, June 1976, 7.

96. TB, 4 Oct. 1940; Cate interview, 27 June 1980; SMCB, Mar. 1970, 6. Zschau was with the Metropolitan and New York City Opera companies. Smith was with the New York City and Dusseldorf Opera companies.

97. Anna Brook Allan interview, 10 July 1979; SMCB, June 1972, 3, 6. The characteriza-

tion of MMM is based upon 20 years of friendship and interviews with many of her students. Among them were Marion Dixon Hogue, 19 Apr. 1975; Mary Ann Cooper Broughton, 29 Mar. 1975; Hardin, 21 June 1980; Page Cole Hoyle, 26 Mar. 1980.

98. Sara E. Jones to MJC, 7 May 1946, SMCA.

99. Lynda Anderson Stone interview, 22 Nov. 1978.

100. TB, 14 Oct. 1960, 27 May 1966; SMCB, Mar. 1966, 5; Hardin interview, 19 July 1979.

101. SMCB, Mar. 1968, 4; TB, 29 Mar. 1963; Mary J. Browne telephone interview, 23 July 1980.

102. SMCB, June 1960, 14; SMCB, Mar. 1963, 7; MMM interview, 21 July 1980; RS interview, 25 July 1980.

103. SMCB, June 1968, 4. Ann Eliza Brewer was the daughter of Charles E. Brewer, for 26 years president of Meredith College.

104. Patricia Connelly to Martha Stoops, Dec. 1981, SMCA.

105. Written from first-hand knowledge of the situations of the women employed during this period and from conversations with RS.

106. Hoyle interview, 26 Mar. 1980; SMCB, June 1966, 5.

107. TB, 12 Feb. 1954; SMCB, Dec. 1967, 48; RT, 3 Nov. 1967.

108. SMCB, Dec. 1960, 6.

109. Helen H. Smith interview, 29 July 1980.

110. TB, 24 Sept. 1943; SMCB, June 1970, 14; SMC, Dec. 1977, 24; MMM interview, 1 Mar. 1980; Doreen Saxe interview, 26 July 1980.

111. Renate H. Thompson interview, 23 Nov. 1981.

112. TB, 4 Oct. 1968; SMCB, Dec. 1968, 3; Saxe interview, 27 July 1980.

113. SMCB, Dec. 1962, 4–5; MMM interviews, 26 July 1980, 7 Jan 1982.

114. TB, 4 Oct. 1957; RS interview, 13 June 1980; MMM interview, 20 July 1979; Jane Augustine Rabon interview, 25 June 1980.

115. SMCB, Dec. 1967, 9; trustees resolutions, SMCA; NO, 19 Nov. 1967; SMM, Dec. 1967, 2. Connelly died in Baptist Hospital, Winston-Salem, as the result of a one-car accident in which he was thrown from his convertible. His funeral was held in the St. Mary's Chapel, and he was buried in Montlawn Memorial Park, Raleigh.

116. SMCB, Dec. 1968, 5.

117. The Tate material was drawn from many sources as well as from a 20–year association as his colleague. TB, 1 Nov. 19 Dec. 1957; Stagecoach, dedication, 1965; Anna DuBose interview, 29 May 1979; Ehringhaus interview, 23 June 1980; Andrea Brown telephone interview, 29 July 1980; John Tate interview, 17 Nov. 1981, MMM interview, 24 July 1980.

118. Ehringhaus interview, 23 June 1980; SMC, June 1978, 4–5.

119. MMM interview, 24 July 1980.


CHAPTER TWELVE

1. RS interview, 20 June 1980.

2. TB, 30 May 1947.

3. Martha Dabney Jones interviews, 12 Aug. 1975, 15 Mar. 1979; Elizabeth Silver Cheshire interview, 1 Mar. 1980; Olivia Lynch Hardin interview, 10 June 1980; Casper Lilley interview, 23 Oct. 1979; Eve Hargrave Smith interview, 3 June 1980; RS interview, 20 June 1980; TB, 12 Oct. 1951; SMCB, Mar. 1948, 2.

4. FM, 4 Nov. 1946, 9 Mar, 1948; SMCB, June 1948, 3.

5. TB, 1 Nov. 1957.

6. The Bluebook, a directory and calendar for the year, was first issued in 1912 by GL. It was absorbed in 1937 by the Student Handbook.

7. FM, 7 Oct. 1947.

8. Ibid., 12 Nov. 1951.

9. TB, 11 Apr. 1952.

10. Rachel Cozart Barwick telephone interview, 14 May 1977.

11. Charter members of the Beacon as listed in TB, 18 Dec. 1948, were Mary Frances

Allen, Patricia Cahoon, Rachel Cozart, Elizabeth Dorris, Barbara Ann Fulton, Alice Hicks, Martha McGuirk, Ann Nicoll, Evelyn Oettinger, Marjorie Penton, Cynthia Perkins, Charlotte Wallin, Lou Ann Watkins, Betty Ann Williamson.

12. *TB*, 22 Oct. 1948.
13. Ibid., 8 Oct. 1948.
14. Ibid., 12 May 1950.
15. Page Cole Hoyle telephone interview, 26 Mar. 1980; Martha Dabney Jones notes, 17 Sept. 1981; SMCA.
16. Salley Digges, "A Tribute to Mrs. Marriott," *SMCB*, June 1949, 25.
17. Cheshire interview, 4 Mar. 1980.
18. Smith interview, 3 June 1980.
19. Banner, *Women in Modern America*, 216.
20. Smith notes, 17 Nov. 1981.
21. *TB*, 30 Sept. 1949; *SMCB*, Dec. 1949, 25; *Stagecoach*, memorial, 1950.
22. Smith interview, 3 June 1980; Hoyle interview, 26 Mar. 1980; *TB*, 22 Mar. 1957; *SMCB*, Mar. 1952, 7.
23. *NO*, 24 Nov. 1946. They were Bettie Gaither and Margo Martin.
24. Hoyle interview, 26 Mar. 1980; Smith interview, 3 June, 1980; Jones notes, 17 Sept. 1981.
25. *SMCB*, Dec. 1970, 47.
26. Ibid., June 1973, 2; *TB*, 27 May 1955; Edith A. Richardson interview, 27 May 1980.
27. *SMCB*, June 1973, 1.
28. Cecil Abernethy, Harriet Hudson, and F. T. Lenfesty, "Report of the Visiting Committee to St. Mary's Junior College, Raleigh, North Carolina, Octber 19–21, 1959," 26, SMCA.
29. Richardson interview, 27 May 1980; *TB*, 28 Feb. 1970.
30. Richardson interview, 27 May 1980.
31. Abernethy, et al., "Report of Visiting Committee," 23.
32. RS interview, 8 Sept. 1981.
33. *TB*, 26 Feb. 1960.
34. FM, 12 Apr. 1961; *SMCB*, Dec. 1961, 14.
35. *Student Handbook*, 1961–62, 12–13; *SMCB*, Dec. 1961, 15.
36. *SMCB*, Dec. 1961, 14.
37. Ibid., June 1962, 2.
38. Abernethy, et al., "Report of Visiting Committee," 26.
39. *SMCB*, June 1964, 22; Betsy Nichols Cooksey to Martha Stoops, 2 Jan. 1980; *SMC*, June 1980, 17.
40. MMM, "Fifty Years at St. Mary's," *SMCB*, Mar. 1965, 5; *TB*, 22 Jan. 1971.
41. TECM, (no day) Sept. 1952.
42. TM, 27 Oct. 1953; *SMCB*, Dec. 1953, 23.
43. *TB*, 14 Feb. 1947; *SMCB*, June 1964, 23.
44. *TB*, 7 Mar. 1958, 28 Feb. 1964.
45. FM, 1 Apr. 1968.
46. Hardin interview, 12 June 1980.
47. FM, 9 Feb. 1959.
48. *TB*, 17 Dec. 1965.
49. Ibid., 9 Mar. 1962.
50. *SMCB*, Dec. 1959, 3; *TB*, 16 Oct. 1959, 22 Apr. 1960, 29 May 1962, 12 Feb. 1965; Hannah Bell Diedrick interview, 7 Apr. 1982. The *Stagecoach*, 1960, listed the Cold Cuts as: Gail Allen, Virginia Anderson, Hannah Bell, Webber Bell, Mary Neal Bolch, Nan Dameron, Frances Douglass, Frankie Davis, Kathy O'Lenic, Judee Metcalfe, Lucy Milward, Lynn Roberson, Margaret Turner, Florence Nash.
51. *TB*, 22 Oct. 1943.
52. Ibid., 7 May 1943; *SMCB*, June 1962, 18; ms. of talk given by Brown to her book club on 26 Mar. 1974.
53. Richardson interview, 28 Nov. 1978.
54. RS interview, 8 Sept. 1981.

55. The gazebo, dated approximately 1645–1700, is said to have been designed by LeNotre, the greatest gardener of his period. A garden bench and a rare marble table, one of three copies extant, were given at the same time by Mr. and Mrs. Julian T. Baker. See notations from Robert C. Wilkins, appraiser, 12 Dec, 1964, SMCA.

56. Richardson interview, 28 Nov. 1978.

57. Ibid., 30 June 1980.

58. *TB*, 17 Jan. 1964; *SMCB*, June 1967, 3.

59. French, *Women's Room*, 545.

60. Mary Perry Grimes was the first recipient of the King medal.

61. Michele Claudine Donovan was the first recipient of the Marian Drane Graham award.

62. Ann Dawson Highsmith, college graduate of 1938, who served as a trustee, died in 1975. See ACM, 8 Oct. 1975.

63. RS interview, 19 Dec. 1980.

64. Margaret Hopkins Downes telephone interview, 6 Apr. 1982.

65. *SMCB*, Dec. 1960, 3; Mary Elva Winston telephone interview, 10 Feb. 1981.

66. *TB*, 27 Sept. 1947; RS reported to the board on 24 Sept. 1947, that the cost of the new entrance and wall was $3,300 and that the alumnae association had paid $1,250. The alumnae raised about $9,000 for the dining room redecoration planned by alumna Elizabeth Thompson. See *SMCB*, Dec. 1940, 31; *TB*, 16 Sept. 1949; ACM, 7 Nov. 1949.

67. *SMCB*, June 1968, 2.

68. RS notes, 8 Sept. 1981.

69. Jane Augustine Rabon, "A Brief History of St. Mary's Alumnae Association," *1980 St. Mary's College Alumnae Directory*, vii.

70. *SMCB*, Dec. 1950, 18.

71. *TB*, 1 Dec. 1961.

72. *SMCB*, June 1969, 2–3, 12.

73. Rabon, "St. Mary's Alumnae Association," xv.

74. Katherine Batts Salley to Martha Stoops, 19 Nov. 1979, SMCA.

75. *SMCB*, June 1958, 12. Elizabeth Montgomery died 8 Nov. 1981, at age 99.

76. *SMCB*, June 1957, 15.

77. AAM, 4 May 1968; *SMCB*, Dec. 1968, 9.

78. *SMCB*, June 1964, 8.

79. *NO*, 26 Mar. 1957; *SMCB*, June 1957, 30.

80. AAM, 2 June 1951; *SMCB*, Dec. 1955, 38–39; *SMCB*, June 1959, 13.

81. *SMCB*, Dec. 1954, 36; Sylvester Green, "Cotten, Elizabeth Brownrigg Henderson," Powell, ed., *Dictionary of North Carolina Biography*, I, 436. Elizabeth Cotten died on 3 Feb. 1975, and was buried beside her husband, Captain Lyman Atkinson Cotten, in Arlington National Cemetery.

82. *SMCB*, June 1955, 36; *SMCB*, June 1958, 11.

83. Ibid., June 1955, 31–32.

84. Ibid., 33.

85. Ibid., Dec. 1956, 11–12; Frances Yarborough Bickett Reeder telephone interview, 16 June 1980.

86. *SMCB*, Dec. 1955, 35.

87. *RT*, 23 May 1957.

88. *SMCB*, June 1953, 40.

89. *NO*, 29 Aug. 1966.

90. *SMCB*, Mar. 1969, 4–5.

91. Ibid., 6. Barbara Howar wrote her autobiography, *Laughing All the Way* (New York: Stein and Day, 1973) and a novel, *Making Ends Meet* (New York: Random House, 1976).

92. *SMCB*, June 1965, 31.

93. *SMCB*, Dec. 1967, 12.

94. *SMCB*, June 1957, 11.

95. Ibid., June 1970, 40.

96. *NCCh*, XLVII (Sept. 1957), 3; *TB*, 4 Oct. 1957, 31 Oct. 1958; *RT*, 16 Oct. 1957; Moultrie Guerry to Martha Stoops, 3 Oct. 1981, SMCA.

97. MMM interviews, 26 July 1979, 23 June 1980; *TB*, 31 Oct. 1958; *SMCB*, Dec. 1961, 8; Moultrie Guerry to Martha Stoops, 3 Oct. 1981, SMCA.

98. *SMCB*, Dec. 1961, 8.

99. "A Self-Evaluation of St. Mary's College," 1959, 50–51, SMCA.

100. *SMCB*, Dec. 1961, 7.

101. Ibid., June 1960, 9.

102. *TB*, 31 Oct. 1958; *SMCB*, Dec. 1958, 4; RS interviews, 2 Dec. 1977, 20 June 1980.

103. Moultrie Guerry to Martha Stoops, 15 Oct. 1981, SMCA.

104. FM, 2 Oct. 1950.

105. TM, 31 Mar. 1960.

106. *SMCB*, Dec. 1967, 5–6; *SMCB*, Dec. 1968, 10.

107. *TB*, 4 Oct. 1968; TM, 25 Nov. 1968; *SMCB*, Dec. 1968, 4.

108. RS interview, 6 June 1980.

109. TM, 15 Oct. 1968.

110. *TB*, 1 Dec. 1961; FM, 5 Feb. 1962; *SMCB*, Mar. 1962, 5.

111. *SMCB*, Mar. 1969, 9; RS interview, 6 June 1980.

112. TM, 28 Oct. 1959.

113. FM, 3 May 1948.

114. Ibid., 2 Nov. 1953.

115. RS interview, 20 June 1980.

116. Ibid.

117. TM, 24 Sept. 1947.

118. *SMCB*, June 1969, 4.

119. FM, 30 Oct. 1950.

120. TM, 28 Feb. 1969.

121. Ibid., 19 Oct. 1954. The classes of 1953 and 1955 gave about half the $2,250 cost of the parlor furniture.

122. TM, 19 Oct. 1954.

123. Trustees Haywood Duke and Arthur Tyler guaranteed the raising of $7,000 to place the 351 new seats in the auditorium. See *SMCB*, Dec. 1956, 8.

124. For the Holt family, see *SMCB*, Mar. 1957, 7, and *TB*, 11 Jan. 1957. The portrait is by Hugo Stevens.

125. FM, 3 Mar. 1952.

126. RS interview, 13 June 1980.

127. The campaign was directed by Winston McClellan of Pierce, Hedrick and Sherwood, Inc., NYC. Costs were not to exceed $18,900. See TM, 2 May 1951.

128. *Saint Mary's and the Challenge of Our Times*, fund-raising brochure, 1952, 2–4, SMCA.

129. Ibid., 2.

130. Ibid., 3, 5; TM, 16 Oct. 1951.

131. Diocesan general chairmen were William H. Ruffin, N. Cortez Green, and W. Beekman Huger.

132. TM, 27 Oct. 1953. Most of the contributions came from the Diocese of North Carolina.

133. RS interview, 20 June 1980.

134. *TB*, 6 Feb. 1953. The architects were Edwards and McKimmon. The entrance hall is a memorial to Sallie Johnson White Ruffin, the gift of her son, William Haywood Ruffin.

135. TM, 18 Jan. 1956.

136. *SMCB*, Dec. 1957, 11. The parlors in Penick Hall were furnished and decorated through a gift from Georgia Wilkins (1881–1959).

137. Holloway-Reeves of Raleigh designed both buildings. See TM, 13 Oct. 1965; *SMCB*, Dec. 1966, 7–8.

138. Sarah Graham Kenan was the daughter of William Rand Kenan of Kenansville and Mary Hargrove of Chapel Hill. In 1912 she married a first cousin, James Graham Kenan, son of St. Mary's alumna Annie Elizabeth Hill. See *SMCB*, Dec. 1966. 10; *NO*, 12 Oct. 1966; *RT*, 12 Oct. 1966.

139. *SMCB*, Mar. 1956, 5; *SMCB*, Dec. 1966, 11; *NO*, 12 Oct. 1966; *RT*, 12 Oct. 1966.

140. *SMCB*, Dec. 1953, 22; *SMCB*, Dec. 1967, 6; RS interview, 20 June 1980.

141. A bequest of about $122,000 came in 1968 from the estate of alumna Mary Bonner Williams Harden.

142. TM, 17 Oct. 1967; *SMCB*, Dec. 1967, 6.

143. TM, 28 Feb. 1969; RS interviews, 11 Feb. 1979, 13 June 1980.

144. RS interview, 13 June 1980.

145. Caroline Dial Penick interview, 27 June 1980; *TB*, 10 May 1957; *SMCB*, Dec. 1956, 3.

146. *TB*, 1 May 1959.

147. TM, 21 Oct. 1952.

148. *JDNC*, 1954, 64.

149. Articles of Amendment to the Charter of Saint Mary's Junior College, 29 Oct. 1959, SMCA.

150. *CCh*, V (Aug. 1914), 8.

151. *SMCB*, June 1968, 18.

152. TM, 13 Oct. 1965; *NCCh*, XL (Oct. 1950), 6.

153. *NO*, 14 Apr. 1981.

154. *SMCB*, June 1973, 7; RS interview, 13 June 1980.

155. TM, 11 Oct. 1966.

156. *TB*, 9 Mar. 1956; *SMCB*, June 1964, 19.

157. By-Laws of Saint Mary's Junior College, TM, 9 Jan. 1968; Certificate of Amendment to Charter of Trustees of Saint Mary's School, A North Carolina Corporation, 22 Apr. 1947, SMCA.

158. By-Laws of St. Mary's Junior College, 1968, SMCA.

159. Executive Council of Diocese of North Carolina to Board of Trustees, St. Mary's Junior College, 13 June 1963, SMCA; Bishop Baker to RS, 24 June 1963, SMCA.

160. TM, 16 Oct. 1963.

161. *JDNC*, 1967, 69.

162. *SMCB*, June 1968, 16.

163. FM, 2 Feb. 1968.

164. *SMCB*, June 1969, 12.

165. TM, 15 Oct. 1968.

166. Ibid., 9 Jan. 1968. Stone died 11 Aug. 1984.

## CHAPTER THIRTEEN

1. FP interview, 3 May 1976.

2. Ibid.

3. *SMCB*, Oct. 1970, 12; *NO*, 21 June 1974; FP to Martha Stoops, 8 June 1982; FP telephone interview, 22 Feb. 1984.

4. *SMCB*, Dec. 1969, 1; *TB*, 21 Nov. 1969.

5. *SMCB*, Dec. 1969, 1; *TB*, 21 Nov. 1969.

6. *TB*, 14 Mar. 1970; FP memorandum to faculty, Mar. 1970, SMCA.

7. FM, 9 Feb. 1970, 2.

8. *SMC*, June 1976, 2.

9. Brick, *Junior College Movement*, 73.

10. *SMCB*, June 1970, 18; TM, 16 July 1970.

11. Brick, *Junior College Movement*, 99. Charter members of Chi Beta Chapter, Phi Theta Kappa were Ann Buddenhagen, Mona Frawls, Rebecca Stallings, Betty Ward, Patricia Hall, Laura Parnell, Mary Anne Kerr, Gail Perry, Helen Pruden, and Linda Glass. See *SMCB*, Mar. 1971, 7.

12. Charter members of the St. Mary's High School Honor Society were Mary Graham Andrews, Ellen Jordan, Marsha McElrath, Mary Ethel Valone, Mary Roberts Blue, Betsy Brooks, Lind Coppage, Meda Lie Doffermyre, Ann Reesman, and Isabel Scott.

13. Helen H. Smith, faculty representative, to some members of the board of trustees, 23 Apr. 1975, SMCA.

14. TM, 24 Apr. 1975.

15. Ibid.

16. Annegret Harnischfeger and Daniel E. Wiley, "The Marrow of Achievement Test Score Declines," Lipsitz, ed., *Test Score Decline*, 5; TM, 24 Apr. 1975.

17. TM, 23 Apr., 8 Jan. 1970.

18. Bergquist et al., *Education of An Age Group*, 27–29.

19. *SMCB*, Dec. 1971, 8.

20. Robert J. Miller interview, 27 June 1980; *SMCB*, Mar. 1973, 1. Robert James Miller is listed in *Who's Who in America*, 1974–75, II, 2160.

21. *NO*, 9 May 1970; TB, 4 Apr. 1970.

22. *SMC*, Dec. 1975, 5.

23. Ibid., June 1976, 3–4.

24. Ethel J. Alpenfels, "Women in the Professional World," Cassara, ed., *Changing Image*, 78, 80; Vivian C. Mason, "Women in Education," Cassara, *Changing Image*, 117; Chafe, *American Woman*, 219.

25. Friedan, *Feminine Mystique*, 353–54, 356.

26. TB, 9 Apr. 1943; *SMCB*, June 1971, 7.

27. *SMC*, June 1976, 7; *SMC*, June 1978, 7.

28. Geraldine S. Cate interview, 15 June 1981.

29. TB, 2 Apr. 1974.

30. RS interview, 13 June 1980; Lou Jones notes, 4 Aug. 1982.

31. *SMCB*, Dec. 1966, 4.

32. Ibid., Dec. 1969, 15. Barnhart in 1972 wrote the words and music to the St. Mary's anthem. Michael Bulley arranged the music.

33. Ibid., Dec. 1970, 15; Hannah P. Scoggin interview, 4 May 1981.

34. *SMCB*, Dec. 1970, 14.

35. Pamela DeVere and Betty Ward were administrative assistants in the alumnae office. Carolyn Westbrook Brown had charge of the registrar's records. Also on the staff were Sealy Cross, Sara Frances Walters, Elizabeth Bynum, Betty Anne Queen, Julia Parsons Pressley, and Laura Norris Raynor.

36. *SMCB*, Dec. 1970, 15.

37. *SMCB*, Dec. 1967, 3; *SMCB*, Dec. 1969, 15.

38. *NO*, 21 June 1974.

39. Ibid.

40. Dell Parker interview, 8 June 1979; Lane Turner, "Reflections of a Four-Year Student," *SMC*, July 1974, 5.

41. TM, 18 Jan. 1973.

42. TB, 16 Oct. 1970.

43. TM, 20 July 1972.

44. Margaret Smith, "You Asked Me What College Life Was Like," TB, 10 Feb. 1975.

45. Gail Perry and Barbara Olechner, "The Belle Tower," TB, 22 Jan. 1971.

46. TB, 5 Feb. 1971.

47. Ibid., 18 Nov. 1971; *SMCB*, Mar. 1972, 1–2.

48. *SMCB*, Mar. 1972, 2.

49. Ibid., 2, 4, 11.

50. TM, 26 Jan. 1972.

51. Anna DuBose interview, 5 May 1979.

52. RT, 22 Feb. 1972.

53. Parker interview, 8 June 1979.

54. RT, 22 Feb. 1972.

55. TB, 24 Feb. 1972.

56. TM, 20 Apr. 1972.

57. Ibid.

58. Ibid., 5 Oct. 1972.

59. *SMC*, July 1974, 5.

60. TB, 23 Jan. 1973.

61. *SMCB*, June 1973, 2. A brass Paschal candlestick was given to the chapel by students, parents, and friends to honor Edith Richardson.

62. FP, ms. of chapel talk to alumnae, 24 Apr. 1976, SMCA.

63. The *Stagecoach*, 1969, lists members of the newly organized vestry as Polly Cozart, Corrine Davidson, Amy Carr, Christy Willis, Ann Highsmith, Walker Holmes, Sherri Graham, Suzanne Green, Ella Davies, and Marion Wolff. Probably the first woman lay reader to be licensed in N.C. to administer the Chalice was Kathleen Noyes, a member of the 1970–72 vestry. She was installed when she was 16 by Bishop M. George Henry, Diocese of Western North Carolina.

64. SMC, June 1975, 4, lists memorial gifts. *SMC*, 6 June 1973, lists the Communion Chalice given in memory of Elizabeth B. Ingram, a student who died 7 Apr. 1972, as the result of an automobile accident.

65. Robert C. Baird telephone interview, 4 June 1981. Later, Baird served St. Christopher's in Garner.

66. TM, 23 Apr. 1970.

67. J. W. S. Davis interview, Aug. 1982. Davis returned as chaplain, 1984.

68. TM, 18 Apr. 1974.

69. SMC, June 1975, 5.

70. TM, 16 July 1970.

71. NCCh, LXI (Feb. 1971), 5.

72. Ibid., LXII (Jan. 1972), 16; JDNC, 1972, 175.

73. Thomas A. Fraser to Martha Stoops, 16 Nov. 1982, SMCA.

74. "An Act to Incorporate the Trustees of Saint Mary's School," *Private Laws of the State of North Carolina, 1897*, c. 86.

75. TM, 17 July 1975.

76. Ibid., 17 July 1971.

77. Ibid., 26 Jan. 1972.

78. Ibid., 18 Jan. 1973.

79. Ibid., 24 Apr. 1975.

80. Steering committee members were James M. Poyner, Mayne Albright, John S. Hill, Lila Spilman Rankin, Katharine Duff Powell, J. Melville Broughton, Jr., J. H. Froelich, Jr., Philip M. Russell, William B. Harrison, Frank H. Kenan, Arthur McKimmon II, James M. Peden, William Ragland, M. Garnett Saunders, and Benjamin S. Willis.

81. TM, 23 Apr. 1970.

82. Ibid., 16 July 1970.

83. Ibid., 22 Apr. 1971, 5 June 1975.

84. SMCB, Dec. 1972, 3–4. Architects for the gymnasium-natatorium were McKimmon and Rogers of Raleigh.

85. Memorial rooms in Ragland are the Henrietta Hunt Towler faculty lounge and the Miriam Morgan Towler classroom.

86. TM, 7 Oct. 1971.

87. Among funds received were grants from the Z. Smith Reynolds, John W. and Anna Hanes, and Sarah Graham Kenan foundations.

88. TM, 5 June 1975.

89. Ibid., 20 Apr. 1972.

90. SMCB, Dec. 1972, 11; TM, 26 Apr. 1973.

91. TM, 18 Apr. 1974.

92. Ibid., 26 Apr. 1973.

93. JDNC, 1969, 69.

94. SMC, Dec. 1973, 2; SMC, July 1974, 2.

95. SMCB, Dec. 1971, 1–2.

96. Ibid., Dec. 1972, 7.

97. SMC, Dec. 1973, 2.

98. Ibid.

99. TM, 18 July, 3 Oct. 1974; SMC, July 1974, 1; SMC, June 1975, 1.

100. SMC, June 1975, 1–2.

101. Alumnae association projects included the sale of Wedgwood plates, the college seal needlepoint kits designed by Charlotte Andrews McCutchen, and the serigraphs executed by Jean Collier. The sale of the old dining room chairs realized $8,000 in 1973. (They cost about $3,500 in 1952.)

102. TM, 18 Apr. 1974.

103. *SMC*, Dec. 1976, 3; Brant Snavely, Executive Director, North Carolina Foundation of Church-Related Colleges, to Martha Stoops, 25 June 1973, SMCA.

104. TM, 5 June 1975.

105. Ibid., 5 June, 5 May 1975.

106. Ibid., 24 Apr. 1975.

107. Ibid., 17 July 1975.

108. Ibid.

109. Ibid., 23 Oct. 1975.

110. Ibid.

111. ACM, 1 May 1970, 13 Jan. 1971.

112. *SMC*, Dec. 1974, 6. Louise Edward Overman was the sixth generation of St. Mary's women: Lucy Williams Boddine (1840s); Ellen Douglas Moore Leach (1867); Sallie Moore Leach Pippen (1902); Ellen Douglas Pippen Townsend (1925); Anne Townsend Overman (1949). Elizabeth Nolan Hubbard was the fifth generation: Sarah Covington Little (1840s); Sarah Covington Little Dowd (early 1860s); Mary Elizabeth Nolan Turner (1921); Marion Nolan Hubbard (1949). Eleanor Hope Maynard was the fifth generation: Eleanor Hope Swain Atkins (early 1860s); Eleanor Hope Atkins Cobb (1880s); Eleanor Hope Cobb Newell (1921); Eleanor Hope Newell (1948). Elizabeth Hinton Cheshire was fourth generation St. Mary's on both sides of her family: Bessie Cain Hinton (1860s); Bessie Hinton Silver (1900); Elizabeth Sprague Silver Cheshire (1947). Elizabeth H. Cheshire was also the great-granddaughter of Annie Webb Cheshire and the granddaughter of Godfrey Cheshire, who attended primary school at St. Mary's.

113. *SMCB*, June 1970, 26–27; *SMCB*, Dec. 1969, 22; *SMCB*, Dec. 1971, 18; *SMCB*, June 1973, 17; *SMC*, June 1975, 10; *SMC*, July 1974, 9; *SMCB*, Dec. 1969, 7; *SMCB*, Mar. 1970, 4; *SMCB*, Mar. 1973, 4.

114. *SMC*, Dec. 1969, 35–36; *SMC*, June 1970, 35; *SMC*, Dec. 1974, 3; *SMC*, June 1979, 6; *SMC*, June 1980, 2, 5.

115. *SMC*, Dec. 1973, 4; *SMC*, June 1979, 2; *SMCB*, Mar. 1973, 2.

116. *SMCB*, Mar. 1971, 2–3.

117. Interviews with three persons who heard the conversation.

118. FP interview, 13 May 1976; *SMC*, June 1976, 1.

119. FP notes for chapel announcement, SMCA.

120. FP interview, 13 May 1976; *SMC*, June 1976, 1.


CHAPTER FOURTEEN

1. JR interview, 5 Aug. 1977.

2. JR's father, William Thomas Rice, became chairman of the board of the Seaboard Coastline Railroad Co. His mother is Jaqueline Palm Johnston Rice.

3. JR interview, 25 June 1982.

4. JR is a member of Phi Kappa Phi, Omricon Delta Kappa National Leadership Fraternity, and Scabbard and Blade National Military Society. He served 2 years at Fort Eustis and was discharged as a captain. He received the master's degree in 1963.

5. JR interview, 5 Aug. 1977; Grace Rice interview, 25 June 1982.

6. The search committee was composed of Eugene B. Hardin, Jr., and Sherwood H. Smith, co-chairmen, Helen A. Barnes, Mary Pride Cruikshank, Llewellyn Faircloth, John S. Hill, June Bourne Long, Nancy O'Herron Rankin, Sallie Lee Walker, Elgiva D. Watson, and Ben S. Willis. See TM, 10 May 1976. JR interview, 25 June 1982; TM, 10 May 1976.

7. Designed by Margaret C. Williams, the large pendant cast in britannia metal bore the seal of the college officially adopted 13 Oct. 1965.

8. *SMC*, June 1977, 1.

9. FM, 6 Feb. 1981.

10. "Long-Range Planning Report," 2.

11. JR interview, 25 June 1982.

12. FM, 1 Sept. 1978.

13. *SMC*, Dec. 1976, 1; *TM* 23 Sept. 1980; JR interview, 25 June 1982.

14. Robert J. Miller interview, 27 June 1980.

15. "Long-Range Planning Report," 1982, SMCA.

16. The Phi Theta Kappa Award for the greatest scholastic improvement in two years was named as a memorial to Georgia Lee Kinsey, a 1981 graduate who was killed in an automobile accident. Elizabeth Lynn Gardner was the first recipient of this award.

17. Karen Lado also placed very high in the regional competition in French.

18. The Morehead scholar was Mary Grady Koonce.

19. Assembly panel by 1980 graduates Kea Capel, Margaret Williams, Cathryn Zevenhuizen, and Garland Waller, 12 Oct. 1981.

20. Informal discussion with 6 male faculty members, 28 Apr. 1982.

21. In 1981 Andrea Brown became vice-chairman and chairman-elect of the junior college section of the N.C. Library Association.

22. 1981–82 library funds amounting to $46.20 per student came from the college budget, a small federal grant, and income from several endowments. The Helen A. Brown endowment reached almost $10,000 by 1982.

23. The collection, cataloged through gifts from John and Catherine Fulenwider, contains first editions, letters (some unpublished), copies of some 30 dissertations, clippings, photographs, a portrait, filmstrips, and video and cassette tapes. The other large Wolfe collections are at Harvard University, the University of North Carolina at Chapel Hill, and at Pack Memorial Library, Asheville.

24. Donors are named on wall plates in the St. Mary's library. They include Richard Walser, Aldo P. Magi, Fred Wolfe, John Fleming, Joan Fleming Cremin, Robert Cremin, and others.

25. Fred Wolfe (Luke in *Look Homeward, Angel*) made a third visit to the college, where he was a great favorite, before his death on 8 Apr. 1980.

26. See Walser, *The Wolfe Family in Raleigh*.

27. The essay contest, including the printing of the winning essay, was sponsored for several years by Catherine G. Barnhart of the English department.

28. The Smedes portraits by William Fields were unveiled in October, 1978, by David Brewster Moore and Sarah Florence Moore, great-great-great grandchildren of Aldert Smedes, at a dedication ceremony in Smedes parlor.

29. JR interview, 25 June 1982.

30. TM, 24 Jan. 1980.

31. Ibid.

32. FM, 17 Mar. 1978.

33. "Self-Study Report," 1979, 188.

34. TM, 24 Jan. 1980.

35. FM, 12 Jan. 1979; JR memorandum to faculty, 31 Jan. 1979, SMCA.

36. "Long-Range Planning Report," 4, 37.

37. FM, 28 Aug. 1981.

38. *SMC*, June 1977, 5.

39. The portrait by Grey Moll was presented in 1973.

40. *SMC*, June 1978, 11. Mary Ruth Haig was buried in Bloomfield, Ind.

41. *SMC*, June 1979, 11.

42. *Caseette*, Sept. 1978, 4; Margaret Williams interview, 17 June 1980.

43. Sallie MacNider Shadrach, great-granddaughter of Charles Peter Mallett (1792–1874) to Martha Stoops, Sept 1976, SMCA. See Rebecca J. Beal, *Jacob Eichholtz, 1776–1842, Portrait Painter of Pennsylvania* (Philadelphia: Historical Society of Pennsylvania, 1969).

44. Zepp, a native of S.C., grew up in Ill. A graduate of Southern Ill. Univ., she lived and studied in Mexico and taught in Ill. and S.C. See *SMC*, June 1980, 5.

45. *Caseette*, fall/winter 1980–81, 5; Helen Smith interview, 12 Nov. 1982.

46. *Caseette*, Mar. 1978, 4; Marjolijn Werman notes, May 1981, SMCA.

47. *Caseette*, Dec. 1977, 6; *SMCB*, Dec. 1971, 10; Elgiva Watson interview, 24 June 1980. Watson served on the advisory editorial committee of the *North Carolina Historical Review*.

48. Saxe's bachelor's and master's degrees were from the Univ. of Durham. *SMCB*, Dec. 1971, 9; *Caseette*, fall/winter 1980–81, 7.

49. *Caseette*, June 1978, 5.

50. Campbell took her master's degree at George Peabody College under a Carnegie fellowship. In Israel she knew missionaries Elmo and Hannah Scoggin. Georgette Campbell interview, 3 Aug. 1982; *SMCB*, Dec. 1971, 9.

51. Alice Greiner and her husband Joe were founding board members of the North Carolina Natural History Society.

52. *Caseette*, spring 1980, 7.

53. Coffey's second trip to the USSR was made at the request of the Russian Academy of Sciences. Janice Coffey telephone interview, 7 June 1982. Her degrees were from Appalachian State Univ. and the Univ. of South Carolina. Wooten-Hawkins's degrees from Hollins College and the Univ. of North Carolina at Greensboro included two master's degrees.

54. Tributes from Ellen Birch, 28 Apr. 1982. Fish retired as colonel, U.S. Army Corps of Engineers. A West Point graduate, he held master's degrees from Harvard and N.C. State Univ.

55. Harry Callahan interview, 23 May 1979.

56. A native of Gastonia, Quinn, a dean of the American Guild of Organists, was known as an organ recitalist. He became choirmaster and organist at the Chapel of the Cross, Chapel Hill, in 1970. He was for 12 years a member of the Liturgical Commission of the Diocese of N.C.

57. Emmett Windham telephone interview, 2 Mar. 1984.

58. JR interview, 25 June 1982; Grace Rice interview, 25 June 1982.

59. The 1982 valedictorian was Jean Huske Schaefer.

60. *SMM*, 1981–82, 7–8.

61. Material on student sub-groups came from interviews with Cynthia Efird, 27 Apr. 1977; Ellyn Faircloth, 4 May 1977; and Anne Sigmon, 7 May 1981; it also came from group discussions on 18 and 27 Mar. 1977, essays on psychology examinations, 1977, and a paper for American history by Margaret Leonard, May, 1981.

62. *New York Times*, 19 Nov. 1978, 1, 35.

63. John Hume interview, Apr. 28, 1982.

64. Resident counselors who served for a number of years were: Elizabeth Duke, Margaret Gentry, Margaret Selph, and Pearl Johnson.

65. TM, 23 Jan. 1981.

66. JR memorandum to trustees, faculty, staff, 3 June 1981. A Virginian, Elizabeth Jones held degrees from Longwood College and the College of William and Mary and had taught for many years.

67. Lane Turner, SGA president, report to trustees, 18 Apr. 1974, SMCA.

68. JR memorandum to trustees, faculty, staff, 1 July 1981.

69. Marcia Jones interview, 30 June 1982.

70. Ibid.

71. JR interview, 5 Aug. 1977.

72. JR to alumnae, 25 Apr. 1981, SMCA.

73. JR, assembly talks to students, 27 Aug. 1979, 25 Aug. 1980.

74. *NO*, 11 Nov. 1979.

75. Student interviews, 20 Apr. 1980.

76. *SMC*, June 1979, 4.

77. The Nancy Elizabeth Marlowe Scholarship was established by her parents, Mr. and Mrs. William A. Marlowe of Wilson, and friends. The first winner was Marilyn Layton Ellerbe.

78. The bell tower was adapted by K. C. Ramsey of Olsen Associates, Inc., of Raleigh from the tower at St. Mark's Episcopal Church, Palatka, Fla. That design was taken from Richard Upjohn, *Upjohn's Rural Architecture* (New York: G. P. Putnam, 1852).

79. Katherine Pate, paper for Martha Stoops's history class, 1980.

80. *TB*, 4 Feb. 1983.

81. Dillard was ordained deacon 1953 by Bishop Penick and priest 1954 by Bishop Baker. He was priest-in-charge at St. Matthew's in Rowan County before entering the Air Force chaplaincy where he served as Episcopal chaplain at the Air Force Academy for 2

years and in Germany for 3 years. He served as rector at St. Paul's, Smithfield, associate rector at Christ Church, Charlotte, as rector of St. Albans, Harlingen, Tex., and of St. John's, Worthington, O.

82. Starke Dillard interview, 6 Sept. 1982; *Caseette,* Summer 1980, 5.

83. *SMC,* June 1980, 1.

84. TM, 26 Jan. 1978.

85. The Elizabeth Strange McNeill Elliott Scholarship was endowed by St. John's, Fayetteville.

86. The gift of $40,000 from St. Paul's, Winston-Salem, was the largest gift ever received from a denominational entity.

87. *SMC,* Summer 1980, 1.

88. W. S. Quinn III, talk in assembly, 3 Nov. 1979.

89. JR interview, 25 June 1982; FM, 6 May 1981.

90. In 1981 Miller was elected vice-president, president-elect of the N.C. Assoc. of Academic Deans.

91. TM, 24 Jan. 1980.

92. Alumnae funds helped finance the refurbishing of the new admissions office. The dean of students office moved to a suite in lower Smedes.

93. Young alumnae working on campus at various times, mostly in admissions, were: Amelia Peden, Jane Bratton, Helen Revelle, Katie Jo Lawrence, Virginia Godwin, Connie Rivenbark, Marina Lynch. Elizabeth Vann administered scholarship funds.

94. "Women's College Regains Appeal," *New York Times,* 19 Nov. 1978.

95. The women department chairpersons involved were Ellen Birch, Mary Oliver Ellington, Mary Ruth Haig, Mary Louise Jones, Dolores Lado, Helen Smith, Nancy Stamey, Martha Stoops, Elgiva Watson, and Margaret Williams. The men were John Tate and August Lawrence.

96. TM, 26 Jan. 1979.

97. Ibid., 24 Jan. 1980. Nola Coggin and Marjorie J. Maddrey assisted Conrad for several years.

98. Funds for some of the campus beautification were given by Mr. and Mrs. William E. Columbus.

99. "Long-Range Planning Report," 55.

100. B. W. Conrad notes, Aug. 1982, SMCA.

101. Barnes and Roche report, 5, 15, SMCA.

102. Henry Read notes, Oct. 1982, 16 Mar. 1984, SMCA.

103. JR interview, 25 June 1982; FM, 29 Oct. 1982.

104. Mr. and Mrs. Sherwood Smith of Raleigh served as co-chairpersons of the West Rock committee.

105. See *SMC,* Sept. 1981, Sept, 1982, *SMC.*

106. Martha Stoops was aided in preparation of material for the nomination of the campus to the National Register of Historic Places by alumna Mary Ann Lee Blackburn, who was then working in the Department of Cultural Resources. The Smedes grant came from the Historical Preservation Fund, U.S. Dept. of the Interior, and was administered by the N.C. Division of Archives and History, of the Department of Cultural Resources.

107. JR address to alumnae, 26 Apr. 1982.

108. TM, 24 Jan. 1980.

109. Members of the college long-range planning committee were Robert Miller, chairperson; B. W. Conrad; Marcia Jones; Robert Simpson; Elgiva Watson; Janice Coffey; Dolores Lado; and Harry Callahan. Members of the board of trustees long-range planning and development committee were: Reba White Williams, chairperson; Jesse Capel; William Clark; Mary P. Cruikshank Clark; Margery Johnson; W. W. Dukes; Thad Eure, Jr.; James Peden; Judith Metcalfe von Seldeneck; Smedes York.

110. Other members of the capital campaign steering committee were Coleman Hardy and Luke Hill Page, alumnae; John Landi, trustee; and Thurman Williams, former trustee.

111. Hardin report, TM, 30 Apr. 1980.

112. Alleen W. Cater interview, 27 Apr. 1980.

113. Elizabeth Morrison Moye and Margaret King Piner were granddaughters of Gertrude Hancock McLennan. Martha Anne Marsh Sigmon was the marshal.

114. *Caseette*, Mar. 1979, 1.

115. The Smedes Associates, established in memory of Aldert Smedes, honors those giving $1,000 or more to the annual fund. Membership in The Order of the Grove is for gifts of $500–$999, and the 1842 Society members pledge $1 for each year of the school's existence.

116. Donors of the matching challenge to excellence funds were Mr. and Mrs. Thomas C. Coxe, Jr., Mr. and Mrs. Frank H. Kenan, Mr. and Mrs. Edwin Pate, Mr. and Mrs. James M. Poyner, Mr. and Mrs. William M. Ragland, Mr. and Mrs. W. Thomas Rice, and Elizabeth Gold Swindell.

117. The first Rabon award went to Anna Tate, editor of *TB*.

118. Sterling Remer interview, 23 July 1982; Remer attended Saint Agnes School, Albany, N.Y., and took a B.A. degree at Utica College of Syracuse Univ.

119. Alumnae bequests were from Sarah Graham Kenan, Alice Walker Dillard and Elizabeth M. Montgomery.

120. Margaret Burgwyn, a Chapel Hill graduate, held a master's degree from Appalachian State Univ. and had experience in teaching and administration.

121. Reba White Williams, commencement address, 1978.

122. *NO*, 25 Oct. 1981.

123. *SMC*, July 1981, 13–14.

124. Ibid., Dec. 1978, 9.

125. Ibid., June 1978, 4; Susan Ehringhaus interview, 23 June 1980.

126. *SMC*, June 1978, 4. Peden was ordained to the priesthood, 6 May 1978, by the Rt. Rev. William G. Weinhauer, bishop of Western N.C.

127. *NO*, 24 Jan. 1981; *SMC*, July 1981, 12–13.

128. *NO*, 28 Jan. 1982.

129. *SMC*, Dec. 1977, 3.

130. *NO*, 3 Feb. 1982.

# BIBLIOGRAPHY

References to articles are cited in full in the notes when first used in each chapter, and they are not included here.

Albright, Raymond W. *A History of the Protestant Episcopal Church*. New York: Macmillan, 1964.

Allen, Sarah. *Ginger Hill*. Winston-Salem, N.C.: John F. Blair, 1973.

Amis, Moses N. *Historical Raleigh with Sketches of Wake County and Its Important Towns*. Raleigh: Commercial Printing Co., 1913.

Arbuckle, John C. *Civil War Experiences of a Foot-Soldier Who Marched with Sherman*. Columbus, Ohio: n.p., 1930.

Avirett, James Battle. *The Old Plantation: How We Lived in Great House and Cabin Before the War*. New York: F. Tennyson Neely Co., 1901.

Bailey, John Lancaster, Papers. Southern Historical Collection. Wilson Library, Univ. of North Carolina at Chapel Hill.

Banner, Lois W. *Women in Modern America: A Brief History*. The Harbrace History of the United States. New York: Harcourt Brace Jovanovich, 1974.

Barrett, John G. *Sherman's March Through the Carolinas*. Chapel Hill: Univ. of North Carolina Press, 1956.

Battle Family Papers. Southern Historical Collection. Wilson Library, Univ. of North Carolina at Chapel Hill.

Battle, Kemp Plummer. *Memories of An Old-Time Tar Heel*. Chapel Hill: Univ. of North Carolina Press, 1945.

Battle, Richard H. *Memorial Address On St. Mary's School and Former Rectors*. Pamphlet. Charlotte, N.C.: Observer Printing House, 1902.

Beach, Helen. *Descendants of Jacob Sebor, 1709–1793, of Middletown, Conn*. N.p., 1923.

Becker, Kate Harbes. *Biography of Christian Reid*. Sacred Heart Junior College, Belmont, N.C., 1941.

Bergquist, A. Bruce, C. Arthur Compton, Richard S. Pieters, Wade C. Stephens, and Harlan P. Hanson. *16–20: The Liberal Education of an Age Group*. College Entrance Examination Board, New York, 1970.

Brick, Michael. *Forum and Focus for the Junior College Movement: The American Association of Junior Colleges*. New York: Bureau of Publications, Teachers College, Columbia Univ., 1964.

Bryan, William Shepard, Papers. Southern Historical Collection. Wilson Library, Univ. of North Carolina at Chapel Hill.

Cameron, Bennehan, Papers. Southern Historical Collection. Wilson Library, Univ. of North Carolina at Chapel Hill.

Cameron Family Papers. Southern Historical Collection. Wilson Library, Univ. of North Carolina at Chapel Hill.

Campion, Nardi Reeder, with Rosamond Wilfley Stanton. *Look to This Day: The Lively Education of a Great Woman Doctor: Connie Guion, M.D.* Boston: Little, Brown and Co., 1965.

Carson Collection. Rare Book Library, The National Cathedral, Washington, D.C.

Cassara, Beverly Benner, ed. *American Women: The Changing Image.* Boston: Beacon Press, 1962.

Catton, Bruce. *This Hallowed Ground: The Story of the Union Side of the Civil War.* Garden City, N.Y.: Doubleday and Co., 1956.

Chafe, William Henry. *The American Woman: Her Changing Social, Economic, and Political Roles, 1920–1970.* New York: Oxford Univ. Press, 1972.

Cheshire, Joseph Blount, Papers. Division of Archives and History, North Carolina Department of Cultural Resources, Raleigh.

———. Proceedings of School Committee of Episcopal School of North Carolina and St. Mary's School papers. Southern Historical Collection. Wilson Library, Univ. of North Carolina at Chapel Hill.

———. St. Mary's College Archives, Raleigh.

Cheshire, Joseph B., ed. *Sketches of Church History in North Carolina.* Wilmington, N.C.: William L. DeRosset, Jr., 1892.

Clark, Walter, ed. *Histories of the Several Regiments and Battalions from North Carolina in the Great War, 1861–65.* Vol. IV. Goldsboro, N.C.: Nash Brothers, 1901.

Clemence, Walter S. Diary. North Carolina Collection. Wilson Library, Univ. of North Carolina at Chapel Hill.

Coates, Albert. *By Her Own Bootstraps: A Saga of Women in North Carolina.* N.p., 1975.

Cobb, Collier, Papers. Southern Historical Collection. Wilson Library, Univ. of North Carolina at Chapel Hill.

Coker, Louise Venable. "The Annals of My College Life." Diary. Private Collection.

Collier, Margaret. *Biographies of Representative Women of the South.* Vol. II. N.p., 1923?

Collier, Susan Elizabeth, Diary. Private collection.

Collins, Anne Cameron, Papers. Southern Historical Collection. Wilson Library, Univ. of North Carolina at Chapel Hill.

Conable, Charlotte Williams. *Women at Cornell: The Myth of Equal Education.* Ithaca, N.Y.: Cornell Univ. Press, 1977.

Coolidge, Jane Toy. *Growing Up With Chapel Hill.* Chapel Hill, N.C.: Chapel Hill Historical Society, 1977.

Coon, Charles Lee. *North Carolina Schools and Academies, 1790–1840: A Documentary History.* Raleigh: North Carolina Historical Commission, 1915.

Cotten, Sallie Southall. *History of the North Carolina Federation of Women's Clubs.* Raleigh: Edwards and Broughton Co., 1925.

Cowan, Thomas, Letters. Southern Historical Collection. Wilson Library, Univ. of North Carolina at Chapel Hill.

Coxe, Emily Badham, and Frances Warfield. *Mother of the Maid.* New York: Rinehart and Winston, 1960.

Creecy Family Papers. Southern Historical Collection. Wilson Library, Univ. of North Carolina at Chapel Hill.

Curtis, Moses Ashley, Papers. Southern Historical Collection. Wilson Library, Univ. of North Carolina at Chapel Hill.

Czarnomska, Marie Elizabeth Josephine, Papers. The Sophia Smith Collection. Women's History Archive, Smith College, Northampton, Mass.

*Daily Progress.* Raleigh, 12 Jan.–3 Mar. 1865.

*Daily Standard.* Raleigh, 1 May 1865.

*Daily State Chronicle.* Raleigh, 5 Apr. 1893.

Davis, Jefferson, Papers. Division of Archives and History, North Carolina Department of Cultural Resources, Raleigh.

Davis, Varina Howell. *Jefferson Davis, Ex-President of the Confederate States of America: A Memoir by His Wife*. Vol. II. New York: Belford Co., 1890.

Dawley, Powel Mills. *The Story of the General Theological Seminary: A Sesquicentennial History, 1817–1967*. New York: Oxford Univ. Press, 1969.

Delta Kappa Gamma Society. *Some Pioneer Women Teachers of North Carolina*. N.p: The Delta Kappa Gamma Society, 1955.

DeRosset Family Papers. Southern Historical Collection. Wilson Library, Univ. of North Carolina at Chapel Hill.

Drake, William E. *Higher Education in North Carolina Before 1860*. New York: Carleton Press, 1964.

Episcopal School of North Carolina Papers. Proceedings of Building Committee. Division of Archives and History, North Carolina Department of Cultural Resources, Raleigh.

French, Marilyn. *The Women's Room*. New York: Jove Publications, 1978.

French, William Glenney, Recollections. Diary and Papers. Southern Historical Collection. Wilson Library, Univ. of North Carolina at Chapel Hill.

Friedan, Betty. *The Feminine Mystique*. 1963. Reprint. New York: Dell Publishing Co., 1973.

Gale and Polk Family Papers. Southern Historical Collection. Wilson Library, Univ. of North Carolina at Chapel Hill.

Goodsell, Willystine, ed. *Pioneers of Women's Education In the United States*. 1931. Reprint. New York: AMS Press, 1970.

Haigh, William Hooper, Papers. Diary. Southern Historical Collection. Wilson Library, Univ. of North Carolina at Chapel Hill.

Halliburton, Cecil D. *A History of St. Augustine's College, 1867–1937*. Raleigh: Edwards and Broughton Co., 1937.

Hanson, Willis T., Jr. *A History of St. George's Church*. Vol. I. Schenectady, N.Y.: n.p., 1919.

Haywood, Marshall DeLancey. *Lives of the Bishops of North Carolina: From the Establishment of the Episcopate in That State down to the Division of the Diocese*. Raleigh: Alfred Williams and Co., 1910.

Henderson, Archibald, Papers. Southern Historical Collection. Wilson Library, Univ. of North Carolina at Chapel Hill.

Henderson, John Steel, Papers. Southern Historical Collection. Wilson Library, Univ. of North Carolina at Chapel Hill.

Hill, Daniel Harvey, Jr., Papers. Division of Archives and History, North Carolina Department of Cultural Resources, Raleigh.

Hines, Wait and Leone, Collection. Division of Archives and History, North Carolina Department of Cultural Resources, Raleigh.

Hitchcock, Henry. *Marching with Sherman*. New Haven: Yale Univ. Press, 1927.

Hofstadter, Richard, William Miller, and Daniel Aaron. *The United States: The History Of A Republic*. Second ed. Englewood Cliffs, N.J.: Prentice-Hall, 1967.

Howard, Oliver Otis. *Autobiography*. The Black Heritage Library Collection. Two vols. 1907. Reprint. Freeport, N.Y.: Books for Libraries Press, 1971.

Howell, Edward Vernon, Papers. Southern Historical Collection. Wilson Library, Univ. of North Carolina at Chapel Hill.

Howerton, Philip H., Papers. Manuscript Department, William R. Perkins Library, Duke Univ., Durham, N.C.

Hughson, Dorothy May. Diary. St. Mary's College Archives, Raleigh.

Ingram, Margaret H. "Development of Higher Education for White Women in North Carolina Prior to 1875." Ph.D. dissertation, Univ. of North Carolina at Chapel Hill, 1961.

Jarratt-Puryear Family Papers. Manuscript Department, William R. Perkins Library, Duke Univ., Durham, N.C.

Johnson, Guion Griffis. *Ante-Bellum North Carolina: A Social History*. Chapel Hill: Univ. of North Carolina Press, 1937.

Johnson, Mary Lynch. *A History of Meredith College*. Raleigh: Edwards and Broughton Co., 1956.

Johnston, Joseph E. *Narrative of Military Operations*. New York: D. Appleton and Co., 1874.

Jordan, Daniel W., Papers. Manuscript Department, William R. Perkins Library, Duke Univ., Durham, N.C.

"Junior League of Raleigh Annual Report, June 1929–June 1930." Junior League of Raleigh, Raleigh, 1930.

Kibler, Lillian Adele. *The History of Converse College, 1889–1971*. Converse College, Spartanburg, S.C., 1973.

Kimberly, John, Papers. Southern Historical Collection. Wilson Library, Univ. of North Carolina at Chapel Hill.

Knight, Edgar W. *Education in the United States*. Boston: Ginn and Co., 1929.

Lay, George William, Papers. Southern Historical Collection. Wilson Library, Univ. of North Carolina at Chapel Hill.

Lay, George W. *Some Additions to the Report of the Rector to the Trustees of St. Mary's School*. Pamphlet. Raleigh: Edwards and Broughton Printing Co., 1918.

Lee, Captain Robert E. *Recollections and Letters of General Robert E. Lee*. New York: Doubleday, Page and Co., 1904.

Lee Papers. Virginia Historical Society, Richmond, Va.

L'Engle, Edward McCrady, Papers. Southern Historical Collection. Wilson Library, Univ. of North Carolina at Chapel Hill.

Lefler, Hugh Talmage, ed. *North Carolina History Told By Contemporaries*. Third ed. Chapel Hill: Univ. of North Carolina Press, 1956.

Lefler, Hugh Talmage, and Albert Ray Newsome. *The History of a Southern State: North Carolina*. Third ed. Chapel Hill: Univ. of North Carolina Press, 1973.

Leslie, Eliza. *Miss Leslie's Behaviour Book: A Guide and Manual for Ladies*. 1859. Reprint. Philadelphia: T. B. Peterson and Brothers, 1972.

Levert Family Papers. Southern Historical Collection. Wilson Library, Univ. of North Carolina at Chapel Hill.

Lewis, Nell Battle. *The Power of Prayer as Set Forth in the Words of Jesus of Nazareth*. Pamphlet. Boston: Little, Brown and Co., 1941.

Lewis, Nell Battle, Papers. Division of Archives and History, North Carolina Department of Cultural Resources, Raleigh.

Lipsitz, Lawrence, ed. *The Test Score Decline: Meaning and Issues*. Englewood Cliffs, N.J.: Educational Technology Publications, 1977.

Littlefield, Milton S., ed. *Hymns of the Christian Life*. N.p.: A. S. Barnes and Co., 1908.

London, Lawrence Foushee. *Bishop Joseph Blount Cheshire: His Life and Work*. Chapel Hill: Univ. of North Carolina Press, 1941.

Long, E. B., and Barbara Long. *The Civil War Day by Day: An Almanac, 1861–1865*. Garden City, N.Y.: Doubleday and Co., 1971.

"Long Range Planning Report." Draft 2. St. Mary's College, Raleigh, 1982. Mimeographed.

Lutz, Alma. *Emma Willard: Daughter of Democracy*. Boston: Houghton Mifflin Co., 1929.

McAdoo, Eleanor Wilson, in collaboration with Margaret Y. Gaffey. *The Woodrow Wilsons*. New York: Macmillan Co., 1937.

MacDowell, Dorothy Kelly. *Dubose Genealogy*. Columbia, S.C.: R. L. Bryan Co., 1972.

McKimmon, Kate, Papers. Division of Archives and History, North Carolina Department of Cultural Resources, Raleigh.

McLachlan, James. *American Boarding Schools: A Historical Study*. New York: Charles Scribner's Sons, 1970.

Massey, Mary Elizabeth. *Bonnet Brigades*. New York: Alfred A. Knopf, 1966.

Meares and DeRosset Family Papers. Southern Historical Collection. Wilson Library, University of North Carolina at Chapel Hill.

Millstein, Beth, and Jeanne Bodin. *We, the American Women: A Documentary History*. Chicago: Science Research Associates, 1977.

Montgomery, Lizzie Wilson. *The St. Mary's of Olden Days*. Raleigh: Bynum Printing Co., 1932.

Mordecai, George W., Papers. Southern Historical Collection. Wilson Library, University of North Carolina at Chapel Hill.

*Morning Post*. Raleigh, 23 Feb. 1899.

Murray, Elizabeth Reid. *WAKE: Capital County of North Carolina*. Vol. I, *Prehistory through Centennial*. Raleigh: Capital County Publishing Co., 1983.

Nash, Ann Strudwick. *Ladies in the Making at the Select Boarding and Day School of the Misses Nash and Miss Kollock, 1859–1890, Hillsborough, North Carolina.* Durham, N.C.: Seeman Printery, 1964.

*News and Observer.* Raleigh, scattered issues 6 Jan. 1885–3 Feb. 1982.

*News Herald.* Winnsboro, S.C., 6 Sept. 1978.

*New York Times.* New York City, scattered issues 31 Dec. 1922–19 Nov. 1978.

*1980 St. Mary's College Alumnae Directory.* Montgomery, Ala.: College and University Press, 1980.

*North Carolina Standard.* Raleigh, scattered issues 6 Jan. 1863–15 Dec. 1874.

*Observer.* Charlotte, N.C., 17 May 1942.

*Observer.* Raleigh, 25 Apr.–8 May 1877.

O'Grady, John. *Levi Silliman Ives: Pioneer Leader in Catholic Charities.* New York: P. J. Kennedy and Sons, 1933.

Paine, Robert Treat, Papers. Southern Historical Collection. Wilson Library, Univ. of North Carolina at Chapel Hill.

Paschal, George Washington. *History of Wake Forest College.* Vol. I, *1834–1865.* Raleigh: Edwards and Broughton Co., 1935.

Porter, Martha Byrd. *Straight Down a Crooked Lane.* Richmond, Va.: Dietz Press, 1945.

Powell, William S. *Higher Education in North Carolina.* Raleigh: State Department of Archives and History, 1970.

Putnam, Emily James. *The Lady: Studies of Certain Significant Phases of Her History.* 1910. Reprint. Chicago: Univ. of Chicago Press, 1970.

*Raleigh Register.* Raleigh, scattered issues 9 June 1840–12 July 1862.

*Raleigh Times.* Raleigh, scattered issues 12 Aug. 1945–22 Feb. 1972.

Raper, Charles Lee. *The Church and Private Schools of North Carolina.* Greensboro, N.C.: Joseph J. Stone, 1898.

"Report of the Visiting Committee, Southern Association of Colleges and Schools, March 1969." St. Mary's Junior College, Raleigh, 1969.

Reid, Elizabeth D. *From Raleigh's Past.* Raleigh: n.p., 1965.

Ridley, Bromfield Lewis. *Battles and Sketches of the Army of Tennessee.* Mexico, Mo.: Missouri Printing and Publishing Co., 1906.

Riley, Jack. *Carolina Power and Light Company, 1908–1958.* Raleigh: Edwards and Broughton Co., 1958.

Ross, Isabel. *First Lady of the South: The Life of Mrs. Jefferson Davis.* New York: Harper and Brothers, 1958.

*Saint Mary's and the Challenge of Our Time.* Fund-raising brochure. N.p., 1952.

St. Mary's College Alumnae Association. Minutes. St. Mary's College Archives, Raleigh.

St. Mary's College Alumnae Association Executive Committee. Minutes. St. Mary's College Archives, Raleigh.

St. Mary's College Board of Trustees. Minutes. St. Mary's College Archives, Raleigh.

St. Mary's College Board of Trustees Executive Committee. Minutes. St. Mary's College Archives, Raleigh.

Salley, Katherine Batts, ed. *Life at St. Mary's.* Chapel Hill: Univ. of North Carolina Press, 1942.

Scott, Anne Firor. *The Southern Lady From Pedestal to Politics, 1830– 1930.* Chicago: Univ. of Chicago Press, 1970.

———. *Two Forays Into Women's History.* Wesleyan College, Macon, Ga., 1974.

*Semi-Centennial Celebration of St. Mary's School, 1842–1892.* Pamphlet. St. Mary's School, Raleigh, [1892].

"A Self Evaluation of St. Mary's Junior College for the Southern Association of Colleges and Secondary Schools." Vol. II. St. Mary's Junior College, 1959.

"Self-Study Report for the Southern Association of Colleges and Schools." St. Mary's Junior College, Raleigh, 1969.

"Self-Study Report for the Southern Association of Colleges and Schools." St. Mary's Junior College, Raleigh, 1979.

Sherman, William Tecumseh. *Memoirs of General William T. Sherman.* Vol. II. 1886. Reprint. Bloomington, Ind.: Indiana Univ. Press, 1957.

Sherrill, William L. *Annals of Lincoln County North Carolina.* Charlotte, N.C.: Observer Printing House, 1937.

Sizer, Theodore R., ed. *The Age of the Academies.* Classics in Education, no. 22, Teachers College, Columbia Univ. Richmond, Va.: William Byrd Press, 1964.

Sklar, Kathryn Kish. *Catherine Beecher: A Study in American Domesticity.* New Haven, Conn.: Yale Univ. Press, 1973.

Smedes, Aldert. *Manual of St. Mary's School, Raleigh.* Raleigh: *Carolina Cultivator,* 1857.

Smedes, Aldert, Papers. Division of Archives and History. North Carolina Department of Cultural Resources, Raleigh.

———. St. Mary's College Archives, Raleigh.

———. Southern Historical Collection. Wilson Library, Univ. of North Carolina at Chapel Hill.

Smedes, Aldert. *She Hath Done What She Could, Or the Duty and Responsibility of Woman.* Sermon. Raleigh: Press of the *Register,* 1847.

Smedes, Bennett, Papers. St. Mary's College Archives, Raleigh.

Smedes, Susan Dabney. *A Southern Planter: Social Life in the Old South.* New York: James Pott and Co., 1900.

Smith, Page. *Daughters of the Promised Land: Women in American History.* Boston: Little, Brown and Co., 1970.

Smith, Peter Evans, Papers. Southern Historical Collection. Wilson Library, Univ. of North Carolina at Chapel Hill.

Sprague, William B. *Annals of the American Pulpit.* Vol. V, *Episcopalian.* 1859. Reprint. New York: Arno Press, 1969.

Sprouse [Stoops], Martha Stennis. "The Development of Research in the Social Sciences as an Academic Function." Master's thesis, Univ. of Wisconsin, 1944.

*State Journal.* Raleigh, 18–25 June 1862.

Stern, Madeleine B. *The Life of Margaret Fuller.* New York: Haskell House Publishers, 1968.

Stock, Phyllis. *Better Than Rubies: A History of Women's Education.* New York: G. P. Putnam's Sons, 1978.

Sullivan, Lou, Papers. Private collection.

Taylor, James M., and Elizabeth H. Haight. *Vassar.* New York: Oxford Univ. Press, 1915.

Ticknor, Anna Eliot, ed. *Life of Joseph Green Cogswell as Sketched in His Letters.* Cambridge, Mass.: Riverside Press, 1874.

Upjohn, Richard, Papers. New York Public Library, New York.

Walser, Richard. *The Wolfe Family in Raleigh.* Raleigh: Wolf's Head Press, 1976.

Warren, Edward Jenner, Papers. Southern Historical Collection. Wilson Library, Univ. of North Carolina at Chapel Hill.

Waugh, Elizabeth Culbertson, ed. *North Carolina's Capital, Raleigh.* Chapel Hill: Univ. of North Carolina Press, 1967.

Wheat, John Thomas, Papers. Southern Historical Collection. Wilson Library, Univ. of North Carolina at Chapel Hill.

Whitaker, Bessie Lewis. *The Provincial Council and Committees of Safety of North Carolina.* James Sprunt Historical Monograph, no. 8. Chapel Hill: Univ. of North Carolina Press, 1908.

White, T. H. *America at Last: The American Journal of T. H. White.* New York: G. P. Putnam's Sons, 1965.

Williams, John W., and William Augustus Williams, Papers. Southern Historical Collection. Wilson Library, Univ. of North Carolina at Chapel Hill.

Wilson, Sidney Ann. *Personae: The History of Peace College.* N.p., 1972.

Winston, Ellen. "A Brief History of the Raleigh Chamber Music Guild." Raleigh Chamber Music Guild, Raleigh, 1973. Mimeographed.

Wood, Maude Talmadge. *Once Apunce a Time.* Athens, Ga.: Classic Press, 1977.

Woody, Thomas. *A History of Women's Education in the United States.* Two vols. 1929. Reprint. New York: Octagon Books, 1974.

Young, Agnes Brooks. *Recurring Cycles of Fashion, 1760–1937.* New York: Harper and Brothers Publishers, 1937.

# INDEX

# THE AUTHOR

Martha Sprouse Stoops was born in 1922 in Staunton, Virginia, the daughter of a Presbyterian minister. Her bachelor's degree is from Mary Baldwin College, where she was a member of the honor society and editor of the college newspaper. She received the master's degree from the University of Wisconsin in 1944 and that year married Robert F. Stoops. They have a daughter and a son.

Her early teaching experience included four years, 1945–1949, at Peace College in Raleigh. After her husband's appointment to the faculty of North Carolina State University brought her back to Raleigh, Martha Stoops taught briefly at North Carolina State University and in 1960 joined the faculty of St. Mary's College, where she taught American history for 25 years. She served as head of the department of social studies, 1970–1973, and then was named St. Mary's College historian.